Song Sheets to Software

A Guide to Print Music, Software, and Web Sites for Musicians

Second Edition

Elizabeth C. Axford

The Scarecrow Press, Inc.
Lanham, Maryland • Toronto • Oxford
2004

SCARECROW PRESS, INC.

Published in the United States of America
by Scarecrow Press, Inc.
A wholly owned subsidiary of The Rowman & Littlefield Publishing Group, Inc.
4501 Forbes Boulevard, Suite 200, Lanham, Maryland 20706
www.scarecrowpress.com

PO Box 317
Oxford
OX2 9RU, UK

British Library Cataloguing in Publication Information Available

Library of Congress Cataloging-in-Publication Data

Axford, Elizabeth C., 1958–
  Song sheets to software : a guide to print music, software, and web sites for
musicians / Elizabeth C. Axford.— 2nd ed.
      p. cm.
  Includes bibliographical references.
  ISBN 0-8108-5027-3 (pbk. : alk. paper)
  1. Music—Computer network resources. 2. Music—United States—History and
criticism. I. Title.
ML74.7.A94 2004
780.26—dc22

2004002488

⊖™ The paper used in this publication meets the minimum requirements of
American National Standard for Information Sciences—Permanence of
Paper for Printed Library Materials, ANSI/NISO Z39.48-1992.
Manufactured in the United States of America.

Contents

Contents

Introduction

The second edition of *Song Sheets to Software* includes completely revised and updated listings of music software, instructional media, including DVDs and Book/Audio CD sets, and music-related Web sites of use to all musicians, whether hobbyist or pro. This book continues to be a great resource for music educators looking for teaching tools and resources for both the private studio and the music classroom. Due to the change in content between the first and second editions, the two books can serve as companion volumes.

New to the second edition is the inclusion of instructional DVDs as well as Book/Audio CD sets produced for music instruction for everything from children's music to high-end professional recording. New sections have been added to the software chapter, including programs available for Drums and Percussion as well as those for Folk and Traditional Instruments.

The idea for this book came to me when I was working with a MIDI sequencing program on my recording project *Merry Christmas Happy Hanukkah—A Multilingual Songbook and CD.*

As my producer and I were editing the keyboard/MIDI performances using the music notation-editing feature, I realized this program was picking up every little nuance of my playing. Every slight off-the-beat was notated as a sixteenth or thirty-second note. So, we quantized. I thought to myself, how could a person who does not read music use this editing feature? I suppose they just don't—they rely on their ear or the other editing features such as the piano roll. This is fine, I thought. Our ears are always the final musical judges anyhow.

Still this puzzled·me. I know many successful musicians and songwriters who would not know their own music if the score were set in front of them. They cannot read it. And how ironic—a MIDI sequencing program with an editing feature that requires the ability to read music, used by musicians, many of whom do not read music! Perhaps I could help fix this situation, I thought.

Remembering not too far back, I was asked by someone who knew I read music if I ever "played by ear." I stopped and thought for a minute—what does she mean? When I am playing the piano, I suppose. Or does she mean, "Can I pick out a tune, add chords to it and improvise?" My answer was "yes" to either question, whichever she had intended. My firm belief is that one ability, either reading music or playing by ear, does not have to exclude the other. Both are important skills for all musicians. And why should we deny ourselves any form of skill or knowledge—or discount that which we have?

In any case, this experience made me evaluate my own musical background, comparing it to those of other musicians I have known. I was fortunate to have piano lessons growing up, study music in college, and acquire a master's degree in music. One thing I know for certain is, in the United States, there is no singular, standard "music background."

Many of us took algebra and geometry in high school, U.S. history, world history, and other college prep courses. Yet, we all come from different experiences in our musical training. Can we pretty much say that we "don't know much about geography" only substitute the word "music" as Sam Cooke so aptly put it in his song *Wonderful World*?

And what in the world *do* we all know about music? Did we all take music courses x, y, and z in high school or college because they were *required*? No. Did we all take private lessons on an instrument? No. Did we all play in a marching band? No. Are there music. flash cards or workbooks for sale in the children's toy section of the drugstore? No. So, where's the common ground? Simple . . . there isn't any.

Music has not been a priority in our American educational system. Budgets and other academic priorities have successfully helped us to fail to learn music in any standardized fashion. So how do we learn it? Where do we go? Simple . . . we scavenge. We find coaches, private teachers, extension courses, junior college classes, songwriting workshops, books, computer software programs, the Internet, *anything* we can to learn music!

Because nobody made learning music a priority for us, we have had to make it a priority for ourselves. And then we wonder why some people bang guitars, make loud, unappealing noises, and call it "music"! Well, they are all "stray musical cats" in my opinion that never had a proper "musical home."

So what do we do? I know what I did. I spent countless hours gathering (scavenging) the information on these pages. It all looks so neat and pretty in its final form, like it was so easy. It was not, by any stretch.

I relentlessly sifted through piles of catalogs, magazines, brochures, whatever I could get my hands on, including pamphlets left on women's restroom sink countertops at trade conventions in Los Angeles. I spent hundreds (maybe thousands) of hours online combing (scavenging) the Internet for worthwhile Web sites.

This book is about learning and teaching music through new and stimulating (and hopefully accessible) means—computers and the Internet. It is intended for anyone who wants to know more about music. We can go to countless Web sites and use any number of music software programs to learn what this music stuff is all about. So, here they are . . . go for it!

And I truly hope this book helps you stray musical cats find a home.

I would like to extend a special "thank you" to those who helped me with this book and who offered their support and encouragement along the way. Thanks especially to my family: my parents, Dr. Roy A. Axford and Anne R. Axford, my brothers Roy and Trevor, my two sisters-in-law Sarah and Cyndi, my nieces Madison and Mackenzie, and my nephew Noah.

1

Song Sheets Yesterday and Today

A Brief History of Printed Music

The musical content of *print music* or *sheet music* has changed along with the history of music itself. Printed music has evolved from the time of the early Catholic monks, the scribes and Gregorian Chant, to its present-day form. Sheet music is a generic term, covering many types of published music, including classical, popular, educational, instrumental, and vocal editions.

If not for the preservation of music through the print medium, centuries of music by the great composers and songwriters could not be performed and listened to today. We would not be able to re-create the great masterpieces of the Medieval, Renaissance, Baroque, Classical, and Romantic eras. We would not know the great songs of Stephen Foster and the Tin Pan Alley composers. We would know nothing of early vocal and keyboard music, symphonies and string quartets, operas and ballets. Before recordings, printed music was the only form of communication, documentation, and reproduction available to composers, musicians, musicologists, and consumers. Print music notation remains an important form of communication among musicians today for computer applications such as graphic music scoring, sequencer editing, and instrument instruction.

Gutenberg developed printing by movable type in the 1450s. Before this, handwritten music manuscripts sold throughout Europe and did so well into the nineteenth century. During this time, more printed music sold than handwritten manuscripts. Music printing developed more slowly than that of literary works as it was more complicated and involved more symbols than the letters of the alphabet.

In the fifteenth century, chant and one-line musical examples in texts were the only music printed by movable type. The staff lines were printed first, then the notes were added. Sometimes this process was done in reverse, with the staff lines being added last. Double impressions were done by first printing the lines and then the notes. A German gradual from around 1473 is the earliest known book of printed music.

Printing from blocks of wood or metal was used into the first half of the sixteenth century, and in some isolated cases, up to the nineteenth century. This system was used for the ninth edition of the *Bay Psalm Book* (1698), the earliest example of music printed in North America. The previous editions did not contain any music.

The first printed mensural music was Ottaviano Petrucci's *Odhecaton* (1501), in choir-book format, in Venice, Italy. The printing was done in three impressions, the first being the staves, next the text, and, finally, the notes. John Rastell was the first to use printing from one impression in London. Pierre Attaingnant, starting in 1527-1528, later developed this process. This system, whereby the note head, stem, and staff lines were combined as a single type unit, was used for part books for the next 200 years by well-known printers in France, Italy, Germany, and Belgium.

In 1752, music from movable type was first printed in America. In the 1750s, J. G. I. Breitkopf further developed the process whereby the music was formed from a type font made up of note heads, stems, and flags, each attached to staff lines.

As music became more complex in florid melodies, keyboard chords, and opera scores, movable type was no longer a suitable process for printing music.

Engraving, where the music notation is drawn with a steel point on a copper plate, or punched onto a pewter plate, came to be the preferred system. Engraving was first used for music printing in the sixteenth century, gradually spreading over Europe in the seventeenth century. Venice was the main center for printed music in the sixteenth century.

Engraving was more common than typography by 1700, with the main music printing centers being Amsterdam, London, and Paris. Vienna became the main printing center later in the eighteenth century. The nineteenth century saw an increased market for printed music, leading to the establishment of music publishers and music stores.

Alois Senefelder invented *lithography* in 1796. It was fully developed by 1850. This chemical process made it possible for music to be written on paper as the preparation for plates. Engraving is still used for the preparation of camera-ready copy.

Most all of today's printing is done by the offset process, using photographic plates prepared from copy from engravings, music typewriters, transfers, composer's manuscripts and, more recently, music notation computer software. The use of computer scoring programs for preparing music notation for the printing process increased considerably during the 1980s and 1990s. The improved features of the programs and the quality of the graphics, along with the use of laser printers, have made it possible for smaller print music publishers to develop and produce their own line of products. Many of the larger print companies have greatly expanded their catalogs with the increased popularity and accessibility of electronic keyboards, multimedia teaching and learning aids, video, and audiocassettes, CDs, and CD-ROMs.

The physical format of printed sheet music has more or less remained constant. This includes *single sheets* printed on one or both sides, *folios* with one sheet folded in half to form four pages, folios with a loose half-sheet inserted to form six pages, double-folios consisting of an inner folio inserted within the fold of an outer folio to make eight pages, and double-folios with a loose half-sheet inserted within the fold of an inner folio to produce ten pages. Print music formats and terms are defined further in chapter 2.

The term *song sheet* refers to popular songs, including words and music. Songwriters, musicians, scholars, collectors, dealers, and hobbyists alike are interested in the history of song sheets. Many collectors of print music do not read music and are as interested in the artwork on the covers as they are in the music itself. Noted print music artists have often been overlooked except by collectors, many of whom frame and display sheet music with attractive covers. Collections may include song sheets with unique and artistic cover designs, or photographs of singers and entertainers, musicals, movies, images from World War I, World War II, pre-1900, and other categories.

Early American Religious, Folk, and Popular Music in Print

Religious Music

The earliest examples of printed music in colonial America included books of psalms, hymns, and spiritual songs from England. These included *The Book of Psalmes: Englished Both in Prose and Metre* (1612) by Henry Ainsworth (1570-1623), the *Sternhold and Hopkins* Psalter (1549, 1553, over 600 different editions from 1562 to 1828), *The Whole Booke of Psalms* (1621, 1667), and *The Whole Booke of Psalms Faithfully Translated into English Metre,* later titled the *Bay Psalm Book* (seventy editions from 1638 to 1773), the first book of any kind to be printed in British North America, with the ninth edition being the first to include printed music.

Other early American publications of note included *An Introduction to the Singing of Psalm-Tunes* (1721) by the Rev. John Tufts (1689-1750), *The Grounds and Rules of Musick Explained* (1721) by Rev. Thomas Walter (1696-1725), *Youth's Entertaining Amusement* (1754) by William Dawson, *Urania* (1761) by James Lyon, *Collection of the Best Psalm Tunes* (1764) and *Sixteen Anthems* (1766) by Josiah Flagg, *Royal Melody Complete* (1767) by William Tans'ur (1706-1783), and the *Universal Psalmodist* (1769) by Aaron Williams (1731-1776). The publications of the 1760s added more than 300 tunes to those already printed in the colonies, quadrupling the tune repertory. Some of the new psalm tunes appeared in more complex musical styles than the three- and four-part harmonizations printed before the mid-1700s.

British publications of note were *New Versions of the Psalms of David, Fitted to the Tunes Used in Churches* ((1696-1828) by Nahum Tate (1652-1715) and Nicholas Brady (1659-1726), and *The Psalms of David Imitated* (1719) and *Hymns and Spiritual Songs* (1707) by Isaac Watts (1674-1748). The latter publication by Watts was the first collection of original, nonbiblical devotional texts used in public worship in British and American Protestant churches, and was very well received. This led to the singing of more hymns and spiritual songs in both public and private worship into the eighteenth century. Watts believed that the texts sung for public worship should not be restricted to psalms and biblical canticles, as many did not have to do with the New Testament or the present circumstances of Christians.

Late in 1770, *The New-England Psalm-Singer: or, American Chorister,* the work of William Billings, was published by Benjamin Edes and John Gill in Boston. At this point in history, no more than a dozen musical compositions by native-born Americans had appeared in print. The Billings collection had 126 pieces, all composed by him, marking its place in the history of American music publication. The original composition of psalms, hymns, and anthems had taken root in America. Thousands of these pieces would be written in the coming decades, establishing the first native school of American composition.

Billings's second collection was the *Singing Master's Assistant*, published in Boston in 1778. It contained seventy-one pieces and had four editions. *Music in Miniature* (1779) was his third book and was a tune supplement for congregational singing. This collection contained seventy-four pieces, of which thirty-one were new tunes he had written, thirty-two were previously published, and eleven were from other composers. *The Psalm-Singer's Amusement* was published by Billings in Boston in 1781 for experienced choirs as opposed to congregational singing or singing-school instruction, with long, complex compositions. *The Suffolk Harmony* (1786) included thirty-two psalm and hymn texts in homophonic settings. Billings's last publication was the *Continental Harmony* in 1794, financially supported by anonymous friends and those who admired him. In early 1782, of the 264 musical compositions published by American-born writers, 226 of them were by Billings. Of the 200 anthems published in America by 1810, over a quarter were written by Billings.

Billings became widely known, and two of his pieces were published in England, the first compositions by an American-born composer to be published abroad. Billings did not see any money from his pieces published in collections compiled by others due to the absence of effective copyright legislation. It was not until 1790 that the first comprehensive federal copyright bill came into place.

Other tune books of the period included *Gentleman and Lady's Musical Companion* (1774) by John Strickney (1744-1827) and *Select Harmony* (1779) by Andrew Law. In the 1780s, tune books abounded. Hundreds of them were published through the first decade of the nineteenth century. These included eclectic anthologies such as *Laus Deo, or the Worcester Collection of Sacred Harmony* published by Isaiah Thomas in 1786. This was the first collection to be printed in America from movable type rather than engraved plates. Similar books included the *Chorister's Companion* (1782) by Simeon Jocelyn and Amos Doolittle, *Select Harmony* (1783) by Timothy and Samuel Green, and the *Federal Harmony* (1784). Daniel Read (1757-1836) was the first American after Billings to publish a collection of his own compositions titled the *American Singing Book* in 1785.

Other tune books from the time following the American Revolution that featured compositions by the compiler included *The New American Melody* by Jacob French (1789), *American Harmony* by Oliver Holden (1792), *Rural Harmony* by Jacob Kimball (1793), *The Psalmodist's Companion* by Jacob

French (1793), *The Harmony of Maine* by Belcher (1794), *The Responsary* by Amos Bull (1795), *New England Harmonist* by Stephen Jenks (1800), *New England Harmony* by Timothy Swan (1801), *The Christian Harmony* by Jeremiah Ingalls (1805), and *Harmonia Americana* (1791) and *Columbian Repository of Sacred Harmony* (1803) by Samuel Holyoke (1762-1820).

The most successful American hymn writer of the nineteenth century was Lowell Mason (1792-1872). In 1821, his famous compilation the *Boston Handel and Haydn Society Collection of Church Music* was published. Even after his death, *The Hymnal of the Methodist Episcopal Church*, published in 1878, contained sixty-eight of his original hymns, along with twenty-two arrangements of tunes by other writers. *The Methodist Hymnal,* published in 1935, contained thirty-two of his original hymns.

Early American Music Education

Mason played an important role in American music education and believed that children should be taught to read music as they were taught how to read. His first book written for children was *Juvenile Psalmist; or, the Child's Introduction to Sacred Music* (1829). Mason was appointed the superintendent of music in the Boston public schools in September of 1838. Boston was the first town in America where music became part of the regular curriculum for children. Other music books for children by Mason included *Musical Exercises for Singing Schools* (1838) and *The Boston School Song Book* (1840).

Later publications by Mason included *The Boston Academy's Collection of Church Music* (1835-1863, twelve editions), *The Boston Academy's Collection of Choruses* (1836), *The Boston Glee Book* (1838), and *The Song-Garden* (1864), the first graded, progressively arranged series of school music books. The market was expanding for instructional music books due greatly to Mason's support of general music literacy. Between 1841 and 1860, *Carmina Sacra* sold over 500,000 copies in thirteen editions. He had become very wealthy by the middle of the century, and was the first American to earn a fortune from music.

William B. Bradury (1816-1868) followed in Mason's footsteps, publishing sixty books for the music education of young children and church choirs between 1841 and 1867. These included *The Young Choir, The Sunday School Choir, The Shawn, The Jubilee,* and *The Devotional Hymn and Tune Book.* Like Mason, Bradbury combined adaptations of European pieces with his own compositions. Over two million copies of Bradbury's publications sold, including 250,000 copies of *The Jubilee.* Mason and Bradbury believed strongly that universal musical literacy was the way to improve the art in America.

Shape Notes

The first collection designed for singing schools used outside of New England was *The Easy Instructor* by William Little and William Smith in 1801. This book utilized a new system of notation called "shape" notes. Shape notes followed the four-syllable solmization system, where the octave was divided into two groups of three notes each, with the seventh note of the scale standing alone. This system was fixed visually by shape-note notation. This proved to be an effective teaching tool among the nonliterate, semiliterate, and newly literate people of the South and West. Many of these collections preserved the pieces sung in the camp meetings of the various populist religious movements of the late 1700s and early 1800s in America.

The Easy Instructor and other early shape-note books contained a New England repertory. By the 1820s, collections represented other parts of the country. These included *Repository of Sacred Music, Part Second* by John Wyeth (1813), *Patterson's Church Music* by Robert Patterson (1813), *Kentucky Harmony* by Ananias Davisson (1815), the *Kentucky Harmony* by Samuel L. Metcalf (1817), and *Missouri Harmony* by Allen D. Carden (1820). These collections came to be called folk hymns or white spirituals, frequently using pentatonic tunes and melodies similar to the ballads, songs, and fiddle and banjo pieces of the region. For pedagogical reasons, the composers drew on the indigenous melodic tradition of the people with whom they lived and worked, writing and arranging in a unique harmonic style. This included few triads and many parallel fifths, unisons, and octaves reflecting oral tradition polyphony and was an American innovation.

Important shape-note collections in the Deep South included *The Southern Harmony* by William Walker (1935), which is said to have sold over 600,000 copies by the time of the Civil War. This collection was used in singing schools, church congregations, and social gatherings. It contained hymns, spiritual songs, and anthems by New England composers of the late 1700s and early 1800s, folk hymns found in early shape-note collections, and new pieces, many written or arranged by Walker, in the melodic tradition of Anglo-Celtic oral-tradition music.

The most successful shape-note book, and most widely dispersed of the 1800s, was *The Sacred Harp* by Benjamin Franklin White (1800-1879), published in 1844, with revised and expanded editions in 1850, 1859, and 1869. *Sacred Harp* singing continued into the twentieth century, with two new editions printed in 1911, one of which was called the *Original Sacred Harp*. Other such collections were *The Hesperian Harp*, compiled by William Hauser in 1848, and *The Social Harp*, compiled by John G. McCurry in 1855. Shape-note music continued with the melodic style of the tunes from oral tradition becoming fixed in musical notation. Still, many learned this music by rote.

Folk Music

Important collections of oral tradition folk songs and ballads printed in America included a five-volume set containing 305 ballads titled *The English and Scottish Popular Ballads* (1882-1898) by Francis James Child (1825-1896), *Folk Songs from Somerset* (five volumes, 1905-1909), and *English Folk Songs* (1920) and *English Folk Songs from the Southern Appalachians* (1917 with 323 tunes, 1932 with 968 tunes) by Cecil J. Sharp (1859-1924). Though brought to America in their original form by immigrants from the Old World, many of these British folk tunes and texts were altered in the course of their oral transmission. Child's collections did not include the British broadsides, which could be traced to the pen of an individual, versus the folk songs, which were transmitted by oral tradition, although more than likely conceived by an individual initially. American ballads and songs are those that originated in the United States and are of completely American character both in text and music, and are sung by both adults and children.

Country dances brought over from England became popular in America. The first collection of dance figures published in the United States was by John Griffith, titled *A Collection of the Newest and Most Fashionable Country Dances and Cotillions* (1788). Thirty similar collections were published in America by 1800. Many publications of the nineteenth century contained both fiddle tunes and dance figures, including *Howe's Complete Ball-Room Hand-Book* (1858) and, also by Elias Howe, *The Musician's Omnibus* (1861).

Popular Music

Popular song was the first music to achieve a typically American character, representing a new style that combined several different national or ethnic styles. The first popular songs performed in America were from England. They were printed and sold as sheet music beginning in the 1780s, arranged for voice and keyboard accompaniment, and usually sung by amateurs for amusement in their parlors. At the turn of the century, Irish and Scottish songs became very popular, many of which were found in *The Irish Melodies* of Thomas Moore (1779-1852), published in Dublin and London from 1807 to 1834. These included *The Last Rose of Summer, Believe Me If All Those Endearing Young Charms* and *The Minstrel Boy*. A collection by Robert Burns (1759-1796) titled *Scots Musical Museum* appeared between 1787 and 1803, and included *Auld Lang Syne, Coming thru the Rye, John Anderson, My Jo,* and *Scots What Hae wi' Wallace Bled*.

Popular in the 1820s, 1830s, and 1840s were songs from operas such as *Away with Melancholy* by Mozart from *The Magic Flute*. Music publishers found a large market for songs based on Italian operatic airs and arias up to the middle part of the nineteenth century. Also popular in America was the German lied. Favorite sheet music items translated into English included songs by Franz Schubert, Franz Abt, and Friedrich Wilhelm Kücken.

Other British songwriters influenced the American market, including Sir Henry Bishop (1786-1855) who wrote *Home Sweet Home*. This was the most popular song of the nineteenth century in the English language, which sold over 100,000 copies in America a year after it was published in 1823 and several million copies before the end of the century. Many of his other songs were successful as well.

John Braham (1774-1856) wrote the most popular duet of the century, *All's Well*, from his opera *The English Fleet in 1342*. Samuel Lover (1797-1868) was the most successful Irish songwriter following Thomas Moore and wrote *Rory O'More* and *The Low-back'd Car*. The son of a German musician, Charles Edward Horn (1786-1849) wrote hundreds of songs, including *Cherry Ripe* and *I've Been Roaming*. The best female songwriter of the century was Claribel-Charlotte Alington Barbard (1830-1869), who wrote *I Cannot Sing the Old Songs*, *Take Back the Heart*, and *Come Back to Erin*.

During the nineteenth century, living standards improved, and many homes could afford both a piano and sheet music and had family members who could sing and play the piano. Many songs were written with the intention of being performed in the home and were arranged with the limitations of amateurs in mind, using simpler vocal lines and piano accompaniments. Publishers also made simpler arrangements of pieces written for professional singers available.

The first person in America to write songs for voice and keyboard was Francis Hopkinson (1737-1791). His *Seven Songs for Harpsichord* was published in Philadelphia in 1788. In a letter to Thomas Jefferson, Hopkinson described himself as an author who composes from his heart rather than from his head. Benjamin Carr (1768-1831) came from London to America in 1793, publishing sixty songs, including some he had written as well as arrangements of traditional songs. His most successful song was *The Little Sailor Boy* (1798), which had the widest distribution of any song in America prior to 1800.

Other immigrant songwriters included James Hewitt, Alexander Reinagle, George K. Jackson, Raynor Taylor, and Charles Gilfert. *The Wounded Hussar* (1800) by Hewitt was one of the most popular sheet music items from 1800 to 1810, dealing with the tragedies of war.

Early American Songwriters

The first important songwriting movement in the United States was centered in New England. Musicians living in and around Massachusetts wrote songs for keyboard and voice following the American Revolution. Forty of these were published in *Massachusetts Magazine*, some were printed in periodicals, and others appeared as separate items of sheet music. Many of these songs were included in *The American Musical Miscellany*, published in Northampton in 1798, and other anthologies. These songs were derived from English pleasure garden and comic opera pieces and had limited distribution.

Oliver Shaw (1779-1848) was the first songwriter born in America to achieve national recognition and spent most of his life in Providence, Rhode Island. Although he became blind early in life, he was a successful organist, singer, teacher, choirmaster, and composer. His most successful songs were *Mary's Tears* (1812), *All Things Bright and Fair Are Thine* (1817), and *There's Nothing True but Heav'n* (1816), which went through six editions in a decade and earned Shaw $1,500 in royalties. Shaw was versed in classical music, and his pieces reflect the balanced, diatonic, symmetrical melodies and harmonies of the simpler works by the great composers of the 1700s.

Great commercial success was achieved by John Hill Hewitt (1801-1890) with the publication of his composition *The Minstrel's Return'd from the War* in 1825. A simple diatonic tune in strophic form with a three-chord keyboard accompaniment, the song was very much in the style of the day. The song remained in print for over half a century and sold all over the country. Its success was a surprise to Hewitt and his brother James, who published the first edition. Because they had failed to obtain a copyright, any publisher could print it without paying a fee or royalties, resulting in a loss of more than $10,000 to the Hewitts.

All of Hewitt's songs were well written, though some were more commercially successful than others. His songs showed the influence of several national schools imported to America. His greatest hit was *Farewell, Since We Must Part* in 1829, reflecting the English style. Other influences included the comic opera style, Italian opera, Swiss and Austrian mountain songs, and the black minstrel songs. Hewitt skillfully assimilated these different national elements into his distinctly American songs, creating new sounding pieces and not imitations. His most popular songs included *Girls Beware* (1832), *Ah! Fondly I Remember* (1837), *The Alpine Horn* (1843), *Eulalie, Mary, Now the Seas Divide Us* (1840), and *All Quiet along the Potomac* (1862). Because the income from his songs was not enough to support his family, Hewitt made a living as a journalist and teacher.

Another songwriter creating characteristically American songs was Henry Russell (1812-1901), the most important and successful songwriter before Stephen Foster. Russell performed his own songs, accompanied himself on the piano, and handled his own business affairs, including advances and publicity. He strove for an emotional response from his audience. One of his most famous songs was *Woodman, Spare That Tree*. Tens of thousands of Americans attended his concerts and purchased copies of his songs. Russell helped to shape indigenous American song and greatly influenced the next generation of American songwriters.

Early American Sheet Music Publishers

The publishing of sheet music in the United States was well established by the early nineteenth century. In 1800, there were several professional music publishers in Philadelphia. By 1820, there were publishers in southern cities as well. Most of the music produced during this time was of English and Irish origin. Not until the 1830s did American songwriters begin to achieve international success.

Engraved plates were used to print most music. Some music was published using *lithography* in the 1820s, but this was not very common until the 1840s. The development of *chromolithography* made it economically possible to do illustrated title pages. Both engraved and lithographed music continued to be issued during this period.

During the Civil War, Confederate imprints were lithographed. These processes required less equipment and materials, including metal, which was in high demand for the war and in short supply for civilians. After the Civil War, there was a large increase in music publishing activity. The *stereotype process* made it possible for publishers to issue large numbers of music for consumption by the masses. This period in popular music history is known as the *Age of Parlor Music*.

Music publishers came to realize the commercial value of printing advertising on the blank pages of sheet music during the rise of parlor music in the 1860s. Entire catalogs of songs and music were printed on the back or inside front covers of publications. By the end of the nineteenth century, lists of songs with melodies or complete pages for the user to "try over on your piano" became standard. Manufacturing companies issued sheet music to advertise their products. During World War I, publishers promoted the war effort by using the margins of the music for slogans.

The *music publishing industry* in the United States was started by entrepreneurship. Before New York City became music publishing's headquarters in the late 1800s, many small music publishers sprang up around the country. For many, music publishing was not their only career. They may have been a local person who owned a printing press. This same printer who printed books, posters, stationery, and advertisements would be asked by local musicians to print sheet music copies of their songs and compositions.

The printer would often make an agreement with the composer whereby the composer and the publisher would share *royalties* based on the number of copies sold. This arrangement would later evolve into the *song contract*. The printer might sell copies of the sheet music in his printed goods store and at the local music store.

Traveling salesmen were hired to sell sheet music throughout a region on a commission basis, along with clothes and household goods. The salesmen would carry sheet music samples as part of his product line and sell the sheet music to the local music store or five-and-ten-cent store. There were some salesmen who could actually play the songs they carried in their cases of sheet music on the piano.

Some of these salesmen became entrepreneurs and set up their own publishing companies. They wrote and published their own songs or acquired new songs from songwriters whose sheet music they had sold previously. These new publishers might look for new songwriters to sign to publishing agreements. Some paid a printer to print their sheet music, and others acquired their own printing presses. In the mid-nineteenth century, publishers issued sacred and secular songs, lieder, opera excerpts, waltzes, marches, and etudes, all from the same catalog.

As folk music has survived through oral tradition, popular music has been promoted as published sheet music, recordings, or performances. One of the main venues for popular song during the early to mid-nineteenth century was the *traveling minstrel show*. The *minstrel song* became the first American genre and was rooted in English comic opera. Created by white Americans, the characters portrayed were black Americans. The music was not related to that of African Americans at the time. Tunes were sung in broken English and were simple, diatonic or pentatonic, with dancelike tempos, supposedly reflecting a primitive music. Music publishers issued many of the popular minstrel show songs in sheet music editions, including *Coal Black Rose*, *Jim along Josey*, and *Long Tail Blue*. Many of the song texts portrayed black people as illiterate, comical, subhuman beings. Some tunes were borrowed or adapted from traditional Anglo-American pieces, with the accompanying instruments playing in a traditional, nonharmonic style. The most famous traveling minstrel troupes were the Virginia Minstrels and Christy's Minstrels, whose first performance was in the 1840s in Albany, New York, moving to New York City in 1846.

In the 1840s, Stephen Foster combined the European American and African American folk traditions. He composed hundreds of songs, including *Oh! Susanna, Camptown Races,* and *The Old Folks at*

Home. Stephen Foster is the father of American popular song and was America's first internationally renowned songwriter.

Composer Profile: Stephen Foster

Stephen Collins Foster was born on July 4, 1826, in Lawrenceville, Pennsylvania, now part of Pittsburgh. That particular Fourth of July marked the fiftieth anniversary of the Declaration of Independence as well as the deaths of the second and third presidents of the United States, John Adams and Thomas Jefferson. Stephen Foster was born the tenth of eleven children but remained the youngest of the family when his younger brother died in infancy.

Foster's very American birth date coincides with his important role in creating songs very near to indigenous American folk songs. The songs brought by ancestors from all over the world were representative of the cultures of their native lands. Although they may have emerged differently, they were still recognizable and not particularly American. The only race that developed a folk-song literature in America was the one which was brought here against its will and brutally exploited: the African American. The African American spirituals and Stephen Foster's songs have sometimes been confused as to authorship.

Active both politically and commercially, the Fosters were prominent people in western Pennsylvania. Stephen was different from the other members of his family. He was a dreamer and loved music. He could pick out tunes on the piano and learned to play the flute and violin. He began to compose as a teenager. Although his parents noticed his talent, they did little to train him in music. The other family members enjoyed music but felt it should not occupy too much of Stephen's time. They believed there was more important work to be done in their own pioneer community, which was beginning to flourish. Stephen promised upon entering boarding school that he would limit his music to a pleasant pastime, not paying any attention to it until after eight o'clock in the evening. Stephen's father wrote in 1841 that his son's leisure hours were all devoted to music, for which he possessed a strange talent.

In 1841, the Foster family moved to Allegheny, Pennsylvania. During the five years that he lived there, Stephen wrote many of his first songs. Stephen's father, William Barclay Foster, became the mayor of Allegheny. During this time, Stephen visited his brother, Morrison, in Youngstown. Morrison went to New Orleans and visited the towns and cities along the Ohio and the Mississippi Rivers. He brought home with him many tales of Southern life. When the two brothers returned to Allegheny, they went many places together, often borrowing from each other and trading between themselves.

Stephen was becoming more and more absorbed in his music. Those who knew him recalled that he was beginning to write songs. His first song published was issued in December of 1844, when he was eighteen, probably written when he was sixteen. He wrote only the music to a poem by George P. Morris, *Open Thy Lattice, Love.* It appeared in a supplement to the *New Mirror* (1843-1844), a Saturday paper edited in New York by Morris and Nathaniel P. Willis.

The song was issued by George Willig of Philadelphia as a two-page song, without a title page, with a heading on the first page listing Stephen's name as "L. C. Foster." The publisher had failed to print Stephen's name correctly on his very first song!

Starting in 1845, a club of young men met twice a week at the Fosters' home. They were known as "The Knights of the S. T. [Square Table]." The club meetings were secret and marked by formal, semi-burlesque rituals. Each of the five members had a fraternal name and was described in a poem written by Stephen, dated May 6, 1845, "The Five Nice Young Men." Along with the writing of personal poems, the most important outgrowth of these meetings was that the group practiced songs. When they had learned all the current popular pieces, Stephen would try writing songs for them himself.

Stephen first wrote *Lou'siana Belle* for the group. They liked it so well, and he was encouraged to write *Old Uncle Ned* for another meeting. His sister, Ann Eliza, claimed later that *Oh! Susanna* was also composed for the club. This type of setting was an early model of the songwriting workshops and open-mics popular around the United States today.

After trying to make Stephen conform to an accepted and conventional pattern, including trying to get him appointed to West Point, his family decided to send him to Cincinnati. His brother Dunning would teach him how to do the bookkeeping for his commission business. At the age of twenty, Stephen sailed down the Ohio River on one of the riverboats he would immortalize in song. He was much more interested in the singing of the black deckhands than adding columns of figures, which he proceeded to do for over three years.

Stephen lived in Cincinnati from the fall of 1846 until early 1850. He was a good bookkeeper and was left in the office with Dunning's partner when Dunning enlisted in the army during the Mexican War. He was primarily interested in writing music and verses, however, and spent much of his spare time getting acquainted with the minstrel performers who might perform his songs in public.

The type of songs Stephen wrote at this time are indicative of the prominent influence that affected his early creative efforts. He thought the songs of the current minstrel shows to be crude and vulgar but, nevertheless, representing something definitely

American. While this was a medium that influenced and affected Foster profoundly, he himself completely reformed it.

Some of the minstrel singers Foster encountered were unscrupulous and took his manuscript copies (which he had given them to perform) to publishers, who, in no time, issued pirated editions.

When he found a publisher to issue *Oh! Susanna* and *Old Uncle Ned*, other firms had already published these songs. It is still uncertain who first printed *Oh! Susanna* and *Old Uncle Ned* and where some of the manuscripts came from.

Because Foster was generous with manuscript copies and because common law copyright protecting the author of a manuscript until publication was apparently not established, the first to present a work at a district copyright office was allowed to take out a copyright.

Of the twenty editions printed of *Oh! Susanna*, some were printed from the manuscript copies Stephen had given to minstrel performers, and others were from transcriptions by those who had heard the song and written out their own versions. This can be seen in the musical and poetic differences between the many editions printed in southern New York, Massachusetts, Maryland, Kentucky, and eastern Pennsylvania.

Foster was credited for authorship on some of the editions of his early songs, but, on most of them, there was no mention of his name.

It is probable that the pirated editions show the variety of uses to which the song *Oh! Susanna* was immediately put: minstrel shows, in some collections of *Negro Songs* as the *Susanna Polka*, and in numerous arrangements with *Easy Variations for the Piano Forte*.

Oh! Susanna is an example of Foster's comic, Ethiopian songs. It was first performed in public at Andrews' Ice Cream Saloon in Pittsburgh on September 11, 1847.

While in Cincinnati, Stephen came in touch with W. C. Peters, a music publisher Stephen's family knew in Pittsburgh. He gave to Peters a number of songs, including *Oh! Susanna*, for either $100.00 or as an outright gift. Foster had no royalty interest, and Peters made a fortune from his early songs. Foster gained only the fame he needed to establish himself as a songwriter.

Oh! Susanna was an overnight hit and was sung by the forty-niners on their way to California. Most of the minstrel troupes sang it at every performance. From this success, two other publishers, Firth, Pond & Co. in New York and F. D. Benteen in Baltimore, offered royalty contracts to Stephen, agreeing to pay him two cents for every copy of his songs sold by them.

Stephen returned to his family in Allegheny, able to prove to them he could make a living as a songwriter. On July 22, 1850, Stephen married Jane McDowell, daughter of a Pittsburgh physician. They honeymooned in New York and Baltimore, then went to live with the Foster family in Allegheny.

Foster published eleven songs during the first six months of 1850, including *Camptown Races*, issued by Benteen. He composed his finest songs during the first six years of his married life. These included: *Old Folks at Home*, 1851; *Massa's in de Cold Ground*, 1852; *My Old Kentucky Home* and *Old Dog Tray*, 1853; *Jeanie with the Light Brown Hair*, 1854; *Come Where My Heart Lies Dreaming*, 1855; and *Gentle Annie*, 1856.

Jeanie with the Light Brown Hair was written for his wife during their separation in 1854. It is an example of Foster's poetic songs and ballads. Due to Stephen's temperament, and Mrs. Foster's possible lack of interest in his songwriting, hoping to make him more of a businessman, their marriage was often strained. They were separated several times, and in the later year, Jane left him when he could no longer support her. He loved his wife and daughter, Marion, dearly and never showed an interest in another woman. He very much wanted them to be happy and enjoy their lives.

In 1851, Foster began to establish transactions on a business basis with E. P. Christy of the famous Christy's Minstrels. He offered Christy the opportunity to be the first performing troupe to perform his songs prior to their being issued by the publisher for a fee of $10.00 on such songs as *Massa's in de Cold Ground* (July 7, 1852) and *Old Dog Tray* (1853) and $15.00 for *Old Folks at Home* (October 1, 1851) and *Farewell My Lilly Dear* (December 13, 1851). Once issued, these songs were announced on the cover as being sung by the Christy Minstrels. Christy had his name alone put on *Ellen Bayne*. These songs were issued by Firth, Pond & Co.

In the case of *Old Folks at Home*, entered for copyright by Firth, Pond & Co. on August 26, 1851, the title page deposited October 1, 1851, stated:

OLD FOLKS AT HOME
Ethiopian Melody
as sung by
Christy's Minstrels
Written and Composed by
·   E. P. Christy

There is no record of any reply from Christy to Stephen's letter of May 25, 1852, in which he asked to receive credit on the title page of his published songs.

Future printings of *Old Folks at Home* continued to list Christy's name as author and composer. When the copyright was renewed by Stephen's widow and daughter, future editions bore his name, beginning in 1879. It is believed that the extra $5.00 Christy paid Foster for the privilege of first performing his songs and having his name appear as a performer of the songs further included being named as author and composer.

The money Foster received from Christy for the privilege of introducing his songs was all Stephen is known to have received for what today is called a performing right. Stephen's income would have been far greater than it was if the copyright laws of the 1850s provided that public performance of a song for profit was the exclusive right of the copyright owner.

Had there been organizations such as ASCAP, BMI, or SESAC to assert this right and collect for him, Stephen would have made much more money from the public performance of his songs.

Though they were not supposed to advertise *Old Folks at Home* as being written by Foster, his publishers were quick to capitalize on his increasing fame. It finally came out that he was the actual composer of *Old Folks at Home* in the February 19, 1853, issue of the *Musical World*, under "Answers to Correspondence."

Foster had a comfortable income from the contracts signed with his publishers. In just over six years, he earned $9,596.96 from Firth, Pond & Co. and $461.85 from Benteen. An annual income just under $2,000.00 was adequate in the 1850s for living comfortably. It did not, however, constitute wealth or anything near what songwriters today would earn with works equal in popularity to those of Stephen Foster.

The Fosters spent a little more than he earned every year, and his accounting books clearly show debts to his landlords and tailors and money borrowed from his brothers Morrison and William. He continued to draw advances from his publishers.

Financial matters reached a crisis level in 1857. Stephen drew a list of what each song had earned and what he estimated each one would bring him in the future. He calculated the thirty-six songs on royalty with Firth, Pond & Co. were worth $2,786.77. He negotiated with them to sell his future rights to those songs for the estimated amount.

They settled with him for about two-thirds of the amount for which he asked. He received $1,500.00 in cash and notes and canceled the amount of $372.28 overdrawn on his previous royalty account. The total sum was $1,872.28. He sold to Benteen for $200.00 the future rights to sixteen songs that had previously earned $461.85.

The following year, a new contract was negotiated with Firth, Pond & Co. He was to compose exclusively for them for two-and-a-half years. He would receive a 10 percent royalty on the retail price of his songs and an advance of $100.00 on each song he wrote—up to twelve per year. This was a better contract than his previous one, but he had already passed his creative peak.

Foster published sixteen songs in the two-and-a-half years of the agreement, earning only $700.00 in royalties. He was again overdrawn at the publishers by nearly $1,400.00 by July of 1860. Once more he sold his future rights to Firth, Pond & Co. for $1,600.00. The overdraft was deducted, and Stephen was paid $203.36.

With this money Stephen moved his family to New York to be in closer touch with publishers and minstrel performers. Firth, Pond & Co. offered him a salary of $800.00 for writing twelve songs a year. The Philadelphia publisher Lee & Walker offered him $400.00 for six songs. His income was guaranteed at $1,200.00 a year.

Upon arriving in New York, Stephen presented to Firth, Pond & Co. *Old Black Joe.* It proved to be only a momentary flash of his former genius. Though he turned out over a hundred songs during his last four years, they were not the quality of his previous work. He collaborated more often with lyric writers as he no longer wrote the words himself.

The salary contracts did not last long, and Stephen began selling songs to other publishers for cash. They were not especially particular about the material as they were glad to have songs bearing his name in their catalog. Stephen spent the cash as soon as he was paid, much of it on liquor. He had become an incurable alcoholic.

After trying to help cure him of his habit, and talk him into leaving the strain and tension of New York, Stephen's wife, Jane, finally left him and moved away to live with her sister. Stephen's brother Morrison spent time with him during the last few years and tried to help him.

Stephen stayed in New York after being invited to move to Cleveland with Morrison. He stayed in New York with his friends who would not try to reform him.

Stephen had an accident while living alone in a lodging house in January of 1864. He was ill and suffering from a fever, possibly tuberculosis. He fell and cut his neck near the jugular vein. He was taken to Bellevue Hospital, where he fainted on the third day and never again regained consciousness.

He died on January 13, 1864, at 2:30 in the afternoon. Morrison and Jane took his body back to Pittsburgh, where it was placed in the family plot in the Allegheny Cemetery.

Vaudeville

The music industry flourished in the latter half of the nineteenth century, mostly through the sale of sheet music, pianos, and organs. Many of the most successful songs of this period were created for and performed in the minstrel shows. Publishers relied on performers to promote their songs and even more so as the minstrel tradition evolved into American vaudeville.

Vaudeville was made up of variety shows featuring entertainers, singers, opera singers, soft-shoe dancers, comedians, comedy teams, contortionists, and animal acts. Vaudeville theaters appeared in cities all over the country. By mid-1869, the first American transcontinental railway was completed. Tens of thousands of miles of railroad tracks were put into place during the next two decades. Entertainers originating in New York City could now travel across the United States and perform in theaters and music halls in most of the country's major cities. This traveling variety show, vaudeville, gave music publishers a constant supply of performers needing new material.

New York City was a busy center for American vaudeville with many theaters, barrooms and dance halls, booking agents, and the industry trade paper the *New York Clipper* located in the district between West 14th and 30th Streets. By 1890, music publishers had also started to locate here, mainly on West 26th, 27th, and 28th Streets. Since this was where the entertainers were, and because they frequently traveled around the country performing songs before large audiences of prospective sheet music buyers, it made sense for the music publishers to be located in the same neighborhood. This area came to be known as Tin Pan Alley. As the theater district moved farther uptown to Broadway, the music publishers also moved to be near the performers and songwriters of the stage. The term *Tin Pan Alley* came to refer to the entire American music industry in the first part of the twentieth century.

Tin Pan Alley

Sheet music continued to be issued in large numbers in the twentieth century, centering on the area of Manhattan known as Tin Pan Alley. Tin Pan Alley refers to 28th Street between 5th and Broadway in New York City. The name comes from the sound made by many songs being played at the same time through open windows, in different keys on poorly tuned pianos. A newspaper reporter by the name of Monroe Rosenfeld is said to have been responsible for the name. Although he did not use the phrase "Tin Pan Alley" in his *New York Herald* article on the publishing houses in the district, he referred to the area as the "Alley" and the noise they collectively created as being "not unlike the sound of tin pans banging together."

Tin Pan Alley gained momentum with the coming of the American industrial revolution, and marked the golden age of the piano in the songwriting world. Musically uneducated tunesmiths fed the fledgling New York publishing houses. During this period, copyright laws were not enforced, and plagiarism was common. The American Society of Composers, Authors, and Publishers (ASCAP) would not be formed for another thirty years. Many songs were sold for very little money, and their success provided the finances needed for the small publishing companies to survive. Songwriters who were tired of selling their hit songs for such small fees eventually became their own publishers.

Tin Pan Alley's most important publishing companies included T. B. Harms, Irving Berlin, Shapiro & Bernstein, M. Witmark & Sons, F. A. Mills, Leo Feist, Inc., Harry Von Tilzer Music Publishing Company, and Jerome H. Remick & Company. Many hit songs came from these publishers, and sheet music became so popular it was issued as supplements to Sunday newspapers.

Some of these music publishing companies were started by the sheet music salesmen who had become publishers. Each of these companies had an office with one or more rooms and a piano. Songwriters were hired to sit in the rooms during the day and write new songs at the piano.

Songs were continually needed, and there was a lot of competition. Musicians and lyricists collaborated all along Tin Pan Alley to come up with new song material. When the Tin Pan Alley songwriter or songwriting team had finished a new song, the publisher would go out and try to convince an entertainer to perform it in his or her act. This process, originating in Tin Pan Alley, came to be known as *song plugging.*

In the early days of song plugging, there were no set rules. The song plugger could be either the publisher himself or a singer hired to persuade the entertainer, the more famous, the better, to perform the number. Once an agreement was reached between the publisher and the entertainer, the publisher would print sheet music of the song. The entertainer's picture would often appear on the cover of the sheet music. This was done both to flatter them and to ensure that the performer would continue using the song in his or her act.

The sheet music was distributed to wholesalers, also known as *jobbers,* throughout the country, with the expectation of orders from retailers. Performers would travel the vaudeville circuit on the train routes throughout the United States, having been booked by Tin Pan Alley booking agents. After performing in a city, the local music store and other stores that sold sheet music would receive requests for copies of the new song that had been performed the night before.

During the 1800s, pianos had become a primary source of entertainment in the home. Sheet music was in high demand. This is almost hard to imagine in today's world of recorded music, where virtually any genre of music can be purchased and listened to, involving no effort to read music or play an instrument on the part of the consumer. During the Tin Pan Alley era, it was the number of copies of sheet music sold that determined whether or not a song was a *hit*, not record sales or a song's position on the Billboard charts.

Sheet music sales rose considerably during this period, and the music publishers profited. Millions of copies of sheet music had been sold by 1910. The most popular songs sold as many as a million copies each *in sheet music*!

Charles K. Harris's *After the Ball* was the first popular song to sell a million sheet music copies in 1893. By 1903, it had sold over ten million copies. During the gay nineties and the early 1900s, sentimental Victorian ballads and clever novelty songs were in vogue. *In the Shade of the Old Apple Tree* and *Little Annie Rooney* were the biggest sellers of this period. Comic songs like George M. Cohan's *So Long Mary* from the musical play *Forty-Five Minutes from Broadway* were also popular.

The advent of the recording industry and the birth of commercial jazz and blues caused a decline in the popularity of the sentimental ballads. Tin Pan Alley came to draw on a variety of new sources, including African American artists and rural American yodelers.

The main source of popular music in America from 1900 through the late 1940s was the Broadway stage. From the Broadway shows came many hit songs by such great songwriters as George and Ira Gershwin, Jerome Kern, Richard Rodgers, Oscar Hammerstein II, Lorenz Hart, and Harold Arlen.

The player piano, the phonograph, radio, and motion pictures gradually brought an end to Tin Pan Alley. As sound became synchronized with film in 1926, the demand for music to accompany the silent films was high. Publishing companies were bought out by the film tycoons and transplanted within the movie companies themselves. Tin Pan Alley came to serve the movie, record, and radio industries.

Tin Pan Alley Composers

Sheet music collectors often collect by composer, searching for representative works of an individual or team of composers. Tin Pan Alley composers who wrote both words and music included Paul Dresser, George M. Cohan, James Thornton, Charles K. Harris, Irving Berlin, Walter Donaldson, and Cole Porter. Irving Berlin occasionally collaborated with others. Walter Donaldson often worked with lyricists. Early Tin Pan Alley composers included Henry Dacre, Paul Dresser, Ed Harrigan and David Braham, Charles K. Harris, Harry Kennedy, Ed Marks and Joe Stern, Kerry (F. A.) Mills, Monroe Rosenfeld, William J. Scanlan, Joseph P. Skelly, and Jim Thornton.

Middle Tin Pan Alley composers included Ernest R. Ball, Irving Berlin, Will J. Cobb and Gus Ed-

wards, George M. Cohan, Raymond Egan and Richard Whiting, Victor Herbert, Ballard MacDonald and Harry Carroll, Edward Madden and Theodore Morse, Andrew Sterling and Harry Von Tilzer, Albert Von Tilzer, Harry Williams, and Egbert Van Alstyne. The late Tin Pan Alley composers included Irving Berlin, Buddy De Sylva, Lew Brown and Ray Henderson, Walter Donaldson, Al Dubin and Harry Warren, Dorothy Fields and Jimmy McHugh, Ira Gershwin and George Gershwin, Jerome Kern, Sam Lewis and Joe Young, Cole Porter, and Richard Rogers and Lorenz Hart.

Music was one of the first professions open to African Americans. *Oh, Dem Golden Slippers* (1870), *Carry Me Back to Old Virginny* (1878), and *In the Evening by the Moonlight* (1879) were written by James A. Bland, one of the first African American composers and influenced by the works of Stephen Foster. Other African American composers include William C. Handy, father of the blues, and Scott Joplin, ragtime master.

Jazz great Duke Ellington wrote *It Don't Mean a Thing, If It Ain't Got That Swing* in 1932, along with many other standard popular jazz tunes. Edward Kennedy composed *Don't Get around Much Anymore* (lyric by Bob Russell) in 1942.

The most active women composers of Tin Pan Alley prior to 1920 were Hattie Starr, the first successful woman composer, Charlotte Blake, Beth Slater Whitson, and Carrie Jacobs-Bond. Dozens of women who occasionally wrote songs included Nora Bayes, May Irwin, Anita Owen, Clare Kummer, Minnie Iris, Dorothy Fields, Mabel Wayne, and Beth Slater Whitson.

Popular Song Sheets without Lyrics

Popular song sheets without lyrics included cakewalks, rags, fox-trots, the hesitation waltz (Boston), Indian intermezzos or ballads, marches, and blues. Also included were dance styles such as the tango. Following are some examples of "music only" popular song sheets.

Cakewalks

Cakewalks were popular in the 1880s and 1890s. The best performing couple of this exaggerated strut received a cake as a prize, thus the name. Occasionally, lyrics were included. Examples of cakewalks include *After the Cakewalk* by Nathaniel Dett (1900), *At a Georgia Camp Meeting* by Kerry Mills (1897), and *Golliwog's Cakewalk* by Claude Debussey (1908). The cakewalk was associated with ragtime rhythm. Although ragtime rhythm was established prior to 1896, the cakewalks were the first music to be published in this rhythm.

Rags

From the cakewalk, ragtime developed into a dance craze that captured the nation unlike any other, reaching its peak in 1913. The ballroom idols of the day were the Irene and Vernon Castle and Maurice Mouret and Florence Walton dance teams. Ragtime rhythm typically includes a syncopated melody played alongside a steady bass beat. Begun in brothels and honky-tonks, ragtime was not originally accepted by the upper class. People came to love the syncopated melodies with the compelling beat.

The most famous ragtime master is Scott Joplin, who composed and performed ragtime piano tunes. Other ragtime composers included James Scott, Joseph F. Lamb, Tom Turpin, Ben Harney, George Botsford, Charles L. Johnson, and Eubie Blake. Hundreds and hundreds of rags were written by scores of writers. Most rags did not have lyrics. The first rag to be published was *Mississippi River* by William Krell in 1897. Rags lead all other categories in song sheet collecting. Some examples of ragtime titles include *Fuss and Feathers, Chills and Fever, Barbed Wire, Holy Moses,* and *Coal Smoke. Alexander's Ragtime Band* by Irving Berlin is not a rag, although he contributed greatly to ragtime music.

Fox-trots

At the peak of the Tin Pan Alley era, the nation was obsessed with new dance creations. Tin Pan Alley composers complied to the demand. The fox-trot was the successor to the rags. Some examples of fox-trot titles are *Frisky, Dr. Brown, Tiddledy Winks, Reuben, Cruel Papa,* and *Tickle Toes.* Fox-trot composers included Lucky Roberts, Chris Smith, Joe Jordon, and Charles L. Johnson.

Hesitations (Boston)

The waltz was once considered to be suggestive and indecent but later earned a position of respectability. By the late 1800s, many people had lost interest in the 3/4 waltz time rhythm. With the coming of the automobile, telephone, and telegraph was a new American rhythm. The new century had little in common with the old country-originated waltz, giving way to the fox-trots, one-steps, and two-steps. To keep the waltz from fading into obscurity, a modified step called the *hesitation* or *Boston* was born. Hesitations were written for the dance idols of the day. The *Lame Duck* hesitation was written for Irene and Vernon Castle. The *Maurice* hesitation was composed for Maurice Mouret of the Mouret and Florence Walton dance team. Unlike the rags and fox-trots, these waltzes were not given humorous titles. Examples of hesitation titles include *Waltz Elaine, Waltz Brune, Old Fashioned Roses, Love Thoughts, Yes and No Valse,* and *Valse June.* The covers were also designed respectably, artistically, and with humor.

Indian Intermezzos and Ballads

In 1903 *Navajo* by Williams and Van Alstyne received national attention. *Silver Heels, Red Wing, Fawneyes, Morning Star, Red Man, Anona, Golden Arrow, Iola, Moon Bird,* and others were published as Indian intermezzos, or short, independent instrumental musical compositions. Lyrics were added to the more popular ones, and the songs became ballads. Because of their popularity, songwriters and publishers produced many Indian songs, calling them intermezzos. The Indian category is a popular field of collecting. The Indian song sheet covers are very attractive, especially the ones of Indian maidens. Other examples of Indian intermezzos and ballads include *Hiawatha* by Neil Moret (1902), *Indian Love Call* by Harbach, Oscar Hammerstein II, and Rudolph Friml (1924), *Kachina-Hopi Girl's Dance* by Albert Van Sand and Arthur Green (1914), and *Oh! That Navajo Rag* by Williams and Van Alstyne (1911).

Marches

Marches were written for every event, including inaugurals, expositions, political campaigns, and wars. John Philip Sousa, the "March King," composed over 150 marches, including the *Washington Post March, The Stars and Stripes Forever, Semper Fidelis,* and *Liberty Bell.* Many march composers were part of the Tin Pan Alley scene. E. T. Paull, Harry J. Lincoln, J. S. Jamecnik, Paul Lincke, and George Rosey (G. M. Rosenberg) are some of the better known march composers. After the turn of the century, march music was published with colorful covers encompassing a variety of subjects, including photographs of presidents and current events.

The Blues

W. C. Handy's 1911 publication of *The Memphis Blues* helped to credit him as the "Father of the Blues." Sorrows were expressed by singing the blues, a twelve-bar refrain with flatted thirds and sevenths. Duke Ellington, Jelly Roll Morton, and Fats Waller all contributed to the blues. Many non-blues songs had a blues title due to their popularity, and Tin Pan Alley profited.

The blues remained popular well into the post-Tin Pan Alley era. Blues singers Gertrude "Ma" Rainey and Bessie Smith became famous for their singing of Tin Pan Alley blues songs. Several blues styles evolved from primitive blues. Tin Pan Alley blues songs numbered in the hundreds.

Dances

To appeal to a variety of tastes in dance styles, it was common among publishers to advertise a song as being suitable for several different dance rhythms. *Tangomania* is a typical example as it could be a one-step, two-step, or tango. Usually the dance step named in the title, regardless of any other dances mentioned, is considered the correct classification. The dance mentioned first would take priority. Other dances include the turkey trot, kangaroo dip, fish walk, Texas Tommy, snake, crab step, grizzly bear, airplane dip, and the waltzes, either syncopated or hesitated. Some examples of one- or two-steps include *Cannon Ball* by Joseph C. Northrop (1905), *Captain Betty* by Lionel Baxter (1914), *Cup Hunters* by Julius Lenzberg (1915), *Fu* by George P. Howard (1919), *Great Snakes!* by Ernest Reeves (1911), *Melody Maids* by W. Leon Ames (1914), *Ole Virginny* by J. S. Zamecnik (1916), *Pepperpot* by Harold Iver (1913), *Pink Poodle* by Charles L. Johnson (1914), *Silhouette One Step* by Harold Bien (1914), *Thanks for the Lobster* by Clarence Jones (1914), *Tsin Tsin Ta Tao* by D. Onivas (1914), and *Yo San* by Al W. Brown (1914). Examples of tangos include *El Irrisistible* by Egbert Van Alstyne (1914), *Everybody Tango* by Paul Pratt (1914), *Pass the Pickles* by Grace LeBoy (1913), *Tangomania* by Egbert Van Alstyne (1914), and *Tom Tom* by Rosardios Furnari (1914).

Composer Profile: Scott Joplin

The "Ragtime Master" Scott Joplin was born November 24, 1868, in Texarkana, Texas. His mother, Florence Givens Joplin, was from Kentucky and had been free from birth. His father, Giles Joplin, was an ex-slave from North Carolina. Slavery ended only five years before Scott Joplin was born. The Joplin family led a very musical home life. The father was a violin player, having performed as a dance musician while he was a slave, and the mother sang and played the banjo. Scott had three brothers and two sisters. The two younger brothers, Will and Robert, both sang. Will also played the guitar and Robert composed. The older brother, Monroe, and sisters Myrtle and Ossie were also musical.

Scott played the guitar and bugle when he was very young. He discovered a piano at a neighbor's house when he was seven and loved playing it. His musical talents soon became obvious to both his father and the neighbors. Giles Joplin managed to scrape together enough money to buy a secondhand square piano. Scott was at the piano day and night.

The ten-year-old Joplin became known through the black community as a remarkable improviser, and rumors spread to the white community about his talent. A German music teacher who had heard him play offered him free piano lessons. The professor also taught him sight-reading, the principles of harmony, classical music and composers, and introduced him to the famous operas. Although his first benefactor's name is unknown, Joplin never forgot him, and in his later years he sent his old, poor, and ailing teacher money.

Scott Joplin's mother Florence died when he was a young adolescent. Friction developed between Scott and his father over learning a trade. This resulted in his leaving home in 1882 when he was about fourteen. His younger brothers Will and Robert followed him a little later. This move brought Scott into the subworld of the American honky-tonk and red-light districts where piano players, both black and white, were in demand. He traveled from Texas to Louisiana and all over the Mississippi Valley states of Missouri, Arkansas, and Kansas.

This region was "the cradle of ragtime. He was now in a different school: adult education for a child. He met hundreds of mainly self-taught musicians and singers, and heard popular music, light classical music, and folk music, old and new, black and white, respectable and not-so-respectable. It would be a prime source of melodic inspiration for the rest of his life. . . . It was a hurrying, exciting world of music, wine, and contraband love, a terrain not cosmopolitan, but still frontier. Its real music was not Strauss nor Waldteufel nor, even, our own Gottschalk. Nor was it the lugubrious teary ballads of the New York Rialto. It was a heady new music called RAGTIME, a dance-song alembicated from the native air, an intoxicant bubbling with the spirit of a wholly American time and place. . . . For a young man marked out to become the greatest composer of this new music, this folk-conservatory was far more valuable than a real conservatory could have been at that moment. It was a world where for the very first time in America black and white musicians were meeting as equals, competing, trading, and borrowing from the musical traditions of their two different races."[1]

Ragtime composition was prominent during the first two decades of the twentieth century. The first ragtime publication was William Krell's *Mississippi Rag* in 1897. This was followed by Tom Turpin's *Harlem Rag* the same year.

By 1899 to 1900, many published compositions with the title "rag" started to appear. The ragtime style was extremely simple and light the first five years. More serious or "high class" rags came out toward the end of the first decade.

The leading composers of ragtime were Scott Joplin, James Scott, Joseph Lamb, Artie Matthews, and Tom Turpin. After 1910, ragtime became a national rage. The major ragtime composers published through the teens, with a few rags published in the early 1920s. By 1925, ragtime composition slowed down considerably due to the commercial exploitation of Tin Pan Alley, giving way to the Jazz Era. There are a limited number of rags recorded "straight." Ragtime was preserved primarily through the printed page and piano rolls, not through recordings.

Scott Joplin became ragtime's special master as it began to take shape in the early to mid-1890s. At the age of seventeen, he arrived in St. Louis just as it was all beginning in 1885. The Mississippi was still a great trade and travel river and was heavy with traffic. The wealth on the river on St. Louis generated one of the most wide open "districts" in the country. The sound of syncopated pianos filled the saloons and cafes, pool halls, and parlors of the ill-famed Chestnut and Market Streets. "Jig piano," as ragtime was first called, was everywhere. Ragtime would come of age during the next eight years, centering mainly in St. Louis and another Missouri city, Sedalia.

Scott Joplin lived in St. Louis from 1885 to 1893, supporting himself by playing in the local honky-tonks. He then moved to Chicago, seeking work there in the clubs, bars, and honky-tonks that sprang up around the 1893 World's Columbian Exposition. Following this, he settled in Sedalia, Missouri, for a brief period, where he played second cornet in the Queen City Concert Band.

He spent the next two years touring with a vocal group he had formed called The Texas Medley Quartet, which included his two younger brothers Will and Robert. During this phase, Joplin began writing his own compositions. He published some of them, namely a pair of waltz songs and three piano pieces. In 1896, his vocal group dissolved and he returned to Sedalia.

This move marked a crucial turning point in Scott Joplin's career. He decided to attend an educational institution for blacks, George Smith College, sponsored by the Methodist Church. There he worked at translating the characteristic ragtime rhythms into musical notation and continued to refine his creative imagination. He composed his first rag, *The Maple Leaf Rag*, and immortalized a club in Sedalia by that name. The Maple Leaf Club became a favorite in Sedalia due to Joplin's piece, attracting the best pianists from all over to play there. Despite this fame, Joplin had difficulty getting the piece published. Both a local firm and a St. Louis publishing house which had bought his original rags turned it down. A break finally came for him in 1899 when a local Sedalia music dealer named Joseph Stark heard *The Maple Leaf Rag* and decided to publish it. This produced instant nationwide success for both Joplin and Stark.

With his newly acquired fortune resulting from *The Maple Leaf Rag*, Stack moved to St. Louis and established an expanded publishing firm. Joplin, newly married, soon followed him there. The two men developed a close relationship despite their differences of age and color. Prosperous from his royalties, Joplin was able to retire from the ragtime world of piano playing, buy a large house, and focus on teaching and composing. He continued to compose rags, and in 1902 brought out *Rag Time Dance*, a folk ballet based on material he had written three years earlier. Not long after this, his first ragtime opera, *A Guest of Honor*, appeared. Neither of these efforts met with much success, and the score to *A Guest of Honor* was subsequently lost and was never found.

Personal problems started to afflict Joplin. His baby daughter died a few months after birth, and strained relations with his wife led to a separation. She had no interest in music. After their breakup, Joplin moved back to Chicago briefly, then to St. Louis and on to New York, all within a year.

He again hit the entertainment circuit, performing in hotels and rooming houses, attempting to sell his new compositions. Joplin sold his pieces to many different publishers over the years and published some himself as well. He remarried happily in 1909, after his first wife had died, and settled into a house on West 41st Street. He later moved uptown to Harlem. He began devoting most of his time to a new opera, *Treemonisha*.

The original production of *Treemonisha* received only one performance during Joplin's lifetime, in Harlem in 1915. Lacking in scenery, costumes, lighting, and orchestral backing, the production was unconvincing. The audience, including potential backers, walked out. This dealt a terrible blow to Joplin's spirit. His health began to fail, and in the fall of 1916, he was taken to Manhattan State Hospital. He still composed occasionally but never recovered. He died in the hospital on April 1, 1917, at the age of forty-nine from complications due to syphilis.

In Joplin's later years, from 1909 on, he was moving toward more varied and interesting structures, almost toward classical forms. This probably was not deliberate or conscious but inevitable. For example, *Magnetic Rag* points toward the sonata form, and *Euphonic Sounds*, the rondo. In ragtime, form was the servant of substance.

As stated by Gunther Schuller: "It has become increasingly clear that 'form' need not be a confining mold into which tonal materials are poured, but rather that the forming process can be directly related to the musical material employed in a specific instance. In other words, form evolved *out* of the material itself and is not imposed upon it. We must learn to think of form as a verb rather than a noun."[2]

Ragtime differs from jazz and other related music because it is a body of written compositions. Where jazz is improvised or arranged music, and in some cases recordings are the only permanent illustration, ragtime is printed music for the piano. This reflects a difference in the orientation of the music. In jazz, the creative process, whether written arrangements or improvisations, involves what is done with the melody and harmony. In ragtime, the creative process involves the writing of the whole piece in all its parts, both horizontal and vertical. In this sense, ragtime is more oriented toward concert music than jazz. Some ragtime is referred to as "early jazz," however.

Ragtime is formal music, originally composed for the piano. It consists of three or four sections, each with its own melody. Improvisation and variation were not often found in classic ragtime, although they did occur in some performances around the turn of the century. Many early jazz pieces, especially Dixieland with its several sections and themes, owe their structures to ragtime.

In ragtime form, the elements of scale, key, and harmony, as well as the instrument itself, came from the "white side." The essential catalytic polyrhythms came from the "black side," going back to earlier Afro-American music and its retentions from African music of the duple and triple polyrhythms. Ragtime added syncopations to the cakewalk rhythm. This was "ragged" time.

The late cakewalk = ONE two THREE four. Ragtime = ONE and a TWO and a THREE and FOUR. Rhythmically, ragtime is characterized by its right-hand rhythmic phrases.

These typical rhythmic phrases are found in all published rags. Sixteenth-note runs stopping on a syncopated beat are common. The left hand is normally in a supporting role "oom-pah" pattern of alternating single notes and chords. The left hand rarely engaged in syncopation.

"James Scott's frequent left-hand syncopation always knows its place—that is, it is inserted in the eighth or sixteenth or perhaps seventh and eighth measures of a strain, where it will not interfere with the orthodox ragtime momentum. This rhythmic phrasing is virtually never more complicated. It is of the essence of ragtime style that it can be trusted not to throw in less regular rhythmic patterns.

One of the surest giveaways of Jelly's (Morton) *jazz*, not ragtime, posture is his hitting the left hand a sixteenth note early. This can be seen in his 'transformation' of the *Maple Leaf Rag* and *Original Rags* by Scott Joplin. No rag written would dream of such a blatant New Orleans crudity. Many of the revivalists fail to get an appropriate rag sound because of left-hand syncopation alone."[3]

Ragtime's conventional form includes the organization of the whole strain, usually sixteen bars divided into four equal parts. Many strains are organized as ABAC—"B" being a semicadence and "C" a full cadence. This organization of tunes carried over into jazz. There are few exceptions to the rule in ragtime, and even fewer in jazz, once the early New Orleans stage was over because of the requirements of improvisation.

Most ragtime compositions are organized on the basis of four strains, either ABCD or ABACD, and less often, ABACDC. In most cases, a repeat will be indicated for all strains, except the return of a strain. Of the thirty-nine Joplin rags, including the collaborations, twenty-seven are ABACD.

Joplin's rags are considered the archetype of the music and are unusually fixed until his later experimental period. In all of Joplin's literature, only two rags, *Euphonic Sounds* and *Palm Leaf Rag*, have less than four themes. Only his first and last rags have more.

Several approaches were used to develop the four-strain structure into a coherent whole. The "A" theme will usually be a straightforward statement, complete in itself, acting as a home base. The "A" theme gives the rag its individuality. The "B" theme is lighter, with a less filled-in treatment. It may begin with an unaccompanied right hand on the dominant. The "B" theme melodic line often has a tendency to soar, so that the effect of returning to "A" reinforces the home base feeling. This is further emphasized by leading off theme "A" with a tonic chord and theme "B" with a dominant chord. In Scott Joplin's *Chrysanthemum*, the "B" strain modulates to the dominant key. In his *Strenuous Life*, he modulates to the dominant chord of the dominant key.

The final two strains function to extend the development of the rag. Where the "B" strain is lighter, strain "C" is slightly darker, often modulating down a fifth in the lower register of the treble. Rhythmically, the "C" strain may have a kind of subdued excitement, which is released in the "D" strain. The "D" strain sometimes returns to the original tonic, as in *Maple Leaf Rag*, but it usually remains in the new key, the subdominant. The "D" strain often has more of a riff quality than the other strains and is generally more relaxed.

Ragtime harmony is based mostly on standard tonic-dominant changes. Extensive use of the common change tonic to submediant to supertonic to dominant back to tonic can be found. Tonic to subdominant is also used. Often, the final four bars will be IV - IV minor - I - VI - II - V - I. In the middle of a strain, the harmony will often move to the mediant minor, then to the dominant, returning to the second half of the strain. These harmonies are similar to those used in early jazz.

Harmonically speaking, everything found in early jazz is found in ragtime, except early jazz placed far more emphasis on the standard blues chorus and internal harmonies appropriate to that series of chord changes. Jazz did not require more complex harmonic resources until well into the 1920s.

One of Joplin's most famous pieces is continually played today by piano players of all levels and ages, *The Entertainer*. It first appeared in 1902, and was dedicated to James Brown and His Mandolin Club. Wandering string groups called "serenaders" performed at this time.

These groups included guitars, mandolins, fiddles, and string bass. They played ragtime, waltzes, and popular ballads in the streets and would join with the piano player when invited indoors. *The Enter-tainer* was popular among these groups.

A quote from his article "Notes on Boogie Woogie" by William Russell in the *HRS Rag* could perhaps also describe the evolution of ragtime and other popular musical forms:

"An amateur is not to be regarded however with condescension. A perusal of the history of music and other arts shows that many important creative innovations have been due to the amateur. Usually in art a new style has its inceptions with the people, and not with cultivated performers."[4]

And if you're considering playing some of Scott Joplin's rags, remember the composer's request:

"Notice! Don't play this piece fast. It is never right to play 'ragtime' fast."

(From the scores.)

Popular Song Sheets with Lyrics

Among the many popular song sheets which included lyrics, the following topics were found:

Alcohol and Prohibition

The subject of alcohol was popular among Tin Pan Alley songwriters and publishers, both pro and con. Many songs were associated with "the bottle."

Some examples include *Budweiser's a Friend of Mine* by Bryan and Furth (1907), *Glorious Beer, Beer, Glorious Beer* by Leggett and Goodwin (1895), *Ida, Sweet as Apple Cider* by Eddie Leonard (1903), *I'm on the Water Wagon Now* by West and Bratton (1903), *Little Brown Jug* by Eastburn, *Prohibition Blues* by Ring Lardner and Nora Bayes (1919), and *What'll We Do on a Saturday Night When the Town Goes Dry* by Bert Kalmar and Harry Ruby (1919).

Blackface

Blackface songs, a result of the presence of African Americans and slavery in the American South, developed from the minstrel shows into a respected musical style in the late Victorian period through the Tin Pan Alley songwriters.

Many of the song titles used the word "coon," which by today's standards is politically incorrect, and some of the caricatures on the covers appear as exaggerated stereotypes. Still, these songs are a part of American musical culture.

Blackface songs were very popular from 1890 to 1910. Some examples include *Ain't Dat a Shame* by John Queen and Walter Wilson (1901), *All Coons Look Alike to Me* by Ernest Hogan (1896), *New Coon in Town* by Paul Allen (1883), *Rufus, Rastus, Johnson, Brown (What You Gonna Do When de Rent Comes Around?)* by Andrew Sterling and Harry Von

Tilzer (1905), and *The Sound of Chicken Frying, Dat's Music to Me* by Chris Smith (1907).

Children

Although not many Tin Pan Alley songs were written about children, those that were had endearing melodies and tender lyrics. Both the song sheet covers and titles were beautiful. Mammy lullabies were very popular. The most famous children's song was *School Days* by Edwards and Cobb (1907). Other examples include *Hush Little Baby, Don't You Cry* by Rosenfeld (1884), *Little Puff of Smoke, Goodnight* by White and Lardner (1909), *Baby Shoes* by Joe Goodwin and Ed Rose (1916), *Sonny Boy* by DeSylva, Brown, and Henderson (1928), *Ten Little Fingers and Ten Little Toes* by Ira Shuster and Ed G. Nelson (1921), *There's No More Buster Brown* by Harry Breen and James Conlin (1908), and *Toyland* by Glen MacDonough and Victor Herbert (1903).

Clothing

The most frequently referred to item of clothing in Tin Pan Alley songs was the "hat," fashioned after the popular Gibson girl hairdos of 1890 to 1910. Mention was also made of pinafores, sunbonnets, bustles, bloomers, peg-bottom trousers, derbies, and raccoon coats. In the field of fashion, Tin Pan Alley perpetuated whatever Paris dictated.

Examples of clothing songs include *Bandanna Days* by Noble Sissler and Eubie Blake (1921), *Bell Bottom Trousers* by Moe Joffe (1943), *Bloomer Girl* by Arlen and Harburg (1944), *Button Up Your Overcoat* by DeSylva, Brown, and Henderson (1928), *Get on Your Sneak Shoes Children* by Gussie L. Davis (1898), *The Gingham Girl* by Fleeson and Albert Von Tilzer, *Keep Your Skirts Down, Maryanne* by King, Sterling, and Henderson (1925), *The Lady in Red* by Dixon and Wrubel (1935), *Let a Smile Be Your Umbrella* by Irving Kahal and Francis Wheeler (1927), *One, Two, Button Your Shoe* by John Burke and Arthur Johnson (1936), *Top Hat, White Tie and Tails* by Irving Berlin (1935), *Where Did You Get That Hat?* by Joseph J. Sullivan (1886), and *Who Threw the Overalls in Mrs. Murphy's Chowder?* by George L. Geifer (1899).

Current Events

Headlines fueled the songs of Tin Pan Alley, including political themes, campaigns, new laws, inaugurals, dedications to political figures or entertainers, expositions, festivals, fairs, roundups, catastrophes, and famous news celebrities. The association of a hit song with a singing or movie star helped to advertise the song. When a photograph of the star appeared on the song sheet cover, it helped to promote the star. Dedication of songs by songwriters was a show of friendship, admiration, or appreciation. "This song is respectfully dedicated to" often appeared near the top border of the song sheet cover, elsewhere on the cover, or on the inside title page. .

Examples include *Goodbye Teddy Roosevelt*, *Meet Me in St. Louis* (1904 World's Fair), *Lewis and Clark Exposition March* (1905, Portland, Oregon), *Panama Canal March and Two-Step* (1914), *The Wreck of the Titanic* (1912), and *Little Colonel*, dedicated to Shirley Temple (1935).

Dixie

"Dixie" geographically includes the entire area south of the Mason-Dixon Line. Hundreds of songs of the Southland, with or without the word "Dixie" in the title, were written during the Tin Pan Alley era. These include *I Want to Be in Dixie* by Berlin and Snyder (1912), *Rockabye Your Baby with a Dixie Melody* by Jerome and Schwartz (1918), and *There's a Lump of Sugar Down in Dixieland* by Bryan, Yellen, and Gumble (1918).

Feminine Names

During the Tin Pan Alley era, "Rose" was the most frequently used female name in a song title. It was a very fashionable name at the time and was conducive to rhyming. Other female names such as "Edna" and "Gertrude" were also popular but were much harder to rhyme. Songs with feminine names in the title were usually love songs written by men and were sometimes humorous.

Female rebellion against Victorianism came with the 1920s. Women wore bobbed hair, shorter skirts, rolled-down stockings, and smoked cigarettes, all symbols of freedom. The "vamp" was a sex symbol capable of getting her wishes and leaving a trail of broken hearts. The lyrics of these songs give an interesting insight into this rebellious time.

Many girls' portraits were used on song sheet covers, and many were very beautifully done. Girls' names frequently used in Tin Pan Alley songs were Rose, Mary, Katie, Sue, Kitty, Maggie, Sally, and Marie. Various other female names included Hannah, Bessie, Lulu, Liza, Jane, Ida, Irene, Peggy, Polly, Lessie, Rebecca, Rosalie, Ruby, and Sandy.

Flowers, Nature, and Animals

The rose, symbolic of love, is found more often than any other flower in flower-related Tin Pan Alley songs. Daisies and violets are the next two most popular. Many song sheet covers show flowers, in particular, the linens. Many dance steps were associated with animals, as the song sheets suggest. These included the grizzly bear, fox-trot, bunny hug, kangaroo hop, and tiger rag, among others.

Examples of flowers, nature, and animal songs include *And the Green Grass Grew All Around* by William Jerome and Henry Von Tilzer (1912),

Cherry Blossoms by Emma I. Hart (1907), *Down among the Sugar Cane* by Cecil Mack and Chris Smith (1908), *Who's Afraid of the Big Bad Wolf?* by Frank E. Churchill and Ann Ronell (1933), *Be My Little Baby Bumblebee* by Stanley Murphy and H. T. Marshall (1912), *When the Mocking Birds Are Singing in the Wildwood* by Lamb and Blake (1905), and *When the Red Red Robin Goes Bob Bob Bobbin' Along* by Harry Woods (1926).

Food and Beverages

Gratification from food was a subject of Tin Pan Alley songs. Examples include *Big Rock Candy Mountain, Blueberry Hill* by Stock, Lewis, and V. Rose (1940), *A Cup of Coffee, a Sandwich, and You* by Billy Rose, Al Dubin, and Joe Meyer (1925), *I'm Putting All My Eggs in One Basket* by Irving Berlin (1935), *Life Is Just a Bowl of Cherries* by Brown and Henderson (1931), *On the Good Ship Lollipop* by Sydney Clare and Richard Whiting (1934), *Oyster, a Cloister, and You* by Richard Connels (1925), *Tea for Two* by Harback, Ceasar, and Youmans (1925), *Yes, We Have No Bananas* by F. Silver and Irving Cohen (1923).

Locations

Songs about locations include Ireland, Hawaii, states, cities, rivers (e.g., the Mississippi River), Broadway, the South, Heaven, and other miscellaneous locations. For almost every state and major city, there is a song title containing its name. Rivers, mountains, and streets were all sources of sentimentality.

Two well-known examples of location songs include Paul Dresser's *Banks of the Wabash* and James Bland's *Carry Me Back to Old Virginny*, which became Virginia's official state song in 1956. Other examples include *For Freedom and Ireland* by Woodward and Mack (1900), *Blue Hawaii* by Leo Robins and Ralph Rainger (1937), *California and You* by Leslie and Puck (1914), *Chicago* by Fred Fisher (1922), *Moonlight on the Colorado* by Billy Moll and Robert King, *Give My Regards to Broadway* by George M. Cohan (1904), and *Cheyenne* by Harry Williams and Egbert Van Alstyne (1906).

Mother

Sentimental feelings having to do with a mother dying or honoring her moral attributes while living were written about in hundreds of "Mother" songs throughout the Tin Pan Alley era. These songs were done so often it sometimes became necessary to remember that mother also divorced, smoked, drank, and even had a sense of humor.

Examples of "Mother" songs include *Always Keep a Smile for Mother* by Converse (1884), *Hand-*

ful of Earth from Mother's Grave by Joseph Murphy (1883), *I Want a Girl Just Like the Girl That Married Dear Old Dad* by Will Dillon and Harry Von Tilzer (1911), *Ireland Must Be Heaven for My Mother Came from There* by McCarthy, H. Johnson, and Fisher (1916), *Mother's Prayer* by Arnstein and Gilbert (1932), *Stories Mother Told* by Frank J. Gurney (1895), *There's Nothing Will Forgive Like a Mother* by Cooper and Wege Farth (1891), and *You've Got Your Mother's Big Blue Eyes* by Irving Berlin (1913).

Novelty Songs

As sentimental songs were the mainstay of Tin Pan Alley, novelty and comical songs helped to break the monotony, developing in the twenties and thirties as signs of the times. Extra verses were added to many novelty songs such as *It Ain't Gonna Rain No Mo'*, with at least a dozen or two extra verses.

Novelty songs included *The Grass Is Always Greener* by Egan and Whiting (1924), *He Used to Be a Farmer but He's a Big Town Slicker Now* by Sterling and Harry Von Tilzer (1919), *Nobody Else Can Love Me Like My Old Tomato Can* by Downs and Baskette (1923), and *Yes, We Have No Bananas* by Silver and Cohn (1923).

Sports and Games

Although our society is very sports oriented, there were few sports-related Tin Pan Alley songs. Most had to do with horse racing and polo or college fight songs and a few about games.

Examples include *Take Me Out to the Ball Game* by Jack Norworth and Albert Von Tilzer (1908), *The Gliders-Skating Waltz* by William Schroeder (1916), and *Checkers* by Edgar Allen and Leo Edwards (1919).

Tearjerkers

Tin Pan Alley songwriters and publishers composed many tragic stories set to music. Some examples include Paul Dresser's *The Convict and the Bird* (1888), *Don't Tell Her That You Saw Me* (1896), *I Wonder Where She Is Tonight* (1899), *Just Tell Them That You Saw Me* (1895), *The Letter That Never Came* (1886), *The Outcast Unknown* (1887), and *The Pardon That Came Too Late* (1891). Songs by Ed Marks and Joe Stern include *Break the News to Mother Gently* (1892), *Don't Wear Your Heart on Your Sleeve* (1901), *His Last Thoughts Were of You* (1894), *The Little Lost Child* (1894), *My Mother Was a Lady* (1896), and *The Old Postmaster* (1900). One more example is Charles K. Harris's *After the Ball* (1892).

Transportation and Communication

Tin Pan Alley made songs about transportation and communication legendary. These songs included the railroad, the automobile, the steamboat, the telephone and telegraph, the United States Postal Department, airborne transportation, walking, the bicycle, the covered wagon, sleigh rides, trolley rides, buggies, rolling chairs, and newspapers.

Railroad songs lent themselves to the hypnotic rhythm of the train's engine moving along the track, such as *Shuffle off to Buffalo, Wabash Cannonball,* and *Casey Jones.*

Any new invention became the subject of a song, such as *I'll Build a Subway to Your Heart,* coinciding with the building of the New York subway system. Many songs about the telephone were written at the time of its invention.

Songs about walking included *Walking My Baby Back Home, Let's Take an Old-Fashioned Walk,* and *Let's Take a Walk around the Block.*

The bicycle became a national pastime in the 1890s. Henry Dacre wrote *Daisy Belle,* also known as *A Bicycle Built for Two.* Postcards and the U.S. mail were other popular Tin Pan Alley song topics, reflected in songs such as *The Postcard Girl* (1908) and those dealing with letters or the United States Postal Department.

War Songs

Tin Pan Alley produced its share of war songs, some pro, some con. With World War I came many songs and emotions, including *Don't Take My Darling Boy Away* and *America, Here's My Boy,* depending on the current political view.

War songs were comical, tragic, and patriotic. During World War I, in order to save paper, the old large-sized song sheets gave way to the present standard size. During the war, songs were printed in four sizes, including large, standard, small, and miniature for the armed forces.

Of the hundreds of songs published during World War I, *Over There* by George M. Cohan (1918) was the most popular. Issued under three different covers, Norman Rockwell's portrayal of soldiers singing by a campfire is considered the most dramatic and unique.

Other examples of war songs include *Gee! What a Wonderful Time We'll Have When the Boys Come Home* by Mary Earl (1917), *Good-by Ma, Good-by Pa* by Herschell and Walker (1918), *Goodbye, Broadway, Hello, France* by Reisner, Davis, and Baskette (1917), *Hello, Central, Give Me No Man's Land* by Lewis, Young, and Schwartz (1918), *I'd Like to See the Kaiser with a Lily in His Hand* by Leslie, Johnson, and Frisch (1918), *Joan of Arc, They Are Calling You* by Bryan, Weston, and Wells (1917), *Just Like Washington Crossed the Delaware,*

General Pershing Will Cross the Rhine by Johnson and Meyer (1918), and *Liberty Bell, It's Time to Ring Again* by Goodman and Mohr (1917).

Song Sheet Cover Art and Artists

Song sheets are collected as much for their covers as for the music itself. Those of Norman Rockwell are the most sought after, and not many were issued.

Over There, Little Grey Mother of Mine, Down Where the Lilies Grow, and the later *Lady Bird Cha Cha Cha* are the four known ones. The scarcity, along with Rockwell's popularity as the *Saturday Evening Post* artist, explains their high price.

Well-known illustrators Archie Gunn, Hamilton King, and James Montgomery Flagg also appeared as song sheet cover artists, and they, too, are rarities. Archie Gunn illustrated the cover of *The American Girl March* by Victor Herbert in the Sunday supplement to the *Examiner.* Hamilton King illustrated the cover of *Peggy O'Neil.* James Montgomery Flagg did the cover of George M. Cohan's *Father of the Land We Love.*

Almost half of all the song sheet covers were unsigned and included many outstanding and artistic covers. The signatures of over 150 different artists are found on large and standard song sheets. These should not be confused with celebrity autographs. Other notable cover artists and photographers include Alpeda, Starmer, J. V. R., Albert Barbelle, Andre Petakacs, Pfeiffer, John Frew, Frederick S. Manning, R. S., Carter/Myers/Pryor, and Gene Buck. Starmer, Barbelle, and R. S. contributed the most on both large- and standard-size song sheets. A new breed of artists emerged in the 1920s with a strong feeling for Art Deco. J. V. R. contributed greatly to this style, creating and signing many striking covers. The signatures of Art Deco artists Wohlman, Perret, Griffith, Leff, Pud, and Lane varied little and can be found easily.

E. T. Paull, composer of marches, arranger, and, later, publisher, produced extremely popular and brilliant five-color lithographed song sheet covers, executed by the A. Hoen Lithograph Company. His songs were advertised on the back side of a standard 1922 reissue as "thirty-seven magnificently lithographed songs by E. T. Paull Publishing Company." All but six of the songs were marches. Almost all were solely Paull compositions, although he collaborated with others on twelve of them. In these cases, he was probably the arranger, as in *Midnight Fire Alarm,* where Harry J. Lincoln wrote the music and Paull the arrangement. Though his covers are more prevalent than Norman Rockwell's, they are considered in the scarce category, often found dirty and torn due to their popularity.

Art Deco (1910 to 1935)

The artistic elements of Art Deco included flower garlands, fruit baskets, popular trees, fountains, nudes, geometric designs, masked harlequins, jesters, clowns, long-legged beautiful women in billowy skirts, deer, flowers, greyhounds, streamlined human figures in exaggerated positions, Cubism, and Egyptian, American Indian, Mexican, and African influences. As Art Nouveau was a revolution against traditional art, Art Deco revolted against its predecessor, Art Nouveau.

Between 1910 and 1920, cover artists such as Starmer, Pfeiffer, R. S., DeTakacs, and Frew played an active role in the development of Art Deco. By the 1920s, new names appeared on Art Deco song sheet covers, including C. E. Millard, Wohlman, G. Kraus, Perret, Politzer, and Griffith. Art Deco is well represented on song sheet covers, both large and standard size. Examples of Art Deco covers in large size include *Cabaret Rag* by Pfeiffer, *The Kangaroo Hop* by F. E. Looney, and *Tiddle-de-Winks* by Starmer. Covers in standard size include *Let Me Call You Sweetheart* by Mary Kidder, *Secondhand Rose* by Wohlman, and *You Said Something When You Said Dixie* by Wohlman.

Cartoonists

Covers by prominent Art Deco era cartoonists such as Opper, Billy DeBeck, Clare Victor, Dwiggins, Swinnerton, Gaar Williams, Paul Fung, George McManus, and Harold Gray are rare. A few examples are *Barney Google* by DeBeck, *Little Orphan Annie* by Harold Gray, and *Seattle Town* by Paul Fung from the comic strip *Dumb Dora.*

Linens

Linens were issued in both large and standard size on a superior quality white, small pebbled surface with a matte finish, distinguishing them from other song sheets. Flowers and landscapes were often found on linen cover designs. Carrie Jacobs-Bond & Sons and Sam Fox Publishing Co. used linens to print sheet music. Linen cover samples include *Basket of Roses* by Fred G. Albers (1913) in the large size, and in the standard size, *Lazy River* by Carrie Jacobs-Bond (1923).

Sunday Supplements

From 1895 to 1908, before microphones, promoters tried to popularize a song by issuing supplemental song sheets in the Sunday newspaper. These Sunday supplements were issued on low-quality paper. Over the years, many became yellowed and brittle. The covers were often drawn by cartoonists on the staff of the newspaper with which they were issued. A popular Sunday supplement artist was H. B. Eddy.

Sunday supplement songs were frequently composed for the newspapers as a good source for musical stars and musical shows. Sunday supplement song cover samples include *American Girl March* by Archie Gunn and *I Caught You Making Eyes at Me* by H. B. Eddy.

Advertising Song Sheets

The Garland Stove Company was the first to use the song sheet as an advertising medium in 1889. The cover was a black-and-white lithograph. Soon to follow was the Bromo Seltzer Company, which used 171 song selections to promote their product, mostly standards and hymns. These were distributed to local pharmacies throughout the country. Anyone could submit a two-cent stamp and a Bromo Seltzer wrapper, and in return select and receive two songs. A prime example of an advertising song sheet was a colored lithograph by Gugler Company, *Wait for the Wagon*, published by the Studebaker Brothers. Free copies were distributed in 1884 for the new year. The cover showed the four Studebaker Brothers, Adams County, Pennsylvania, where they were born, and a horse-drawn wagon of folks celebrating New Year's. On the back side was printed a four-verse parody of *Wait for the Wagon* titled *A Carol of the Studebaker Wagon*, with information promoting it. In 1941, a free song sheet titled *Honeymoon for Three* advertised the new Chevrolet, the third party being the new car. *Miss Samantha Johnson's Wedding Day* was covered the most by advertisers. Twenty different advertisers used every available border space. In some instances, parts of the music were blocked. Advertising song sheets published by the companies themselves, or expressly for the companies, are hard to find. Using song sheets as a promotional scheme was quite successful and continued throughout the Tin Pan Alley era and even later. More advertising song sheet samples include *Cable March and Two Step* by the Cable Piano Company (1903), *Song of the Great Big Baked Potato* by the Northern Pacific Railroad (before 1918), and *Way Down upon the Suwannee River* by the Southern Railway System (1921).

Cowboy and Action Westerns

The fascinating wild west was depicted in some song sheet covers, including the colorful action westerns reminiscent of Russell and Remington. Western song sheet covers include *Cheyenne*, *In the Land of the Buffalo*, and *Santa Fe Song* by Starmer.

Songs in Musicals, Silent Films, Talkies, Radio, and Records

Musicals

The earliest form of American entertainment, the minstrel shows, originated in the 1840s. By the 1880s, variety shows took over, followed by operettas, vaudeville, the follies, revues, scandals, and others, evolving into Broadway musicals. These musical entertainment forms became interwoven with Tin Pan Alley. Each contributed to the continuation of the show and its songs.

Musicals were advertised on the covers of song sheets. Samples of musical shows advertised on pre-1920 song sheets include George M. Cohan's *Hello Broadway* and Victor Herbert operettas, including *Naughty Marietta*.

The Ziegfeld Follies, which ran from 1907 until 1943, was one of the most famous musical shows. Irving Berlin's *Music Box Revues* ran from 1921 to 1924. Other famous shows included George White's *Scandals*, the *Greenwich Village Follies*, Jack Norworth's *Odds and Ends*, the *Hippodrome Shows*, Earl Carroll's *Vanities*, Schubert's *Passing Shows*, the *Wintergarden Shows*, and the *Broadway Brevities*. Major producers of the period included Daniel Arthur, Richard Carle, Charles Dillingham, Lew Fields, Joe Hertig, Klaw and Erlander, George W. Lederer, Oliver Morosco, August Pitou, Henry Savage, Mort Singer, and Whitney.

Before radios and phonographs, minstrel shows, stage shows, and vaudeville were the only avenues of song plugging available to music publishers. Not unlike today, the association of a song with a star performer ensured its success. Every publisher or song plugger used any means available to convince a star to include a song in his or her repertoire. This included anything from giving expensive gifts such as jewelry to giving up a percentage of the song's royalties. This was "payola" in its early stages.

Songs and singers were dependent on each other for survival. Songs were made successful by a star performer's rendition, and singers became successful by introducing great songs. "Sung with great success by," "prominently featured by," "introduced and sung by the phenomenal," "triumphantly featured by," and "sung with tremendous success by" were phrases used along with a star's photograph on many song sheet covers from the late 1800s through the early 1900s.

Blackface songs were the end result of the minstrel shows and were very popular at this time. Blackface song entertainers overwhelmed audiences with the power of their throaty tenor voices. In the minstrel shows, a carryover from the Civil War, the entire cast consisted of male members who personified the popular caricature of the African American in song and dance. They frequently worked in pairs, such as Primrose and West. The culmination of this impersonation came in the early 1900s with the legendary performer Al Jolson. Stars who were successful prior to and after the age of movies, phonograph, and radio included Al Jolson *(Bring Along Your Dancing Shoes)* and Sophie Tucker *(Darktown Strutters' Ball)*.

Songs of the Silent Films

In 1895, Ed Marks came up with the idea, with the help of an electrician, to photograph actors and actresses in subsequent portrayals of episodes from his tearjerker song *Little Lost Child*, cowritten with Joe Stern. These photographs were placed on slides and projected through a lantern onto a screen as the song was being sung. This was an instant success, and the lantern slide and *Little Lost Child* became synonymous. The silent movie and the theme song followed, as did the synchronization of musical score and film and, later, the *talkies*.

In 1926, Warner Brothers purchased a device called the *Vitaphone,* which synchronized a wax sound recording with a film projector. That same year, Warner Brothers produced the movie *Don Juan* with a musical score. Al Jolson sang the songs in *The Jazz Singer* in 1927. The first all-talking film, *Lights of New York,* was produced in 1928 by the Warner Brothers Vitaphone process. William Fox used a similar device called *Movietone.* Silent movie theme song covers advertised the movie from which they came. The film stars were normally shown on the cover as well as the film company and the producer. These songs were often dedicated to the stars by the songwriters.

The first movie theme song to gain national popularity was *Mickey* from Mack Sennett's 1918 film of the same name, starring Mabel Normand. This song was issued in three different sizes, with the star Mabel Normand in three different cover poses. The large- and small-sized song sheets were published in 1918. The standard sized one was issued in 1919. A second standard-sized publication with Mabel Normand in yet another pose was also published, making four total distinct song sheet covers.

Some song sheets were definitely designated as a theme song or introduced in a motion picture and are collected as such. Other silent film song sheets are collected by the stars pictured on the covers. These covers often stated that the photograph was reproduced by permission of the film company with which the star was affiliated.

Any song sheet marked *Vitaphone* or *Movietone* came from a movie that at least had partial sound. By 1930, there were no more silent films; however, Charlie Chaplin produced two such films at a later date.

Songs of the Talkies, Radio, and Records

In the post-silent screen era, radios and phonographs were becoming popular among the American people. The piano was almost completely ignored, and the player piano came to be considered out of style. Not only did pianos take up a lot of space, but a person had to work at learning how to play it. Turning a radio knob or phonograph crank was much easier and could produce many sounds at once from all over the world. "Successfully featured by" was still used on song sheet covers during the 1920s, in combination with a star and the song, but was soon replaced by "introduced by" or "as featured in."

Eventually, it was hard to distinguish if a song sheet cover star was associated with radio, film, or a record.

Some stars were popular in all three mediums, including Al Jolson, Eddie Cantor, and Sophie Tucker. The movie performers took over the song sheet covers, providing a gallery of collectible stars. Along with individual performers, famous band leaders or entire bands were being featured on the covers of song sheets.

Because they were instrumental in making so many popular hit songs, the most sought-after covers are those featuring Al Jolson, Charlie Chaplin, Shirley Temple, and Eddie Cantor. There are many covers featuring Al Jolson, Rudy Vallee, Bing Crosby, Sophie Tucker, and Ruth Etting. Bing Crosby, Shirley Temple, and Kate Smith were part of the Tin Pan Alley era early in their careers, but their greatest popularity was achieved later. Individual songs were often issued with several different stars on the covers. For example, *Bye, Bye, Blackbird* was issued with four separate covers, all identical, except for the star photographs of Gus Edwards, Frank Richardson, Olive O'Niel, or the Angelus Sisters.

Tin Pan Alley's cut off date is usually considered to be the early 1930s. Shirley Temple was born on April 23, 1928, and her first movie was produced in 1932. In 1928, Walt Disney produced his first animated cartoon, *Plane Crazy,* marking the beginning of the Disney dynasty. From the 1933 Walt Disney film *Three Little Pigs* came the first song written for an animated cartoon, *Who's Afraid of the Big Bad Wolf?*

Song sheets associated with Walt Disney and Shirley Temple are among the most sought after of those published in the post-Tin Pan Alley era, along with those issued during World War II. News, political, and exposition songs have also been popular with collectors. The post-Tin Pan Alley song sheet covers show many star celebrities from radio, records, and film.

Collecting Song Sheets

Song sheets are most valuable when they're in mint condition. If the sheet music has been damaged or reduced in size, the monetary value goes down. Sheet music is best kept in unsealed plastic bags, allowing it to breathe. The paper used for song sheets before 1900 and for the Sunday supplements was easily perishable, and requires extra care.

When determining the value of a song sheet, the following criteria are considered: age, composer's popularity, performer(s), scarcity, cover artist, category, early or late issue, condition, and identical songs with different covers or performed by different stars. Individual songs were sometimes issued under several different covers, and the same cover design may have been used for different performing artists. The best resource for current prices is *The Sheet Music Reference and Price Guide* by Anna Marie Guiheen and Marie-Reine A. Pafik. Songs are cross-referenced alphabetically by cover artists, performers, composers, and by miscellaneous categories. Many pictures of actual sheet music covers are included.

Using mint condition as the standard from which to work, the following guidelines should be followed when determining the value of a song sheet. Mint condition means near music store condition, with an absence of names, smears, tears, or frays and is valued at 100 percent. If there is a music store stamp, but the condition is otherwise mint, the value is 90 percent of the mint condition value. If the owner's name appears in ink, but the condition is otherwise very good, the value is 75 percent. A sheet with carefully trimmed edges but otherwise very good condition is valued at 65 percent. Sheets with a separated cover but otherwise in very good condition are worth 55 percent. Dog-eared or slightly frayed sheets are worth 50 percent. Torn, somewhat smeared, or badly frayed sheets are worth 25 percent. Dirty, badly torn, or incomplete sheets are valued at 10 percent.

Song sheet covers show America's character and history. Those who collect song sheets do so both for the music and for the cover design. The collector may have an interest in certain composers, stage shows, theme music from the silent movies, Walt Disney, the various dances and rhythms of the era, locations, communications, political issues, news songs, sad songs, songs about mother, or novelty songs. Those who collect by cover may do so for the cover artists, Art Deco designs, advertising song sheets, or favorite categories. Song sheets are sometimes collected as a part of other antique collections.

Song sheets are seldom in mint condition as they were used frequently when the song was in vogue. The majority of music published prior to 1900 had covers decorated with black-and-white engravings. The pre-1900 black-and-white engravings consisted of fine lines. The name of the engraving or lithograph company was ordinarily placed somewhere near the bottom of the song sheet.

There are two basic sheet music sizes. Prior to 1917, with a few exceptions, all music was published in the large 13- x 10-inch size. From 1920 onward, all music was published in the standard 12- x 9-inch size. Dimensions in both instances could vary as much as an inch. The transition period from 1917 to 1919 was during World War I. As in any war, resources were needed for the war effort. This included paper. During this time, music was published in four different sizes, those being large, standard, small, and

miniature. The small 10- x 7-inch was to help further the war effort. A miniature version 4- x 5-inch was distributed free to those in the armed services.

Because all popular music was published in the standard size from 1920 on, it is possible to date a late or early issue of a song sheet by its size, especially if the first release was prior to 1917. The first issue of *In My Merry Oldsmobile* was in 1905 and was large sized. A revival of the song reissued after 1926 was in the standard size.

"Now try this over on your piano" was a stock phrase used extensively by publishers to advertise current song issues, which were printed on the back cover or on the inside of the front cover. These current song samples had their copyright dates listed just below a printed line of the song.

First release issues are often difficult to determine. Copyright transfers can be a clue. William C. Handy's *Memphis Blues* was first published by Handy, but the copyright was later transferred to Theron C. Bennett and then again to Joe Morris Publishing Company. W. C. Handy's original publication is subsequently classified as a rare imprint.

First release songs or imprints, like first edition books, are highly valued. Whatever the reason for the copyright transfer, it is often the one and only clue to a first release. At the bottom of the title page, that being the first page of song, the copyright date of the song appears. This normally indicates the publication date of the song. If the copyright has been transferred, the original owner's date of copyright is listed first. Below this is listed the new copyright owner and date.

Successful marches, intermezzos, and waltzes prompted publishing companies to call in lyricists, changing the musical compositions into singable ballads, and thus requiring recopyrighting in the new form.

Occasionally, songs were sold to another company, which would supply the lyrics and publish the song as a ballad. This also required a copyright transfer. Songwriters would sometimes publish their own songs either because they were unable to interest a publisher or because they wished to reap the profits. If a song achieved any degree of success, publishing companies eagerly sought a copyright transfer.

Identifying the date of a song sheet publication can be difficult. There has been more interest in the printing and publishing of music in the eighteenth and early nineteenth centuries than in the publications from 1825 to the Civil War. Copyright dates are not universal in the publications before the enactment of the first U.S. copyright law in 1871.

Because music was engraved on plates, publishers often kept the plates in storage for long periods of time, printing new copies as the stock ran low. They would sometimes sell plates to other publishers who may not have bothered changing the original copyright information on the plates. A plate number can sometimes be used to identify an approximate date of publication, but that depends on how much is known about the engravers or publishers.

Care and Repair

One of the difficulties of caring for sheet music collections is that music was intended to be used, and people did just that. The sheet music may have been stored on a music rack or in a piano bench, but it was usually played or sung and, therefore, came to show signs of wear and tear. Some pieces survived better than others.

Much of the music printed from engraved plates in the nineteenth century is in fairly good condition because the paper was usually made of rags rather than wood pulp and was a little thicker than paper used for other purposes. Music printed on cheap paper made of wood pulp becomes very brittle in a short period of time.

To preserve sheet music items, they are often placed in acid-free folders, in acid-free boxes with low light conditions, in climate-controlled stacks. Albums are a good place for storage and easy viewing of song sheets, consisting of plastic envelopes sized to fit the music. Before filing, framing, or inserting into an album, it is a good idea to go over a song sheet with a soft, dry cloth to remove dirt.

Attempting to remove an ink signature by erasure or ink eradicator will only leave a white area. Watercolors can sometimes be used effectively to color the white worn or creased areas noticeable on the darker covers. A pencil signature can be carefully removed with a gum or rubber eraser. Tape carefully applied can be used to repair torn song sheets.

Many song sheets had an insert sheet. If this is missing, the value decreases, and the pages are no longer numbered consecutively. Missing inserts can be combined with incomplete copies. Before the 1920s, nearly all pianos came with a stool. Sheet music cabinets rather than benches were used for storing sheet music.

After the 1920s, pianos came with benches which could accommodate standard-sized sheet music. If a new piano was purchased, the borders of large size song sheets were sometimes cut off with scissors, leaving the music intact. Cut-down song sheets show cut off designs and lettering on the covers and were usually not cut straight.

The large size song sheets were generally considered more attractive than the standard size covers for several reasons. Pre-1920 era artists used the entire color spectrum, with no preference for any particular color.

The 1920 or 1930 era frequently used orange-blue, orange-green, orange-black, and orange-purple combinations. As the movie and record industries emerged, portraits of singers and movie stars were placed wherever they would gain exposure, including song sheet covers.

Song sheets came to serve the movie and record industry, and thus the decline in artistic covers. This was true somewhat in the pre-1920 era when vaudeville, minstrels, and stage shows were sometimes advertised on sheet music covers. But the trend became more common in the 1920s and 1930s. Simplicity of life in the 1930s was reflected in the sterile quality of interior design. This could also be seen in song sheet cover designs.

Framed song sheets complement any room and decor, and the decorating possibilities are endless. Simple frames matching or coordinating with a color in the cover art itself work best. Song sheets can be framed in pairs or sets, and may thematically compliment a room.

Song sheets have sentimental as well as monetary value and can hold a special meaning in the heart of the collector.

The Print Music Business Today

The music publishing industry was greatly affected by the new technology of the early twentieth century. Initially, the U.S. Copyright Act, on which publishing principles are based, was not keeping up with the rapid growth of technology, not unlike the situation today with Internet technology. Before the U.S. Copyright Act of 1909, there was confusion as to what should be owed to publishers by the piano roll manufacturers. The new law established that the publisher would receive two cents for each of his songs appearing on a piano roll or recording manufactured by these quickly growing American industries.

Beginning in the 1920s, recordings and radio had become important new forms of entertainment in the home. Many vaudeville entertainers had become radio stars. Publishers wanted the new radio stars to perform their songs on the radio, with the anticipation of greatly increased sheet music sales. Still more profits could be made from record sales of their songs sung by the stars.

Before the end of the 1920s, the addition of sound to film was another technological advancement creating major changes in the world of Tin Pan Alley. On October 6, 1927, the first movie musical, *The Jazz Singer*, starring Al Jolson, opened. This was the first film to use songs and moving pictures on the big screen, and it was a hit at the box office. This success caused Hollywood to turn to Broadway, and Broadway to Hollywood.

Many stars and songwriters, now in demand by Hollywood studios, headed for California. Motion picture companies began purchasing entire publishing companies from the original owners. Sheet music became a less important part of the music industry as sound recordings became prominent after World War II.

By the early 1950s, many publishers started to *job out* the printing portion of their business to companies that specialized in printing sheet music for many different publishers, including song folios, band, orchestra, and choral arrangements. This new practice led to today's *print publishers.*

Print publishers own few or no copyrights, with the exception of original material composed for teaching method books or choral productions, and the copyrights on their particular arrangements of popular or public domain songs. They print and distribute music on behalf of the publishers that hold the copyrights on the music material printed, and share in the income earned from the print sales. Very few music publishers today have their own print departments. The print business today is a much smaller part of the music industry than it was in earlier times, but it remains an important one.

By the time of Elvis Presley in the 1950s, the songwriters who had been an important part of Tin Pan Alley were writing primarily for Broadway and film, or had been replaced by younger songwriters whose songs were those with which newer audiences identified. Very few songwriters of Tin Pan Alley's heyday made the transition to rock music. Older songwriters who adapted to the new styles of popular music in the 1950s survived in the music industry. New York still had many music publishers, the new ones of which specialized in rock and pop music.

By the early 1960s, the music publishing industry followed the youthful dance crazes that were popular all over the country. The Hollywood film industry did so as well. Many publishers moved into the recording industry, signing acts to record songs composed by the publisher's staff writers. The new independent record/publishing companies achieved much success.

In 1964, the Beatles brought their songs to America, written by themselves. American publishers were not ready for this. Unlike Elvis Presley who needed songwriters, popular music acts of the middle 1960s began to write their own material.

Many publishers tried to convince the self-contained acts that it was still necessary to sign over their publishing rights to properly promote and administer their songs. Not knowing how they were going to get their songs recorded, publishers signed the artists who had recording contracts and got the publishing rights to all the songs on their albums. Many well-known acts signed away the publisher's share to publishers who did little more than profit from their work.

Many of the self-contained acts began to realize the importance of publishing. They set up in-house publishing companies with the help of entertainment attorneys and managers, consisting of song catalogs written and recorded by themselves. When recordings were sold, instead of paying the publishing royalties to an outside publisher, the record company paid them to the publishing company owned by the self-contained act.

Many of the jobs that used to be the publisher's now belonged to the record company. In the Tin Pan Alley era, it was the publishing company's job to print, distribute, and promote sheet music. When recordings came to dominate home entertainment after World War II, it became the record company's responsibility to press, distribute, and promote records. As a result of this, if a self-contained act wanted to sign a recording contract with a label, the act also had to sign a publishing agreement with the label's in-house publishing company. This is how many record companies became owners of the important popular music publishing catalogs of the 1950s through the 1970s. Similar deals are made less frequently today. Usually record labels will ask for only a percentage of the publishing as opposed to all of it.

The music publishing industry is very much alive today in New York City and Los Angeles. Publishers resembling those of Tin Pan Alley, with staff writers and song pluggers who take their songs to artists and producers on a daily basis in an effort to get them recorded, are found today on Music Row in Nashville, Tennessee. Other publishing and recording centers in the United States include Miami, Seattle, Minneapolis, Chicago, Memphis, Philadelphia, Boston, and Muscle Shoals, Alabama. There are other regions throughout the United States where publishers and print music publishers do business. For the songwriter who does not perform, there are still many performers who do not write and need new songs.

Music publishers today have started doing developmental deals with up and coming artists/songwriters who do perform. Rather than signing a songwriter to compose songs for others to record, many publishers look for singer/songwriters or self-contained acts that the publisher can take into the recording studio, walk away with a polished demo or master recording, and shop to a major record label. The publisher gets all or part of the publishing rights to the songs written by the artist in exchange for paying for the demo and production costs and helping to secure the record deal. By becoming involved in producing self-contained artists, many music publishers have survived in an industry that is constantly changing.

In recent years, music publishers have begun buying in and selling out. At one point in time, music publishing was an industry of several dozen major companies, each of which owned thousands of copyrights, and hundreds of smaller companies, each of which owned one to several hundred copyrights. The Hollywood film industry started buying up publishing companies in the early part of the twentieth century because it was an easy way to acquire many readily available songs.

Since that time, the number of publishing companies has risen and fallen considerably. While new companies are constantly emerging, new and old companies are being bought and incorporated into larger ones. The 1980s and 1990s, and into the new millennium, saw an unprecedented amount of buying and selling among music publishers. Songwriters and their songs have become part of huge catalogs, often with little priority being given to their work among thousands of other copyrights.

While performing artists, with rare exceptions, tend to come and go, great songs stand the test of time. In earlier days, they were marketed as sheet music. Today, music publishers have many ways to market songs, resulting in many different sources of income. While copyright laws and technology continue to change, it is still the music publisher that owns, promotes, and administers songs. Chapter 2 discusses the print music market today, including royalties, copyright laws, and legal issues, as well as print music formats and terms.

Notes

1. Rudi Blesh, "Scott Joplin: Black American Classicist," in *Scott Joplin Collected Piano Works* (Miami, FL: Warner Bros./CPP/Belwin, 1971), 15.

2. Gunther Schuller, "The Future of Form in Jazz" in *Saturday Review*, January 12, 1957, 62.

3. Guy Waterman, "Ragtime," in *Jazz*, ed. by Nat Hentoff and Albert McCarthy (New York: Rinehart, 1959), 47-48.

4. William Russell, "Notes on Boogie Woogie," in *Frontiers of Jazz*, ed. by Ralph de Toledano (New York: Ungar, 1962), 64.

2

Print Music Royalties, Copyright Laws, Formats, and Terms

Print Music Royalties

Before the invention of the phonograph, music publishers earned the majority of their income from the sale of printed music. Over one hundred songs sold over one million copies of *sheet music* from 1900 to 1910. Today, music publishers exploit songs in many different ways, including recordings, music videos, music for movies and television, music for the Internet and video games, music for the theater, and commercials for radio and television.

The demand for sheet music fell substantially with the coming of these new media. Today, *music print publishers* deal primarily in printed music. Many also offer instructional media in the form of audio CDs, cassettes, videos, DVDs, and CD-ROMs. Only a few major music print publishers are in operation, often acting as distributors for the smaller ones. A list of music print publisher Web sites can be found in chapter 4 under "Music, Print Music, and Music Book Publishers."

The print department of a publishing company will be in-house only if the publishing company is large. Very few publishers today have their own print departments. Instead, the copyright-owning publishing companies farm out their print work to print publishers who specialize in printing sheet music, folios, band and choral arrangements, and any other printed editions of songs. Whether the print department is in-house or not, it is the job of the copyright-owning publishing company to authorize the printing of music. It is the job of the print department or print publisher to account to the royalty department the amount of printed music that has been sold.

Print royalties are earned from the sale of printed editions of songs. This was the original source of income for music publishers and songwriters in the early days of music publishing. Although print royal-

ties are not usually as great as mechanical, synchronization, and performance royalties, printed editions of songs are still an important part of music publishing.

Print publishers must acquire the rights to create printed editions of songs. They attempt to make exclusive deals with copyright-owning publishers. Exclusive deals give the print publisher the right to create printed editions of all the songs in the publisher's catalog for a given length of time. For song publishers, the major points of negotiation for agreements with print music companies include the advance, the royalties, and the term.

One print publisher may own the print rights of a large number of copyright-owning publishers at one time. The rights the print publisher acquires can include the rights to print sheet music, folios, and arrangements for bands, orchestras, and choirs. The print publisher usually pays an advance to the copyright-owning publisher in exchange for these rights. A percentage of royalties the print publisher earns from sales of the printed editions is then paid to the publisher.

It is the publisher's responsibility to see that, once a song has become successful, it is made available in printed editions and is properly distributed. This includes use of the song in sheet music, songbooks, folios, and marching band or choral arrangements. Of the different types of printed editions available, sheet music is the most frequently published.

Songwriters earn a percentage of the retail-selling price of each copy of sheet music sold, depending on the print royalty agreement in the songwriter contract. Payment for use of a song in songbooks and folios is either a one-time fixed sum or a percentage of the retail-selling price of editions sold containing the song. The royalties from print music are usually split between the music publisher and the songwriter fifty-fifty, but some deals may vary. It is possible for a songwriter to discuss with the print publisher directly appropriate uses for a song in various print formats, deriving more income from the song in its printed versions.

Copyright Laws

Copyright law moral rights are of European origin, historically Roman, and reflect an early appreciation of the fact that the work of an artist is inseparable from the artist's soul. The work is an extension and representation of the person who created it, reflecting their inner spirit and vision, and projecting the artist's personality. The *Statute of Anne* was a 1709 British law recognized as the first true copyright law anywhere in the world. Copyright is a form of protection provided by the laws of the United States to the authors of "original works of authorship," including literary, dramatic, musical, artistic, and certain other intellectual works. This protection is available for both published and unpublished works.

A copyright gives the owner the exclusive right to reproduce, distribute, perform, display, or license his or her work. The copyright owner also has the exclusive right to produce or license derivatives of his or her work. A work must be original and in a concrete "medium of expression" to be covered by copyright law. Under the current law, works are covered whether or not there is a copyright notice and whether or not the work is registered.

United States Copyright Law

The U.S. Copyright Act is federal legislation enacted by Congress to protect the writings of authors under its constitutional grant of authority. The federal agency in charge of administering the act is the Copyright Office of the Library of Congress. Evolving technology has led to many changes in the meaning and interpretation of the word "writings." The copyright act now includes architectural design, software, the graphic arts, motion pictures, sound recordings, and Internet technology. Copyrighted works on the Internet include music, news stories, software, novels, screenplays, graphics, pictures, and e-mail. Copyright law protects the majority of the items on the Internet.

The first United States copyright act was the Copyright Act of 1790, granting copyright protection for books, maps, and charts. The first United States copyright act to grant copyright protection for musical works was the Copyright Act of 1831. The Copyright Act of 1909 called for a general revision of copyright law in the United States. It was the first law to recognize the *mechanical right*, originally licensed by publishers for works used in *piano rolls*, the first widely accepted means of recording songs. The 1909 law also helped to strengthen the *performance right*.

To prevent any one manufacturer of piano rolls from monopolizing the industry with the only recording of a popular song, Congress enacted the Compulsory Mechanical License in the Copyright Act of 1909. This law stated that once a copyright owner had recorded a song for public distribution, or had given permission to someone else to record the song, anyone could record that song as long as they followed certain procedures, including paying a royalty of two cents per recording to the copyright owner. The copyright owner, therefore, controlled the first recording of a work, but anyone willing to pay the two-cent mechanical royalty to the copyright owner could record the song.

As the phonograph came to replace piano rolls in the first half of the twentieth century, and recordings started to sell in the millions, music publishers gladly accepted the two-cent per recording mechanical royalty, half of which went to the composer. Music publishers and songwriters made millions of dollars by the 1950s and 1960s at the fixed mechanical royalty rate of two cents per recording. The mechanical royalty rate remained the same until the new Copyright Act of 1976.

On October 19, 1976, President Gerald R. Ford signed into law a new and long overdue revision of United States copyright legislation. Copyright Revision Bill S.22 became Public Law 94-553 and was the first completely new copyright law since 1909. Congress took twenty-one years to approve the modern copyright law, which began revision in 1955. Provisions of the new statute became effective January 1, 1978, superseding the Copyright Act of 1909, which remained in force until the new enactment took effect.

Most of the elements of the Compulsory Mechanical License of the 1909 act were retained in the Act of 1976, with "mechanicals" referring to all recorded media, including vinyl records, tapes, CDs, music boxes, and MIDI disks played only in audio format. The mechanical royalty rate was raised from two cents to two and three-quarter cents or one-half cent per minute of playing time, whichever was greater. The Copyright Royalty Tribunal, a panel established to review royalty rates on compulsory licenses of all types, would periodically review the rate.

Although this panel no longer exists, increases in compulsory royalties have been revised under the jurisdiction of the copyright office and continue to be subject to revision. This involves negotiation between copyright owners and users and requires approval of the copyright office. The mechanical royalty rate from 2004 through 2005 is 8.5 cents per recording and is the maximum rate allowed by statute.

Occasionally lower mechanical rates are negotiated between copyright owners and record companies, especially in the commercial music industry. MIDI disks with computer codes other than audio, for example, those that can print scores, and CD-ROMs that contain visual images, are not covered by the Compulsory Mechanical License, and a separate fee must be negotiated between the copyright owner and the producer of the MIDI disk or CD-ROM.

The 1976 law established a single national system of statutory protection for all copyrightable works, whether published or unpublished. Common law, which gave a work protection under the common laws of the various states before it was published, was superseded by the single national system effective January 1, 1978.

Notice of Copyright

The new law does call for published copies of music to contain the notice of copyright; however, omission or errors in the notice of copyright do not immediately result in the copyright becoming public domain. The copyright notice on any tangible work, be it printed or recorded, should include (1) the symbol, either the letter "C" in a circle "©," the word "Copyright," or the abbreviation "Copy," (2) the first year of publication of the work, and (3) the name of the copyright owner of the work, or its abbreviation; in the case of compilations or derivative works using previously published material, the date of first publication may be used and/or the new date; examples: Copyright 2001 Elizabeth C. Axford; © 2001, 1992 Piano Press. A copyright notice should appear on all copies of a piece of music, even if it has not been registered with the U.S. Copyright Office.

Duration of Copyright

By the Copyright Act of 1976 and the subsequent Copyright Term Extension Act passed in 1998, the duration of copyright provides for the following terms: (1) works published before 1923 are in the public domain; (2) works published between 1923 and 1963 have an initial term of twenty-eight years and must be renewed for an additional sixty-seven-year term for a total of ninety-five years; (3) works published between 1964 and 1977 have an initial twenty-eight-year term plus an automatic sixty-seven-year second term for a total of ninety-five years; (4) works published after 1977 have a term of the life of the author plus seventy years, or in the case of works with multiple authors, seventy years after the death of the last surviving author.

Fair Use

There are limited exceptions to the exclusive rights of copyright owners for certain types of "Fair Use." These include such use by reproduction in copies or phonorecords or by any other means for purposes such as criticism, comment, news reporting, teaching, scholarship, or research and are not considered an infringement of copyright.

There are four factors, which are used in determining a Fair Use. These include (1) the purpose and character of the use, including whether such use is of a commercial nature or is for nonprofit educational purposes; (2) the nature of the copyrighted work; (3) the amount and substantiality of the portion used in relation to the copyrighted work as a whole; and (4) the effect of the use upon the potential market for or value of the copyrighted work. The fact that a work is unpublished does not influence a finding of Fair Use if it is made by considering all the above factors.

This first factor takes into account the following three subfactors: (1) commercial nature or nonprofit educational purposes; (2) preamble purposes, including criticism, comment, news reporting, teaching, scholarship, or research; and (3) degree of transformation.

The second factor acknowledges the fact that some works are more deserving of copyright protection than others and attempts to determine where the work is in the spectrum of worthiness of copyright protection.

The third factor looks at the amount and substantiality of the copying in relation to the copyrighted work as a whole. The critical determination is whether the quality and value of the materials used are reasonable in relation to the purpose of copying and is not a pure ratio test. The quantity, as well as the quality and importance, of the copied material must be considered.

The fourth factor considers the extent of harm to the market or potential market of the original work caused by the infringement, taking into account harm to the original, as well as harm to derivative works.

Photocopying of Print Music

Regarding the photocopying of print music, the Fair Use guidelines include (1) emergency copying to replace purchased copies which for any reason are not available for an imminent performance, provided purchased replacement copies shall be substituted in due course and (2) for academic purposes other than performance, single or multiple copies of excerpts of works may be made, provided that the excerpts do not comprise a part of the whole which would constitute a performable unit such as a section, movement, or aria, but in no case more than 10 percent of the whole work; the number of copies shall not exceed one copy per pupil.

Under the Fair Use guidelines, the following are expressly prohibited: (1) copying to create or replace or substitute for anthologies, compilations, or collective works; (2) copying of or from works intended to be "consumable" in the course of study or teaching such as workbooks, exercises, standardized tests and answer sheets, and like material; (3) copying for the purposes of performance except for emergency copying to replace purchased copies as outlined in (1) of the Fair Uses; (4) copying for the purpose of substituting for the purchase of music, except as in Fair Uses (1) and (2); and (5) copying without inclusion of the copyright notice which appears on the printed copy.

It is important to note that copyright protection is not related to the print status of a piece of music. Permission must be granted for copying a piece of out-of-print music. Photocopying a piece of out-of-print music is as much an infringement of copyright as copying one that is in print. Check the copyright notice for the date and subsequent duration of copyright on any piece of music that is out of print.

Other uses requiring permission from the publisher include photocopying works from collections, extra parts for bands, or choral or speaking parts for musicals. Most contests prohibit the use of photocopies and require that an original copy of the music be provided to the judges.

Public Domain

Public domain is the repository of all works that for any reason are not protected by copyright and are free for all to use without permission. Works in the public domain include items that by their very nature are not eligible for copyright protection such as ideas, facts, titles, names, short phrases, and blank forms.

The public domain contains all works which previously had copyright protection but which subsequently lost that protection. An example includes all works published before January 1, 1978, that did not contain a valid copyright notice. Owners of works published between 1978 and March 1, 1989, that did not contain a valid copyright notice were given a five-year grace period in which to correct the problem before their work was placed into the public domain.

The public domain contains all works for which the statutory copyright period has expired. Any work published before 1964 in which the copyright owner failed to renew the copyright is considered public domain. Copyrightable works may enter the public domain if the copyright owner grants the work to the public domain.

Some aspects of a piece of music may be protected by copyright, while other parts are in the public domain. For example, although a piece of music and its lyrics may be in the public domain, a specific recording of the music may be protected by copyright. Anyone wishing to use that recording would be required to get a master recording license from the holder of the recording rights.

Furthermore, some parts of a piece of music, for example, the melody, may be in the public domain, while other parts, say the lyrics, may be protected by copyright. The rights to a specific recording may be held by someone different from the holder of the rights to the music, lyrics, or arrangements.

Performing Rights Organizations

ASCAP, BMI, and SESAC are licensing organizations that collect performance royalties (radio airplay, TV broadcasts, Web casts, etc.) through licensing fees, which are then distributed to the organizations' members, including artists, songwriters, lyricists, and composers. More detailed information on these organizations can be found at their respective Web sites.

ASCAP, BMI, and SESAC are excellent resources for identifying the copyright holder for any given piece of music, or of a particular recording of a piece of music. These organizations have Web sites with searchable databases, making it possible to find the rights holders to any piece of music in question. These Web sites, along with many others with information on copyrights and current copyright issues relating to the Internet, are listed in chapter 4 under "Copyright, Legal, and Tax Information-Performing and Mechanical Rights-Government Grants."

Compulsory Mechanical License

Artists may record a *cover version* of any song through a compulsory mechanical license. A compulsory mechanical license is authorized by copyright law and issued by the Copyright Office. This license can be secured without the permission of the copyright owner and allows the licensee certain use rights of copyrighted material. All compulsory licenses, however, have many conditions, restrictions, fee payment requirements, and liabilities inherent to their use that are defined by copyright law. Information on procedures that must be followed to obtain such a license may be received from the Copyright Office or its Web site.

Who Can Claim a Copyright

(1) The author of the work; (2) Anyone to whom the author has assigned his or her rights of ownership to the copyright; (3) In the cases of a work made for hire, the employer rather than the employee, or creator, is regarded as the author and can claim copyright. Only those authorized people are permitted to sign the copyright application form.

Copyright Registration and Forms

Copyright registration is a legal formality intended to make a public record of the basic facts of any given copyright. Although registration is not required for protection, the copyright law provides several advantages to encourage copyright owners to register their work.

Registration establishes a public record of the copyright claim. Before an infringement suit may be filed in court, registration is necessary. If made before or within five years of publication, registration will establish evidence in court of the validity of the copyright and of the facts stated in the certificate. If registration is made within three months after publication of the work or prior to an infringement of the work, statutory damages and attorney's fees will be available to the copyright owner in court actions.

Otherwise, only an award of actual damages and profits is available to the copyright owner. Copyright registration allows the owners of the copyright to record the registration with the U.S. Customs Service for protection against the importation of infringing copies.

The Copyright Office supplies various application forms for copyright registration. *Form PA* is for works in the performing arts, including published and unpublished musical works, any accompanying music, motion pictures, and other visual works. This form does not cover sound recordings. *Form SR* is for sound recordings and includes published songs. *Form TX* is for nondramatic literary works, including all types of published and unpublished works. The form covers lyric books and also poems that may be used as lyrics. *Form RE* is for renewal registrations. *Form CA* is for correction of an error in a copyright registration or to amplify the information given in a registration. Most applications for copyright will be made on Form PA, and are then issued a PA copyright number. These forms may be obtained for free by writing: Copyright Office, Library of Congress, Washington, D.C. 20559-6000 or call (202) 707-3000, or visit the Web site.

To register a work for copyright, send the following in the same package to the Register of Copyrights, Copyright Office, Library of Congress, Washington, D.C. 20559-6000: (1) a properly completed application form; (2) a nonrefundable filing fee for each application; (3) a complete recording (cassette, CD, etc.) of the work or a lead sheet or complete score; (4) a complete lyric sheet, if applicable.

Prior to 1978, songwriters had to submit lead sheets of their work for copyright registration. Because many songwriters could not notate music, this requirement was changed in the Copyright Act of 1976 to allow recordings such as demo tapes to be used instead. It is important to keep a copy of any submission, as the one submitted to the Copyright Office will not be returned.

For the copyright registration of musical works, the new law allows for one complete copy or recording of an unpublished work to be submitted. For a published work, two complete copies or recordings of the best edition of the work must be submitted.

More than one song per application may be registered as a "collection" under a single title. This is an economical means to protect two or more songs under the same copyright registration number. If there is interest in a particular song by a publishing, production, or recording company, it is best to register it separately.

Assignment of Copyright

This states that the writer assigns or transfers the copyright ownership of a musical composition to a publisher. Under copyright law, this may be done in full or in part. Exclusive rights, that is, rights that may be exercised only by a single person or company in copyright, are divisible.

Copyright Infringement of Musical Compositions

A copyright registration certificate does not guarantee originality of a song. It is evidence of the approximate date of a song's creation. This information and registration certificate is necessary in order to file a lawsuit against an alleged infringer of a composition in federal court. A lawsuit in federal court as opposed to state court provides for stipulated damages and in some circumstances for tripling those damages.

Before January 1, 1978, an original work that had not been published was protected under the common law without requiring the filing of a copyright claim. In the event an infringement occurred regarding an unregistered composition, one would bring a lawsuit in the state court under common law. To prove plagiarism or copyright infringement, one had to prove substantial similarity between the songs and that the alleged copier had access to the song.

Copyright infringement cases involving musical works deal initially with similarity. Substantial similarity between two compositions brings up the possibility of an infringement. Despite the popular misconception, there is no rigid standard for the exact number of duplicate bars that will constitute an infringement. If substantial similarity is found, then the element of "access" must be considered to determine if the alleged copier had access to the song. Access may include anything from hearing a song played on the radio to seeing a written lead sheet of the song.

The Audio Home Recording Act of 1992

This act allows for the digital copying of copyrighted music. It is generally acceptable to make one copy of copyrighted music, provided it is for personal use and not for distribution to others. Fees are built into the sales of all blank digital media and digital recorders, which are collected and distributed to copyright holders. The act requires a built-in fee of 3 percent to be added to all blank digital tapes and of 2 percent to be added to all digital recording devices. The fees are collected and distributed to copyright holders, including record companies, publishers, performers, and songwriters. Included in the act was the requirement of the inclusion of a Serial Copy Management System (SCMS) circuit to be included in all digital recorders. The circuit allows users to make copies of copyrighted works but not to make second-generation copies, or copies of copies.

The Digital Performance Rights in Sound Recording Act of 1995

This act gives copyright owners of sound recordings the exclusive right, with some limitations, to perform the recording publicly by means of a digital audio transmission. This act extends the provision for compulsory mechanical licenses to include downloadable music.

The Digital Millennium Copyright Act of 1998

This act states that without permission from a song's owner, it is illegal to make copyrighted music available online for unlimited distribution. This law also puts specific limitations on the length of public broadcasts, the types of song and artist announcements, and the frequency and sequence of songs played.

Print Music Formats

Print music publishers license the rights to print, package, and distribute music from the publisher, copyright owners, or administrators. Printed music falls into two main categories: *popular* and *educational*.

Popular Print Music

Popular music includes pop songs, rhythm and blues, dance, rock and roll, adult contemporary, alternative, country, new age, jazz standards, gospel, contemporary Christian, and other radio hits that appear on the charts. They are printed as single *song sheets* and collections of songs in *songbooks* or *folios*.

Popular print music includes *sheet music, mixed folios,* or collections of songs by a variety of artists around a theme such as *Hits of the Sixties,* or *Country Song Hits of the Nineties, matching folios,* those that match a specific record album, movie, TV show, or Broadway musical and have the same cover art or photo, and *personality folios,* which include collections of an artist's or group's songs or greatest hits.

Major publishers of popular music will not print sheet music for a song unless it has become a *hit single* as a recording, and has more than likely been on the *Billboard Hot 100 Chart* or is a *Top 100 Album.* Print publishers will often publish various *arrangements* of popular songs, in addition to a sheet music version that matches the key and style of the original recording.

Not all hit songs are considered marketable as sheet music. Because printing costs are high, print publishers will print only those songs that have made it to the top of the popular song charts, are well suited as piano/vocal/guitar arrangements, or those that have become standards over time. For example, a popular groove-oriented dance tune with two chords may never be released as sheet music as the arrangement would be "thin" and the demand would more than likely be minimal.

Sheet music buyers are often musicians who want to learn how to play songs for performances such as weddings, casuals, or piano bars, music teachers and students, or hobbyists on their instrument. The sheet music section of a local music store will usually include racks of current hits and many standards from all eras.

Current popular print music formats include *Piano/Vocal/Guitar, Easy Piano, Five-Finger Piano (Very Easy), Guitar Tablature, E-Z Play,* and *Fake Books.* Piano/Vocal/Guitar arrangements consist of three staves, with the top line including the melody line and song lyrics. Sometimes the song lyric is written all the way through on multiple pages. In some cases, only the first verse, chorus, and bridge are written out, with any additional lyrics typed on the last page and direction signs instructing the player to repeat certain sections. Above the top line will appear guitar chord symbols either as alphabet letters or actual tablature.

The bottom two lines of a Piano/Vocal/Guitar arrangement will include a treble and bass clef with a piano accompaniment (indicated by a brace joining the two lower staves), that may or may not include the song melody. It is usually the Piano/Vocal/Guitar arrangement that most closely resembles the original recording. When these arrangements are written in the same key, as they often are, they can actually be practiced along with the original recording.

Easy piano arrangements consist of two staves, usually treble and bass clef, and include the song melody, a simple piano accompaniment, the song lyric, and chord symbols above the top staff. Because these are "easy" piano arrangements, they are sometimes not in the same key as the original recording and are often in the "easy" keys of C, F, or G major, or a related relative minor key.

Five-finger piano arrangements are written on two staves, usually treble and bass clef, and include only the song melody as single notes played between the two hands, with a few accompaniment notes, and in easy keys. Song lyrics and simple chord symbols may be included.

Guitar tablature books are written for guitarists and include the guitar chords, song lyrics, and, occasionally, guitar solo transcriptions. Fake books include only the melody line, lyrics, and chords of a song and are usually used by professional performing musicians who can improvise around the tune at a glance. E-Z Play books are similar to fake books, but the print is usually larger and the actual note names are printed on the note heads. They are frequently used for playing the organ or electronic keyboards with one-finger chord accompaniment functions.

While some popular songs work well as piano arrangements, especially those which are "piano-based," meaning the piano was used substantially in the original recording, others do not. For example, a student will have a hard time playing a heavy metal guitar song on the piano, especially if there is no clearly defined melody line, and the original recording is comprised primarily of melodic fragments and guitar riffs. Similarly, a "piano-based" song might not lend itself well to guitar chord strumming or finger-picking patterns.

The popular songs that sell the most as sheet music editions are those that cross over into a variety of instrumental markets. A recent example of a major sheet music seller is the theme from the movie *Titanic* by James Horner, *My Heart Will Go On*. Melodically, this song adapted to many different instrumental arrangements. Other examples of extremely popular sheet music sellers include *Theme from Love Story*, *Theme from Ice Castles*, *The Rose*, *Music Box Dancer*, and any of the twentieth-century popular songs that have become standards.

Educational Print Music

Although many arrangements of popular songs can be found in educational print music, especially piano and guitar methods and those for school bands and orchestras, chart action is not a factor when considering original educational material.

Educational print publishers look for work that fits into their publishing program and is appropriate for those who use their music, such as private teaching studios, school and church choirs, and school bands or orchestras. Unlike popular song publishers, choral, religious, and educational print music publishers want a fully written arrangement included in a submission package. A print music publisher needs every note of the arrangement to be legible, clear, and complete. Composers and arrangers must be familiar with the capabilities of school age performers or church musicians.

Educational print music includes choral, band, orchestral and instrumental ensemble arrangements, and *instrumental method* or *how-to books*. There are companies who print both popular and educational music, those who produce just popular music, and those that fall into various areas of educational print music, such as piano methods or band and orchestra. There are religious print publishers who publish sheet music, books, and choral music, and distribute primarily to churches and religious bookstores.

Educational and religious print companies accept original songs suitable for choral arrangement, in some cases requesting 2-, 3-, or 4-part harmony. When submitting a choral piece to a print publisher, it is a good idea to also send a recording of the piece being performed by singers in the age group for which the arrangement is intended, such as elementary or high school students. This will show that the notes in the arrangement are within the singing range of the particular age group. Look for material similar to the composition and direct submissions to that publisher. Submissions should be made to someone on the choral publisher's editorial staff. It is a good idea to call before submitting to get a contact name.

Other educational print publishers look for original piano, jazz band, concert band, marching band, or instrumental ensemble pieces. Instrumental arrangements for high school marching and jazz bands and college or community orchestras make up a large market. Submissions of band and orchestra arrangements to potential print publishers are made in the same format as submissions of choral arrangements.

When submitting an arrangement for a marching band, the piece needs to be in 4/4, 2/4, or 6/8 time (march tempo) on a full score lead sheet. Do not send the individual parts that each musician reads. The publisher will want to hear a recorded performance of the arrangement by a high school band or community orchestra. The cover letter should be similar to the one used for a choral arrangement submission.

Arrangements

Many music educators have done some arranging for their students. The issue of copyright must be considered before making an arrangement. An arrangement of a copyrighted work done without permission from the copyright owner is considered an infringement of copyright.

One of the five exclusive rights granted to copyright owners is "the right to prepare derivative works based on the copyrighted work." A derivative work is defined as any adaptation of a copyrighted work. In music, derivative works include arrangements, transcriptions, simplified editions, adaptations, translations of texts, orchestrations, and instrumental accompaniments to vocal publications and parody lyrics. Permission must be granted before arranging, adapting, simplifying, editing, or translating a copyrighted work.

To obtain permission to make an arrangement, it is first necessary to identify the copyright owner. The copyright notice at the bottom of the first page of a printed sheet music edition provides this information, or the credits on a CD label or insert. This information can also be obtained from ASCAP, BMI, or SESAC, with the exact title and writer information. Always check the copyright date. If the work was published before 1923, it is in the public domain and permission is not necessary to make an arrangement.

After locating the copyright owner, it is necessary to write and request permission to make an arrangement of the work. It is important to be specific and provide as much information as possible, including the type of arrangement, the number of copies or parts, who will be performing the arrangement, who will actually be making the arrangement, and whether or not the arrangement will be sold.

It is also important to note if the arrangement is to be used for one occasion only, or if it will be performed regularly. The more information provided, the better the chance of getting a response from the publisher. This information is necessary for them to decide if permission should be granted to make the arrangement, and whether or not to charge a fee.

A copyright owner is not obligated to grant permission to make arrangements. For example, if the type of arrangement suggested has already been done, the publisher may deny the request. If the request is within reason, the copyright owner will grant permission to arrange and may or may not charge a fee.

The copyright owner will always require a copyright notice to be shown on an arrangement and will specify how it should be stated. In the case of an instrumental arrangement, the copyright notice should appear on the score and all the accompanying parts.

If permission to arrange is denied, then an arrangement should not be done as the arranger could be sued for copyright infringement.

Publishers consider the sale of unauthorized arrangements a serious copyright infringement. Several popular music publishers have successfully sued jazz and marching band arrangers who have sold unauthorized arrangements, resulting in stiff fines and penalties from the courts.

One more important point: arrangements themselves are copyrightable and may not be adapted or orchestrated without permission, even if the basic work is in the public domain.

Adaptations

An adaptation of a work can range anywhere from a complete orchestration to changing several notes in one part of a choral work. Permission must be obtained to adapt a musical work in any way.

Any adaptation which may result in lost sales for the publisher, or which changes the character of the work, requires permission from the copyright owner. This includes instrumental accompaniments to vocal or choral works.

One Fair Use that covers adaptations is the case of printed copies that have already been purchased. They may be edited or simplified, as long as the fundamental character of the work is not distorted or the lyrics changed, or lyrics added if there were none.

The general principle of Fair Use will help to determine whether or not permission should be requested to adapt a work.

Transcriptions

Prior to transcribing a copyrighted musical work or arrangement from one format to another, for example, from a chamber ensemble to a piano duet, permission must be obtained from the copyright owner

of the work. Parody lyrics, altered texts, and translations also require permission from the copyright owner.

Writing, Arranging, and Copying

Writing, arranging, and copying can be a good source of income for musicians skilled in these areas. This includes writing lead sheets, full arrangements, and scores. It is a good idea to network at recording studios, jingle agencies, music schools and conservatories, music stores, music trade conventions, and songwriter groups to meet the people who need these services. Transcribers, arrangers, and specialists on their instrument can have lucrative print music careers.

Lyric Sheets

A lyric sheet is a sheet of paper containing the typed lyrics or words to a song. The purpose of the lyric sheet is to make the lyrics of a song accessible to the listener and to avoid the possibility of misheard lyrics. When submitting songs to song publishers, it is essential that a lyric sheet be included with the song demo.

Lyric sheets should be typed or computer generated on standard-sized paper (8.5- x 11-inch) with the title at the top. The song title should be in capital letters. The chorus should be in capital letters or indented, or both. It is also acceptable to type all the lyrics in capital letters, and type the title and chorus in boldface caps. In either case, the style should be consistent.

The lyric should be centered from top to bottom and symmetrically aligned with the margins. Set the lyrics up so that the parts of the song stand out. The way a lyric is set on the page should clearly indicate the sections of the song. Labeling the verse, chorus, and bridge is optional but not necessary. It is also not necessary to retype a chorus that has identical wording. Typing "Chorus" or "Repeat Chorus" or "Chorus Repeats" is sufficient.

A lyric sheet should be as clean and uncluttered as possible. It is not necessary to insert chord changes over the lyrics or the melody note names. Handwritten lyric sheets or a typed lyric sheet with handwritten chord notations look unprofessional. Never make ink or pencil corrections on a lyric sheet. If there are errors, retype the lyric sheet.

Besides the lyrics themselves, the only information the lyric sheet needs to contain is the copyright notice and the name, address, phone number, and E-mail address of the songwriter(s). If the lyric sheet is typed on plain paper, this information should appear at the bottom of the page, at least two spaces below the copyright notice.

Using letterhead stationery gives a more professional look to a lyric sheet, although lyrics typed neatly on plain white paper are perfectly acceptable.

Most word processing programs can generate a letterhead each time a lyric sheet is printed. It is easy enough to purchase special paper, for example, "gray marble" to add a letterhead to, with each separate printing of the lyric sheet. This can help the writer to avoid the cost of having stationery specially printed and having leftover, unused, or shelf-worn paper.

Custom printed or typed cassette, J-card or CD labels, envelopes, and address labels also look much more professional than handwritten ones. The songwriter should be prepared with multiple copies of lyric sheets for demo and recording sessions as well as song pitching opportunities.

Lead Sheets

Lead sheets communicate the melody, chords, and lyrics of a song in written format. Before the Copyright Act of 1976, songwriters were required to submit a lead sheet with any song sent in for registration with the United States Copyright Office. As of the new law effective January 1, 1978, a cassette recording and lyric sheet are considered sufficient documentation for copyright registration.

Lead sheets are no longer required as part of the copyright registration process, nor are they appropriate or necessary to send as part of a song submission package to a song publisher. They may still be used for copyright purposes, however. It is not necessary to submit a complete piano arrangement of the song. The melody line, lyrics, and chords are sufficient. There is also the argument that a paper copy of a song may have a longer shelf life than a magnetic tape. CDs are also more durable than a cassette tape for the purpose of copyright registration.

A lead sheet is musical manuscript handwritten, engraved, or computer generated on five-line staff paper. Lead sheets made on ten-stave paper are easier to read than those done on twelve-stave paper. If the melody notes and rests are written in pencil, mistakes can be easily erased and corrected. There are many computer software notation programs available that can produce lead sheets as well as complete scores in a variety of formats. These are listed in chapter 3 under "Notation, Scoring, and Transcription Software."

A properly formatted lead sheet should include the following:

(1) The song's title and the author(s) of the words and music; (2) contact information, including name, address, telephone number, e-mail address, and/or Web site; (3) copyright notice on the first page, even if the song has not been registered with the Copyright Office; (4) the style or tempo of the music should be placed above the first measure such as "waltz" or "moderately"; (5) a treble clef sign as all lead sheets are written in the treble clef; (6) the key signature, indicated by accidentals after the treble clef sign; (7) the time signature directly after the key signature; (8) vertical bar lines separating the measures; (9) notes below the third line should have stems going up and on the right side; notes on or above the third line should have stems going down and on the left side; (10) even spacing; (11) complete measures; each measure must contain the exact combination of note and/or rest values as indicated by the top number of the time signature; (12) the lyric typed below the musical staff with each word or syllable placed directly under the note it corresponds to; for a sustained note such as a tie or whole note, insert the word or syllable directly under the note and draw a straight line from the bottom of the last letter of the word or syllable to the beginning of the next note or rest; (13) chord symbols should be written in their proper places above the musical staff, above a particular note, rest, or beat; (14) measure or rehearsal numbers; (15) section breaks.

It is important to keep a master copy of a lead sheet, sending out only duplicate copies. The three basic techniques for reproducing lead sheets and other music manuscripts include the diazo process white-print reproduction, photocopying, or photo-offset reproduction.

The diazo process white-print reproduction is the most flexible method of manuscript reproduction. Copies come in many sizes, they can be printed on one or both sides, and they may be bound in many ways. Paper with a special diazo chemical coating is used for this process. The transparent master copy of a work, preferably dense, black engrossing ink printed on a special kind of onion skin paper referred to as deschon or vellum, is placed in contact with the paper and is then exposed to ultraviolet light, then developed in ammonia fumes. The copies come out as black print on white paper.

Photocopying is the reproduction of copies by photocopying machines. It is a convenient method to use because of the availability of photocopying machines and the most economical when only small quantities are needed. Two-sided prints can be punched and bound with a plastic binding. Photocopying machines can reproduce 8.5- x 11-inch and 11- x 17-inch copies as well as color copies for covers.

Photo-offset reproduction or offset printing is the most economical process to use when over five hundred copies of a work are needed. In this process, the manuscript is photographed and a printing plate is made from the photographic negative. This plate is then mounted on a rotary press, inked, and the image is printed onto a rubber blanket on the press. The resulting copies are clear and professional.

For more information and prices on reproduction techniques, consult a music copyist or printer listed in the yellow pages under *Music Copyist, Music Manuscript Reproductions,* or *Music Printers and Engravers,* or in advertisements in trade magazines or online.

Those unable to write or generate a computer lead sheet can seek the help of someone who knows how to notate music. They can sing, present on cassette tape, or play the song on an instrument to a music copyist or stenographer, arranger, musician, music teacher, or friend who is able to write a lead sheet. A fee will be charged for the transcription of the melody onto paper and the notation of the chord symbols and lyrics. Professionals can be found in the yellow pages under *Music Copyists, Music Arrangers, Music Teachers,* or in the trade magazines or online.

Many arrangers will use a lead sheet when writing out the musical parts of a song. While some parts are worked out intuitively or by ear, other songs are recorded by groups of musicians who read off charts. In writing out the charts, the arranger works from the original lead sheet of the song. It is best if the lead sheet is written as uncomplicated as possible so that a vocalist or musician can interpret the song without becoming confused.

A lead sheet can be helpful in the demo-making process of a song, especially when hiring musicians who do not know the song. However, experienced musicians will usually make a spontaneous *head arrangement*, using only a chart showing the chord changes written over the lyrics on the lyric sheet.

In Nashville, charts using the Nashville Number System are used with session players. These charts include the chords written as Arabic numerals that can easily be transposed to any key. A work-tape of a song demonstrating the suggested style and groove is helpful for a demo-recording session. A great song demo is useful for communicating the song's intended interpretation to a publisher or producer. Despite all the technological advancements in computer-generated lead sheet production, in today's market, it is still the recorded demo that sells the song.

If a song is going to be recorded by an artist for commercial release, it is a good idea to supply the producer with a full lead sheet, showing melody, chords, rhythms, and lyrics, in addition to a quality song demo. The degree to which the songwriter's ideas are adapted in the final recording can vary considerably. Having strong ideas initially, such as a strong intro lick or groove pattern, will best help to influence the final outcome of the production.

Only if a popular song is a hit will sheet music be printed. At this stage, it is very important that the music publisher be supplied with an accurate lead sheet to use as a reference. Most music publishers want the sheet music to be like the final recording, reflecting the creative changes that took place in the studio.

The most important quality of a professional-looking lead sheet is legibility. The musical notation must be accurate. The notes must add up to the correct number of beats per measure, and the stems must face the right direction. The lyrics should be clearly written and accurately placed under the appropriate notes.

Many successful singer/songwriters do not play an instrument or know how to write songs down. Many of the great jazz and blues artists did not use writing to communicate their songs and arrangements to others. They learned by listening and played by ear. This method is used by many pop and rock musicians today. It is not necessary to know how to notate music in order to create it. Writing down music is simply another form of communication and documentation, another skill. A good natural ear can create great music with or without this skill.

Lead sheets may be used to teach songs to others, especially for songwriters who can't sing on key. Lead sheets are a convenient reference on the songwriter's piano or shelf. Having a lead sheet makes it possible to play a song on the spot, be it for pleasure, to share with others or to rework the song. Tunes or parts of a tune may be written out then returned to later when the writer is inspired to finish it.

A tape recorder is a powerful songwriting tool and can be used as an auditory notebook. Using a tape recorder gives the songwriter an opportunity to review his or her ideas as well as a way to communicate ideas to a collaborator or other musicians working on a song. Synthesizers, drum machines, sequencers, MIDI devices, and music software have created many new possibilities for musical experimentation and home recording for the songwriter. Chapters 3 and 4 list many of the options available.

Chord Charts

The standard lead sheet format is not always necessary. Many instrumentalists find a chord chart to be sufficient, even preferable. A chord chart must clearly show the chords and when they change. Typing out the complete lyric of the song and placing each chord symbol directly above the word or syllable where the change occurs accomplishes this.

Some chord charts are written out using rhythm-figure notation or slash marks. These marks use the same system of open and filled-in noteheads and stems, flags, and beams as standard notation, except that the quarter-note slash mark is usually drawn without a stem. When the rhythm is consistent, only quarter-note slashes are used. Important riffs or musical hooks can be indicated in standard notation. Stops, pushes, or anticipated rhythms can be written in as well as chords that change off the beat. This type of chord chart can be used by any instrumentalist and by singers when the lyric is added.

The Nashville Number System

Most Nashville musicians substitute Arabic numerals in place of chords or note symbols when making musical notations. This quick and effective system has become standard. Using this method, musicians can hear a song one time, write out the numbers, and then play it. If the key of the song is too low or too high for the singer, the musicians can easily transpose or change key while using the same number chart.

Tablature

When tablature is used, musical notes are represented on a staff in which the staff lines depict the strings of the instrument played, usually the guitar. This is in contrast to a normal staff where the lines represent musical tones. Bends, slides, pops, hammers, and strums are represented by different symbols and are displayed according to the position and sequence in which they are performed.

Reading and Writing Music

There is no mystery to reading and writing music, and it is not a difficult task to become musically literate. It is simply a matter of practice. Usually a person who plays an instrument is familiar with notes, chords, and their names. Those who play or sing entirely by ear will need some help writing down music. In either case, it is a good idea to become familiar with the accepted formats. There are many useful Web sites and music software programs available for learning basic music theory and notation skills. Many of these are listed in chapters 3 and 4 under "Music Theory Fundamentals," "Aural Skills and Ear Training," "Rhythm Skills," and "Music Theory and Composition–Notation–Ear Training."

Sample Templates

A demo with sample templates from the notation software program *Finale*, used by publishers, composers, arrangers, and songwriters for preparing scores, can be downloaded at www.finalemusic.com.

Print Music and Copyright Terms

Abridgment of Music Removing or changing parts of a song to create a new arrangement.

Administration When a songwriter retains ownership of the copyright and assigns a portion of the publisher's share of rights to a publisher in exchange for its services in administering the copyright.

American Society of Composers, Authors, and Publishers (ASCAP) Founded in 1914; the first performing rights organization in the United States.

Arrangement A new and different version or adaptation of the lyrics, melody, instrumental, or vocal parts of a song; a new orchestration of an instrumental; an orchestration to which new ideas are added; an enhancement of the performance of a song.

Arranger One who orchestrates or adapts a musical composition by scoring for voices or instruments other than those for which it was originally written.

Author One who creates or originally writes the lyrics and/or music to a musical composition; the author's name.

Blanket Performing License A license purchased from a performing rights organization; licensee obtains the performance right for all works written and/or published by all the members of the organization.

Broadcast Music, Inc. (BMI) U.S. performing rights organization; founded in 1939.

Broadcast/Public Performance License The right to broadcast a copyright on radio, television, Internet streaming, or to perform it in concert; issued to broadcasters, arenas, and clubs; issued by performing rights organizations (ASCAP, BMI, SESAC); rate varies by usage.

Catalog A collection of all the songs owned by a music publisher.

Chromolithography Lithography adapted to use multicolored inks.

Collaborator Cowriter; person(s) with whom musical works are written.

Compose To write a musical work.

Composer A person who composes.

Composition An intellectual and artistic creation of music; a musical work.

Contractor Anyone who is under contract or works for another under contract; an independent contractor; a music contractor.

Contracts Written legal agreement between two or more parties.

Copublishing When a songwriter transfers part of the copyright and assigns all or a part of the publisher's share of the rights to a publisher for an advance.

Copy Reproduction of an original work; to reproduce an original work; work ready to be printed.

Copyist Person who copies music from a lead sheet or score in written or computer manuscript form.

Copyright Infringement A violation of any of the exclusive rights granted by law to a copyright owner.

Copyright Owner Owner(s) of any or all exclusive rights granted under copyright law.

Cowriter Collaborator.

Derivative Works Based on one or more preexisting works; arrangement, dramatization, transcription, orchestration, or simplified edition; a derivative or sample license issued by the publisher is required.

Distortion Any changing of the fundamental character or melody of a copyrighted work.

Dramatic Work Performing arts work such as a play, musical play, opera, or ballet, which is primarily dramatic in nature.

Electrical Transcription The right to use a copyright as background music on an airplane, electronic game, Karaoke system, or jukebox; an electrical transcription license issued by the publisher is required.

Engraving The production of music notes, letters, or illustrations by means of incised lines on a metal plate.

Exclusive Rights The specific rights granted under copyright law to a copyright owner or his licensee.

Exempt Performance A public performance covered by one or more of the limitations placed upon the performance right by the Copyright Act of 1976.

Fair Use A limitation placed on an exclusive right of a copyright owner.

First Sale Doctrine A portion of the U.S. Copyright Act stating that anyone who purchases a recording may then sell or otherwise dispose of that recording; the seller may not keep, sell, or give away any other copies.

First Use The right to record and commercially release a copyright for the first time; a first use license issued by the publisher to a company or individual commercially releasing the copyright is required; fee is negotiable.

Fixed The way in which music is fixed is legally separated into two classes: (1) sound recordings, including records, CDs, and tapes; (2) all others, including material copies such as printed copies, and audiovisual copies such as video, and motion picture synchronizations; a work's physical existence where it is embodied in a tangible medium of expression; the fixation must be done by, or under the authority of, the author; the embodiment must be sufficiently permanent or stable to permit it to be perceived, reproduced, or otherwise communicated for a period of more than transitory duration; a fixed work is in contrast with a "non-fixed" work as a piece that is memorized or a work that is performed or played from memory.

Folio A collection of songs of printed sheet music; the songs may be by a particular artist or group, or by a number of different artists.

Full Publishing When a writer transfers the copyright and assigns all of the publisher's share of the right to a publisher, usually in exchange for an advance.

Grand Rights Another name for performance rights in dramatic works.

Harry Fox Agency, Inc., The For the licensing of recordings of copyrighted musical works.

Head Arrangement A spontaneous arrangement of a musical work where a musician plays from memory, experience, and habit.

Independent Contractor A person or business who performs a service for another under verbal or written contract, as opposed to a person who works for wages or salary or an employee; contractor retains control of the means, method, and manner of production or execution concerning the work or service contracted; neither the contractor nor the contractee may independently terminate the contract before completion of the work by the contractor; an independent contractor is not, by tax law, considered to be an employee.

Instrumental A composition written for a musical instrument; a musical performance involving only musical instruments; a recorded performance of a musical instrument.

License A contractual permission to act; given by written agreement granted by an authority that is legally authorized to grant such permission; a grant of one or more of the exclusive rights of copyright owners by the owner of that right to another party.

Literary Work A nondramatic work of prose or poetry.

Lithography The process of printing from a flat surface such as stone or a metal plate; the surface on which the image is printed is ink receptive and the blank area is ink repellant.

Lyric License License to print lyrics.

Lyric Sheet A page with only the lyrics or words to a song.

Lyricist A person who writes the words to a song.

Lyrics The words of a song.

Mechanical Reproduction License The right to mechanically reproduce a copyright on a CD or tape, or to digitally download it to a hard drive; a mechanical license is issued to record companies by a publisher or license clearance agency such as the Harry Fox Agency.

Mechanical Right One of the exclusive rights granted to copyright owners; the right to record the copyrighted work.

Music Manuscript A set of symbols used to fix a musical composition in written manuscript form; the music notation symbols are placed on a five-line staff and convey the meter, key, notes, rests, etc., of a musical composition.

Music Publishers Association of the U.S. An association of publishers of primarily serious and/or educational music.

Musical Play A dramatic work, such as a musical, musical comedy, or operetta, incorporating music as an integral part of the work.

Musical Work A term used in copyright law that refers to the actual notes and lyrics used in a song.

National Music Publishers Association An association of publishers of primarily popular music.

No Electronic Theft Act The No Electronic Theft Act of 1997 amends the U.S. Copyright Act to define "financial gain" to include the receipt of anything of value, including the receipt of other copyrighted works.

Nondramatic Work A work of the performing arts, such as a musical work, which is not dramatic in nature.

Nonexempt Performance A public performance which falls under the purview of the performance right.

Orchestra Large group of musicians performing on brass, woodwind, string, and percussion instruments; may include the piano or unique instruments not usually associated with the western European orchestra; genre-specific orchestras include the klezmer and tango orchestras, consisting of traditional and ethnic instruments.

Orchestral Sketch Linear form of writing music; harmonic content shown with symbols.

Orchestration Written music for orchestra separated into performance parts for specific instruments.

Orchestrator A person who transcribes a musical composition for orchestra with performance specifications.

Original Material Song, lyrics, or music written or composed by an individual or group of individuals.

Original Work Independently created work of authorship.

Out-of-Print Music A music publication which is no longer available for sale; the copyright on a musical work does not expire when the work is placed out of print.

Parody Lyrics Any lyric which replaces the original lyric of a vocal work.

Performance Right One of the exclusive rights granted to copyright owners; the right to publicly perform the work.

Performing Rights Organization An organization which administers the performance rights in musical works for its publisher and writer members; in the United States, these are ASCAP, BMI, and SESAC.

Print To make a copy by use of a machine that prints or transfers print from an inked or carbon surface, or applies ink, carbon, or other printing material to paper.

Print License Defines the agreement to assign the print rights of a copyrighted work; the assignment is made by the legal owner of the print right, or his representative (licensor), to another (licensee); usually assigned to, and administered by, the music publisher.

Print License Fee The monetary compensation paid to a print right licensor to obtain a print license; the payment is a negotiated rate.

Print Publisher One who issues a printed edition of a work; may or may not be the copyright owner of the work.

Print Right The right, authorized by copyright law, to reproduce a copyrighted work in printed form; one of the exclusive rights granted to copyright owners, that being the right to print copies of the work.

Print Royalties The standard royalty paid on all printed sheet music collected and distributed by publishers; the compensation paid to a copyright owner for the printed use of his work in, for example, song folios and sheet music; if the work has been assigned to a music publisher by the songwriter(s) who created the work, the royalty is paid by the music publisher to the songwriter(s); the amount paid is proportionate to the license fees received by the publisher from its print publisher licensees or from the sales gross if the publisher is printing and publishing in-house; the royalty rate paid is defined by the songwriter/publisher contract.

Public Domain The absence of copyright; a work is in the public domain if no copyright is claimed on the work or if the copyright on the work has expired; arrangements of works in the public domain are copyrightable.

Public Performance To perform or display a work at a public place live or by any device or process capable of transmitting or recording an image of a performance or display.

Published Work A work which has been distributed to the public in copies or recordings by sale, rental, lease, or lending.

Publishing License Defines the agreement to assign the publishing rights of a copyrighted work; assignment is made by the legal owner or licensor of the publishing; publishing licenses include the print license, mechanical license, compulsory license, purchase license, transcription license, and synchronization license.

Publishing Rights The administration of a copyright divided into two parts: the writer's share (50%) and the publisher's share (50%); publishing rights can be assigned without transferring ownership of the copyright; ownership of a copyright can be transferred without assigning publishing rights.

Register of Copyrights The director of the United States Copyright Office.

Rental Music Music distributed through the rental of scores and/or parts rather than through the sale of copies; a rental work is considered a published work, and is granted the same copyright protection.

Reproduction Right The exclusive right, granted by copyright law, to reproduce a copyrighted work in copies of phonorecords, piano copies, CDs, cassette tapes, and all fixed material objects that can be perceived, reproduced, or otherwise communicated.

Reversion Clause A statement requiring the publisher to provide a release of a commercial recording on the national level within a specified period of time; if this requirement is not met, the contract terminates and all rights revert to the songwriter.

Right of Attribution Concerns the right of the creator to be known as the author of his/her work, the right to prevent others from being named as the author of his/her work and the right to prevent others from falsely attributing to him/her the authorship of work which the author has not written.

Right of Integrity Concerns the right to prevent others from making deforming changes in the author's work, the right to withdraw a published work from distribution if it no longer represents the views of the author, and the right to prevent others from using the work or the author's name in such a way as to damage his/her professional standing.

Role of the Publisher The primary publisher functions are authorizing the use of a copyright, collecting income generated by the copyright, protecting the copyright against illegal use, and promoting the copyright.

Royalties Payment made to a composer by an assignee or copyright holder for each unit or copy sold of the composer's work; royalty income sources, according to the contractually agreed-upon amount, include mechanical, which covers CD, tape, and album sales; sheet music sales; sync licenses for synchronization of music to film, movie videos, etc.; background music for elevators and similar uses; special licenses such as commercial, merchandising, etc.

Royalty Rates In the royalty rates section of a song contract, the percentage rate of royalty payment for various uses of the song.

Royalty Statement An accounting statement made by the user licensee to the licensor or by the copyright assignee; statement shows the dates and sources of income, itemized deductions and costs, total sales, royalty rates, and royalties owed and paid out; sent out quarterly by registered mail.

Self-Publishing The act of carrying on the duties of a music publisher by oneself.

SESAC The smallest of the three performing rights organizations in the United States.

Sheet Music Printed music that is sold to the public.

Single-Song Contract Where a publisher signs one song; term is typically for the duration of copyright; common with new writers.

Small Rights Performance rights in non-dramatic works.

Software Publishers Association Publishers of computer software.

Song Dex Index system that lists the writer, publisher, copyright proprietor, lyrics, and melody line of various songs.

Song File A publisher's checklist and data sheet for an individual song that is part of its catalog; file contains various information, including the song name, the songwriter(s) name(s), the date of the songwriter/publisher contract, royalty income distribution dates, when and to whom mechanical licenses were granted, when and to whom compulsory licenses were granted, when and to what performance rights society a publisher registration card was sent, the date of copyright, the copyright registration number, and the song's status as published or unpublished.

Song Registration The act of establishing a written record to substantiate the ownership and date of ownership of a song.

Song Rights All the legal rights in a musical composition that may be sold or assigned.

Song Royalties Royalties received from the sale of the rights to a song from performance, publishing, compulsory, jukebox, or derivative work licenses.

Song Shark Any person who charges a fee to publish a song; anyone who profits by exploiting the ignorance of a novice songwriter.

Songwriter's Biography Form A form kept by a music publisher with information concerning one of their contracted or affiliated songwriters; includes the songwriter's name, professional name, address, address of a close relative, birth date, birthplace, citizenship, driver's license (state and number), social security number, music organization affiliates, union membership, spouse's name, children's names, published songs, and other publishers of the songwriter's music.

Stereotype Process A solid metal duplicate of a relief printing surface that is made by pressing a molding material such as wet paper pulp against it to make a matrix; molten metal is then poured into the matrix to make a casting, which may then be faced with a harder metal to increase durability.

Subpublishing When a publisher licenses the copyright and the publishing rights associated with the copyright to a third party to administer; used most often when dealing with foreign territories; subpublisher receives a percentage of the publishing share.

Synchronization Right The right to affix, or synchronize, a musical work in an audiovisual work such as a film or video; the right to use a copyright by "syncing" it up with a visual picture, such as in film or television; a synchronization or sync license is issued to a film or TV production company by the publisher or license clearing agency.

Union Contractor Union musician that performs supervisory functions for a recording session; contractor that employs union labor.

Universal Copyright Convention An organization of nations, all of which agree to provide copyright protection in their countries to copyright works from all member nations; the United States is a member.

Unpublished Work A work which has not been distributed to the public in copies or recordings by sale, rental, lease, or lending; unpublished works may be protected by copyright.

WIPO The World Intellectual Property Organization; negotiates treaties that help make copyright laws more consistent between nations; the WIPO treaties, negotiated in 1996 by more than one hundred countries, make it possible to fight piracy worldwide, regardless of the location of the copyright holder or the infringer.

Work for Hire When a writer is hired or contracted to write for a company or other second party; often utilized in jingles, corporate themes, and some TV and film uses; the employer is the copyright owner.

3

Software, CD-ROMs, Instructional DVDs, and Book/Audio CD Sets for Musicians

The purpose of this chapter is to help sift through the maze of music software brochures and catalogs currently available, providing an easy-to-use sample listing of products. Over eight hundred music software programs, CD-ROMs, instructional DVDs, and Book/Audio CD sets are listed and organized by category, then alphabetically. The manufacturer company Web site, if available, appears in parentheses immediately following the product title. The annotations list product features as well as system specifications (SYSTEM SPECS). It is important to check these before purchasing to make sure the product is compatible with the computer operating system being used.

Some products are available for Windows only or for Macintosh only. Some are sold in platform specific versions although they are available for both operating systems. Hybrid CD-ROMs work on both Macintosh and Windows platforms. More programs are now available as online downloads, and fewer programs are available as floppy disks.

Version numbers and years, which may be included in the software title, are not necessarily included here. Please consult the manufacturer's Web site for the latest version of a program and any available upgrades. If no Web site is listed, either the company is no longer in business, or there is no active URL. The product(s) may still be available, however, through distributors, online retailers, and/or site-licensed multimedia labs or libraries. No product endorsements are intended, and any choice of purchase is left to the discretion of the consumer.

New to this edition of *Song Sheets to Software* is the inclusion of music instructional DVDs and instructional Book/Audio CD sets, both of which can be played on most computers with newer operating systems. While music performance and documentary DVDs can offer valuable insights, there are simply too many available to mention all of them here. Similarly, there are by now many Book/Audio CD sets available for practice and self-instruction, too voluminous to mention all of them here. The best way to stay current on available titles is to frequently visit the Web sites of the companies who offer these formats, and/or the online retailers who sell them.

The programs listed here include those for scoring and notation, composition and songwriting, professional or home studio recording, sequencing applications, digital audio recording and editing, CD burning, multimedia, MIDI file libraries, sample sounds and loops, software synthesizers, plug-ins, and MP3-related software. Many of these programs overlap in function.

There are also programs listed for computer-assisted instruction (CAI), including children's music software, music theory fundamentals, aural skills, rhythm skills, music appreciation, music history, composers, jazz, blues and rock, piano, guitar, vocal, drums, traditional instruments, band and orchestra instruction, and band, choir, and studio management.

The products listed are available online from the manufacturers directly, in music or school libraries, in multimedia labs, at computer software trade shows, and through online and offline computer product retailers and catalogs. Not surprisingly, new titles will appear as this book is being printed, and some may go out of print.

To stay current on new music software products, it is a good idea to consult music trade and recording magazines, attend music industry conferences, and to regularly browse the Internet.

By searching on the Internet under "music software" at any of the major search engine sites, thousands of related Web sites can be accessed. Many titles are available as downloadable freeware, shareware, or demo ware. The best way to stay current on new titles, new versions, and upgrades is to visit software company Web sites often.

Product support, company e-mail addresses, phone numbers, and street addresses can be accessed from their respective Web sites. In many cases, products can be ordered and/or downloaded from the software company's Web site. Some music software retailers offer discounts when purchasing several titles at once, or "bundles," which may or may not include related hardware items such as keyboards or MIDI interfaces. Discounts are frequently given to teachers and to educational and religious institutions. It is a good idea to inquire about these. When purchasing a single software title as an individual for private use, one will usually pay the retail list price, possibly at a discount, depending on the retailer.

Working with music software programs, CD-ROMs, Instructional DVDs, and Book/Audio CD sets is a creative and effective way to improve musicianship skills and general knowledge about music. Many music instructors use these resources in their private studios as well as in teaching labs and multimedia centers. Some students own their own copies for home use. There is no reason why an individual couldn't obtain the titles that interest him or her, begin learning on their own, and consult an instructor when necessary.

Children's Music

Adiboo (www.knowledgeadventure.com): Allows children to learn using their natural talents and interests; Adiboo is a space alien anxious to share his knowledge and enthusiasm; explores Music, Melody and Rhyme as well as Nature, Animals and Planets and Mazes, Numbers and Puzzles; musical concepts explored include sounds, musical scales, notes, tones, pitch, instruments, rhythm, repeating rhythm, combining rhythm and melody, matching rhyme and melody, and musical styles; children are encouraged to develop their own rhythm patterns and record their own voices; for ages two to six. SYSTEM SPECS: Macintosh: System 7.6.1 or higher, Power PC 601 running at 120 MHz, 32 MB available RAM, 256 color monitor, 12x CD-ROM drive; Windows: 95/98, P133 or higher, 32 MB RAM, SVGA 256 color, 12x CD-ROM, 16-bit sound card.

Adventures in Music with the Recorder CD-ROM (www.ubi.com/US): Sixty interactive lessons for teaching students the recorder; covers reading music, rhythm, harmony, and other important musical concepts; students can download songs from the Internet and upload songs they have written; encourages creativity; free recorder included; for ages seven and up. SYSTEM SPECS: Windows.

Adventures in Musicland CD-ROM (www.ecsmedia.com): Animations; colorful graphics; general music program; listening skills; music nota-

tion; White Rabbit serves as a guide; Music Match tests identification of musical symbols, notes, rests, and instruments; Sound Concentration tests aural memory skills, including various sounds, single notes, intervals, triads, and scales; in Melody Mix-Up students duplicate a melody with pitches from a major triad, pentatonic scale, or the major scale; in Picture Perfect students identify instruments, musical signs, or composers; can save scores in the Hall of Records; characters from Carroll's *Alice in Wonderland*; for beginners, grades K-6. SYSTEM SPECS: Hybrid.

Animusic DVD (www.clearvue.com): Review basic music vocabulary with colorful animated programs; computer-generated graphics of instruments perform seven different songs, using light and movement to help illustrate pitch, length of note, tones, and more; music is catchy; impressive graphics. SYSTEM SPECS: Instructional DVD.

Arthur's Preschool (The Learning Company): Helps children make the transition to a more structured learning environment; two CD set; academic or creative play; music activities are on the second CD; for ages two to eight. SYSTEM SPECS: Macintosh: PowerPC or faster, 16 MB RAM, 40 MB HD, 4X CD, 256, 640 x 480, System 7.5; Windows: P75 or higher, 16 MB RAM, 40 MB HD, 4x CD, 256, 640 x 480, Win 95/98.

Barney: On Location All Around Town (www.hasbrointeractive.com): Barney, B.J., and Baby Bop take children to visit the Bakery, Park, and the town's Firehouse, each with games and sing-along songs; for beginners, ages two to five; SYSTEM SPECS: Windows: 95/98, P166 MHz, 32 MB RAM, 60 MB HD, 8x CD-ROM, 2 MB Win 95/98 SVGA video card, Win 95/98 sound, DirectX 7.0 (included).

Buddy Brush and The Painted Playhouse (www.ideasthatplay.com): Interactive coloring book designed to help young children use shapes, colors, sounds, and eye-to-hand coordination; innovative, interactive musical painting adventure; introduces children to computer-based skills with the fun of mixing colors and solving interactive musical puzzles; for ages two to five. SYSTEM SPECS: Macintosh: OS System 7.5 or higher, 120 MHz Power PC or faster, 16 MB RAM, 8x CD-ROM drive, 20 MB HD; Windows: 95/98, P100 MHz, 16 MB RAM, 8x CD-ROM, 20 MB HD.

Children's Guitar Method Volume 1 (www.melbay.com): By William Bay; supplements the method of the same title for teaching guitar to young children; integrates chord playing with note reading; student starts with easy one finger chord forms and strums accompaniments to numerous songs; note reading is then introduced; features Ron Wheeler's cartoon artwork. SYSTEM SPECS: Instructional DVD.

Children's Songbook CD-ROM (Forest Technologies): Fifteen traditional songs from around the world; each recording is accompanied by an animated illustration, lyrics, notation, and background information; instrumental version of each song so children can sing along; games teach children to recognize music and lyrics; historical and cultural information about each song; for beginners, ages six to twelve. SYSTEM SPECS: Hybrid.

Cloud 9 Music (www.ecsmedia.com): Educational music software; CD-ROM; based upon recent research in accelerated learning techniques; children explore pitch, duration, and rhythm in four different scenarios; Freeform Flyer leaves small clouds at various altitudes to assist learning about pitch through unstructured compositional techniques; Pitch Pilot concentrates on understanding relative pitch differences; Head To Tail offers intros, verses, and endings of a variety of compositions that children can freely arrange into their own compositions; Rhythm Drops explores beats and rests. SYSTEM SPECS: Hybrid.

Fortune Cookie Basic Skills CD-ROM (www.wrldcon.com/maestro/): Basic skill development for piano, vocal, and instrumental students; nine learning modules; tutorial explanations; drill and practice sequences; optional speech for prereading and special needs users; for ages five to six. SYSTEM SPECS: Macintosh; Windows.

Jazz-A-Ma-Tazz (www.clearvue.com): CD-ROM; lively introduction to one of the fundamental styles of music; popular children's songs, including *Twinkle, Twinkle Little Star* and *Oh Susanna*, are performed with a jazz twist. SYSTEM SPECS: Hybrid.

Juilliard Music Adventure CD-ROM (www.clearvue.com): Quality musical production and animation; interesting and enjoyable alternative application for music classes in the computer lab; elements of music woven into a magical adventure-style game; enables children to learn about music according to appropriate criteria established by the National Standards for Arts Education report. SYSTEM SPECS: Hybrid.

Jump Start Baby with Baby Ball (www.knowledgeadventure.com): The ball is big and sits on the desk in front of your child; rather than clicking a mouse or striking a key on the keyboard, baby pushes down on the oversized ball and gets the same effect; in "Let's Make Music" section, Teddy's on the drums, Monkey plays the flute, Bunny toots the horn, and Kitty plays the violin, joined together, on stage, to play music; for beginners. SYSTEM SPECS: Macintosh: PowerPC/100 MHz, 4x CD-ROM, 8 MB RAM, 15 MB HD, 256 colors, 13-inch monitor, System 7.5; Windows: 95/98, 486/66 or faster, 2x CD-ROM, 16 MB RAM, 15 MB HD, SVGA 256 colors, MPC-compatible sound, mouse, available serial port for Baby Ball.

Jump Start Learning Games Music (www.knowledgeadventure.com): Role-playing game

for children; music fundamentals; the Land of Music is being threatened by Sir Sour Note; when child and Hopsalot collect all the sour notes by playing the games, they can defeat Sir Sour Note; explore four different Lands of Music World; learn rhythm patterns and simple melodies; recognize the different sounds instruments make; for ages two to eight. SYSTEM SPECS: Macintosh: Power Macintosh, 12M RAM, 15M hard drive, System 7.5, CDx4; Windows: 95, 486/66, 16M RAM, 15M hard drive, CDx4.

Jump Start (www.knowledgeadventure.com): Introduces toddlers, 18 months to 3 years, to the alphabet, numbers, colors, musical instruments, and 200+ vocabulary words; Musical Waterfall lets little ones explore music; print thirty-two-page printable workbook; easy-to-load program with color and bold animations; audio is clear; for beginners, ages two to five. SYSTEM SPECS: Macintosh: Power PC 90 MHz, System 7.5.3, 32 MB RAM, 15 MB HD, 4x CD-ROM drive, 256 colors, 13-inch monitor; Windows: 95/98: P90, 16 MB RAM, 15 MB HD, 4x CD-ROM drive, 640 x 480 x 256 color SVGA.

Junior Beat (Aludra Software): Music program that is fun for the whole family; mix sounds to create musical masterpieces; up to twelve channels of sound mixing in Real Time; hundreds of sound effects; professional music samples tailored for kids; record voices directly into the program; for ages four to eight. SYSTEM SPECS: Windows.

Kid Riffs (IBM): Program designed to promote the exploration of musical instruments and the different "building blocks" of music; allows the explorer to choose from over 100 musical instruments and special effects and to hear small portions, or riffs, of everything from "Old McDonald" to Mozart; game is divided into five areas: Concert Castle, Instrument Inn, Mirror Mansion, Rhythm Room, and Scale Shack; each area explores such things as pitch, scale, rhythm, and tempo; the child can record his or her own compositions; separate areas to explore different aspects of music; on-screen help from the main character, Kid Riff; "click-by-click" guide; quick reference guide; develops familiarity with musical terms and instruments; for ages four to eight. SYSTEM SPECS: Windows.

Kidtunes (www.pianopress.com): Includes thirty songs by twenty-eight singer-songwriters from the United States and Canada; fun and delightful mixture of musical styles (folk, bluegrass, country, rock); children's and adult's voices; over seventy minutes of family friendly entertainment; recorded and produced in Nashville and in other studios around North America; tunes are easy to listen to and sing along with, and appeal to all ages; Rock 'n' Roll Teachers, School Is Cool, and Addicted to the Dictionary. SYSTEM SPECS: Book and Audio CD.

Lamb Chop Loves Music CD-ROM (Philips Media): Shari Lewis and Lamb Chop introduce kids to the world of music; animated storybook based on the children's classic The Musicians of Bremen; learn the shapes and sounds of more than fifty instruments; fun musical activities; disk features a video of Shari Lewis and Lamb Chop; comes packaged with a Lamb Chop finger puppet; for beginners, ages three to seven. SYSTEM SPECS: Hybrid.

Lego Friends for Children (www.lego.com/eng/interactive): Town of Sunnyvale and band members in Tuff Stuff—Mimi, Joolz, Emma, and Anita; Tuff Stuff is working on a stage show and needs help putting it together—the music, the dance, and the stage decoration; start working on music by listening to samples of the instruments played by different band members; drag sound samples from each instrument onto the cells of the musical sequence; play and adjust until it sounds right; process to choreograph a dance routine is similar; head over to the Auditorium and decorate the stage backdrop for the show; move between Anita's basement, the Bedroom, Tina's Café, and different locations for band practice and performance; each location has stories in it, which involve dialogue between band members and sometimes their brothers and friends; main screen shows town with all its locations; buttons at the bottom to access the Scrapbook, Mobile Phone, and Camera; pictures can be taken at any time, and the images can be dragged from the filmstrip into the Scrapbook; clicking on the phone gets a message related to a story in progress, suggesting what to do next; Scrapbook/Diary is a place for recording pictures, events, and thoughts about them; after composing music, choreographing dance steps to go with it, and designing backdrops for the show, Tuff Stuff is invited to perform at the Auditorium, in front of a screaming audience; multiple users with password protection; thirteen stories that play randomly; instruction manual; CD includes Loose Chippin's music video; for ages four to eight. SYSTEM SPECS: Macintosh: 200 MHz Power PC, MAC OS 8.1 or higher, 30 MB free hard disk space, Quicktime 4.0 and Sound Manager 3.0; P200 MHz with MMX, Windows: 95/98/2000 only, 4x speed CD-ROM or DVD drive, 32 MB RAM, 30 MB HD, DirectX 7.0a, DirectDraw video card (640 x 480 16-bit high color), DirectSound sound card.

Lego My Style for Children (www.lego.com/eng/interactive): Invites preschoolers to a play date in a Duplo environment; provides a positive learning experience allowing each user to experiment with various learning styles to find those best suited to his or her development; 3D graphics with bold colors; LEGO characters; noncompetitive format; tailored to individual needs; five animal friends representing visual, musical, kinesthetic, linguistic, and analytical learning styles; four learning landscapes include music, math, language, and art; users earn Lego bricks for admission to magic toy room; users become teachers after achieving competence; for ages two to five. SYSTEM SPECS: Macintosh: 200 MHz Power PC, MAC OS 8.1 or higher, 30 MB free hard disk space, Quicktime 4.0 and Sound Manager 3.0; P200 MHz with MMX; Windows: 95/98/2000 only, 4x speed CD-ROM or DVD drive, 32 MB RAM, 30 MB HD, DirectX 7.0a, DirectDraw video card (640 x 480 16-bit high color), DirectSound sound card.

Lenny's Music Toons (Paramount Interactive): Edutainment game; play several games with musical persuasion; many humorous things in penguin Lenny's house can be activated; can turn on the TV and see advertisements, news reports, and MPTV (Music Penguin TV); cartoon graphics. SYSTEM SPECS: Windows: 4 MB RAM, super VGA color monitor, 20 MB hard disk space, CD-ROM recommended.

Magicbaton Jr. (PFU Limited): By moving the mouse, children can "conduct" one of seven songs; can control the tempo as well as instrument solos and accompaniments; can also create own animations and set them to music; simple interface; bright graphics; three modes of play include melody, rhythm, edit; for ages two to eight. SYSTEM SPECS: Windows.

Making More Music CD-ROM (Voyager): Follow-up to Making Music CD-ROM; introduces standard music notation; children act as composer, performer, and audience; includes drawing notes on an animated screen, experimenting with different instruments, and putting together sections of a score; games; music-making tools; covers musical heritage of Western culture. SYSTEM SPECS: Hybrid.

Making Music CD-ROM (Voyager): By author/composer Morton Subotnick; "to allow children to experience what composing music is like before they are training on a musical instrument"; uses a graphic approach; no manual, other than installation instructions; overview to learn about all of the program's capabilities; all instructions are available through spoken online help; five work areas; students manipulate sounds with the mouse, choosing from the instrument palette in the main composition space; other creative areas include Building Blocks, Flip Book, and Melody and Rhythm Maker; students learn about repetition, sequence, inversion, retrograde, and sectional forms as composition tools; scales screen where the composer may select from major, minor, pentatonic, chromatic, whole tone, or "your own" scales; scales are shown as a series of stair steps; game area where users compare short tunes to determine if they are same-different, higher-lower, faster-slower, forward-backward, upside-down, etc.; sharpens aural skills; students may save, retrieve, modify, or play back their work; no score or grade, except in the games section; aims to foster creativity, even before the student learns to play or read music; takes thought and listening; can learn a great deal about the basic elements of composition—rhythm, melody, combining sounds, timbre, and form—using only auditory skills as a guide; ability to manipulate sounds and pitch sets extends beyond that of traditional instruments; a true composing space for children; presents the components of music visually and aurally; for children of any age; for all musicians, ages six to ten (possibly preschool students). SYSTEM SPECS: Hybrid.

Mary-Kate and Ashley's Dance Party of the Century (www.acclaim.com): Learn popular dances from various eras from the past century; Mary-Kate and Ashley "cut a rug" from each time period, including the Charleston from the 20's and the Hustle from the 70's; dances can be seen from either a full-shot demonstration or zoomed in to study the movements of the feet; other activities include: party planning, memory testing games on the dances, and costume area and scrapbook pages to print out for photo memories; eight dances from eight eras; cute outfits; printable activities; no text options; interface is simple to use; dances can be learned with no instructions. SYSTEM SPECS: Windows.

MIDIsaurus (www.town4kids.com): Award-winning edutainment; musical dinosaur introduces music with animation, games, and songs to play and sing; on-screen keyboard; MIDI keyboard optional; user friendly; eight-volume CD-ROM series; 510 activities; read, play, compose, and appreciate music; from simple to basic to advanced concepts; relates graphics or animated sequences with sound; instructions on screen and read aloud; thorough grounding in music fundamentals; for private teacher and schools; accounts for up to 250 students; Volumes 1-8; CD-ROMs include Notation, Rhythm, Instruments, and Composers; for ages four to eleven. SYSTEM SPECS: Hybrid.

Mr. Drumstix (www.howlingdog.com): Allows children to sing along to a variety of kids' tunes karaoke-style, compose their own music, play on-screen instruments, and enjoy music learning games; Howler, the animated drum-playing dog, performs any songs containing drums; in the Song Window, kids can simply select a song or opt to click on buttons to randomize the instruments and songs; can play and edit individual parts of the songs or experiment with tempo; composing music involves selecting instruments and notes and placing them on a grid; musical compositions can be played back, looped, and even dragged to the drum window, the keyboard, or the song window to change an existing song; learning games involve such things as listening to melodies and choosing the higher/lower notes, counting the number of notes played, and identifying the instrument used; designed to test pitch and timbre discrimination, sound and memory skills, and knowledge of basic chord types; CD-ROM version includes four

extra song packs; Karaoke-style sing-along; JukeBox mode allows continuous automatic play; playable on-screen instruments: guitar, piano, drums; educational games that teach important music concepts; drums and melodies can be played "live" on the computer keyboard; songs can be exported to MIDI file; three difficulty levels; for ages four to eight. SYSTEM SPECS: Windows.

Mrs. G's Music Room CD-ROM (http://creativeware.com): Fundamentals of music theory; interactive learning activities; songs; games; five rooms with corresponding game or exercise; covers the musical staff, clef signs, notes in the music alphabet and on the staff, time values, bar lines, measures, time signatures (2/4, 3/4, and 4/4), rhythm patterns, and exercises. SYSTEM SPECS: Hybrid.

Peter and the Wolf CD-ROM (www.clearvue.com): Narrated by Jack Lemmon; story; classic piece performed in its entirety by the Prague Festival Orchestra; animation; select stories, pictures, or sound. SYSTEM SPECS: Macintosh: 60830 processor or better, 4 MB RAM, System 6.0.7 or later; Windows: 386 processor or better, 4 MB RAM, Windows 3.1 or later, SVGA monitor.

Piano Mouse Goes to Preschool CD-ROM (www.pianomouse.com): Introduces young children to beginning theory, including the musical alphabet, notes, patterns, and instruments; preschoolers also learn about the lives and music of four great composers; easy to use; fully narrated. SYSTEM SPECS: Hybrid.

Progressive Young Beginner Guitar 1 (www.learntoplaymusic.com): By Andrew Scott and Gary Turner; illustrated by James Stuart; for young beginning guitarists; very easy arrangements of over twenty favorite children's songs; introduces five notes and four easy chord shapes; illustrated in full color. SYSTEM SPECS: Book, Audio CD, and Instructional DVD.

Radio Disney Music Mix Studio CD-ROM (www.radiodisney.com): Enables kids with no prior musical abilities to mix their own voices using a standard Windows: microphone; variety of different background tunes; Mix Your Jam, Record Your Voice, and Make a Video; activate different filters that sound like a robot or singing into an echo chamber; illustrate sounds with video that includes Disney graphics; optional MP3 player; files can be saved as MP3 files and sent over the Internet. SYSTEM SPECS: Windows.

Ricky Recorder (Gvox): Learn about the recorder; covers parts; playing posture and instrument care; twelve interactive lessons; thirty-two exercises; instant feedback; for ages six to eleven. SYSTEM SPECS: Windows.

Sesame Street Music (www.mattel.com): Presents musical concepts that motivate and encourage the child to expand his or her horizons in a child-friendly atmosphere; eight fun-filled activities; familiar Sesame Street characters; includes Studio 543, where children can choose from six songs and Elmo and Grover dance to the music; World of Music teaches children about different instruments; Ernie's World, where Ernie is in a mischievous mood and invites his friends over to sing their favorite songs; for ages two to five. SYSTEM SPECS: Windows.

Sim Tunes (Maxis): Children choose and draw from the color palette, then listen as the Bugz quartet dances on the screen, triggering bursts of light and sound; each Bug has its own unique sound and animations; variety of playing levels, from basic menus for simple tunes to an advanced menu for complex creations; paint area; forty Bugz choices; forty different stamps; helps kids discover their creative abilities; for ages eight and up. SYSTEM SPECS: Windows.

Smack-a-Note (www.ecsmedia.com): Music games covering staff note reading, solfege, and piano key names; can set skill levels; works in keys of C, F, G, D, and B-flat; Solfege game; Note Names game in treble, bass, or grand staff; Keyboard Names game with or without accidentals; for beginners, ages one to six. SYSTEM SPECS: Hybrid.

Song Library (www.ecsmedia.com): Offers over 500 new songs for children of all ages—preschool, elementary, and children's chorus; acclaimed by recognized leaders in Orff, Kodaly, Dalcroze, Suzuki, Gordon, and children's chorus; comprehensive resource includes art songs for young children, many songs in modes and unusual meters, songs for choral performance, songs for musicals, songs for children's church choir, and much more; song lyrics include folk rhymes from twenty-seven different cultures and poems of forty-five distinguished poets; teachers can browse electronically to find songs that meet their educational priorities, as well as search by difficulty, tonality, meter, and vocal range to find songs that meet children's musical needs; manual process of going through stacks of music and numerous songbooks to find appropriate songs for various groups of children has been streamlined; provides a full library of quality songs for children of all ages; see the notation; hear the songs; print copies. SYSTEM SPECS: Hybrid.

Sophia's Dreams (www.clearvue.com): CD-ROM; listening skills; Sophia is a cat character; match melodies that are the same; over fifty characters; over 150 melodies; music appreciation; score-keeping. SYSTEM SPECS: Macintosh: PowerPC processor or better, 8 MB RAM, System 7.1 or later; Windows: 486/66 MHz processor or better, 8 MB RAM, Windows 95 or later.

Spy Fox: Operation Ozone (Humongous Entertainment): Huge hairspray space station is blasting vile vapors in the ozone, putting Earth at the mercy of the sun's rays; Poodles Galore unleashes her plot to corner the sunscreen market; it's up to SPY Fox and his friends to "can" Poodles and save the planet; fun new characters; several alternate game paths; mini games; eleven original SPY songs for computer or Audio CD player, lyrics included; detailed graphics; clear audio; edutainment game teaches children problem-solving skills while reinforcing listening skills, letters, and numbers; CD-ROM; for ages four and up. SYSTEM SPECS: Macintosh: 132 MHz Power PC, System 7.5.5, 32 MB RAM, 4x CD-ROM; Windows: P133, 95/98/2000/ME, 32 MB RAM, 4x.

Super Duper Music Looper for PC (http://mediasoftware.sonypictures.com): Fun and exciting way for kids to create music on their PCs; for kids ages 6 to 10 and beyond; can be used at home for furthering a child's musical experiences, or by schools for exploring the fundamental basics behind music creation; packed with instruments and sound effects; kids can record their own vocals, e-mail songs to; pick from nine instruments, mix them together and create a complete song in minutes; animations as they dance to the music; create music with recordings of actual musicians; over 700 studio-quality sounds and instruments, including drums, keyboards, guitars, horns, percussion, and more; Cool FX effects and other sounds; plug in a mic and record vocals. SYSTEM SPECS: Windows 9x, Me, 2000, or XP.

Teach Yourself Keyboard for Young Beginners (www.teachyourselftoplay.com): By Gary Turner; easy-to-follow introduction to keyboard playing for young beginners; covers basics of melody and chord playing using simple arrangements of favorite children's songs; entertaining full-color illustrations along with each song. SYSTEM SPECS: Book, Audio CD, and Instructional DVD.

Teach Yourself Piano for the Young Beginner (www.teachyourselftoplay.com): By Gary Turner; introduction to the piano for young beginners; covers the basics of melody and chord playing using simple arrangements of favorite children's songs. SYSTEM SPECS: Book, Audio CD, and Instructional DVD.

Teach Yourself Young Beginner Guitar (www.learntoplaymusic.com): For beginning guitarists; easy-to-follow introduction to guitar for young beginners; covers the basics of melody and chord playing using simple arrangements of favorite children's songs; entertaining full-color illustrations along with each song. SYSTEM SPECS: Book, Audio CD, and Instructional DVD.

The Adventures of Elmo in Grouchland (www.mattel.com): Elmo's adventure begins in Elmo's room where kids will have fun playing Hide, Draw, and Seek; the singing Stenchmen, who guard the dump, want Elmo to listen to all of their songs; they won't let him pass until he helps them finish their music contraption so they can make beautiful noises; children will listen to a sound, find the object that makes that sound in a pile of dirt, and then give it to one of the Stenchmen; easy and hard levels; original songs; five games; ten different screens; for ages two to eight. SYSTEM SPECS: Windows.

The Land Before Time Kindergarten Adventure (Sound Source Interactive): Features six activities and a few extras; Musical Shapes Part I has children match stone shapes to the rock they came from; Musical Shapes Part II is more challenging as kids match pictographs of objects and animals to their live counterparts; both Part I and II are musically activated by correct choices; Sharptooth Gulch encourages eye-hand coordination as kids use arrow keys to maneuver, Ducky or Chomper, 'left', 'right', 'forward' and 'back,' across land, water, and tar strips while trying to avoid prowling Sharptooths; Adventure Stories allows children to Read or Write; Jungle Jam lets children experience Jazz, Reggae, Ambient, Somba, and the Piano while adding their own improvisations using the drum, musical selections, nature sounds, or mystery melodies; as kids click on a few piano keys to make the improvisation happen they are surprised by Little Foot and friends who pop out to see what's going on; Living Valley wants kids to paint with animations while listening to music; with Creature Cards children design and print cards with pictures of their favorite Land Before Time characters; includes an arcade-style game; Prehistoric Pinball; Going Home can be played by up to five players; upon completion of any adventure, kids may view a Movie Clip; interactive animations and sound components; for ages four to eight. SYSTEM SPECS: Macintosh: Power PC, System 7.5 or better, 2x CD-ROM drive, 16 MB RAM, 12 MB HD; Windows: 95, 486/66, 2x CD-ROM drive, 8 bit sound card, SVGA (640 x 480 color), 16 MB RAM, 12 MB HD.

The Magic School Bus in Concert Activity Center (Microsoft): Creative look at the science of sound; explore volume and the way varying lengths of waves change a sound in the Wild Waves Experiment; test skill at sequencing sounds in the Sound-Off Memory Game; experiment with how sounds change when made in varying environments (e.g., blowing a whistle in the bathroom, a canyon, or a box) with the Acoustamatic or playing all kinds of instruments with characters from the series on the Sound Stage; animated clips in every activity explain various aspects of sound vibrations, waves, how various musical instruments work, how sound travels through the ear, and much more; Noisy Game Show; Wild Waves Experiment; Sound Mixer; The Acoustamatic; Scrambled Sounds; The Sound Stage; The Power of Sound Game; The Sound-off Memory Game; eight activities; different difficulty levels; open, play and structured activities; for ages four to eight. SYSTEM SPECS: Macintosh: iMac, iBook, PowerPC, 233 MHz, OS 8.1+, 16 MB RAM (32 if

OS 9.1+), 256-color, 15 MB HD, 4x CD-ROM; Windows: 95+, P133, 16 MB RAM, 15 MB HD, 4x CD-ROM, Super VGA, 256-color, 16-bit sound.

Thinking Things 1 (Edmark): Auditory discrimination; visual relationships and patterns; melodic and rhythmic dictation; audio and visual memory; for Pre-K-3. SYSTEM SPECS: Hybrid.

Thinking Things 2 (Edmark): Strengthen listening skills and auditory memory; jamming machine; audio and visual memory; for grades 2-5. SYSTEM SPECS: Hybrid.

Tigger (www.disneyinteractive.com): Features five activities, including games, puzzle-solving, and musical creativity; player is taken to the navigation screen where each of the activities is represented by a scene from that area of the 100-Acre Wood accompanied by a verbal description of the object of the game or activity in question; launch any of the activities by clicking on a highlighted area; Spot the Dot is a connect-the-dots game; Tigger's Travels is a straightforward board game for two players (or play against the computer) in which Pooh and Tigger compete to be the first one back to Pooh's house; Tigger's Bushels of Fun is a matching game for one or two players; Turtle Hurdles is a code-breaking puzzle game; Tiggerific Tunes allows the player to compose a song performed by an orchestra of Pooh and friends; choose from a variety of instrument sounds and pitches; a sound is assigned to each square of a grid; when composition is complete, the child can play it back by having Tigger bounce across the grid, activating each sound as he hops over it; reinforces cognitive skills and creativity; three difficulty levels; one- or two-player games; for ages four to eight. SYSTEM SPECS: Windows: P166 MHz, DirectX compatible, 32 MB RAM, 95/98/ME, 60 MB HD, 8x CD-ROM, 16-bit 2 MB video card, 16-bit sound.

Winnie the Pooh for Kindergarten (www.disneyinteractive.com): Christopher Robin is off at school, so Pooh Bear has his own classmates Tigger, Rabbit, Owl, Roo, Eeyore, and a kindergarten-age computer user; six learning activities; print projects; graduation ceremony once all key skills have been mastered; targets twenty-five key kindergarten skills; adjustable levels of difficulty; progress reports; printable workbook sheets; for ages four to eight. SYSTEM SPECS: Macintosh: System 7.6.1, PowerPC 75 MHz, 24 MB RAM, 30 MB HD, 640 x 480 with 256 colors, 4x CD-ROM drive; Windows: 95/98, Pentium 90 MHz or faster, 16 MB RAM, 30 MB HD, 4x CD-ROM drive, 256 color PC.

Winnie the Pooh for Toddlers (www.disneyinteractive.com): Includes Winnie the Pooh and his friends; offers six activities; French and Spanish vocabulary; "Who Likes To" game tackles the skills of observation, thinking, memory, and listening; in "Popping Balloons for Pooh" child has to pop balloons to bring Pooh and his friends back down to the ground; each balloon has a color, number, shape, or letter associated with it; as balloons are popped, the narrator explains the importance of each element associated with the popped balloon; "Making Opposites" teaches the opposites of words or actions; children can sing along with "Pooh's Learning Jamboree"; in "Owl's Magnificent Machine" children hear the name of the object first, then it is translated into Spanish or French; "Pooh's Print and Learn" lets children print pictures, flash cards, and coloring pages; can also create personalized bookmarks and I.D. tags; graphics and animation; for beginners, ages two to five. SYSTEM SPECS: Macintosh: OS 7.6+, 24 MB ram, 25 MB free hard drive space, 256 color display, 16-bit sound; Windows: 95/98, P90+, 16 MB RAM, 30 MB free hard drive space, 4x CD-ROM, 256 color video, 16-bit sound.

Music Theory Fundamentals

3 2 1 Music Match (www.clearvue.com): CD-ROM; challenges students with interactive matching games and enhances listening skills; students are presented with six melodies, three of which are the same, another matching pair, and one that stands alone; must sort them correctly into three containers; soccer balls, aliens, ancient Egyptians, and a chicken laying eggs are a few of the humorous characters users meet; presents a wide variety of keys, tonalities, and meters; program teaches essential listening and theory skills while entertaining students. SYSTEM SPECS: Macintosh; Windows.

Clef Notes (www.ecsmedia.com): In a drill, students use the mouse or arrow keys to move the note to match the indicated note name; student must successfully complete ten tries in a row to place a designated note on the treble, bass, tenor, or alto staff; student is prompted to try again if a mistake is made until the correct answer is given; help menu shows the name for all notes on a particular staff; timed games encourage students to improve the speed at which they accurately identify notes on the staff; students choose note names by selecting from a musical alphabet displayed at the bottom of the screen; at the end of each game a screen displays the percent of correct answers and the time in seconds; program automatically makes a record for each student tracking the time and score for the first and last game and an average for all games played; Hall of Fame displays top ten scores; student may choose one clef or all clefs; instructor may view or print the roster or individual records; program is copy protected; a backup copy cannot be made; for all music students ages six to fourteen; reading skills. SYSTEM SPECS: Hybrid.

Computer Activities (www.pbjmusic.com): Prep-2 and Levels 3-4 on two separate disks; note identification; half and whole steps; intervals; major/minor five-finger positions; triads; scales in C, F, G, D, and B-flat major and A minor; 2/4, 3/4, 4/4, and 6/8 meters; eighth notes; cadences; major key signatures; scales; key signatures in A, E, D, G, C, and B-natural and harmonic minor; major and minor intervals; major and minor triads and inversions; diminished triads; primary and secondary triads; dominant seventh chords; rhythm including 2/2, triplets, sixteenth notes; analysis of repetition, sequence, and imitation in music. SYSTEM SPECS: Hybrid.

Dolphin Don's Music School (www.dolphindon.com): Nine games, each with ten skill levels that can be set up for treble, alto, tenor, or bass clef; in Read Notes students identify notes on the staff; in Hear Notes two notes are played and student identifies the second; a one-measure rhythm is shown with one hidden note in Rhythm Read; in Hear Rhythm a short rhythm is played and student selects the correct written version from the three displayed; in Read Keys students identify the correct key for the key signature shown; Interval and Chord games are similar; games may be paused; examples may be replayed or wrong answers tried again, but timer continues to run; final score and the highest recorded score are displayed; games begin by clicking on the Start button; computer counts backward from ten; points are scored equal to the amount of time left when the player enters a correct answer; answers are selected from a multiple-choice list or group of possible notes; a large Yes appears for correct answers, along with a rippling chime sound; in hearing drills, the correct response is played again as reinforcement; for wrong answers, a visual No, Try Again appears; each game advances to the next level upon achieving a score of ninety or more points; progress tallied by giving a rank, which has both a number and an ocean-related name such as Seaweed or Octopus; highest rank is Dolphin; students can view their scores any time; teacher can view or print all students' scores by entering a password; maximum of fifteen players is recorded; a well-sequenced program; complete set of theory and ear-training skills for the young student; for music students ages six to ten; reading skills; rhythm skills; video resolution is restricted to 640 x 480 pixels; most all multimedia computers default to higher resolutions, requiring users to reset the video and restart Windows. SYSTEM SPECS: Windows: 386SX, 4 MB RAM, 6 MB hard drive, MIDI soundboard, can be used with headphones or speakers.

Dynamics and Tone (www.clearvue.com): CD-ROM; Elements of dynamics and tone; keynote; scale; chords; piano; forte; tone color; changing use of these elements in different style periods shown with examples. SYSTEM SPECS: Hybrid.

Early Music Skills (www.ecsmedia.com): Introduces beginning students to four basic musical concepts: line and space recognition, numbering lines and spaces on the staff, direction of melodic patterns, and steps and skips; multiple-choice answers; if a MIDI keyboard is used, answers are played on the keyboard; for beginners, grades K-3. SYSTEM SPECS: Hybrid.

Echos (www.ecsmedia.com): Sight-reading skills, rhythm and note reading; students echo musical examples of notes from bass C to treble C on the staff, and rhythms up to eighth notes at the keyboard; dotted quarter notes in Level II; ability to identify key signatures up to five flats and sharps is assumed; six sharps and flats for Level II; sight-reading/ear-training combination; students hear each example before they play it; wrong notes are highlighted; student is given three tries to play correctly; when played correctly, the program gives a praise word; if played incorrectly three times, program states, No, but let's go on; holds up to fifty names and passwords; keeps record of last time student used program only; gives percentage of correct responses for each section; Music Reading, Sight-Reading Boxes, and Mystery Boxes; repetition of musical examples; for students ages ten to eighteen. SYSTEM SPECS: Windows.

Elements of Music (www.ecsmedia.com): Beginning music program for children or adults; random drills; includes naming major and minor key signatures and naming notes on the staff or keyboard; progress tests and reports for each drill; instructor file for access to student records; for beginners, grades K-adult. SYSTEM SPECS: Hybrid.

Essentials of Music Theory Levels 1-3 (www.alfred.com): Interactive way to learn music; for classroom or individual instruction; CD-ROM; exercises reinforce concepts; narration, musical examples, and animations; ear-training exercises with acoustic instruments and scored reviews; Glossary of Terms; spoken pronunciations; audio and visual examples of each term; scorekeeping; record keeping; custom tests; separate Vocal, Piano, and Gold editions available; for ages eight to adult. SYSTEM SPECS: Hybrid.

Explorations: Music Fundamentals (www.mhhe.com/catalogs/1559346981.mhtml): Music fundamentals course with textbook and computer software; intended for students with no previous knowledge of music or computers; covers note recognition, intervals, diatonic melody, rhythm and meter, triads, voice leading, key signatures, seventh chords, scales (major, three forms of minor, and modal), and chord function; textbook provides written explanations, suggested activities for exploring musical elements on the computer, creative exercises, written exercises, and a step-by-step guide on using the software program and MIDI keyboard; software explores each musical subject; practice sessions and tests separated into written theory skills and ear-training skills; students enter musical information using the computer by writing notation with the mouse, entering answers by clicking on interval names, solfege and so

on, and playing music on a MIDI instrument or the on-screen keyboard; practice session mode includes detailed feedback; in test mode, students respond to a series of questions and are told how many have been attempted and how many were correct; Music Editor for music writing assignments and compositions; can collect test scores; automatic record keeping; easy-to-use comprehensive music fundamentals program; adult beginners may use the software and textbook for self-instruction; tool bar for entering music notation; choice of solfege or musical alphabet for identifying melodies; exploration mode for learning each subject; for music students, ages ten to adult; listening skills; rhythm skills; music notation. SYSTEM SPECS: Macintosh.

Explorations in Music (www.kjos.com): By Joanne Haroutounian; comprehensive theory series which integrates ear training, listening lessons, compositions, and analysis; seven levels of work/textbooks span beginning through advanced levels of theory; carefully sequenced writing and listening assignments; series parallels the Music Teacher's National Association and affiliated state organizations' theory guidelines; can be used with all piano or instrumental methods and in all class situations; CD and cassette recordings available with each Student Book provide recorded examples for ear training and musical analysis using examples of piano and instrumental solo, chamber, and orchestral literature; Teacher's Guides give teaching tips, learning objectives, and Extend and Excel enrichment activities to fit the needs of each student. SYSTEM SPECS: Books with Audio CDs.

Functional Harmony (www.ecsmedia.com): Drill packages; displays grand staves with four-voice chords; key signatures provided; select answers by moving cursor through boxes identifying chord types; covers borrowed and altered chords, diatonic sevenths, and secondary dominants; cannot hear sound on a single-voice Apple II computer; MIDI keyboard required to hear sound; in Section 1, the user practices analyzing basic chords in major or minor keys and in root position or inversions; Section 2 presents diatonic seventh chords; Section 3 presents secondary dominants; Section 4 covers borrowed and altered chords; instructor may select the number of problems in each quiz; when using the MIDI option, the chord displayed on the screen will play through the audio device to aid in chord identification; for high school students and above. SYSTEMS SPECS: Hybrid.

Gary Ewer's Easy Music Theory CD-ROM (www.musictheory.halifax.ns.ca/): Veteran teacher, composer, and arranger; twenty-five critical music theory lessons on double CD-ROM set; complete music theory course; over 600 pages of materials. SYSTEM SPECS: Book and Hybrid CD-ROMs.

Harmonic Chord Progressions CD-ROM (www.ecsmedia.com): Designed to help the user in analysis of functional harmony; includes root position chords, inverted chords, and the V7, embellishing sixth chords and the V7, diatonic sevenths, and cadence patterns; over 200 chord sets; practice analyzing chords, harmonic dictation, and aural identification; user must detect quality of chord sounded harmonically as well as position and voicing of chord; correct answer given at end of example; for advanced students, high school to college. SYSTEM SPECS: Hybrid.

MacGAMUT (www.macgamut.com): Drill and practice in aural identification and notation skills; includes Intervals, Scales, Chords, Melodic and Harmonic Dictation; easy to use; interaction with computer is done with mouse; can control the number of times a student may hear a particular example; printout of student statistics; for high school to college music students. SYSTEM SPECS: Hybrid.

MiBAC Music Lessons I and II (www.MiBAC.com): Comprehensive music theory and ear-training program; eleven drill types: Note Names, Circle of Fifths, Key Signatures, Major/Minor Scales, Modes, Jazz Scales, Scale Degrees, Intervals, Note-Rest Durations, Intervals Ear-Training, and Scales Ear-Training; each drill has five to eight levels of difficulty; user can choose to work with treble, bass, alto, or random choice of clefs; in some drills, students enter answers by clicking on a note on the on-screen keyboard or by playing a key on a MIDI keyboard; in other drills, students enter answers by clicking an answer button with the mouse; students may select any of the eleven drills as well as the level of difficulty by clicking one of eleven buttons at the top of the screen; correct answers are displayed in several ways; for example, a black diamond shape appears above an answer box for a correct answer and the number of correct responses, the number of tries and a percentage score are shown on the screen throughout the exercise; incomplete drills show a zero percent; complete drills show a score for each level and an average score for all levels for that drill type; requires no previous musical background. SYSTEM SPECS: Macintosh; Windows.

Multimedia Music Theory CD-ROM (www.voyetra.com): Self-paced course used interactivity; animation; audio examples to help understand and appreciate the fundamentals of music; eight lessons cover the Nature of Sound, Melody, Harmony, Tonality, Notation, Rhythm, Harmony and Texture, and Form and Style; learn the language of music in the Music Glossary; click on a term to hear how it is pronounced and see its definitions; for all ages beginner to advanced. SYSTEM SPECS: Windows.

Music Ace (www.harmonicvision.com): CD-ROM; includes Music Ace and the Music Doodle Pad; colorful graphics; animated conductor named Maestro Max teaches music fundamentals from the staff through key signatures and scales; six students may be enrolled at one time; students select their name, then one of the twenty-four lessons or twenty-four correlating games; instruments may be presented in treble and bass, treble only, or bass only; lesson control buttons include: skip forward, skip backward, volume control, pause/resume, and a game button; each lesson and game has several sections to complete to win the game; games include "The ABC's of the Piano Keyboard," "The ABC's of the Treble Staff," "Half Steps and Whole Steps," and "Introduction to Major Scales"; "Lesson Progress Tracking" shows how many times a user has completed each lesson section; "Game Progress" screen shows if a game was won as well as the total score; "High Scores" section allows users to see who has the highest score on each of the twenty-four games; with the "Music Doodle Pad" users can listen to and change sample melodies or create and hear their own; sample songs are selected and played by clicking the "Jukebox" button; new melody can be created by dragging a "face"; melodies can be heard on six different instruments: piano, guitar, oboe, trumpet, marimba, and synthesizer; each "face" sings as it is played; introduction to music fundamentals; for beginning music students ages eight to adult. SYSTEM SPECS: Hybrid.

Music Ace 2 (www.harmonicvision.com): CD-ROM; second title in series; standard notation, rhythm, melody, key signatures, harmony, intervals, and more; Maestro Max; choir of Singing Notes; over 2,000 musical examples; new instruments; introduction to music fundamentals and theory; twenty-four comprehensive lessons; games; composition tool; tracks progress through lessons and games; Music Doodle Pad. SYSTEM SPECS: Hybrid.

Music Ace Starter Kit CD-ROM (www.harmonicvision.com): Introduces music students to the basics of rhythm, pitch, listening, and the keyboard; requires no previous musical experience or instrument; designed by music educators; contains twelve selected lessons from Music Ace and Music Ace 2; will challenge, engage, and motivate music students and help them succeed by mastering important music concepts and skills; easy to use, self-paced learning; complements traditional music instruction; appropriate for students of any instrument; create and play music; compatible with General MIDI keyboards (optional). SYSTEM SPECS: Hybrid.

Music Flash Cards (www.ecsmedia.com): Important music material in a drill-and-practice format; nine lessons; Section 1 includes names of notes, rhythm values, and rhythm value equivalents; Section 2 includes major scales, minor scales, modal scales, and key signatures; Section 3 includes intervals and basic chords; user evaluation displayed at the end of each lesson; for beginner to early advanced, grades K-9. SYSTEM SPECS: Hybrid.

Music Lab (www.musicwareinc.com): Music Lab Melody and Music Lab Harmony are programs that teach music literacy—the ability to hear, read, write, and to understand music; learning process involves practicing real musical tasks with immediate feedback to build success and confidence; teaches skills interactively, paced according to the individual's capability at progressive achievement levels from beginner to advanced; all student work monitored instantaneously; help, including the right answer is one click of the mouse away; Music Lab Melody teaches the ability to read and write music, to know and sing melodies that are notated, to know and be able to perform rhythms, and to notate musical sounds that are heard, thought, or remembered; software "reads" a student's singing voice with the help of computer's sound card and a microphone to ensure that a student can match pitch, interval, and melody; Music Lab Harmony teaches the ability to recognize, read, and transcribe intervals and chords and to hear and understand harmony and harmonic progressions; with a MIDI keyboard, Music Lab Harmony also trains the student to play and improvise harmonic progressions at the keyboard; complete curriculum; addresses all the crucial skills that make up music literacy and combines these skills into real musical ability; personalized; drills skills while providing immediate feedback; monitors progress; in quiz mode, the musical problems are exactly the same as in practice mode, but all Help is shut down and all student work is scored and retained; recommended for anyone ages twelve to adult. SYSTEM SPECS: Macintosh; Windows 95 or higher; Pentium 1 CPU or better; 16 MB RAM, 6 MB hard disk space, Sound Blaster compatible Sound Card, VGA Monitor, microphone, MIDI keyboard.

Music Lab Harmony for Windows (www.musicwareinc.com): Recognize, read, and transcribe chords; master aural and symbolic techniques of harmonization; learning activities are interactive with immediate feedback; remedial help; each level consists of eight game-like tutorials called modules; Name: aural recognition; Analyze: visual recognition and naming; Sing: vocal harmonic and reading skills; Echo: builds keyboard ability to mimic music; Play: keyboard performance from music symbols; Notate: traditional harmonic systems; final two modules, Read and Write, summarize all skills. SYSTEM SPECS: Windows.

Music Lab Lite (www.musicwareinc.com): Tutoring sight-reading, singing, and writing music; complete skill development system paced according to student's capability; through microphone, software reads student's singing voice to develop pitch matching and sight-reading skills; practice with immediate feedback; covers rhythm, ear training, writing, and performance skills interactively; includes eight units: Sing (pitch), Notes (solfege), Names (pitch recognition), Echo (rhythm reading), Notate (rhythm writing), Read, and Write (combine all skills into sight-

singing and melodic dictation); beginner to advanced, ages seven and up. SYSTEM SPECS: Hybrid.

Music Reading (www.clearvue.com): Evaluation and teaching tool; users listen to specific tonal or rhythm patterns and match them with the correct symbolic representation; students can check answers and save scores; five levels; supplement to instrumental lessons. SYSTEM SPECS: Hybrid.

Music Terminology (www.ecsmedia.com): Five programs for improving student's knowledge of music terminology; includes: Glossary of Terms, Categories of Terms, True/False Test, Multiple-Choice Test, and Fill-In Questions; programs randomly select questions from a pool of over one hundred terms; summary of terms to be reviewed is displayed at the end of each program; for beginner to intermediate, grades 5-12. SYSTEM SPECS: Hybrid.

Music Theory Drill and Practice (www.wrldcon.com/maestro/index.html): Topic specific; three traditional drill and practice programs for upgrading skills in naming notes, recognition of intervals, and identifying chromatic structures; advanced. SYSTEM SPECS: Macintosh; Windows.

Music Theory Series Levels 1 and 2 (www.wrldcon.com/maestro/index.html): Two tutorial programs to teach an actual course in music fundamentals; electronic equivalent of a fundamentals or theory method which would accompany most keyboard, band, orchestra, or choral programs; for grades 3-7. SYSTEM SPECS: Macintosh; Windows.

Musica Analytica Advanced Music Theory Software (www.ertechsoft.com): Integration of music notation, multimedia elements, auto grading, and help for students; create multimedia documents with tool palettes; convert documents into assignments, tests, or tutorials; covers fundamentals to part writing, voice leading, and chord progression treatment; class management; MIDI playback. SYSTEM SPECS: Macintosh.

Musical Stairs (www.ecsmedia.com): Introduction to interval reading; screen displays an interval in the treble or bass clef; student reproduces the interval at the MIDI keyboard; ten problems in each session; scoring is based on the number correct out of ten; Hall of Fame for the top ten scores; covers intervals within one octave on the white keys; for beginners, grades K-3. SYSTEM SPECS: Hybrid.

Musiq (www.adventus.com): Music strategy game enhances aural perception and knowledge of all common musical devices. SYSTEM SPECS: Windows 95, 98, ME, 2000, or XP, Pentium 150 MHz or better, 32 MB RAM for Win95, 64 MB for Win98 and up, 8x CD-ROM, minimum high color (16-bit color) display at 800 x 600 resolution, 100 percent Sound Blaster compatible sound card.

Musique (www.ecsmedia.com): Self-paced exercises for theory instruction; ear-training and theory drills present immediate feedback; maintain achievement scores for student and instructor; includes interval and chord analysis, harmonic dictation, aural identification of chord function within a chord series, keyboard topography, note placement, scales and modes, and over one hundred basic music terms; for advanced, high school to college. SYSTEM SPECS: Hybrid.

Musition (www.risingsoftware.com): Educational music theory package; drill-based teaching; covers Scales, Intervals, Instrument Range, Note Reading, Advanced Clefs, Key Signatures, Scale Degrees, Symbols, Terms, Musical Concepts, Chord Recognition, Meter Recognition, Rhythm Notation, and Transposition; customize to needs; set up tests; define contents of test; extensive reporting features; twenty built-in reports. SYSTEM SPECS: Windows.

Note Speller (www.ecsmedia.com): Players identify words created by on-screen staff notation; each game has a ten-example quiz; clef options include treble, bass, grand staff, alto, and upper or lower ledger lines; game speed options are adagio, moderato, or allegro; word length can be short (three to four letters) or long (up to seven letters); user clicks the on-screen Answer button, the example disappears and the user types the correct spelling of the notational word with the computer keyboard or plays the alphabetical spelling of the word on a MIDI keyboard; Continue button is clicked when finished; if word is spelled correctly, points are awarded based on the time it takes to answer; negative points are given if an incorrect answer is given; higher points for using faster game speeds, but not for using longer words or ledger lines; if the user runs out of time on an example but gives a correct answer, no points are awarded; no second rides for incorrect answers; up to ten student names can be listed in the Hall of Fame; four Halls of Fame include Treble, Bass, Treble and Bass (grand staff), and Alto; Help menu includes the sayings Every Good Boy Does Fine, Great Big Dogs Fight Animals, and All Cows Eat Grass for identifying grand staff lines and spaces; alphabetical spelling also appears to the right side of the staves; alphabetical note identification; easy to use; on-screen graphics; for beginners, grades K-6. SYSTEM SPECS: Hybrid.

NotePlay (www.alfred.com): Learn how to read music; thirty-six levels from beginning to advanced; composes an exercise game; try to beat the clock; at top levels will be playing chords and counterpoint and will be ready for sheet music of almost any level of difficulty. SYSTEM SPECS: Windows.

Piano Mouse Music Theory FUNdamentals (www.pianomouse.com): CD-ROM; basic foundation for beginning music students; introduction to keyboard basics; sixteen lessons and games; review tests and games; four ear-training lessons; introduction to basics; keyboard, pitch, and musical alphabet; treble clef and bass clef notes; note and rest values;

time signature and counting; sharps, flats, and naturals; enharmonic notes, half steps, and whole steps; five finger pattern. SYSTEM SPECS: Hybrid.

Practica Musica (www.ars-nova.com): Comprehensive music-literacy training for middle-school through adult students; includes textbook, Exploring Theory with Practica Musica, with tutorial and references to specific activities; to reinforce classroom and studio learning or to be used as an independent study package; each learning activity has four levels of difficulty; includes Pitch Matching, Reading and Dictation; Rhythm Matching, Reading and Dictation; Pitch and Rhythm Reading and Dictation; Scales and Key Signatures; Interval Playing, Spelling, and Ear Training; Chord Playing, Spelling, and Ear Training; Chord Progression Ear Training; Melody Writing and Listening; students can select the musical elements they wish to practice in one of several clefs; answers are entered with a MIDI keyboard, an on-screen keyboard, or guitar fretboard or computer keyboard; assumes a certain level of musical skill for students at Level One of each activity; difficulty of exercises presented changes with the student's success; students earn points toward a mastery goal; shows student progress toward goal during each practice session; points are displayed in a colored box that matches a chart on the title page of the program when student masters an activity; instructors can create custom exercises using the Melody Writing activity or by using Songworks; Student Files can be used if multiple students use the program on one computer; Student Disks and site licenses, which include additional Instructor Options, are available for multiple computers with or without a network; complete music theory and ear-training package; interactive as it responds to and corrects input and it is customizable; supports QuickTime Musical Instruments (Mac) and Sound Blaster compatible sound cards (PC); OMS and USB MIDI are supported; for beginner to advanced, middle or high school and college theory courses. SYSTEM SPECS: Macintosh; Windows.

Rhythm and Melody (www.clearvue.com): Science of sound; rhythm; theme and variation in melody; developments in instruments and musical styles from all periods with examples. SYSTEM SPECS: Macintosh; Windows.

Smack-A-Note (www.ecsmedia.com): CD-ROM; speed up note recognition and reflexes; note-letter critters creep out across the screen; "smack" if they match the note displayed on a music staff; includes Solfege option. SYSTEM SPECS: Hybrid.

Symbol · Simon (www.ecsmedia.com): Teaches music symbols and terms; game-based drill format; sound effects and graphics use a nautical metaphor; two games, each divided into two levels; drills symbols, terms, rhythm values, time signatures, and note names; "Invention Island" presents multiple-choice lists to show a series of symbols; in

"Hatch Match," cabin windows and portholes match symbols with their definitions; installation instructions and trouble-shooting procedures for sound and MIDI cards; online help; Reference displays definitions and examples of all terms and symbols used in the program; students sign in with their name and a password; program functions involve using a mouse or other pointing device; video game format; Hall of Fame records highest scores; when sound option is activated, a pirate voice is heard; for elementary music students, beginners, grades 3-6. SYSTEM SPECS: Windows.

Theory Games (www.alfred.com): Learn important music theory concepts; each game covers a different topic, from note names and intervals to musical terms and rhythms; to be used with Alfred's Basic Piano Library; may also be used with other methods; games include: Name That Key, Note Names Race, Chord Name Race, Cross the Road, Melodic Intervals, Counting Game, Scale Game, Carnival Fun, Invader, and Composer Game; for beginners, all ages. SYSTEM SPECS: Macintosh; Windows.

Aural Skills and Ear Training

Audiation Assistant (www.clearvue.com): Comprehensive drill-and-practice CD-ROM; through a variety of exercises, users will listen to, respond to, and evaluate tonal and rhythm patterns from digital audio sound clips; students progress through five skill levels as they practice tonal patterns in four tonalities and rhythm patterns in nine meters and five rhythm functions; follow-up quizzes will test user progress. SYSTEM SPECS: Macintosh: 68040 Processor (PowerPC recommended), 12 MB RAM, System 7.1, and 6 MB free hard disk space; Windows: Pentium/66 MHz processor (100 MHz recommended), 12 MB RAM, Windows 95, and 6 MB free hard disk space.

Aural Skills Trainer (www.ecsmedia.com): Intervals; basic chords; seventh chords; student records; diagnostic information; progress reports; completion scores; advanced. SYSTEM SPECS: Hybrid.

Auralia (www.risingsoftware.com): Aural training course; includes Cadences, Chords, Chord Progression, Cluster Chords, Interval Recognition, Interval Singing, Jazz Chords, Meter, Pitch, Rhythm Dictation, Rhythm Elements, and Scales; each subject area has several levels of difficulty; lower levels for beginners; testing features; give test a name, save, and use again; for beginner to advanced, ages twelve and up. SYSTEM SPECS: Macintosh; Windows.

Ear Challenger (www.ecsmedia.com): Listening skills, hand-eye coordination; pitches are played by the computer, each represented by a different color key; student plays back pitches on the MIDI keyboard; correct answer is shown in response to right or wrong answers; helps student develop good listening

habits; students visualize the notes and hear the intervallic movement among the pitches; seven levels of difficulty based on the number of pitches presented; students advance at their own pace; one or two players may play at the same time; Hall of Fame records student scores; self-explanatory; quick and easy installation; aural-visual music game designed to increase player's ability to remember a series of pitches as they are played by the computer; for beginners, all ages. SYSTEM SPECS: Windows.

Ear Training Coach (www.adventus.com): Well-rounded and entertaining combination of assessment and constructive activities, graded by year of music study; carefully selected supply of music content; ear-training and sight-reading tests; interactive activities; five disk series that will take the student through a 10-grade curriculum in ear training and sight-reading. SYSTEM SPECS: Windows.

Ear Training Expedition Part 1 and Part 2 (www.trailcreeksystems.com): Tutorial introductions; practice drills; listening skills games; high and low pitch recognition; ascending and descending note patterns; recognizing major and minor triads and scales; identifying intervals; general theory concepts. SYSTEM SPECS: Windows.

Earmaster Pro (www.earmaster.com): Ear-training tutor; graded exercises; design own course; covers intervals, scales, chords, rhythm, and melody. SYSTEM SPECS: Windows.

Earmaster School (www.earmaster.com): Premium edition of Earmaster Pro; extra features for classroom use; customized reports; overview results. SYSTEM SPECS: Windows.

ECS Music Tuner (www.ecsmedia.com): Includes a metronome and tuner; automatic note sensing in real time; broad chromatic range; transpose function to shift entire scale to match instruments not in the key of "C"; Music Metronome helps users play more accurately in tempo. SYSTEM SPECS: Windows.

Hearmaster (www.emagic.de): Music theory and ear-training program; graphic interface; intervals, chords, and melodies; exercises for hearing and playing randomly generated rhythmic patterns; statistical record of learning progress; can fit individual needs such as degree of difficulty and musical style; for beginner to advanced, middle school to college. SYSTEM SPECS: Windows 95.

Play It By Ear (www.alfred.com): Emphasizes learning to recognize, identify, and play single notes, melodies, scales, chords, and intervals; six predefined levels; may customize to fit specific needs; visual feedback with on-screen keyboard or guitar fret board; tracks progress; ear-training/dictation program appropriate for beginning theory classes through advanced college classes. SYSTEM SPECS: Windows.

Super Ear Challenger (www.ecsmedia.com): Aural-visual game designed to increase a student's memory of a series of pitches played by the computer; based on a twelve-note chromatic scale, a major scale, and a minor scale; each pitch is represented visually by a color on the on-screen keyboard; for beginner to intermediate, all age groups. SYSTEM SPECS: Macintosh.

The Art of Listening Interactive CD-ROM (www.clearvue.com): Develop active listening skills; interactive CD-ROM; numerous types of music and sound; explanations of terms such as melody, harmony, timbre, and rhythm; many examples from numerous forms; for beginners, grades 4-9. SYSTEM SPECS: Hybrid.

Toon Up (www.ecsmedia.com): Covers intonation; users choose between a carnival game or a more traditional instrument, for example, the violin, to try to get pitches in tune; for beginner to intermediate, grades K-6. SYSTEM SPECS: Windows.

Tune-It II (www.ecsmedia.com): Practice in matching pitches; graphic-representation of stringed instrument fingerboard; two pitches are played, second one sounding out of tune with the first one; student adjusts the second pitch until it matches the first one; pitch differences are finer for the more difficult exercises; student score record keeping; for beginner to advanced, grades K-6. SYSTEM SPECS: Macintosh.

Rhythm Skills

Challenge Musicus (www.ecsmedia.com): Second title in series; rests are introduced; 9/8, 12/8, 7/8, and 7/4 meters; understanding of the relative lengths of notes and rests as well as combinations of tied notes; move note blocks of rhythms to complete lines of music; hear completed lines played at end of game. SYSTEM SPECS: Windows.

Feel It! (www.clearvue.com): Cultivate students' musical awareness by teaching fun games of rhythm; uses the principles of the Dalcroze method; each game is taught in progressive order with one skill building upon the next, aiming toward a specific goal; two compact disks contain music specifically designed for the book, incorporating the activities with rhythmic sound. SYSTEM SPECS: Book/Audio CD; Hybrid.

Musicus (www.ecsmedia.com): Students complete measures in a given meter with music blocks; student completes as many lines within a given time frame as possible; five levels of difficulty; players are not required to understand the rhythmic notation, only to fit the blocks of notes into a given space; falling note blocks of rhythm must be put into measures of specific meters; student selects the space for the note block to fall by pressing a button; another note appears at the top of the screen for placement; each game is timed and the speed that notes fall can be adjusted at the beginning of each session; total points are accumulated by completing lines of rhythms with the note blocks; each note offers a different point value that is added to the total score; user has the option to hear their completed rhythmic lines at the end of the game; for elementary to middle-school students; rhythm game. SYSTEM SPECS: Hybrid.

Rhythm Ace (www.alfred.com): Comprehensive rhythm-training program; jazz or classical library; create and save rhythmic patterns; three exercise types: reading, dictation, or custom; twelve predefined levels; notation includes whole notes and rests to sixteenth notes and rests, quarter and eight-note triplets, dotted notes and ties, simple and compound meter; for beginners to advanced, ages twelve and up. SYSTEM SPECS: Windows.

Rhythm Factory (www.ecsmedia.com): Rhythmic notation; audio voice explanations; keywords; Time and Notation sections; Beat Machine; Beat Splitter; Tempo Warehouse; Paint Shop; Part Shop; Inventory Time; Pattern Shop; evaluation and feedback; learning activities; time tests; quizzes; puzzles; for ages eight to fourteen. SYSTEM SPECS: Hybrid.

Rhythm Performance (www.ecsmedia.com): Test for tapping a steady beat and rhythm patterns; standardized for children ages four to twelve; screening tool; research and assessment. SYSTEM SPECS: Windows.

Super Musicus (www.ecsmedia.com): To help learn time values of notes; whole, half, quarter, eighth, sixteenth, and triplets; combinations of tied notes of equal values and tied notes of unequal value or dotted notes; how these note values relate to different musical meters, including 6/8 and 5/4; follow-up to Musicus. SYSTEM SPECS: Hybrid.

Tap-It (www.ecsmedia.com): Aural and visual rhythmic examples at four levels; each level includes three levels of difficulty and seven tempo choices; students play rhythms at the computer keyboard; quiz and percentage scores are given at the end of each level; automatic scorekeeping is available; final quiz is considered the "All-Pro" level; ear training and sight-reading; for beginners, all age groups. SYSTEM SPECS: Hybrid.

Tap-It II (www.ecsmedia.com): Sequel to Tap-It; more difficult rhythm patterns; syncopation, eighth, and sixteenth note values; actual note heads are introduced; online help menu; each of three levels includes new rhythms; Tutorial; Listening and Tapping; Reading and Tapping; each level has a quiz of twenty measures; seven different tempo settings from 54 to 144 for practice; full record keeping; for intermediate to early advanced. SYSTEM SPECS: Hybrid.

Piano and Keyboards

21st Century Americana Intermediate Piano Solos with General MIDI Accompaniment (www.melbay.com): By Elisabeth Lomax;

includes folk songs collected by John and Alan Lomax; variety of styles for solo piano, including soft rock ballad, fandango, lullaby, new age, blues, and more; complete lyrics; melodies in lead sheet format; historical notes; suggestions for related study topics; for historians and pianists; solos may be performed independently, with the enclosed CD, or with included part for second piano; companion CD features MIDI-generated accompaniments for pieces with piano included and without. SYSTEM SPECS: Book and Audio CD.

Absolute Beginners: Keyboard DVD (www.msc-catalog.com): DVD tutor; step by step; exercises; play along with professional backing track; learn how to maintain posture and playing position, read basic music notation, play with hands separately and then together, and perform songs; includes a thirty-two page booklet matching the exercises on the DVD. SYSTEM SPECS: Book, Audio CD, and Instructional DVD.

Alfred's Piano Library (www.alfred.com): Library of piano methods assists teachers in introducing the piano through a sequenced presentation of technical concepts and a variety of musical compositions; piano methods for children under age seven: Music for Little Mozarts, Alfred's Basic Prep Course; piano methods for children ages seven to nine: Basic Piano Course, Later Beginner, All-in-One Course, Sacred All-in-One Course, Group Piano Course; piano methods for children ages ten to fifteen: Chord Approach, Jazz/Rock Course, Electronic Keyboard Course, Group Piano Course; piano methods for ages sixteen and up: Adult Piano Course, Adult All-in-One Course, Adult Jazz/Rock Course, Chord Approach, Chord Approach Electronic Keyboards, Electronic Keyboard Course. SYSTEM SPECS: Books, Audio CDs, and MIDI accompaniment disks.

An Introduction to Musical Styles—Keyboard Instructional DVD (www.warnerbrospublications.com): Learn the essentials of keyboard playing in many different popular styles, including blues to rock to Latin to funk; covers posture, technique, chords structure, inversions, arpeggios, basic theory, and more. SYSTEM SPECS: Instructional DVD.

Anyone Can Play Piano (www.melbay.com): By Beth Adams; for beginners and amateur players; learn chord formulas, chord progressions, left-hand accompaniment techniques, and right-hand melody work; no previous knowledge of music necessary; free instructional booklet; forty-five minutes. SYSTEM SPECS: Instructional DVD.

Bastien Piano Library/Bastien Piano Basics (www.kjos.com): Elementary piano method with accompanying MIDI disks and audio CDs. SYSTEM SPECS: Books/MIDI Disks/Audio CDs.

Berklee Press (www.berkleepress.com): Berklee Instant Keyboard—Play Right Now!; Berklee Practice Method: Keyboard; Hammond Organ Complete—Tunes, Tones and Techniques for Drawbar Keyboards; Solo Jazz Piano—The Linear Approach. SYSTEM SPECS: Books and Audio CDs.

Century of Jazz Piano CD-ROM (www.halleonard.com): Dick Hyman; history of jazz piano; CD-ROM; re-creates styles of sixty-three pianists; 103 tunes; over five hours of music; twenty-one rare historical videos; over one hundred historical photographs; more than 500 pages of documentation by Joel Simpson, Dick Hyman, and others; biographies; stylistic analyses; discographies; complete bibliography. SYSTEM SPECS: Hybrid.

Clavisoft Book/Disk Accompaniments (www.yamahamusicsoft.com): Book/disk collections; "You are the Artist"; educator collections; disk orchestra collection; complete instrumental accompaniments. SYSTEM SPECS: MIDI compatible keyboard or computer.

Cuetime Smartkey for Disklavier Pianos (www.yamahamusicsoft.com): Control tempo of prerecorded instrumental background by how fast or slow user plays at the keyboard; mixed genre song selections. SYSTEM SPECS: Yamaha Clavinova digital pianos; Smartkey equipped Disklavier pianos.

Discover Blues (www.fjhmusic.com): Comprehensive approach for the beginning blues player; instruction in improvisation and theory; pieces with improvisation options, blues technique, and blues ear training. SYSTEM SPECS: Book and Audio CD or Book and MIDI Disk.

Early Keyboard Skills CD-ROM (www.ecsmedia.com): CD-ROM; helps teach keyboard positions; five different sections drill the student; show the note letter for a pressed key; show the staff position for a pressed key; drill on which key matches a given note letter; drill on which key matches a given staff position; drill on which note letter corresponds to the presented key. SYSTEM SPECS: Hybrid.

Electronic Keyboards (www.voyetra.com): Software companion for MIDI musical keyboard; piano lessons on CD; dynamic, well-rounded multimedia environment for learning basic piano keyboard skills; comprehensive overview of MIDI technology and the history of keyboard instruments; perform with the interactive MIDI Songbook; bonus tutorial "Understanding MIDI and Synthesis" offers information on how PC's and keyboards generate sound and make music; record performances and compositions in the "Recording Station." SYSTEM SPECS: Windows.

FJH Orchestrated MIDI Accompaniments (www.fjhmusic.com): Orchestrations for Piano Adventures and PreTime to BigTime Piano Supplementary Library; feature instrumentation of marching band, Baroque chamber group, jazz ensemble, chamber orchestra, rock group, etc.; exposure to the sounds of ensembles; can play along; General MIDI format offers teachers and students option of modifying tempos without changing pitch; isolate parts, solo, or mute selected instruments to match individual practice needs. SYSTEM SPECS: Books/MIDI Disks/Audio CDs.

Frances Clark (www.burtnco.com): "Music Tree" elementary piano method with accompanying MIDI disks and audio CDs. SYSTEM SPECS: Books/MIDI Disks/Audio CDs.

Frederick Harris Music Series for Piano (www.frederickharrismusic.com): Celebration Series; The Piano Odyssey; Celebrate Piano!; Composer Library; Souvenirs for Piano; introductory piano repertoire and method books. SYSTEM SPECS: Books, Audio CDs, and MIDI Disks.

Hal Leonard DVDs (www.halleonard.com): Play Piano Today!; Beginning Keyboard Volume One. SYSTEM SPECS: Instructional DVDs.

Hal Leonard (www.halleonard.com): Elementary piano method with accompanying MIDI disks and audio CDs. SYSTEM SPECS: Books/MIDI Disks/Audio CDs.

Heritage Music Press Accompaniments (www.lorenz.com/heritage.html): Accompaniments for Piano Discoveries and works by Carol and Walter Noona. SYSTEM SPECS: Books/MIDI Disks/Audio CDs.

Homespun Tapes Instructional DVDs (www.halleonard.com): DVDs for learning piano include Learn to Play Gospel Piano and A Pianist's Guide to Free Improvisation. SYSTEM SPECS: Instructional DVDs.

Isong CD-ROMs (www.halleonard.com): Teaching tool; animated score and tab; interactive sheet music; synced instructor video; arrangements in varying levels of difficulty; virtual keyboard; tempo control; looping with exact cueing; classical piano; artists. SYSTEM SPECS: Hybrid.

Jazz Piano Masterclass for Windows (www.pgmusic.com): Interactive piano lessons; illustrates basic skills to the beginning pianist; enhances skills of more advanced pianists; includes over sixty topics such as Roots and Shells, Block Chords, Stride Piano, Playing the Blues, Scales, Common Progressions, Improvisation, and more; practice exercises; backing tracks; eleven tunes included in the program; over five hours of verbal instruction; nearly one hundred exercises; practice tip for each exercise; multimedia features. SYSTEM SPECS: Windows.

Keyboard Arpeggios (www.ecsmedia.com): Covers key signatures, notes, and fingerings in major and minor two-octave arpeggios; designed to review arpeggio performance and fingerings; students enter correct fingering, then play the requested arpeggio on the MIDI keyboard; program is presented in five parts: Instructions, Hand-over-Hand Triads (major and minor), Major Triads (two octaves), Minor Triads (two octaves), and a Final Quiz; two-octave triads are presented to the user for both right-hand and left-hand fingerings; final exams record percentage scores; top ten scores are listed; evaluation is stored in student records for the instructor; for beginners to intermediate, grades 3-7. SYSTEM SPECS: Hybrid.

Keyboard Blues (www.ecsmedia.com): Simple blues chords; twelve-bar blues; practice playing and hearing chord changes, first with the music, then without; drill-and-practice section scores student's knowledge of simple blues chords; student creates an original solo with a computer accompaniment; student evaluation and record keeping; requires MIDI; for beginners, grades 4-8. SYSTEM SPECS: Hybrid.

Keyboard Chords (www.ecsmedia.com): Tests students' knowledge of major and minor triads in all positions; one note of a triad is provided and student answers by spelling the triad or playing the triad on the keyboard; percentage scores are recorded; presents qualities of simple chords; composed of a tutorial on major, minor, diminished, and augmented chords; chord spelling drill; keyboard drill; test; drill-and-practice programs allow user to select the inversion (root, first, or second) and the clef (treble or bass) for the drill; score is displayed after student correctly answers ten consecutive items; test randomly selects the inversion and clef for each item, and the student's score is displayed; student evaluation and record keeping; for intermediate to advanced pianists, all age groups. SYSTEM SPECS: Hybrid.

Keyboard Coach (www.halleonard.com): CD-ROM; in-depth video sequences and helpful learning aids; play in a wide variety of styles; more than 150 lessons that cover: Play Tunes—learn to read music notation, rhythms signs and symbols, and play in pop, dance, rock, country, and classical styles; Play By Ear—develop ability to learn and play songs by listening and watching; Play Solos—learn to play solos, develop hand coordination, and master keyboard's on-board features; Play Cool Songs—apply techniques learned while performing songs by famous artists; Play Cool Band Trax—discover how to play with other musicians. SYSTEM SPECS: Windows.

Keyboard Extended Jazz Harmonies (www.ecsmedia.com): Sequel to Keyboard Jazz Harmonies; designed to teach students to identify and build ninth, eleventh, and thirteenth chords; tutorial presents option to hear each chord played through MIDI synthesizer keyboard; four sections are included in the lesson: Visual Chord Recognition, Aural Chord Recognition, Chord Symbol Drill, and Chord Spelling Drill; final quiz included; student record keeping allows instructor to monitor progress; for advanced, all age groups. SYSTEM SPECS: Hybrid.

Keyboard Fingerings (www.ecsmedia.com): Drill program; combines scale construction reviews with fingering practice; major, natural, and harmonic minor scales presented in standard and special fingerings for student review and practice; for both the right and left hands; single staves are used, with treble for the right-hand exercises and bass for the left hand; students enter scale fingerings, then play the same scales correctly at the MIDI keyboard; help is available; automatic scorekeeping; student roster and scores are available for printout; Hall of Fame provides top scores; computer judges the accuracy of the scale performance in each section and on the final test; for beginners to intermediate. SYSTEM SPECS: Windows.

Keyboard Intervals (www.ecsmedia.com): Designed to help music students learn to play major, minor, diminished, and augmented intervals; must be able to read music and play notes on a keyboard; student evaluation and record keeping; for intermediate students, all ages. SYSTEM SPECS: Hybrid.

Keyboard Introductory Development Series (KIDS) (www.ecsmedia.com): Four disk series for very young beginners; Zoo Puppet Theater introduces learning correct finger numbers for playing the piano; Race Car Keys teaches the layout of the keyboard by recognizing solfege syllables or note names; Dinosaurs Lunch teaches notes on the treble staff; Follow Me asks the student to play notes after hearing them; computer graphics; designed to correlate with Yamaha Music Education System Primary One Course; for grades K-3. SYSTEM SPECS: Hybrid.

Keyboard Jazz Harmonies CD-ROM (www.ecsmedia.com): Teaches chord symbols, seventh chord recognition, and chord spelling; basic knowledge of traditional harmonies and musical intervals required; tutorial; four drills and quizzes; final quiz uses MIDI to provide aural chord examples; advanced, all ages. SYSTEM SPECS: Hybrid.

Keyboard Kapers (www.ecsmedia.com): Provides staff-to-keyboard drills for pitch identification, melodic dictation and sight-reading; scores are kept for correct answers per clef; no automatic record keeping; consists of three challenging piano keyboard games: Keyboard Clues plots a note on the grand staff and requires that the note be played on the keyboard; ?Mystery? Notes presents one note visually and aurally, then asks the student to identify other notes(s) played by the computer; Kwik Keys is a timed game requiring the student to play back notes presented on the screen as quickly as possible; two levels of difficulty and Halls of Fame; scores are displayed; for beginner to intermediate, all age groups. SYSTEM SPECS: Hybrid.

Keyboard Note Drill (www.ecsmedia.com): Designed to increase speed in identifying notes randomly placed on the bass and treble staves; musical keyboard used to allow for selection of correct answers; twenty notes must be identified to complete each session; summary score presented at the end of each session; response time can be adjusted to the level of difficulty; for beginners, all age groups. SYSTEM SPECS: Hybrid.

Keyboard Speed-Reading CD-ROM (www.ecsmedia.com): Sight-reading program flashes groups of notes on a monitor; students then play notes on a MIDI keyboard and are graded for speed and accuracy; completion time can be set by the user; Hall of Fame records top ten scores; for beginner to intermediate, all ages. SYSTEM SPECS: Hybrid.

Keyboard Tutor (www.ecsmedia.com): Provides tutorial and drill for students beginning to learn note location on the grand staff; presents exercises for learning elementary keyboard skills, including knowledge of names of the keys, piano keys matched to notes, notes matched to piano keys, and whole steps and half steps; each lesson allows unlimited practice of the skills; for beginning keyboard students, all age groups. SYSTEM SPECS: Hybrid.

Master Blues Solos (www.pgmusic.com): Includes thirty full tunes with Pop/Rock/Jazz Blues piano solos in the style of the great Blues pianists Jelly Roll, DrJ, MontyA and more; gives a foundation for many styles of music; includes comping examples along with easy, medium and difficult soloing styles; all solos are integrated with an on-screen piano display and notation; can see and hear note-for-note exactly what is being played; can loop any portion of a solo, slow a solo down, or step through a solo one note at a time; can print solos out for further study; all tunes are done in standard MIDI and Band-in-a-Box MGU formats with either solo piano or a complete band arrangement (drums, bass, guitar and piano soloing; stand-alone product; includes files in Band-in-a-Box format for Band-in-a-Box users. SYSTEM SPECS: Windows.

Master Composer Library Books and Audio CDs (www.kjos.com): Selected and edited by Keith Snell; new editions of the most popular piano teaching repertoire; includes works by J. S. Bach, Bartók, Beethoven, Burgmüller, Chopin, Clementi, Debussy, Diabelli, Grieg, Gurlitt, Haydn, Kabalevsky, Kuhlau, Lynes, Mendelssohn, Mozart, Scarlatti, Streabbog, and Tchaikovsky; Sonatina Collections; First Sonata Album; Quiet Classics. SYSTEM SPECS: Books and Audio CDs.

Masterwork Library (www.alfred.com): Standard piano repertoire edited with high musicological standards; artistic covers with reproductions of classic paintings to reflect the spirit of each composer and musical period; publications are prepared from original sources, first printings, or the most reliable sources from the composer; musically accurate editions; prefaces give historical and stylistic context for the pieces; high-quality engraving and printing. SYSTEM SPECS: Books and Audio CDs.

Music Dynamics Sight-Reading Software (Paul Renard Music): Learn to read and play standard piano sheet music; designed for those who have never been able to sight-read; for the beginning sight-reader; includes a foundation in music theory;

see music as a series of interval patterns; transmit musical patterns to hands; will catch mistakes and correct through entire course; tracks progress of multiple users; musical glossary; interval training section. SYSTEM SPECS: Hybrid.

Musicians Institute (www.halleonard.com): Dictionary of Keyboard Grooves—The Complete Source for Loops, Patterns and Sequences in All Popular Styles; Funk Keyboards—The Complete Method—A Contemporary Guide to Chords, Rhythms, and Licks; Keyboard Technique; Keyboard Voicings—The Complete Guide; Music Reading For Keyboard—The Complete Method; RandB Soul Keyboards—The Complete Guide; Salsa Hanon—50 Essential Exercises for Latin Piano. SYSTEM SPECS: Books and Audio CDs.

Note Detective (www.ecsmedia.com): Helps beginning students locate notes on grand staff and keyboard; graphic tutorial and game series designed to help students develop keyboard skills; Section 1 introduces beginners to basic concepts such as high and low sounds, the musical alphabet, and staff note reading; Section 2 helps students develop fluent music reading skills; practice in note reading on the grand staff, ledger line recognition, interval recognition, and reading sharps and flats; letter name answers are entered at the computer keyboard and notes at the computer MIDI keyboard; Sherlock provides guidance and instructions throughout the program; automatic scorekeeping for up to fifty student records; records provide information only on levels completed; for beginning keyboard students of reading age and above, grades K-5. SYSTEM SPECS: Hybrid.

Performance Practices in Baroque Keyboard Music DVD (www.alfred.com): Composers in the Baroque period (1600-1750) produced some of the greatest and most exciting keyboard music; looks at conventions and knowledge that help the performer create a more historically informed performance; practical aid to today's performers and teachers; basic touches, articulations, dynamics and ornamentation are discussed in detail; includes a lecture on the history of Baroque dance and the relationship between dance movements and the performance of keyboard music; dances broken down into component steps for learning by the viewer; nine of the most popular court dances (minuet, sarabande, gigue, allemande, bourrée, polonaise, courante, gavotte and rigaudon) performed to Dr. Hinson's keyboard accompaniment by dancers in Baroque costume; approx. 107 minutes. SYSTEM SPECS: Instructional DVD.

Performance Practices in Classical Piano Music DVD (www.alfred.com): Dr. Maurice Hinson; piano music by composers in the Classical Period including Beethoven and Mozart; historical context. SYSTEM SPECS: Instructional DVD.

Performance Practices in Early 20th Century Piano Music (www.alfred.com): Covering music from approximately 1890 to 1914; Dr. Maurice Hinson; music by Bartók, Debussy, Joplin, Grainger, Hindemith, MacDowell, Coleridge-Taylor, Satie, Schoenberg, and more; performed in context of the performance challenges and stylistic explorations of the period; approx. one hour. SYSTEM SPECS: Instructional DVD.

Performance Practices in Romantic Piano Music DVD (www.alfred.com): Piano repertoire of the Romantic era is explored; Dr. Maurice Hinson examines the performance practices of the era and discusses the influence that literature and art had on the composers of the period; dance forms, nationalistic influences, pedaling, dynamics, ornamentation, Italian terms, and tempo markings are covered in depth, along with interesting historical anecdotes about the composers; one hour. SYSTEM SPECS: Instructional DVD.

Piano and Keyboard Method CD-ROM (www.emediamusic.com) On-screen instructor is Irma Irene Justicia, MA, of the Juilliard School of Music; learn the skills needed for sight-reading and playing music; method is song based; MIDI accompaniments; quizzes reinforce skills learned; feedback to help students correct any mistakes made while playing; 250 lessons. SYSTEM SPECS: Hybrid.

Piano Literature Series (www.kjos.com): Edited by James and/or Jane Bastien; introduction to the master composers of the Baroque, Classical, Romantic, and Contemporary eras; VOLUME 1: Bach, Kabalevsky, Schumann, Beethoven, Bartók, Spindler, Mozart, and Shostakovich, Levels 2–4; VOLUME 2: Bach, Bartók, Schumann, Kabalevsky, Clementi, Beethoven, and Rebikoff, Levels 4–5; VOLUME 3: For the intermediate grades; Grieg, Bach, Burgmüller, Beethoven, Kirnberger, Tchaikovsky, Kuhlau, Kabalevsky, eleven others, Level 5–6; VOLUME 4: For the early advanced grades; Chopin, Schubert, Schumann, Kabalevsky, seventeen others, Level 6; all the music from Piano Literature, Volumes 1–4 available on CD; listening to a musical performance enhances and reinforces the emphasis on phrasing, touch, dynamics, and balance provided during lessons; performed by Diane Hidy. SYSTEM SPECS: Books and Audio CDs.

Piano Press (www.pianopress.com): Kidtunes; Merry Christmas Happy Hanukkah—A Multilingual Songbook and CD with MIDI accompaniments; Pieces for Piano series; audio samples on Web site. SYSTEM SPECS: Books and Audio CDs.

Piano Repertoire Series (www.kjos.com): Edited by Keith Snell; Prep-Level 10; CD recordings available for each level; each CD includes the music of all three books at each level; Preparatory Level and Level One are included on one CD; piano interpretations by pianist Diane Hidy closely follow the editions as a practical example for students. SYSTEM SPECS: Books and Audio CDs.

Piano Suite Basic (www.adventus.com): Customizable and expandable tools; interactive voice tutor; continuous feedback; in-depth interactive theory lessons; large musical repertoire; personal and musical biographies of over 150 composers and performers; compositions can be exported to MIDI format and made available on the Internet; contains one hundred musical pieces covering Classical, Jazz/Blues, Country, Pop/Rock, Children's, Folk/Traditional, and more. SYSTEM SPECS: Windows.

Piano Suite Premier (www.adventus.com): Customizable and expandable tools; record music; display and print musical notation; add own composition with a photo to Learning Library repertoire; includes Piano Player: supervised piano practice with audiovisual feedback; Library: over 400 pieces from Pop/Rock, Classical, Folk, and Jazz/Blues; sixty-five licensed songs; animation, lyrics, and voice recordings; Theory Thinker: hundreds of narrated, step-by-step theory lessons with practice exercises to teach notation, sight-reading, and playing skills; Composers Corner: compose, edit, and print music; pieces can be saved to a custom library and learned by others; Personal Profile: individual performance records to review progress; tracks results of every piece practiced or game played for any number of users; History Happens: biographies of famous composers and performers; free add-on Adventus Internet Music Studio. SYSTEM SPECS: Windows.

Pianosoft Solo and Pianosoft Plus Collections (www.yamahamusicsoft.com): Artists; Broadway; children's; Christmas; classical; contemporary; country; international; jazz; movie and TV themes; pop; sacred; standards; accompanist; educational. SYSTEM SPECS: Yamaha or compatible keyboard with disk player.

Play Piano (Interactive Digital Design—Midisoft): Multimedia; nine levels of difficulty; three modules: demo, learn, or practice; optional theory lessons; videos of professional pianists performing some of the forty classical and rock/pop selections; best used as a practice aid under a teacher's direction; for keyboard students, ages eight to adult. SYSTEM SPECS: Windows, CD-ROM, 8 MB RAM, 18 MB hard disk space, MIDI soundboard, MIDI keyboard, VGA color monitor, headphones or speakers.

Progressive Beginner Keyboard Audio CD and DVD (www.learntoplaymusic.com): By Gary Turner; for all types of electronic keyboards; for the complete beginner; covers note reading, finger technique, using the automatic accompaniment function, and playing chords with the left hand. SYSTEM SPECS: Book, Audio CD, and Instructional DVD.

Progressive Beginner Piano Audio CD and DVD (www.learntoplaymusic.com): By Gary Turner; for the complete beginner; covers note reading, music fundamentals, finger technique, and play-

ing chords with the left hand; includes many well-known songs in a variety of styles. SYSTEM SPECS: Book, Audio CD, and Instructional DVD.

Ricochet (www.ecsmedia.com): Innovative music game; in Ricochet Random, play highlighted keys after random balls ricochet off piano keys on computer screen; number of balls and movement speed will increase at higher level of difficulty; in Ricochet Melody, choose a melody from a play list and try to play the notes before the ball leaves the screen; tempo can be changed. SYSTEM SPECS: Windows.

Step One: Play Piano (www.msc-catalog.com): Designed for the learner to understand the keys and play scales and chords for any keyboard; audio tracks allow listener to hear correct sounds while DVD presentation demonstrates proper hand and finger positioning. SYSTEM SPECS: Book, Audio CD, and Instructional DVD.

Step One: Teach Yourself Keyboard DVD (www.msc-catalog.com): Learn the keys and play scales and chords for any keyboard; audio tracks allow listener to hear correct sounds while the DVD presentation demonstrates proper hand and finger positioning; chapter menus and more for easy navigation through the lessons. SYSTEM SPECS: Book, Audio CD, and Instructional DVD.

Teach Me Piano (www.voyetra.com): Over 150 lessons; over 100 exercises; beginners learn basic techniques; advanced players reinforce musical skills; Keyboard Lessons include note reading in treble and bass clefs, rhythm and timing, finger numbering and finger positions, key signatures, time signatures, scales, and chords; keeps records; Songbook organizes songs; Trainer Screen for practice; Performance Screen to play with full accompaniment; Musician's Reference for commonly used musical terms; includes MediaCheck; for beginner to intermediate, ages ten to adult. SYSTEM SPECS: Windows.

Teach Me Piano Deluxe for Windows (www.voyetra.com): Play, practice, perform and compose songs on the computer; instruction in music theory; learn about the history of keyboards; have access to tools for composing, arranging, and recording music; The Piano Room is the main screen from where the student can access all of the programs; divided into six sections with more than 150 lessons; covers a full spectrum of keyboard-playing skills, including notation, rhythm and timing, finger positions, key signatures, time signatures, scales, and chords; learn how to play more than seventy-five popular songs and proper playing technique; students can maintain their own progress reports as they learn to play; with the Song Book, easily access songs learned by title, style, composer, or level of difficulty; choose a song and go either to the Trainer Screen to practice or to the Performance Screen to play with background accompaniment; can print the music to play later on; import MIDI files into the Songbook to perform; Musician's Reference introduces theory; describes musical notation, definitions, and musical terms, and serves as a reference guide; set up music system with SoundCheck and check the operation of MIDI keyboard, microphone, audio playback, and more; video lesson on how to connect MIDI keyboard to PC; record songs with Recording Station; MIDI and digital audio recording studio to create MIDI songs with PC and MIDI keyboard; record songs with multiple MIDI instruments and add vocals or acoustic instruments; import MIDI files from piano lessons and create your own variations; create background tracks with Jammin' Keys "auto-accompaniment" program; choose a style, then add fills, solos, drums, accompaniment, sound effects, and more; test music skills with Music Games, including reading skills, knowledge of general music topics, and ability to recognize rhythm patterns with arcade-style games; includes Music Quiz, Note Blaster, and Rhythm Master; learn the basics of MIDI music; reviews the technology of digital music and MIDI—the "language" used to control synthesizer keyboards and make electronic music; learn about MIDI and WAV files, analog vs. digital synthesis, and much more; learn about the history of keyboards; guided tour of the origins and development of keyboard instruments from the Baroque harpsichord to the modern synthesizer. SYSTEM SPECS: Windows.

Teach Yourself Keyboard Audio CD and DVD (www.learntoplaymusic.com): By Gary Turner; for all types of electronic keyboards; covers basics of reading music and playing melodies; contains diagrams showing fingerings for automatic chordal accompaniment and a lesson on left-hand fingering as it applies to the keyboard. SYSTEM SPECS: Book, Audio CD, and Instructional DVD.

Teach Yourself Piano Audio CD and DVD (www.learntoplaymusic.com): By Gary Turner; for beginning pianists; learn to read and play piano music; learn chords, chord progressions, and over twenty-five songs using a range of two octaves; classical, folk, pop, rock, and blues. SYSTEM SPECS: Book, Audio CD, and Instructional DVD.

Teach Yourself to Play Piano CD-ROM (www.alfred.com): Uses same teaching approach as the best-selling book; interactive, audiovisual format; for beginners of all ages; learn the notes of the entire keyboard, how to form the most important scales and chords, basic rhythms, and how to play expressively and with feeling; exercises reinforce technique as follow along with music on screen; with interactive song player can change tempos, adjust audio levels, and record performance; video of an instructor teaching and demonstrating lessons; customizable ear-training program. SYSTEM SPECS: Hybrid.

The Beginner Piano MasterClass CD-ROM (www.pgmusic.com): Master pianist Miles Black; illustrates basic keyboard skills and theory; specifically designed for the beginner piano or keyboard student; helps develop skills on its own or as a valuable addition to any existing course of study. SYSTEM SPECS: Windows.

The Blues Pianist (www.pgmusic.com): Large library of original blues tunes performed by top studio musicians; wide variety of styles: Boogie Woogie, Slow/Fast Boogies, Jazz Blues, New Orleans Style, Chicago Blues, and more; styles made famous by Pete Johnson, Albert Ammons, Jelly Roll Morton, Jerry Lee Lewis, etc.; Trivia and Guess the Song games; notes; biographies; all levels can use the games and biographies; advanced, all ages. SYSTEM SPECS: Macintosh; Windows.

The Blues Piano MasterClass CD-ROM (www.pgmusic.com): Master pianist Miles Black; designed to illustrate basic skills to the beginner Blues pianist; first twenty lessons deal with blues history, basic blues form, simple chord construction, and learning to improvise a simple blues melody over a few basic blues styles; blues piano styles included are boogie, barrelhouse, rag blues, jazz blues, rock blues, and more. SYSTEM SPECS: Windows.

The Latin Pianist (www.pgmusic.com): Over fifty tunes played on MIDI keyboard by Rebecca Mauleon-Santana; authentic Latin and Salsa piano songs and styles: Conga, Cumbia, Merengue, Son, Mambo, Cha-Cha-Cha, Guaracha, Samba, Partido Alto, and more; on-screen piano keyboard shows what pianist is playing; slow down piece or step through chord by chord; learn music note for note watching notes on screen; load MIDI files for further study; advanced. SYSTEM SPECS: Macintosh; Windows.

The Modern Jazz Pianist (www.pgmusic.com): Top jazz/studio pianists play over fifty jazz standards in a wide variety of styles; on-screen piano keyboard shows exactly what is being played; slow down piece or step through chord by chord; learn the music note for note by watching the piano notes on the screen; load MIDI files into programs for further study; Music Trivia and Guess the Song games; program notes; biographies; music dictionary and more; all levels can use the games and biographies; advanced. SYSTEM SPECS: Macintosh; Windows.

The New Age Pianist (www.pgmusic.com): Collection of solo piano compositions inspired by the natural world; covers New Age piano music; full range of piano techniques presented; over four hours of music; song memory, biographies, and information on important New Age musicians; advanced, all ages; all levels can use the games and biographies. SYSTEM SPECS: Macintosh; Windows.

Ultimate Beginner Series Blues Keyboards (www.warnerbrospublications.com): Instructor Henry Brewer teaches how to play twelve bar progressions, triplets, shuffle beats, inversions, turnarounds, blues scales, and blues licks; includes examples using a band that will help demonstrate the lessons. SYSTEM SPECS: Instructional DVD.

Ultimate Beginner Series Jr. Basic Keyboards (www.warnerbrospublications.com): Learn how to start playing the keyboard; learn the notes, how to play basic melodies, and about the keyboard. SYSTEM SPECS: Instructional DVD.

Ultimate Beginner Series Keyboard Basics (WEA): Covers the basics of keyboard playing, finding notes, positioning one's body, using both hands simultaneously, major and minor chords and scales, basic improvisation, and more. SYSTEM SPECS: Instructional DVD.

Ultimate Beginner Series Rock Keyboard (www.warnerbrospublications.com): Instructor David Garfield; compiles Volumes 1 and 2 of previously released programs; study minor seventh chords, the dorian mode, improvisation, and playing in a band; introduces the blues form, dominant seventh chords, rock and roll style, and how to select sounds and create a part. SYSTEM SPECS: Instructional DVD.

Virtuoso (www.yamahamusicsoft.com): Artist-oriented recordings for reproducing pianos, digital keyboards, and multimedia computers. SYSTEM SPECS: Yamaha Disklavier, Yamaha Clavinova, PianoDisk, Roland KR and HP Series, Baldwin Concert Master, and Kurzwel Mark Series.

Yamaha General MIDI Compatible Style Disks (www.halleonard.com): Yamaha ROM Cartridges include: 60s Pop; Amy Grant—Heart In Motion; Big Band—Volume I; Christmas Hits; Classical and Folk; Contemporary Pop; Country and Western; Country Sound; Dancefloor; Eric Clapton; Jazz; Latin—Volume I; Latin Ballroom; Latin Pop; Pops of The 60s and 70s; Rock N' Roll; Songs of The 60s; Soul; Sting; The Beatles—Greatest Hits I; The Beatles—Greatest Hits II; The Beatles—Greatest Hits III; The Best Of Elvis Presley; The Best Of Marvin Hamlisch; Traditional Dance. SYSTEM SPECS: General MIDI Compatible.

Yamaha Musicsoft for Disklavier and Clavinova (www.yamahamusicsoft.com): Music software, accessories, and digital downloads. SYSTEM SPECS: Digital piano, portable keyboard, or synthesizer; Disklavier; Clavinova.

You Can Teach Yourself Piano DVD (www.melbay.com): By Matt Dennis; taught by L. Dean Bye; accompanies book of same title; teaches basic music reading skills; essential technique and theory for playing in all contemporary keyboard styles; technical and theoretical concepts; graded material; ear training and modern harmony. SYSTEM SPECS: Instructional DVD.

You're the Star! (Turbo Music): General MIDI performances and print; songbook/CD-ROM disk series; MIDI accompaniments; change tempo and keys; create own orchestration and mix; improvise solos; for computers and instruments with disk drives and a digital keyboard; some with E-Z play notation. SYSTEM SPECS: Hybrid.

Guitar and Bass

50 Licks Series (www.halleonard.com): Guitar technique DVDs; 50 Licks Blues Style; 50 Licks Country Style; 50 Licks Jazz; Style; 50 Licks Rock Style. SYSTEM SPECS: Instructional DVDs.

Absolute Beginners: Bass Guitar DVD (www.msc-catalog.com): DVD tutor; step by step; exercises; play along with professional backing track; learn how to tune bass, pluck the strings using fingers or a pick, and read basic notation and bass tab; practice scales and arpeggios; play first complete bass lines along with a band; includes thirty-two page booklet containing all the music examples shown on the DVD. SYSTEM SPECS: Book, Audio CD, and Instructional DVD.

Absolute Beginners: Guitar DVD (www.msc-catalog.com): DVD tutor; step by step; exercises; play along with professional backing track; learn how to tune guitar; develop techniques using fingers or a pick; practice sense of rhythm; play essential chord shapes; perform first complete guitar solo; includes thirty-two page booklet matching the exercises on the DVD. SYSTEM SPECS: Book, Audio CD, and Instructional DVD.

Acoustic Guitar (MGI Interactive): CD-ROM; for beginners, all ages; how to buy a guitar; how to use the capo; chords, harmony, and rhythm; accompaniments; vocal playbacks; picking and fingerstyle techniques; basic exercises. SYSTEM SPECS: Windows.

An Evening with John Abercrombie (www.alfred.com): Intimate session with leading jazz guitar artist; host Jody Fisher covers improvising over standards, guitar synthesis, use of scales, and composition. SYSTEM SPECS: Instructional DVD.

An Evening with Tal Farlow: Jazz Guitar (www.alfred.com): Jazz guitar legend Tal Farlow with Jody Fisher in a candid, entertaining, and instructional interview; topics of discussion include chord/melody arranging, flat-five substitutions, soloing over ii-V-I, and more; Tal talks about his influences and the great players that he's performed and recorded with; running time: one hour, five minutes. SYSTEM SPECS: Instructional DVD.

An Introduction to Musical Styles—Bass Instructional DVD (www.warnerbrospublications.com): Learn how to play the bass in many different styles: hard rock, blues, funk, or basic rock; shows such skills as posture, technique, tuning, chords, changing strings, common bass lines and figures, and practice exercises. SYSTEM SPECS: Instructional DVD.

An Introduction to Musical Styles Ultimate Beginner Xpress Electric Guitar (www.warnerbrospublications.com): Teaches basics of playing an electric guitar; learn posture, tuning, changing strings, chords, arpeggios, power chords, and more. SYSTEM SPECS: Instructional DVD.

Anyone Can Play Blues Guitar DVD (www.melbay.com): By Vern Juran; for the beginning to intermediate guitarist; learn blues chord progressions; variety of blues strumming and picking patterns; basic blues scales; lead guitar techniques; combination rhythm and lead playing; basics of slide guitar and open tuning; no music reading required but student should understand basic chords and strumming. SYSTEM SPECS: Instructional DVD.

Anyone Can Play Bottleneck Blues Guitar (www.melbay.com): By James Van Nuys; designed for the beginning slide guitar player; will also help intermediate player develop bottleneck technique; learn standard and alternate tunings, reading slide tablature, basic left- and right-hand technique, and classic bottleneck blues riffs; free tablature booklet of examples from the video included. SYSTEM SPECS: Instructional DVD.

Anyone Can Play Electric Bass DVD (www.melbay.com): By Scott Miller; designed for people who want to play bass in a small group or ensemble; presents all the most common musical forms; learn bass techniques for rock, country, pop, and other popular music styles; no music-reading ability required; free instructional booklet included. SYSTEM SPECS: Instructional DVD.

Anyone Can Play Fingerstyle Guitar DVD (www.melbay.com): By Paul Hayman; lessons derived from easy-to-learn method which doesn't require student to read music; learn basic accompaniment patterns; alternating bass styles; fingerstyle classics; free instructional booklet. SYSTEM SPECS: Instructional DVD.

Anyone Can Play Guitar Chords (www.melbay.com): By Vern Juran; learn the most commonly used chords; split-screen viewing; learn how the chords are fingered and how they should sound; learn major, minor and seventh chord forms and diminished and augmented chord shapes on first four frets of fingerboard; thirty minutes. SYSTEM SPECS: Instructional DVD.

Anyone Can Play Guitar Volume I (www.melbay.com): By Vern Juran; for beginning acoustic and electric guitar students; practical, easy-to-learn approach; no previous knowledge of music necessary; teaches tuning, the parts of the guitar, how to hold the guitar and pick, and proper right and left hand positioning; numerous close-ups and diagrams both on-screen and in accompanying booklet; learn to strum basic chords for four folk songs and two blues progressions; free instructional booklet. SYSTEM SPECS: Instructional DVD.

Anyone Can Play Popular Chord Progressions (www.melbay.com): By Vern Juran; for the beginning guitarist who already understands and uses chords in first position; learn standard chord changes used in thousands of folk, country, blues, and rock songs, and in the development of faster chord changing; helps songwriters to write better songs; learn to play all the friendly guitar keys; booklet included. SYSTEM SPECS: Instructional DVD.

Bass Basics DVD (www.clearvue.com): Offers beginning bass players key information that will help them excel as musicians; features renowned master bassist, writer, and teacher Beaver Felton; covers stringing and tuning the instrument, setting up bass and amp, practicing proper technique, and basic scales; practice routines and technical exercises; Felton discusses music terminology, ear training, rhythmic and harmonic theory, and neck familiarization; students are invited to play along and practice with the guest guitarist and drum tracks. SYSTEM SPECS: Instructional DVD.

Bass Method (www.emediamusic.com): Beginning level CD-ROM; 114 step-by-step lessons by renowned bass instructor John Arbo; full-motion video with multiple angles and close-ups; over 200 songs and exercises; triads; fills; syncopation; creating a bass line; multitrack recorded audio; variable-speed MIDI; bass-only and no-bass options; songs by the Grateful Dead, Bob Dylan, and others; animated fretboard; automatic tuner; recorder and metronome. SYSTEM SPECS: Hybrid.

Beginning Blues Guitar (www.alfred.com): Comprehensive collection of blues guitar lessons from outstanding blues guitarist Matt Smith; important blues concepts are explained such as 8- and 12-bar blues forms, phrasing concepts and improvisation along with techniques, including bending and vibrato; close-ups of hands, split screens, and opportunities to improvise with a real blues band; running time: one hour, thirty-one minutes. SYSTEM SPECS: Instructional DVD.

Beginning Delta Blues Guitar DVD (www.alfred.com): Teaches basic chords and strums for playing the blues; learn authentic blues tunings and basic chord forms; teaches Delta slide guitar technique; includes performances by Fruteland Jackson, an authentic Delta blues master; on-screen graphics, close-ups of the hands, and other video techniques; diagrams and examples in standard music notation, and TAB appear on screen to make learning easier. SYSTEM SPECS: Instructional DVD.

Beginning Electric Slide Guitar DVD (www.alfred.com): Learn slide guitar with Texas guitarist Kirby Kelley; easy-to-understand, friendly, laid-back approach; get started playing slide; most important slide tunings are introduced; includes a step-by-step explanation of basic slide techniques such as muting, vibrato, and more; close-ups, music, and

TAB on screen; other video techniques; classic licks; running time: fifty-four minutes. SYSTEM SPECS: Instructional DVD.

Beginning Jazz Guitar (www.alfred.com): Collection of jazz lessons based on the best-selling book by Jody Fisher; step-by-step lessons cover basic chords, jazz chord-scales, the major scale, and basic jazz improvisation; includes live performances by guitarist Jody Fisher; opportunities to practice improvising with a real jazz combo. SYSTEM SPECS: Instructional DVD.

Beginning Rock Guitar: Lead and Rhythm (www.alfred.com): Includes lessons on improvising with the blues scale, hammer-ons, pull-offs, slides, vibrato, bending, and more; basic lessons on open chords, bar chords, and power chords; R and B style riffs, shuffle, and straight-eighth playing; many music examples in standard music notation and TAB. SYSTEM SPECS: Instructional DVD.

Berklee Press (www.berkleepress.com): A Modern Method for Guitar—Volume 1; A Modern Method for Guitar—Volume 2; Berklee Instant Guitar—Play Right Now!; Berklee Practice Method: Bass; Berklee Practice Method: Guitar; Instant Bass—Play Right Now!; Jim Kelly's Guitar Workshop; Modern Method for Guitar (French Edition); Modern Method for Guitar (Spanish Edition); More Guitar Workshop; Rock Bass Lines; Slap Bass Lines; The Guitarist's Guide to Composing and Improvising; Voice Leading for Guitar—Moving Through the Changes. SYSTEM SPECS: Books and Audio CDs.

Beyond Power Chords (www.artistpro.com): By Leo Cavanagh; covers intermediate and professional guitar techniques; number of chords used will increase dramatically; gives means to play all types of chords including major, minor, seventh, and more in all keys; includes 85-track audio CD with almost 300 examples performed by the author. SYSTEM SPECS: Book and Audio CD.

Blues Guitar (MGI Interactive): CD-ROM; standard blues progressions; blues scales; improvisations and licks; music theory, chords, and scales; endings; walking blues technique; daily exercises; intermediate; for all ages. SYSTEM SPECS: Windows.

Blues Guitar Legends CD-ROM (www.emediamusic.com): Learn how to play classic blues songs from the masters; music notation is highlighted as songs play; animated fretboard displays fingerings in real time; learn to play ten blues classics, including Stevie Ray Vaughan's Crossfire, Robert Cray's Smoking Gun and B.B. King's The Thrill Is Gone from the original master recordings; variable-speed MIDI tracks; simplified chord versions for beginners; full note-for-note transcriptions and biographical material. SYSTEM SPECS: Hybrid.

CD-ROM Guitar Chord Finder (www.msc-catalog.com): See and hear every chord played on the virtual guitar neck; standard music nota-

tion and chord boxes for each; 350 most-used chords fully illustrated; how to tune guitar. SYSTEM SPECS: Hybrid.

Classic Rock Guitar (www.ubi.com/US): Over eighty lessons and 180 exercises for eight acoustic song arrangements; full-screen zooming and lesson looping; two digital tuners; digital metronome; songs include: Hey Joe, Blackbird, No Woman, No Cry, Sweet Home Alabama, Dust in the Wind, Wild World, Life by the Drop, and Blowin' in the Wind. SYSTEM SPECS: Windows 3.1 or 95, 486 DX 66 MHz or better, 4 MB RAM or better, 256 color SVGA, MPC compatible sound card, 2x CD-ROM driver or better, mouse.

Complete Blues Guitar Instructional DVD (www.melbay.com): By Mike Christiansen; accompanies book of same title; covers basic concepts in blues guitar; performance level blues solos and techniques. SYSTEM SPECS: Instructional DVD.

Complete Jazz Guitar Method Volume 1 and 2 (www.melbay.com): By Mike Christiansen; combines all material previously presented in two-volume video set; parallels book of same title; guides guitarist through barre chords, dead-string chords, bass-string chords, comping, chord inversions, altered seventh chords, major scales, concept of tonal centers, chord construction, ways of connecting chord forms, chord embellishment, transposition, chord substitution, blues progressions, pentatonic and blues scales, sequencing, diminished chords and the diminished scale, augmented chords, and the whole-tone scale; also presents Latin rhythms, the Dorian and Mixolydian modes applied separately and in combination, improvising over the ii-V-I progression in various keys, the Lydian, Aeolian, Phrygian, Locrian, and Super Locrian modes, "targeting" of chord tones, guide tones, phrasing, constructing a solo, secondary arpeggios, the Parker Cycle, improvising around a melody, quartal harmony as applied to the blues, chord substitution using quartal harmony, single-note soloing using fourths, and concept of moving geometrical chord shapes from one fret to another, or from one set of strings to another; hands-on demonstrations. SYSTEM SPECS: Instructional DVD.

Doc's Guitar Jam (Vestapol Videos): Flatpicking guitar legends gathered at the Merle Watson Festival in Wilkesboro, North Carolina, in 1992 play some of country music's most beloved and challenging songs on their stringed instruments; joining Doc Watson are Tony Rice, David Grisman, Jack Lawrence, and others. SYSTEM SPECS: Instructional DVD.

Flamenco Guitar Step-By-Step Volumes 1, 2, and 3 (www.melbay.com) Flamenco guitar video instruction series produced entirely in Spain; for those who already have a command of basic classic guitar technique; insights on sitting and hand positions; thumb/index technique; the "picado," the "picado falseta," and the "golpe;" demonstrates various "rasgueos" executed with and without the thumb and presents the "tango" and "soleas" rhythms; booklet included with English and Spanish text and music in notation and tablature; tracks in four languages: Spanish, English, French, and Japanese. SYSTEM SPECS: Instructional DVDs.

Frank Gambale Chopbuilder for Guitar (www.warnerbrospublications.com): Master guitarist takes students on a ten-round workout designed to build up performance muscles; learn how to develop ears and fingers to build up guitar chops. SYSTEM SPECS: Instructional DVD.

Fun With the Guitar (www.melbay.com): By Mel Bay and Joe Carr; beginner's video teaching simple chords, strums, and songs; for guitarists of any age. SYSTEM SPECS: Instructional DVD.

Guitar for the Absolute Beginner DVD (www.alfred.com): Instructor is Susan Mazer; learn basic chords, strumming power chords, finger picking, and improvising; play along with easy songs; close-ups of hands, split screens, and music examples on screen; running time: fifty minutes. SYSTEM SPECS: Instructional DVD.

Guitar Method (www.emediamusic.com): Beginning guitar CD-ROM; 155 comprehensive lessons cover basics; chord strumming, playing melodies and fingerpicking; over seventy songs, including hits from artists such as Bob Dylan, Grateful Dead, and Steve Miller; over thirty videos; over three hours of audio from guitar instructor/national performer Kevin Garry, PhD; animated fretboard; multitrack audio for hit songs; variable-speed MIDI tracks to slow down any song or exercise; learn songs in either guitar tablature or standard music notation as the notes on the screen highlight and fingering is displayed on the animated fretboard; built-in automatic tuner to interactively tune guitar; digital metronome; recorder with playback; Internet song guide; 250-chord dictionary. SYSTEM SPECS: Hybrid.

Guitar Songs (www.emediamusic.com): Learn to play hit songs in all styles, including rock, blues, country, classical, and folk genres; variable-speed MIDI track for slowing down music; separate audio tracks, including no guitar, guitar only and bass only; over twenty songs made famous by artists such as Eric Clapton, Melissa Etheridge, Heart, Willie Nelson, Bonnie Raitt, Santana, Talking Heads, Stevie Ray Vaughan, The Who; song playing tips are included for both bass and guitar players; animated fretboard shows bends and vibrato in addition to fingering positions in real time; automatic tuner and metronome; options for guitar tablature or standard notation available on each song. SYSTEM SPECS: Hybrid.

Guitar Toolbox (www.emediamusic.com): Guitar accessory tool; integrates a built-in automatic tuner, metronome, recorder, and chord dictionaries onto one CD-ROM; automatic tuner analyzes sound for each guitar string, then visually displays if sharp or flat until exactly in tune; prerecorded reference notes; 900-chord dictionary displays variations of each chord for three positions on the guitar neck; simplified 250-chord dictionary displays fingering charts and features audio playback for chords played in the first position; digital metronome helps work on picking speed and develops rhythm and timing; built-in recorder to record playing; save and retrieve recordings for future playback. SYSTEM SPECS: Hybrid.

Guitar Workshop (www.lorenz.com): Platform for song packs and interactive lesson modules in a variety of skill levels and styles; guitar tutorial; fretboard finger positions; music window with score, tablature, chord frames, and performance notes; keyboard; lesson window; metronome; alternate tunings; user song entry. SYSTEM SPECS: Windows 3.1, 16-bit sound card, VGA color monitor, 486/33 MHz recommended; supports MIDI synthesizers.

Guitropolis (www.alfred.com): Teaches guitar; humor; musical game play; award-winning game design; live video; solid guitar techniques for the beginning guitarist; licks; chords; popular melodies. SYSTEM SPECS: Hybrid.

Hal Leonard Guitar and Bass CD-ROMs (www.halleonard.com): Electric Guitar Coach; Guitar Coach; Intermediate Guitar Coach—Cool Songs, Solos, and Skills for All Guitarists; J. S. Bach—Inventions—Transcriptions for 2 Four-String Electric Basses; Play Guitar with Ross Bolton; Play Rock Guitar with Keith Wyatt. SYSTEM SPECS: Hybrid.

Hal Leonard Guitar and Bass DVDs (www.halleonard.com): Basic Guitar and String Set Up; Bass Day 1998; Beginning Bass Volume One; Beginning Guitar Volume One; Fender Presents Getting Started on Acoustic Guitar; Fender Presents Getting Started on Electric Guitar; Flea—Instructional DVD for Bass; Fretboard Roadmaps; Hal Leonard Guitar Method; Jim Kelly's Guitar Workshop; Jimi Hendrix—Learn to Play the Songs from Are You Experienced; Play Bass Today!; Play Guitar Today!; Playing in the Style of the Fender Stratocaster Greats; Slap Bass—The Ultimate Guide; Victor Wooten and Carter Beauford—Making Music; Victor Wooten: Live at Bass Day 1998. SYSTEM SPECS: Instructional DVDs.

Homespun Tapes Instructional DVD Series (www.halleonard.com): DVDs for learning guitar include: Muriel Anderson's All-Star Guitar Night; Norman Blake's Guitar Techniques; An Introduction to Open Tunings and Slide Guitar; Learn to Play the Songs of John Denver; Easy Steps to Guitar Fingerpicking; The Guitar Style of Richie Havens; The Blues Guitar of Keb' Mo'; Learn to Play Bottleneck Blues Guitar; Learning to Flatpick; Roger McGuinn's Basic Folk Guitar; The Tony Rice Guitar Method;

You Can Play Guitar. SYSTEM SPECS: Instructional DVDs.

Interactive Guitar Chords CD-ROM (www.melbay.com): By Ralf Fiebelkorn; more than 775 chord voicings presented in videos; easy-to-use interface and "View-in-View" displays; watch each chord played, fingered on the fretboard, diagrammed; section on music theory; tuning guitar; creative use of chord voicings. SYSTEM SPECS: Windows: 486 DX2 Processor or better, 16 MB RAM, 4x CD-ROM drive, VGA display capable of 800 x 600 resolution in 256-color mode, 16-bit sound card, speakers, Windows 3.1 or later.

Intermediate Guitar Method CD-ROM (www.emediamusic.com): CD-ROM; learn to play lead guitar and more; take your playing beyond basic chords and melodies; new techniques demonstrated in over 175 lessons; full-motion video; variable-speed MIDI; recorded audio; animated fretboard; lead guitar skills; rhythm and fingerstyle chapters; lessons on improvisation; scale directory provides fingerings, recordings and variable-speed MIDI for over 200 scales; automatic tuner; digital metronome; recorder and 1000-chord dictionary with audio playback. SYSTEM SPECS: Hybrid.

Isong CD-ROMs (www.halleonrd.com): Teaching tool; animated score and tab; synced instructor video; varying levels of difficulty; virtual fretboard; tempo control; looping with exact cueing; classical guitarists. SYSTEM SPECS: Hybrid.

Jazz Guitar (MGI Interactive): Chord progressions; improvisational techniques; harmony theory; chords; scales; blues scales; daily exercises; for intermediate, all ages. SYSTEM SPECS: Windows.

Jazz Guitar Masterclass Interactive (www.pgmusic.com): Illustrates basic skills to the beginning guitarist; enhances skills of more advanced guitarists; sixty lessons, including Chord Voicings, Inversions, Right-Hand Techniques, Comping, Scales, Modes, Arpeggios, Common Progressions, Improvisation, Chord Melodies, and more; each lesson has an accompanying exercise and a practice tip; ten program tunes feature common chord progressions in a variety of styles and tempos; reference sheets and practice backing tracks; integrates interactive audio lessons with on-screen guitar display and notation. SYSTEM SPECS: Windows.

Just Enough Bass Instructional DVD Kit (www.melbay.com): Instructional package for beginning electric bass guitar; includes DVD, interactive CD-ROM, and portable book/CD set; DVD Video introduces the instructors, shows how they got started, what it is like to perform, what music means to them, and how to buy first gear; learn basic techniques; play with band in interactive Virtual Jam Session; CD-ROM contains over fifty bass lessons; learn the twelve-bar structure, how to play with a steady beat, and bass lines for country, soft rock, heavy

metal, jazz, pop, rap, and funk; AudioBook pocket reference manual works with Audio CD; over fifty lessons; match tracks in book to tracks on CD player and follow along. SYSTEM SPECS: Macintosh: 120 MHz Power PC processor, Mac OS 8.1 or later, 64 MB RAM, 8x CD-ROM drive, 800 x 600 monitor resolution, 16-bit color depth, external speakers recommended; Windows: 166 MHz Intel Pentium processor or compatible, Windows 95/98/ME/2000/XP, 64 MB RAM, 8x CD-ROM drive, 800 x 600 monitor resolution, 16-bit color depth, sound card and speakers.

Just Enough Guitar Instructional DVD Kit (www.melbay.com): Instructional package for beginning guitar; includes DVD, interactive CD-ROM, and portable book/CD set; DVD Video introduces the instructors, shows how they got started, what it is like to perform, what music means to them, and how to buy first gear; learn basic techniques; play with band in interactive Virtual Jam Session; CD-ROM contains over fifty guitar lessons; animated content includes chord charts, twelve-bar blues structure, lead boxes, and video tips taught by fifteen-year-old guitarist Andrew; AudioBook pocket reference manual that works with Audio CD; contains over fifty lessons; match tracks in book to tracks on CD player and follow along. SYSTEM SPECS: Macintosh: 120 MHz Power PC processor, Mac OS 8.1 or later, 64 MB RAM, 8x CD-ROM drive, 800 x 600 monitor resolution, 16-bit color depth, external speakers recommended; Windows: 166 MHz Intel Pentium processor or compatible, Windows 95/98/ME/2000/XP, 64 MB RAM, 8x CD-ROM drive, 800 x 600 monitor resolution, 16-bit color depth, sound card and speakers.

Learning Guitar for Dummies (Anchor Bay Entertainment): By Jon Chappell; presents an easy method for learning to play guitar; step-by-step method does not require viewer to read music; shows how to play in tune and in rhythm, how to form chords, fingerpick, and strum in different patterns; demonstrates how to apply these techniques in actual songs; leads the viewer through a number of popular favorites. SYSTEM SPECS: Instructional DVD.

Martin Simpson Teaches Alternate Tunings (www.alfred.com): Virtuoso performer and composer Martin Simpson demystifies open and altered tunings with book and DVD; teaches how the important tunings relate to each other and to standard tuning; available chord forms in each tuning; Open G, D, and C tunings, DADGAD, suspended fourth modal tunings, and more are explained; diagrams and examples are shown in standard music notation and TAB. SYSTEM SPECS: Instructional DVD.

Mastering the Guitar Class Method Level 1 (www.melbay.com): Tool for teacher who is teaching a guitar class; pedagogical information regarding techniques such as holding position, strumming, playing single-note melodies, and improvisation are demonstrated; how to set up and rehearse a guitar ensemble. SYSTEM SPECS: Instructional DVD.

Modern Guitar Method Grade 1 (www.melbay.com): For building the harmonic knowledge and technique needed to play any style; guitarist learns basic notes on the guitar, single note playing, thirds, triads, chords, and chord progressions; student will play solos, duets, scales, and chords in the keys of C, A minor, G, and E minor while learning to read musical notation; follows along with book of same title (sold separately); offers added instruction and tips along with split-screen right- and left-hand views of exercises, solos, and duets; music is shown on screen (in notation only); can use video without book, but book is recommended; 105 minute video. SYSTEM SPECS: Instructional DVD.

Musicians Institute Press Publications (www.halleonard.com): Book and Audio CD sets for learning guitar and bass include: Advanced Guitar Soloing—The Professional Guide to Improvisation; Advanced Scale Concepts and Licks for Guitar—Private Lessons; Arpeggios for Bass—The Ultimate Reference Guide; Bass Fretboard Basics—Essential Scales, Theory, Bass Lines and Fingerings; Bass Playing Techniques—The Complete Guide; Chord Progressions for Guitar—101 Patterns for All Styles from Folk to Funk!; Classical and Fingerstyle Guitar Techniques; Contemporary Acoustic Guitar; Creative Chord Shapes—Guitarist's Guide to Open-String Chord Forms; Essential Rhythm Guitar—Patterns, Progressions and Techniques for All Styles; French Diminished Scale For Guitar; Funk Guitar—The Essential Guide; Grooves for Electric Bass—Essential Patterns and Bass Lines for All Styles; Guitar Basics—Essential Chords, Scales, Rhythms and Theory; Guitar Fretboard Workbook—A Complete System for Understanding the Fretboard For Acoustic or Electric Guitar; Guitar Hanon—Private Lessons; Guitar Soloing—The Contemporary Guide to Improvisation; Harmonics—Guitar in the Style of Lenny Breau, Ted Greene, and Ralph Towner; Latin Bass—The Essential Guide to Afro-Cuban and Brazilian Styles; Latin Guitar—The Essential Guide to Brazilian and Afro-Cuban Rhythms; Modes for Guitar; Music Reading for Bass—The Complete Guide; Music Reading for Guitar; Odd Meter Bassics—A Comprehensive Source for Playing Bass in Odd Time Signatures; Outside Guitar Licks—Lessons and Lines for Taking Your Playing Over the Top; Practice Trax for Guitar—Musicians Institute Press; The Art of Walking Bass—A Method for Acoustic or Electric Bass; The Diminished Scale for Guitar; The Guitar Lick·tionary; The Musician's Guide to Recording Acoustic Guitar; Rhythm Guitar—The Complete Guide. SYSTEM SPECS: Books and Audio CDs.

Play Blues Guitar (www.playmusic.com): CD-ROM; instruction by master blues guitarist Keith Wyatt; includes four songs and lessons for playing the solo and rhythm guitar parts of each; multitrack music video of a band playing the songs; instruction in four classic blues styles: the twelve-bar medium shuffle, the slow blues, the minor-key blues, and the eight-bar blues; over one hundred minutes of video and animation; forty interactive MIDI practice sessions and more; for intermediate to advanced, all age groups. SYSTEM SPECS: Windows.

Play Guitar (www.playmusic.com): CD-ROM; intensive one-on-one guitar instruction; lessons proceed step by step; play basic chords and scales; play original songs that follow each lesson; music theory; for beginners, all ages. SYSTEM SPECS: Windows.

Play Rock Guitar (www.playmusic.com): CD-ROM; videos, songbooks, and MIDI; intensive one-on-one guitar instruction; features four classic rock songs: Crossroads, Little Wing, Freeway Jam, and Black Magic Woman; interactive multimedia links rock guitar technique lessons to the songs; play great rock riffs note for note; watch a demo and take a lesson at the same time; features Keith Wyatt; learn scale patterns, phrasing techniques, and musical concepts; for intermediate to advanced, all age groups. SYSTEM SPECS: Windows.

Plugged-In Volume 1: The Next Generation in Guitar Instruction Tutorial (www.ubi.com/US): Interactive guitar tutorial; songs by some of rock's all-time greats and the licks that made them famous; intermediate guitarists go step by step through eight guitar classics; songs chosen for style and stature; arrangements presented in a challenging acoustic format; over 180 exercises in over 70 lessons; digital tuner; scrolling music; tablature and lyrics; customize each lesson through looping riffs, rewind and fast forward features, and zooming in full screen to see strumming and fingering up close. SYSTEM SPECS: Macintosh; Windows.

Progressive Beginner Bass Instructional DVD (www.learntoplaymusic.com): By Gary Turner; for beginning bassists; introduction to playing electric bass; essential techniques and music fundamentals as applied to bass playing. SYSTEM SPECS: Book, Audio CD, and Instructional DVD.

Progressive Beginner Classical Guitar (www.learntoplaymusic.com): By Brett Duncan; for beginning guitarists; introduction to classical guitar playing; introduces chords, scales, arpeggios, and essential techniques for both hands; includes pieces by Tarrega, Giuliani, Sor, Carcassi, etc. SYSTEM SPECS: Book, Audio CD, and Instructional DVD.

Progressive Beginner Guitar Instructional DVD (www.learntoplaymusic.com): By Gary Turner; for beginners; covers melody and chord playing using standard notation and tablature; introduces essential techniques and music fundamentals; includes chords and melodies of many well-known songs in a variety of musical styles. SYSTEM SPECS: Book, Audio CD, and Instructional DVD.

Progressive Guitar Method—Bar Chords (www.learntoplaymusic.com): By Gary Turner; beginner to advanced; introduces useful bar, rock, and jazz chord shapes used by rock/pop/country and blues guitarists; includes major, minor, seventh, sixth, major seventh, minor seventh, suspended, etc.; bar chords discussed in detail; suggested bar chord rhythm patterns including percussive strums, dampening, and sixteenth note rhythms. SYSTEM SPECS: Book, Audio CD, and Instructional DVD.

Progressive Guitar Method—Chords (www.learntoplaymusic.com): By Gary Turner; beginner to advanced; open, bar, and jazz chord shapes of frequently used chord types; chord progressions to practice and play along; tuning; how to read sheet music; transposing; the capo; easy chord table, chord formula, and chord symbol chart. SYSTEM SPECS: Book, Audio CD, and Instructional DVD.

Progressive Guitar Method—Fingerpicking (www.learntoplaymusic.com): By Gary Turner; beginner to advanced; introduces right-hand fingerpicking patterns that can be used as an accompaniment to any chord, chord progression, or song; covers alternate thumb, arpeggio, and constant bass style used in rock, pop, folk, country, blues, ragtime and classical music. SYSTEM SPECS: Book, Audio CD, and Instructional DVD.

Progressive Guitar Method—Lead DVD (www.learntoplaymusic.com): By Gary Turner; beginner to advanced; covers scales and patterns over the entire fretboard so can improvise against major, minor, and blues progressions in any key; learn licks and techniques used by lead guitarists, such as hammer-ons, slides, bending, vibrato, pick tremolo, double notes, slurring, and right hand tapping. SYSTEM SPECS: Book, Audio CD, and Instructional DVD.

Progressive Guitar Method—Rhythm DVD (www.learntoplaymusic.com): By Gary Turner; for beginning guitarists; introduces open chord shapes for major, minor, seventh, sixth, major seventh, minor seventh, suspended, diminished, and augmented chords; learn to play over fifty chord progressions, including twelve-bar blues and turnaround progressions. SYSTEM SPECS: Book, Audio CD, and Instructional DVD.

Progressive Guitar Method Book One (www.learntoplaymusic.com): By Gary Turner and Brenton White; for beginning guitarists; basics of guitar; how to read music; covers notes on each of the six strings and basic elements of music theory; how to play melodies and chord arrangements of many well-known traditional, rock, blues, ragtime, and folk songs. SYSTEM SPECS: Book, Audio CD, and Instructional DVD.

Progressive Guitar Method Book One—Supplement (www.learntoplaymusic.com): By Gary Turner; over seventy well-known songs with chord symbols; can be used alone or with Progressive Guitar Method Book 1; contains eight more lessons, including information on major scales, keys, triplets, 6/8 time, sixteenth notes, syncopation, etc. SYSTEM SPECS: Book, Audio CD, and Instructional DVD.

Progressive Guitar Method Book One—Tab (www.learntoplaymusic.com): By Gary Turner and Brenton White; comprehensive, lesson by lesson introduction to the guitar; covers notes on all strings, reading music and tablature, picking technique, and basic music theory; well known traditional, pop/rock, folk, and blues songs. SYSTEM SPECS: Book, Audio CD, and Instructional DVD.

Pumping Nylon (www.alfred.com): Based on Scott Tennant's best-selling book; classical guitarist's technique workout; includes Pumping Nylon daily warm-up routine; subjects covered include nail shape and care, arpeggios, and tremolo; music examples are shown on screen; close-ups of hands and split screens make concepts easy to understand; running time: one hour, fifty-seven minutes. SYSTEM SPECS: Instructional DVD.

Ramble to Cashel—Celtic Fingerstyle Guitar Volume 1 (www.melbay.com): Irish and Scottish music adapted to fingerstyle by Martin Simpson, Steve Baughman, Pierre Bensusan, Duck Baker, Tom Long, Pat Kirtley, and El McMeen; follow in the footsteps of Scottish guitarist Davey Graham, who developed the D-A-D-G-A-D tuning, now the predominant tuning for Irish guitarists; features performances of Believe Me If All These Endearing Young Charms; Waters of Tyne; Shepherd's Delight; Lowlands of Holland; Bony Crossing the Alps; Ramble to Cashel; Cullen Bay; Murtagh McKann; Flamorgan Air; and many more. SYSTEM SPECS: Instructional DVD.

Richie Sambora Interactive Guitar CD-ROM (www.enteractive.com): Features Richie Sambora, lead guitarist of Bon Jovi; teaches different riffs and techniques; play lead with the band; rock star shares his photo collection, popular music videos, personal interviews, and more; includes tuner, scale charts, chord dictionary, and over forty rock guitar techniques; interactive multimedia; user-friendly. SYSTEM SPECS: Windows.

Rock Bass (www.alfred.com): Features Joe Bouchard, formerly of Blue Öyster Cult; step-by-step approach; includes how to play with a guitarist and drummer; opportunity to jam with a professional rock band; special section on how to create a bass solo; close-ups of the hands, split screens, and other video techniques. SYSTEM SPECS: Instructional DVD.

Shred Is Not Dead (www.alfred.com): Master shredder Terry Syrek; chop-building exercises for playing mind bending, super-fast, sweep picking licks; covers creative uses of the pentatonic scale and other scales. SYSTEM SPECS: Instructional DVD.

Signature Licks (www.halleonard.com): Learn trademark riffs and solos from guitar legends; The Allman Brothers Band; Black Sabbath; Freddie King; Lennon and McCartney; Stevie Ray Vaughn; T-Bone Walker; Muddy Waters. SYSTEM SPECS: Instructional DVDs.

Step One: Play Guitar (www.msc-catalog.com): Learn how to play notes, chords, and chord progressions; learn proper playing techniques on the CD and DVD; chapter menus and more for easy navigation through the lessons. SYSTEM SPECS: Book, Audio CD, and Instructional DVD.

Step One: Teach Yourself Guitar (www.msc-catalog.com): Learn how to play notes, chords, and chord progressions while using the book and accompanying audio tracks; teacher demonstrates proper playing techniques on DVD; chapter menus and more for easy navigation through the lessons. SYSTEM SPECS: Book, Audio CD, and Instructional DVD.

Teach Me Blues Guitar (www.voyetra.com): Method; video clips; animation; voice-overs; classic blues riffs, solos, and songs; comes with picks, chord dictionary, and software-based tuning system; for beginners and advanced players. SYSTEM SPECS: Windows.

Teach Me Guitar (www.voyetra.com): Shows how to play chords and songs with videos, intuitive charts, and diagrams; online instructor demonstrates techniques; talks user through lesson; animated fretboard shows neck fingerings in real time; control tempos or loop sections to learn songs at own pace; play with virtual backup band; comes with picks, a chord dictionary, and software-based tuning system; for beginners and advanced players. SYSTEM SPECS: Windows.

Teach Me Rock Guitar (www.voyetra.com): Vidoes, charts, and diagrams; animated fretboard shows fingerings on the guitar neck in real time; control tempos or loop sections; learn songs at own pace; jam and play along with band; comes with picks, chord dictionary, and software-based tuning system; for beginners and advanced players. SYSTEM SPECS: Windows.

Teach Yourself Bar Chords Instructional DVD (www.learntoplaymusic.com): For beginners; contains the most useful bar chord shapes for every type of chord; includes major, minor, seventh, sixth, major seventh, minor seventh, suspended, ninth, etc.; section on reading sheet music, chord symbols, and jam along progressions. SYSTEM SPECS: Book, Audio CD, and Instructional DVD.

Teach Yourself Bass Instructional DVD (www.learntoplaymusic.com): By Gary Turner; for beginning bassists; introduces fundamentals of both left- and right- hand technique; covers music reading using standard notation and tablature; scales, arpeggios, riffs, and how to create bass lines. SYSTEM SPECS: Book, Audio CD, and Instructional DVD.

Teach Yourself Blues Guitar Instructional DVD (www.learntoplaymusic.com): By Brett Duncan; for beginning blues guitarists; covers blues rhythm guitar playing, involving open chords, and movable chord patterns, together with classic blues triplets and shuffle rhythms; teaches lead guitar playing. SYSTEM SPECS: Book, Audio CD, and Instructional DVD.

Teach Yourself Classical Guitar Instructional DVD (www.learntoplaymusic.com): By Brett Duncan; for beginning guitarists; introduces basics of reading music; variety of left- and right-hand techniques introduced; learn pieces through study of chords and arpeggios as well as notes. SYSTEM SPECS: Book, Audio CD, and Instructional DVD.

Teach Yourself Fingerpicking Guitar DVD (www.learntoplaymusic.com): For beginning fingerpicking guitarists; right-hand fingerpicking techniques and patterns which can be applied to any chord or chord progression; covers basics of fingerpicking accompaniment styles. SYSTEM SPECS: Book, Audio CD, and Instructional DVD.

Teach Yourself Guitar Instructional DVD (www.learntoplaymusic.com): By Gary Turner; for beginning guitarists; introduction to playing the guitar; types of guitars available; basic chord shapes and chord progressions; covers standard music notation, guitar tablature, and basic music theory. SYSTEM SPECS: Book, Audio CD, and Instructional DVD.

Teach Yourself Guitar Chords Instructional DVD (www.learntoplaymusic.com): For beginning guitarists; easy to use chord dictionary containing the most useful open, jazz, and bar chord shapes of all the most commonly used chord types; includes special sections on tuning, reading sheet music, transposing, and using a capo. SYSTEM SPECS: Book, Audio CD, and Instructional DVD.

Teach Yourself Lead Guitar Instructional DVD (www.learntoplaymusic.com): For beginning guitarists; comprehensive introduction to lead guitar playing; demonstrates essential techniques and scales; learn important rhythms, note bending, slides, hammer-ons, pull-offs, and right-hand tapping. SYSTEM SPECS: Book, Audio CD, and Instructional DVD.

Teach Yourself Rhythm Guitar Instructional DVD. (www.learntoplaymusic.com): For beginning guitarists; introduction to chords and rhythm guitar playing for the complete beginner; learn to play over fifty chord progressions, including twelve-bar blues and turnaround progressions; learn a variety of rhythm patterns. SYSTEM SPECS: Book, Audio CD, and Instructional DVD.

Teach Yourself Rock Guitar Instructional DVD (www.learntoplaymusic.com): By Brett Duncan; for beginning guitarists; introduces popular rock guitar techniques; covers important bar chords along with two string rock chords and other movable chord shapes; teaches techniques such as slides, hammer-ons, pull-offs, and string bending. SYSTEM SPECS: Book, Audio CD, and Instructional DVD.

Teach Yourself Slap Bass Instructional DVD (www.learntoplaymusic.com): By Peter Gelling; for beginning slap bassists; slapping, popping, left-hand hammers, slides, bends, ghost notes, and double stops; scales, arpeggios, and fingering. SYSTEM SPECS: Book, Audio CD, and Instructional DVD.

Teach Yourself to Play Guitar CD-ROM (www.alfred.com): CD-ROM uses the same teaching approach as the best-selling book; interactive audiovisual format; for beginners of all ages; learn to read standard music notation and TAB; perform songs in a variety of styles; play chords, scales, and cool licks on either acoustic or electric guitar; exercises reinforce technique as follow along with music right on screen; interactive song player to change tempos, adjust audio levels, and record performance; videos of an instructor teaching and demonstrating lessons; bonus games reinforce concepts; customizable ear-training program; interactive guitar tuner. SYSTEM SPECS: Hybrid.

The Art of Acoustic Blues Guitar: Ragtime and Gospel (www.msc-catalog.com): By Woody Mann; book and DVD package; showcases the songs and techniques of two of the most fundamental and exciting styles of traditional fingerstyle guitar playing as exemplified by the legendary virtuoso Reverend Gary Davis; illustrates how the music of one of America's greatest guitarists offers a complete lesson in the beauty and subtleties of ragtime and gospel guitar playing; includes music and instruction for six full blues tunes. SYSTEM SPECS: Book and Instructional DVD.

The Art of Acoustic Blues Guitar: The Basics (www.msc-catalog.com): By Woody Mann; covers basic techniques; capture the essence of traditional blues styles; exercises, tunes, and clear explanation in print and on video; practical ways to develop fundamental techniquel offers insights into the musical logic of blues guitar; includes music and instruction for six full blues tunes. SYSTEM SPECS: Book and Instructional DVD.

The Blues Guitarist (www.pgmusic.com): Music programs containing studio recordings of performances; listen to session players perform blues music; learn riffs, licks, and tricks; each instrument (guitar, piano, bass, and drums) recorded on a separate track; listen to each part independently; multimedia features; study arrangements; hear music; play along

with top studio musicians. SYSTEM SPECS: Windows.

The Gospel Guitar of Rev. Gary Davis (www.melbay.com): Century of different techniques, styles and ideas; many musical formats such as blues, ragtime, folk, gospel, marching songs and Tin Pan Alley hits; four full-length video lessons; Ernie Hawkins teaches fourteen of Rev. Davis's most requested and famous gospel guitar arrangements; rare footage of Rev. Davis playing; detailed rundown of each arrangement, analyzing the structure and timing of each phrase, verse and chorus and replaying everything slower on a split screen with close-ups of both hands; comprehensive eighty-page tab/music booklet included; almost six hours of instruction. SYSTEM SPECS: Instructional DVD.

The Guitar MasterClass for Windows (www.pgmusic.com): Master Guitarist Oliver Gannon; illustrates basic guitar skills and theory; specifically designed for the beginner guitar student; helps develop skills on its own or as a valuable addition to any existing course of study. SYSTEM SPECS: Windows.

The Guitar of Chet Atkins (www.melbay.com): Taught by CGP (Certified Guitar Player) Chet Atkins; for intermediate and advanced fingerstyle guitarists; performs and describes in detail, phrase by phrase, the playing of nine of his classic arrangements; with split-screen techniques can carefully study left- and right-hand movements; eighty-four-minute DVD; booklet is not included, but may be downloaded from guitarvideos.com. SYSTEM SPECS: Instructional DVD.

The Guitar of Elizabeth Cotton (www.melbay.com): Elizabeth Cotten (1893-1987) occupies a unique niche in American finger-picked guitar; composer of the perennial favorite Freight Train; taught herself to play left-handed on her older brother's guitar, which was strung right-handed, leaving her playing left-handed, and upside down as well, picking alternating bass with her index finger and melody with her thumb; lived with and worked for the Seeger family; exceptional attention to details of phrasing and voice leading; strong improvisatory element; includes rare film footage of Elizabeth Cotten performing the songs that are taught; accompanying booklet includes TAB/standard notation transcriptions and song lyrics; 102 minutes. SYSTEM SPECS: Instructional DVD.

The Guitar of Mississippi John Hurt Volumes One and Two (www.melbay.com): Musician of his time and place; played within a tradition but with own subtleties of touch, phrasing, and use of the guitar; famous for fingerpicking in alternating bass style; employed omitted beats or syncopated runs rather than sticking to an unvaried alternation; was comfortable playing in a variety of keys; instruction in John Hurt's repertoire; songs chosen to showcase his playing in different keys; rare documentary silent film footage; accompanying booklet includes TAB/standard notation transcriptions and song lyrics. SYSTEM SPECS: Instructional DVDs.

The Master Flatpick Guitar Solos (www.pgmusic.com): Fully-featured interactive music program with professional flatpick arrangements of fifty-one songs; each song features a Flatpick guitar solo played by top studio musician Marty Cutler, as well as accompanying piano (comping), bass, drums, and strings. SYSTEM SPECS: Windows.

The Master Jazz Guitar Solos (www.pgmusic.com): Interactive music program with professional jazz quartet/quintet arrangements of fifty songs; each song features a jazz guitar solo played by a top studio musician; accompanying piano (comping), bass, drums, and strings; almost five hours of jazz guitar soloing; on-screen guitar fretboard shows exactly which notes and chords are being played; guide notes for typical positions for the key; note names to help learn the fret/string positions; large library of jazz solos; all solos are mainstream playing based on typical chord progressions; most use eighth notes or triplets; each song contains six full choruses; hear solos, slow them down, or step through one note at a time; solos may be printed out; notation also contains TAB; advanced looping features; loop a number of bars, what is on screen, or entire song; adjust tempo or key. SYSTEM SPECS: Windows 3.1, 95/98, NT, 16 MB RAM, PC sound card or MIDI module, CD-ROM drive; Macintosh: MacOS 7.6 or later, 4 MB RAM, 6 MB available hard drive, MIDI module or QuickTime, CD-ROM drive.

The Rock Guitarist (www.pgmusic.com): Music programs containing studio recordings of performances; listen to session players perform rock music; learn riffs, licks, and tricks; each instrument recorded on a separate track; listen to each part independently; multimedia features; study arrangements; hear music; play along with top studio musicians. SYSTEM SPECS: Windows.

The Sor Studies (www.pgmusic.com): Classical guitar performances of 121 of Sor's studies for guitar; music notation and chord symbols on-screen; audio performance; on-screen guitar, fretboard, and fingering; print a high-resolution copy; three CD-ROMs; biography of Sor; historical time line; multimedia features. SYSTEM SPECS: Windows.

Ultimate Beginner Series Acoustic Guitar Basics (WEA) Interactive, step-by-step guide to basics of acoustic guitar playing; topics covered include tuning up quickly, changing guitar strings, playing all keys using bar' and capo chords, playing widely used chords, and more. SYSTEM SPECS: Instructional DVD.

Ultimate Beginner Series Bass Basics DVD (www.warnerbrospublications.com): Covers basics of bass playing; includes lessons on tuning up, right-handed and left-handed techniques, changing strings, creating blues bass lines, picking and fretting, playing with a drummer, and more. SYSTEM SPECS: Instructional DVD.

Ultimate Beginner Series Blues Guitar Keith Wyatt (www.warnerbrospublications.com): First steps in learning to play blues guitar; instructor Keith Wyatt teaches intros and endings, slow blues, sweet blues, and phrasing; includes both tablature and examples using a band that will help demonstrate the lessons. SYSTEM SPECS: Instructional DVD.

Ultimate Beginner Series Electric Guitar Basics (WEA) Step-by-step guide; basics of the electric guitar are covered, including tuning up, playing the most ubiquitous and widely used chords, basic techniques of strumming, cleaning, and picking, and some other specialized skills. SYSTEM SPECS: Instructional DVD.

Ultimate Beginner Series Jr. Learn Basic Guitar (www.warnerbrospublications.com): Learn how to start playing the guitar; learn the fretboard, basic chords and strumming patterns. SYSTEM SPECS: Instructional DVD.

Ultimate Beginner Series Jr. Learn Bass Basics (www.warnerbrospublications.com): Learn how to start playing bass guitar; learn the fretboard, basic melodies, basic rhythms, and how to get in the groove. SYSTEM SPECS: Instructional DVD.

Ultimate Beginner Series Rock Guitar Nick Nolan (www.warnerbrospublications.com): Compiles Volumes 1 and 2 onto a single DVD disk; includes scales and chords, picking and bending techniques, and equipment in Step One; Step Two shows more sophisticated techniques. SYSTEM SPECS: Instructional DVD.

Ultimate Beginner Xpress Acoustic Guitar (www.warnerbrospublications.com): Over two hours of lessons; topics covered include posture and technique, tuning, changing strings, chords, strumming patterns, arpeggios, finger picking, and more. SYSTEM SPECS: Instructional DVD.

You Can Teach Yourself Blues Guitar (www.melbay.com): Companion video to book of same title; in-depth look at basics of acoustic blues guitar; blues progression, blues chords, strum patterns, how to accompany a blues song, 6/8 blues, minor blues, power chords, movable chords, barre chords, the blues scale, turnarounds, fill-ins, the capo, double stops, blues licks, bass line accompaniments, 12/8 blues, blues techniques, how to build and play an improvised solo, and fingerpicking blues; dozens of blues solos and nine new blues songs. SYSTEM SPECS: Instructional DVD.

You Can Teach Yourself Classic Guitar (www.melbay.com): Learn to play classic guitar in all basic keys; solos ranging from Renaissance to twentieth century compositions; masterpieces by Sor, Carcassi, Carulli, Diabelli, Giuliani, Bach, Handel, and Dowland; studies for playing in the second, third, fourth, and fifth positions; "hands on" method. SYSTEM SPECS: Instructional DVD.

You Can Teach Yourself Country Guitar (www.melbay.com): For beginners and intermediate players; how to tune guitar; basic major, minor, and seventh guitar chords; guitar accompaniment strums from current country hits; all songs and examples from the book; basic flatpick technique; how to use a capo; easy play-along country songs. SYSTEM SPECS: Instructional DVD.

You Can Teach Yourself Electric Bass (www.melbay.com): Useful information for the working bass player; thorough and easy to understand; covers popular bass techniques like slap and pop and hammering. SYSTEM SPECS: Instructional DVD.

You Can Teach Yourself Guitar DVD (www.melbay.com): Popular guitar method; easy to understand; moves at a slow, steady pace; play chord accompaniments in seven primary guitar keys; learn to strum blues chords and begin to play fingerstyle backgrounds; ninety-minute video. SYSTEM SPECS: Instructional DVD.

You Can Teach Yourself Rock Guitar (www.melbay.com): Extended length video; William Bay teaches essential elements of contemporary rock and blues guitar; rock rhythm and rock solo techniques are shown; solo, power chords, barre chords, licks, improvising, scales and rhythm chord progressions shown in keys of E, G, D, A, C, F, and B flat; for each key, solos and studies are contained in various positions on the guitar fingerboard. SYSTEM SPECS: Instructional DVD.

Folk and Traditional Instruments

Anyone Can Play Bluegrass Banjo (www.melbay.com): Teaches the basics of bluegrass banjo playing to the beginning student with no previous music experience; discussion of Scruggs style banjo playing; brief introduction to melodic-style playing; Bluegrass standards such as Cripple Creek, Lonesome Road Blues, Little Maggie, Bury Me Beneath the Willow, and many others; free instructional booklet. SYSTEM SPECS: Instructional DVD.

Anyone Can Play Country Fiddle (www.melbay.com): Designed to teach beginners of any age how to play country fiddle; no previous musical experience needed; learn basics of bowing, fingering, chord playing, shuffle bowing, and several famous fiddle tunes; free instructional booklet; forty-five minutes. SYSTEM SPECS: Instructional DVD.

Anyone Can Play Harmonica DVD (www.melbay.com): By Phil Duncan; different techniques and styles taught including folk, gospel, country, and blues; requires ten-hole diatonic harmonica pitched in key of C; free instructional booklet; thirty minutes. SYSTEM SPECS: Instructional DVD.

Anyone Can Play Mandolin DVD (www.melbay.com): By Paul Hayman; designed for beginning mandolin students; teaches fundamentals of mandolin chord strumming, single-note melody picking, and explains tablature; does not require any previous musical experience or note-reading ability; learn several well-known bluegrass songs in both strumming and picking styles; free instructional booklet. SYSTEM SPECS: Instructional DVD.

Basic Blues Harmonica Method DVD (www.melbay.com): By David Barrett; accompanies the book and CD Basic Blues Harmonica Method; large charts, diagrams, and many playing examples. SYSTEM SPECS: Instructional DVD.

Clawhammer from Scratch Volumes 1 and 2 (www.melbay.com): By Dan Levenson; brief history of the five-string banjo; covers the parts of the banjo, holding the banjo, right- and left- hand styles and basic clawhammer strum; strum is broken down into the steps of the finger and thumb; based on Dan's Meet the Banjo program; assumes no prior experience; using one tune, Spotted Pony, student is guided through chords, scale, and individual notes of tune; tips and frequently asked questions; two-page pamphlet included. SYSTEM SPECS: Instructional DVDs.

Conjunto Button Accordion DVD (www.melbay.com): By Joe Torres; the three-row button accordion gives Tex-Mex music its unique sound; learn to play in the authentic Norteno style; basic scales and chords; step by step; overview of Spanish music terminology used by conjunto musicians. SYSTEM SPECS: Instructional DVD.

Fun With the Banjo (www.melbay.com): By Joe Carr; chords, strums, and songs; beginner's course for five-string banjo; concert C tuning. SYSTEM SPECS: Instructional DVD.

Fun With the Mandolin DVD (www.melbay.com): By Joe Carr; teaches material in book of same title; twenty-two songs; tuning and hand positions briefly discussed; 4/4, 3/4, and 2/4 rhythm chord accompaniments in C, G, and D Major; chords are shown in picture diagram form. SYSTEM SPECS: Instructional DVD.

Fun With the Ukulele (www.melbay.com): By Mel Bay; taught by Joe Carr; simple chords, strums, and songs; beginner's course for ukulele in C tuning. SYSTEM SPECS: Instructional DVD.

Homespun Tapes Instructional DVDs (www.halleonard.com): Bluegrass Fiddle Boot Camp; The Sam Bush Mandolin Method; Classic Bluegrass Banjo Solos; Essential Techniques for Dobro; Essential Techniques for Mandolin; Tony Trischka's Essential Practice Techniques for Bluegrass Banjo; Lead Singing and Rhythm Guitar—Finding Your Bluegrass Voice. SYSTEM SPECS: Instructional DVDs.

Nitty Gritty Surround DVD (www.Aixrecords.com): John McEuen, Jimmy Ibbotson, Jennifer Warnes, Laurie Lewis, Tom Rozum, and the String Wizards; play their favorite music from years as recognized performers; recorded for DVD with the 96/24 process with four cameras and five-channel surround sound; technology puts viewer on stage with them as they perform; rehearsal night; artist interviews backstage; background on historic Hanford Fox Theater where recorded; winner of the Diskus Award for "Best DVD-Audio Disk of 2002" and "Best of Show" at the first Surround Music Awards. SYSTEM SPECS: DVD.

Power Pickin' Volume I—Up the Neck Backup for Bluegrass Banjo DVD (www.melbay.com): By Bill Evans; visual method for learning the basic techniques used to play bluegrass banjo accompaniment in up the neck positions; step-by-step approach appropriate for all levels of pickers; tab booklet included; techniques covered include vamping with variations, 3/4 time backup, roll patterns based on chord forms, classic backup licks, two finger backup for slower songs, and bluesy backup styles. SYSTEM SPECS: Instructional DVD.

Step One: Play Harmonica DVD (www.msc-catalog.com): All-in-one package for learning to play the harmonica; guidebook; practice with accompanying audio tracks; DVD features demonstration with an expert; chapter menus and more for easy navigation through the lessons. SYSTEM SPECS: Book, Audio CD, and Instructional DVD.

Step One: Teach Yourself Harmonica DVD (www.msc-catalog.com): Guidebook; practice along with accompanying audio tracks; DVD features demonstration with an expert; chapter menus and more for easy navigation through the lessons. SYSTEM SPECS: Book, Audio CD, and Instructional DVD.

Teach Yourself to Play Harmonica CD-ROM (www.alfred.com): Interactive program designed for beginners with no prior musical experience; packaged with a free Hohner Harmonica; includes licks in the style of The Beatles, Bob Dylan, and Stevie Wonder; demonstrates chording, single-note playing, advanced techniques, and more. SYSTEM SPECS: Hybrid.

The Interactive Blues Harp Workshop (www.melbay.com): By Steve Baker; CD-ROM; starting from beginners level; multimedia tutorial program features play-along tracks and more than 100 exercises with loop function; covers the basics to advanced playing techniques; background information about the history of the harp; most important players; how to tune and repair harp; recommended recordings, mics and amps; graphics, audio files, pictures, and text files. SYSTEM SPECS: Windows: PC 486/66 MHz or better, 16 MB RAM minimum, Windows 3.x or better, 2x CD-ROM drive, SVGA display capable of displaying more than 256 colors using 640 x 480 resolution, 16-bit sound card.

You Can Teach Yourself Banjo DVD (www.melbay.com): By Janet Davis; for five-string bluegrass banjo; teaches tuning, how to read tablature, roll patterns, chords, licks, and other basic information needed to play bluegrass and melodic-style banjo; explains first twenty-two lessons from book of same title; demonstrates examples slowly and at regular speed; can be used by itself to learn by ear, or with tablature found in companion book; companion book purchased separately; sixty minutes. SYSTEM SPECS: Instructional DVD.

You Can Teach Yourself Blues Harp (www.melbay.com): Taught by Phil Duncan; play rhythm chords; designed to be used with book of same title; demonstrates selected examples from book; student is guided in developing ability to hear blues progressions and styles; helps student develop ability to handle demands of most blues music. SYSTEM SPECS: Instructional DVD.

You Can Teach Yourself Dobro DVD (www.melbay.com): By Janet Davis; presents several popular styles used in playing the Dobro, including bluegrass, old time, blues, country, and Hawaiian; no previous musical knowledge needed; tunes included are: Good Night Ladies, Dark Hallow, Jon Henry, Dixie, and many more; presented in G tuning with tablature only; companion book recommended. SYSTEM SPECS: Instructional DVD.

You Can Teach Yourself Dulcimer DVD (www.melbay.com): By Madeline Macneil; companion to book of same title; covers tuning, scales, strumming, fingering, chord studies, alternate tunings, use of capo, and noter; demonstrates dulcimer arrangements. SYSTEM SPECS: Instructional DVD.

You Can Teach Yourself Fiddling DVD (www.melbay.com): By Craig Duncan; complements first seventeen lessons of companion text; covers tuning, holding fiddle and bow, left-hand position, basic A, D, and G scales, shuffle bowing, slurs, double stops, and tunes, including Liza Jane, Shortening Bread, Going to Boston, and Bile Them Cabbage Down. SYSTEM SPECS: Instructional DVD.

You Can Teach Yourself Hammered Dulcimer (www.melbay.com): By Madeline Macneil; companion to book of same title; information on playing hammered dulcimer; tuning, major and minor keys, duplicated notes, repeated notes, modulations, walking bass lines, chromatic notes, drone harmony, back-up chords, interval harmony, and more; arrangements of twenty-five tunes. SYSTEM SPECS: Instructional DVD.

You Can Teach Yourself Harmonica (www.melbay.com): By Phil Duncan; guides viewer through solos and techniques in companion book; fifty minutes. SYSTEM SPECS: Instructional DVD.

You Can Teach Yourself Mandolin (www.melbay.com): By Dix Bruce; play-along examples and tunes; basics of mandolin and mandolin playing; accompanying self and others; common chords and useful strums; reading simple melodies; playing mandolin folk songs; musical examples and tunes written in standard notation and tablature; diagrams principal chords used on mandolin; Chord Appendix; drawings and photographs of vintage instruments. SYSTEM SPECS: Instructional DVD.

You Can Teach Yourself Uke DVD (www.melbay.com): By William Bay; teaches basics of uke playing; how to hold the uke; strum in different time signatures; fifty-eight ukulele songs in keys of C, G, D, F, and Bb; step-by-step instruction; C tuning. SYSTEM SPECS: Instructional DVD.

Drums and Percussion

Absolute Beginners: Drums DVD (www.msc-catalog.com): DVD tutor; step by step; exercises; play along with professional backing track learn how to set up drum kit; tune drums; read drum music; understand rhythm; coordinate bass drum, snare, hi-hat, rash, and ride cymbals; perform first drum part; includes a thirty-two page booklet with exercises matching the DVD. SYSTEM SPECS: Book, Audio CD, and Instructional DVD.

Alfred's Drum Method Instructional DVD (www.alfred.com): Alfred's Drum Method, Books 1 and 2 prepare beginning players for all styles of snare drum and percussion performance; Book 1 contains eighty pages of sequential instruction covering rudimental studies, roll studies, contest solos, and bass drum and cymbal technique; also includes twenty-three solos suitable for recitals and contests; Book 2 covers additional rudimental studies, tonal properties of the snare drum, theme and variations, musical forms, solos and duets; also covers traditional rudimental style, corps style (by Jay Wanamaker), orchestral style, accessory instruments, and multiple percussion techniques; videotapes include demonstrations of all the rudiments and accessory instruments, plus solo performances by the authors. SYSTEM SPECS: Instructional DVD.

An Introduction to Musical Styles Ultimate Beginner Xpress Drums DVD (www.warnerbrospublications.com): Body posture, proper stick technique, basic grooves, fills, rhythms, and more. SYSTEM SPECS: Instructional DVD.

Anyone Can Play Drum Set (www.melbay.com): By Gene Holter; designed for anyone who wants to learn to play drum set; learn popular techniques used in modern music; step-by-step process; no previous musical experience necessary; learn rock, swing, jazz, and country styles; drum music reading, counting, and proper drum setup; free booklet. SYSTEM SPECS: Instructional DVD.

Berklee Press (www.berkleepress.com): Instant Drum Set—Play Right Now!; Berklee Practice Method: Drum Set; Beyond the Backbeat; Brazilian Rhythms for Drum Set and Percussion; Mastering the Art of Brushes; Rudiment Grooves for Drum Set. SYSTEM SPECS: Books and Audio CDs.

Buddy Rich The Lost West Side Story Tapes (www.voyetra.com): Recorded in 1985; state-of-the-art audio mix; 4.0 Channel Dolby Digital and DTS Digital Surround tracks; solos of selected performers; track selection menu; additional commentary by Dave Weckl and Gary Reber; includes interviews, behind-the-scenes footage of Buddy, and more. SYSTEM SPECS: Instructional DVD.

Classic Drum Solos and Drum Battles (www.voyetra.com): Presents fifteen jazz drumming legends in extended solos; filmed over the last five decades; uncut solos from big band legends Sonny Payne, Rufus Jones, Buddy Rich, Sam Woodyard, and Louie Bellson; small group giants Art Blakey and Joe Morello; rare drum battles include meetings between Gene Krupa and Cozy Cole, Buddy Rich and Ed Shaughnessy, Chico Hamilton, Gene Krupa, and Lionel Hampton; Elvin Jones, Sunny Murray, and Art Blakey. SYSTEM SPECS: Instructional DVD.

Complete Modern Drum Set DVD (www.melbay.com): Companion to Complete Modern Drum Set Book; challenging material for the intermediate to advanced drummer; special effects have been removed and sound track has been encoded in Dolby Digital stereo; twenty-one play-along tracks; CueLink; metronome; jazz, Latin, rock, RandB, African, and more; Frank Briggs presents masterful performances and cutting edge concepts such as metric modulation, displaced beats, polyrhythms, etc.; complete performances of Red Moon, Home, Along the Mohawk, Sketch/Electric, and more; over 115 minutes of drumming; hear what patterns sound like in context. SYSTEM SPECS: Instructional DVD.

Drum Basics (www.clearvue.com): For beginners; watch and listen to established player Larry Bright; learn proper hand positions, exercises to build "in the pocket" playing, rolls, solos and fills, snare two and four ghost notes, hi-hat patterns, timing exercises, and more; sound advice and guidance. SYSTEM SPECS: Instructional DVD.

Hal Leonard DVDs (www.halleonard.com): Beginning Drums Volume One; Buddy Rich—At the Top; Classic Drum Solos and Drum Battles; Classic Drum Solos and Drum Battles—Vol. 2; Classic Jazz Drummers; Drummers Collective 25th Anniversary Celebration.and Bass Day 2002; Getting Started on Drums; John Blackwell—Technique, Grooving and Showmanship; Learn to Play the Drumset; Modern Drummer Festival 2000; Play Drums Today!; Snare Drum Basics; Steve Jordan—The Groove Is Here; Steve Smith—Drum Set Technique/History of the U.S. Beat. SYSTEM SPECS: Instructional DVDs.

How to Play Drums from Day One (www.melbay.com): By Jim Payne; basics of rock and blues drumming; assigns singing drum sounds or solfege syllables to five basic components of drumset; addresses holding the sticks, playing the bass drum, and traditional notation and singing syllables of the hi-hat, bass drum, cymbals, and toms; rock and blues tunes with various grooves and tempos; awareness of song form; on-screen samples in both standard notation and drum sounds. SYSTEM SPECS: Instructional DVD.

Just Enough Drums DVD Kit (www.melbay.com): Instructional package for beginning drum set; includes DVD, interactive CD-ROM, and portable book/CD set; DVD Video introduces instructors, shows how they got started, what it is like to perform, what music means to them, and how to buy first gear; Learn basic techniques; play with band in interactive Virtual Jam Session; CD-ROM contains over fifty drums lessons; Gavin, Ben, and Nikki teach how to get set up and start jamming; learn twelve-bar structure, rolls, fills, and how to play beats for funk, jazz, rock, rap, pop, and more; AudioBook pocket reference manual works with Audio CD; contains over fifty lessons; match tracks in Book to tracks on CD player and follow along. SYSTEM SPECS: Macintosh: 120 MHz Power PC processor, Mac OS 8.1 or later, 64 MB RAM, 8x CD-ROM drive, 800 x 600 monitor resolution, 16-bit color depth, external speakers recommended; Windows: 166 MHz Intel Pentium processor or compatible, Windows 95/98/ME/2000/XP, 64 MB RAM, 8x CD-ROM drive, 800 x 600 monitor resolution, 16-bit color depth, sound card and speakers.

Marco Minnemann Extreme Drumming (Music Video Distributors): Reveals many tricks and tips to becoming a successful drummer; five live band performances included featuring Steve Hamilton (Earthworks) on piano; solo drumming material. SYSTEM SPECS: Instructional DVD.

Mike Portnoy Liquid Drum Theater DVD (www.voyetra.com): Two-disk DVD set featuring two bonus, live performances by Dream Theater and Liquid Tension Experiment; over twenty minutes of new footage; full-length commentary by Mike; camera switching option allows the viewer to "direct" four studio performances; photo gallery, and more. SYSTEM SPECS: Instructional DVD.

Modern Drummer Festival 2000 Highlights (www.voyetra.com): Don Brewer, Vinnie Colaiuta, Horacio "El Negro" Hernandez with Marc Quinones, Akira Jimbo, Hilary Jones, Paul Leim, Dave Lombardo, and Billy Ward; first-ever DVD for musician's market; combines all of the material from both video highlights releases; 170 minutes of performances, clinics, and interviews; instant access to each performance and clinic; superior sound and picture. SYSTEM SPECS: Instructional DVD.

Musicians Institute (www.halleonard.com): Book and Audio CD sets for learning drums include: Afro-Cuban Coordination for Drumset—The Essential Method and Workbook; Blues Drumming—The Drummer's Guide to Blues Drumming Styles and Grooves; Brazilian Coordination for Drumset—The Essential Method and Workbook; Chart Reading Workbook for Drummers; Drummer's Guide to Odd Meters—A Comprehensive Source for Playing Drums in Odd Time Signatures; Encyclopedia of Reading Rhythms—Text and Workbook for All Instruments; Funk and Hip-Hop Drumming—Essential Grooves, Fills and Styles; Latin Soloing for Drumset; Working the Inner Clock for Drumset. SYSTEM SPECS: Books and Audio CDs.

Progressive Beginner Drums DVD (www.learntoplaymusic.com): By Peter Gelling; for beginning drummers; explains and demonstrates essential sounds and techniques used in modern drumming styles; includes music fundamentals, coordination and rhythm studies, and making effective use of the whole drum kit. SYSTEM SPECS: Book, Audio CD, and Instructional DVD.

Rock Drums for Beginners DVD (www.alfred.com): Correlates to the method book Rock Drums for Beginners; author shows the concepts and techniques discussed in the book; step-by-step, easy-to-understand approach; teaches how to set up and tune drums; covers two methods of holding sticks and basic stroke technique; close-ups of the hands and feet, split screens, and other video techniques. SYSTEM SPECS: Instructional DVD.

Steve Smith Drumset Technique: History of the U.S. Beat (Music Video Distributors): Four-and-a-half-hour-drum tutorial from one of the most accomplished drummers in the country; two disks; disk 1 concentrates on hand and foot technique; disk 2 on the history and evolution of the drum kit. SYSTEM SPECS: Instructional DVD.

Teach Me Drums (www.voyetra.com): Step-by-step instruction; start with the basics of setting up and tuning; learn to play beats, fills, grooves, and special techniques; with standard DVD format can learn with the convenience of watching a movie and the interactivity of using a software program; can use a computer or a standard DVD player; rewind, loop, and review sections; progress chart keeps track of multiple students; learn at own pace with clear illustrations, diagrams, and charts. SYSTEM SPECS: Instructional DVD.

Teach Yourself Drums Instructional DVD (www.learntoplaymusic.com): By Peter Gelling; for beginning drummers; introduces basics of playing rock, funk, blues, jazz, and other popular styles; exercises for developing independence between all four limbs; lesson on how to play in a band. SYSTEM SPECS: Book, Audio CD, and Instructional DVD.

Tim Alexander (www.halleonard.com): Former Primus drummer Tim "Herb" Alexander; combination of his songs and commentary; navigates his way through a variety of techniques. SYSTEM SPECS: Instructional DVD.

Ultimate Beginner Series Drum Basics (www.warnerbrospublications.com): For the beginning drummer; provides all the basics: How do you hold a drumstick? What is the drummer's function within the framework of a band? How do you play a simple drum fill and basic rock and blues beats? SYSTEM SPECS: Instructional DVD.

Ultimate Beginner Series Jr. Learn Basic Drums (www.warnerbrospublications.com): Learn how to play the drums; learn how to hold the drumsticks, what each drums is, some basic patterns, and how to get in the groove. SYSTEM SPECS: Instructional DVD.

You Can Teach Yourself Drums DVD (www.melbay.com): By James Morton; useful information; for the beginning drummer of any age; progressively introduces drumset basics from setup and basic sticking patterns to rock and funk grooves and fills involving syncopation; sixty-seven minutes. SYSTEM SPECS: Instructional DVD.

Vocal—Choral—Singing

Audio Mirror (www.ecsmedia.com): CD-ROM; practice singing and matching pitches using the latest in technology; listens to notes in real time and determines the note being sung and how sharp or flat the note is in cents; set the sensitivity of the program to compensate for various mic level inputs and impedances; record keeping is included so progress can be tracked and performance evaluated; for all ages. SYSTEM SPECS: Windows.

Born to Sing (www.vocalpowerinc.com): By Elisabeth Howard and Howard Austin; founders of the Vocal Power School in Los Angeles; step-by-step demonstrations, orchestrated tracks, and over 300 song phrases and exercises; TECHNIQUE section covers: breath support, vibrato, range, resonance, falsetto, head voice, chest voice, smoothing out the "break" between registers, volume control, projection, holding notes and long phrases, and more; STYLE section covers: pop, rock, country, blues, RandB, Broadway, phrasing, improvisation, personal style; SUPER VOCALS gives licks and tricks for every style; SING-AEROBICS is a thirty-minute daily workout; High and Low voice; warm up at home or in car. SYSTEM SPECS: Book and Audio CDs.

Contemporary Singer Book and Audio CD (www.berkleepress.com): Berklee Guide; elements of contemporary vocal technique; learn how to, use and protect voice properly; develop stage presence, microphone technique, stamina, range, and sound. SYSTEM SPECS: Book and Audio CD.

CopyScat (www.pgmusic.com): Remove vocals from an audio track, then record your singing overtop; loop sections of a song together to compare your singing with that of the original recording. SYSTEM SPECS: Windows.

ECS Music Tuner (www.ecsmedia.com): Software tool designed to help student play or sing in tune; sing or play any note; program shows if playing is sharp or flat in real time; range is +/- 50 cents; if pitch is outside of this range, program displays the next musical half step; for musicians of any skill or age. SYSTEM SPECS: Windows-MPC2, Windows 95, 8 MB RAM, SVGA display, 3.5-inch disk drive, 4 MB free hard drive space, Windows compatible sound card, microphone, full duplex Sound Blaster drivers recommended.

Global Voices in Song CD-ROM (www.globalvoicesinsong.com): Aural and visual model of vocal music from different cultures; interactive CD-ROM with music and cultural information; resource guide; supplementary audio CD and videotape; for multicultural and choral studies; all ages. SYSTEM SPECS: Hybrid.

Harmony Vocals—The Essential Guide (www.halleonard.com); by Mike Campbell and Tracee Lewis; learn to sing harmony; instructors at Hollywood's Musicians Institute; building harmonies; reading music; scales, chords and intervals; stage and studio techniques; drills for the advanced singer; includes eighteen songs in pop, rock, blues, funk, soul, and country styles; CD with ninety-nine full-demo tracks. SYSTEM SPECS: Book and Audio CD.

How to Train Singers (www.clearvue.com): Explain proper vocal care to students with step-by-step instructions and examples; instructors learn essential warm-ups and exercises that help loosen all parts of the voice and work the muscles used in singing; other topics covered are singing techniques, the relationship of anatomy and physiology to singing, breath support, body alignment, vocal problems, the singing of vowels and consonants, and more; for beginning and advanced singers. SYSTEM SPECS: Book and CD-ROM.

I'm Not Crazy, I'm Vocalizing Audio CD (www.vocalizing.com): By Karen Oleson, founder of VoiceTech; warm-up exercises; helpful adjunct to teaching; mini vocal lesson before each exercise; twenty-minute warm-up exercise recording with vocal guide; twenty-minute warm-up on own with horn guide; instruction booklet includes musical notation and guidance for each exercise, along with tips on vocal health care; car bumper sticker. SYSTEM SPECS: Booklet and Audio CD.

JamRam CD-ROM Songbook Series (www.halleonard.com): Eight fully orchestrated MIDI song files; Roland Sound Canvas soft-synth tone generator driver with over 300 instrument sounds; 16-track recorder/sequencer; songbook with melody, guitar chord frames, and lyrics. SYSTEM SPECS: Windows 95/98, Pentium-based processor, 16 MB RAM, 7 MB hard drive space, 640 x 480 or higher display, 16-bit stereo; double-speed CD-ROM drive, 8-bit sound card.

Just Enough Vocals Instructional DVD Kit (www.melbay.com): Instructional package for beginning vocals; includes DVD, interactive CD-ROM, and portable book/CD set; DVD Video introduces instructors, shows how they got started, what it is like to perform, what music means to them, and how to buy first gear; learn basic techniques; sing with band in interactive Virtual Jam Session; CD-ROM contains over fifty vocal lessons; Allen, Anna, Aron, Daniel, Lillian and SaBella, teach how to use voice, find range, and learn to sing different styles of music; includes karaoke-style practice tracks; AudioBook pocket reference manual works with Audio CD; contains over fifty lessons; match tracks in Book to the tracks on CD player. SYSTEM SPECS: Macintosh: 120 MHz Power PC processor, Mac OS 8.1 or later, 64 MB RAM, 8x CD-ROM drive, 800 x 600 monitor resolution, 16-bit color depth, external speakers recommended; Windows: 166 MHz Intel Pentium processor or compatible, Windows 95/98/ME/2000/XP, 64 MB RAM, 8x CD-ROM drive, 800 x 600 monitor resolution, 16-bit color depth, sound card and speakers.

Karaoke Maker (www.replayinc.com) Remove or reduce vocals in real time from any wav file; change pitch in real time without changing the tempo; automatically convert MP3 files to wav format; digitally copy tracks from any audio CD to wav files; display and scroll lyrics as the song is playing; remove or reduce vocals in any wav file and save the results; change the pitch of any wav file and save the results; load a wav file of any size, regardless of available computer memory; loop an entire song or just sections; supports customized play lists. SYSTEM SPECS: Windows 95, 98, NT 4.0, or later.

Kool Karaoke (www.koolkaraokestudio.com): CD-ROM; adjustable tempo and pitch, melody and volume control; changeable lyrics display; over fifty popular songs; download songs; for all ages. SYSTEM SPECS: Windows.

Learn to Sing! (www.clearvue.com): Teach students the basic vocal sounds of blues, country, funk, jazz, rock, and more; comprehensive collection of resources; includes a DVD, CD-ROM, audio CD, and book; relates vocal techniques through step-by-step lessons and interactive activities in a peer-to-peer format; for beginning singers; includes instructions about how to buy gear, how to set up, how to practice major and minor scales, and more; CD-ROM includes over fifty vocal lessons; how to use voice; how to find range; how to sing in different musical styles; full-color book and CD contain more lessons

and allow flexibility to practice; offers students Web resources for additional research and advice. SYSTEM SPECS: Macintosh: PowerPC/120 MHz processor, 64 MB RAM, and System 8.1-10; Windows: Pentium/166 MHz processor, 64 MB RAM, Windows 95, 98, ME, 2000, or XP, and sound card.

Musicians Institute (www.halleonard.com): Sightsinging—The Complete Method for Singers; The Musician's Guide to Recording Vocals; Vocal Technique. SYSTEM SPECS: Books and Audio CDs.

Pop Singers Warm-Up Kit Book and Audio CD (www.thesingersworkshop.com): By Lis Lewis; vocal instruction for pop singers; companion CD with a dozen warm-up exercises specific to men and women; each exercise begins with a sung example, then piano plays exercise; includes warming up lower and upper voices, connecting the two voices, loosening the throat, placing the sound forward, relaxing the tongue, breath and volume control, increasing vocal range, pitch accuracy, stabilizing tone, and more; book shows practical objectives of each exercise and gives helpful pointers for success. SYSTEM SPECS: Book and Audio CD.

Progressive Beginner Singing DVD (www.learntoplaymusic.com): For beginner to intermediate; for anyone who wants to learn to sing or sing better; essential information on breathing, posture, and tone production; introduction to the basics of reading and understanding music and copying melodies by ear; performing in public, overcoming nerves, and microphone technique; perform many well-known songs in a variety of styles. SYSTEM SPECS: Book, Audio CD, and Instructional DVD.

Scat! Vocal Improvisation Techniques (www.clearvue.com): Learn the fine art of vocal improvisation from renowned jazz vocalist and music professor Bob Stoloff; comprehensive set includes rhythmic and melodic exercises, transcribed solos, vocal bass lines and drum grooves, and more; CD features call-and-response exercises, demonstration solos, and sing-along chord patterns in Latin, jazz, and hip-hop styles. SYSTEM SPECS: Book and Audio CD.

SHOWTRAX (www.halleonard.com): Background tracks; choral CDs of popular music, holiday music, show tunes, traditional music, and more; arranged for SATB, etc. SYSTEM SPECS: Audio CDs.

Sight Singing Made Simple Book and Audio CD (www.halleonard.com): Solfege; hear sounds music symbols represent; for home or school; over sixty exercises; for vocal and choral studies; audio CD. SYSTEM SPECS: Book and Audio CD.

Singer's First Aid Kit Book and Audio CD (www.thesingersworkshop.com): By Lis Lewis; book and vocal warm-up CD; twenty-minute Singer's Warm-Up; use on the way to rehearsals or gigs, at the recording studio, or at home; warm up before voice lesson; protect vocal instrument and keep it stronger and healthier; book includes chapters on recording, rehearsing, performing, auditions, vocal health, and more; The Singer's Troubleshooting Guide gives insider tips needed to be successful. SYSTEM SPECS: Book and Audio CD.

Singing for the Stars (www.alfred.com): By famed LA-based vocal and opera coach Seth Riggs; speech level singing and master classes; complete index and table of contents; vocal therapy and technique for singing; lecturer and teacher; consultant; performer. SYSTEM SPECS: Book and Audio CDs.

Song Express Instructional DVDs (www.warnerbrospublications.com): Learn songs from all genres; large selection of standards. SYSTEM SPECS: Instructional DVDs.

Teach Yourself to Sing (www.alfred.com): CD-ROM; covers the basics of singing, including breathing, posture, warming up, and more; discusses the mind/body connection to singing; easy and comprehensive approach to reading music; covers rock, jazz, blues, and other popular styles; can transpose accompaniment to any key. SYSTEM SPECS: Hybrid.

Teach Yourself to Sing — 10 Easy Lessons (www.learntoplaymusic.com): For beginning vocalists; learn the basic principles of singing; covers vocal tone, vocal control, breathing, posture, microphone technique, performance ideas, etc. SYSTEM SPECS: Book, Audio CD, and Instructional DVD.

The Bach Chorales (www.pgmusic.com): Performance of Bach's four-part Chorales; professional choral ensemble; detailed multimedia history; each voice (soprano, alto, tenor, and bass) recorded on a separate track; listen to independently; interactive program; vocal music; history of Bach; time line. SYSTEM SPECS: Windows.

The Barbershop Quartet for Windows (www.pgmusic.com): Music program; favorite barbershop songs; interactive multimedia history of barbershop singing in America; each voice (tenor, lead, baritone, and bass) recorded on a separate track; listen to each part independently; study arrangements; hear music; sing along; made with the assistance of the Society for the Preservation and Encouragement of Barbershop Quartet Singing in America, the leading authority in America. SYSTEM SPECS: Windows.

The Pop Singer's Warm-Up Kit (www.clearvue.com): Book and CD focus on essential instruction for the pop singer; activities cover fundamental exercises: warming up the lower and upper voice, connecting the two voices, loosening the throat, controlling breathing and volume, increasing range, stabilizing tone, and many others; CD features a sung example followed by a piano version to which students can practice; book gives practical objectives

of each exercise and offers valuable pointers. SYSTEM SPECS: Book and Audio CD.

The Vocal Visions Warm-Up CD (www.vocalvisions.net): By Ellen Johnson; for soloists, choirs, bands, studio musicians, and anyone who sings; seventeen exercises designed for all levels; instruction booklet included; CDs made for male high or low voice, female high or low voice; helps get voice ready to perform; increases musicianship skills. SYSTEM SPECS: Book and Audio CD.

Vocal Practice for Performance DVD (www.clearvue.com): Instructor is Donna McElroy, Berklee Professor, Grammy nominee, Dove Award winner, and vocalist; singers learn how to use whole bodies to enhance sound by watching McElroy work with a student one-on-one; McElroy also demonstrates the use of different muscle groups, provides lifestyle tips, and illustrates simple, everyday exercises that can help cultivate and protect vocal power. SYSTEM SPECS: Instructional DVD.

Voice-Tradition and Technology: A State-of-the-Art Studio (www.clearvue.com): Voice pedagogy, voice and science; findings of medical and scientific researchers to enhance traditional voice training in the studio; interactive CD-ROM and book; techniques; feedback; special challenges. SYSTEM SPECS: Hybrid.

Worship Studio (Interactive Digital Design — Midisoft): Create music for hymns and choir; lead sheets; orchestral scores; record and play back; comes with 1,000 hymns; add notes, symbols, lyrics, and instrumentation; print out music; MIDI keyboard required. SYSTEM SPECS: Windows.

Studio, Choir, Band, and Orchestra Practice and Management

3D Dynamic Drill (www.pyware.com): Drill design software used by high schools, colleges, universities, and corps around the world; fast drawing and animating drill program; count-to-count technology; view, edit, or print any count of the drill at any time; with Morph feature can create transitions by morphing existing formation instead of re-creating formations from scratch; Time Track process removes the limitation that requires all transitions to begin and end at the same time; Follow-the-Leader function; with Rewrite can rewrite drill in seconds; on-screen help; Stride Zone; unlimited drawing tools; reduced editing of symmetrical shapes; resize a drill any time to reflect current band size; animated color with music; position numbers or labels; flexible instructional printouts include drill book; cast sheet; design props; hash marks; measuring tape and compass; measurement tool (Mac only); coordinates printed by performer; animation tempos. SYSTEM SPECS: Macintosh: 16 MB RAM, System 7 or 8, 14-inch color monitor; Windows.

3D Java Drill Design (www.pyware.com): New innovative features with highly requested features contained in earlier versions; upgrade; cross compatibility; can operate on any computer that supports Java including Windows, NT, Unix, and Macintosh; 3D Java data files are not downward compatible to Original 3D and Virtual 3D; complete control of grid design; grid designs can be saved as .GRD files and used in any 3D Java drill file; specialized drawing and editing tools are implemented as 3D Java Plug-Ins; plug-in sets include Military Style Editing Tools, Pageantry Tools, Showband Style Editing Tools, and many more; animated drills can synchronize to MIDI files and to CD recordings of live performances; labels or position numbers can be automatically positioned along the curvature of shapes or places manually; design a drill backwards; Charting Aid program; with Static Charts drills can be designed without animation capabilities for idea books where each page is an unrelated chart and for creating a library of standard charts used by a performing group such as a school name or logo; Static Chart can be copied and pasted into a drill file that has animation capabilities; improved Drill Rewrite; special Internet distribution features for professional drill designers; drill files can be locked internally to read only, not print, view first eighty counts, and display the designer information such as name and phone number; customer can download from Internet and review drill for purchase; drill can be unlocked by customer with password provided by drill designer. SYSTEM SPECS: Macintosh: System 8 or greater, 400 MHz machine or greater, 64 MB RAM; Windows: Windows 95/98/NT, 400 MHz machine or greater, 64 MB RAM.

3D Virtual Dynamic Drill Design (www.pyware.com): Analyze every aspect of drill; view every count of drill for collisions, excessive strides, and visual voicing, including phasing and balance of actual music through MIDI capabilities; for use in marching techniques class; students can turn in projects on disk; grade and return with built-in multimedia report for review; NCAA hashes; perspective view; changing of performer colors and symbols during animation; measurement tool; unlimited drawing tools; props; flexible instructional printouts; new features added in Version Two include largest stride indicator, fixed intervals, mixed intervals, additional rewrite features, additional print layout options, additional labeling features, show/hide shapes. SYSTEM SPECS: Macintosh: System 7 or 8, 16 MB RAM, 14-inch color monitor; Windows.

Alfred Enhanced CDs (www.alfred.com): Can be played in a conventional audio CD player; can also be used in a computer CD-ROM drive; follow along with the musical notation and record while playing along; twenty-three Alfred book titles with enhanced CDs. SYSTEM SPECS: Windows.

Amadeus Al Fine (www.pyware.com): Pitch-to-MIDI device; use wind instruments for input with Amadeus Tutor, notation software, or instructional courseware; hardware box that converts microphone input of any wind instrument into standard MIDI data; compatible with any software that normally uses a MIDI keyboard as a way of input; any notation program will operate with Amadeus for transcribing a performed passage into notation on the computer. SYSTEM SPECS: Macintosh; Windows.

Amadeus Tutor (www.pyware.com): Assessment and evaluation software; works with Amadeus Al Fine; develop a curriculum for students; Graphic Tuner: graphically displays, assesses, and compares the intonation perception and performance of students individually or in groups; Scale Drills: practice and assessment application for developing and testing student's knowledge and performance of any scale type; Finger Module: contains fingering and alternate fingerings for most instruments; Pitch Pong: game for ear training and pitch detection; Practice Monitor: practice a solo as Amadeus plays the accompaniment; listens and assesses, showing an accuracy grade for rhythm and pitch on each measure. SYSTEM SPECS: Macintosh; Windows; requires Amadeus Al Fine to work.

Anyone Can Play Violin DVD (www.melbay.com): By Coral White; self-guided beginner's violin course; designed for anyone of any age; no previous musical experience necessary; teaches basics for all types of performance, from classical to country; step-by-step process compatible with Suzuki pedagogy; instrument care, tuning, positioning, note reading, playing pizzicato on open strings, fingering, and use of the bow; instructional booklet included; sixty-five minutes. SYSTEM SPECS: Instructional DVD.

Artistry in Strings (www.kjos.com): By Robert S. Frost and Gerald Fischbach with Wendy Barden; beginning string methods; fifty-six page string method for the classroom or private studio; comprehensive approach includes music theory, composition, listening exercises, ensemble performances, and interdisciplinary studies; many music styles are featured, including classical, jazz, country, rock, and folk music from a variety of cultures around the world; note reading; artistry with the bow; rhythm charts feature creative rhythmic word associations; note values and rhythm patterns; "Swingercises" emphasize left- and right-hand technical development; solos, duets, rounds and orchestrated arrangements; bow strokes such as martelé are introduced and reinforced; scales, thirds, and arpeggios in the keys of D, G, and C Major are included in the back of each part book; multiple image photographs, graphics, and artwork; complete Teacher's Score and Manual with

Enrichment CD containing excerpts of symphonic classical music and world folk music; full-length recordings of the four ensembles featured in the book; articles; worksheets; separate books available for all string instruments. SYSTEM SPECS: Books with Audio CDs.

Audio File (Doubleware Productions): Record records, CDs, and cassettes; recall any recording or song in collection; information about each includes title, performer, music type, recording media, record label, and more. SYSTEM SPECS: Windows 3.1 or 95, 386 or better, 4 MB RAM, 2 MB hard disk space.

BandQuest Series (www.halleonard.com): CD-ROMs; A+: A Precise Prelude and an Excellent March; American Composers Forum; Alegre; City Rain; Grandmother Song; Hambone; New Wade 'n Water; Old Churches; Ridgeview Centrum; Spring Festival. SYSTEM SPECS: Hybrid.

Berklee Press (www.berkleepress.com): Berklee Practice Method: Alto and Baritone Sax; Berklee Practice Method: Tenor and Soprano Sax; Berklee Practice Method: Trombone; Berklee Practice Method: Trumpet. SYSTEM SPECS: Books and Audio CDs.

Canadian Brass (www.halleonrad.com): Beginning Trumpet Solos (Piano/Trumpet); Easy Trumpet Solos (Piano/Trumpet); Intermediate Trumpet Solos (Piano/Trumpet). SYSTEM SPECS: Books and Audio CDs.

Church Music Master for Windows (www.churchmusicmaster.com) Visual interface for organizing church music program; customizable; free demo download. SYSTEM SPECS: Windows.

Computer Music: An Interactive Documentary (Digital Studios): Educational CD-ROM; covers computer music for middle-school through college-age students; sounds created by digital instruments; over two hours of movies and animation that demonstrate key concepts in digital audio, MIDI sampling, sequencing, editing, and composition; pioneers in computer music; career advice from professionals; Lab Annex allows students to make their own instruments, experiment with WAVEforms, and edit a composition. SYSTEM SPECS: Hybrid.

Crowd Pleasers (www.halleonard.com): For bands without time or resources to put together complicated field shows; each CD-ROM set offers three arrangements by well-known arrangers, easy-to-learn drills; view and print; Complete Set; Crowd Pleasers Nos. 1-10. SYSTEM SPECS: Macintosh; Windows.

De Haske Play-Along Book/CD Packages (www.halleonard.com): Alto Saxophone and Romance; Clarinet and Romance; Euphonium and Romance; Flute and Romance; Oboe and Romance; Pini Di Roma; Ponte Romano; Tenor Saxophone and Romance; Trombone and Romance; Trumpet and Romance. SYSTEM SPECS: Books and Audio CDs.

Digital Music Mentor CD-ROM (www.ecsmedia.com): For classroom or private in-struction; teacher records exercises or tunes for study; student can study away from the lesson time by hearing how the piece is supposed to sound and then record their version of the piece; teacher can review and discuss with the student; all ages. SYSTEM SPECS: Hybrid.

Director's Communication Kit for Band (www.halleonard.com): Text-only computer disk includes over thirty-five letters, brochures, and guidelines for parents and administrators; recruitment retention; advocacy and more; for all band programs. SYSTEM SPECS: Macintosh; Windows.

Do It! Play In Band: A Beginning Band Method (www.clearvue.com): Twenty-six CDs and books; helps students learn unique role of every instrument in the band; CDs allow students to discover the rich diversity among American, Latin American, African, European, and Far Eastern musical styles; books include details about phrasing, rhythm, tempo, style, tone quality, emotion, history, and culture; teacher's resource edition contains a 550-page guide with a complete musical score, a compact disk with exercises for group instruction, and resources to align materials with National Standards for Music Education. SYSTEM SPECS: Books and Audio CDs.

Drill Quest (www.drillquest.com): Automatic matching and animation; easy-to-read charts; unlimited number of symbols; perspective view; free site license; multimedia; stand-alone drill player; extensive editing capabilities; charting assistants; customize symbol colors; pit area; toll-free phone support. SYSTEM SPECS: Macintosh; Windows.

ECS Music Suite (www.ecsmedia.com): Includes a metronome and tuner; tuner offers fast, automatic note sensing in real time with a broad chromatic range and a special transpose function to shift the entire scale to match instruments not in the key of "C"; metronome turns computer into a device to assist users in playing more accurately "in tempo." SYSTEM SPECS: Windows 95, MPC2, 8 MB RAM, SVGA Display, microphone, Creative Labs Sound Blaster sound card (no compatibles), Full Duplex SoundBaster Drivers (recommended).

Essential Elements 2000 Band Director's Communications Kit CD-ROM (www.halleonrad.com): Letters focusing on music advocacy, the importance of the arts in the schools, and the benefits of musical study in the development of the child; additional letters written specifically for band; time savers for the busy band director. SYSTEM SPECS: Hybrid.

Expressive Conducting (Weins): Interactive, multimedia presentation of the conductor's skills and gestural grammar; video clips; moving animations; begins with the most basic gestures; progresses to complications faced by professionals; fourteen chapters; program coordinated with textbook; for the classroom or independent study; approximately 500 video clips; 200 animations; author is an experienced teacher of counducting and a choral/orchestral conductor at Wheaton Conservatory of Music; two CDs; program will AutoRun (AutoStart) from CD or may be installed to hard drive; installer checks for adequate space and provides required version of QuickTime as necessary. SYSTEM SPECS: Hybrid.

FastForward Series (www.musicsales.com): Instructional series; all instruments. SYSTEM SPECS: Books and Audio CDs.

FastTrack Series (www.halleonard.com): Instructional series; standard and pocket size; all instruments and vocal; Spanish editions. SYSTEM SPECS: Books and Audio CDs.

Hal Leonard DVDs (www.halleonard.com): Play Alto Sax Today!; Play Clarinet Today!; Play Flute Today!; Play Trumpet Today! SYSTEM SPECS: Instructional DVDs.

Intonation Trainer (www.finalemusic.com): Teaches students how to listen for and eliminate intonation beats; learn which notes on instrument are flat and which are sharp; learn to anticipate pitch problems and how to solve them. SYSTEM SPECS: Hybrid.

Jump Right In: The Instrumental Series (www.clearvue.com): Twenty-eight books and twenty-eight CDs for band instruments; instruct beginning musicians to learn sounds before they play them; encourage students to recognize sounds by ear, to build music vocabulary, and to read music; students will learn to carry a tune and keep a steady beat; will discover embouchure, posture, hand position, and articulation; students can listen and play along with the compact disks, which feature folk songs and melodies from many cultures and time periods; student books contain arrangements of over forty songs; materials include national standards and suggestions for measurement and evaluation; teacher's guide contains lesson plans and teaching suggestions. SYSTEM SPECS: Books and Audio CDs.

Master Music Manager (Manager Software): Music library; membership files; personnel directory; inventory/uniform manager; recordings library; for all choral and instrumental educators; access commands by pulling down menu bar or clicking on buttons; datafile capacity limited only by the amount of hard disk space. SYSTEM SPECS: Macintosh; Windows.

Music Admin Pro (www.ecsmedia.com): Intuitive program which handles all administrative aspects of running a music department, a band program or instrument tuition; access and cross-reference any information on students, parents, teachers, ensembles, progress reports, hire, instruments, resources, lesson charges, teacher pays, purchases, etc., from one relational data file; Ensemble Module produces ensemble lists and mailing labels as well as tracks each student's activities through the years; Student Progress Reports Module sends reports home with one-step mailing labels; Instrumental Music Time-Tabling Module automated to change some or all lesson times each week with lesson timetables produced for the week, term, or semester; Instrument Hire Module; external and internal examination records section; Teacher Pay Module with automated calculations based on the teacher's students, activities, and rates; one-click New Year changes increasing student year, deleting final year students, erasing old timetable records, etc.; Automated Invoicing Module for charges to parents for lessons and/or student purchases; Teacher Resource Library Module easily obtains lists of all owned resources by topic area, ensemble, grade, and so on; student practice time and room allocation; teacher room allocations; mail merging; To Do Lists; Student Medical Records for tours and excursions; Uniform Allocation; Locker assignment and an Accession Register; comprehensive and easy to use; reports and lists can be viewed on the screen, printed or exported to programs such as Word, Excel, etc.; manual is concise and written in plain English for the novice computer user; Help files are on most screens and there are many automated tasks; state-of-the art professional database engine that can be networked. SYSTEM SPECS: Macintosh; Windows.

Music Administrator (www.pyware.com): Modifiable database including student files, music library, equipment and uniform inventory, general ledger; predesigned file templates. SYSTEM SPECS: Macintosh version 7 or 8, 2 MB RAM.

Music Directors Assistant (Interactive Digital Design—Midisoft): Management tool for all types of music directors; organize music program; event calendar; record keeping for instrument inventory, recordings, and literature; plan rehearsals; manage room schedules, equipment, and more. SYSTEM SPECS: Macintosh.

Music Ministry Manager (Manager Software): Data management system for church musicians; includes modules for music library, recordings, personal directory, music inventory, and personnel; generates customized memo forms and letterhead; will dial phone numbers with a mouse and modem. SYSTEM SPECS: Macintosh; Windows.

Music Office (www.pyware.com): For record keeping, including student grades, student addresses, music in music library, fund-raising, or uniform and equipment inventories; maintenance and accounting; export data function in file menu; copy to/from floppy feature so files can be easily transferred between computers; added font options allowing better control of fonts during printing; added restore function to revert a data file easily to a backup; additional backup security to protect work. SYSTEM SPECS: Windows 3.1/95/98, 16 MB RAM.

Music Terminology for Bands, Orchestra, and Choirs (www.ecsmedia.com): Covers fundamental music terminology; includes dynamics, tempo markings, stylistic expression markings, music symbols, key signatures, scales, and string terminology; final test of fifty questions and record keeping included; for beginner to intermediate, grades 5-12. SYSTEM SPECS: Hybrid.

Musical Performance Art Collection: Volume 1 (J Graphics): CD-ROM collection of musicians, instruments, musical symbols, humorous musical characters and instruments, musical borders and themes on music; for music teachers and computer graphic artists; includes Concert, Jazz, Marching Band, Musical Borders, General Music, and Just Instruments; 1-inch illustrations; over 250 line art illustrations; import, place, or insert into page layout and word processing applications that support TIFF graphic formats for both Mac and PC/Windows platforms; images are sharp, black-and-white line art drawings that can be colorized; all MPAC illustrations are copyrighted and may not be duplicated or copied for unauthorized distribution in any form; can be used freely only by the original registered user for the purpose of publication in non-commercial use on a single computer; licensing is required for commercial use. SYSTEM SPECS: Macintosh; Windows.

RCI Music Library CD-ROM (RCI Software): Organize and track performances; create program notes; catalog composers; keep track of music and instrument loans; access music library by title, composer, arranger, or accompaniment; keep track of concert and recital dates; order music from publishers; keep track of robes and uniforms; print customized reports. SYSTEM SPECS: Macintosh; Windows.

Sibelius Instruments (www.sibelius.com): Guide to orchestral and band instruments; interactive encyclopedia of instruments, bands, orchestras, and ensembles; complete information on every orchestral and band instrument, with full details of their characteristics, how to write for them, and hundreds of high-quality recordings; explains about different orchestras, bands, and ensembles, including their historical development and repertoire; extensive quiz; for schools, colleges, universities, teachers, students, composers, and arrangers; over fifty instruments, from alto clarinet to xylophone; over twenty types of band, orchestra, and ensemble, from string quartet to marching band; instrumental writing and playing techniques such as range, bowing, mutes, glissandi, harmonics, mallets, and multiphonics; lesson plans, student assignments, and recommended listening; quiz with 500 listening and general questions. SYSTEM SPECS: Macintosh: Mac OS 8.6 or later (including OS X), 32 MB+ free RAM (128 MB total RAM for OS X), 170 MB free hard disk space, CD-ROM drive; Windows: Pentium II, Windows 95/98/Me/2000/XP/NT4 or later, 32 MB+ RAM, 170 MB free hard disk space, CD-ROM drive.

Sibelius Notes (Teaching Tools) (www.sibelius.com): Educational resources to help teach music in the classroom; covers all levels, K-12; ready-to-use exercises and worksheets; covers notation, composing, and more; dozens of music files on CD-ROM; includes guides for teachers and students. SYSTEM SPECS: Macintosh; Windows.

Sibelius Starclass (www.sibelius.com): Lesson plans and resources for the elementary and primary school; 180 ready-to-use lesson plans which support MENC and QCA standards; includes full explanations of musical concepts for nonspecialist teachers; hundreds of music clips and printable pictures; ninety-nine-track audio CD to play in class; classroom resource; well-presented and impressively structured lesson plans; saves hours of preparation. SYSTEM SPECS: Macintosh; Windows.

SlowBlast! and SlowGold for Windows (www.slowgold.com): Help students practice difficult musical passages; slows music down; play along or transcribe riffs and tunes at own speed instead of at full pace; master difficult phrases. SYSTEM SPECS: Windows.

SmartMusic Studio (www.smartmusic.com): CD-ROM; practice program for woodwinds, brass players, and vocalists; improvement in the ability to perform solo repertoire comes from working with accompaniment; provides accompaniment and follows player; metronome; practice loops; vocal warm-ups; vocal and instrument microphones included; foot pedal; practice with 20,000 professional accompaniments featuring authentic basso continuo, full orchestra, jazz piano combos, and rock/pop bands; accompaniments to over 50,000 skill-building exercises; subscribe online. SYSTEM SPECS: Hybrid.

Standard of Excellence Practice and Assessment Software (www.onlineamadeus.com): From Pyware; use in the classroom for evaluation or testing; use at home for practice; use as a stand-alone product or through the Internet; uses Online Amadeus, PC, and microphone; students play predesigned exercises from the Kjos series Standard of Excellence Books 1, 2, or 3 or any musical passage created with the Online Amadeus Tutor; once the exercise or passage is selected, the student plays and the computer objectively evaluates the pitch and rhythmic accuracy of that performance; Online Amadeus assigns a numerical grade from 1 to 100, and displays those results on a graph; instant feedback designates problem areas; students can upload their results to an Instructor database either in the classroom or via the Internet; includes the name of the student, the exercise or passage practiced, overall score and breakdown by points of rhythmic and intonation accuracy; instructors view and monitor every student's practice and progress; print out results for grading or for parents and administrators; use the Standard of Excellence Practice and Assessment Software or design own lessons with the Online Amadeus Tutor. SYSTEM SPECS: Windows 95 thru Windows 2000, 32 MB

RAM, Pentium I 133 or faster, MIDI capable sound card, external microphone.

Step One Series (www.musicsales.com): Instructional series; all instruments. SYSTEM SPECS: Books and Audio CDs.

The Music Maid (www.signature5.com): Tool for creating music worksheets, exams, and answer keys; for use in individual lessons or classrooms, with or without an instrument; focus is primarily on keyboard skills, but can be adapted for use with any instrument; topics include: note names, interval or chord qualities, seventh chords, scales, key signatures, rhythmic exercises, and harmonic progressions; can create specific worksheets; exercises can be written on a grand staff, single staff, or single line for rhythmic exercises; single-line staffs default to treble clef; can be changed to bass, tenor, or alto clef; text can be edited and displayed in any font size or style; worksheets can be created for ear training, sight-reading, harmonization, and composition; remedial exercises in note reading, interval or chord identification, and harmonic analysis; can save custom exercises; harmonic progressions are voice-leading and analysis exercises in choral style; can create an answer key on command for any worksheets; exercise menu displays frequently used exercises; manual is easy to read; begins with four tutorials that create sample worksheets; provides installation directions; user support is available from the publisher through e-mail or toll-free number; for music teachers; free download. SYSTEM SPECS: Macintosh, System 6, or higher.

The Teacher's Apprentice for Music Theory (Creative Software): Create question and answer sessions for interactive testing; create printed music tests; keep student records of progress; two different work areas, one for the teacher and one for the student; customize the program by adding, editing, or deleting questions; add custom graphics and basic aural capabilities to the questions; can create written tests and computer online interactive tests; can use the questions that come with the program or create them; database to keep records on students' progress; multiple levels of questions; can review or print any questions that were missed during the testing session; students can monitor scores and view a graph that shows progress made; last twenty scores are saved for future reference. SYSTEM SPECS: Macintosh: 68020 or better, 4 MB RAM free, 8 MB recommended, System 7.0 or higher, 13-inch monitor recommended; Windows: 386SX or better, Windows 3/1 or better, 6 MB RAM.

Timesketch Editor (www.ecsmedia.com): For listening to and analyzing music with computer; create teacher-developed listening lessons with any audio CD; for fundamentals courses, appreciation courses, or music history courses at any level; annotated listening format can be applied to classes, activities, and music performance. SYSTEM SPECS: Hybrid.

TrackNotes CD-ROM for Windows (www.virtualstudiosystems): Track management software; custom studio configuration; supports up to sixty-four multitracks, plus 2,048 virtual tracks; signal path tracking; digital image viewer; artist, musician, musical instrument, and audio equipment documentation; studio asset tracking and valuation; wide variety of printed reports, including several versions of Track Sheets. SYSTEM SPECS: Windows.

Ultimate Beginner Series—Alto Sax (www.warnerbrospublications.com): Takes the novice alto saxist from opening the case through assembling the instrument, proper breathing, forming the embouchure, producing a sound, holding the instrument, correct posture, basic theory, learning notes, playing a song, and basic maintenance; includes demonstrations of good tone and proper technique; contains everything needed to get one started on the alto sax. SYSTEM SPECS: Instructional DVD.

Ultimate Beginner Series—Cello (www.warnerbrospublications.com): Takes student from opening the case to playing a simple tune; learn the history of the instrument, instrument maintenance, the proper way to hold the instrument, simple finger patterns, bowing, plucking methods, and how to develop a rich full tone; for the new student or as a refresher course at the intermediate level. SYSTEM SPECS: Instructional DVD.

Ultimate Beginner Series—Clarinet (www.warnerbrospublications.com): Takes the novice clarinetist from opening the case through assembling the instrument, proper breathing, forming the embouchure, producing a sound, holding the instrument, correct posture, basic theory, learning notes, playing a song, and basic maintenance; includes demonstrations of good tone and proper technique; contains everything needed to get one started on the clarinet. SYSTEM SPECS: Instructional DVD.

Ultimate Beginner Series—Flute (www.warnerbrospublications.com): Takes the novice flautist from opening the case through assembling the instrument, proper breathing, forming the embouchure, producing a sound, holding the instrument, correct posture, basic theory, learning notes, playing a song, and basic maintenance; includes demonstrations of good tone and proper technique; contains everything needed to get one started on the flute. SYSTEM SPECS: Instructional DVD.

Ultimate Beginner Series—Trombone (www.warnerbrospublications.com): Takes the novice trombonist from opening the case through assembling the instrument, proper breathing, forming the embouchure, producing a sound, holding the instrument, correct posture, basic theory, learning notes, playing a song, and basic maintenance; includes demonstrations of good tone and proper technique; contains everything needed to get one started on the trombone. SYSTEM SPECS: Instructional DVD.

Ultimate Beginner Series—Trumpet (www.warnerbrospublications.com): Takes the novice trumpeter from opening the case through assembling the instrument, proper breathing, forming the embouchure, producing a sound, holding the instrument, correct posture, basic theory, learning notes, playing a song, and basic maintenance; includes demonstrations of good tone and proper technique; contains everything needed to get one started on the trumpet. SYSTEM SPECS: Instructional DVD.

Ultimate Beginner Series—Viola (www.warnerbrospublications.com): Takes student from opening the case to playing a simple tune; learn the history of the instrument, instrument maintenance, the proper way to hold the instrument, simple finger patterns, bowing, plucking methods, and how to develop a rich, full tone; for the new student or as a refresher course at the intermediate level. SYSTEM SPECS: Instructional DVD.

Ultimate Beginner Series—Violin (www.warnerbrospublications.com): Introduction to playing the violin; covers basic topics from instrument care to playing techniques; also covers the history of the instrument, the proper way to hold the instrument, simple finger patterns, bowing and plucking methods, and various techniques that allow the player to develop own distinctive tone; for beginners and novices. SYSTEM SPECS: Instructional DVD.

Virtual Virtuoso for Violinists (www.webcom.com/virtvirt/): Practice software for violinists of all levels. SYSTEM SPECS: Windows 3.1 or higher, 4 MB RAM, sound card or external MIDI module, 3.5-inch diskette drive, 1 MB hard disk space.

When Music Works Instructional DVD Series (www.berkleepress.com): Basic Afro-Cuban Rhythms; Beginning Improvisation: Motivic Development; Building Your Music Career; Modal Voicing Techniques; Rockin' Grooves; Shred Metal Chop Builder; Vocal Practice for Performance. SYSTEM SPECS: Instructional DVDs.

WinBand and WinChoir (Music Data Management Software): Complete student, parent, and booster records; individual fund-raising accounts with automatic tab and project totals; grade tabulations; complete music library information; equipment and uniform inventory; shortcut keys. SYSTEM SPECS: Macintosh: minimum of 68040 with 4 MB or better, 8 MB hard disk space, System 7 or better, 14-inch monitor; Windows: 486 with 4 MB RAM or better, 6 MB hard disk space, Windows 3.1 or better.

WinEnsemble (Music Data Management Software): For scheduling solo and ensemble festivals; make complete schedules and reports; automatic scheduling of events; flexible start, break, and event interval times; random or specific time scheduling; automatic matching of event type to judge; labels for comment sheets; mailing labels for participating schools and judges; imports data from WinBand, WinChoir, or WinEnsemble. SYSTEM SPECS: Macintosh: minimum of 68040 with 4 MB or better, 8 MB hard disk space, System 7 or better, 14-inch monitor; Windows: 486 with 4 MB RAM or better, 6 MB hard disk space, Windows 3.1 or better.

Worship Assistant (www.churchassist.com): For anyone who plans, organizes, and manages worship services, concerts, holiday productions, etc.; keep track of worship songs; plan worship services and musical productions; present song lyrics using a video projector; manage worship teams, choir members, and more. SYSTEM SPECS: Windows 98, Me, 2000 or XP, 200 MHz processor (500 MHz recommended), 32 MB RAM (64 MB recommended), mouse and printer, CD-ROM drive (if purchased on CD-ROM).

Jazz, Blues, and Rock

Berklee Press (www.berkleepress.com): A Guide to Jazz Improvisation; A Guide to Jazz Improvisation (Bass Clef Instruments); A Guide to Jazz Improvisation (Bb Instruments); A Guide to Jazz Improvisation (Eb Instruments); Arranging for Large Jazz Ensemble; Blues Improvisation Complete (Bb Instruments); Blues Improvisation Complete (C Bass Instruments); Blues Improvisation Complete (C Instruments); Blues Improvisation Complete (Eb Instruments); Jazz Composition—Theory and Practice; Modern Jazz Voicings—Arranging for Small and Medium Ensembles. SYSTEM SPECS: Books and Audio CDs.

Elements of the Jazz Language (www.warnerbrospub.com): Comprehensive book on jazz analysis and improvisation; elements used in jazz improvisation are examined in recorded solos; suggestions are made for using each element in the jazz language; specific exercises are provided for practicing the element; ideal environment for developing fluency with the jazz language; for intermediate to advanced, ninth grade and up. SYSTEM SPECS: Book and Audio CD.

Joy of Improv (www.halleonard.com): Twelve to twenty-four-month foundation course for music improvisation on all instruments; fifty-two lessons; emphasize practice rather than theory; strengthens all aspects of playing, including technique, theory, and ear training; organized for beginning and intermediate players having some basic music reading skills and at least a year of experience playing any musical style; experience real-time synthesis of feeling, hearing, and playing. SYSTEM SPECS: Book and Audio CD.

Hal Leonard DVDs (www.halleonard.com): Breakthrough to Improv: The Secrets of Improvisation—Freedom for All Musicians; Dizzy Gillespie—A Night in Chicago; Gordon Goodwin's Big Phat Band—Swingin' for the Fences; Joe Lovano—Improvisation—Developing a Personal Approach; The Ladies Sing the Blues. SYSTEM SPECS: Instructional DVDs.

MiBAC Jazz (www.MiBAC.com): MiBAC (Music Instruction By A Computer) breaks jazz into four main styles; each of these main styles has three different tempo subgroups that can be mixed and matched with any of the other styles or groups; many playing options; manual includes a tutorial that covers all twelve styles; how to type in chord progressions; printing charts; tempos and transposition; based on the basic blues progressions; user can experiment with the rhythm section, intros, voicings, and chord alternations; section on printing and setup; last section is a complete reference for all of the commands used; detailed discussions on the twenty-eight possible chord combinations; tool for developing jazz improvisational skills; practice examples; play with a jazz combo on any tune; can play in any key, at any tempo; comes with twenty-three jazz styles, including 4/4 and Ballad, Swing, Bebop, Rock Shuffle, Bossa Nova, Samba, Slow 12/8, and Two Beat; for all music students, intermediate to advanced, ages fifteen to adult. SYSTEM SPECS: Macintosh; Windows.

MIDI Jazz Improvisation Volumes I and II (www.ecsmedia.com): Instruction and practice in jazz improvisation for all instruments; jazz ensemble is played through MIDI synthesizer and records student's solo keyboard improvisation; each exercise is organized into eight separate tracks: Bass Line, Chords, Melody, Riff or Counter Melody, Scale Study, Sample Improvised Line, Drums (Vol. II only), and User Solo; Volume I covers ii-V-I progressions and twelve-bar blues; Volume II covers advanced materials and assumes student knowledge of scales and basic improvisation techniques such as harmonic substitution and complex ii-V-I progressions; knowledge of MIDI operation is essential; detailed learning sequence provided to give students guidance and goal-oriented practice; for middle-school through adult keyboard students. SYSTEM SPECS: Hybrid.

Musicians Institute (www.halleonard.com): Book and Audio CD sets for learning jazz and rock include: A Modern Approach to Jazz, Rock and Fusion Guitar; An Approach to Jazz Improvisation—A Step-by-Step Guide for All Musicians; Basic Blues Guitar—Essential Progressions, Patterns and Styles; Blues—Workshop Series; Blues Hanon—50 Exercises for the Beginning to Professional Blues Pianist; Blues/Rock Soloing for Guitar—A Guide to the Essential Scales, Licks and Soloing Techniques; Classic Rock—Workshop Series; Jazz Guitar Chord System; Jazz Guitar Improvisation; Jazz Hanon; Jazz-Rock Triad Improvising for Guitar; Modern Rock Rhythm Guitar—A Guide to the Essential Chords, Riffs, Rhythms and Grooves; Rock Lead Ba-

sics—Techniques, Scales and Fundamentals for Guitar; Rock Lead Guitar—Techniques, Scales, Licks, and Soloing Concepts for Guitar; Rock Lead Performance—Techniques, Scales and Soloing Concepts for Guitar; Rock Lead Techniques—Techniques, Scales and Fundamentals for Guitar; Slap and Pop Technique for Guitar; Texas Blues Guitar—Private Lessons. SYSTEM SPECS: Books and Audio CDs.

Oscar Peterson Multimedia CD-ROM (www.pgmusic.com): Fourteen complete audio/video performances by Oscar Peterson; ten MIDI transcriptions of his famous blues performances; signature CD-ROM; integrates interactive audiovisual performances with on-screen piano display and notation; see and study exactly what the master is playing; musical journey through his life and career; comprehensive multimedia autobiography with audio and video clips; exclusive photographs from Oscar Peterson's private collection. SYSTEM SPECS: Windows.

Oscar Peterson Note for Note Transcriptions Book (www.pgmusic.com): Transcriptions of Oscar Peterson's jazz piano performances; authorized volume of eighteen full-length transcriptions all taken directly from original recordings; selected and approved by Oscar Peterson. SYSTEM SPECS: Book and Audio CD.

Robben Ford—The Blues and Beyond (www.warnerbrospublications.com): Innovator in contemporary jazz fusion reveals his advanced concepts for improvising and comping; learn from one of the modern master of blues. SYSTEM SPECS: Instructional DVD.

Robben Ford—Playin' the Blues (www.warnerbrospublications.com): Famed blues and jazz guitarist teaches his favorite blues scales and phrases along with his unique fingerings. SYSTEM SPECS: Instructional DVD.

Saxophone Lessons with Alan Neveu (Parakeet): Twenty multimedia saxophone lessons; finger technique, embouchure, articulation, reeds, vibrato, intonation, time, repertoire, and more; lessons on soprano, alto, tenor, and baritone sax playing specifics; multimedia experience; movie clips; CD-quality sounds; color photos; music notation; rich text. SYSTEM SPECS: Macintosh; Windows.

The Complete Monterey Pop Festival DVD (www.clearvue.com): Revisit the spirit and music of the 1960s; monumental DVD collection; documents the 1967 Monterey International Pop Festival; three-DVD set features classic and rare footage taken by D. A. Pennebaker; first disk contains the legendary 1968 concert film of the festival, highlighting the performances of such greats as The Who, Jimi Hendrix, and Ravi Shankar; second disk includes "Jimi Plays Monterey" and "Shake! Otis at Monterey"; both provide detailed looks at the sets of Jimi Hendrix and Otis Redding; third disk offers two hours of amazing outtake performances and showcases the

Byrds, Buffalo Springfield, Quicksilver Messenger Service, Simon and Garfunkel, the Mamas and the Papas, and others; DVD features include crisp digital picture and sound, audio commentaries, photographs, and trailers. SYSTEM SPECS: Instructional DVD.

The History of Jazz CD-ROM (www.clearvue.com): History of jazz; performers; jazz from different cities; 1900s to present; interactive; shows how jazz was created by the descendants of the slaves brought from Africa; preserves the spirit and beat of African drum music; includes jazz music legends Louis Armstrong, Dizzy Gillespie, Scott Joplin, Duke Ellington, Benny Goodman, and others; for beginner to intermediate, grades 4-college. SYSTEM SPECS: Hybrid.

The Instrumental History of Jazz CD-ROM Set (www.clearvue.com): History of jazz; audio CD and CD-ROM; ragtime; Dixieland; swing through twentieth century; roots of instrumental jazz; twenty-two audio tracks; archival photos; video clips; different types of jazz; virtual time line; fifty-six-page book with text and photos. SYSTEM SPECS: Macintosh; Windows.

The Jazz Channel Presents DVDs (www.clearvue.com): Familiarize students with some of the greatest names in contemporary jazz; highlighting famed performances at Black Entertainment Television Studio II; each program includes a candid interview and features the artist performing some of his or her most memorable songs; thirteen DVDs; titles include B. B. King, Ben E. King, Bobby Womack, Brenda Russell, Chaka Khan, Earl Klugh, Freddie Jackson, Herbie Hancock, Jeffrey Osborne, Keiko Matsui, Kenny Rankin, Lou Rawls, Soul Conversation: Mark Whitfield and JK. SYSTEM SPECS: Instructional DVDs.

The Jazz Saxophonist (www.pgmusic.com): Music program with studio recordings of great jazz saxophone music; learn riffs and tricks; each instrument (sax, piano, bass, and drums) recorded on a separate track; listen to each part independently; multimedia features; study arrangements; hear music; play along with top studio musicians; tips and techniques; integrates multitrack audio, MIDI, chord symbols, and music notation. SYSTEM SPECS: Windows.

The Jazz Soloist (www.pgmusic.com): Jazz quartet arrangements of fifty songs per volume; each song features a jazz solo played by jazz musicians, piano comping, bass, and drums; over three hours of jazz soloing on each volume; MIDI files; for intermediate to advanced, high school and up. SYSTEM SPECS: Macintosh: 4 MB RAM, System 6 or 7, MIDI interface, synthesizer/module with guitar, bass, and drum sounds, 2 MB hard disk space; Windows: 4 MB RAM, sound card or MIDI system with guitar, bass, and drum sounds, 2 MB hard disk space.

The Rock Saxophonist for Windows (www.pgmusic.com): Music program with studio recordings of great rock and roll saxophone music; learn riffs and tricks; each instrument recorded on a separate track; listen to each part independently; multimedia features; study arrangements; hear music; play along with top studio musicians; tips and techniques; integrates multitrack audio, MIDI, chord symbols, music notation, and chord progressions. SYSTEM SPECS: Windows.

Music Appreciation, Music History, World Music, and Composers

Apple Pie Music: The History of American Music (Lintronics Software Publishing): CD-ROM multimedia reference and anthology; contains over 400 songs, over 300 pictures, 54 chapters of interactive text; covers the Colonial Era, the Expansion Era, and the Industrial Era; divided into Folk Music, Popular Music, and Religious Music; cursor appears over any text that can be copied; set of hierarchical menus for navigation; Hotwords are used to indicate titles of songs that can be played, reference to related areas, names of instruments, or names of composers or lyricists; Music Alley is a special search and indexing system that allows songs to be located based on specific criteria and then played; includes a selected bibliography and discography; for all musicians, ages ten-adult. SYSTEM SPECS: Windows Multimedia PC or Windows 3.1, super VGA, CD-ROM, sound card, 4 MB RAM.

Art and Music (www.clearvue.com): Interactive series; exploration through history from the medieval era through surrealism; shows parallels between art and architecture and music; humanities in a new light; series of eight includes the following titles: THE MEDIEVAL ERA: the art, architecture, and music of the era were created for and governed by the Church; evolution of art and music during Medieval times; THE RENAISSANCE: Renaissance artists and composers, influenced and inspired by the new humanistic philosophy, developed new forms and techniques from painting with oils to four-part polyphony; THE BAROQUE: examples of the dramatic effect of art from Caravaggio to Rembrandt; the energetic, expressive style of music from Frescobaldi to Handel; the drama of opera; THE EIGHTEENTH CENTURY: developments in painting and sculpture parallel music's changing styles; comic opera, Viennese classical style, emerging Romanticism; art and music of the French Revolution; comparison between the works of David and Beethoven; THE ROMANTIC ERA: Berlioz's Requiem and Delacroix's Liberty Leading the People; numerous works of music and art that are related; IMPRESSIONISM: Impressionist art and music; parallels between the artist's use of color and light and the composer's use of instrumentation; THE TWENTIETH CENTURY: significant artistic developments; abstraction in art and atonality in music emerge, followed by Fauvism and Cubism; SURREALISM: parallels between the artistic methods of Ernst, Magritte, and Dali and the musical works of Satie, Bartok, and Cage; all titles are in hybrid format; for intermediate to advanced, grades 7-college. SYSTEM SPECS: Hybrid; Macintosh: 68030 or better, 256 colors recommended, 8 MB RAM, System 7.0 or later, 2x speed CD-ROM or better; Windows: 486 DX/25 or better, 8 MB RAM, VGA or better, sound card, 2x speed CD-ROM or better, Windows 95.

Barrage: The World on Stage DVD (www.clearvue.com): Combining Celtic, East Indian, big band swing, and American folk music; concert presentation fuses song, dance, and theater; highlights resourceful stringed instruments; upbeat blend of different cultures and musical styles. SYSTEM SPECS: Instructional DVD.

Beethoven Lives Upstairs DVD (www.childrensgroup.com): Best-loved and best-selling of all Classical Kids stories; arrival of an eccentric boarder turns a young boy's life upside down; Ludwig van Beethoven has moved in upstairs; at first Christoph resents their new tenant but slowly he comes to understand the genius of the man, the torment of his deafness, and the beauty of his music; in the end he is won over by the music and true incidents from the great composer's life. SYSTEM SPECS: Instructional DVD.

Borodin Quartet: Concert Master Class DVD (www.clearvue.com): Internationally renowned A. P. Borodin Quartet and V. A. Berlinsky; complete live concert; presents interviews with the classical music celebrities in the quartet and provides an inside look at the people associated with the world-famous group; rehearsal footage; behind-the-scenes glimpse at concert preparation; rare archival video recordings. SYSTEM SPECS: Instructional DVD.

CD Time Sketch (www.ecsmedia.com): To facilitate listening and analyzing music; create listening lessons with any audio CD; for fundamentals and appreciation courses, or music history courses at any level; annotated listening format can be applied to classes and activities and the music performance curriculum; glossary of terms includes dynamics, tempo markings, stylistic expression markings, music symbols, and standard musical terms. SYSTEM SPECS: Windows.

Classical Music Series CD-ROMs (Voyager): Includes Beethoven's Symphony No. 9, Mozart's Dissonant String Quartet, and Schubert's Trout Quintet; Pocket Guide: single screen overview of the symphony; play any major section instantaneously; Close Reading: running commentary across the whole composition, measure by measure play through, or search and browse at own pace; Composer's World: sets the music in a historical and cultural context;

Games: test newly acquired expertise; Comprehensive Glossary: terms and definitions. For beginner to advanced, eighth grade and up. SYSTEM SPECS: Macintosh.

Classical Orchestra Notes for Windows (www.hoptechno.com): Almost 2,000 program notes, many with complete vocal text in their original language with English translations; 500 text-audio links; read about a piece and hear music examples of timeless masterpieces; CD-ROM; full-text search; portraits of over 500 composers; picture library and text covering scores of instruments; hypertext classical glossary with hundreds of music terms; information on the world's greatest conductors and music directors. SYSTEM SPECS: Windows.

Exploring Music Book and Compact Disk (www.clearvue.com): Familiarizes students with the diversity of Western music; comprehensive book and compact disk set; sharpen listening skills; analyze details and overall effects of classical music, traditional world music, folk, pop, and jazz; reproducible worksheets with questions, activities, and discussion ideas to enhance aural perception, music theory comprehension, and music appreciation; answer key included; for intermediate and advanced music students; to supplement music instruction; concepts covered include instrument identification, rhythm and pitch recognition, music reading, arrangement, and more. SYSTEM SPECS: Book and Audio CD.

Exploring Music Two (www.clearvue.com): Multimedia program; furthering the ideas and skills targeted in the popular program Exploring Music, the book and compact disk set prompts students to listen critically to short pieces and then to answer questions about musical elements, including instruments, time signatures, rhythm patterns, pitch, themes, and more; students explore world music and jazz, as well as many classical masterpieces: Mozart's Domine Jesu, Copland's Appalachian Spring, Britten's Young Person's Guide to the Orchestra, and others; to build a greater understanding of and appreciation for the beauty and complexity of music. SYSTEM SPECS: Book and Audio CD.

Gramophone Classical Good CD Guide DVD (www.msc-catalog.com): Edited by Emma Lilley; over 3,500 reviews of classical CDs and DVDs written by the critics of Gramophone; each review is clearly rated so that readers can see at a glance the best disks in each repertoire area; includes suggested basic library, composer biographies, and critics' appraisals of the world's finest musicians; includes CD sampler of music by favorite composers. SYSTEM SPECS: Instructional DVD.

Great Composers: Their Lives and Music CD-ROMs (www.clearvue.com): Six-volume multimedia presentation about the lives of composers; to supplement music education of grade-school through high-school students; text, images, audio, animation, and video; hear composers' works behind the script; users highlight multiple-choice answers; tally of user answers; multiple-choice answers test the student on the time period in which the composer lived; includes a dictionary and encyclopedia; click on blue or green words in the text for explanations of terms; scorekeeping feature; for a group studio or study at home; Volume 1: Johann Sebastian Bach, Robert Schumann, Sergei Rachmaninoff; Volume 2: George Frideric Handel, Frideric Chopin, Claude Debussy; Volume 3: Wolfgang Amadeus Mozart, Felix Mendelssohn, Antonin Dvorak; Volume 4: Ludwig van Beethoven, Edvard Grieg, Howard Hanson; Volume 5: Franz Joseph Haydn, Pyotr Ilich Tchaikovsky, Maurice Ravel; Volume 6: Franz Schubert, Johannes Brahms, Johann Strauss; traces the lives and music of the great composers; interactive multimedia programs; tells composers' life stories from their first musical training to their greatest achievements; highlights musical selections; chronicles the events that influenced their music; explains characteristics that identify their work; for all music students, ages six-eighteen. SYSTEM SPECS: Hybrid; Macintosh: 68030 or better processor, 8 MB RAM, System 7 or later, 2x speed CD-ROM or better; Windows: 486 DX/25 or better, 8 MB RAM, VGA or better, sound card, 2x speed CD-ROM or better, Windows 95.

Hansel and Gretel (www.halleonard.com): 1954 feature set to Englebert Humperdinck's classic 1893 opera; stop-action animation and hand-sculpted dolls and sets create fantasy legend; Grammy nominated; over thirty scene selections; composer biography; story synopsis; seventy-two minutes. SYSTEM SPECS: Instructional DVD.

Instruments of the Symphony Orchestra CD-ROM (www.clearvue.com): Select instrument and view summary of its history and development; identify instruments by appearance, sound, and musical capability; how to hold and play each instrument; music; colorful photography; detailed narration; for beginners, grades 7-12. SYSTEM SPECS: Macintosh; Windows.

Mozart's The Magic Flute Story (www.halleonard.com): English narration; sung in the original German; story of Prince Tamino and Princess Pamina, young lovers who use the powers of a magic flute to battle the forces of evil that threaten to keep them apart; lavish opera; forty-two minutes. SYSTEM SPECS: Instructional DVD.

Music and Culture (www.clearvue.com): CD-ROM covers the music and traditions of Polynesian, African, and North American Indian peoples; instruments, vocal music, and dance; authentic recordings and graphics; audiovisual presentation with text linked to an encyclopedia and glossary; multiple-choice questions for quizzes; identifies the four major

instrument groups classified by ethnomusicologists; for beginners to intermediate, grades 7-college. SYSTEM SPECS: Hybrid; Macintosh: CD-ROM, 68030/25 MHz, color monitor, System 7.0, 8 MB RAM; Windows: 386/33 MHz, Windows 3.1, 8 MB RAM, VGA color monitor.

Music Appreciation Intermediate Level (www.clearvue.com): Two interactive CD-ROMs; periods of music; composers; instruments; hands-on activities; video clips; archival images; quizzes; encyclopedia; dictionary; teachers guide; Presentation Manager. SYSTEM SPECS: Macintosh; Windows.

Music Composer Quiz CD-ROM (www.ecsmedia.com): Twenty questions randomly selected from a pool; users have three chances to answer a question correctly before the answer is displayed; instructor may edit or print any of the one hundred quiz questions; feedback is given at the end of each quiz session; student records are retained; for grades 6-college. SYSTEM SPECS: Hybrid.

Music Conservatory (www.voyetra.com): CD-ROM; covers music history, theory, instruments and composers; musical journey through time, listening to symphonic masterpieces; learn about the lives and works of great composers from the Baroque period through the twentieth century; acquire an understanding of music theory; introduction to notation, rhythm, tonality and harmony; audio and video demonstrations of more than seventy-five of the world's most popular orchestral instruments; musical glossary with definitions and pronunciation of more than 250 musical terms and concepts. SYSTEM SPECS: Windows.

Music History Review: Composers CD-ROM (www.ecsmedia.com): Test knowledge of composers; Renaissance to twentieth century; select quiz from ten categories; multiple-choice format; feedback; coordinated with A History of Western Music, 4th ed., by Grout and Palisca (published by W. W. Norton); student records; for beginners, grades 6-college. SYSTEM SPECS: Hybrid.

Music Mentor (Interactive Digital Design—Midisoft): Covers melody, rhythm, harmony, timbre, texture, and form; how composers combine elements; on-screen buttons; integrates history, composers, and creativity; thirteen centuries of musical style; learn how different instruments sound; complete multitrack studio (sequencer) to make, record, edit, and print music; for beginners to advanced, ages twelve and up. SYSTEM SPECS: Pentium PC or greater, Windows 9x/XP, 64 MB RAM, SVGA graphics adapter and monitor (800 x 600 with 256 color minimum), 15 MB hard disk space, Windows/DirectX 8.1 supported sound card or MIDI device (sound card required for digital sound), mouse, any MIDI instrument (optional), CD-ROM drive.

Piano Mouse Meets Great Composers (www.pianomouse.com): CD-ROM; introduction to the lives and music of eight great composers from the Baroque, Classical, and Romantic periods; biographies; games. SYSTEM SPECS: Hybrid.

The Global Songbook (www.clearvue.com): Book and CD-ROM; journey through the music of nine countries from the Brazilian rain forest, through South Africa to Indonesia; gives children a peek at other cultures through their songs; translated into English. SYSTEM SPECS: Hybrid.

The History of Folk Music CD-ROM (www.clearvue.com): Information about the European and African influences on the development of American folk music; five sections: Roots of American Folk Music, Country Music, Black Folk Music, Folk Music in History, and Folk Music in History, Part II; tracks the roots of American folk music from early Native American music, to the music of new settlers, to country music, and to African American music; in-depth surveys; includes aural examples of folk instruments, singing, and chanting; spoken text between the examples; color pictures showing costumed groups singing, playing different instruments, and dancing; main program runs through the musical examples and spoken text; click on different icons to access extra information and references, question and answer sections, and quizzes; Intro to Power CD answers questions about how to access other areas of the program such as references, printing, and quizzes; Question and Answer icon takes user through several multiple-choice questions; when an incorrect choice is made, the correct answer is shown, and the reasons why; preparation for the seven timed quizzes; score and the correct answers are given at the end of each timed quiz; quiz topics include Ethnic and Cultural Aspects, Important People, and Styles of Music; quiz scores are automatically recorded; information can be printed; references given for more in-depth research; clicking the Magnifying Glass icon enlarges the picture on the screen; helps users see instrument and costume details; CD is installed each time it is used; addition to any American music history curriculum; offers technical support; for all music students, ages ten to adult. SYSTEM SPECS: Hybrid; Macintosh: 68030/25 MHz, System 7, color quickdraw, 4 MB RAM; Windows: 386/20 MHz, Windows 3.1, 4 MB RAM, VGA color monitor.

Timesketch Series (www.ecsmedia.com): CD-ROMs; each sketch includes a recording and a form analysis of the piece; for use in music fundamentals, music appreciation, and music history courses; listening lab or private studio; for all grade levels. Includes Portrait of Bach, Toccata and Fugue in D Minor; Portrait of Beethoven, Symphony No. 5; Portrait of Brahms, Symphony No. 3; Portrait of Mozart, Symphony 40; Portrait of Schubert, Unfinished Symphony; Portrait of Dvorak, New World Symphony; Pathetique Sonata, Beethoven; Piano Concerto, Beethoven; Brubeck Sketches No. 1, Jazz Series; Miles Davis Sketches No. 1, Jazz Series; Grainger Sketches No. 1, Lincolnshire Posey. SYSTEM SPECS: Hybrid.

Traditional Music of Africa Books and Audio CD (www.clearvue.com): Acquaints students with the rich history and culture of Africa through thirty-six tracks of traditional African music; text details the relationship between music and society; highlights musical instruments; describes the importance of the human voice and rhythm in African music; geographical and historical information about Kenya, Lamu Island, Somalia, Ethiopia, Burundi, and other areas of Africa; interdisciplinary lesson; musical tracks recorded in remote and private locations; insight into tribal and community life; includes audio CD, ten books, and activity guide with reproducible worksheets, discussion ideas, preapproved Web links, and more. SYSTEM SPECS: Books and Audio CD.

Traditional Songs from Singing Cultures (www.clearvue.com): Explores the musical heritage of cultures around the world; collection of twenty songs; features maps, cultural information, and activities to enhance the listening experience; gives students a greater understanding of the music that has developed in different cultures. SYSTEM SPECS: Book and Audio CD.

Traditional World Music Book and Audio CD (www.clearvue.com): Musical exploration of geography, culture, and history through a variety of regions; audio CD includes twenty diverse recordings carefully selected to showcase the various characteristics of each culture and tradition; covers details of fourteen countries; each chapter of book describes musical history, influences, instruments, and performance details; descriptive analysis of each musical piece includes information from regions as diverse as the Andes, Spain, India, Tibet, Egypt, and others; interdisciplinary lesson; can be used both in music classes and area studies; classroom bundle includes audio CD, ten books, and activity guide with reproducible worksheets, discussion ideas, preapproved Web links, and more. SYSTEM SPECS: Books and Audio CD.

World Beat Fun: Multicultural and Contemporary Rhythms Book and Compact Disk (www.clearvue.com): Interactive book and CD set; features different world music styles and contemporary themes; varying difficulty levels for students of all ages; allows students to hear and see notes and rhythms; encourages the use of different instruments; reinforces learning through rote and reproducible handouts; helpful notations for students; contains easy-to-follow teaching suggestions; play along with the seven tracks; students learn to maintain a steady beat; discover cultural music awareness; reinforce note values and rhythm reading; perform call-and-response rhythms as ostinatos, and more; for grades K-8. SYSTEM SPECS: Book and Audio CD.

Composition, Songwriting, Accompanying, and Music Industry

A Zillion Kajillion Rhymes and Cliches (www.eccentricsoftware.com): Thesaurus for rhymes; for songwriting, poetry, parodies, plays on words, jingles, product names, and more; enter word and will produce a list of rhyming words. SYSTEM SPECS: Macintosh; Windows.

Band-In-A-Box (www.pgmusic.com): Award-winning software; type in the chords for any song using standard chord symbols (like C, Fm7 or C13b9), choose the style, and Band-in-a-Box does the rest; automatically generates a complete professional quality arrangement of piano, bass, drums, guitar, and strings in a wide variety of popular styles (jazz, pop, country, classical, and more); "MIDI-file to Style Wizard" automatically converts a MIDI file (.MID) to a Band-in-a-Box Style (.STY); wizard has plenty of options to make simple to advanced styles from a MIDI file without any knowledge of the StyleMaker required; twice as many instruments as previous versions; support for General MIDI 2 standard (GM2); GM2 support adds 128 new instruments to Band-in-a-Box styles and songs, including ukulele, mandolin, twelve-string guitar plus many new and improved piano, organ, guitar, brass and string sounds; many new styles using the new instruments; updated versions of previous styles; hear new instruments with new and existing styles; included Roland VSC3 synth supports the new GM2 instruments, as do most newer modules/sound cards; a similar instrument from the existing 128 General MIDI sounds can be substituted; enhanced the Guitar Window by adding fret display support for other instruments, including mandolin, ukulele, and banjo; authentic chord voicings and melody display on the fretboard for all of the new instruments; StyleMaker has been enhanced with support for GM2 instruments, so can make styles that use the new instruments and have correct instrument voicings displayed on the fretboard; option for standard guitar chord diagrams to be included in the notation display, lead sheet, and printout; choose from Folk, Pop, or Jazz Guitar Chord Diagrams; bass players can see bass tablature and correctly displayed bass parts on the new bass fretboard; program's user interface has been enhanced, with a single dialog for all program options and song settings, right mouse support, simplified menu, additional hot keys and more; all of the styles are enhanced; improved or updated every Band-in-a-Box style with the newest StyleMaker features, including guitar and other fretted instrument voicings, consistent volume levels, edited patterns and more; many of these styles and new demo songs are included with the Band-in-a-Box version 12 upgrade; new options for song navigation during playback, including "One-More-Time" feature that allows fine control over the song looping during live performance; can load and play an entire MIDI file in Band-in-a-Box, including interpreting the chords with the Chord Wizard; harmony notation display has been enhanced; harmonies can now be displayed on the lead sheet window (or printed) with separate notation tracks for each harmony voice; view each harmony on a separate track, or view or print a single harmony voice; print harmony charts for band, or use for sight-reading practice to read or play a harmony voice along with the melody. SYSTEM SPECS: Macintosh; Windows.

Band-In-A-Box Soloist Disk Sets (www.pgmusic.com): Soloist Disk Set No. 2, Killer Jazz Soloing; No. 3, Specialty Jazz Soloing; No. 4, Rock Soloing; No. 5, Bluegrass; No. 6, Killer Pop and Older Jazz; No. 7, Blues, Pop, Funk, and More; No. 8, Killer Jazz Waltz and Jazz Fusion; No. 9, Blues Guitar, Country Piano, Pop Eighths, and Pop Swing Sixteenths. SYSTEM SPECS: Macintosh; Windows.

Band-In-A-Box Styles Disk Sets (www.pgmusic.com): Styles Disk Set No. 4, Jazz, Country, Pop, and More; No. 5, Jazz, Ethnic, and More; No. 6, Latin and Jazz; No. 7, Country and Pop; No. 8, Jazz, Ethnic, and More; No. 9, Latin and Salsa; No. 10, Pop and Rock; No. 11, Classical and Classical MIDI Fakebook; No. 12, Country, Swing, Rock, Waltz, Boogie; No. 13, Euro-Techno; No. 14, Jazz, Fusion; No. 15, Nashville Country; No. 16, All Blues; No. 17, Unplugged; No. 18, Praise and Worship; No. 19, Most Requested; No. 20, Southern Gospel; No. 21, Top 40; No. 22, 60s British Invasion; No. 23, Contemporary Country; No. 24, Guitar and More; No. 25, Vintage Jazz; No. 26, Classic Country; No. 27, Jazz n' Pop; No. 28, Smooth Jazz; No. 29, Top 40 Country; No. 30, World Fretboards; No. 31, Country Rock; No. 32, Alternative Contemporary; No. 34, World Styles; No. 35, Requested Jazz; No. 36, Rock On! SYSTEM SPECS: Macintosh; Windows.

Cakewalk Guitar Tracks 2 Software (www.cakewalk.com): Easy control; audio tools; multiple effects; easy portable studio console simplifies recording, punch-in, looping, drum tracks, simultaneous effects and more; special edit view makes moving around song ideas as simple as drag and drop; designed to be as easy to use as a multitrack cassette recorder or tape deck; musical scratchpad for guitarists and singer/songwriters; play backup to eight simultaneous tracks of digital audio; cut, copy, and paste audio clips with the click of a mouse; mix tracks with real-time effects; add vintage analog warmth with amp simulation; save music as a wav file, burn it to CD, or put it on the Internet; MP3 ready. SYSTEM SPECS: Windows 95/98.

Cakewalk Guitar Tracks Pro Software (www.cakewalk.com): Thirty-two track studio for guitar players and performing songwriters; familiar multitrack "portable studio" interface; all the benefits of PC-based, digital recording, and editing; thirty-two-track digital recorder; guitar amp simulator; high-quality effects; software-based drum loop generator; chromatic-tuner; complete drum loop library; use any guitar or microphone and PC; save as MP3 or export to WAV to burn CDs; record songs fast; plug and play; professional editing and mixing tools; supports up to 24-bit/96 KHz audio; ideal for guitarists and performing songwriters; free ReValver SE guitar amp simulator; built-in chromatic tuner; Fruityloops Express drum loop generator; ACID-format audio loops. SYSTEM SPECS: Windows 98/Me/2000/XP.

Camps V4.2 (www.campspro.com/win4/): Generates new melodies, bass lines, drum patterns, chord patterns, and chord progressions from scratch; loads standard MIDI files; reharmonizes melodies. SYSTEM SPECS: Windows 95/98/NT or later.

CD Looper (www.replayinc.com): Learn to play any song directly from computer's CD player; can slow down any audio CD two, three, or four times without changing pitch; learn songs note for note; set loop points anywhere within a track; can set a loop point for every two-bar phrase; loop options can play each loop once, twice, or continuously, pausing between each loop or user-settable amount of time; highlight multiple loops and loop an entire section. SYSTEM SPECS: Windows 95, 100 percent compatible Sound Blaster sound card, 8 MB RAM.

CD Looper Pro (www.replayinc.com): Upgrades CD Looper with select sampling resolution; 8 bit or 16-bit; select either mono or stereo recording; improved slow-down algorithms; improved speed-up by percentage algorithms; visually see the WAVE file for the note grabber. SYSTEM SPECS: Windows 95, 100 percent compatible Sound Blaster sound card, 8 MB RAM.

Composer Notes (www.ecsmedia.com): CD-ROM; includes Teacher's Guide; explains instrumentation and composition to student composers using both traditional and electronic instruments; allows users to play over 500 recordings from orchestral, jazz, and contemporary musicians in a variety of formats: from their own computer, with included MIDI files using a sequencer, or from a CD player with the included audio CD; topics covered include arranging, texture, tempo and meter, musical form and structure, melody, motifs, phrases, MIDI, ensemble writing, and writing for strings, woodwinds, brass, and rhythm instruments; teachers also can use the program to generate related worksheets for distribution in the classroom. SYSTEM SPECS: Hybrid.

Contracts for the Music Industry (www.songwriterproducts.com/software.htm): SPIN contracts, including a wide variety of performance, collaboration, work-for-hires, copyright release, barter agreements, session agreements, various logs, jingle contact sheet, advertisement music production agreement, etc.; devised by attorneys and are legal and binding; CD-ROM, instructions and hard copies in hard back three-ring binder; formatted in Microsoft Word and Word Perfect. SYSTEM SPECS: Macintosh; Windows.

Decomposer (www.replayinc.com): Advanced filtering program; filter out a single instrument or sections of instruments from any digital audio file. SYSTEM SPECS: Windows.

Financial Management for Musicians (www.artistpro.com): By Certified Public Accountants Gaines and McCormack; for working musicians; manage band's income and expenses; create budget for touring, recording, and major purchases; help with the income tax process; learn how to legally write off equipment purchases, touring expenses, and issue 1099 forms to band members; includes CD-ROM containing Excel and Lotus spreadsheet templates of budgeting examples. SYSTEM SPECS: Book and Hybrid CD-ROM.

Gigorama (www.giglogic.com): Book gigs and appointments; produce ready-to-sign contracts; generate and print financial reports; build and save favorite song/setlists; create musician/contacts databases; develop equipment inventory database; fill out and print copyright forms; run own private/virtual network; import over a thousand clubs and venues; unlock and personalize; customize instrument categories; drag-n-drop to copy a gig on calendar; use customizable business letter templates; backup and restore data; send and receive files; auto-copy and calculate repeat gigs. SYSTEM SPECS: Windows.

Guitar   Playing   for   Songwriters (www.garytalley.com): DVD by Gary Talley, guitar player for The Box Tops; unique, effective, and streamlined approach to teaching guitar especially designed for songwriters; fun and innovative three-lesson, fifty-five-minute instructional video. SYSTEM SPECS: Instructional DVD.

Home   Concert   (www.timewarptech.com): Play a piece of music on a MIDI instrument, reading the music off the computer screen, while music's accompaniment is synchronized to playing; play solo part on keyboard; plays the accompaniment, following the player's timing, tempo, and dynamic changes. SYSTEM SPECS: Macintosh; Windows.

How to Find Gigs That Pay Big Bucks (www.halleonard.com):   Advice from music industry heavy-hitters; Kevin Eubanks, musical director for Tonight Show band, shares thoughts on getting major work as a musician in today's market; guitarist Richie Sambora talks about critical elements to launching a music career; Kevin Cronin (REO Speedwagon), Eric Schenkman (Spin Doctors), and Joe Satriani give inside scoop about finding good-paying gigs, agents, and learning from mistakes; Carnival Cruise Lines supervisor J. B. Buccafusco gives ideas on how to get booked on cruise ships; Steve Schirripa, former entertainment director for Las Vegas Riviera, gives insight into casino bookings nationwide; tips from concert and festival promoters, studio musicians, and talent buyers; thirty-eight minutes. SYSTEM SPECS: Instructional DVD.

How To Mic A Band For Ultimate Live Sound (www.msc-catalog.com): Professional mic techniques and placement for vocals, guitars, bass, horns, and percussion; learn about room acoustic variations, setting up a final mix, effects usage, compressors, gates, types of PAs, and microphones; full mixer explanation included. SYSTEM SPECS: Instructional DVD.

Jammer Hit Session (www.soundtrek.com): 256-track single-port MIDI sequencer with built-in studio musicians; 100 assorted band-style grooves, intros, breaks, stops, holds, and endings in a wide variety of styles; fifty drum styles, harmony composers and more. SYSTEM SPECS: Windows 3.1/95/98/NT.

Jammer Live (www.soundtrek.com): Interactive virtual professional backup band that jams to chord changes in real time and interacts with melodies upon command; captured the feel of top pros; photograhic user interface; professionally recorded style riffs in a wide variety of styles; "state of the art" graphic style editor for styles. SYSTEM SPECS: Windows.

Jammer Pro (www.soundtrek.com): Virtual studio musicians ready to improvise, harmonize, exchange ideas, and lay down original tracks; control the style of each musician on each track; over 200 band styles; complete control over player styles, note ranges, velocities, and transitions; blend multiple styles together; 25-track MIDI studio located in the PC; six-part harmony; load and save individual drum styles; automatic fades and crescendos; "Real Feel" composition engine; 32-bit graphic user interface. SYSTEM SPECS: Windows.

Jammer Pro Band and Drum Styles Volumes 1-4 (www.soundtrek.com): Vol. 1: over seventy assorted professional band-style grooves, intros, breaks, stops, holds and endings for ballads, fast jazz swing, moderate swing rock, slow guitar blues, slow randb, upbeat country, reggae, swing, and hip hop; plus 100 assorted professional drum styles including jazz, rock, blues, and country beats with dynamic drum fills; Vol. 2: over seventy assorted professional band-style grooves, intros, breaks, stops, holds and endings for pop-rock, bossanova, boogie woogie, jazz fusion, new age, upbeat soul, slow country swing, funk-rock swing, and easy listening; plus 100 assorted professional drum styles, including Latin, jazz, and rock beats with dynamic drum fills; Vol. 3 over seventy professional band-style grooves, intros, breaks, stops, holds, and endings for contemporary jazz, slow rock, moderate rock, upbeat rock swing, upbeat Latin rock, mambo, salsa, merengue,

techno dance, and gospel waltz; plus 100 drum styles including Latin, jazz, rock, funk, and country beats with dynamic drum fills; Vol. 4 over seventy assorted professional band-style grooves, intros, breaks, stops, holds, and endings for medium alternative rock, upbeat alternative rock, pop funk, inspirational, 50s RandB swing, country rock, Irish jig, Irish reel, big band swing, and big band ballads; plus 100 assorted drum styles, including rock, ballad, fusion, hip-hop, and dance beats with dynamic drum fills.

Jammer Songmaker (www.soundtrek.com): 256-track single-port MIDI sequencer with built-in studio musicians; 200 assorted band style grooves, intros, breaks, stops, holds, and endings in a wide variety of styles; 50 drum styles, harmony composers, and more; upgradeable to Jammer Pro SYSTEM SPECS: Windows 3.1/95/98/NT.

Jammin' Keys (www.voyetra.com): Creates original MIDI music; wide variety of styles, including rock, jazz, Latin, and more; 128 general MIDI instruments; virtual five-part band adds backups and riffs; compose music by clicking the "Jam Grid," the on-screen music keyboard, or use an external keyboard; professional-sounding fills and endings; more than thirty-five sound effects files to use with the drum pads; record song as a MIDI file and load it into a sequencing program; includes a video tutorial and media check diagnostic utility. SYSTEM SPECS: Windows.

Killer Demos (www.halleonard.com): By Bill Gibson; shows how to produce great demos at home; goes step-by-step through the recording process; covers everything from equipment selection to mixdown. SYSTEM SPECS: Instructional DVD.

Lyricist (www.virtualstudiosystems.com): CD-ROM; word processor designed for lyricists, musicians, songwriters, and poets; includes rhyming dictionary, spell checker, thesaurus, chord charting and editing, chord wizard, online file copyright, programmable text styles, Web link button, database-oriented storage, album categorization, and more. SYSTEM SPECS: Windows 95, 98, 2000, ME, NT, XP, 32 MB RAM, 486/33 or higher IBM compatible, 55 MB available hard disk space, SuperVGA Monitor running at High Color (16-bit) and 1024 x 768 resolution or higher.

MasterWriter (www.masterwriter.com) CD-ROM; collection of tools for songwriters; rhyming dictionary with over 100,000 entries; pop-culture dictionary with over 11,000 icons of American and World Culture; dictionary containing over 35,000 phrases, idioms, clichés, sayings, and word combinations; *Rhymed-Phrases Dictionary* with over 36,000 entries; *Alliterations Dictionary* in existence; *American Heritage Dictionary* and *Roget's II Thesaurus*; state-of-the-art database to keep track of all lyrics, melodies and information related to the songs written; stereo Hard Disk Recorder for recording melodic ideas; Songuard online date-of-creation Song Registration Service; over 250 tempo adjustable MIDI Drum Loops; Word Processing. SYSTEM SPECS: Hybrid.

Musician's ToolKit CD-ROM (www.indie-music.com): By Suzanne Glass; forty-six full-length articles covering writing, recording, music marketing, radio, and more; written by a respected industry veteran; fill out and print copyright forms right from computer desktop; ninety easy-to-use templates for flyers, letterhead, business cards, special events, press releases, and more; edit and print; Music Fonts to use with any program on computer; Print Music Papers: manuscript, tablature, and percussion paper printed from computer; Cool Musician Software (PC only): selection of thirteen freeware and shareware programs just for musicians; how to buy and sell musical gear at online auctions; thirty+ page seller's guide; free auction software; Industry Directory links to 23,000+ music contacts, including media and record labels. SYSTEM SPECS: Hybrid.

MusicMaker (www.halleonard.com): Play fifteen pop hits with five options: One Key Play: tap out timing to play melody along with backing track; Jamtrax: play any key; Drum Along: choose between four kits to drum along with tracks; Quiz: take a musical quiz; Melody Play: play melody on keyboard. SYSTEM SPECS: Windows.

Number Chart Pro Software (http://members.aol.com/numchart/): Custom font enables users to create any sized professional Nashville Number System song charts; computer-generated charts can be archived, updated, e-mailed. SYSTEM SPECS: Macintosh; Windows.

Rhyme Wizard (www.rhymewizard.com): CD-ROM; over 100,000 words and phrases, all with cross-references to near rhymes; tool for any songwriter, poet, jingle writer, advertiser, student, or anyone who enjoys rhyme, poetry, or limericks and who uses a computer; created by a songwriter and a teacher; type in a word or phrase and click. SYSTEM SPECS: Hybrid.

Rock Rap 'n Roll (www.clearvue.com): CD-ROM; original music combined with a unique interactive interface; user can produce professional quality music; music in program was recorded using professional vocalists and musicians; ten separate genre/sound studios; students can modify and manipulate sounds and record vocals or sound effects to add to the mix. SYSTEM SPECS: Macintosh; Windows.

Secrets of Songwriting Success CD-ROMs (www.jaijomusic.com): Jai Josef's live seminar on two-CD-ROM set; author of *Writing Music for Hit Songs*; live clips of actual workshops; text; graphics; interactivity; links to useful resources. SYSTEM SPECS: Macintosh; Windows.

SetMaker (www.sweetwater.com): Freeware application; make set lists; key field; filter songs by key; new key column in every set list; open multiple set lists simultaneously; drag and drop between set lists; print all songs in the songs window; songs in the songs window are saved with every modification; print preview print jobs; more control over final printed output; backwards compatibility with SetMaker 1.0/1.1 set lists; "song manager" allows songwriter to keep "database" or "list" of song information; data are automatically saved with program and can be categorized, filtered, and manipulated in useful ways; set list creator allows songwriter to quickly select songs from database, put them in a set list, and print out a list of songs to use for live performance, general reference, etc.; create and save unlimited number of sets. SYSTEM SPECS: Macintosh; Windows.

Songster Software (Songster): Songwriting and lyric writing software; pitch list; song profile; lyrics; contacts; track sheet; import sound files; calendar; schedules; royalty statements; copyright forms and more. SYSTEM SPECS: Macintosh; Windows.

Songworks II (www.ars-nova.com): Notate compositions on multiple staves with up to eight voices per staff; invents tune ideas and suggests chord progressions; with Active Listening, can perform one part of a composition while computer plays the others; explore polyphony; learn a part in a choral piece; experience being part of a music ensemble; can export music to an AIFF, MIDI, or PICT file for use on multimedia projects; MIDI compatible; MIDI not required; Macintosh 16-bit sound. SYSTEM SPECS: Macintosh; Windows.

The Complete Music Business Office (www.artistpro.com): Includes over 125 essential contracts and forms for conducting music and entertainment industry business; includes United States Government documents for filing copyrights; CD-ROM containing contract library for use with Windows and Macintosh computers. SYSTEM SPECS: Book and Hybrid CD-ROM.

The Lead Sheet Bible Book and Audio CD (www.halleonard.com): Guide to writing lead sheets and chord charts; by Robin Randall and Janice Peterson; book/CD package for singer, songwriter, or musician who wants to create a lead sheet or chord chart that is easy-to-follow; CD includes over seventy demo tracks; covers: song form, transposition, considering the instrumentation, scales, keys, rhythm, chords, slash notation, and other basics, beaming, stemming, syncopation, intervals, and chord symbols; includes sample songs, common terms, and important tips for putting music on paper. SYSTEM SPECS: Book and Audio CD.

The MIDI Fakebook (www.pgmusic.com): Hundreds of favorite tunes; load songs into Band-in-a-Box and play or sing along; create own arrangements on computer; learn traditional jazz and improvisational skills with Soloist feature; 300 songs in a variety of styles; Traditional/Original Jazz and Pop, fifty songs; Classical, 200 songs; Bluegrass, fifty songs. SYSTEM SPECS: Macintosh; Windows.

The Professional Musician's Internet Guide (www.artistpro.com): Learn about opportunities for musicians to market and sell music on the Internet; addresses various technical issues musician face preparing and uploading music to a Web site; details on how to get online companies to sell music; how to upload music using Mac and Windows computers; accompanying CD-ROM provides simple HTML templates and audio test files in various Web-ready formats to test Web audio files. SYSTEM SPECS: Book and Hybrid CD-ROM.

The Recording Industry Sourcebook (www.artistpro.com): Music business and production directory; music industry contact information; contains over 12,000 listings in eighty categories; searchable CD-ROM of book's data is included. SYSTEM SPECS: Book and Hybrid CD-ROM.

The Songwriter's Survival Kit (www.craftofsongwriting.com): By Danny Arena, Sara Light, Fett, and Nancy Moran; four cassette tapes or two CDs; over two hours of tips, ideas, and practical "prescriptions" to heal songwriting ailments, strengthen creative muscles, and lead to success. SYSTEM SPECS: Cassettes or Audio CDs.

The Songwriter's Workshop: Melody (www.berkleemusic.com): By Jimmy Kachulis; teaches fundamental techniques behind today's hit songs; easy-to-follow exercises; develop melodies that express unique spirit of lyrics; choose notes, rhythm, and section structures to effectively express lyric meaning; write memorable choruses and verses that work together as a complete song; follow examples and tips from professional songwriters; practice songs with accompaniment on play-along CD. SYSTEM SPECS: Book and Audio CD.

Visual Arranger (www.clearvue.com): CD-ROM; create and compose; classroom tool allows students to write, arrange, and play music on computers; chord progression templates; "Smart Arranger" speeds up or slows down tempos; built-in styles include rock, jazz, and reggae; preprogrammed phrases, instruments; digital mixer; users can enter favorite songs and play along. SYSTEM SPECS: Windows.

You Can Write Hits, Volumes 1 and 2 (www.jasonblume.com): Writing Hit Melodies with Jason Blume, Volume 1: Topics: The Power of Repetition; Using Short Phrases; Repeating Rhythms; Magic Moments; Writing A Cappella; Prosody; Appropriate Range, Signature Licks; Varying Your Rhythms and Keeping Them Fresh; Rewriting; seven new exercises and more. Writing Hit Lyrics with Jason Blume, Volume 2: Topics: Writing for Yourself vs. Other Artists; Developing Great Titles and Concepts; Focusing Your Lyrics; Writing "Melody-Friendly" Lyrics; Finding a Market for Your Talent;

Evoking Emotion with Action, Detail and Imagery; Writing Strong Opening Lines; Bridges; five new exercises and more. SYSTEM SPECS: Audio CDs.

Notation, Scoring, and Transcription

Amadeus Opus Lite (Sincrosoft): Entry-level program; up to sixteen staves; eight parts per staff; cross-staff beaming; easy to use; automatic or manual functions, including spacing of notes, staves, systems, and bar lines; dialog windows; playback includes dynamics, tempos, and articulations. SYSTEM SPECS: Macintosh; Windows.

Autoscore Deluxe (www.wildcat.com): Same as Autoscore Professional but does not have pitch bend tracking, volume tracking, customizable instrument filters, or direct connection with popular music programs. SYSTEM SPECS: Windows 3.1, 95, 98, or ME, Windows compatible soundcard, Pentium class processor, 16 MB RAM.

Autoscore Professional (www.wildcat.com): Pitch-to MIDI converter; converts sound into written music, ready to edit, play back, or print; tracks pitch bend and volume; MIDI transcriptions of instrumental solos; records vibrato; comes with microphone. SYSTEM SPECS: Windows 3.1, 95, 98, or ME, Windows compatible soundcard, Pentium class processor, 16 MB RAM.

Autoscore Studio (www.wildcat.com): Turns signing or playing into written music; compose music with a sequencer or notation program without a MIDI keyboard; software-based audio-to-MIDI converter; sing or play an instrument and the musical notes immediately appear on computer screen; instrument filters, such as male voice, female voice, wind instruments, string instruments, etc.; reference tones for tuning up prior to recording; Volume Tracking and Pitch Bend Tracking are also included in the Studio version of Autoscore. SYSTEM SPECS: Windows 3.1, 95, 98, or ME, Windows compatible sound card, Pentium class processor, 16 MB RAM.

CD Sheet Music (www.cdsheetmusic.com): Printable scans of sheet music on CD-ROM for piano, vocal, opera, choral, organ, strings, woodwinds, guitar, full scores.; no MIDI files; all have a Table of Contents; cannot be used with other notation software; drawn from standard available public domain editions. SYSTEM SPECS: Hybrid.

CD-ROM Sheet Music—Artist Songbooks (www.halleonard.com): Each song in piano/vocal/guitar arrangements; view and print music; hear a MIDI playback; transpose to different keys; titles include Beach Boys; Blink 182; Classical Themes; Motown; Rock Guitar Tab; Rodgers and Hammerstein. SYSTEM SPECS: Hybrid.

CD-ROM Sheet Music—Manuscript Paper (www.halleonard.com): Variety of staff paper for composing and arranging; print staff paper right from Mac or PC; single-line paper; guitar and bass tablature paper; grand staff paper; guitar or keyboard with vocal paper; viewable with Adobe Acrobat Reader on screen and printable; includes music basics; music notation guide; guitar, bass, and drum notation legends; instrument ranges, standard articulations, and transpositions for jazz bands and orchestras and more; installation instructions. SYSTEM SPECS: Hybrid.

Desktop Sheet Music (Interactive Digital Design—Midisoft): Real-time input; drum notation; embed graphic images in score; lead sheets; scores; parts; add clip art, photos, and lyrics to sheet music; for every instrument. SYSTEM SPECS: Windows.

Encore (www.passportdesigns.com): Transcribe and edit print music; used for motion picture scores, orchestral arrangements, choir songbooks, and teaching music in schools; includes guitar tablature with fret position for up to eight strings in any tuning; customizable toolbar; percussion staff for notating complex percussion parts; zoom in and out; tempo window, color, bank select, and on-screen keyboard. SYSTEM SPECS: Macintosh; Windows.

Finale (www.finalemusic.com): Create more and edit less; save time forming musical ideas or building curriculum; from musical inspiration to printed results; four easy steps to sheet music; easy score set-up; select instruments or voices and the key and time signatures and score is set up automatically; or use one of sixty-eight professional templates; six ways to enter notes; select a note; click it onto the staff; notes space automatically; notate while playing a solo acoustic instrument; type notes on computer keyboard with or without MIDI.; notate while playing using a MIDI keyboard; scan printed sheet music; opens automatically with SmartScore Lite; import MIDI or Internet files; imports Encore files; plays music as it should be performed, even if enter notes manually; with included SmartMusic SoundFont, trumpet staves sound like violins and flutes sound like flutes; dynamics and expressions are interpreted; choose a variety of musical styles and customize the playback parameters; print the whole score or parts; publish on the Internet on Web page or to Finale Showcase, a free Web site for sharing music; save music as an audio file and create CDs; new Templates; more than twenty-five free new templates centered around the guitar and other fretted instruments; ensembles include Classical Guitar Quartet, Rock Power Trio, Dixieland Band, and Jazz Quintet; optional features include MIDI interface, MIDI input and/or playback device, printer, scanner, higher-quality computer microphone. SYSTEM SPECS: Macintosh: OS 10.1.5 and higher (some features require OS 10.2) or 9.0.4—9.2.2, CD-ROM drive, 800 x 600 minimum monitor resolution, 128 MB RAM minimum (depending on OS), 200 MB hard drive space required for software and user manual; Win-

dows: 98, 2000, NT, Me, XP (import and export of EPS files supported under Windows 98, NT, and Me only), CD-ROM drive, 800 x 600 minimum monitor resolution, 128 MB RAM minimum (depending on OS), 200 MB hard drive space required for software and user manual.

Finale Allegro (www.finalemusic.com): With Setup Wizard can select instruments, add key and time signature, tempo marking and pick-up measure, then sets up score automatically on any page size; play directly into Allegro from a MIDI keyboard, import a MIDI file or use MicNotator feature to play in single note melodies directly from electric guitar, brass or woodwind instrument; provides an accurate transcription of performance; edit all MIDI data; transpose, add lyrics, chord symbols, and guitar fingerboards; place dynamics, articulations, and slurs; instant guitar charts, drum mapping, and part extraction; every nuance of performance is saved; tempo variations, crescendos, staccatos, and attacks all play and watch music scroll; post scores on the Web; optional features include MIDI interface, MIDI input and/or playback device, printer, scanner, higher-quality computer microphone. SYSTEM SPECS: Macintosh OS 7.6.1 through the latest version of OS 9 (9.2.2), works under OSX in classic mode provided that MIDI and printing hardware (and associated software drivers) are compatible with the OSX classic mode, CD-ROM drive, 32 MB RAM minimum (depending on OS), 64 MB RAM recommended, 40 MB hard drive space required for software and user manual; Windows 95, 98, 2000, NT, Me, XP, CD-ROM drive, 32 MB RAM minimum (depending on OS), 64 MB RAM recommended, 40 MB hard drive space required for software and user manual.

Finale: An Easy Guide to Music Notation (www.berkleepress.com): CD-ROM by Thomas Rudolph and Vincent Leonard; resource for learning to use Finale; step-by-step instructions; for both novice and experienced Finale users; understand and master all of Finale's capabilities; detailed guide; 750+ pages. SYSTEM SPECS: Hybrid.

Finale Guitar (www.finalemusic.com): Choose from over fifty fretted instruments, hundreds of keyboards, percussion, brass, voices, and more; type in from computer keyboard; MIDI Step Time combination of computer and MIDI; import and notate all sequence and MIDI files; scan sheet music; with MIDI Real-Time can notate while playing using any MIDI; with Acoustic Real-Time can notate single-line melodies while playing acoustic instrument; edit all MIDI data; every nuance of performance plays back; tempo variation, crescendos, staccatos, and attacks all play as music scrolls; publish music on the Web for free at Finale Showcase, the world's gathering place for sharing great sheet music; more than twenty-five free new templates centered around the guitar and other fretted instruments; ensembles include Classical Guitar Quartet, Rock Power Trio, Dixieland Band, and Jazz Quintet. SYSTEM SPECS: Macintosh: OS 8.6 through the latest version of OS 9 (9.2.2), works under OSX in classic mode provided that MIDI and printing hardware (and associated software drivers) are compatible with the OSX classic mode, 64 MB RAM minimum, 128 MB RAM recommended, 70 MB hard drive space required; Windows: 98, 2000, Me, XP, 64 MB RAM minimum, 128 MB RAM recommended, 70 MB hard drive space required.

Finale Notepad (www.finalemusic.com): Improved palette and background graphics; interface-lift; can choose to view staves in concert pitch or transposed for transposing instruments; new engraver Smart Slurs; can change crescendo hairpins to decrescendos and vice versa by dragging; share files between Windows and Macintosh users; cross-platform fonts automatically translate upper-ASCII text such as accents, umlauts, and hard spaces to appropriate characters in Windows; create own accompaniments; play them in SmartMusic; configure and save NotePad files for customizable part playback in SmartMusic with the Intelligent Accompaniment feature; free download. SYSTEM SPECS: Macintosh: OS 8.6 through the latest version of OS 9 (9.2.2), works under OSX in classic mode provided that MIDI and printing hardware (and associated software drivers) are compatible with the OSX classic mode, 32 MB RAM minimum, 64 MB RAM recommended, 20 MB hard drive space required; Windows: 98, 2000, NT, Me, XP, 32 MB RAM minimum, 64 MB RAM recommended, 20 MB hard drive space required.

Finale Notepad Plus with MIDI (www.finalemusic.com): Turn any standard MIDI file into sheet music; use MIDI files from sequencer or access from Internet MIDI files; all the features of NotePad, plus the ability to save as, import, and export MIDI files. SYSTEM SPECS: Macintosh: OS 8.6 through the latest version of OS 9 (9.2.2), works under OSX in classic mode provided that MIDI and printing hardware (and associated software drivers) are compatible with the OSX classic mode, 32 MB RAM minimum, 64 MB RAM recommended, 20 MB hard drive space required; Windows: 98/2000/NT/Me/XP, 32 MB RAM minimum, 64 MB RAM recommended, 20 MB hard drive space required.

Finale Plug-In Tools (http://tgtools.de): Provides over forty powerful extensions to Finale; tools menu; easier music entry; lyrics enhancements; faster spacing corrections; layout tools; detailed feature list "Music" menu; "Spacing" menu; "Layout" menu; align/move dynamics; print multiple files for Windows; new spacing; "Lyrics" menu; "Miscellaneous" menu. SYSTEM SPECS: Hybrid.

Finale PrintMusic! (www.finalemusic.com): Create, play back, and print publisher-quality sheet music, up to twenty-four staves; QuickStart Video

Tips show basics on computer screen; Setup Wizard helps select instruments/voices, then sets up score automatically; MicNotator accurately enters notes played on acoustic instrument; with Simple Entry Palette can hear notes when "clicked" into place; use HyperScribe to enter notes from MIDI keyboard; Speedy Note Entry "clicks" in notes from computer keyboard or MIDI keyboard; click PLAY button and watch music scroll as it plays with selected instrumentation; print sheet music; post music for others to view, play, transpose, or print; "Save as Web Page" for own site or "Publish to Finale Showcase" a free Web site service available to PrintMusic! registered users; optional features include MIDI interface, MIDI input and/or playback device, printer, scanner, higher-quality computer microphone. SYSTEM SPECS: Macintosh: OS 7.6.1 through the latest version of OS 9 (9.2.2), works under OSX in classic mode provided that MIDI and printing hardware (and associated software drivers) are compatible with the OSX classic mode, CD-ROM drive, 32 MB RAM minimum (depending on OS), 64 MB RAM recommended, 40 MB hard drive space required for software and user manual; Windows 95, 98, 2000, NT, Me, XP, CD-ROM drive, 32 MB RAM minimum, 64 MB RAM recommended, 40 MB hard drive space required for software and user manual.

Igor Engraver (www.noteheads.com): Offers the professional engraver control over all aspects of the notation of music; easy to use for beginners; cross-platform scores can two cross-platform installs for use on two computers; movies show how basic procedures in Igor Engraver work; advanced movie shows more advanced features such as lyrics input, coloring, tablature, and Internet publishing; playback capabilities include interpretation of trills, arpeggios, and more. SYSTEM SPECS: Macintosh: OS 8.5 or later; Windows: 98, 2000.

IntelliScore (www.intelliscore.net): Convert WAV to MIDI, MP3 to MIDI, CD to MIDI; compose MIDI music by singing or playing any instrument; helps remove vocals for karaoke singing; record MIDI directly into sequencer software using voice or any acoustic instrument; generate cell phone ringtones in conjunction with Mobile Music or other ringtone conversion program; view notation from music; see chord names and key; change individual notes, swap instruments, transpose, etc.; polyphonic: WAVE, MP3, CD, and live music can contain several notes at a time, even chords. SYSTEM SPECS: Windows.

Mosaic (www.motu.com): State-of-the-art music desktop publishing software for Macintosh; provides a WYSIWYG environment in which user can produce publication-quality music notation, from lead sheets to full orchestra scores; includes real-time MIDI recording and playback, as well as step-record and mouse and keyboard note entry; supports standard

MIDI file format; unlimited voices, staves, and voices per staff; unlimited Undo/Redo; multiple views feature; see the same music formatted differently in separate windows, such as a transposed staff in an instrument part and the same staff at a smaller point size in concert pitch in the conductor score; all in the same file and linked dynamically; flexible page formatting directly on the page; "click-and-drag" placement of over 160 musical symbols; reshape slurs, ties, dynamics and more; word-processing-style lyric entry with automatic text flow through music; engraver spacing, cross-staff beaming, all forms of musical transposition, check rhythm and range commands, and complex meters; graphic user interface adheres to Macintosh software design conventions; easy sound selection of built-in sounds in MIDI synthesizers using pop-up menus; supports multiport MIDI interfaces such as the MIDI Express XT and MIDI Timepiece AV. SYSTEM SPECS: Macintosh.

Music Write Series (www.voyetra.com): Starter Kit; Songwriter; Maestro; compose, play, edit, and print music on PC; create and print sheet music; connect MIDI keyboard to PC, play the keys, and see the music transcribed on the screen; use mouse to edit compositions with drag-and-drop ease; copy, paste, insert notes, chords and ties, add lyrics and copyright info to sheet music; see the notes on PC screen; hear it played on MIDI synthesizer or PC soundcard; print sheet music for others to play; listen to compositions played by a MIDI Orchestra; compose with an orchestra of different instrument sounds; edit every nuance; print a score that represents exactly how song will sound when played by other musicians; printed music makes it easier to compose and rehearse with sheet music with each part written out; printout options include the whole score or just the drum notation and the second harmony. SYSTEM SPECS: Windows.

MusicTime Delux Notation Software (www.passportdesigns.com): Make music with computer using soundcard or MIDI instrument; create and print music with lyrics, text and guitar chords on up to sixteen staves; write and arrange music for rock bands, piano and vocals, jazz combos, choirs, marching bands, and other small ensembles. SYSTEM SPECS: Macintosh; Windows.

My Sheet Music (www.ecsmedia.com): CD-ROM; over 350 printable titles from Platinum series; twenty-eight interactive lessons; watch and hear music play; printable Chord Book, Manuscript Paper, Music Dictionary, and Exercise Books, including Hanon and Bach; Adobe PDF files can be printed over and over; can transpose music to a different key; choose another instrument such as clarinet or alto saxophone and the score will automatically change to give a special arrangement for the instrument of choice; popular with schools, churches, teachers, students, and the home hobby musician; can slow the music down or speed it up; click anywhere on score to begin playing from that point; transpose the music up or down into any key; create arrangements of all scores for most instruments; print out new arrangements. SYSTEM SPECS: Hybrid.

Photoscore (www.sibelius.com): Professional and MIDI versions; scans and reads printed music into Sibelius; requires Sibelius; edit or transpose score; play back score; transpose parts; print. SYSTEM SPECS: Macintosh; Windows.

Play Music (www.notationtechnologies.com): Music composition software available; no music theory knowledge needed; user-friendly interface guides through the composition process; click on instrument sound (up to twenty-four at one time) and will play back song with those sounds; add lyrics and text; select a note, click on the desired area of score and the notes will appear; can use any MIDI keyboard or MIDI instrument to insert notes and play back song; play keyboard and Play Music will write the notes; play composition back as a violin, guitar, bass, flute, tuba, steel drum, or any sound; record live or by using step entry to create songs; can use a computer soundcard to choose from over 128 sounds to play back song; save song as a MIDI file to use with other music software programs; import MIDI files; edit MIDI files; includes over thirty templates to create new scores. SYSTEM SPECS: Windows 95/98 or NT, Pentium processor, 16 MB RAM, Sound Blaster compatible audio card, CD-ROM drive, 13-inch monitor, 800 x 600 resolution, recommend 32 MB RAM, 17-inch monitor, and 1024 x 768 resolution.

QuickScore Copyist (www.sionsoft.com): Music notation tool for creating musical examples; treats notes, staves, clefs, and other musical characters as graphical elements; put musical objects on the page regardless of musical rules; create small excerpts to be included in work that is predominantly text; create very complex scores which are difficult to create using software which must follow musical rules; works with existing QuickScore files; save scores as .BMP, TIFF, or .EPS files and incorporate them into Microsoft Word, Corel WordPerfect, Corel Draw, Adobe Illustrator, Adobe PageMaker, and many other types of documents. SYSTEM SPECS: Windows.

QuickScore Elite (www.sionsoft.com): Mix inputs; record whole tracks or fragments of tracks in real time, step time, or while tapping own beat; mix volume, pan, and other controllers in real time; use .WAV digital audio files; look at music from all angles; score, piano roll, controller, event list, and song views; edit using comprehensive set of tools, including intelligent filters; create notation with text, lyrics, grace notes, drum notation, guitar chords, engraver spacing, multiple voices, hundreds of symbols, flexible note and staff spacing, adjustable braces and brackets, and more; cross-staff beaming with adjustable split point, six-string guitar tablature notation and multiple undo; share MIDI; play using any Windows-compatible sound card or MIDI interface; score templates; fast and easy note entry and integrated, intuitive environment. SYSTEM SPECS: Windows 95, 98, ME, NT, 2000 or XP, 64 MB RAM, 16 MB hard disk space; Windows-compatible sound card or MIDI interface is optional.

QuickScore Elite Level II Notation Software (www.sionsoft.com): Up to forty-eight tracks; editing windows include Score, Piano Roll, Controller, Event List, Song, Track Sheet, Mixer, and Comments; comprehensive set of standard editing commands in all editors including Cut, Copy, Paste, and Undo; complete control over all MIDI events; rich set of notation editing commands, including transpose chromatically or in the key, adjust enharmonic note spellings, assign notes to different voices or staves, automatically set the duration of notes to fit musical passages, and more; global graphic arranging options to cut and paste sections of songs; intelligent edit filters; loop editing; Real-time and step-time recording or record while tapping tempo from MIDI keyboard; Real-time sixteen-channel MIDI mixer controls which respond to all MIDI controllers, including volume and velocity; Punch In/Out; SMPTE/MTC and Midi Clock synchronization; optional automatic quantization of real-time recording; input and controller filters for real-time recording; playback through MIDI and all popular sound cards included; scrolling playback with synchronized window display; repeats and first and second endings automatically play; interactively edit in full-score, single-track, piano-roll, song-overview, event-list, or graphic controller formats as the music plays; play standard WAVE digital audio files; Track Sheet to mute or solo tracks and change sounds; up to ninety-six staves; independently adjust the characteristics of song title, track name, headers, footers, copyright information, four sets of lyrics, six sets of text, bar and page numbers; complete set of symbols, including groupings, fingerings, articulations, slurs, repeats, crescendos, decrescendos, dynamics, line and box drawing; all standard clefs including five-line and single-line percussion clefs; import and export standard MIDI files; export Copyist files; export Tiff, BMP, EMF, and EPS files; record and play back multiple tracks of digital audio; synchronize with digitized movie clips. SYSTEM SPECS: Windows 95, 98, ME, NT, 2000 or XP, 64 MB RAM, 16 MB hard disk space; Windows-compatible sound card or MIDI interface is optional.

Roni Music Downloadable Software Programs (www.ronimusic.com): AMAZING SLOW DOWNER: Learn new songs and techniques while listening to repeated parts of songs; provides, means to slow down music so it can be learned in real-time by playing it from a CD, MP3, WAV, AIFF (Mac only), or WMA (Windows only) file; increase music speed to up to twice normal rate; make pitch adjustments in semi-tones at full or lower speed; set loop points using keyboard shortcuts. MIDI SOFTWARE: Sweet MIDI Player and Sweet Sixteen MIDI Sequencer; software implementation of an arpeggiator often found on older synthesizers called Sweet MIDI Arpeggiator: computer version of an intelligent harmonizer called Sweet MIDI Harmony Maker; Sweet Little Piano lets user play sound card from the computer keyboard. AUDIO COMPANION: Three different programs in one: one to grab audio from CD (CD Ripper), one for processing MP3, WMA and WAV files (Batch Processor), and an audio recorder (Audio Splitter) for recording audio from line-in input of soundcard (with auto-split function for easy recording of vinyl records, etc). MUSICIAN'S CD PLAYER: Works like Amazing Slow Downer but does recording of desired section first; intended for slower/older Windows computers; available for download. SYSTEM SPECS: Macintosh; Windows.

Scorch (www.sibelius.com): Software for viewing, playing, customizing, printing, and saving scores from the Internet; free download. SYSTEM SPECS: Macintosh; Windows.

Sibelius (www.sibelius.com): Professional quality notation program; notate, edit, play back, and publish every kind of music; fast and easy to use; clear, instant graphics; Flexi-time MIDI input; Expressive and SoundStage playback; PhotoScore Lite music scanning plug-in included; write other plug-in features with ManuScript language; search and edit score using filters; includes guitar tab, nested tuplets, drum kit notation, figured bass, and other specific notations; export graphics in a variety of standard file formats; add music to posters, covers and exams, papers, books, and magazines; plays back score through sound card or MIDI equipment; reads and plays all standard markings; score reformatting and part extraction; add scores to Web site; concise manual; Platinum Edition plug-ins check for redundant dynamics, suspect mutes, pedaling, and errors in the full score. SYSTEM SPECS: Macintosh: G4/G3/iMac/fast PowerMac, Mac OS 7.1 to 9.2, 15 MB+ free RAM (20 MB+ recommended, 32 MB+ for scanning), CD-ROM drive, 40 MB+ free hard disk space, some features require printer, MIDI keyboard, Internet access, TWAIN-compatible scanner; Windows: Pentium or fast 486 (Pentium II or faster recommended), Windows 95, 98, Me, 2000, XP, NT4 or later, 32 MB+ RAM (64 MB recommended for scanning), CD-ROM drive, 40 MB+ free hard disk space, some features require printer, sound card, MIDI keyboard, Internet access, scanner.

Sibelius G7 (www.sibelius.com): Software for writing songs and playing better guitar; write tab, chords, lyrics, and notation; learn songs and riffs with the on-screen fretboard; publish music on the Internet. SYSTEM SPECS: Macintosh; Windows.

Sibelius Internet (www.sibelius.com): Solution for publishing sheet music online; used by top publishers and retailers, including Yamaha, Hal Leonard, Music Sales, Boosey and Hawkes, and J. W. Pepper. SYSTEM SPECS: Macintosh; Windows.

SmartScore (www.musitek.com): Integrated music scanning, scoring, and MIDI sequencing; advanced recognition intelligence; plays back repeats, dynamics, and articulation; displays contrapuntal voices with direct voice-to-MIDI channel linking; automatic instrument assignments according to number of staves; playback continuity; intelligent control of instrumental parts; creates scores using mouse, keyboard, MIDI instrument, MIDI file, or scanner input; control over page layout, spacing, and irregular systems; part and voice separation; notation-to-MIDI-to-notation implementation; import standard MIDI files to display, transpose, or print out scores; Pro Edition; SongBook Edition; Piano Edition; MIDI Edition; Guitar Edition. SYSTEM SPECS: Macintosh: OS X—any computer that runs OS 10.2 (Jaguar) or later, OS 8/9—System 8.2 with QuickTime 3.0 or later; PowerPC or better, 32 MB RAM (recommended) and 16 MB disk space; Windows: Win 9x, 2000, NT, ME, XP, Pentium 120 or better, 24 MB RAM and 16 MB disk space.

The Finale Notepad Primer: Learning the Art of Music Notation with Notepad Book and CD-ROM (www.clearvue.com): Easy-to-follow program; will enable student to work with any composition for editing, formatting, and reorganization; applicable for both original works and existing; book is full of exercises, projects, and tips. SYSTEM SPECS: Macintosh: PowerPC processor, 32 MB RAM, and System 7.6.1-10; Windows: Pentium processor, 32 MB RAM, Windows 95, 98, ME, NT, 2000, or XP, and sound card.

The Vivaldi Studio (www.vialdistudio.com): Suite of products working together; combination of music notation software, thousands of interactive digital sheet music, interactive digital teaching, and music notation scanning software from the leading music company in Italy, Allegroassai.com; ten years of development; successful test markets in Italy and Europe. VIVALDI PLAYALONG: music play-along and notation software designed by musicians for musicians; makes practicing easier by slowing down or speeding up playback to learn to play a piece more easily; designed by musicians who know how to take advantage of all the benefits of using digital sheet music. VIVALDI PLUS: notation software for teachers and everyone else; includes software, Viva score digital sheet music, learning and teaching templates; designed by music teachers who are practicing musicians for the average user of music notation; enables basic music editing software; can open, view, edit, play, and print Viva Digital Scores of any type and complexity. VIVALDI GOLD: designed by composers for composers to be easy to use, intuitive, and powerful; quickly, accurately, and intuitively write music. VIVALDI SCAN: Optical Music Recognition engine; rhythm checking and note validation tools; correct errors; add text and fingering. SYSTEM SPECS: Macintosh: PowerPC Processor, System 7.x-9.x; Windows 95, 98, ME, NT, 2000, XP.

Transcribe (www.seventhstring.demon.co.uk/): Software to help transcribe recorded music; use to work out a piece of music from a recording in order to write it out or play it, or both; copy recording to computer's hard disk as a sound file then use Transcribe instead of a cassette machine and a piano; offers many features aimed at making the transcription job smoother and easier, including the ability to slow the music down without changing its pitch and to analyze chords and show what notes are present; does not attempt to do the whole job of processing an audio file and putting out musical notation; spectrum analysis feature is very useful for working out hard-to-hear chords; must still use ear to decide which of the peaks in the spectrum are notes being played, which are harmonics, and which are the result of noise and broad-spectrum instruments such as drums; no interest in MIDI files; deals with audio sample data files; not an editor; reads, plays, and records audio files but does not modify them; downloadable shareware. SYSTEM SPECS: Macintosh: System 7.5 or higher, running on a Power PC or 68020 with Sound Manager 3; separate version for Mac OS-X; Windows: Windows 95, 98, 2000, NT, ME, XP, sound card.

Transkriber (www.reedkotler.com): Play music to learn on computer CD player or on an external CD or tape player hooked up to the sound card; record music using the recording panel; play music back at 3/4, 2/3, 1/2, 1/3, 1/4, or 1/26 of the original speed without changing the pitch; phrase selection to focus on one part of the music at a time; slow down algorithms, tuning, and smoothing filters; reinforce or remove certain frequency bands from the music to better focus on the part being transcribed; adjust the pitch to match the recording exactly; transpose the sound up or down as much as an octave; pitch generator identifies which note is being played on the recording; for beginning to advanced transcribers. SYSTEM SPECS: Macintosh; Windows.

Digital Audio Recording and Editing—MIDI Sequencing— CD Burning—Multimedia— MIDI File Libraries—Sample Sounds and Loops—Software Synthesizers— MP3 Software

ACID Loops for Windows (mediasoftware.sonypictures.com): High-quality sound files for use with ACID; store special data to optimize time stretching/compressing and pitch change features;

standard .WAV sound files with extra data; royalty free; includes Essential Sounds Vol. 2, Funky Extremes 1, Street Beats, Voices of Native America, Cyclotonic Resonator, Pandoras Toolbox, Rads Drum Construction Kit, Vortexual Amplitude, Funky Extremes 2, Sytonic Generator; Loop Starter Kits; Loop Bundles; 1,001 Sound Effects. SYSTEM SPECS: Windows.

ACID Pro (mediasoftware.sonypictures.com): Loop-based music creation tool that allows professionals to produce original, royalty-free music; create own songs, remix tracks, produce 5.1 surround audio mixes, develop music beds, score own videos, and create music for Web sites and Flash animations; intuitive and easy to use; powerful enough for professional production; huge assortment of loops in multiple genres; compose using unlimited tracks of audio and MIDI, import and Beatmap complete songs; saves to a variety of formats such as WAV, WMA, RM, AVI, and MP3; apply VSTi soft synths, create 5.1 surround mixes, and perform video scoring; create resonant sweeps, dramatic fades, EQ changes, and effects by utilizing automation parameters and envelope control; automated effects such as Resonant Filters, Track EQ, and Flange/Wah Wah/Phase; includes over 20 DirectX audio Plug-Ins such as Amplitude Modulation, Chorus, Delay, Distortion, Flange, Noise Gate, Reverb, and more; display and edit MIDI files in a piano roll format, just like a sequencer; with MIDI piano roll editor can draw new notes, and graphically edit MIDI parameters; record MIDI tracks into ACID project using external MIDI devices, or add events using MIDI step recording; MIDI tracks time stretch to any tempo, and can be rendered with effects like audio tracks; content CD containing more than 350 multi-genre music loops and dozens of projects from Sony Pictures Digital's Loops for ACID collection; genres include: Dance, Hip-Hop, Techno, Industrial, Pop, Rock, Jazz, Ambient, Orchestral, and more; get 5.1 surround projects and alternate time signature loops. SYSTEM SPECS: Windows 98SE, Me, 2000, or XP.

ACID XPress for Windows (mediasoftware.sonypictures.com): Music creation tool; pick loops, paint them into a track, and play them back; download sample songs from mediasoftware.sonypictures.com, or use any of the Loops for ACID or Loop Starter Kit libraries; matches tempo and pitch automatically; publish song on ACIDplanet.com, or stream it from own Web site; "pick, paint, and play" style interface; entry-level software. SYSTEM SPECS: Windows.

Adobe Audition (www.adobe.com): Professional audio editing environment; for audio and video professionals; offers advanced audio mixing, editing, and effects processing capabilities; flexible workflow; ease of use; precise tools; free upgrade for Cool Edit Pro 2 users. SYSTEM SPECS: Windows: 400 MHz processor (2 GHz or faster recommended), Windows 98 Second Edition, Windows Millennium Edition, Windows 2000, or Windows XP Professional or Home Edition, 64 MB RAM (512 MB or more recommended), 55 MB available hard-disk space (500 MB recommended for installing optional audio clips), 800 x 600 color display (1,024 x 768 display recommended), stereo sound card (multitrack sound card recommended), CD-ROM drive, speakers or headphones recommended, microphone (optional); additional requirements for the Multichannel Encoder—for multichannel WMA import: Windows XP; for surround preview: Microsoft DirectX 8.0 and a multichannel sound card and DirectSound driver.

Audioactive Player (www.audioactive.com): MP3 player and encoder software. SYSTEM SPECS: Windows.

Audiocaster (www.sekd.com): Radio broadcasting automation program; noncommercial radio stations, local stations, schools, universities, hospitals, health resorts, and military institutions are potential users. SYSTEM SPECS: Windows.

Audiocatalyst (www.xingtech.com): MP3 player and encoder software. SYSTEM SPECS: Macintosh; Windows.

AudioDesk (www.motu.com): Full-featured audio workstation software package for Mac OS X; 24-bit/192 KHz recording and real time, 32-bit effects processing; includes multitrack audio editing, sample-accurate placement of audio, complete virtual mixing environment with up to sixty-four stereo busses, automated mixing, graphic editing of mix and effects automation, scrubbing, trimming, spotting, crossfades, support for third-party MAS effects plug-ins, unlimited digital track bouncing (including effects and automation, and much more; does not place artificial restrictions on the number of tracks user can work with; unlimited audio tracks; view audio tracks in a single, unified mixer; configure up to twenty effects inserts per audio channel, and thirty-two stereo busses; automatable, effects parameters with five advanced automation modes, beat-synchronized effects and sample accurate editing of automation data; automation system features rich set of user interface technologies such as event flags for discrete events and spline tools for manipulating control points; automation parameters displayed in real world values such as decibels and milliseconds; includes dozens of real-time DSP effects with easy to use graphical controls and complete automation; two-, four-, and eight-band EQ, tube-simulation and distortion effects with the flexible.PreAmp-1 plug-in, reverbs, a compressor, a synthesizer-style multimode filter, echo and delay effects, chorus, phaser, flanger, and more. SYSTEM SPECS: Macintosh OS X.

AudioStation (www.voyetra.com): Run multimedia PC like a home stereo system; intuitive, hardware-style interface unites MIDI, WAV, and CD functions; edit MIDI and digital audio WAV files; group files into playlists for automated playback; play audio CDs with CD-ROM drive and create custom playlists of songs; includes dozens of MIDI music and digital audio files; diagnostic program to help fix common multimedia setup problems. SYSTEM SPECS: Windows.

AudioSurgeon (www.voyetra.com): Record, edit, transform, convert, manipulate, and burn music to CD; get inside digital music files for customization and control; optimize loudness, remove unwanted sections, fade out songs, remove hiss, use sound effects, and more; convert music files to and from multiple file formats, including MP3, WMA, and WAVE; audio recording, editing, and CD burning tool; digitally record songs to PC hard drive; view music as a graphical waveform showing every peak and valley in the sound; zoom in and change every nuance then burn it back to CD; companion to any music jukebox program and digital music on a PC, portable or network audio player; restore and preserve cassette and vinyl record collection; remove pops, clicks, and hiss from original recordings then convert into digital audio files on PC; create voice and music backgrounds for multimedia presentations; mix music and voice-overs together to create professional-sounding audio clips to complement PowerPoint and other visual applications; include transforms like echo, volume scaling, fades, reverse, and more; paste in sound effects and use processing to shape finished presentation; highly customizable mixer; customize faders, hide unnecessary options, control multiple sound card mixers, create own mixer applications for different functions, like recording vinyl, MP3 playback, Internet chat, and more; record and edit music and sound samples; create sample loops for drums, rhythm parts, voices, and more; loop control feature to edit nuances of audio file; import finished sample into sequencer program or other audio sampler; customize desktop with WAV sound effects, or create greeting messages for PC answering machine. SYSTEM SPECS: Windows.

Be a DJ (www.warnerbrospublications.com): Parts One and Two; the late Jam Master Jay shows off his tricks. SYSTM SPECS: Instructional DVD.

Berklee Press (www.berkleepress.com): Electronic and Digital Instruments; Producing in the Home Studio with Pro Tools; Turntable Technique—The Art of the DJ. SYSTEM SPECS: Books and Audio CDs.

Big Fish Audio Sample CDs and CD-ROMs (www.bigfishaudio.com): Quality sample libraries since 1986; can find extensive selection of sample library and sound effects products from around the world; all products are license free; no clearance forms or additional licenses are required; Big Fish sounds are featured in hundreds of charting songs and top film scores; products contain Loops/Performances and/or Sounds; formats include: Akai, Audio E-mu, GigaSampler, Kurzweil, Mac (AIFF)/SampleCell, MPC 2000, Roland, SoundFont, Soundscan, TC, and WAV; Big Fish Audio Listening Centers at music stores nationwide, including Guitar Center, Sam Ash Music, Mars Music, Manny's Music, West L. A. Music, Bananas at Large, Veneman Music, and others; extensive selection of disks; can audition before buying. SYSTEM SPECS: Macintosh; Windows.

Bitheadz (www.bitheadz.com): Primary Applications—Unity Session Software Synth & Sampling Environment Mac; Unity DS-1 Digital Software Sampler/Editor Mac/PC; Unity AS-1 Digital Software Synthesizer/Editor Mac/PC; Unity Synth Expander 1 Additional Synths for Unity or Stand Alone Use Mac; Phrazer Loop Composition Software Mac; Phrazer LE Sample Loop Arranger Mac; Osmosis Software Sample Converter Mac/PC; Unity Player Digital Software Sample Player Mac/PC; Voodoo Digital Drum Machine Mac/PC; Retro Lite Digital Synthesis Player Mac/PC. Unity Based Sound Modules—Unity Topaz Kits Software Drums Kits Mac; Ultimate Acoustics Software Gibson Guitars Mac; Black & Whites Software Piano Module Mac/PC; Unity Discrete Drums Studio Drum Kits Mac; Tubes, Tines & Transitors Software Vintage Keyboard Module Mac/PC; Pop Drums Vol. 1 Contemporary Drum Loops Mac/PC; Tempo Tantrum Breakbeat Loop Module Mac/PC; Harry Sharpe Guitars Guitar Loop Module Mac/PC; Steve Reid's Global Percussion Software Percussion Module Mac/PC; Miroslav Vitous MINI Symphonic Orchestral Samples Mac. Loop Based Content— Phrazer Smart Loops Bass Guitar Loops Mac; Phrazer Smart Loops Drum & Percussion Loops Mac; Phrazer Smart Loops Electric Guitar Loops Mac; Phrazer Discrete Drums Studio Drum Loops Mac; AfroCuban Percussion Tropical Rhythm Module Mac; Phrazer Underground Beatz Vol. 1 Mac; Phrazer Underground Beatz Vol. 2 Mac. SYSTEM SPECS: Macintosh; Windows.

BPM Force (www.steinberg.net): Bundle by Steinberg and Waldorf; unique combination of a top sequencer with first-class instruments and filters; for dance producers; includes Cubase SL sequencer and the A1 synth for hammering bass lines; Waldorf Attack delivers the beats; percussion synthesizer integrates analog drum sounds of the 80s and the club drums of the 90s in VST System; Waldorf PPG Wave 2.V, the second coming of a synth legend as a VST instrument, gives synth pads to manic techno sounds; Waldorf D-Pole, with five filter types can morph any acoustic drum loop into a heavy-duty dance groove; BPM Force; Cubase SL PC; Cubase SL MAC; Waldorf Attack; Waldorf PPG Wave 2.V; Waldorf D-Pole. SYSTEM SPECS: Macintosh; Windows.

Cakewalk Express 8 (www.cakewalk.com): Turn PC into a music recording studio; inexpensive;

record any instrument, voice, or the on-screen Virtual Piano; supports two tracks of audio along with MIDI; edit and mix tracks quickly and easily; prints notation; support for simultaneous projects; Real-time audio and MIDI effects. SYSTEM SPECS: Windows 95/98/NT, Pentium 120 MHz, 16 MB RAM, Windows-compatible MIDI interface required for MIDI recording.

Cakewalk Home Studio 2004 for Windows (www.cakewalk.com): Record, edit, mix, and master; centralized audio and MIDI recording; loop-based composition tools; built-in DXi soft synths; ReWire 2.0 support; DirectX audio effects; compose and print sheet music; graphical editing tools; create video soundtracks; support for real-time DirectX effects, DXi and ReWire software synths, MIDI FX plug-ins, and ACID-format audio loop technology; ReWire support to integrate Home Studio 2004 with Project5, Reason, and other ReWire synths; simultaneously record whole band with support for multichannel audio cards; record up to 24-bit/96 KHz audio; easier soft synth implementation; click and drag to paint drum tracks with new pattern brush and Drum Editing Grid; Pyro Express CD maker and WAV ripper; support for all Windows compatible audio hardware through WDM, MME, or ASIO; record unlimited audio and MIDI tracks; mix with real-time audio and MIDI effects; plug and play DXi soft synths; create loops fast; supports ACID-format, MP3, WAV, WMA, and MIDI files. SYSTEM SPECS: Windows 98SE/Me/2000/XP.

Cakewalk Home Studio 2004 XL (www.cakewalk.com): For the musician, project studio producer, or dance/remix artist looking for more value; provides all the capabilities of Home Studio 2004, plus additional DirectX plug-ins, a DXi Sampler, and an additional CD of audio samples. SYSTEM SPECS: Windows 98SE/Me/2000/XP.

Cakewalk Loop Libraries for Windows (www.cakewalk.com): Variety of loop libraries to help maximize creative potential. CAKEWALK LOOPS: Cakewalk partnered with leading producers of major-label club remixes, including X-Mix, PowerFX, and Smart Loops to bring a series of top-notch, prerecorded, royalty free, ACID-format audio content that spans many genres; for use with any Cakewalk PC program that opens WAV files; optimized for use in SONAR. POWERFX ONLINE LOOP LIBRARY: filled with thousands of loops, sound effects, and samples available for download. SMART LOOPS LOOP LIBRARIES: ACID-compatible loops in audio (.wav) format; for use with any Cakewalk PC program that opens WAV files; optimized for use in SONAR. SYSTEM SPECS: Windows.

Cakewalk Music Creator for Windows (www.cakewalk.com): Complete desktop studio; intuitive controls; loop-based tools; DXi soft synths; DirectX audio effects; compose and print sheet music;

graphical editing tools; create video soundtracks; plug in any instrument or microphone and press Record; for musicians, music enthusiasts, singer/songwriters, bands, choir groups, music teachers and students, PC hobbyists; connect any instrument to PC; record audio and MIDI tracks using any instrument, vocals, or audio loops; write music for CDs, sheet music, home videos, and the Internet; includes free Pyro Express CD Maker and WAV Ripper, Virtual Sound Canvas DXi soft synth, Dreamstation DXi soft synth, ACID-format audio loop library. SYSTEM SPECS: Windows 98/Me/2000/XP.

Cakewalk Music Creator Pro for Windows (www.cakewalk.com): Centralized audio and MIDI recording; loop-based composition tools; perform with DXi soft synths; mix with DirectX effects; compose and print sheet music; graphical editing tools; create video soundtracks; turn PC into a multitrack recording studio; record self or whole band in 24-bit/96 KHz, DVD-quality audio; combines professional recording, mixing, and audio effects with integrated ACID-format looping tools, software synthesizers, audio CD burning, and more; record unlimited tracks of audio and MIDI; mix with real-time audio and MIDI effects; perform with DXi software synthesizers; create loops fast; includes ACID-format loop library; audio CD burning and ripping; record whole band with support for multi-channel audio cards; easy soft synth implementation; click and drag to paint drum tracks with new pattern brush and Drum Editing Grid; Pyro Express CD maker and WAV ripper; support for all Windows compatible audio hardware through WDM, MME, or ASIO; 24-bit/96 KHz recording/playback requires compatible audio hardware. SYSTEM SPECS: Windows 98SE/Me/2000/XP.

Cakewalk Plasma (www.cakewalk.com): Create loop-based music and remixes; create DJ effects; use deep progressive synth sounds; make music videos soundtracks; create own music and remixes with the same loops, beats, synths, and effects used by DJs and remix artists; record, edit, arrange, and mix music; record keyboards, vocals, live turntable scratches, CD samples, or any other sound source; click-and-drag looping; multitrack recorder; joystick-controlled DJ effects mixer; software synths; audio effects; CD loop library created by leading Dance, Techno, and Hip Hop producers; includes free Plasma FXPad joystick-controlled DJ FX plug-in, DreamStation DXi and Triangle DXi soft synths, bonus CD Dance and Hip Hop loop library, and Pyro Express CD maker and WAV ripper. SYSTEM SPECS: Windows 98/Me/2000/XP.

Cakewalk Project5 Soft Synth Work Station (www.cakewalk.com): PSYN Virtual Analog Synth; DS864 Digital Sampler; VELOCITY Drum Sampler; PULSE Drum Synthesizer; Cyclone DXi Groove Sampler; Spectral Transformations; pattern and loop-based tools; expand and customize;

workflow innovations; samples and loops; song examples; complete studio environment for electronic musicians; experiment, create, and perform music using integrated sequencers, software synths, samplers, audio and MIDI effects, and audio looping tools all in one workstation; advanced capabilities for synth layering, real-time pattern genesis, and triggering; live-performance audio engine; customize and expand studio with additional plug-ins; supports any Windows-compatible audio hardware; studio-quality instruments and effects; pattern-based sequencers and processors; ACID-compatible audio looping tools; Real-time, live-performance; open environment (ASIO, DX, DXi, MFX, ReWire client, WDM, VST, VSTi). SYSTEM SPECS: Windows 2000/XP.

Cakewalk Pyro (www.cakewalk.com): Complete system for recording, playing, and organizing favorite digital music; custom audio editing; noise wizard; CD labeling; comparison chart; rip and burn responsibly; make MP3s, burn and share mix CDs of favorite music; digitize and clean up old LPs or cassettes; archive important data files; burn professional-quality CDs of favorite songs; turn CDs into MP3s, WAV, or WMA files; back up valuable files to data CD; convert LPs and cassettes into CDs or digital files; clean audio to remove clicks, crackles, pops, hiss, and hum from LPs, cassettes, and low-quality MP3s; rip individual songs or entire albums; locate and organize all music files on PC; create megamixes and smooth transitions by overlaying and cross-fading songs; superior sound quality with 64-bit EQ; downloads song titles and artist info from Gracenote/CDDB. SYSTEM SPECS: Windows 98, Me, 2000, XP.

CD Architect for Windows (mediasoftware.sonypictures.com): Produce professional audio CDs to Red Book specification; stand-alone version; full PQ code editing; trim events from full-length media and add as new tracks; import regions from Sound Forge software as tracks; master audio by applying over twenty real-time DirectX effects to events and the master output; disk-at-once CD burning; drag-and-drop operations; complex crossfades and DJ-style megamixes; generate multiple takes of a song; create live-style CDs with audio in the time between tracks; apply volume envelopes and event ASR envelopes; create hidden tracks; supports many drives, including FireWire and USB devices. SYSTEM SPECS: Windows 98SE, Me, 2000, or XP.

Computer Music Starter Kit for Windows (www.voyetra.com): Turns multimedia PC and MIDI keyboard into a desktop music system; connect MIDI cable to sound card's joystick port, plug in MIDI keyboard, and load CD-ROM; ready to play; includes MIDI Orchestrator Plus sequencer program; record, edit, and play MIDI music; print sheet music; Jam Grid interactive music utility; multimedia course on MIDI and music synthesis; variety of songs. SYSTEM SPECS: Windows.

Creative Music Production: Joe Meek's Bold Techniques (www.artistpro.com); By veteran music journalist Barry Cleveland; legendary British producer and technical innovator Joe Meek behind the hits "Telstar" and "Have I the Right?"; details on methods that led to influential hits; explores professional career in depth, equipment used, and effect his work had on people around him; audio CD containing Meek's "I Hear a New World" album. SYSTEM SPECS: Book and Audio CD.

Critical Listening and Auditory Perception (www.artistpro.com): Sharpen skills of evaluating sound quality; five CDs narrate entire course; hundreds of illustrations elaborate on text. SYSTEM SPECS: Book and Audio CDs.

Cubase (www.steinberg.net): Virtual studio for Mac or PC; all Cubase versions are developed for musicians by musicians; intuitive handling with professional, expandable capabilities. CUBASE SL: for both engineers in project studios and newcomers to home recording; VST and ASIO interfaces; has set standards in sequencing; unlimited Undo and Redo and Offline Process History; Sample Accurate Automation; Virtual Instruments and VST Effects; MIDI Plug-ins; VST System Link; free updates; Mackie Control (1.5 MB PDF); features overview; Cubase SL and Cubase SX (210 kB PDF). CUBASE SX 2.0: music creation and production system; music workstation unites the proven and the pioneering in one program; features and innovations such as new VST audio engine, freeze function for VSTi's, 32-bit floating point audio resolution, real multichannel surround, Stacked Recording, and more. CUBASE XlTC: native music production suite; complete music production suite that includes Cubase SX and the high-end TC Works Native Bundle 3.0 collection of six virtual effects. STEINBERG STUDIO CASE: complete music producers' collection; for beginners, cross-graders, hobby musicians, and users of Cubase SX and/or VST System Link; includes a sequencer and five VST instruments. THE SL EDITION: Cubase SL and HALion VST sampler encompassing both Cubase SL and Steinberg's HALion virtual sampler; complete music production package for project studios. THE WALDORF EDITION: collection of instruments and filters; three Waldorf plug-ins include the PPG Wave 2.V classic wavetable synthesizer, the Attack drum synthesizer, and the first-rate D-Pole filter. V-STACK: virtual instrument rack for VST System Link; 32-bit virtual instrument rack for PC that expands VST System Link network by adding 16 VST instrument slots; as a stand alone application, V-STACK works as a "live" station for VST instruments. SYSTEM SPECS: Macintosh; Windows.

Dart (www.dartpro.com): Digital audio recording and restoration software; CD-Recorder software; complete audio toolkit for PC; record audio, apply restoration processing; make music CDs in computer's CD-R or CD-RW drive; record from a compact disk or stereo; clean up digital recordings using DeHiss and DeClick DirectX plug-ins; enhance audio using nine-band equalizer; Volume Control and Fade In/Fade Out features; organize tunes into playlists; write an audio CD that can be played in any CD player; SureThing Lite CD Labeler included; batch file conversion; converts WAV or MP3 to CD audio format; connect to the Internet and add artist, title, and other CD track information to the online CDDB music database; erase CD-RW disks for reuse; free updates from Dartech via the Internet. SYSTEM SPECS: Windows, CD-R, or CD-RW drive required for burning audio CDs.

Deck (www.bias-inc.com): Advanced digital audio workstation for music, audio-for-picture, Internet audio, 5.1 surround mixing, and more; Mac-based multitrack digital audio workstation; professional audio solution for film or video; spot effects, edit dialogue, process soundtracks, record ADR-style voiceovers and craft complex mixes to stereo or complete 5.1 surround while in perfect sync to a Quick-Time movie or DV clip; for music production; up to four real-time effects plug-ins per track; editing platform; audio tools include surround mixing; multimedia development for video games, the Web, and presentations; intuitive user interface; many available plug-ins. SYSTEM SPECS: Macintosh.

Digital Music Starter Kit for Windows (www.voyetra.com): Digital Audio and MIDI sequencing software; Digital Sound Gallery II library of digital music samples; drag and drop; MIDI adapter cable connects PC to any MIDI-compatible digital musical instrument. SYSTEM SPECS: Windows.

Digital Orchestrator for Windows (www.voyetra.com): Turns PC into a complete desktop recording studio; unlimited tracks of MIDI; four tracks of digital audio; editing features and ability to print sheet music; on-screen video tutorials; intuitive interface; record, copy, paste, and mix MIDI and digital audio tracks; add digital FX; integration of MIDI and digital audio. SYSTEM SPECS: Windows.

Digital Orchestrator Plus for Windows (www.voyetra.com): Create music enhanced with vocals and other acoustic sounds; MIDI and digital audio technology; MIDI sequencer; multitrack digital audio; digital audio effects; music notation; video tutorials; demo files; digital sound clips; MIDI drum tracks; multitrack MIDI and digital audio recorder/editor; control up to 256 MIDI Channels; extensive help; MIDI/WAV Sync; digital sound effects processing; drag-and-drop user interface displays MIDI and digital audio tracks together; record, zoom edit, move, mix, or copy MIDI and digital audio tracks.

SYSTEM SPECS: Windows 486 DX2/66 MHz, Windows 3.1 or Windows 95, 8 MB RAM, 10 MB hard disk, sound card with 16-bit digital audio record/playback capability, onboard MIDI synthesizer, double speed CD-ROM or faster.

Digital Orchestrator Pro for Windows (www.voyetra.com): More than 1,000 tracks of MIDI and digital audio; works with PC and sound cards; prints sheet music; desktop music production; multitrack digital audio recording and feature-rich MIDI sequencing; zoom, edit, move, mix, or copy sections of the song with a few simple mouse movements; merge tacks by dragging one on top of the other; add digital sound effects processing; transcribe and print professional quality sheet music from MIDI tracks. SYSTEM SPECS: Windows.

Digital Performer (www.motu.com): Integrated digital audio and MIDI sequencing production system; provides a comprehensive environment for editing, arranging, mixing, processing, and mastering multitrack audio projects for a wide variety of applications; simultaneously record and playback multiple tracks of digital audio and MIDI data in a totally integrated, creative environment; does not place artificial restrictions on the number of tracks user can work with; unlimited audio and MIDI tracks; supports a wide range of audio hardware, including TDM (Pro Tools), Direct I/O, ASIO, Sound Manager, and MOTU audio interfaces; supports high-resolution 24-bit/192 KHz audio; view MIDI and audio tracks in a single, unified mixer; configure up to twenty effects inserts per audio channel, and thirty-two stereo busses; automatable, effects parameters with five advanced automation modes, beat-synchronized effects, and sample accurate editing of automation data; automation system features a rich set of user interface technologies such as event flags for discrete events and spline tools for manipulating control points; automation parameters are displayed in meaningful real world values such as decibels and milliseconds; includes dozens of real-time DSP effects with easy-to-use graphic controls and complete automation; two-, four-, and eight-band EQ, tube simulation and distortion effects with the flexible PreAmp-1 plug-in, three reverbs, two noise gates, including the MasterWorks Gate with real-time lookahead gating, two compressors, a synthesizer-style multimode filter, echo and delay effects including a surround delay, chorus, phaser, flanger, Sonic Modulator, and more; supports multiple processors; fully compatible with all MOTU Audio System plug-ins, including those from third-party vendors; includes a built-in waveform editor that provides a pencil tool for removing clicks and a loop tool for defining loops for sampler; auto edit cross-fades;. sampler integration allows user to transfer audio from project to sampler with a drag and drop operation; sampler appears as a device inside Digital Performer; can seamlessly share data; PureDSP functions provide independent control over the duration and pitch of audio files with exceptional sound quality; tempo-conform drum loops, add vocal harmony or even gender-bend vocal tracks; audio editing is accurate to a single sample; edit MIDI with a resolution of 1/10,000.000 PPQ (pulses per quarter); when used with a USB MOTU MIDI interface, provides MIDI timing resolution to within a single MIDI byte, under one third of a millisecond; with Multirecord MIDI recording, can record on an unlimited number of MIDI tracks simultaneously; three continuous controller editing modes, creating continuous controller streams for the automation of MIDI instruments is flexible and intuitive; movie track and Quicktime support integrates Digital Performer with the video world, enabling user to see instantly how edits relate to picture; individually zoomable tracks, flexible window arrangement, and navigation tools allow for trouble-free manipulation within projects; provides many flexible editors, including Sequence Editor, Graphic Editor, Event List, Drum Editor, and QuickScribe notation; list-editing or graphical style display; score layout, or extensive drum-programming; fine-tuning of single MIDI events, or massive changes of entire sections; QuickScibe notation window lets user print out whole score or individual parts; continuous scrolling moves the music under the wiper, which stays fixed to the center of the window; provides a choice of four panner plug-ins, including a localizing room simulator; each audio track can be assigned to any surround sound format, from LCRS up to 10.2; panning movements can be automated using automation system; include complete surround submixes or record the output of a surround reverb with surround tracks; master multichannel mix with a broad assortment of variable channel effects processors, including the MasterWorks Limiter. SYSTEM SPECS: Macintosh.

DJ Style (www.warnerbrospublications.com): "Mixing and Remixing": mixing and remixing as a DJ; by acclaimed DJ KNS; includes tips on beat matching, blending vocals, working with beats, bars and breaks, and more; "DJing in a Band": DJs KNS and Ucada give the lowdown on being the turntable guru in a band; included are tips on scratching, creating beats, understanding bars and breaks and more; "DJing with CDs": learn all the techniques of DJ-ing with CDs from DJ Gerald "World Wide" Webb; master such areas as scratchable and non-scratchable CDs, beat matching techniques, creating loops, and matching beats and breaks. SYSTEM SPECS: Instructional DVDs.

Easy CD and DVD Creator (www.roxio.com): Digital Media Suite; rip, play, edit, organize, and burn digital music with AudioCentral; preserve memories in electronic albums, create photo slide shows, print or e-mail photos with PhotoSuite Limited Edition; make DVD movies with professional transitions and animated menus to play on home DVD player with DVD Builder; create personalized disk labels with Label Creator; save large data projects to multiple disks with Creator Classic or copy personal disks with Disk Copier; fully integrated product! SYSTEM SPECS: Windows.

Echoview Pro for Windows (http://www.mirage1.u-net.com): Integrated suite of interactive music calculating tools for musicians, sound engineers, and producers; 32-bit package; freeware; download from the Internet; delay time calculator; delay time grid; metronome; tap tempo utility; chord cue; song length calculator; stopwatch; sample calculator; synthesisers; printing features. SYSTEM SPECS: Windows 95, 98, or NT.

Edirol Plug-In Software Synthesizers (www.edirol.com): HQ Hyper Canvas: GM2 plug-in software synthesizer; HQ Orchestral: orchestral instruments; HQ Super Quartet: plug-in software synthesizer, set of four contemporary music instruments; VSC-MP1: Virtual Sound Canvas Multi Pack stand-alone software synthesizer with two plug-in versions (DXi and VST Instruments). SYSTEM SPECS: Macintosh; Windows.

Emagic Software Instruments (www.emagic.de): Sounds as Bits and Bytes; take full advantage of the capabilities of native sound synthesis and processing; excellent sound quality at minimal latency values, ergonomically designed interfaces, and seamless integration into the Logic system; authentic playability in every software instrument, ensuring an intuitive workflow. ES1: virtual synthesizer for the Logic series. ES2: innovative software synthesizer, combining warmth of additive synthesis with advantages of digital synthesizer techniques. EVP73: offers legendary electric piano sounds of Fender Rhodes in a VST2.0 plug-in. EVP88: authentic recreations of legendary Rhodes, Wurlitzer, and Hohner pianos. EXS24 mk II: software sampler, integrated into digital mixing desk of Logic. EXSP24: software sample player for VST2.0 compatible host software. EVB3: authentic Hammond B3 organ sound created as vintage software instrument for Logic 5 and higher. EVD6: Hohner Clavinet recreated as vintage software instrument for Logic 5 or higher. HOST TDM ENABLER: makes it possible to use Emagic software instruments on DirectConnect-compatible ProToolsMIX and HD hardware systems with the HostTDM-compatible host software of user's choice. SYSTEM SPECS: Macintosh; Windows.

Emagic Sound Libraries (www.emagic.de): Stacked sounds and complex sound variations; load into EXS24 sampler or EXSP24 sample player, and create own high-quality sounds. XTREME ANALOG: extremely fat sounds of renowned classic analog synths. XTREME DIGITAL: sounds of unparalleled richness from an expensive digital synthesizer or workstation. XTREME HIP HOP: most comprehensive sound resource for HipHop. SYSTEM SPECS: Macintosh; Windows.

Emagic Studio Tools (www.emagic.de): Help increase efficiency in every professional studio from signal processing to device editing libraries. EVOC20: plug-in package with classic polyphonic vocoder, formant filter bank, and pitch tracking vocoder. SOUNDDIVER: Universal sound editor and librarian. WAVEBURNER: professional audio CD mastering and burning program. EPIC TDM: plug-in collection for TDM. SPACE DESIGNER: reverb plug-in to produce realistic room sounds and unique reverb effects. SYSTEM SPECS: Macintosh; Windows.

ESB TDM (www.emaigc.de): Emagic System Bridge TDM is link between DSP world of TDM system, and computer's previously unexploited native CPU processing resources; allows Logic's native audio engine to be routed into the TDM mixer; enables all Logic tracks, native, and VST plug-ins (Mac OS 9) or Audio Unit plug-ins (Mac OS X), including Audio Instruments, to be used in conjunction with TDM system DSPs; also enhances functionality of EXS24 by allowing it to be inserted into the Aux channels of Logic Platinum's TDM mixer. SYSTEM SPECS: Macintosh; Windows.

Essentials of Music for Audio Professionals (www.artistpro.com): Music fundamentals for engineers, producers, directors, editors, managers, and audio/video recording professionals; music theory, musical notation, arrangements, and scores; rhythmic and pitch notation, musical expression, sound production, melody and musical form, harmony and harmonics, sound in space, modes, scales, chords, intervals, and more. SYSTEM SPECS: Book and Audio CD.

FLStudio 4 (www.cakewalk.com): Europe's leading electronic music creation tool; now with audio recording; complete virtual studio; latest version of Fruityloops; hybrid product that combines sound generation and emulation with song creation; runs as a DXi soft synth; can plug it directly into SONAR, Project5, Home Studio, Music Creator, or Plasma; The Fruityloops Edition and The Producer Edition; The Producer edition includes everything found in the Fruityloops edition, plus audio recording and editing capabilities. SYSTEM SPECS: Windows 95/98/Me/2000/XP.

Freeamp Player (www.freeamp.org): MP3 player software. SYSTEM SPECS: Windows; Linux.

FreeMIDI (www.motu.com): Complete MIDI operating system for the Macintosh OS 9; automatically installed with all Mark of the Unicorn music software products; automatically detects what type of MIDI interface is connected to the Macintosh serial or USB ports, automatically detects what MIDI devices are connected to interface, and provides a graphical representation of their MIDI studio; also provides pop-up sound lists for over 100 popular MIDI synthesizers as well as generic support for any General MIDI device; includes advanced features such as interapplication communication, multiple application real-time synchronization, and support for Digidesign's Sample Cell Nubus card. SYSTEM SPECS: Macintosh.

Freestyle (www.motu.com): First trackless sequencer with instant music notation; create compositions intuitively using ensembles, players, takes, and arrangements; dozens of drum riffs; notate performances as played; see music on screen exactly as it will print; built-in support for dozens of popular MIDI instruments, including any General MIDI device; provides both tape recorder and drum machine style composing. SYSTEM SPECS: Macintosh; Windows.

Gigastudio (www.nemesysmusic.com): Offshoot of GigaSampler; redesigned user interface; real-time effects; support for sixty-four MIDI channels; bundled audio editing software; up to 160 streaming disk-based voices depending on processor and hard drive speed; comes with a 1-GB grand piano multisample; compatible with GigaSampler-format sounds, and the Akai S1000/S3000 library, E-mu Sound-Fonts, and WAV files; timing latency is in the 3-8-ms range. SYSTEM SPECS: Windows.

Hal Leonard DVDs (www.halleonard.com): DJ's Complete Guide; Home Recording Magazine's 100 Recording Tips and Tricks; Hudson DVD Sampler—The Finest Multimedia for Musicians; Setting Up Your Surround Studio; Shaping Your Sound with Microphones, Mixers and Multitrack Recording; Shaping Your Sound with Signal Processors; Turntable Technique—The Art of the DJ. SYSTEM SPECS: Instructional DVDs.

Hip-Hop Ejay (www.voyetra.com): Create and mix hip-hop tracks; CD-ROM; drag audio loops, samples, and sound effects into eight-track sequencer; sounds color-coded by category; bass loops; drum beats; raps; scratches; keyboards; effects; create a WAVE or MP3 file; burn to a CD. SYSTEM SPECS: Windows.

Hypercard (www.apple.com): Development tool for multimedia presentations and computer-based classroom materials; automatically integrates text, graphics, video, sound, spoken text, and links. SYSTEM SPECS: Macintosh.

Infinity DSP Sample Looping Tools (www.antarestech.com): Macintosh-based DSP tool kit designed to be used in conjunction with current sample editor; uses DSP technologies to automate and improve the looping process; loop everything from solo woodwinds to huge synth stacks with dramatic improvements in quality and speed; preserves the "liveness" of samples because it has a looping tool appropriate for every type of sound; with Real Time Loop Adjust can move the loop points during real-time playback and locate the best loop points by ear; SPR Looper automatically creates seamless loops in chorused and ensemble sounds while preserving the exact sound color and stereo image of sample; resulting loop data can be automatically merged with attack portion of sample; with Synthesis Looper can control the frequency domain sidelobe energy of the loop and selectively smooth out lumpy sounding frequencies in chorused and ensemble sounds; new sound is more stable and loop repetitions are less noticeable; with Rotated Sums Looper can randomly layer multiple copies of loop data to homogenize the sound while preserving original loop points; Freeze Looper creates perfect loops in sounds like winds, brass, and other solo sounds that have a clear harmonic series; Cross-fade Looper with Smart Auto-Scan is an enhanced cross-fade tool with an intelligent loop point scanner to find the best loop point automatically; full support for 24-bit files; support for 88.2 KHz and 96 KHz playback via the Sound Manager; full 32-bit floating point audio processing; unlimited Undo/Redo nesting; support for the AIFC file format; compatible with any Macintosh Sound Manager compatible hardware; reads and writes stereo and mono sound files in Sound Designer, AIFF, and AIFC file formats. SYSTEM SPECS: Macintosh OS 9.x.

Internet Music Kit (www.wildcat.com): Add music to Web page in three easy steps; create music with hundreds of professional quality musical phrases; combine phrases into a song in a variety of music styles; convert music with Webtracks technology to play music immediately when Web page is accessed; embed music by streamlining the process of placing music on Web page with an automated embed wizard; includes a multitrack sequencer and professional layout features for Web page design. SYSTEM SPECS: Windows.

Kantos Audio Controlled Synthesizer (www.antarestech.com): Software-based synthesizer; alternative to conventional controllers; controlled by audio; analyzes incoming audio and instantaneously extracts pitch, dynamics, harmonic content, and formant characteristics; this information is used to control the Kantos 1.0 sound engine in ways not possible with a conventional MIDI synth; provides a combination of traditional synthesizer functions and new functions unique to audio control; two Wavetable Oscillators, Pitch Constraint and Quantization Control, Noise Source, three Resonant Multimode Filters, two Chorus Generators, Timbral Articulator, two Envelope Generators, two LFOs, Modulation Matrix, Gate Generator, Noise Gate, Delay Line, Mixers, A Cool UI; available for RTAS (Mac and PC), VST (Mac and PC), MAS (Mac), and DirectX (PC). SYSTEM SPECS: Macintosh; Windows.

Kyma (www.symbolicsound.com): Integration with Sentech motor mix; features motorized faders; high-level user interface includes library of useful factory settings, time line for performance automation and new effects and synthesis algorithms; includes

Capybara hardware system with 96 MB of RAM and four channels of 24-bit, 100 KHz I/O. SYSTEM SPECS: Macintosh; Windows.

Liquid Audio (www.liquidaudio.com): Digital music distribution and downloads; player; streaming audio; MP3 and WAV compatible; CD burning. SYSTEM SPECS: Macintosh; Windows.

Live Music (www.msc-catalog.com): By Eugene Medvedev and Vera Trusova; for the professional musician and the home-hobbyist; comprehensive reference contains notes, tips, and tricks to turn a personal computer into a virtual studio with the ability to create an entire musical project; methods outlined include making live recordings with SAWPro, creating a home studio based on Cool Edit Pro, arranging music with Cubase, and processing sound with virtual exciters; tips on creating "live" MIDI sound; various music software features, with special attention given to non-destructive editing and mastering an AUDIO CD with WaveLab and T-Racks; CD-ROM included contains files with settings and presets; tutorial for several programs discussed in the book. SYSTEM SPECS: Book and CD-ROM.

Logic Audio (www.emagic.de): Software system offers flexibility, reliability, and precision; functionality and ease of use in a powerful, yet economically priced, package; up to forty-eight audio tracks in stereo or mono, up to sixteen instrument channels, four inserts, and eight sends per channel using eight stereo or mono busses, twenty-eight high-quality effect plug-ins, live input support, and twelve audio outputs; includes track-based automation system and superior POW-r dithering found in more powerful versions of the Logic line; development of Logic Audio is accompanied and inspired by a constant dialogue with professional music producers of all styles. SYSTEM SPECS: Macintosh; Windows.

Logic Audio Gold (www.emagic.de): Conceived for price conscious project studios that wish to offer professional quality without using exclusive digital audio hardware; versatile tool for demanding MIDI/audio production with DTP quality notation editing, and printing; inexhaustible variety of editing options available in linked Event, Matrix, Score, and Hyper editors and in the Environment and Arrange window; difference when compared to the larger, more expensive, Platinum version is primarily the lack of support for TDM audio hardware; maximum track count of sixty-four stereo or mono audio tracks and virtually unlimited MIDI tracks; digital audio hardware systems offering up to 24-bit/96 audio resolution are fully supported; can be supplemented with up to sixty-four extra native audio tracks; generous quantity of Emagic effect plug-ins included; solution for desktop computers and self-contained mobile laptop studio. SYSTEM SPECS: Macintosh; Windows.

Logic Audio Platinum (www.emagic.de): Flagship software for computer-based music production; combines composition, notation, and audio production facilities in one comprehensive product; most powerful program of the Logic series designed to meet the needs of professional musicians and producers; unique combination of intuitive usability, freely configurable user interface, comprehensive MIDI and audio editing possibilities; polished film and sync features; ergonomic workflow and maximum productivity; offers superb sound quality with precise 32-bit signal processing, surround sound digital mixer (up to 7.1), sample-accurate automation, and over fifty high-quality audio effect plug-ins; maximizes performance through optimizations for Macintosh systems that feature velocity engine and/or multiple processors; opens the door to expansion of the Logic system with ProTools hardware, providing a highly integrated music production tool, supporting sample rates up to 192 KHz, and a dynamic resolution of up to 24-bit. SYSTEM SPECS: Macintosh; Windows.

Lounge Lizard EP-2 Electric Piano (www.applied-acoustics.com): Re-creation of the classic electric piano sound; includes key release model for greater realism; choose between the original pickup model acclaimed for its "growl and bite," or new secondary model specifically designed for crystal clean tones; all effects modulation and stereo delays sync to host tempo; support for MIDI program change for hands-free operation; new browser interface makes finding presets easy; optimized DSP engine for three times greater CPU performance; support for Digidesign's RTAS plug-in format for Pro Tools 6.x; support for OS X; create reproductions of classic electric piano sounds; all of the various parameters can be pushed beyond the range of their hardware equivalents, opening up new sonic possibilities; mallet module has parameter controls for the material properties of the mallet head (stiffness), the striking force, and the audible noise the impact creates; with stiffness parameters can change the mallets material from felt tip to solid steel, as well as how the stiffness changes in response to the information received from the keyboard; force parameters regulate how hard the mallet hits the tone bar and how this changes in response to the keyboard; with noise parameters can adjust the volume and color of the sound of the mallets impact, and how this is altered by the keyboard; fork module is comprised of two elements, the tone bar and the tine; pickup module greatly effects the overall tone of color; symmetry parameter adjusts the pickup's vertical position in relation to the tine; distance parameter adjusts how far the pick is from the fork; wah effect; sync parameter allows the modulators (LFOs) for the wah, phaser, and tremolo, as well as the stereo delays to sync to host tempo when used as a VST, DXi, or RTAS plug-in; phaser alters a signal by removing frequency bands from its spectrum; onscreen controls; tremolo effect; high-quality stereo delay modeled after classic analog delay boxes; total integration with sequencing applications such as Dxi, RTAS (Under OS X), and VST instrument plug-in. SYSTEM SPECS: Macintosh: Mac OS X.2 800 x 600 or resolution, G3 processor, 128 MB RAM, ASIO, CoreAudio, CoreMIDI, RTAS, and VST compatibility; Windows: Windows 98, ME, 2000, XP, 800 x 600 or higher resolution, P III 500 MHz processor, 32 Mb RAM, ASIO, DirectX, DXI, EASI, MME, VST, and WDM compatibility.

MACAST (www.macast.com): Audio multimedia player; plays a variety of sound formats, including MP3, MP2, CD Audio, MP1, and Internet streaming audio in the form of Shoutcast and Icecast; hear music through two types of plugins, Visual and BLRs; designed for PowerPC only. SYSTEM SPECS: Macintosh 7.5.

Making Music with Your Computer (www.artistpro.com): Detailed instruction for using computer to create music; MIDI orchestration, musicianship, understanding and using music technology; anatomy of styles, including example scores to demonstrate the use of computers and synthesizers to create music in a variety of modes; audio CD demonstrates concepts used throughout the book; for anyone using a computer for hard disk, MIDI, recording, composing, or orchestrating music. SYSTEM SPECS: Book and Audio CD.

Master Tracks (www.passportdesigns.com): Sixty-four tracks with track looping; step entry and real-time entry; automated punch-in; OMS support; easy to use; graphic user interface offers several views of a musical piece; any section can be deleted, moved, or copied with cut and paste edits; supports SMPTE; synchronize music to film, video, multimedia presentations, or multitrack audiotape; automatically adjust tempo to fit a specific length of time or precisely match a visual event; graphic note editor; event list editor; support for Quicktime internal synthesizer; looped overdub and record for drum machine-style recording. SYSTEM SPECS: Macintosh; Windows.

MIDI Kit CD-ROM (Interactive Digital Design—Midisoft): Multitrack digital audio recording; MIDI sequencer; print entire score or selected tracks; connect keyboard, drum machine, or other MIDI instrument with included cable; unlimited tracks; free MIDI set-up video; real-time notation; virtual music sheet highlights notes during playback. SYSTEM SPECS: Windows.

MIDI Quest (www.squest.com): CD-ROM; Editor/librarian; easy to use; supports over 600 instruments and sixty manufacturers; fast tips online help; comprehensive sound auditioning tools; all functions are active while playing; extensive sound sorting capabilities; sophisticated patch organization and editing for banks; store sound and banks from different MIDI devices together; "Sound Checker" has complete graphic MIDI systems analysis; uses advanced graphic editing. SYSTEM SPECS: Windows.

Midisoft Studio 2002XP (Interactive Digital Design—Midisoft): First award-winning, notation-based sequencing product for Windows; create, record, and edit both MIDI and digital audio; easy-to-use interface features; WYSIWYG (what you see is what you get) display and drag-and-drop visual editing of all music symbols, markings, and expressions; intelligent notation automatically positions and beams notes according to meter, time, and key signature; music symbols positioned using engraver spacing standards; Music Score, Piano Roll, Event List, and Wave View provide several different alternatives for entering music; all views are synchronized so that changes in one view are immediately updated in all other views. SYSTEM SPECS: Pentium PC, or greater, Windows 9x/SE/ME/2000/XP, 16 MB RAM (64 with Windows 98), SVGA graphics adapter and monitor, 15 MB hard disk space, Windows /DirectX supported sound card or MIDI device (sound card required for digital sound), mouse, any MIDI instrument (optional), CD-ROM drive.

MP3 Music On The Internet (www.msc-catalog.com): Guide for all musicians and music consumers who want to understand the possibilities of MP3; answers key questions: How does MP3 work? Where can you download MP3s? Which system software and player do you need to encode and play back MP3s? SYSTEM SPECS: Book and CD-ROM.

Music Master (www.datasonics.com.au/) Control the power of the Roland VS-880 digital workstation from a computer; on-screen control; record and edit audio and MIDI in one integrated environment; cut and paste; full editing; completely automated mix; control of effects; interface via MIDI; simple connections without SCSI; infinite undo/redo on all MIDI and audio functions; synchronizes with the VS-880 via MTC and MMC; full control of EQ and Mix parameters; each VS-880 track shows the virtual track selected; automated mixdown of mixer parameters, including faders, mutes, sends, EQ, and Master controls; use of faders and pans on Music Master or VS-880. SYSTEM SPECS: Windows.

Musicator (www.musicator.com): Sixteen tracks hard disk recording; thirty-two parts per system; general MIDI compatible; supports multiple sound cards; mixdown audio parts to single track; create song sheets and large scores; record, view, edit, and mix audio and MIDI data; enter notes with a MIDI keyboard; quantize notation without affecting underlying MIDI data; sync to SMPTE/MTC; use multiple MIDI devices; export notation to PageMaker and other DTP programs; automatically inserts rests, ties, and beams whenever notes are entered, moved, or deleted; prepare scores; extract parts. SYSTEM SPECS: Windows.

MusicMatch (www.musicmatch.com): MP3 player and encoder software; MP3 and WAV compatible; CD burning. SYSTEM SPECS: Windows.

Native Instruments Music Software Programs (www.nativeinstruments.de): SYNTH LINE: REAKTOR 4: modular sound design studio allows users to design, construct and edit own synthesizers, samplers, drum machines, effects, and more; extensive library of finished instruments. REAKTOR SESSION: smaller brother of REAKTOR; can load any instrument made with REAKTOR; hundreds of synths, samplers, drum machines, step sequencers, effects, and live performance machines. ABSYNTH 2: Semi-modular synthesizer with multiple synthesis techniques; high-performance envelope control, breathtaking sound spectrum, and over 700 factory sounds. B4 ORGAN: perfect emulation of the most legendary organ of all time with all the functions of the original, including the rotating speaker cabinet; additional new features like fine-tuning. FM7: Powerful and uncomplicated FM-synthesizer with a much expanded synthesis architecture and groundbreaking sonic potential; can load and reproduce all presets from the DX Series predecessors. PRO-53: Authentic emulation of one of the most legendary analog synths of the 80s; creates powerful, warm virtual-analog sounds; additional effects section and other new features. SAMPLING LINE: KONTAKT: Powerful and extremely versatile sampler; ease of use; large range of functions; extensive instrument library; popular sample libraries. KOMPAKT: Streamlined sampler based on KONTAKT's sample engine; loads all popular sample library formats and provides exceptional effects, filters, and modulation possibilities. INTAKT: intuitive sampler for loop-based productions; slice and rearrange loops, change tempo without affecting pitch or timbre, and add effects, filters, and modulation. BATTERY: sampler designed especially for drum samples, offering quick and complete control over fifty-four sample cells and many sound parameters; loads all popular sample libraries and comes with a Drumsound Library. DJ LINE: TRAKTOR DJ STUDIO 2.0: Professional DJ software for the live mixing of MP3s and audio CDs on two virtual decks; allows for tempo synchronization, loops on the fly, cue points, and mix recording. TRAKTOR DJ: digital DJ mixing of MP3s and audio CDs; includes all the basic functions of TRAKTOR DJ Studio. TRAKTOR DJ Player: free software for the playback and blending of MP3s and audio CDs on the PC; can also load special DJ mix files made with TRAKTOR DJ or TRAKTOR DJ Studio. EFFECTS LINE: VOKATOR: High-end vocoder and vocoding-based synthesizer/granular sampler; extremely high resolution and vast modualtion abilities. NI-SPEKTRAL DELAY: effects software allows user to invade the frequency domain itself, with up to 1,024 frequency bands that can be individually affected, resulting in unusual effects. VOKATOR: suite of vocoding tools; puts an FFT-based vocoder, a sophisticated synthesizer, and a granular sampler at user's disposal. PRO TOOLS EDITION: STUDIO COLLECTION: Software bundle consisting of the B4 Organ, PRO-52, and BATTERY; supports RTAS and HTDM for perfect integration with Pro Tools; for Mac only. NI-SPEKTRAL DELAY PTE: especially for Pro Tools optimized version of NI-SPEKTRAL DELAY with RTAS and HTDM support; for Mac only. SOUND LINE: ABSYNTH SOUNDS VOLUME 1: includes 256 new ABSYNTH presets, ranging from evolving atmospheres, acoustic sounds, innovative synths, to basses, pads, drums, and rhythmic patterns. REAKTOR ELECTRONIC INSTRUMENTS: contains seven versatile new and high-professional instruments for REAKTOR; three synthesizers, three effects, and a drum machine. FM7 SOUNDS VOL. 1: 256 new presets for the powerful FM synthesizer; includes pads, looped sequences, synth sounds, drums and percussion. BATTERY STUDIO DRUMS: sampling CD-ROM (2x), including more than 1.1. GB of acoustic drum samples in high-end quality; for BATTERY and KONTAKT. SYNTHETIC DRUMS: sampling CD-ROM including more than 1,800 samples of electronic drum sounds in thirty-two drum kits; for BATTERY and KONTAKT. B4 TONEWHEEL SET VINTAGE COLLECTION: software extension provides B4 Organ with sounds of a Farfisa Compact, a Vox Continental, and a Harmoniums; aging of the B4 sounds. SYSTEM SPECS: Macintosh; Windows.

Neato CD Labeler Kit (www.neato.com): Design on any computer; print on any laser or inkjet; apply with precision; includes assortment of CD/DVD labels, jewel case inserts, media labels, and inserts; Neato applicator; MediaFace media labeling design software; templates for most major design software; digital background art for labels; jewel cases and other media labeling needs in black and white or color; all copyright free. SYSTEM SPECS: Hybrid.

Nuendo System (www.steinberg.net): Next generation of digital workstations on PC or Mac, laptop, or desktop; innovative tools optimize workflow in audio or post production. NUENDO 2.0: media production system; created to perform any task within the media industry; delivers a complete media production system; designed with needs of user in mind and meeting demands of working professionals in all genres of audio production. NUENDO DOLBY DIGITAL ENCODER: AC-3 encoder for Nuendo; offers full functionality and quality of original Dolby hardware in one easy-to-use export dialog. NUENDO POWERCORE: Nuendo 2.0, TC Powercore, and TC Surround Verb; combination of advanced media production software with world-famous, top-quality PCI-powered plug-in suite; world-class mixing and production environment on Mac or PC. URBAN ATMOSPHERES: real 5.1 audio surroundings of urban locations; unique, authentic surround environments contain top-quality recordings of urban sound-

scapes; versatile and well-structured package contains ninety-five scenes from twenty-five locations; presented in AIFF format on nine DVDs. SYSTEM SPECS: Macintosh; Windows.

Onyx (www.ntonyx.com): Sequencer and arranger functions are combined; arranger has advanced features; controllers and other events are visualized by different colors and are shown in the Main and Orchestrator Measure panes and in the Piano-Roll; uses Onyx MIDI FXs; Onyx Orchestrator Style (OOStyle) can be created from any MIDI file or from recorded MIDI tracks; keeps performance nuances, including Velocity accents, Pitch Bend, Volume, Pan, other controllers, Tempo and Meter changes; with Musical Object Morphing (MOM) technology can transform any music object such as a song into another according to that style; large OOStyle library; orchestrator; Intelligent Auto-harmony (IAH). SYSTEM SPECS: 500 Mhz processor, Windows-compatible sound card, 128 MB RAM, 30 MB Hard disk space for program installation, Windows 98SE/Me/2000/XP.

PC Virtual Digital Audio Workstation With SAWStudio, Nuendo and Samplitude Producer (www.msc-catalog.com): By Eugene Medvedev and Vera Trusova; turn PC into a Digital Audio Workstation; SAWStudio, Nuendo, and Samplitude Producer programs give user new capabilities for creating audio productions; from traditional multitrack sound recording to sound design and music constructing; compatibility with a wide range of hardware; can work with a regular multimedia sound card or professional equipment; create multitrack audio production for DVD video and DVD audio formats; CD-ROM with complete projects, presets, audio tracks, and preferences is included. SYSTEM SPECS: Windows.

Peak (www.bias-inc.com): Stereo audio editing, processing, and mastering application; sound design for film, video, or multimedia; rapid-fire broadcast editing; music production; create dance loops and remixes; Internet streaming; convert vinyl records to CDs, ultra-portable AAC (MP4) or MP3 files; craft soundtracks; fix audio problems for digital video; burn replication-ready audio CDs. SYSTEM SPECS: Macintosh.

Performer (www.motu.com): MIDI sequencing and production tool; provides a comprehensive recording, playback, and editing environment for a large variety of applications; allows user to record and playback digital audio and MIDI data in a totally integrated, creative environment; award-winning multitrack sequencer design, combined with new digital audio capabilities, provide user with unprecedented flexibility and control; replaces racks full of recording gear; get the capabilities of a multitrack digital recording system, including a digital mixer, reverb, effects, EQ, and compression; integrated with award-winning sequencing capabilities. SYSTEM SPECS: Macintosh.

PowerTracks Pro Audio for Windows
(www.pgmusic.com): Professional, fully featured
digital audio and MIDI workstation; for musicians,
students, and songwriters; integrated digital
audio/MIDI recording; 32-bit version; supports Real
Time DirectX Effects for live playback and monitoring; includes effects; up to four chained plug-ins can
be used at once; Chord Wizard; load in any MIDI file,
PowerTracks MIDI sequence file, or a work-in-
progress, and the Chord Wizard will intelligently fig-
ure out the chords and display them in the Notation
Window and the new Chords Window; PG Dynamics;
PG Echo-Chorus; PG Flanger; PG Five Band EQ;
PG Ten Band EQ; PG Reverb; PG Peak Limit; Mixer
Window; Track Effects Inserts allow up to four effects
to be inserted directly into a track's signal path, so
each individual track can have its own effects; LED
VU meters with clipping indicator and peak-hold with
gradual peak fallback; 24-bit/96 KHz audio file format
is supported; Recordable audio track mixer moves for
Volume, Pan, Aux1, and Aux2; automated mixes for
audio tracks using MIDI controller events in the event
list; user determined order for the Audio Output ports
in the Audio Drivers dialog; 1-Track Stereo Audio;
each audio track can play either stereo or mono;
Audio I/O Latency Delay keeps audio play-
back/recording in sync with software MIDI synthesizers; Audio I/O Thread gives three different choices for
audio playback and recording priority; paste audio
tracks into the current song from the scrap buffer with
the Load Scrap command; 32-bit Floating Point
Processing in the audio signal path; Track data is
automatically re-channeled to the MIDI channels in
the Tracks view with the new "Automatically Re-
channel track data when saving to a .MID" option;
user-determined order for MIDI Output Ports in MIDI
Driver Setup dialog; "Use Existing Channel" check-
box in the Other Staff Options dialog will intelligently determine the channel number of inserted
notes; clicking on a lyric or a chord in the Big Lyrics
window plays the song from that location; Jazz notation font gives a "handwritten" look to notes, symbols, chords, and titles; multiple track Leadsheet window notation display; can print multiple tracks of
notation; Scrub Mode in the Notation window will
play the notes in the notation as drag mouse horizon-
tally over window; slanted beams in notation window, which indicates whether the general direction of
a phrase is upward or downward in pitch; New Section Text events let user place a text event at any
location on the staff window; Beat Resolution settings in Notation Window; multiple levels of
Edit|Undo, user-selectable from 1 to 100;
Copy/Cut/Paste commands have an option to work
on Chord Symbols; Lyrics window automatically
switches to Chord mode when lyrics are not present;
[Find] button in the Custom File Selection dialog to
search for a file within the current folder; Favorite

Folders button in the Custom File Selection dialog to
quickly change the current folder by selecting from a
list of "favorite" folders; Preferences dialog with
"tabbed pages" gives access to user preferences; "Big
Piano" piano settings option for sizable on-screen
piano keyboard display; main toolbar displays the
number of megabytes and the percentage of disk space
free on the hard drive. SYSTEM SPECS: Windows
9x, ME, NT, 2000, XP, 16 MB RAM, 75 MB hard
drive space, PC Sound card or MIDI module.

Pro Guide: The Perfect Music PC
(www.msc-catalog.com): By Rainer Hain; definitive
hands-on book; make music on PC, record it digitally, and burn it to CD; basic knowledge, trouble-
shooting, and Pro tricks; includes CD-ROM with PC
tools, software, demos, and music shareware.
SYSTEM SPECS: Book and CD-ROM.

**Pro Tools LE Software Features for
Music Production** (www.digidesign.com): Pro
Tools LE software is included with Digi 002, Digi
002 Rack, and Mbox; serves as the interface between
user, computer, and Pro Tools LE hardware; simplicity, power, and flexibility. AUDIO: Input and output
quality of Pro Tools LE systems is superior; Pro
Tools LE software supports up to thirty-two tracks of
professional-quality 24-bit/96 KHz audio and enables
user to define quality of audio, to import and export
popular audio file formats, and to manage all audio
files at all times. MIXING: Pro Tools LE software
makes mixing music smooth, quick, and enjoyable;
Edit and Mix windows; access to all tools available in
a traditional home/project studio and more; automate
every facet of up to thirty-two guaranteed audio and
256 MIDI tracks; incorporate Digidesign and Development Partner plug-ins; use ReWire-compatible
audio applications such as Propellerhead's Reason and
Ableton Live, as well as outboard gear; multiple levels of Undo provide a back door, and Pro Tools LE
software's total recall capability enables user to go
back and forth between any number of projects without losing any mixer settings. MIDI: Full MIDI sequencing capabilities; record, edit, and mix up to 256
MIDI tracks alongside audio; user-friendly, powerful
MIDI sequencer is integrated directly into the Pro
Tools application; MIDI events and sequences are
manipulated as easily as audio in Pro Tools software,
in most cases sharing the same editing and mixing
tools; import and export MIDI data from both software and hardware sources; support for Windows XP
or full integration of Mac OS X's Core MIDI Services, MIDI Time Stamping, Groove Quantize, Restore Performance, and other enhancements.
EDITING: Edit window within the Pro Tools LE
interface; adjust every aspect of both audio and MIDI
tracks; Time Trimmer included in the Pro Tools LE
6.1 software; easily and instantly change the tempo of
audio files and loops. PLUG-INS: Plug-ins, add-on
software-based tools that work in conjunction with

Pro Tools, are an important part of the Pro Tools platform; do everything from adjusting dynamics of performance to adding effects to tracks to sound design; open plug-ins within Pro Tools software interface; use presets, customize settings, interact via MIDI, and/or automate a given plug-in's activity within a mix; RTAS and AudioSuite. RTAS (Real-Time AudioSuite) plug-ins provide real-time processing and can be assigned to as many tracks as are within system; RTAS plug-ins are often the same as those found in professional TDM systems, except use computer's processing power instead of specialized TDM hardware; AudioSuite plug-ins are non-real-time plug-ins that enable user to create new audio files with the effect chosen printed to that file; can recover original file at any time. COMPATIBILITY: Pro designed to serve as hub of user's music-making universe; any session can be seamlessly moved between both Windows- and Macintosh-based Pro Tools LE and/or TDM systems while retaining all automation, track configurations, MIDI data, and plug-in assignments; Pro Tools LE systems share the same user interface as the professional TDM systems, everything learned using Pro Tools LE is transferable to Pro Tools TDM systems; Pro Tools 6.1 software's support for ReWire, Propellerhead/Steinberg's technology for transferring audio data between software applications, enables user to take advantage of ReWire-compatible music creation applications; develop sounds or sequences in the likes of Propellerhead Reason, Ableton Live, and Native Instruments' products, and use them directly in Pro Tools session; sonic palette will increase. MASTERING: Pro Tools LE software features many tools that allow user to master projects; editing capabilities and plug-ins used in tandem with Pro Tools software interface enable user to make necessary fine adjustments to final mix in order to achieve perfect combination of warmth, presence, and balance; supports a real-time "bounce to disk" feature that reads and prints all automation information, allowing user to incorporate various outboard gear, and provides mono or stereo output of final mix. SYSTEM SPECS: Macintosh; Windows.

Pro Tools LE Software Features for Post Production (www.digidesign.com): Pro Tools LE software is included with Digi 002, Digi 002 Rack, and Mbox; serves as interface between user, computer, Pro Tools LE hardware, and desktop video production gear. DV TOOLKIT OPTION: DV Toolkit for Pro Tools LE converts a Pro Tools LE system into a desktop audio-for-video powerhouse; DV Toolkit is a software bundle that enables user to easily sweeten and augment the audio content of desktop video projects; with DV Toolkit, can open up a project file (OMF or AAF) from applications such as Avid's Xpress DV on either Windows XP- or Mac OS X-based Pro Tools LE system, record new audio such as voice-over and Foley, clean up existing audio

such as unwanted background noise, replace audio such as faulty on-camera dialog, and even add own music tracks; DV Toolkit complements Pro Tools LE's standard feature set to give full control over projects; two primary DV Toolkit features: Time Code functions and specialized plug-ins; Time Code functions enable user to edit audio to picture with frame accuracy, making it easy to spot sound effects; Because Pro Tools software is inherently sample accurate, can easily achieve difficult audio edits with precision; specialized plug-ins such as Synchro Arts' VocALign Project and Digidesign's DINR LE (AudioSuite) complete the picture, readily assisting in audio clean-up chores. AUDIO: Input and output quality of Pro Tools LE systems is superior; Pro Tools LE software supports up to thirty-two tracks of high-fidelity 24-bit/96 KHz audio and enables user to define quality of audio, to import and export popular audio file formats, and to manage all of audio files with Pro Tools LE 6.1 software and the DV Toolkit option, can easily import and export OMF and AAF sequences, allowing user to transfer audio from desktop video workstation for further sweetening. MIXING: Edit and Mix windows; automate every facet of up to thirty-two guaranteed audio and 256 MIDI tracks; incorporate large variety of high-quality Digidesign and Development Partner plug-ins and make use of ReWire-compatible audio applications such as Propellerhead's Reason and Ableton Live, as well as outboard gear to make music tracks; multiple levels of Undo provide a back door; Pro Tools LE software's total recall capability enables user to go back and forth between any number of projects without losing any mixer settings. MIDI: Pro Tools LE software's MIDI capabilities are suited to music composition for picture; full MIDI sequencing, allowing user to record, edit, and mix up to 256 MIDI tracks; MIDI events and sequences are manipulated as easily as audio in Pro Tools software, in most cases sharing the same editing and mixing tools; import and export MIDI data from both software and hardware sources; support for Windows XP or full integration of Mac OS X's Core MIDI Services, MIDI Time Stamping, Groove Quantize, Restore Performance, and other enhancements. EDITING: Edit window within Pro Tools LE interface; adjust every aspect of both audio and MIDI data; use same tools as major film studios to tweak sounds, change pitch of vocal, rearrange sound effects, record new audio such as voice-over and Foley, clean up unwanted background noise, replace dialogue, and more; Time Trimmer included in Pro Tools LE 6.1 software; easily change the tempo of audio files and loops. PLUG-INS: Plug-ins, add-on software-based tools that work in conjunction with Pro Tools, are an important part of the Pro Tools platform; plug-ins facilitate everything from removing unwanted background noise to automatically replacing dialog to sound design; open plug-ins within

Pro Tools software interface; use presets, customize settings, and/or automate a given plug-in's activity within a mix; Pro Tools LE-compatible plug-ins take two forms: RTAS and AudioSuite. RTAS (Real-Time AudioSuite) plug-ins provide real-time processing and can be assigned to as many tracks as are within limits of system; RTAS plug-ins are often the same as those found in professional TDM systems, except that they use computer's processing power instead of specialized TDM hardware; AudioSuite plug-ins are non-real-time plug-ins that enable user to create new audio files with effect chosen printed to that file; recover original file at any time. COMPATIBILITY: Any session can be seamlessly moved between both Windows- and Macintosh-based Pro Tools LE and/or TDM systems while retaining all automation, track configurations, MIDI data, and plug-in assignments; Pro Tools LE systems share the same user interface as the professional TDM systems; everything learned using Pro Tools LE is transferable to Pro Tools TDM systems; Pro Tools 6.1 software's support for ReWire, Propellerhead/Steinberg's technology for transferring audio data between software applications, enables user to take advantage of popular, ReWire-compatible music creation applications; develop sounds or sequences in the likes of Propellerhead Reason, Ableton Live, and Native Instruments' products, and use them in Pro Tools session; sonic palette will increase dramatically. DELIVERY: In addition to providing tools to compose, record, edit, and mix projects, Pro Tools LE software also handles delivery of finalized audio to compatible video solutions such as Avid's Xpress DV; Pro Tools LE 6.1's optional DigiTranslator 2.0 utility handles the transfer of AAF or OMFI sequences to and from video application; once in Pro Tools, editing capabilities and plug-ins used in conjunction with the Pro Tools software interface enable user to make necessary fine adjustments to final mix to achieve perfect combination of warmth, presence, and balance; export AAF or OMFI sequence, using DigiTranslator 2.0, to preferred picture workstation for final output or layback to tape. SYSTEM SPECS: Macintosh; Windows.

Pro Tools Software (www.digidesign.com): Pro Tools software has become the industry standard for audio production; used with Digidesign hardware; for both music and post production professionals to achieve all of their production tasks within one easy-to-use interface; unique balance of power and simplicity; suited to those just getting into digital audio production for the first time; Pro Tools software takes two forms, TDM and LE, both of which ship with their respective hardware components; latest Pro Tools TDM software works in conjunction with Pro Tools|HD hardware to provide audio professionals with an exhaustive, extensible, high-powered feature set, capable of managing massive mixes as well as complex audio/video interactions; Pro Tools LE

software works in tandem with LE hardware, Digi 002, Digi 002 Rack, or Mbox, to give the home and project studio community affordable access to achieving professional results; furthers possibilities by enabling user to integrate third-party hardware and software into production environment; seamless Avid picture workstation support; ReWire compatibility; makes process of audio production as efficient, effective, and fun as possible; Pro Tools TDM Software for Music Production; Pro Tools TDM Software for Post Production; Pro Tools LE Software for Music Production; Pro Tools LE Software for Post Production. SYSTEM SPECS: Macintosh; Windows.

Pro Tools TDM Software for Music Production (www.digidesign.com): Pro Tools TDM software is included with all Pro Tools|HD systems; serves as the interface between user, computer, and Pro Tools TDM hardware, providing power, flexibility, and ease of use. AUDIO: In conjunction with Pro Tools|HD hardware, Pro Tools software offers audio production freedom; support for up to 24-bit/192 KHz audio files; play back up to 128 simultaneous tracks with no dropped samples; control all aspects of audio; fidelity is protected throughout production process; import and export popular audio file formats; with Pro Tools TDM 6.1 software's DigiBase Pro file management utility can manage the whereabouts of all audio files in sessions. MIXING: Edit and Mix windows; gives ears and eyes access to all of the tools, including a large-format mixer, effects racks, and more; automation, visual control over mix, and large selection of plug-ins; comprehensive, easy-to-use mixing environment available; massive mixes comprised of up to 128 simultaneous audio tracks can be managed without audio degradation; control surface options such as ProControl and Control|24; total session recall. MIDI: Full MIDI sequencing capabilities; edit and mix up to 256 MIDI tracks alongside audio; supports the import, creation, and export of MIDI data; extensive MIDI editing and manipulation capabilities; MIDI events and sequences manipulated as easily as audio in the same Edit window; full integration of Mac OS X's Core MIDI Services, as well as support for Windows XP, MIDI Time Stamping, Groove Quantize, Restore Performance, and other enhancements, offers increased flexibility and solid performance; native ReWire support in conjunction with a wide array of TDM- and RTAS-compatible instruments. EDITING: Using a single screen; Edit window within the Pro Tools interface; adjust every aspect of both audio and MIDI data at sample-level resolution; trim waveforms, reprocess regions of audio, pitch-correct, replace drum sounds, and rearrange song sections; nonlinear approach to editing; Beat Detective allows for multitrack rhythm analysis and repair. PLUG-INS: Plug-ins facilitate everything from dynamics to effects to sound generation; a wide range of

Digidesign Development Partner plug-ins that emulate favorite classic studio gear, such as the LA-2A or 1176 compressors; apply quality effects to mix without the need for expensive vintage hardware; to use plug-ins, open them within the Pro Tools software interface; utilize presets, customize settings, and/or automate a given plug-in's activity within a mix; can use large selection of industry's best professional plug-ins; Pro Tools|HD-compatible plug-ins take four forms: TDM, HTDM, RTAS, and AudioSuite; TDM plug-ins are uniquely powerful because they utilize dedicated, power-on-demand hardware rather than relying on limited resources of host computer; TDM plug-ins are afforded more processing power than is available in any competing system; Pro Tools software supports HTDM and RTAS plug-ins, empowering user to efficiently exploit native power of computer for more real-time processing options; Audio-Suite plug-ins, based on Digidesign's file-based, non-real-time plug-in format, allow user to create new audio files with processing permanently intact; the original audio remains untouched. SURROUND SOUND: Pro Tools|HD systems include comprehensive surround mixing capabilities; no need to leave Pro Tools application for surround music production mixing; Pro Tools TDM software mixes in every popular surround format, including LCRS, 5.1, and 7.1 as well as developing multiple surround formats concurrently. COMPATIBILITY: Designed to serve as the hub of audio production; any session can be seamlessly moved between both Windows- and Macintosh-based Pro Tools TDM and/or LE systems while retaining all automation, track configurations, MIDI data, and plug-in assignments. MASTERING: Add finishing touches to projects via mastering; editing capabilities and plug-ins used along with Pro Tools software interface enable user to make necessary fine adjustments to final mix in order to achieve perfect combination of warmth, presence, and balance; supports real-time "bounce to disk" feature that reads and prints all automation information, allows incorporation of various outboard gear, and provides mono, stereo, or surround output of final mix, which can then be delivered in a variety of digital audio file formats. SYSTEM SPECS: Macintosh; Windows.

Pro Tools TDM Software for Post Production (www.digidesign.com): AUDIO: Freedom in post production arena, including support for up to 24-bit/192 KHz audio files; play back up to 128 simultaneous tracks of audio with your Pro Tools|HD system with guarantee of no dropped samples; control all aspects of audio; fidelity is protected throughout production process; import and export popular media including, AAF and OMF sequences with DigiTranslator 2.0 option; with Pro Tools TDM 6.1 software's DigiBase Pro file management utility, manage audio files associated with post sessions. MIXING: Pro Tools TDM systems have revolutionized the process

of mixing; any sound treatment is possible and no nuance is compromised; Pro Tools TDM components work seamlessly with host Windows or Macintosh computer; Edit and Mix windows; gives ears and eyes access to all of the tools; large-format mixer, effects racks, and more; up to a guaranteed 128 simultaneous audio tracks; automation, visual control over mix, and large selection of the plug-ins; comprehensive, easy-to-use mixing environment for post production; massive mixes comprised of up to a guaranteed 128 simultaneous audio tracks can be managed without audio degradation; professional control surface options ProControl and Control|24; hands-on control; total session recall; all routing, automation, mixer, and effects settings remain. MIDI: full MIDI sequencing capabilities; edit and mix up to 256 sample-accurate MIDI tracks alongside audio; supports the import, creation, and export of MIDI data, as well as offering extensive MIDI editing and manipulation capabilities; sequence music tracks without having to leave the digital domain with ReWire applications such as Propellerhead's Reason, Ableton's Live, or the many powerful TDM and RTAS plug-ins available for Pro Tools; MIDI events and sequences can be manipulated as easily as audio, in most cases sharing the same tools for editing audio; full integration of Mac OS X's Core MIDI Services, support for Windows XP, MIDI Time Stamping, and other enhancements offer increased flexibility. EDITING: Edit window within Pro Tools interface; adjust every aspect of both audio and MIDI data at sample-level resolution; trim waveforms, reprocess regions of audio, change the pitch of a vocal, edit audio to picture with time code accuracy, rearrange sound effects on a whim, record new audio such as voice-over and Foley, clean up unwanted background noise, replace dialogue; non-linear approach to editing; sound-to-picture editing capabilities; nearly every major motion picture is edited with Pro Tools. PLUG-INS: Plug-ins, add-on software-based tools that work in conjunction with Pro Tools, are paramount to the Pro Tools platform, directly contributing to the creation of the best mixes possible; plug-ins enable user to take care of everything from removing unwanted background noise to automatically replacing dialogue; simply open plug-ins within the Pro Tools software interface; employ presets, customize settings, and/or automate a given plug-in's activity within a mix, all of which are recallable at any time; Pro Tools|HD-compatible plug-ins take four forms: TDM, HTDM, RTAS, and AudioSuite;. TDM plug-ins are uniquely powerful because they utilize dedicated, power-on-demand hardware rather than relying on the limited resources of the host computer; TDM plug-ins are afforded much more processing power than is available in any competing system; Pro Tools software supports HTDM and RTAS plug-ins; AudioSuite plug-ins, based on Digidesign's file-based, non-real-time plug-in format, allow user to create new audio files with the processing permanently intact; original audio remains untouched. AVID INTEROPERABILITY AND NETWORKING: Pro Tools TDM software includes powerful, cross-platform Avid interoperability; support for the following is included: AVoption|XL for playback of Avid Meridien video files from systems such Avid Symphony, Media Composer|X, and Xpress NT; FilmFrame for 24P/25P support; Digi-Translator 2.0 option for AAF and OMFI interchange; and Avid Unity MediaNetwork shared storage for dynamically storing and sharing high-bandwidth, high-resolution media; Pro Tools TDM software also includes support for the following: AVoption, increased pull up/pull down and PostConform with Digidesign's SYNC I/O, QuickTime DV playback via FireWire or computer monitor, remote nine-pin deck emulation, and 24-bit sessions using IDE hard drives; some post features are not available for both Windows and Macintosh platforms. SURROUND SOUND: Pro Tools|HD systems include comprehensive surround mixing capabilities, eliminating the need to leave the Pro Tools application for many specialized post production projects; Pro Tools TDM software enables user to mix in every popular surround format including LCRS, .5.1, and 7.1 as well as to work in several surround formats simultaneously. COMPATIBILITY: Pro Tools is designed to serve as the hub of user's audio production universe; any session can be moved seamlessly between both Windows- and Macintosh-based Pro Tools TDM and/or LE systems while retaining all automation, track configurations, MIDI data, and plug-in assignments. DELIVERY: tools needed to compose, record, edit, and mix projects; deliver finalized audio post in nearly any format; with the DigiTranslator 2.0 option, AAF or OMFI sequences can be exported to preferred picture workstation for final output or layback to tape. SYSTEM SPECS: Macintosh; Windows.

Professional Microphone Techniques (www.artistpro.com): Microphone usage for dozens of different instruments as well as vocals, amplifiers, Leslie cabinets, and more; audio CD to hear different effects of microphone placement techniques in real time. SYSTEM SPECS: Book and Audio CD.

ProStart: Cubase SX/SL Mixing And Mastering (www.msc-catalog.com): By Craig Anderton and Christian Deinhardt; practical book helps reader improve arranging, mixing and mastering skills, using Cubase SX/SL; basic introduction into sound engineering; numerous tips and tricks to help user improve results; for both beginners and advanced users; CD-ROM includes a demo version of Cubase SX and audio examples. SYSTEM SPECS: Book and CD-ROM.

ProStart: Cubase SX/SL Reference (www.msc-catalog.com): By Mark Wherry; workshop shows how to use some of Cubase SX's features in context including using key commands, mixing in the Project window, using insert and send effects, VST instruments and MIDI plug-ins, and getting the tempo right when importing audio loops; enclosed CD-ROM includes a demo version of Cubase SX and support material to accompany the introduction. SYSTEM SPECS: Book and CD-ROM.

ProStart: Cubase SX/SL Workshop (www.msc-catalog.com): By Mark Wherry; first guide book available that covers Steinberg's Cubase SX and SL; easy-to-read explanations; hands-on tutorials; opens with a complete song walkthrough from first basics to the finished master, showing how to record, edit, and mix both audio and MIDI; second part of the book features workshops on some of Cubase's more advanced features, including hitpoints, surround sound, video, hardware mixing controllers, VST System Link, and using ReWire with applications such as Propellerhead's Reason; includes full coverage of Windows XP and Mac OS X versions; provides information for Cubase VST 5 and Logic Audio users who are moving over to Steinberg's next generation music production software; enclosed CD-ROM features a demo version of Cubase SX, resources to accompany the tutorials in the book, and a selection of freeware VST plug-in effects and instruments. SYSTEM SPECS: Book and CD-ROM.

ProStart: Logic Audio (www.msc-catalog.com): Covers all of Logic's audio facilities; complements the Emagic Reference manual; includes information on all Logic versions up to, and including, Logic 6; includes topics such as using the Track Automation system, using insert and send effects, mixing, bouncing, VST instruments and plug-ins, audio handling, sample editing, EQ-ing, synchronization, and integration with other applications and hardware plus more; for beginners and advanced users; enclosed CD-ROM includes plug-in and application demo versions, utilities, and support material; information on computer and audio hardware; extensive collection of Internet links. SYSTEM SPECS: Book and CD-ROM.

PTHD Extension (www.emagic.de): Emagic PTHD Extension connects Logic Platinum 5 and Pro Tools HD hardware; form uniquely powerful system, providing superlative audio quality and generous I/O capabilities; access to ever-increasing number of exciting DSP plug-ins; add optional Emagic System Bridge TDM (ESB TDM) to expand creative potential with native synthesizers and plug-ins ES2 and EXS24 or VST2-compatible (Mac OS 9) or Audio Unit (Mac OS X) plug-ins. SYSTEM SPECS: Macintosh; Windows.

Quick Start Series (www.msc-catalog.com): Books and CD-ROMs; helps musicians understand home recording, MIDI, SONAR, Reason, Cubase, Fruity Loops, audio mastering, CD burning, music publishing online, and more; illustrated, easy-to-understand books answer questions about a variety of music topics; valuable tips and troubleshooting skills; accompanying CD-ROMs feature audio examples, demo songs, MIDI software, MP3 software, and more. SYSTEM SPECS: Books and CD-ROMs.

Quicktime (www.apple.com/quicktime): Extensive support for 3GPP, including video, audio, text, and native .3gp file format support; import, export, and play back .3gp files, .mp4 and .mov files; enhanced MPEG-4 and H.263 video codecs, enhanced AAC (Advanced Audio Coding) audio codec, AMR (Adaptive Multi-Rate) audio codec, 3G Text importer and exporter, and user-friendly 3GPP export dialog to aid in the creation of 3GPP-compliant files. SYSTEM SPECS: Macintosh; Windows.

Reality (www.seersystems.com): CD-ROM; professional software-based synthesizer for Pentium PC; create and play multiple synthesis types simultaneously and at different sample rates; 16-part multitimbral with up to 128-note polyphony; multiple patches and synthesis types; access any library of sounds and samples by loading as WAV files. SYSTEM SPECS: Windows.

RealOne Player (www.real.com): Streaming audio and video player; vTuner software; RealAudio stations. SYSTEM SPECS: Macintosh; Windows.

Reason (www.propellerheads.se): Stand-alone music station; in the shape of a classic studio rack; samplers; analog synths; mixers; step-time drum machines; effects; real-time multitrack sequencer; full automation of all fader and control movements; patching and routing possibilities; full synchronization with other MIDI equipment; total recall; setup and sounds saved with song; self-contained song format; AIFF and WAV file export; ASIO; MME; DirectX and Soundmanager support; 500 MB of high quality samples; REX files; kits and patches; CD-ROM. SYSTEM SPECS: Macintosh; Windows.

Reason Adapted (www.propellerheads.se): Slimmed-down version of Reason; powerful package of versatile sound tools; not as big as Reason. SYSTEM SPECS: Macintosh; Windows.

Rebirth (www.propellerheads.se): Total integration with Steinberg Cubase VST 2.0; up to eighteen individual audio channels direct to VST; alternative drum machines available; virtual software instrument; includes two synthesizers and two drum machines; inspired by the legendary TR-808, TB-303, and TR-909, originally created by Roland Corporation; unique sounds and visual images reborn through digital simulation by Propellerhead software; distortion units, PCF, compressor, shuffle, and digital delay; quirks and subtle qualities of analog synths, coupled with convenience of modern computers; minimum of cables; integration with sequencer software; complete, front panel automation; real-time audio streaming; no external samplers or special cards required; mixer section with panning, level, effect, and distortion; audio quality: 16-bit, 44.1 KHz output stereo export of stereo AIFF or Wave audio files; MIDI clock synchronization to external hardware. SYSTEM SPECS: Macintosh; Windows.

Record Producer (www.voyetra.com): Turns MIDI-equipped PC into a desktop music production studio; record song using MIDI and digital audio tracks, edit, and play back; compose multitrack songs with MIDI keyboard and live instruments; add lead vocals, background harmony; process with professional sounding effects; for creating demos or fully mastered CD quality recordings; layer guitars, drums, and other instruments; dozens of digital audio tracks to record drums, guitars, keyboards, bass guitars, sound effects, and more; wide variety of audio and MIDI files; drum loops, keyboard riffs, guitar leads, etc.; MIDI composition tools; play back. SYSTEM SPECS: Windows.

Recording Station (www.voyetra.com): Create songs with MIDI and digital audio; two digital audio tracks; ten MIDI tracks; video tutorial; includes MIDI drum tracks and songs; load and play; scrolling lyrics display; MIDI portion of song played by sound card's synthesizer or an external MIDI synthesizer; digital audio is played by the sound card's WAV audio hardware. SYSTEM SPECS: Windows.

Recycle (www.propellerheads.se): Audio processing tool for drum loops and grooves; uses a technique called slicing to "atomize" loops; once a loop has been sliced, it is transmitted to user sampler and mapped to keyboard; can also be sent to Steinberg Cubase VST as an audio part; from there the final audio is played back; automatically slaves tempo of any drum groove to sequencer tempo; layers grooves originally recorded in different tempi; groove quantizes loops as fast and simple as with any MIDI recording; sends different sounds in the groove to different sampler outputs; removes and/or replaces sounds without altering the feel; transmits and receives samples from most popular samplers; Windows and Macintosh specific features. SYSTEM SPECS: Macintosh; Windows.

Reload (www.propellerheads.se): Utility for loading Akai S1000//S3000 sound disks; can also convert them into ReFills with NN-XT patches. SYSTEM SPECS: Macintosh; Windows.

Rewire (www.propellerheads.se): The audio cable of the virtual studio; lets user connect virtual instruments to each other. SYSTEM SPECS: Macintosh; Windows.

SampleHeads (www.sampleheads.com): Audio sampling CDs and CD-ROMs for all popular sampler formats, including AKAI, Roland, E-MU, SampleCell, GigaSampler, .WAV files; downloadable SoundFonts, GigaSampler, SampleCell and .WAV files for immediate purchase and download; 100 percent copyright free. SYSTEM SPECS: Macintosh; Windows.

Samplitude 2496 (www.sekd.com): Search for audio with energy in various frequency bands; effects can be applied to individual audio clips; MIDI sequence editing and enhanced track count. SYSTEM SPECS: Windows 95, 98, NT, 2000.

Screenblast ACID for Windows (http://mediasoftware.sonypictures.com): Loop-based music creation program; create songs instantly from prerecorded; make own music or remixes, add soundtracks to videos, or burn own songs onto CD; create pro-sounding music by controlling the volume, panning, and effects on each track; export creations to portable devices; interactive tutorials covering topics such as: CD burning, fading in/out, using pan and volume envelopes, splitting events, pitch-shifting, tempo-matching, and more; included sample project; "Get Media" button accesses hundreds of professional quality loops, sound effects, and video clips directly from Screenblast.com to use; support for import, editing, transcoding, and export of Windows Media 9 video format, WAV, MP3, and many other popular formats; powerful audio editor. SYSTEM SPECS: Windows 98SE, 2000, or XP.

Shaping Your Sound (www.artistpro.com): Two-DVD set; by Tom Lubin; Shaping Your Sound With Signal Processors teaches how to understand compressors and gates and how to use them to shape the dynamics of any instrument by emphasizing or diminishing the attack, sustain, or release of each note; learn how to create custom flanging, delay, phasing, echo, and chorusing effects, when to use them and when not to use them in recordings; learn to use EQ to open up the sound of recordings and make room for each instrumental texture while discovering various types of EQ curves and devices with the techniques professional engineers use to shape the space where the sound happens; Shaping Your Sound with Microphones, Mixers and Multitrack Recording teaches how to best mike, record, and mix drums, guitars, pianos, horns, vocals, strings, and more; professionally build a song, step by step, through the tracking and overdubbing process with dozens of musical examples and demonstrations; learn fundamental characteristics of analog tape and professional multitrack recorders and the techniques to make top quality recordings; explore the inside of the recording console and learn to route signals through mixer to get the best sound. SYSTEM SPECS: Instructional DVD.

Software Synthesizers—The Definitive Guide to Virtual Musical Instruments (www.halleonard.com): By Jim Aiken; CD-ROM; authoritative guide; concise explanations of sound synthesis techniques; Reason, Reaktor, Kantos, Absynth, Attack, Live, Fruityloops, and more than two dozen other applications; physical modeling and FM synthesis, filters and envelope generators, using MIDI, sampled loop libraries, and more. SYSTEM SPECS: Hybrid.

Sonar 2.2 (www.cakewalk.com): MIDI sequencing; digital recording; integrated multitrack recording, editing, mixing, and delivery of audio and MIDI; audio loop construction and editing; Cyclone DXi groove sampler; DXi soft synths; automatable DirectX audio effects; professional MIDI editing and sequencing; Real-time MIDI FX; Global control surface support; ReWire 2.0 integration; advanced project management. SYSTEM SPECS: Windows 98SE, Me, 2000, XP.

Sonar 2.2 XL (www.cakewalk.com): Provides all of the capabilities of SONAR, plus additional 64-bit mastering plug-ins and an advanced DXi drum synth/sampler. SYSTEM SPECS: Windows 98SE, Me, 2000, XP.

Sonique (http://sonique.lycos.com): MP3 player and encoder software; supports all audio formats. SYSTEM SPECS: Windows.

Sound Advice on Compressors, Limiters, Expanders & Gates (www.artistpro.com): Compressors, limiters, gates, expanders, and other dynamics processors for creating recordings that sound professional; step-by-step instruction; audio examples. SYSTEM SPECS: Book and Audio CD.

Sound Advice on Developing Your Home Studio (www.artistpro.com): Learn proper way to set up gear; equipment connection, selection, and placement; cables; patch bay; monitors; acoustics. SYSTEM SPECS: Book and Audio CD.

Sound Advice on Equalizers, Reverbs & Delays (www.artistpro.com): Techniques and examples designed to help mixes come alive; understand how the controls on equalizers and effects processors work; step-by-step equalization guidelines for recording and mixing guitars, bass, drums, keys, vocals, and other popular instruments; learn how to use reverbs and delays to set music in a controlled, blended, and dimensional space; how to craft and shape each sound. SYSTEM SPECS: Book and Audio CD.

Sound Advice on Microphone Techniques (www.artistpro.com): Microphone selection and technique; how the three most common microphone designs work and how to use them; which microphones are recommended for different instruments and voices and why. SYSTEM SPECS: Book and Audio CD.

Sound Advice on MIDI Production (www.artistpro.com): MIDI sequencing; supporting acoustic recording; synchronizing equipment; practical applications of MIDI keyboards, sound modules, effect processors, recorders, mixers, triggers, and controllers. SYSTEM SPECS: Book and Audio CD.

Sound Advice on Mixing (www.artistpro.com): Mixing techniques; audio examples; build a mix from the ground up; how to set up a mix. SYSTEM SPECS: Book and Audio CD.

Sound Forge for Windows (mediasoftware.sonypictures.com): Digital audio editor; includes set of audio processes, tools, and effects for recording and manipulating audio; for audio editing, audio recording, effects processing, streaming content creation, and more; DirectX plug-in effects automation; automated time-based recording and audio threshold record triggering; VU/PPM meters for RMS playback and record monitoring; enhanced Spectrum Analysis tools; white, pink, and brown noise generators; clipped peak detection and marking; Media Explorer; Sound Forge project file creation; support for 24 fps DV video files and more. SYSTEM SPECS: Windows 2000, or XP.

Sound Forge Studio for Windows (http://mediasoftware.sonypictures.com): Edit files in real time and hear changes immediately; record, edit, and process audio using PC; record from a CD, microphone, LP, cassette, or musical instrument; edit recording using a wide range of tools and effects; includes dozens of editing tools, including: cut, paste, move, delete, mute, reverse, crossfade, trim, normalize, fade, pan, resample, enhance, insert silence, and more; includes 10-band EQ, reverb, delay, distortion; supports many popular audio and Web formats, including WAV, Windows Media Audio and Video, QuickTime, RealAudio, and MP3; create streaming media for the Web; sound effects library of over 1,000 professional-quality sound clips; royalty-free library. SYSTEM SPECS: Windows 98SE, Me, 2000, XP.

SoundDiver (www.emagic.de): Comprehensive MIDI Editor and Librarian software; support for more than 500 MIDI devices; new editors constantly being developed; edit every parameter, and catalog, store, and organize patches. SYSTEM SPECS: Macintosh; Windows.

SoundSoap (www.bias-inc.com): Audio cleaning solution; removes noise from digital video or digital audio files; works stand-alone or as a plug-in for most VST or DirectX host programs; reduces tape hiss, buzzing and hum, rumble, and most other types of background noise; one-step "Learn Noise" button; intuitive controls for more professional results. SYSTEM SPECS: Macintosh; Windows.

Soundsuite (www.voyetra.com): Audio Power Pack for Multimedia PC; AudioStation; VideoStation; ImageStation; AudioView; MIDI Orchestrator; Jukebox; MIDI Screen Saver; Audio Calendar; Say It; Sound Events; SoundScript; VoiceNet; Level Controller; MIDI Orchestrator Plus; Music Gallery; Additional Files and Utilities. SYSTEM SPECS: Windows 3x or 9x.

Speedsoft Vsampler (www.vsampler.com): 24-bit/96 KHz, sixteen-part multitimbral DXi sampler and synthesizer; up to sixty-four stereo voices; easy-to-use interface; play live via any MIDI instrument or play back MIDI tracks from Cakewalk program; DXi format integrates into SONAR +, Plasma +, Home Studio 2002 +, Music Creator 2002 +, Fruityloops 3.0 +, and other DXi-compatible applications. SYSTEM SPECS: DXi compatible host application, Windows 98/ME/2000/XP, Windows-compatible sound card, 200 MHz processor (Pentium III or Athlon recommended), 32 MB RAM (128 MB or more recommended), 25 MB hard disk space for program installation.

Steinberg Sounds and Loops (www.steinberg.net): High-end sound libraries especially crafted for Cubase, Nuendo, and HALion; inspiring, top-quality audio material in a variety of formats. HALION STRING EDITION—VOLUME 1: symphonic string orchestra instrument and library; symphonic strings collection; orchestral string section with playability, unique, warm character, and a natural ambience. HALIONIZED: creative sound libraries for Steinberg's HALion; Wizoo. MiXtended, Latin Percussion, and Technoid Guitars; developed especially for HALion; no conversions necessary; load and play. PRIMESOUNDS: online library; subscription grants access to an ever-expanding pool of sounds and samples; download only the samples needed that fit into audio project; pay once a month with unique subscription payment system. URBAN ATMOSPHERES: real 5.1 audio surroundings of urban locations; unique, authentic surround environments contain top-quality recordings of urban soundscapes; contains ninety-five scenes from twenty-five locations; presented in AIFF format on nine DVDs. WIZOOSOUNDS.COM: professional sample instruments online; inexhaustible resource for new sounds and instruments; either download sounds or compile own sound collection, which is then burned onto CD. SYSTEM SPECS: Macintosh; Windows.

Steinberg Virtual Effect Processors (www.steinberg.net): For sound design, mastering, or restoration; expand production environment by adding effects and dynamics; open VST architecture. GRM TOOLS VOLUME 1: sound manipulation plug-in collection for VST GRM Tools consists of four unique effect processors with extremely flexible, high-quality algorithms; Shuffling, Comb Filters, Band Pass, PitchAccum. GRM TOOLS VOLUME 2: sound manipulation plug-in collection for VST; second collection of GRM Tools offers four effect processors: Reson, Doppler, Freeze, and Delays. KARLETTE: tape delay emulation; an authentic emulation of an analog tape echo unit; set volume, feedback, and panning for up to four delays. NUENDO TC SURROUNDVERB: surround reverb for Steinberg's Nuendo; offers Nuendo users a 5.1 reverb in TC Works quality; three frequency bands, various room editors, and filters offer maximum flexibility. STEINBERG SURROUND EDITION: eight-channel surround plug-ins; offers six different real-time effects, each one specially designed for surround sound production; up to eight channels can be accessed at once. THE STEINBERG MASTERING EDITION: complete mastering solution; contains six top-quality plug-ins. VOICEMACHINE: Real-time voice transformer; effect plug-in can create up to four additional voices, change melodies, or correct intonation while maintaining natural vocal characteristics. WARP VST: amp modeling; virtual effect processor turns computer into a guitar amplifier; combine three landmark amplifiers with any of three classic speaker cabinets on computer. SYSTEM SPECS: Macintosh; Windows.

Studio (Interactive Digital Design—Midisoft): Record, edit, and compose music with MIDI; record and edit WAVEform audio, including vocals; print sheet music; MIDI tracks limited only by computer memory; add lyrics synced to music; highlight notes during playback. SYSTEM SPECS: Windows.

SuperFreq (www.bias-inc.com): Paragraphic equalizer; "Aquafied" user interface for control over every parameter; graphic display of EQ; Carbon Event-driven OS X plug-in; sports OS X's distinctive "Aqua" interface; one of the first Mac OS X-native plug-ins; works within any Carbonized VST host application such as BIAS Deck 3.5, Peak 3, or Peak LE 3; also works under Mac OS 8.5 through 9.2.x. SYSTEM SPECS: Macintosh.

SurReal (www.seersystems.com): Brings audio quality of professional music synthesizers and samplers to the personal computer; add piano, brass, percussion, guitar, bass, classic synth, techno, ambient, and other musical instruments and sounds; makes sound card sound better; sixty-four-note polyphony; up to sixteen channels; control panel for each channel; five forms of synthesis include sample playback, FM, physical modeling, analog, and modal; built-in sequence player; wide variety of sounds; full GM patch set; eight GS drum kits. SYSTEM SPECS: Windows.

Tassman Sound Synthesis Studio (www.applied-acoustics.com): Modular instrument and sound design environment based on physical modeling; large collection of instruments and sound design tools; Physical Modeling synthesis uses no sampling; calculates the sound played in accordance to the controls it receives; fifty pre-patched instruments; over 1000 presets; includes classic analog and FM instrument emulations; realistic acoustic instruments, including various drums and chromatic percussion, string instruments, an electric piano, tonewheel and pipe based organs, and more; complete with the nuances and subtleties that would be unattainable with a sample based solution; instruments which allow importing of own samples; can utilize them as would any other tone generators; result is unique hybrid constructions; Drag and Drop Access: The Browser; At the Controls: The Player; Create and Customize: The Builder; Total Integration: Plug-ins; total integration with sequencing applications such as DXi, MAS, and VST instrument plug-in; available to Pro Tools users with the release of the RTAS version for OS X.

SYSTEM SPECS: Macintosh: Mac OS9.x/OSX.2 (recommended), G4 Processor, 128 Mb RAM, 800 x 600 or higher screen resolution, ASIO supported sound card (recommended for OS 9.x), MIDI keyboard (recommended); Windows: PC Win98, SE, 2000, ME, XP, PIII 500 of better processor, 128 MB RAM, 800 x 600 or higher screen resolution, Direct X or ASIO supported sound card, MIDI keyboard.

Techno Ejay (www.voyetra.com): Create songs in techno, drum 'n bass, trance, and acid jazz; more than 3,000 samples; sixteen tracks per song. SYSTEM SPECS: Windows 95, 98, ME or NT 4.0.

The AudioPro Home Recording Course Volumes I, II and III (www.artistpro.com): Includes everything necessary to start recording; basics on mixer, signal processing, and microphones; detailed information on recording guitars, drums, and percussion; illustrations and audio examples; wiring, impedance, and stereo imaging; recording bass guitars, vocals, pianos, and synths; digital hard disk recording, MIDI sequencing, mastering with computers, CD-R technology and more; glossary of common terms used in recording; two CDs of audio examples. SYSTEM SPECS: Books and Audio CDs.

The DJs Guide to Scratching DVD (www.wrnerbrospublications.com): Canadian DJ P-Love; covers all aspects of becoming a good DJ including the unique vocabulary and different types of scratching equipment; teaches how to become the reigning king or queen of the dance party while having a great time; contains interviews with other DJ's and an overall introduction to Montreal DJ culture. SYSTEM SPECS: Instructional DVD.

The Mix Reference Disk Deluxe Edition (www.artistpro.com): Collection of audio test signals; professional toolkit for any pro audio or multimedia application; audio tracks include: alignment tones, frequency sweeps, one third octave EQ bands, pink noise, sine/square/triangle waves, A-440 tuning reference, SMPTE time code, and guitar tuning notes; multimedia tracks include L/R channel IDs and audio clips in .WAV and .AIF formats at various sampling and bit rates. SYSTEM SPECS: Audio CD.

Toast Titanium (www.roxio.com): Comprehensive, all-in-one DVD and CD burner software; create, organize, share, and store all digital content on CDs or DVDs; preserve and share music, data, photos, and video on CD or DVD; Turn digital photos into a video slide show CD or burn iMovie productions onto Video CDs that are playable on most DVD players; turn scratchy LPs and cassettes into CDs; convert MP3s into professional audio CDs or burn them on MP3; protect valuable data on CDs or share it with Windows PC users; print custom labels and cases for new CDs; burning companion to iMovie, iTunes, and DVD authoring software. SYSTEM SPECS: Toast 5 for Macintosh OS 9; Toast 6 for Macintosh OS X.

Toast with Jam (www.roxio.com): Arrange and master pro audio CDs; suite includes three award-winning applications—Toast 5 Titanium: for CD or DVD burner—audio, video, photo and data; will burn final master CD; Jam 5: arrange tracks and build 100 percent Red Book-compliant audio CD; create dynamic cross-fades between tracks, edit PQ subcodes, set the gain for each channel of each track, cleanly trim tracks, and more; BIAS Peak LE VST: use non-destructive waveform editing tools to improve and add special effects to music; enhance vocals with concert reverb, soften dynamic peaks, and create other effects with included VST plug-ins; tool for pro musicians archiving a gig; for garage bands ready to go pro; for DJs that need a smooth track to track transition. SYSTEM SPECS: Macintosh OS X.

Tune 1000 (www.halleonard.com): General MIDI files; sound-alike arrangements; songs of top artists; lyrics display; backup vocal parts; 157 titles in catalog. SYSTEM SPECS: General MIDI-compatible keyboard.

Twiddly Bits Standard MIDI Files (www.keyfax.com): Standard MIDI files; real musicians playing real instruments; hundreds of riffs, runs, patterns, grooves, and licks; sequences can be cut and pasted; drums, keyboard, guitar, horn section, and more. SYSTEM SPECS: Macintosh; Windows.

Ultimate MP3 and CD Manager for Windows (www.voyetra.com): Create, organize and play digital music on PC; "Rip" CDs into MP3s for convenient listening on computer or portable devices; "Burn" custom mix CDs; listen to Internet radio broadcasts from around the world; automates the encoding and organizing process; transfer CD collection to computer; with AudioStation's MP3 or Windows Media compression modes can store thousands of songs on a typical hard drive; AutoGain automatically corrects changes in volume levels on songs recorded from different CDs, for a consistent listening experience; play digital music downloaded from the Internet; listen to radio broadcasts in Windows Media and MP3 formats; use CD-R Drive to create audio CDs that play on standard CD players; with data recording mode can fit more than 150 songs in MP3 or Windows Media compressed formats to play on the latest generation of MP3 CD players; turn PC into digital jukebox; sort music by artist, genre, album, title, song length, and more; take personalized music collections along; make personalized CD library of favorite tunes; custom-mix CDs for trips, parties, events or for fun. SYSTEM SPECS: Windows.

Unisyn (www.motu.com): Provides comprehensive sound management features available on the Macintosh and Windows, including seamless integration with Performer; editor/librarian; modify a sound, in Unisyn using graphic envelope controls and faders, while getting instant feedback within the context of music as Performer plays the sequence; generate entire banks of new sounds with a click of the mouse using Blend, Randomize, and Copy/Paste Parameter features; share bank names with Performer and other FreeMIDI-compatible software for accurate pop-up sound lists; can store thousands of sounds and recall them instantly using database-style search criteria. SYSTEM SPECS: Macintosh; Windows.

USB Music Studio Kit (www.voyetra.com): Play songs on music keyboard; mix and edit on PC; Plug-N-Play capabilities and convenience of USB; USB MIDI Cable; overdub additional instruments; edit; mix; print sheet music; Setup Utility; includes Record Producer Music Software; hundreds of music loops; MIDI music files; "musical templates" to quickly create songs by providing drum patterns, instrument melodies and more; paste together to create background patterns of bass lines, drum beats, and melodic loops; wide variety of styles, including rock, funk, dance, techno, blues, and more; includes bonus software. SYSTEM SPECS: Windows.

VAZ Modular (www.software-technology.com): Can run sixteen separate synths at once, each with up to sixteen-note polyphony and up to 255 modules; includes sample-playback module, several types of filters, support for DirectX, VST, and ASIO, and arpeggiator, pattern sequencer, MIDI control of on-screen sliders and delay, chorus, phaser, flanger, and reverb effects. SYSTEM SPECS: Windows 95/98.

Vbox (www.bias-inc.com): Audio DSP solution for music, Internet audio, audio-for-picture, broadcast, DJ'ing, and more; create, manage, store, and recall huge numbers of VST plug-ins; for use in music, audio-post, sound for the Web, or multimedia; powerful, unique effects matrix; combine, route, and mix multiple plug-ins, up to hundreds per channel; manage signal processing needs, since Vbox stores and recalls combinations, routings, and parameters for each plug-in; use as a stand-alone application or run it fully integrated in any VST host program, including Steinberg Cubase, Emagic Logic, and others; work with audio files or even live feeds; can use for DJ'ing, broadcasting, and theater sound. SYSTEM SPECS: Macintosh; Windows.

Vegas (mediasoftware.sonypictures.com): Video editing, audio production, compositing, titling, and advanced encoding on the PC platform; intuitive interface; powerful video and audio production tools; integrated solution for digital video, audio recording, editing and mixing, streaming content creation, and surround sound production; for professional multimedia production; apply high-quality transitions, filters, credit rolls, and text animations; create sophisticated composites, keyframe track motion and pan/crop with unlimited tracks and flexibility; provides real-time previewing of effects and transitions from time-line without needing to render; advanced color correction and scene matching using three-wheel primary and secondary color correction filters; view video levels using video scopes, including Waveform, Vectorscope, Parade, and Histogram monitors; supports HD editing and rendering along with native support for 24p DV; unlimited tracks, 24-bit/96 KHz audio support, record input monitoring, effects automation, time compress/expand, and more; ships with over thirty studio-quality real-time DirectX effects, including, EQ, reverb, noise gate, time compress/expand and delay; for digital video production, TV soundtracks, Web content creation, radio and broadcast, and mixing 5.1 surround soundtracks. SYSTEM SPECS: Windows 98SE, Me, 2000, or XP.

Virtuosa Gold for Windows (www.mp3-converter.com/virtuosa.htm): MP3 player and encoder software. SYSTEM SPECS: Windows.

VST Instruments (www.steinberg.net): From classic synthesizers to powerful samplers and drum machines; wide range of instruments offer the advantages of Virtual Studio Technology, including sample accurate timing, automation, and seamless integration into Cubase or Nuendo. D'COTA MULTIPLE SYNTHESIS VST INSTRUMENT: Combines three types of synthesis into one VSTi; offers an editing environment that lets user utilize its triple synthesizing power. GROOVE AGENT: Virtual drummer plays dozens of drum styles; exemplary handling concept makes it easy to come up with drum grooves. HALION 2.0: HALion VST sampler offers top-quality Waldorf filters, surround support, thirty-two-stage envelopes, superior GIGA import, and more. HALION STRING EDITION—VOLUME 1: Symphonic string orchestra instrument and library; symphonic strings collection; top-quality orchestral string section; playability, unique, warm character, and a natural ambience. LM•4 MARKII: 32-bit VST drum module with the LM•4 Mark II; precision timing, eighteen pads with twenty velocity zones and drum sample package. MODEL•E: Classic analog synthesizer; classic synth sounds for virtual studio; deep basses, smooth analog filter sweeps, and lead lines; program own sounds or use presets. PLEX: Restructuring synthesizer by Wolfgang Palm; synthesizer based on a novel synthesizing process; limitless possibilities in varying and creating sounds. THE GRAND: Steinberg's virtual concert piano; superb sound quality and playing characteristics of a high-quality concert piano with a rich and realistic sound. VB 1: Virtual bass synthesizer; freeware VST instrument; covers all basses from authentic bass guitar sounds to pumping acid synth bass-lines. VIRTUAL GUITARIST: Rhythm guitarist for computer; VST instrument that produces just about any guitar sound, including heavy LA riffs, funky Wah guitar and many more. VIRTUAL GUITARIST "ELECTRIC EDITION": Rhythm guitarist and guitar effect board for VST Systems; virtual electric guitarist; based on real recordings, the twenty-nine players offer a large range of sounds, styles, guitars, amps, and effects. WALDORF ATTACK: Percussion synthesizer; brings the drum sounds of the 80s and 90s into the twenty-first century VST world; stunning drums and percussion; create polyphonic bass and lead sounds. WALDORF PPG WAVE 2.V: Classic wavetable synthesizer; software recreation of a synth classic; wavetable synthesis; generate dynamic soundscapes. XPHRAZE: Phrase synthesizer; brings together powerful sound shaping and real-time polyphonic phrase creation; offers virtually unlimited sound-shaping and real-time modulation capabilities. SYSTEM SPECS: Macintosh; Windows.

Wave Lab Essential (www.steinberg.net): Digital audio editing for project studios; offers a range of digital audio editing features, from CD writing functions to comprehensive mastering possibilities; based on award-winning WaveLab 4.0 technology; fast and flexible audio editor; Real-time VST and DirectX audio plug-ins; audio and data CD burning; powerful audio montage; innovative, clip-oriented editing system; MP3 encoding/decoding; label editor for creating CD covers. SYSTEM SPECS: Windows.

WaveBurner Pro (www.emagic.de): Professional 32-bit audio CD mastering and burning; advanced version of Eddy award-winning WaveBurner; cost-effective mastering and burning solution for 100 percent Red Book compatible CDs, using SCSI and FireWire CD burners; extensive range of functions; clearly laid out user interface; professional mastering tools. SYSTEM SPECS: Macintosh.

WaveLab (www.steinberg.net): WaveLab 4.0; professional audio editing and mastering software for Windows PCs; easy-to-use stereo editors; wealth of mastering features; powerful editing tools; array of new, high-quality virtual effect processors; comprehensive CD burning capabilities, real-time audio file analysis, and batch processors; supports samplers, ASIO, WDM, a vast range of file formats as well as file resolutions of up to 32-bit IEEE/192 KHz; real-time input and output monitoring; Audio Montage window; nondestructive editing concept; latest update, WaveLab 4.01, offers almost fifty additional new features; 32-bit floating point processing up to 192 KHz; Audio Montage features; real-time audio processing plug-ins; professional sampler support and CD writing; integrated batch processing; audio database. SYSTEM SPECS: Windows.

Winamp (www.winamp.com): MP3 player software; MP3 and WAV compatible; plug-ins. SYSTEM SPECS: Windows.

Windows. Media Player (www.microsoft.com): Streaming audio and video; MP3 and WAV compatible; supports RealAudio and RealVideo formats. SYSTEM SPECS: Macintosh; Windows.

XAudio MP3 Player (www.Xaudio.com): MP3 player software. SYSTEM SPECS: Unix.

Xing MP3 Encoder (www.xingtech.com): MP3 encoder software. SYSTEM SPECS: Windows.

Xmms (www.xmms.org): MP3 player software. SYSTEM SPECS: Linux; Unix.

Plug-Ins

5.1 Surround Plug-In-Pack for Windows (http://mediasoftware.sonypictures.com): Encode ACID PRO 4.0 and Vegas 4.0 surround mixes to Dolby Digital AC-3 multichannel 5.1 files and burn to DVD for playback on audio systems that support multichannel 5.1 surround audio; includes: Sony Pictures Digital AC-3 Encoder Plug-In; Sony Pictures Digital AC-3 DVD Burner; supports both 5.1 and stereo AC-3 encoding. SYSTEM SPECS: Windows 98SE, Me, 2000, or XP.

Acoustics Mirror Software for Windows (http://mediasoftware.sonypictures.com): Imparts the acoustics of real environments, signal processors, and microphones onto sound files; can simulate responses from large concert halls to the sound of an old microphone. SYSTEM SPECS: Windows.

Alien Connections ReValver for Windows (www.cakewalk.com): Build own virtual guitar rack; arsenal of modules, including preamps, filters, effects modules, power amps, speaker simulators, and room simulators; many guitar tones; effect for wringing unique sonic characteristics out of vocals, organs, drums, and other instruments; can be used in any program that supports DirectX plug-ins; is an upgrade from ReValver SE found in SONAR 2.0 and 2.0 XL, SONAR 1.0 XL, and Guitar Tracks Pro; primary difference between ReValver SE and the full version of ReValver is in the number of modules one can access; ReValver SE offers two modules each of preamps, speakers, power amps, and effects; full version has between thirteen and twenty of each kind. SYSTEM SPECS: Windows.

Analog Tube Modeling Plug-In (www.antarestech.com): Tools to create a wide range of modeled analog tube effects; models the effect of a high-quality analog tube preamp; two tube models for a variety of sonic effects; OmniTube allows applying the tube effect to the entire signal; superb sound quality; DSP efficient; use simultaneously on dozens of tracks. SYSTEM SPECS: Macintosh: RTAS, MAS and VST, Macintosh with a PowerPC processor running OS 9.x (RTAS, VST, MAS) or OS X (RTAS, VST), host program that supports the appropriate plug-in architecture, Tube RTAS OS X requires Pro Tools 6 TDM or LE and OS 10.2.3. or later; Windows: PC RTAS, VST and DirectX, PC running Win 98, ME, NT, 2000, or XP (as required by host program), host program that supports the appropriate plug-in architecture.

Apogee UV22 Encoder (Steinberg Mastertools): Available for Soundscape SSHDR1, Mix-treme, and R.Ed digital audio workstations. SYSTEM SPECS: Windows 95/98/NT.

Arboretum Plug-Ins (www.arboretum.com): Creators of video editing and audio plug-ins processing software for multimedia content creation, sound design, mastering, post production, sound restoration, for both professionals and hobbyists; Hyperprism: real-time sound design software (Mac, Windows); Ray Gun: clean up noisy records and tapes (Mac, Windows); Ionizer: professional noise reduction and mastering system (Mac, Windows); Restoration-NR: high-resolution hiss removal plug-in (Windows); Harmony: pitch and harmony processor (Mac); Realizer Pro: Internet DSP solutions for online listening and authoring (Mac, Windows). SYSTEM SPECS: Macintosh; Windows.

Auto-Tune (www.antarestech.com): The next generation of the worldwide standard in professional pitch correction; new features; new interface; for MAS, VST (Mac), TDM, RTAS (Mac and PC), and DirectX. (TDM and RTAS versions now compatible with Pro Tools|HD). SYSTEM SPECS: Macintosh; Windows.

Batch Converter Plug-In for Windows (mediasoftware.sonypictures.com): Time-saving utility for converting tens, hundreds, or thousands of sound files to a different format; for a multimedia developer needing to support different computer platforms and compression formats, or a sound engineer requiring a specific sample rate; reduces the process to a few simple mouse clicks; installs within Sound Forge. SYSTEM SPECS: Windows.

BBE Sonic Maximizer DirectX Plug-In (www.bbesound.com): Now offered as a DirectX plug-in; can download or order on CD; adds brilliance, depth, detail, and definition to music in SONAR, Cakewalk Pro Audio, Cakewalk Home Studio, Cakewalk Guitar Studio, Cakewalk Guitar Tracks, Cakewalk Club Tracks, Cakewalk Professional, Pyro, Cakewalk Express, and other products that support DirectX plug-ins; BBE technology compensates for phase shifting between high, low, and mid frequencies, while augmenting sound to compensate for tendency to lose extreme high and low frequency range during recording and playback; result is restored brilliance of original live sound. SYSTEM SPECS: Windows: IBM PC or compatible (486 or higher), Windows 95, 98, ME, 2000, 2 MB of free hard-disk space, 16 MB RAM, 256-color VGA video or better, host application supporting DirectX plug-ins.

Cakewalk Audio FX 1, 2, and 3 (www.cakewalk.com): DirectX audio plug-ins for digital audio; add real-time, 32-bit, audio processing to Windows music applications; AudioFX1 includes a compressor/gate, limiter, expander/gate, and dynamics processor; with AudioFX2, can simulate amplifiers and tape simulation to add to tone; with AudioFX3, can create custom reverb in any environment.

SYSTEM SPECS: Windows 95/98: Pentium 120, 16 MB RAM, CD-ROM Drive; Windows Me/NT/2000/XP: Pentium 120, 32 MB RAM, CD-ROM Drive.

Cakewalk VST Adapter (www.cakewalk.com): Add support for VST effects and instruments to Cakewalk software; available for download; adds support for VST audio effects and instruments to Cakewalk software or any DirectX compatible application; converts VST format plug-ins to DirectX and DXi format; gives sample-accurate automation with identical audio fidelity; no additional latency and almost no additional CPU resources are required; opens studio up to hundreds of available freeware and shareware VST effects plug-ins and VSTi software synths and expands sonic palette; offers identical internal processing and sound quality as VST hosts; negligible CPU hit; key benefits for SONAR users: using the VST Adapter in the SONAR/DirectX environment adds functionality to VST plug-ins unattainable in other VST host applications; no limit on the number of simultaneous soft synths or automatable parameters; sample-accurate envelope automation; Project5 already adds VST support to system; owners of earlier versions of Cakewalk software without DXi support (e.g., Cakewalk Pro Audio 9) can use the Cakewalk VST Adapter to gain access to VST audio effects, but cannot access VST instruments. SYSTEM SPECS: Windows.

Drawmer Dynamics TDM (www.drawmer.com): Plug-in for Pro Tools; includes gating, compression, and limiting; increases the number of instantiations per DSP chip, doubled from two to four; expander/compressor/limiter plug-in based on Drawmer's DL241 Auto Compressor and DL251 Limiter. SYSTEM SPECS: Windows.

Drum Tools (www.musiclab.com): Combining SlicyDrummer and Fill-in Drummer together in one download; MIDI drum track generating tools. SYSTEM SPECS: Windows.

DSP•FX Plug-Ins (www.dspfx.com): StudioVerb; AcousticVerb; Optimizer; Aural Activator; Stereo Pitch Shifter; Multi-Tap Delay; Analog Tape Flanger; Multi-Element Chorus; Parametric EQ; Auto-Panner; Tremolo; Stereo Widener; gives PC-digital audio workstation users access to real-time effects processing with pro studio quality; works in real time with Cakewalk Pro Audio, Cubase VST, Sound Forge, WAVElab, Samplitude, and other high-end programs. SYSTEM SPECS: Windows.

ExpressFX 1 DirectX Audio Plug-Ins (http://mediasoftware.sonypictures.com): Collection of four streamlined effects; designed especially for use with Sound Forge XP 4.5 and ACID Music 1.0; each effect provides parameter adjustments to give control over sound processing; works with any DirectX-compatible host program; available for purchase as a downloadable product; features four discrete plug-ins: Distortion, Flange/Wah-Wah, Reverb, and Stutter; installs into and operates in any program that fully supports DirectX Plug-Ins. SYSTEM SPECS: Windows 9x, Me, NT 4.0, 2000, or XP.

ExpressFX 2 DirectX Audio Plug-Ins (http://mediasoftware.sonypictures.com): Collection of four streamlined effects designed especially for use with Sound Forge XP 4.5 and ACID Music 1.0; each effect provides parameter adjustments to give control over sound processing; works with any DirectX-compatible host program; available for purchase as a downloadable product; features four discrete plug-ins: Amplitude Modulation, Chorus, Delay, and EQ; installs into and operates in any program that fully supports DirectX Plug-Ins. SYSTEM SPECS: Windows 9x, Me, NT 4.0, 2000, or XP.

Fill-in Drummer (www.musiclab.com): Perfect basic rhythm part with pro quality drum fills, breaks, intros, and endings; full integration with FXpansion's DR-008 drum sampler; about 600 pro quality dynamic drum fills, intros, endings; Importing User drum fills; Intelligent Fill Modifying system; fill variations at a mouse click; advanced dynamics control; automated crescendo/decrescendo; swing control; combining drum fill with basic rhythm; real time and undestructive edits; graphic feedback of all edits; Event Edit; Snap to Grid. SYSTEM SPECS: Any sequencer with support of MIDI Plugins (MFX) technology, Windows.

Guitar Rhythm Pattern Library (www.musiclab.com): Collection of numerous guitar accompaniment rhythm patterns classified by various musical categories, such as meter, tempo, rhythmic feel, guitar technique, and music style; specially prerecorded for use only with Rhythm-'n'-Chords plug-ins. SYSTEM SPECS: Windows.

JVP Voice Processor for Windows (www.antarestech.com): Combines de-essing, compression, gating, EQ, and delay effects to produce a variety of vocal sounds; all in one DSP-efficient TDM plug-in. SYSTEM SPECS: Windows.

Logic Plug-Ins (www.emagic.de): Native audio editing; new proprietary Plug-Ins; 32-bit floating point precision for audio formats up to 24-bit/96 KHz; sophistication of underlying algorithms; best circuit design concepts known today modeled digitally to provide tools of uncompromising quality. DELAY: Tape Delay, Stereo Delay. EQ: Channel EQ. DYNAMICS: Compressor, Expander, Noise Gate, Enveloper, DeEsser, Multipressor, Limiter. DISTORTION: Distortion 2, Overdrive and Distortion, BitCrusher, Clip Distortion, Phase Distortion. FILTER: Autofilter, Fuzz Wah. MODULATION: Modulation Delay, Phaser, Tremolo, Ensemble, Rotor Cabinet, Spreader, Scanner Vibrato. REVERB: SilverVerb, GoldVerb, PlatinumVerb, EnVerb. SPECIAL: Spectral Gate, Pitch Shifter, SubBass, Denoiser, Exciter, Stereo Spread. Detailed information regarding which program version contains which plug-ins can be found in the Comparison Charts at the EMagic Web site. SYSTEM SPECS: Macintosh; Windows.

MachFive (www.motu.com): Intelligent file management; sound bank management remembers where sounds are located; optimized for browsing and loading libraries; multi-gigabyte libraries are quickly and efficiently scanned; sampler that is also a real plug-in; collaborate across platforms; compatibility with all sample libraries; multitimbral performance; synthesis engine; built-in multichannel waveform editor; support for 24-bit 192 KHz audio; surround-capable sampler; integrated tuner; drag and drop; modulation and tempo sync; integrated multieffects. SYSTEM SPECS: Macintosh; Windows.

Master X3 (www.tcelectronic.com): Virtual incarnation of Finalizer, the standard mastering processor in the pro audio field; supports Pro Tools 24 Mix and HD and can operate at sample rates up to 96 KHz; available for MacOS 9.x and Windows; expedites the mastering process by integrating several phases of mastering into a single interface; features multiband processing with expansion, compression, and limiting separately for each band; high-quality uncorrelated dithering; intuitive user interface; "Target Curves" providing a global processing style for all bands in all modules; interaction between bands fine tuned by applying "Target Factors" which determine frequency focus of each processing module; "Soft Clipping" provides "analog" sound whenever desired; three-band processing with adjustable crossovers; Expander; Compressor; Limiter; Dithering (uncorrelated); Look-Ahead feature of up to 10 ms; Adjustable Digital Ceiling with accuracy of up to 0.05 dB; Hi-Res Metering with selectable Hold Modes; Consecutive Clippings counter; supports Pro Tools 24Mix and HD systems. SYSTEM SPECS: Macintosh: PowerMac G3 or G4 equipped with Pro Tools 24Mix according to Digidesign's requirements; Windows: PC equipped with Pro Tools 24Mix or HD according to Digidesign's requirements.

Microphone Modeler (www.antarestech.com): Mics can sound like other, better mics; available for TDM, MAS, VST, RTAS and DirectX. SYSTEM SPECS: Macintosh.

Multiband Dynamics Tool (www.antarestech.com): Complete creative control over dynamics; DSP plug-in for Digidesign's TDM environment; uses a unique graphic interface to give control over the musical character of the processor itself; can emulate any existing compressor, limiter, or expander; applications include mastering, post production, broadcast, track sweetening, sound effects, sample editing, or any other application where top-, quality dynamics processing or dynamic EQ is needed; up to thirty separate thresholds and ratios; configure compressors, expanders, limiters, reverse gain effects,

or any possible combination of these; one, three, or five individually adjustable spectral bands; create dynamic EQs, de-essers, spectral enhancers; avoid "pumping" and "breathing;" uses special algorithms in multiband mode to give a greater than 144 dB dynamic range and imperceptible passband coloration; up to 1,028 sample "look-ahead" allows MDT to track difficult material; Clip Sentry high-speed digital limiter prevents clipping by reducing gain only when clipping is about to occur; zero attack and release times allow MDT to be used as a peak limiter with customizable sonic characteristics ranging from subtle tube leveling to hard-wall crunch; continuously variable Offset Levels allow the input offset levels to be continuously adjusted so the band levels are, on the average, even with one another; eliminates major source of sonic coloration previously inherent in multiband compressors; processes 16-bit or 24-bit sound files with an internal 56-bit accumulator; audiophile-quality sound in stereo or mono; buttons, sliders and the Settings Menu are automated under Pro Tools 4.0 or later; using TDM pagetables, MDT can be controlled by external control surfaces, including the JL Cooper CS-10, Peavey PC 1600, Digidesign ProControl, and Mackie HUI; Pro Tools|24 MIX compatible. SYSTEM SPECS: Windows: PowerPC running a TDM-compatible host program.

Muon Electron (www.muon-software.com): Combines the warmth, power, and range of a classic analog synth with innovative and flexible architecture; create huge, complex sounds and control them dynamically; three powerful 64-bit oscillators with pulse-width modulation and sync to hit deep bass or crystal highs without distortion, noise or digital artifacts; two independent multimode resonant filters capable of being linked together, split apart, re-routed into each other or cross-faded from one type to another; two user-assignable LFOs, plus envelope generators and MIDI performance controllers for modulation madness; over sixty parameters; user interface features include the XY Controller; multimode filterbank with unique morphing cross-fader; each filter can be fed with up to three modulation signals each. SYSTEM SPECS: Macintosh: MacOS 8.5/higher or Mac OS-X, 400 MHz G3 or G4, 128 MB RAM, compatible host program; Windows: PIII400 processor, 64 MB RAM, 16-bit sound card.

Muon Tau Pro (www.muon-software.com): Create lead riffs and basslines; took classic monosynth design of the Tau, added a second oscillator, PWM, sync, ring modulation, and an effects engine; two 64-bit waveform oscillators with eleven waveforms each; pulse-width modulation; sync and ring modulation; no noise or digital artifacts; lowpass resonant filter, with 1dB Classic, 2dB Hi-Q and 36 dB Phat modes; built-in FX unit for warm overdrive, chorus, flange and vintage-style delay effects; full MIDI control, SYSTEM SPECS: Macintosh: MacOS 8.5/higher or Mac OS-X, 300 MHz G3 or G4, 128 MB RAM, compatible host program; Windows: PIII300 processor, 64 MB RAM, 16-bit sound card.

Native Bundle (www.tcelectronic.com): For the new Version of Native Bundle 3.0, all existing plug-ins have been completely rewritten in order to achieve even better sound and system performance; new preset handling on all plug-ins; includes all Hi-End processing tools for VST; covers all needs for equalization, dynamic processing (including de-essing), reverberation, limiting and maximizing; tools are performance optimized so they work in multitrack environment; intuitive user interfaces; supports the Apple Audio Unit Plug-In format; users of Native Bundle 3.0 can download the free AudioUnit update. SYSTEM SPECS: Macintosh OS X.

Native Instruments: Reaktor 3 (www.msc-catalog.com): By Len Sasso; official Reaktor book approved by Native Instruments; guided tour of Reaktor's approach to sound design; Reaktor's basic operation; twenty-two of Reaktor's most popular factory Ensembles; step-by-step instructions for building basic and advanced synthesizers, samplers, sequencers, and effects processors; CD-ROM featuring all Reaktor Ensembles and Instruments described in the book plus fifty-seven audio tracks. SYSTEM SPECS: Book and CD-ROM.

Native Performance Verb for Macintosh (www.tcelectronic.com): TC-Quality reverb to any OS X VST recording, editing, or mastering environment; easy to operate user interface; Rooms, Halls, Churches, Cathedrals, and Spring Reverb presets allow user to simulate the environment; for simulating acoustic spaces for DV productions; integrates with SparkME and SparkLE; original SPARK reverb technology; supports MacOS X VST-compatible host application; In, Out, and Mix controls; Decay times up to five seconds; nine different room sizes. SYSTEM SPECS: MacOS X (10.1 recommended); VST-application, that is MacOS X compatible (SparkME, SparkLE).

Native Reverb (www.tcelectronic.com): Intuitive user interface; Color, Diffuse, and Shape; integrate all aspects of reverb tail sound design into a highly graphical interface; permanent ROM presets within the plug-in provide the important basic kinds of reverbs; can be quickly and simply edited and saved into custom user presets. SYSTEM SPECS: Windows.

Noise Reduction for Windows (http://mediasoftware.sonypictures.com): Analyzes and removes background noise such as tape hiss, electrical hum, and machinery rumble from sound recordings; separate click removal and vinyl restoration tools for specific conditions included. SYSTEM SPECS: Windows.

PSP 84 (www.pspaudioware.com): High-quality processor, capable of producing a wide variety of delay-based effects; two independent delay lines operating with variable sampling rate and precise tape saturation algorithm with adjustable gain; allows for convincingly sounding simulation of tape delay, including effects resulting from tape speed instability; filtration section consisting of three second order switchable resonant filter types can be used to process input, feedback, or wet signal adjustable slope of filter ranges from a gentle curve; useful for simulating high-frequency absorption typical for tape delay and wet signal equalization to an extremely steep curve with a high cutoff frequency peak; all wah-wah and resonance effects easily available; delay line sampling rate and filter cutoff can be modulated by any of the 5 LFO waveforms that are automatically synchronized to the sequencer tempo or envelope follower with adjustable sensitivity and attack/release; contains fully functional reverb unit with simplified settings tuned to exactly reproduce the sound of classic spring and plate reverberators. SYSTEM SPECS: Macintosh: Mac OS X v. 10.0 or later, MacOS v. 8.6 or later, VST or RTAS compatible host application, G3 300 MHz, 256 MB RAM memory settings on Mac, High Color S-VGA, 1024 x 768; Windows: Windows 95, VST or DirectX compatible host application, 128 MB RAM, Pentium 200 MHz, High Color S-VGA, 1024x768.

PSP Plug-Ins (www.pspaudioware.com): Develops high-quality audio processors and effects plug-ins; supportive tool during mixing or mastering; PSP VINTAGEWARMER: digital simulation of analog-style, multi-band compressor-limiter. LEXICON PSP 42: digital stereo delay and phrase sampler. PSP VINTAGEMETER: provides professional VU and PPM metering for mono and stereo tracks; PSP MIXPACK: to add rich, detailed, warm, lively, and punchy sound to tracks. PSP STEREOPACK: plug-ins designed for creating, expanding, improving, controlling, and analyzing quality of stereo audio signals. PSP PIANOVERB: reproduces special kind of reverberation originally provided by piano strings. SYSTEM SPECS: Macintosh; Windows.

QSound (www.qsound.com): Audio processing technologies; transform music and sound effects into realistic, multidimensional audio; set of three plug-in tools providing mono-to-wide-3D, stereo-to-3D and mono-to-positional 3D effects; extends the capability of standard stereo systems; optimized for Cakewalk Pro Audio. SYSTEM SPECS: Windows.

Rhythm-'n'-Chords (www.musiclab.com): MIDI FX plug-in; for Cakewalk or Cubase; create rhythm guitar parts in MIDI format; enter chord symbols into measures and select rhythm pattern; guitar part is ready; create professional sounding guitar accompaniment MIDI tracks; create sophisticated harmonic progressions; fit guitar parts into arrangements; learn the sounding of various chords and main principles of chord construction and voices leading. SYSTEM SPECS: Windows.

SlicyDrummer (www.musiclab.com): Tool for instant creation of drum loops by combining individual drum instrument patterns; provides user with a unique way to quickly construct drum loops by selecting the appropriate prerecorded pattern for each individual drum instrument from the library; includes a large library of MIDI patterns for a number of drum instruments (kick, snare, hi-hat, ride cymbal) and percussions (conga, cowbell, tambourine, maracas, hand clap); patterns are prerecorded in such a way that they can be easily combined to make up professionally sounding drum loops; full integration with FXpansion's DR-008 drum sampler; can be loaded in to any pad of DR-008 as a sequencer module and performs drum loop by triggering appropriate MIDI note from host sequencer or external MIDI keyboard; Event Edit; insert/delete/drag individual beats right inside the plug-in window, allowing to fully edit the prerecorded patterns or create own from scratch; Snap to Grid; up to thirty-two triplet resolution available, that makes it easy to edit beats. SYSTEM SPECS: Windows.

Sonic Timeworks for Windows (www.sonictimeworks.com): Equalizer V1-LP for DirectX; ReverbX; EqualizerV1; CompressorX; Delay 6022; Reverb 4080L; Phazer Model 88; Mastering EQ; Mastering Compressor; ReverbX RTAS; ChannelX RTAS; CompressorX RTAS; Pulsar/Scope Pro Reverb; Pulsar/Scope VintagEQ Series; Pulsar/Scope CompressorX; Mastering Compressor's for Scope/Pulsar; SharcOne for Scope/Pulsar. SYSTEM SPECS: Windows.

Sound Bridge (www.alesis.com): Latest version for Alesis QS-series synths; enables user to map individual sounds into a single multisampled instrument; can download software from Alesis Web site. SYSTEM SPECS: Macintosh; Windows.

Spark XL (www.tcelectronic.com): Real-time digital audio editor; represents the state-of-the-art, all-inclusive version of SPARK technology; a complete mastering and editing environment; includes the FX MACHINE and all its Plug-Ins; SPARK FX MACHINE; SPARK FX MACHINE Instrument; Compressor & Limiter; MaxIt; Bandpass; Cut Filter; Resonance Filter; Tape Delay; one and three Band EQ; Expander; TCO-Oscillator; TCF-Filter; TCA-Amplifier; TCSeq-Step Sequenzer; TCK-Virtual Keyboard; FuzzSat; Grainalizer; Touch Wah; Sonic Destructor; Sonograph; Metergraph; Denoiser; Declicker. SYSTEM SPECS: Macintosh OS X.

Spectrum Analysis Plug-In (mediasoftware.sonypictures.com): Offers Sound Forge users a powerful method of analyzing vital frequency content in digital recordings; powerful analysis capability of the two graphic formats: Spectrum Graph and the Sonogram display; installs within Sound Forge. SYSTEM SPECS: Windows.

Style Enhancer Micro 2.0 (SEM2.0) (www.ntonyx.com): MIDI FX plug-in created for use with Cakewalk software; based on Performance Modeling, a unique technology developed by NTONYX to allow users to introduce a MIDI-sequence of live sounding music into their projects; analyzes MIDI-sequences and changes controller commands such as Velocity, Volume, Pitch Wheel, Expression, and other commands; result is simulation of live musician playing real instrument, as well as an interesting character to the performance; MIDI data processing software. SYSTEM SPECS: Windows.

TC Tools (www.tcelectronic.com): Includes three essential processing tools for Pro Tools 24Mix and HD; studio-quality Reverb, Chorus, and Parametric EQ Plug-Ins in 24-bit; now support Pro Tools 24Mix and HD and are able to operate at sample rates up to 96KHz; available for MacOS 9.x; MEGA REVERB for your Pro Tools PCI, 24 and Pro Tools 24Mix system; adds Initial Reflection and Tail Balance Faders; intuitive user interface; graphic representation and easy control of the parameters; runs on Pro Tools 24Mix systems with up to two independent Plug-Ins running on one DSP; also supports Pro Tools 24 and Pro Tools PCI; Reverb algorithms core 1 and 2 from the TC M5000; New Diffusion and Tail Tuning; Six room shapes, modeled after real rooms: Hall, Fan, Prism, HorseShoe, Small and Club; Three-Band Tail; Seperate Early Reflections and Tail Controls; Hi-Cut Filter; True Stereo processing; 100 presets; 24/96 processing; Modulation Multi-FX.

VeloMaster (www.musiclab.com): MIDI FX plug-in; real-time MIDI dynamics processor with an interactive graph; works with note velocity; modify the dynamics of MIDI track or MIDI keyboard with visual feedback; manipulate interactive velocity curve of plug-in to modify dynamics of track; use like a compressor, limiter, expander, or gate for MIDI; use as adjustable velocity curve for MIDI keyboard. SYSTEM SPECS: Windows.

Voice Tools (www.tcelectronic.com): Plug-in bundle for Pro Tools 24Mix; includes Intonator, used for pitch correction and Voice Strip virtual channel strip with compressor, de-esser, EQ, low-cut filter/gate, and SoftSat; can be used to emulate sound of analog gear. SYSTEM SPECS: Windows.

WaveArts (http://wavearts.com): Plug-ins include Power Couple; TrackPlug; MasterVerb; WaveSurround Pro; WaveSurround for Winamp; WaveSurround for the RioPort Audio Manager; tools for sound processing. SYSTEM SPECS: Macintosh; Windows. .

Waves Plug-Ins (www.waves.com): Native Plug-Ins: AudioTrack; C1; C4; Doppler; De-Esser; Enigma; L1; Maxx Bass Bass Enhancer; MetaFlanger; MondoMod; PAZ; Q10 bands Paragraphic EQ; Renaissance Compressor; Renaissance Equalizer; Renaissance Reverb N; S1 Stereo Imager;

SuperTap; TrueVerb; UltraPitch. TDM Plug-Ins: AudioTrack; C1Compressor, Gate, Expander; C4; DOPPLER; De-Esser; ENIGMA; L1; Maxx Bass Bass Enhancer; MetaFlanger; MondoMod; PS22 Psuedo Stereo; PAZ; Q10 bands Paragraphic EQ; Renaissance Compressor; Renaissance Equalizer; Renaissance Reverb; S1 Stereo Imager; SuperTap; TrueVerb; UltraPitch. SYSTEM SPECS: Macintosh; Windows.

XFX1 DirectX Plug-In for Windows (http://mediasoftware.sonypictures.com): Six plug-in effects: Simple Delay, Multitap Delay, Reverb, Chorus, Pitch Shift (maintaining correct tempo or speed), and Time Compression (maintaining correct pitch); create multieffects within Sound Forge; with real-time previewing. SYSTEM SPECS: Windows.

XFX2 DirectX Plug-In for Windows (http://mediasoftware.sonypictures.com): Six plug-in effects: Graphic Equalizer (ten-band), Parametric Equalizer (four Filter Modes), Paragraphic Equalizer, Graphic Compressor, Multiband Limiter, and Noise Gate; hear results as screen setting change; for mastering and CD prep. SYSTEM SPECS: Windows.

XFX3 DirectX Plug-In for Windows (http://mediasoftware.sonypictures.com): Amplitude Modulation, Gapper-Snipper, Flange-Wah-Wah, Vibrato, Distortion, and Smooth-Enhance; optimizes editing time by allowing real-time previews; as parameters for an effect are modified, the result is heard immediately; use with any Windows audio editor that fully supports DirectX Audio plug-ins, including Sound Forge. SYSTEM SPECS: Windows.

4

Web Sites for Musicians

The Web sites listed in this chapter are all music related, or are in some way of practical use to musicians. They are organized by category, then alphabetically. Most of the **URLs** *(Uniform Resource Locators)* or *Web addresses* begin with **http://**, meaning *hypertext transfer protocol.* This is the protocol by which computers exchange information on the *World Wide Web,* or **www.** A Web address also includes the host's name, that being the name of the server location or computer from which the information is being received, a two- to three-letter designation for the type of server it is on, the directory path, sometimes followed by one or more subpaths, and a file name. There are six three-letter codes used in the United States to indicate the type of server or domain: **.com** = commercial, **.edu** = educational, **.gov** = government, **.net** = network, **.org** = nonprofit organization, and **.mil** = military. Addresses outside the United States may have a two-letter code at the end of the server location, such as **.uk** (United Kingdom) or **.au** (Australia).

A *home page* is the starting point on a Web site, which is often composed of many Web pages. A home page usually includes a table of contents, logos, photos, and links to other pages on the Web site. Most of the Web sites included in this chapter have information about the company, product, or organization, bios, a description of services, goals, or projects, answers to frequently asked questions or *FAQs,* images, graphics, sound, contact information, and links to related Web sites on the Internet.

Search engines, also known as *Web searchers* and *search directories,* are a great help in finding information on the Web. By choosing a category or subject heading, or submitting a word or descriptive phrase, one can locate any type of information. The search engine retrieves lists of related hypertext links. Because these lists can often be very long, it is important to sift through them, deleting unwanted, outdated, or unnecessary links. Some search engines help to narrow or refine a search, and some will eliminate duplicate site listings. Setting *bookmarks* or *favorites* saves the trouble of typing in the URL each time a Web site is accessed, making it possible to quickly find and click on to frequently visited sites. An extensive list of search engines can be found in this chapter (see "Search Engines").

In trying to locate music-related Web sites of interest and of value, a lot of "sifting" was done before choosing those listed in the forty-eight categories that follow. Although some Web sites could be listed under more than one category, each one is listed only once, under what was believed to be the most appropriate category. As with music software programs, URLs are subject to change and discontinuation. As this book is being printed, new Web sites will appear, and some will expire. If any topic of interest, such as a particular artist or composer, is not listed here, simply do a search on any of the available search engines. It is important to regularly use a search engine to find the most current information available. Happy Web surfing!

Artists

To find any artist's Web site, simply type his or her name into a search engine and click on the link(s). Look for the "Official Web Site" among the fan sites. Signed artist Web pages can also be found at their record label's Web site.

Ballet—Ballroom and Modern Dance

American Ballet Theater www.abt.org/default.asp Performances; dancers; education and training; contact information.

Ballet www.Ballet.co.uk/ UK dance Web site and discussion group.

Ballet Alert! www.balletalert.com Ballet in America and around the world; information on ballets, companies, and dancers; ballet talk for fans; dancer of the week; weekly quiz; photos; interviews; articles about ballet.

Ballet and Dance Art www.danceart.com E-zine for dancers; feature articles; chat and message boards; interviews with famous dancers; advice from teachers.

Ballet on the Net www.cyberdance.org Companies; colleges; schools; news; education; programs.

Ballet-DANS Library Listings www.chebucto.ns.ca/Culture/DANS/Library/ballet.html Ballet books, videos, CDs, and tapes.

Ballroom Dance Music Resource-Dance Plus www.danceplus.com Ballroom dance supply company; strict-time ballroom dance CDs from all over the world.

Critical Dance www.criticaldance.com Moderated bulletin board; news articles; interviews with dance celebrities; performance reviews; extensive links.

Dance Books Online www.dancebooks.co.uk/ Books, CDs, videos, and DVDs on dance and human movement.

Dance Links dancer.com/dance-links/ Large collection of dance-related links.

Dance Magazine www.dancemagazine.com Magazine on dance music.

Dance USA www.danceusa.org Programs and publications; meetings; facts and figures; members.

Dancer Online www.danceronline.com Dance magazine; columns; reviews; links.

Dancetv.com www.dancetv.comindex.html Ballroom dance Web site.

DanceWeb www.danceWeb.co.uk/ Interactive directory; searchable database for all sorts of dance-related information.

English National Ballet www.ballet.org.uk/ UK's premier touring ballet company; news; performances; resources.

Lotus www.lotusarts.com Music and dance multicultural studio.

New York City Ballet www.nycballet.com/nycballet/homepage.asp Repertoire; dancers; educational resources; schedule; tickets.

Nutcracker Ballet www.nutcrackerballet.net/ History of the Nutcracker Ballet; music; links; movies; information on performances.

Russian Classical Ballet www.aha.ru/~vladmo History; outstanding choreographers; ballet teachers; ballet dancers; musicians; education; photo gallery.

The Art of Ballet www.artofballet.com/classics.html Ballet; dance information; photos; clip art; ballet class; performing arts; adult beginners; instructional; classics; MIDI; famous ballets; steps; exercises; stretching tips; recommended books and videos; links.

The International Guild of Musicians in Dance www.dancemusician.org Membership; publications; conferences.

The Joffrey Ballet of Chicago www.joffreyballet.org Leading ballet company; performs the finest ballets from the great choreographers of the twentieth century.

The National Ballet of Canada www.national.ballet.ca/home.php Repertoire; tickets; subscriptions; artists; performances.

The National Ballet School www.nationalballetschool.org School of ballet.

Twyla Tharpe www.twylatharp.org Famous choreographer.

USA International Ballet Competition www.usaibc.com Official International Ballet Competition site in the United States.

Voice of Dance www.voiceofdance.com Online resource for dance; insights; calendar.

Booking—Touring—Gigging— Clubs and Venues

American Bed & Breakfast Association www.abba.com Regional directory of B and Bs.

Amtrak www.amtrak.com Train schedules and reservations.

Artist Couch Exchange www.couchexchange.org Place where touring indie artists can find a couch to crash on when passing through an area; in turn offer a couch to other artists coming through their hometown.

Atlanta Entertainment www.atlantaentertainment.com/ATLANTA/ By date, type, and venue; attractions; tickets; events.

Barnes & Noble www.barnesandnoble.com Chain store venue; list of stores nationwide; contact the community relations coordinator.

Billboard International Talent & Touring Directory
www.billboard.com/bb/directories/index.jsp
Includes over 27,000 listings; artists; managers;
venues; instrument rentals; booking agents;
security services; staging and special effects;
hotels; all in one easy-to-use reference source.

Borders Books and Music
www.borders.com/stores/index.html Chain store
venue; list of stores by state, including contact
information, phone, address, directions; contact
the community relations coordinator.

Club Connexion www.clubconnexion.com UK clubs.

ClubPlanet.com
www.clubplanet.com/default.asp?site=14 New
York music clubs.

Clubs Index www.clubsindex.com Nightclub
database.

CNN Airport cnn.com/airport Flight information;
travel news; weather.

CNN Weather cnn.com/WEATHER Four-day
forecasts for towns in the United States and many
cities around the world.

CNN: Travel Guide www.cnn.com/TRAVEL Travel
journalism and multimedia.

Coffee House Music www.coffeehousemusic.com
Unique collection of "coffee house" music on
CD; displays; audio samples.

Coffee House Tour www.coffeehousetour.com
Comprehensive resource and tour guide.

Cowboys.com: Night Clubs
www.cowboys.comnightclubs.htm Information
on horses, cattle, tack, guest ranches, rodeos,
country music, dancing, Southwestern art,
Western wear, collectibles, food, events,
classified ads, and more.

Digital City: Austin-Bars & Clubs
home.digitalcity.com/austin/bars Inside bars and
clubs; event planner; features.

EF Performing Arts Tours www.efperform.com Bring
performers on tour.

Expedia www.expedia.com Booking and issuing of
airline tickets.

Foreign Languages for Travelers
www.travlang.com/languages Online
multilingual phrase book.

Gig America
www.gigamerica.com/Band/pages/band_home.asp
Find a band, find a show, find a venue, FAQ.

Gig Magazine www.gigmag.com Webzine.

Gig Masters www.gigmasters.com Indie music.

Gig Page www.gigpage.com Interactive; add, edit, or
delete a gig; page is immediately updated online;
choose colors; annual fee.

Gig Swap www.gigswap.com Free networking tool
for bands and musicians; intuitive database-driven
site to help bands easily find and communicate
with each other worldwide; offers a community-
building tool or forum for direct contact between
artists to network and expand their touring base.

GigMan www.dedocsoft.com Database designed for
freelance musicians, band leaders, and agents.

GigMaster www.shubb.com/gigm.html Software;
lists, organizes; for every aspect of gigging.

Gig-O-Rama www.giglogic.com Software for
working musicians.

Gigs Online www.gigsonline.com Find a musician,
join a band, get a gig, gear, lessons, advice,
books, CDs, interviews, resources, and more.

HouseConcerts.com www.houseconcerts.com
Venues; singer-songwriters; hosting concerts;
photos; press; links; featured artists.

HouseConcerts.org www.houseconcerts.org
Grassroots phenomenon where both world class
musicians and developing local talent perform in
the comfortable intimacy of private homes and
similar nontraditional spaces; online guide.

LA Music Scene www.lamusicscene.com Bands;
forum; articles; clubs; calendar; links.

Las Vegas Bars, Pubs, and Night Clubs
www.lvindex.comvegas/nite.htm LasVegas bars
and nightclubs; bars with live music.

Las Vegas Leisure Guide www.mesquite-
nv.comlvnight.htm Las Vegas nightlife.

Lastminute.com www.lastminute.com UK live music
resource; tickets to London shows.

London Clubs
www.londonnet.co.uk/ln/out/ent/clubs.html
Regularly updated guide to London's best clubs
from dance music to retro; club listings; venues;
reviews; previews; free tickets.

Los Angeles Bars and Dance Clubs
weekendevents.com/LOSANGEL/lamusic.html
Club guide.

Map Quest www.mapquest.com Road maps online.

Maps On Us www.mapsonus.com Interactive maps.

Ministry of Sound www.ministryofsound.com Dance
Webzine; MP3s; news; reviews; club listings.

Musi-Cal www.musi-cal.com Concert calendar
listing dates for musicians and venues; all genres.

National Weather Service www.nws.noaa.gov
Weather disaster warnings.

Night Clubs USA www.nightclubsusa.com Databases
of nightclubs in the United States.

NYCE Clubs nyceclubs.com/clubs/ Club guide.

Oakwood www.oakwood.com Entertainment
housing; corporate housing.

On Stage Magazine onstagemag.com Live
performance magazine for bands and musicians;
interviews popular artists on the realities of
touring and the business; source for new
performance product information and reviews.

Peak Performance Tours
www.peakperformancetours.com Touring Web
site for performing musicians.

*Performance Magazine-International Touring
    Talent Weekly Newspaper*
    www.performanceclassified.com Subscription
    includes fifty-one weekly magazines and ten
    yearly directories; artist tour itineraries, news
    features, box office reports, international news
    and market reports, information about personnel
    and companies in the touring industry;
    Performance Series of Directories includes
    *Talent/Personal Managers;
    Clubs/Theaters/Colleges; Concert
    Productions; Facilities; Booking Agencies;
    International; Country Talent; The Black Book*
    phone and fax guide; *Manufacturers/Production
    Personnel.*

Pollstar www.pollstar.com Subscription includes
    weekly magazine plus five biannual directories;
    weekly magazine has tour itineraries, music
    industry news, box office summaries, *Concert
    Pulse Charts* for album sales and radio airplay in
    nine formats; directories include *Talent Buyers &
    Clubs, Concert Venues, Concert Support
    Services, Agency Rosters, Record Company
    Rosters;* individual directories available
    separately; mailing labels available for an
    additional fee.

Power Gig www.powergig.com Book gigs.

Rand McNally www.randmcnally.com Directions.

Roadie.net www.roadie.net True stories from roadies
    on the road.

Roadsideamerica.com www.roadsideamerica.com
    Unusual tourist attractions.

Russ and Julie's House Concerts www.jrp-
    graphics.com/houseconcerts.html Chance to
    experience music in a warm and intimate
    environment; opportunity to meet performers and
    have them sign their CD; social evening of
    friends and neighbors; upcoming concerts; past
    performers.

Sdam.com www.sdam.com San Diego bands; local
    music scene.

SetMaker
    www.sweetwater.com/download/?download=setm
    aker Free software for gigging musicians.

SFX.com www.sfx.com Live entertainment; all
    genres; buy tickets online.

South Florida NightLife
    www.floridagoldcoast.com/nightlife/index.htm
    Nightclubs; bars; dancing; clubs; pubs; listings
    of nightclubs organized by region and format.

Southwest Airlines Internet Specials
    www.southwest.com Weekly e-mail listings of
    special fares; online reservations.

Talent & Booking www.talentandbooking.com Talent
    and booking directories; record labels; A & R
    contact/artist roster; public relations firms.

Teen Night Spots in LA
    home.inreach.com/chucky/rockwell/clubs.html
    Clubs for teens.

The Bomp Bookshelf
    www.bomp.com/BompbooksRoad.html On the
    road, roadies, tour stories, etc.

The John F. Kennedy Center for the Performing Arts
    www.kennedy-center.org Information on the
    performing arts center.

The Musician's Guide to Touring and Promotion
    www.musicianmag.com or
    www.musiciansguide.com Lists agents, bands,
    clubs, labels, lawyers, press, fan magazines,
    radio stations, music stores, and more.

The Palace www.hollywoodpalace.com Famous
    Hollywood venue.

The Rough Guide www.travel.roughguides.com
    Budget travel advice.

The Universal Currency Converter
    www.xe.net/currency Count in foreign
    denominations.

The Weather Underground www.wunderground.com
    Weather updates.

This Is London www.thisislondon.co.uk Guide to the
    city; nightclubs.

Time Out www.timeout.com Clubbing.

Tour Baby www.tourbaby.com Regional
    performances by independent artists.

Touring and Gigging
    www.cops.co.uk/gigging_biz_page.html Finding
    and approaching venues, promotion, touring
    abroad, and more.

TravelASSIST Magazine travelassist.com Online
    magazine; bed and breakfast directory.

Travelocity www.travelocity.com Full-service online
    travel agent.

United States Chamber of Commerce
    www.uschamber.com/default Information on
    United States cities and locals.

United States Gazetteer www.census.gov/cgi-
    bin/gazetteer Maps of the United States.

Universal Currency Exchange www.xe.net/ucc
    Exchange money.

Washington, D.C. City Pages: Entertainment: Clubs
    www.dcpages.com/Entertainment/Clubs/
    Washington, D.C. clubs.

World Clubs Net www.worldclubs.net Guide to clubs
    around the world.

Worldwide Guide to Hostelling www.hostels.com
    Travel cheap.

Brass and Woodwind Instruments

A Physical Approach to Playing the Trumpet
    www.trumpetbook.com Method book for
    trumpet players.

A Tutorial on the Fife beafifer.com Tutorial book and CD with seventy-five lessons keyed to CD tracks; forty-nine tunes of varying difficulty; tips on how to buy a new fife or recondition an old one.

AAIIRR Power AcoustiCoils for Brass and Woodwinds www.dmamusic.orgacousticoils Produces enhanced response for all brass and woodwind musical instruments.

Anaheim Band Instruments www.abimusic.com Brass and woodwind specialists.

Bands of America www.bands.org Presenter of educational events for high school bands.

Bandstand www.bandstand.com.au/intro.html Specialists in brass and woodwind instruments; catalog; repairs and maintenance; links.

Blas-Basen Music Publishing www.blas-basen.se/ Brass, woodwind, symphonic band.

Borodi Music www.borodimusic.com Brass and woodwind instruments; repairs.

Brass www.bymt.org.uk/brass.htm Information on brass instruments.

Brass Band World www.brassbandworld.com Webzine for bands.

Brough's Books www.dropbears.comb/broughsbooks/music/wind _instruments.htm Books on playing, maintaining, technique and history of brass and woodwind instruments.

Calicchio Brass Musical Instruments www.calicchio.com Hand-crafted horns.

Charles Double Reed Company www.charlesmusic.com Reeds.

Chartier www.chartierreeds.com Reeds.

Custom Music Co. www.custommusiccorp.com Tubas; euphoniums; trumpets; trombones; bassoons; oboes; brass winds.

E. M. Winston Band Instruments www.emwinston.com Band instruments; orchestra instruments; stands; sax straps; recorders; percussion; educational toys; mouthpieces.

Emerson Musical Instruments www.emersonflutes.com Emerson flutes.

Empire Brass Sheet Music www.empirebrass.comsheet.html Brass arrangements.

Flute World www.fluteworld.com Flutes; piccolos; sheet music; accessories.

Flute.net Publications www.flute.net/publications Works for flute choir.

Gemeinhardt www.gemeinhardt.com Flutes and piccolos.

Giardinelli www.giardinelli.com Band and orchestral instruments and accessories.

Horn Place www.hornplace.com Online catalog of music instruction books, CDs, videos, and

software for tenor saxophone, alto saxophone, baritone saxophone, soprano saxophone, flute, trombone, and trumpet.

Jason DuMars Engraving www.saxophone.org Information; resources; links.

Jim Laabs www.jimlaabs.com/bandinstruments/bandinstrum ents.htm Brass and woodwind instruments.

John Myatt www.myatt.co.uk/ UK woodwind and brass instrument specialists.

John Packer Ltd. www.johnpacker.co.uk/about/default.asp Woodwind and brass specialists.

Jones Double Reed Products www.jonesdoublereed.com Jones; Meason; Pisoni; Daniel's.

Jupiter Band Instruments Inc. www.jupitermusic.com Jupiter Brass & Woodwinds; Ross Mallet Instruments.

Leblanc www.gleblanc.com Wind instrument manufacturer and distributor.

Let's Play the Recorder www.frontdsk.com/lptr Designed for classroom instruction as well as for individual use; Macintosh; Windows.

Lighthouse Media Group www.lighthousemediagroup.com Tips and Techniques videos for repairing band instruments, string, and percussion.

Maggio System for Brass www.maggiomusic.com A book for trumpet, trombone, French horn, and tuba; available in five languages.

Matthew's Music www.matthewsmusic.nl Vintage saxophones.

Melbourne Brass and Woodwind Center www.brassnwoodwind.com.au/ Australian dealership.

Mouthpiece Express.com www.mouthpieceexpress.com Mouthpieces and accessories for brass and woodwind instruments.

Music by Arrangement www.musicbyarrangement.co.uk/index.html Music for orchestras, bands, and ensembles; specially arranged for the instruments available.

National Association of School Music Dealers www.nasmd.com Trade association dedicated to sales, rental, and service of band and orchestra instruments, accessories, and published music.

Nine-Note Recorder Method members.aol.comPG9Note Book and CD to teach children to read music and play the recorder; duets and trios for classroom instruction.

Oberloh Woodwind and Brass Works www.oberloh.com Repairing and rebuilding.

Osmun Music www.osmun.com Brass and woodwind instruments; accessories.

Rayburn Musical Instrument Company www.rayburn.com Brass, woodwind, and string instruments; new and used; accessories.

Recorder Music Publishers
www.iinet.net.au/~nickl/music.html
Comprehensive directory of publishers and
retailers of music for the recorder.

Recorder Teacher www.theshops.co.uk/childsplay
Software program for learning to write and read
music and to play the recorder; Windows.

Rico International www.ricoreeds.com Reeds;
mouthpieces.

Secondwind www.secondwind.co.uk New and used
brass and woodwind instruments.

Selmer www.selmer.com Saxophone makers.

Sheet Music for Baritone Horn
www.trombonepuppy.com/cat68.html List of
items in the category.

Sheet Music for Baritone Saxophone
www.saxpuppy.com/cat46.html or
www.saxspot.com/cat46.htm List of items in the
category.

Sheet Music for Bassoon
www.bassoonspot.com/cat28.htm List of items
in the category.

Sheet Music for Soprano Saxophone
www.saxpuppy.com/cat71.html or
www.saxspot.com/cat71.htm List of items in the
category.

Sheet Music for Tenor Saxophone
www.saxpuppy.com/cat43.html or
www.saxspot.com/cat43.htm List of items in the
category.

Sheet Music for Tuba
www.trombonepuppy.com/cat61.html or
www.trombonespot.com/cat61.htm List of items
in the category.

Softwind Instruments www.softwind.com
Synthophone MIDI Sax.

Sonic Implants
www.sonicimplants.com/Products/brasswoodwin
d.htm Brass and woodwind implants.

SR Mouthpieces www.srtechnologies.com SR
Technologies; SR Mouthpieces.

Tap Music Sales www.tapmusic.com Woodwind and
brass instrument recordings on compact disks,
tapes, records, and videocassettes; imported and
artist produced; publishes sheet music.

The American Music Center
www.amc.net/resources/library/subsearch/b.html
Scores for brass and woodwind instruments.

The Bandstand Ltd. www.bandstand.ab.ca Wind
instrument specialists.

The Bate Collection of Musical Instruments
www.ashmol.ox.ac.uk/bat/visinf.html Collection
of historical woodwind, brass, and percussion
instruments.

The Brass and Woodwind Shop
brassandwoodwind.ca/repairs.html Canadian
dealership.

The Clarinet Pages www.woodwind.org/clarinet/
Clarinet pedagogy; equipment; hints; tips and
techniques.

The Horn Guy www.hornguy.com Band instruments;
trumpet; trombone; flute; clarinet; saxophone;
sales and repair.

The L.A. Sax Co. www.lasax.com Saxophones;
horns.

The Music House www.musichouse.com Band and
orchestra rental program.

The Woodwind and the Brasswind www.wwbw.com
Music store; large selection of musical
instruments and accessories.

Trombone USA www.trombone-usa.com Over 4,000
trombonists listed; links.

Verne Q. Powell Flutes Inc. www.powellflutes.com
Handmade metal flutes; handmade wooden flutes
and piccolos; clarinet reeds; alto sax reeds; tenor
saxophone reeds; pads.

Westwind Brass www.westwindbrass.org San Diego-
based brass quintet; performances; recordings;
concert calendar; education.

Wind Player www.windplayer.com Webzine.

Wind Shop www.angelfire.com/biz/thewindshop/
Repair services.

Windband www.windband.co.uk Specialists in
woodwind, brass, folk, and early musical
instruments, including bagpipes, banjos,
bassoons, clarinets, concertinas, flutes, folk
instruments, mandolins, and saxophones.

Windcraft Limited & Dawkes Music Limited
www.windcraft.co.uk or www.dawkes.co.uk
Woodwind and brass instruments; accessories;
mouthpieces; spares; repair materials and tools.

Woodsy's Brass, Woodwind, and String Instruments
www.woodsys.com/winds.htm Band and
orchestra department.

*Woodwind, Brass, and Percussion Instruments of the
Orchestra*
www.music.indiana.edu/~l631/skei.html William
and Gayle Cook Music Library, Indiana
University School of Music; bibliographic guide.

Zachary Music www.zacharymusic.com Clarinet,
trumpet, trombone, flute, and saxophone.

Children's Music

A to Z Kids Stuff www.atozkidsstuff.com Name That
Tune; link to the American Symphony Orchestra
League; instruments; lesson plans and games.

America's Story—Children's Songs
www.americaslibrary.gov/cgi-
bin/page.cgi/sh/kidsongs History and stories
about children's songs.

Babyuniversity.com www.babyuniversity.com
Songs and more; All About Baby; Family Fun;
Home Life; Holidays; Just for Laughs.

Best Children's Music.com
www.bestchildrensmusic.com Children's music for parents and teachers.

Buck Howdy www.buckhowdy.com Cowboy songs for kids; activities; store.

Burl Ives www.burlives.com Classic American balladeer; songs for children; gospel; holidays.

Children's Music www.childrensmusic.co.uk UK-based Web site for children's music.

Children's Music Network www.cmnonline.org Music for children; information; resources; links.

Children's Music Web www.childrensmusic.org Nonprofit organization dedicated to music for kids; resources; information; links; guide to children's music online; children's concert calendar; database of musicians; children's radio list; RealAudio children's music programming; music education.

Children's Music Workshop
www.childrensmusicworkshop.com Instrumental music instruction to public and private schools throughout the greater Los Angeles area.

Children's Television Workshop www.ctw.org Children's educational programming; includes *Sesame Street*; games; stories; art; music.

Coloring.com www.coloring.com Coloring pages online.

Creating Music www.creatingmusic.com By Morton Sobotnick; online creative music environment for children of all ages; place for kids to compose music, play with musical performance; music games and music puzzles.

Creating Music www.creatingmusic.com Elementary-age students enjoy exploring and creating music; Morton Subotnik.

Daniel's French Children's Music
www.abcdaniel.com Children's songs performed in French and English.

Data Dragon www.datadragon.com Learn about and listen to different instruments; reading music; musical genres; links.

Disney www.disney.com All things Disney; music; graphics.

Disney Interactive www.disneyinteractive.com Disney multimedia products.

Dr. Toy www.drtoy.com Guide to children's products; links; awards.

Four Fish Fly Free www.4fishkids.com Videos for children five to ten.

Free Children's Music by David Jack
www.davidjack.com Kid's singing star David Jack; free MP3s, audio samples.

Go-Go-Diggity www.go-go-diggity.com Music and books for children ages zero to six.

Hasbro Interactive www.hasbrointeractive.com Children's music instructional media.

Horace Hopper's Musical Adventures
preschoolmusic.com Teaches the preschooler how to play twenty-three simple songs and phrases on the keyboard.

Hunk-ta-Bunk-ta Music www.hunktabunkta.com Music for children by platinum-selling and award-winning singer/songwriter Katherine Dines; CDs; songbooks; performances; workshops.

Ideas That Play www.ideasthatplay.com Children's music instructional media.

In the Land of Staff www.landofstaff.com Children's book series that teaches music theory with a new method employing audiovisual concepts with CDs; for primary grades.

International Kids' Space www.kids-space.org Purpose is to make a difference in the future educational use of the Internet, in learning and motivation, and in understanding people and ourselves; On Air Concert.

JazzKids Music Program www.jazzkids.com Useful information about jazz.

Judy and David judyanddavid.com/cma.html Online songbook of children's songs.

KIDiddles Mojo's Musical Museum: Complete Song List www.kididdles.com/mouseum/allsongs.html Lyrics to hundreds of children's songs and lullabies; stories; games; contests; search for a song by title.

Kid's Domain Children's Music Software Reviews www.kidsdomain.com/review/kdr/_music-index.html Product reviews and information.

Kids Camps www.kidscamps.com Directory of camps.

Kids Domain www.kidsdomain.com Informative children's Web site including a variety of activities; product reviews.

Kids Entertainment www.kidsentertainment.com Children's entertainment; music; links.

Kids Games www.kidsgames.org Games for first-through twelfth-graders; links.

Kids Games and More www.1st-in-kids.com/kids-music.html Children's music, past and present.

KidsCom www.kidscom.com Creative Web site for kids.

Kids-Space.org www.kids-space.org Performances and compositions by and for kids from all over the world.

Kidtunes www.pianopress.com/kidtunes.htm Thirty songs by various children's performing artists; accompanying songbook and activity guide.

Kindermusk www.kindermusik.com Early childhood music instruction.

Knowledge Adventure
www.knowledgeadventure.com Children's music instructional software.

Kool Songs www.koolsongs.com Personalized children's songs.

Laura's MIDI Heaven www.laurasmidiheaven.com/Kidsshtml MIDI files of many children's songs.

Lego www.lego.com/eng/interactive Children's music instructional media.

Lori Diefenbacher Music for Children www.diefenbacher.com/lori Music for children's education in nature, intercultural, and early childhood; lesson plans.

Makin' Music Rockin' Rhythms www.makin-music.com Nationally acclaimed children's music on tape and CDs.

Mama Lisa's World www.mamalisa.com/world/ Children's songs and rhymes of all nations.

Mattel www.mattel.com Children's music instructional media.

MIDI Page of Children's Songs www.punkyschildcare.com/musicmidi_page.html MIDI file of many children's songs.

MIDIsaurus Software www.Town4kids.com/us_ecom

Mister Rogers' Neighborhood www.pbs.org/rogers Online version of the TV series; popular children's program.

Music for Young Children www.myc.com Music education program for children.

Music Together www.musictogether.com Early childhood music workshops.

Music4KidsOnline www.music4kidsonline.com Everything musical for children.

Musik Garten www.musikgarten.org Early childhood music education workshops.

NIEHS Kids' Pages www.niehs.nih.gov/kids/musicchild.htm or www.niehs.nih.gov/kids/music.htm MIDI files and lyrics to children's songs.

NNCC Music and Movement Activities www.nncc.org/Curriculum/cc21_music.movement.html Music and rhythm activities for children.

Nursery Rhymes www-personal.umich.edu/~pfa/dreamhouse/nursery/rhymes/ Alphabetical listing of nursery rhymes.

Nursery Songs www.nursery-songs.com/songs_and_engravings.htm Lyrics and pictures to many nursery songs.

PBS Jazz Kids www.pbs.org/jazz/kids/ Children's jazz Web site.

PBS Kids Web Site pbskids.org Links to many children's television programs.

Play and Teach www.playandteach.com Fun and educational materials for children.

Play Music www.playmusic.org Introduces kids aged seven to eleven to the instruments of the orchestra using games, animations, audio, and more.

Preschooleducation.com www.preschooleducation.com/song.shtml Music and songs.

Radio Disney www.radiodisney.com Children's instructional software, DVDs, videos.

Raffi www.raffinews.com Well-known children's recording artist.

San Francisco Symphony Kids Site www.sfskids.org Instruments of the orchestra; music lab; family and children's concerts.

San Jose Children's Musical Theater Online www.sjcmt.com Musical theater that's young at heart.

Screen It! www.screenit.com Source of entertainment reviews for parents.

Songs for Scouts www.macscouter.com/Songs/index.html Includes some good old campfire songs, silly songs, and chants and songs for leaders.

Strike a Chord www.strikeachord.com Dynamic, interactive, character building music program for elementary students produced and presented by Karl and Jeanne Anthony.

The Children's Group www.childrensgroup.com/bindex_ie.html Award-winning classical music for children, including *Classical Kids, Song of the Unicorn, The Mozart Effect Music for Babies, The Mozart Effect Music for Children.*

The New York Philharmonic Kidzone www.nyphilkids.org Musician's Lounge; Composers Gallery; Composers Workshop.

The Teacher's Guide to Children's Songs www.theteachersguide.com/ChildrensSongs.htm Lyrics and MIDI files to children's songs.

Town4Kids www.town4kids.com MIDIsaurus music education software for children.

Toys to Grow On www.ttgo.com Musical instruments for kids.

Twin Sisters Productions Inc. www.twinsisters.com/about/powermusic.asp Educational products for children.

Yahooligans www.yahooligans.com Web guide for kids; music links and more.

Young Composers www.youngcomposers.com Web site for publishing musical compositions of kids, teens, and young adults.

Classical Music and Composers

All Classical Guide www.allclassical.com Explore classical music; search by composer/performer, work title/keyword, or album title; top composers listed by period and genre.

American Composers Forum www.composersforum.org Arts service organization which provides grants, fellowships, recordings, and other services for composers of contemporary music; national programs; regional chapters.

Arsis Press: Music by Women Composers www.instantWeb.com~arsis Publisher of concert and sacred music by women composers; music for chorus, solo voice, keyboards, and chamber ensembles.

Artek Recordings—Classical www.artekrecordings.com Range of classical music that spans traditional and well-known repertoire and rarely heard masterpieces from little-known composers.

BBC Music Magazine www.bbcmusicmagazine.com Classical music reviews; reviews by subject; search by composer; search by type of music: orchestral, opera, choral and song, chamber instrumental.

Cadenza www.cadenza.org Resources and information for classical and contemporary music and musicians; program note library; musicians; concerts; glossary; MIDI diary.

Central Links Resource for Research on Composers www.lib.duke.edu/music/resources/classical_inde x.html Information on classical composers; composer home pages; chronologies and necrologies; national and regionally oriented pages; organizations and centers for scholarly research; electronic journals and newsletters; genre-specific pages; databases.

Clásica www.clasica.com Online guide to classical music performance and recordings; news; reviews; links to classical music-related sites.

Classical Archives www.classicalarchives.com Thousands of classical music files to listen to or download; over 1,500 works arranged alphabetically by composer; public domain files.

Classical Composer Home Pages www.skdesigns.com/internet/music/composer.ht m Links to information on composers.

Classical Composers Database www.classical-composers.org/cgi-bin/ccd.cgi?comp=_phome Ever-growing list of composers; over 2,000 entries; links and contributions accepted.

Classical Is Cool www.classicaliscool.com Classical music information and fun; list of classical music radio stations, program listings, concert schedules, MP3 files, and more.

Classical Link www.classicallink.com CD reviews; features; composers; subscriptions; LudwigRadio; LudwigVanWeb.com.

Classical Music www.classical-music.net Over 2,100 recordings from Baroque to Contemporary.

Classical Music Hall of Fame www.americanclassicalmusic.org Dedicated to honoring and celebrating the many facets of classical music in the United States; seeks to recognize those who have made significant contributions to classical music.

Classical Music History Timelines on the Web . . . The History Beat www.search-beat.com/composer.htm Classical music history time lines; composer history resources.

Classical Music Online www.scapecast.com/onworld/CMO Online resource dedicated exclusively to classical music.

Classical Music Pages w3.rz-berlin.mpg.de/cmp/classmus.html Variety of information on music in the Western culture.

Classical Music UK www.classicalmusic.co.uk Links, videos, CDs, concerts, and jobs; guide to classical music Web sites in the UK.

Classical Music Web Ring www.orchestranet.co.uk/ring.html Chain of classical music Web sites; add site to the largest classical music Web ring on the Internet.

Classical Musical MIDI Page www.classicalmidi.gothere.uk.com/page20.htm Classical pieces to download; accompaniments.

Classical Net www.classical.net/music Features more than 2,500 CD reviews; 5,800 files; over 4,000 links to other classical music Web sites.

Classical Piano MIDI Page www.piano-midi.de/ Composers of classical piano music; MP3s.

Classical Search www.classicalsearch.com Classical music search engine.

ClassicalUSA.com classicalusa.com Resources; search; reviews; links.

ClassicWeb www.classicWeb.com Classical links.

Directories at Classical Music UK www.classicalmusic.co.uk Concerts; videos; CDs; jobs; site reviews and links.

Early Music FAQ www.medieval.org/emfaq/misc/ Early music links and resources; recordings; concerts; performers.

Early Music News www.earlymusic.org.uk Event listings, concerts, and festivals for Baroque, choral, Renaissance, and early music; promotes the understanding and enjoyment of early music and historically informed performance.

Early Music on the Web . . . The Classical Music Beat www.search-beat.com/earlymusic.htm Classical music history Internet links; time lines; composer history resources on the Web.

Early Women Composers/Artists/Poetry music.acu.edu/www/iawm/pages Annotated CD discography of music by women composers born before 1760 with bibliographic sources; MIDI files; notes on music publishers; illustrated by historical women artists.

Essentials of Music www.essentialsofmusic.com Music facts and information; from Sony Classical and W. W. Norton; basic information eras; terms; composers; audio examples.

Global Music Network www.gmn.com Classical music; downloads; streaming audio.

Gramophone www.gramophone.co.uk UK classical music Web site and magazine.

Impulse Classical Music Website www.impulse-music.co.uk Pages on contemporary classical composers and performers; photographs; biographies; reviews; downloadable musical tracks.

International Alliance for Women in Music (IAWM) music.acu.edu/www/iawm/home.html A community archive for women composers and women in music topics.

LudwiVanWeb.com Links Page www.ludwigvanweb.com/navigation/1,1270,3-1,00.html Comprehensive variety of classical music links.

Meet the Composer www.meetthecomposer.org Information on composers.

MIDIWorld.com Classical midiworld.com/classic.htm Classical music MIDI files listed by composer.

MIDIWorld.com Composers midiworld.com/composers.htm Alphabetical listing of links to composer information and MIDI files.

Music Resources on the Internet www.skdesigns.com/internet/music Free music graphics; links to regional symphony orchestras and music organizations.

Musical Online-Classical Music Directory www.musicalonline.com Classical music directory; music education; music instruction; virtual concert hall; online music directory listing service and Web page design source for artists, musicians, and performers; resource for locating professional musicians and companies; listings of opera singers and instrumentalists as well as composers and conductors; opera companies and orchestras are indexed.

Naxos: Composers Biographies and Their Works www.naxos.com/qcomp.htm Links to information on composers and their works in alphabetical order; classical music record label.

NPR Performance Today www.npr.org/programs/pt/ Features; stations.

OrchestraNET www.orchestranet.co.uk UK classical music Web site; Internet orchestra guide.

REC Music Foundation www.recmusic.org Promotes new classical music composers, primarily through the development of new computer tools.

Society of Composers, Inc. www.societyofcomposers.org Home page; members; performers; recordings.

Sony Classical www.sonyclassical.com Artists and new releases; sound clips; tour schedules; upcoming releases.

Symphony Orchestra Schedules www.hoptechno.com/symphony.htm Links to major symphony orchestra home pages.

The Classical Music Department of the WWW Virtual Library www.gprep.org/classical/ Links to classical music information.

The Classical Music Navigator www.wku.edu/~smithch/music/index2.htm Basic library of notable works; geographical roster; index of forms and styles of music.

The J. S. Bach Home Page www.jsbach.org Extensive biography; tour of Bach's life in Germany; catalog of complete works; bibliography; recommended recordings; other Bach resources on the Web; Bach discussion list.

Ubisoft www.ubi.com/US Computer games.

Vox Music Group www.voxcd.com Catalog of classical compact disks and recordings.

Worldwide Internet Music Resources www.music.indiana.edu/music_resources/outline.html William and Gayle Cook Music Library Indiana University School of Music; links to information on many music topics.

Yahoo Classical Music Artists dir.yahoo.com/Entertainment/music/artists/by_genre/classical/ By instrument; composers; conductors; ensembles; opera; orchestras; vocal.

Yahoo Classical Music Index dir.yahoo.com/Entertainment/music/genres/classical/ Links to a variety of classical music sites.

Young Concert Artists, Inc. www.yca.org Home page; roster of artists; concerts.

Computer and Electronic Music—MIDI—Software

AABACA www.aabaca.com Digital pianos, keyboards, software, and sound solutions; distributor; educational bundles; workshops.

Aardvark www.aardvarkaudio.com *Direct Pro* integrated recording system; hardware and software; support; suppliers.

ABC2Win abc2win.com Integrated shareware music notation program; supports writing and editing of tunes, file management, and playback; view tunes as publication-quality music; registration enables printing.

Acon Digital Media Acoustica www.aconas.de/english/index.html Audio editor for Windows 9x/NT.

Adaptec www.adaptec.com Adaptec has teamed with Sonic Solutions to deliver two new software products—*MyDVD Video Suite* and *MyDVD Media Suite*. *MyDVD Media Suite* enables users to create CDs and DVDs containing music, movies, and multimedia; *MyDVD Video*

Suite makes it simple to record and share videos on CD or DVD.

Adobe Audition www.adobe.com New version of Cool Edit Pro.

Akai www.akai.com Consumer electronics; founded in 1929 in Tokyo, Japan; quality home entertainment products specializing in the audio and video arenas.

AKG Acoustics www.akg.com Microphones; headphones; sound processing equipment; mixers; news; distributors; links.

AKoff Sound Labs www.akoff.com *Music Composer* is music recognition software which performs Wave to MIDI conversion; recognizes polyphonic music from microphone (other Wave input or file) and converts it into MIDI sequences.

Alesis www.alesis.com ADAT and recorders; performance FX tools; power amplifiers; studio mixers; electronic drums; signal processors; synthesizers; studio monitors; new products.

Alesis Semiconductor Inc. www.alesis-semi.com Alesis Semiconductor products.

Algorithmix www.algorithmix.com *Sound Laundry* and *Easy Tools* software for cleaning and mastering old recordings; download demos; *AlgoRec* is an add-on program to all CD recording programs.

A M G www.amguk.co.uk Longest established producer of sample CDs in the UK; preview studio; downloads.

Analog Modular Systems, Inc. www.analogsynths.com Supplier of vintage analog instruments; synthesizer service and restoration.

Analog Samples www.analogsamples.com Samples online.

Antares www.antarestech.com Digital signal processing software; *Auto-Tune* automatic and graphical intonation correction for voices and solo instruments; *Infinity* sample looping program for Macintosh; *Multiband Dynamics Tool* five-band dynamics controller; *JVP Voice Processor* de-esser, compressor, three-band EQ and Delay FX processor for vocals; *Tube* analog tube modeling plug-in; *Kantos* audio-controlled synthesizer; *Antares Microphone Modeler*; details of software; demos to download; technical support; news; links.

Antex Electronics www.antex.com Digital audio products; *Media Director*; audio for digital broadcast; satellite receivers.

Anvil Studio www.anvilstudio.com Windows freeware program to multitrack record, compose, and edit with audio and MIDI.

Aphex www.aphex.com Microphone preamplifiers; aural exciters; dynamics processors; effects pedals; modular products; audio interfaces.

Apogee Electronics Corp. www.apogeedigital.com *Master Tools; Session Tools;* developer of digital audio software and hardware; product information; download manuals; updates; news.

Apple Computer Inc. www.apple.com News; hardware; software; Made4Mac; education; pro; support; where to buy; iTunes Music Store.

Applied Acoustics www.applied-acoustics.com *Lounge Lizard EP-2 Electric Piano.*

Applied Research and Technology www.artroch.com Pre-amps; compressors; equalizers.

Arboretum Systems Inc. www.arboretum.com Developer of digital audio software for Macintosh and PC; access and download manuals; new products; download demos and plug-ins; newsgroup; *Hyperprism; Ray Gun; Ionizer; Restoration-NR; Harmony; Realizer Pro.*

Arturia www.arturia.com *Moog Modular V; Storm;* virtual home studio for music composition, both modular and real time; virtual instruments, sequencers, synthesizers, and effects; French.

ASM Audio www.voyce.com/asm/index.html Program for mixing together several tracks of digital audio in real time; 32-bit Windows application; requires Windows 95 or NT; uses Microsoft's DirectX sound engine—DirectSound.

Association of Shareware Professionals www.asp-shareware.org Trade organization for independent software developers and vendors.

Audible Magic www.audiblemagic.com Provides innovative technology, applications, and information services to traditional and digital media industries.

Audio Compositor home.att.net/~audiocompositor MIDI-to-WAV file renderer suitable for professional applications; multitimbral real time software wavetable synth; sophisticated patch editor which understands SoundFonts, DLS and KRZ files, and its own instrument bank format; file converter for all types listed; librarian for sample collection in .WAV format.

Audio Ease www.audioease.com Macintosh audio software; *Altiverb; Barbabatch; VST Wrapper V3; the Nautilus Bundle; Rocket Science Bundle; Peter Pan; Audio Ease Freeware.*

Audioactive Player www.audioactive.com MP3 player and encoder software.

Audix www.audixusa.com Vocal microphones; professional instrument microphones.

AuReality midiworld.com/AuReality/index.htm *Building Blocks; QE and QE; Kai'cku; AIM (Automated Instrumental Musician); Reaktor Library.*

BBE Sound www.bbesound.com *Sonic Maximizer* plug-in; bass pre-amp.

BeOS www.lebuzz.com Started in February of 1999 to cover the Be Operating System as a platform on which to do professional audio work; reports news on a daily basis, covering every nuance of BeOS audio.

Bias Inc. (Berkley Integrated Audio Software Inc.) www.bias-inc.com Macintosh digital audio software; *Peak VST, Peak TDM, Peak LE, Peak DV, Deck, Freq, SuperFreq, SoundSoap, Vbox,* and *Vbox SE;* product information; news; updates; downloads.

Big Fish Audio www.bigfishaudio.com Large selection of sample CDs; sample libraries.

BitHeadz www.bitheadz.com Software synthesizers; primary applications; Unity-based sound modules; loop-based content; updates; manuals; miscellaneous; FAQs; subscribe to user's group; e-mail tech support; updates; hardware compatibility; shop online; upgrade form.

Bomb Factory www.bombfactory.com BF Essentials; Classic Compressors LA-2A and 1176; Classic Compressors LA-3A; Fairchild 660; JOEMEEK; moogerfooger Analog Effects; Pultec EQP-1A; SansAmp PSA-1; Tel-Ray Variable Delay; Voce Spin and Chorus/Vibrato.

Bose www.bose.com Speaker manufacturer; sound technologies; product information; sound reproduction; car audio systems; new developments.

Byte www.byte.com Online magazine about hardware and computer technology.

Cakewalk www.cakewalk.com *Cakewalk* digital audio recording and sequencing software and related products; plug-ins; Windows.

Capella Music Software www.metatone.com.au/ Score entry, note processing, and publishing; MIDI sequencing; scanning of sheet music for arrangement using Capella2002; tutorial software; create playlists of scores or extractions onto CD.

Celemony Software www.celemony.com *Melodyne;* news; support.

Cinram www.cinram.com Media duplicator; design templates.

Circuit City www.circuitcity.com Electronics retailer.

Clavia www.clavia.com Digital musical instruments; Nord Lead Synthesizer; Nord Rack; Nord Modular; ddrum4; Nord Electro; downloads; brochures; manuals; press; awards; history; FAQs.

CLEARVUE/eav Inc. www.clearvue.com Maker and distributor of educational music software products; CD-ROMS; DVDs.

CNET news.com.com Technology news Web site.

CNet Shareware.Com shareware.cnet.com Source of shareware for all computer platforms; not music specific.

CNMAT Home Page Center www.cnmat.berkeley.edu Center for New Music and Audio Technologies; at the University of California, Berkeley; showcases creative interaction between music and technology.

Computer Music Journal www.mitpress.mit.edu/catalog/item/default.asp?s id=8C4B13AA-2B39-4983-ABD9-568392D0C71A&ttype=4&tid=15 Quarterly journal; topics relating to digital audio signal processing and electro-acoustic music; software and hardware; aesthetics of contemporary music.

Computers and Music www.computersandmusic.com Retailer of audio hardware and software.

Creamware www.creamware.de/en/Home/gate.asp Products; Overview; Noah; SCOPE Fusion Platform; Additional Software; Additional Hardware; AD/DA Converters; CLAN; Broadcasting Systems; Volkszämpler.

Creative www.americas.creative.com *Sound Blaster;* MP3 players; speaker systems; music and PC keyboards and more.

Creative Synth www.creativesynth.com Reviews; technical tips.

Crescit Software Incorporated www.crescit.com Software tools for lighting for professional and educational needs; film and studio software; pro audio and sound effects software.

Crown International www.crownaudio.com Amplifiers; microphones.

CrusherX-Live www.crusher-x.de Vapor algorithm enables creating very complex waves; can be used as a synthesizer or as a versatile effect unit; creates unusual sounds with oscillators, WAV files, and real-time inputs.

Cybercorder skyhawktech.com Provides VCR-like recording for radio shows or any audio input.

Cycling '74 www.cycling74.com *Pluggo; Radial; Max/MSP; Jitter; M;* record label.

Dart www.dartpro.com Digital audio restoration technology.

Datasonics www.datasonics.com.au *Music Master; Mastering Music; VS Pro.*

Dbx www.dbxpro.com Signal processing; equalizers; pre-amps; online resources.

Deepsound Sample Calculators deepsound.net/calculation.html Sample calculators to help sampler users deal with time-stretching, pitch-shifting, delay times, etc.

Denon www.denon.com Speakers and car stereo systems; home audio CD and DVD players; pro audio products; news; links; FAQs; dealers.

Depopper www.droidinfo.comsoftware/depopper Software to get near CD quality from vinyl disks; minimizes clicks, scratches, and noise without removing treble sounds.

Digidesign www.digidesign.com Developer of *Pro Tools* direct-to-disk recording system, workstation, software, and plug-ins; product information; news; support; Macintosh; Windows.

Digigram www.digigram.com Digital audio solutions for public address and pro sound installations, and broadcast and media production companies worldwide; innovative networked audio devices, computer sound cards, and audio management software.

Digital Ear www.digital-ear.com/digital-ear/index.html Makers of audio to MIDI conversion software.

Digital Music Corp. www.voodoolab.com *Voodoo Lab Pedal Effects* for electric guitar; *Ground Control System.*

Digitech www.digitech.com Guitar and studio effects; resources; artist pages; sound community; FAQs.

Discogs www.discogs.com Database of electronic music;14,583 labels;153,950 releases;100,813 artists;100% user-built.

Discovery www.discoveryfirm.com Sample CDs and CD-ROMs.

Dissidents www.dissidents.com Develops software for audio, music, and multimedia applications for Windows and Amiga computers.

DJ-Media www.dj-media.com Audio and video resource; links.

Dod www.dod.com Products; manuals; FX pedals; multieffects; signal processors; graphic equalizers; effects processors; press; outlet stores; FAQs.

Dolby Laboratories www.dolby.com Develops audio signal processing systems; manufactures professional equipment to implement technologies in the motion picture, broadcasting, and music recording industries; invented noise reduction; site includes new information, press releases, Dolby news, statistics, cassettes, technical information, movies and cinema, home theatre, multimedia, cinema products, professional products, literature, Dolby digital, DVD, company information, people, career opportunities, and trademark information.

Download.com www.download.com Freeware; shareware.

Drawmer Dynamics TDM www.drawmer.com Dynamic signal processing.

Drum Tools www.musiclab.com Plug-ins.

DVCPRO Errorchecker www.errorchecker.de Software tool to report the OnTape error rate of DVCPRO and DV tapes.

East West Sounds www.soundsonline.com Sample sounds superstore; search by category or format; downloads.

Easy Mix perso.wanadoo.fr/easymix/info1.htm For mixing with a turntable.

Eccentric www.eccentricsoftware.com *A Zillion Kajillion Rhymes and Cliches.*

Echo Corp. www.echoaudio.com Products; sales; support; downloads.

Edirol www.edirol.com Desktop media production tools.

Ego Systems Inc. www.esi-pro.com Audio, MIDI, studio equipment.

Electronic Arts Research autoinfo.smartlink.net/ray GSMP or Genetic Spectrum Modeling Program; Fractal Melody Generator; MIDI files and Wave files; download software.

Electronic Music Foundation (EMF) www.emf.org Materials and information for understanding the history and development of music technology; links.

Electronic Musical Instruments 1870-1990 www.obsolete.com/120_years Vintage electronic music instruments; links.

Electronic Scene www.electronicscene.com Electronic music network.

Electronisounds.com www.Electronisounds.com Loops and samples.

Emagic www.emagic.de *Logic* sequencer and *Logic Audio* hard disk recording software for Macintosh and PC; *SoundDiver* librarian/editing program; technical support; instruments; studio tools; hardware; sounds; education.

Emu Systems www.emu.com Samplers; sound modules; command stations; keyboards; digital audio; support; *Ensoniq.*

Etcetera www.etcetera.co.uk UK source for computer music products.

European Imaging and Sound Association www.eisa-awards.org/home.htm European editorial multimedia organization; annual EISA awards.

EveryMac www.everymac.com Complete guide to every Macintosh, Mac Compatible, and upgrade card in the world; technical, configuration, and pricing details.

Evolution Electronics www.evolution.co.uk/ Ekeys; keyboards; controllers; software; products; distributors; downloads; support; evolution.

Fostex www.fostex.com Hard disk recording systems; multitrack recorders; digital effects; product information; FAQ and Tips; distributors; partners.

Free On-Line Dictionary of Computing wombat.doc.ic.ac.uk/foldoc/index.html Dictionary of computer terms.

Frontier Design Group www.frontierdesign.com
Dakota; Wave Center PCI; Tango 24; Montana;
Sierra.

Fruityloops www.fruityloops.net Loop creating tool;
started as a drumloop creator; evolved into a
complete loop and song creating package; can
hold an unlimited number of samples and
channels; play stand-alone or by triggering MIDI
equipment.

Gallery Software www.demon.co.uk/gallery
Digidesign software partner; hardware utilities;
accessories for Digidesign products; information;
software updates and demo versions.

Global Music www.globalmusic.com Mobile Vision
Sound; content library; songs, ringtones, games,
and video for mobile phones and handheld
devices.

Glowing Coast Technology
www.glowingcoast.co.uk/index.htm *Audio
Suite*; multitrack digital audio workstation;
integrated group of audio waveform editing tools.

Glyph Technologies Inc.
www.glyphtech.com/site/home_intro.html
Founded in 1993 to be a bridge between the A/V
production industry and the computer storage
industry; dominant provider of data storage
solutions to the United States and European
digital audio recording and post production
industries.

GoldWave www.goldwave.com Digital audio editor
for Windows; Multiple Document Interface for
editing dozens of files in one session; large file
editing, up to 1 GB in size; configurable RAM;
real-time oscilloscopes.

Greytsounds www.greytsounds.com CD-ROMs,
floppy disks, synth patches, and audio CDs;
electronic delivery for some synth patches with
Internet orders; over 2,000 Sampling and MI
products for over 70 different keyboards.

Groove Maker www.groovemaker.com
Groovemaker; Loops.

Groovestyle www.groovestyle.com Sound banks for
soundcards and Yamaha samplers; Madplayer.

Guillemot www.guillemot.com Sound cards;
speakers; support; links.

Hands-on-MIDI www.hands-on-midi.com MIDI and
MIDI Karaoke files; MP3 backing tracks; band
arrangements; digital sheet music.

Hinton Instrument Links
www.hinton.demon.co.uk/#links Design and
manufacture equipment for use in professional
automation applications in the recording, film,
broadcast, and entertainment industries.

Hitsquad.com Software Titles
www.hitsquad.com/smm/alphabetic/a/ or
www.hitsquad.comsmm/ Large list of music
software titles listed alphabetically; links to

information, system requirements, and
downloads; freeware; shareware; commercial
titles.

Hobbes Internet Timeline
www.zakon.org/robert/internet/timeline/ Trace
the history of the Internet.

Hopkins Technology
www.hoptechno.comclassic.htm *Classical Notes*
CD-ROM.

Hosa Technology Inc. www.hosatech.com Cables and
adapters.

Howling Dog Systems www.howlingdog.com Guitar-
oriented MIDI software; *Power Chords*.

Hudson Music www.hudsonmusic.com Music
instructional DVDs.

Hyperreal Music Machines
www.hyperreal.org/music/machines/ General
music; MIDI and equipment sites; manufacturer
sites; publications; retailers; dealers.

I/O MUG www.iomug.org Internet Only Macintosh
Users Group; links to Macintosh Web sites,
companies, and software.

ILIO Entertainments www.ilio.com Virtual
instruments, sample CDs, and CD-ROMs;
loops; sounds; software and tools for the modern
musician.

Imaja www.imaja.comlisten/index.html *Listen* ear-
training program.

Impulse Tracker v75.vweb.citenet.net/it/
Downloads; history; FAQ.

IntelliScore www.intelliscore.net Convert MP3 and
WAV files to MIDI; convert music from a CD to
a MIDI file; MIDI-enable any musical
instrument, even voice; helps remove vocals for
karaoke singing.

International Game Developers Network
www.igdn.org Membership; FAQs.

Iomega www.iomega.com Zip drives; data storage;
online storage.

JBL www.jbl.com Speaker manufacturer.

Kable Keepers www.kablekeepers.com *Wrap-All
Straps*.

Key Trax www.keytrax.com Audio library;
musician's community; music portal.

Keyfax Software www.keyfax.com *Twiddly.Bits*
MIDI sample series; *Phat Boy;* demos.

Kid Nepro www.kidnepro.com Developer of sounds
for many instruments; catalog; soundlists; synth
patches; digital samples.

Lexicon www.lexicon.com Digital effects;
multiprocessor effects; MIDI reverberators; power
amps; demos; downloads; upgrades; technical
support.

Lintronics www.lintronics.de Specialist for analog
synthesizers; MIDI interfaces and modification
upgrades; repairs for Moog, ARP, SC, and
others.

LiveUpdate www.liveupdate.com/crescendo.html *Crescendo Max.*

Logic Users www.logicuser.net/group Home of the world wide group.

Looper's Delight annihilist.com/loop/loop.html Information on making and using loops.

Lynx Studio Technology Inc. www.lynxstudio.com Lynx ONE; Lynx TWO; digital audio interfaces.

Mac Music www.macmusic.org/home/?lang=EN&vRmtQjp AznOhM=1 Music on the Macintosh; large set of links; freeware; shareware; downloads; resources.

Macintosh MIDI User's Internet Guide www.aitech.ac.jp/~ckelly/mmuig.html Collection of information and links for the Macintosh musician; updates and new products.

Mackie www.mackie.com Mixers; Desktop Studio Tools; studio monitors; recorders; speakers; amplifiers.

Macromedia www.macromedia.com Studio MX; Flash MX; Dreamweaver MX; ColdFusion MX; Director MX; FreeHand MX; Breeze; Contribute; Central; Fireworks MX; Authorware 7.

Macware macware.erehwon.org/Audio-Midi.html Downloadable shareware and freeware.

Macworld macworld.zdnet.com Information for Macintosh users.

Magix Entertainment Corp. www.magix.net *Magix Music Maker; Artist Pools; MP3 Maker; Audio Video Composer; Magix Music Studio; Sound Pools; Notation; Music Maker Videojam; Magix Dance Maker; Guitar Workshop; PlayR; Live Act.*

Magma www.magma.com PCI Expansion products; products for OEMS.

Making Waves www.makingwavesaudio.co.uk/ Original music production software.

ManyMIDI www.manymidi.com Synthesizer sound libraries.

Mark of the Unicorn www.motu.com Developer of *Performer* and *Digital Performer* sequencer and digital audio recording software; one of the first high-end MIDI sequencers for Macintosh.

Master Bits www.masterbits.com CD-ROMS; sample data.

M-Audio www.m-audio.com Consumer audio; pro-audio and MIDI; software.

Maz Sound Tools www.maz-sound.com Large collection of MOD/S3M/XM/IT tracking software; *Mazzive Injection* sample CDs; free samples in .WAV format; downloads; links; software synthesizers; MP3 players and encoders.

McAfee www.mcafee.com Virus protection software; *VirusScan; Virex.*

MDA-VST www.mda-vst.com Digital audio freeware.

MediaMation Inc. www.mediamat.com Entertainment systems integrator; designs and implements creative solutions for complex interactive shows, rides, exhibits and theaters; software and hardware products.

MetaSynth www.uisoftware.com Synthesis and sound design software; downloads.

MGI Interactive www.midi-classics.com/p4665.htm Interactive guitar instructional software.

Microboards Technology www.microboards.com CD and DVD duplication equipment.

MIDI at Warp Speed www.dinosoft.it/~midistation MIDI Station Sequencer for OS/2.

MIDI Auto-Accompaniment Section ourworld.compuserve.com/homepages/michaelbri ck MAAS auto-accompaniment software; virtual keyboard; song arranger; real time chord recognition; up to sixteen fingered and ten two-finger chord types; MIDI controls.

MIDI Editor perso.magic.fr/llebot MIDI manager; works with any MIDI device; design editor windows; two help files; English and French versions; presets for Alesis, Casio, Emu, Kawai, Korg, Roland, Sequential, Yamaha; information; demo to download.

MIDI Farm www.midifarm.com MIDI and music site; news; audio recording; press releases; free MIDI files; music software; FTP site; connection to MIDI and digital audio sites on the Internet; product updates; demos.

MIDI Hits www.midi-hits.com Large catalog; MIDI, MP3, and Audio CD formats; medleys, current hits, and piano only; pay for downloads.

MIDI Loops www.midiloops.com/copyrite.htm Site licensing MIDI files for use on the Internet; information about copyright and MIDI music; use of MIDI music under copyright; permission to use files, MIDI files, and shareware.

MIDI Manufacturers Association (MMA) www.midi.org Source for information on MIDI technology; up to date MIDI specifications; issues unique manufacturer IDs; licenses logos that identify MMA standards.

MIDI Mark www.midimark.com Sounds and samples.

MIDI Quest www.squest.com CD-ROM; editor/librarian.

MIDI Solutions www.midisolutions.com Pedal Controller; MIDI-powered products.

MIDI Workshop www.midiworkshop.com Music technology workshops and information; information about music software.

MIDI World midiworld.com Collection of MIDI and music-related information; basics; synthesizers; software; sounds; links; files; lab; marketplace; PC and Macintosh; downloads; archive of MIDI files; links to music software and hardware companies.

MidiMan www.midiman.net M-Audio; manufacturer of MIDI interfaces for Macintosh and PC; digital and audio patch-bays; digital-to-analog converters; synchronizers; line mixers; MIDI accessories; product information; FAQs; drivers and utilities to download.

MidiNotate by Notation Software, Inc. www.notation.com/midinotate.htm Converts MIDI files to printable sheet music; can be viewed on screen while highlighted notes play.

MIDI-OX MidiOx.com MIDI utility; free downloads.

MidiSoft www.midisoft.com/idd/DesktopDefault.aspx?tabindex=0&tabid=1 Music creational and educational software.

MidiSyn planeta.clix.pt/acesteves/MidiSyn/MSynMain.htm MIDI to WAVE file converter.

Millennium Music Software www.millennium-music.biz/home/?res=800&actualres=800&ref= Online UK retailer of audio technology.

MiniDisc.org www.MiniDisc.org Community portal.

Minimusic www.minimusic.com/index.html Music software and hardware for Palm.

Mining Company MIDI Music midimusic.miningco.com/index.htm MIDI basics; where to find online.

Minnetonka Audio Software www.minnetonkaaudio.com Surround Sound authoring tools.

Mixman www.mixman.com *Mixman Studio;* demos; support.

Monolith Media www.monomedia.com Audio and video system design; proposal generation software package.

Moog Music www.moogmusic.com Robert Moog is one of the original synthesizer developers; information on current products, including the Minimoog and modular synths; archive of older, classic instruments; products; support; dealers.

MOTU-MAC Mailing List www.unicornation.com Mailing list for users.

Muon www.muon-software.com Audio software.

Music Data Management. Software www.winband.com WinBand; WinChoir; WinEnsemble.

Music Loops www.MusicLoops.com Royalty-free music loops and sound effects.

Music Software at Harmony-Central www.harmony-central.com/Software Online listing of music software products by platform; downloads.

Musicator www.musicator.com PC software program; complete musical workstation for notation, sequencing, and audio recording.

MusicTech.com www.musictech.com College for music technology.

Musitek www.musitek.com *SmartScore* for Windows and Macintosh; fully integrated music scoring, MIDI sequencing, and music scanning with advanced recognition technology; for copying music, composing, or importing MIDI.

Muzical Wizard www.mclink.it/personal/MC3796/ Free download.

Native Instruments www.native-instruments.com *Reaktor; Vokator;* products; synth line; sampling line; effects line; DJ line; Pro Tools edition; sound line; support; community.

Navigator Systems www.hiretrack.com Developer of software for use by entertainment industry equipment rental companies.

Neato www.neato.com Media labeling products; CD labels, jewel case inserts, DAT tape J-cards and labels, audiocassette J-cards and labels, zip disk inserts and labels.

Needle Doctor www.needledoctor.com Large selection of needles cartridges, turntables, and phono accessories.

Nemesys Music Technology Inc. www.nemesysmusic.com Gigasampler; NCS44; Gigastudio; Nemesys Soundware.

Newtronic www.newtronic.com High-end tools for MIDI programmers; dance and electronic music; MIDI files; sample CDs; MIDI programming books, software, and synthesizer sounds.

Northstar Productions www.northstarsamples.com Digital sample CD-ROMs.

Norton AntiVirus www.norton.com Virus protection program.

Novation www.novationusa.com/nov_route/docs/front/front2.htm or www.novationuk.com Tech support; FAQ; products; support; distributors.

Ntonyx www.ntonyx.com Process MIDI files to add human performance characteristics; *Onyx Arranger; Style Enhancer.*

Nullsoft www.nullsoft.com *WinAmp* and other product downloads.

Omnirax www.omnirax.com Professional studio furniture.

Palm Pilot www.palmpilot.com Personal digital assistant handheld computer.

Partners in Rhyme www.partnersinrhyme.com Royalty-free music, loops, sound effects, and MIDI files; Macintosh; Windows.

Passport Designs www.passportdesigns.com Developer of *Encore, MusicTime,* and *Master Tracks Pro* MIDI sequencers for the Macintosh and Windows.

Patchman Music www.patchmanmusic.com Over 787 sound banks.

PBJ Music www.pbjmusic.com/activities.html *Computer Activities* software by music teachers for music students; Windows.

Peavey Electronics www.peavey.com Musical instruments manufacturer; guitars, amps, drums, and keyboards; product information.

Peter Solley Productions www.petersolleyproductions.com MIDI file sequences for sale.

PG Music www.pgmusic.com Developer of *Band-In-A-Box* accompaniment software; *Power Tracks Pro;* software for pianists and guitar players; news; updates; demos; information; technical support; reviews; press releases; links.

PlayPro Software Inc. www.playprosoft.com *Interactive Guitar, Interactive Bass.*

Pocket Fuel www.pocketfuel.com Download loops.

Polyhedric Software www.polyhedric.com/software ACE of WAV; WAVmaker; Gsound 22; Virtual Sampler SDK; Mellosoftron; MIDInight Express.

Power On www.poweronsoftware.com *Now Up-to-Date and Contact.*

Power Technology www.dspfx.com Developer of *DSP/FX* digital audio DirectX plug-ins for PC; information about effects; magazine reviews; user comments; press releases; download a demo.

PowerTracks www.powertracks.com Sequencer for Windows from PG Music; up to forty-eight tracks of digital audio with effects, EQ, and panning; third party plug-in support.

Professional Sound Projects www.psp.l.pl Audio processors and effects plug-ins.

Propellerhead www.propellerheads.se *Reason; ReBirth; Recycle; Reload; Rewire; Refills.*

Pro-Rec www.pro-rec.com Synthesizer sounds; sample CDs; MIDI files.

Prosoniq www.prosoniq.com Developer of *SonicWorx* software for Macintosh and digital audio plug-ins for *Cubase VST.*

ProSound Web www.prosoundWeb.com Pro audio community.

PSP www.pspaudioware.com Plug-ins.

Purple Audio www.purpleaudio.com Audio equipment manufacturer.

Q Up Arts www.quparts.com/cgi-bin/cp-app.cgi Sample collections for computers and samplers.

Q-Sound Labs www.qsound.com Supplier of 3D audio solutions for the Internet, PC/multimedia, consumer electronics, and health care marketplaces.

QuickShot www.quickshot.com Developer of peripherals for electronic/multimedia entertainment.

Radikal Technologies www.radikaltechnologies.com SAC-2K Software Assigned Controller.

Radio Shack www.radioshack.com Audio equipment; batteries, parts, and accessories; phones; keyboards.

Radix Services www.radix.co.uk/radsamp *Radsamp* PC Sample Player; supports vari-speed, looping, and volume for each channel; demo for download.

Rapco.com www.rapco.com Electronics.

Replay www.replayinc.com *CD Looper; Decomposer.*

RetroActive Audio Sampler www.flytools.com Records audio that has already happened.

Roland www.rolandus.com Electronics manufacturer; keyboards; digital pianos; synthesizers; studio workstations; sound modules; and more.

Roxio www.roxio.com *Toast; Toast with Jam; Easy CD and DVD Creator.*

Rubber Chicken Software Co. www.chickensys.com *Translator* sample converter.

SampleHeads www.sampleheads.com Real sound sample libraries; copyright free.

SampleTank www.sampletank.com Software sound module; combines sophisticated sampler/synth engine with high-quality multisampled sounds into a VST instrument; for Cubase, Logic, or any VST compatible MIDI sequencer; natural and synthesized sounds.

Samson www.samsontech.com Equalizers; loudspeakers; headphones; microphones.

Saw Studio www.sawstudio.com/SAWStudio.htm Digital editing software.

Sectionz.com www.sectionz.com Community of electronica artists; platform for musicians who are interested in learning about the construction and philosophies of the electronic medium; informative content; direct interaction with their peers; members receive peer feedback, educate one another about the electronic music industry, and compose collaborative tracks online.

Seer Systems www.seersystems.com Developer of real-time software synthesizer for the PC, *Reality.*

SEK'D www.sekd.com Software for recording and CD-mastering; analog and digital audio cards.

Sennheiser Electronic Corp. www.sennheiserusa.com Microphones; headphones; wireless solutions; audiology.

Shadow Pickups www.shadow-pickups.com Pickups; pre-amps.

Shareware Music Machine www.SharewareMusicMachine.com or www.hitsquad.comsmm Over 4,400 music software titles available to download; world's largest music software site; software categories include: audio editors, audio players, audio recording, audio restoration, business application, SCD burner, SCD player, SCD rippers, collecting and cataloging, computer-aided music,

CSound drums and percussion, ear training, effects, format converters, guitar, jukebox and multiformat karaoke, label printing, metronomes, MIDI players and utilities, MIDI sequencers, miscellaneous, mod trackers and players, MP3, MPEG, multitrack recording, music calculators, music tuition, notation, oscilloscopes, patch editors and librarians, plug-ins, radio production, remixing and DJ software, samplers, software synthesizers, sound cards, device drivers, sound fonts, spectrum analyzers, streaming audio, media, tuners, video and multimedia, and wavetable emulators.

Simtel.Net www.simtel.net/simtel.net Collection of shareware, freeware, and public domain software.

Sion Software www.infoserve.net/quickscore or www.sionsoft.com *QuickScore Elite* and *Copyist;* award-winning music composition, arranging, notation, MIDI sequencing, and recording software; links.

Software Publishers Association www.spa.org Software and Information Industry Association.

Software Technology www.software-technology.com Retailer and supplier of computer products.

Sonic Emulations www.sonicemulations.com Digital audio content.

Sonic Implants www.sonicimplants.com Sound libraries, audio software and music for PC and synthesizer.

Sonic Reality sonicreality.com Sample libraries on CD-ROM and audio CD.

Sonic State www.sonicstate.com News; views; events; links to synthesizer sites; Macintosh and PC software to download; chat.

Sonic Timeworks www.sonictimeworks.com Digital audio software.

Sonomic www.sonomic.com Sample and sound effects downloads.

Sonorus Inc. www.sonorus.com STUDI/O; STUDI/O-Sync Backplate; MEDI/0; AUDI/O AES-8; AUDI/O 24; Audi/O Modular/8.

Sony www.sony.com Electronics; music and more.

Sony Pictures Media Software mediasoftware.sonypictures.com Acquired products developed by *Sonic Foundry,* including *Sound Forge* wave edit software for PC; *Acid; Acid Loops; Vegas;* digital audio plug-ins and utilities; product information; technical support.

Sound Blaster www.soundblaster.com Transform PC or Notebook into a stereo system.

Sound Central www.soundcentral.com Computer audio samples; MIDI files; freeware; shareware.

Sound Quest Inc. www.squest.com *MIDI Quest; Infinity; SQ MIDI Tools; Solo Quest.*

Sounder www.sounder.com Software for creating interactive music.

Sounds Logical www.soundslogical.com *WaveWarp.*

Sounds Megastore www.voxoo.comsounds-megastore/indexsms.html Selections of professional samples.

Soundtrek www.soundtrek.com Developer of *Jammer* and *Jammer Pro;* product information; demos; MIDI files to download.

Speedsoft Vsampler www.vsampler.com Audio software.

Spin Audio Software www.spinaudio.com Company that develops audio signal processing plug-ins and supplementary tools for computer-based audio production.

SRS Labs www.srswowcast.com/demonstrations.asp Invents technologies and audio techniques that make products sound better.

Stage Research, Inc. www.stageresearch.com Developer of SFX for Windows 98/NT; to aid the sound designer and the sound technician in creating, maintaining, and executing sound effects, music, and show control for a live entertainment environment.

Starland www.starland.co.uk UK-based retailer.

Steinberg www.steinberg.net Leading music software manufacturer; professional audio systems and technologies; *Cubase; Rebirth RB-338;* information on products; demos; software updates; drivers; free plug-ins; dealers; equipment; hints; sound card information.

Storecase Technology Inc. www.storecase.com *Data Express; Data Silo; Rhino Jr.; Data Stacker; Infostation;* data storage products.

Stormware www.stormware.cz Software devlopment.

Studio Electronics www.studioelectronics.com Synth products; support; downloads.

Summit Audio www.summitaudio.com Pre-amps; compressors; Eqs.

Super Loops www.SuperLoops.com Drum loops and samples on CD.

Sweetwater Sound www.sweetwater.com Music technology supplier and retailer.

Swiftkick Productions www.swiftkick.com Developer of the *Environment Toolkit* book and disk; tools for customizing Logic Environment to MIDI studio; descriptions of advanced features; *ET4* quarterly electronic journal.

Swissonic America www.swissonic.com AD24; DA24; AD96; AD8; AD8 Pro; USB Studio; USB Studio D; AD8 Fire Wire; converters.

Symbolic Sound www.symbolicsound.com Hardware and software for computer-based digital audio; *Kyma.*

Synchro Arts www.SynchroArts.co.uk *VocALign Project; ProTools* plug-ins; information; downloadable demos.

Synth Museum www.synthmuseum.com Vintage synth resource.

Synth Zone www.synthzone.com Synthesizer resources on the Internet; links to manufacturer and user group sites; music and audio software; MIDI, synthesizer, and electronic music; electronic keyboards and effects.

Tascam www.tascam.com Multitrack reel-to-reel recorders; data storage products; consumer audio equipment; mixers; DATs; product information; FAQs; technical support; list of repair centers; *Ministudio; Portastudio;* pro audio division of TEAC Corporation.

TC Electronic www.tcelectronic.com High-end signal processors for the studio, PA, and broadcast industries; product information; software updates; distributor lists; manuals to download; news; press releases; employment opportunities; *Powercore Firewire; Reverb.*

Terzoid www.terzoid.com *NoiZe* for Windows universal MIDI patch editor/librarian.

TG Tools tgtools.de Finale plug-ins.

The Center for Computer Research in Music and Acoustics (CCRMA) ccrma-www.stanford.edu/ News and events; information; overview.

The Online Directory of Electronic Music members.tripod.com~emusic/index.html Links to electronic music sites.

The Sonic Spot www.sonicspot.com Comprehensive library of computer music and audio resources.

Thinkware www.thinkware.com Audio, MIDI, and video solutions; distributor of computer music hardware and software.

Third Wave Media www.thirdwavemedia.com Audio CD, Video CD, CD-ROM, and DVD replication.

Time and Space www.timespace.com Sample CDs, CD-ROMs, virtual instruments, and software.

Total Recorder www.highcriteria.com/products.htm Universal sound recording tool; captures sound being played by other sound players, either from a file or from the Internet; records audio from CD, microphone, line-in; converts any sound formats to WAVE.

T-RackS 24 www.t-racks.com IK Multimedia; analog modeled, stand-alone software dedicated to audio mastering; built with actual physical models of tube circuitry; updated to support 24-bit file processing; complete workstation made of four discrete processors; state-of-the-art six band parametric EQ; classic stereo tube compressor/leveler; multiband master stereo limiter; soft-clipping adjustable output stage.

Tran Tracks www.trantracks.com MIDI files; rhythm, groove, and style disks.

Trycho Tunes www.trycho.com MIDI sequences; all genres.

Tune 1000 www.midi-classics.com/tune1000.htm General MIDI sequences.

Turtle Beach www.turtlebeach.com Connected audio solutions.

U&I Software www.uisoftware.com Unique music software products.

Ueberschall www.ueberschall.com Sample CDs; sound libraries.

Unitec Products Corp. www.unitecproducts.com Case manufacturer.

Universal Audio www.uaudio.com/index_1.html Vintage analog recording tools; plug-ins.

Universal Sound Bank www.universalsoundbank.com Audio CD and CD-ROM sample sound libraries.

VAZ Modular www.software-technology.com Synthesizer sounds.

Vestax www.vestax.co.uk Mixers; turntables; merchandise.

Vintage Synth www.vintagesynth.com Vintage synthesizers; links to over 500 vintage and new synthesizers.

Vinyl to CDR Processing Software www.wavecor.co.uk/ganymede.html Support for Wave Corrector; application for removing vinyl clicks, ticks, and plops from wave recordings of vinyl records prior to transfer to CD.

Voicecrystal www.voicecrystal.com Developer of sounds and voices for synthesizers on floppy disk, CD, and RAM cards; sample CDs and music software; product information; sound clips to download; mailing list.

Wave Arts wavearts.com Plug-ins.

Wave Distribution www.wavedistribution.com High-end audio processing.

Wave Mechanics Inc. www.wavemechanics.com *UltraTools; Sound Blender; Speed; Pitch Doctor; Pure Pitch;* designs and manufactures DSP plug-ins for audio professionals.

Waveform www.Waveform.dk Database of samples to freely download.

Waves www.waves.com Digital audio software and plug-ins for Macintosh and PC; list of products and platforms supported; demos to download; free software updates; tips; FAQ; links.

Wired News www.wired.com/news High-tech news.

Wizoo www.wizoo.com Music books, sounds, samples, and music software.

World Wide Woodshed www.worldwidewoodshed.com *Slow Gold; Slow Blast!* .

Yamaha Corporation of America www.yamaha.com Music manufacturer of keyboards, drums, guitars, Clavinovas, Disklaviers, receivers, stereos, tuners, pro-audio, mixers, brass, woodwind, recorders, and software.

Yamaha Music Soft www.yamahamusicsoft.com
Yamaha music software products.
ZDNET.com shopper-zdnet.com.com/4007-3669_15-
0.html?tag=dir Information on computer
products; reviews; current music software prices.

Conferences and Showcases— Festivals and Fairs

All American Music Festival www.bandfest.com
Provides an unforgettable experience for students
from around the world; concert bands, marching
bands, jazz bands, orchestras, choral groups,
color guard, drill teams, dance groups, and other
performance groups.
American Music Conference www.amc-music.com
National nonprofit educational association
founded in 1947; dedicated to promoting the
importance of music, music-making, and music
education to the general public; goal is to build
credibility for music and music education,
especially at an early age, and to expand that
portion of the population that enjoys and makes
its own music.
Appel Farm Festival www.appelfarm.org Held the
first Saturday in June in Elmer, NJ.
Arts Midwest www.artsmidwest.org Enables
individuals and families throughout America's
heartland to share in and to enjoy the arts and
cultures of our region and the world.
*Association for the Promotion of Campus Activities
(APCA)* www.apca.com Annual conference in
early March; trade show; showcases performance
types interested in the college market.
Association of Performing Arts Presenters (APAP)
www.artspresenters.org Annual conference in
mid-January in New York City; regional
conferences include (1) early September: Western
Arts Alliance Association, (2) mid-September:
Midwest Arts Conference, (3) late September:
Southern Arts Exchange.
Atlantis Music Conference www.atlantismusic.com
Held in Atlanta, GA.
Audio Engineering Society (AES) Convention
www.aes.org Held in New York City.
Augusta Heritage Center Music Camp
www.augustaheritage.com Held in August in
Elkins, WV; vocal week; festival.
Billboard Music Conferences
www.billboardevents.com/billboardevents/index.j
sp Billboard events.
Calgary Folk Music Festival
www.calgaryfolkfest.com Held in July in
Calgary, Alberta, Canada.
Canadian Music Week www.cmw.net Annual music
conference in early March; trade show; showcase;
all genres.

Chamber Music Northwest www.cmnw.org One of
the leading festivals of chamber music in North
America; festival musicians have international
solo and ensemble careers.
City Stages www.citystages.org Held in May.
CMJ Music Marathon & Music Fest www.cmj.com
Fall conference and showcase in New York City
clubs and at the Lincoln Center; all genres of
music; subscription available to journal; college
radio chart reports.
Common Ground on the Hill
www.commongroundonthehill.com Held in July
at Western Maryland College, Westminster, MD;
workshop; festival.
Consumer Electronics Show www.cesWeb.org
January in Las Vegas.
Country Music Showcase International, Inc.
www.cmshowcase.org Directory; event calendar.
Country Showdown www.countryshowdown.com
Judged country music artist showcases; annual
local, state, regional, and national winners
compete for cash and a recording contract.
Country Stampede Music Festival
www.countrystampede.com Four days of country
music in June in Kansas and Kentucky.
Dawson City Music Festival www.dcmf.com Held in
July in Dawson City, Yukon, Canada.
Durango Songwriters Expo durangosong.com Annual
event held in Colorado; blend of music business
seminars and workshops, song listening/critique
sessions, live songwriter showcases, and a live
hit-writer concert to close the event.
EAT'M www.eat-m.com Emerging Artists and
Talent in Music; annual conference and festival
held in May.
Edmonton Folk Music Festival www.efmf.ab.ca Held
in August in Edmonton, Alberta, Canada.
Falcon Ridge Folk Festival www.falconridgefolk.com
Held in July in New York.
Fan Fair www.fanfair.com Held in Nashville in June.
Festival Finder www.festivalfinder.com
Comprehensive guide to music festivals in North
America; search by genre, date, location,
performer, or festival name.
Festivals of Music www.festivalsofmusic.com
Adjudication festivals for vocal and instrumental
ensembles.
Festivals.com www.festivals.com Information on
music festivals.
GrassRoots Festival www.grassrootsfest.org Held in
July; Cajun, Zydeco, stringband, African music,
and more; over forty bands on four stages over
four days.
Heritage Festivals/Bowl Games of America
www.heritagefestivals.com Band, choir, and
orchestra festivals.

High Sierra Music Festival www.hsmusic.net Held in July in California.

Independent Music Conference www.indiemusicon.com Conference; trade show; showcases; all styles of commercial music; in Philadelphia in the fall.

International Association of African American Music (IAAAM) www.IAAAM.com Presents series of educational seminars; conference tour sponsorship; concert production.

International Bluegrass Music Association (IBMA) www.ibma.org Annual week-long trade show, showcase, and festival in early October; showcase new and established bluegrass acts; membership required.

Kerrville Folk Festival www.kerrville-music.com Annual folk event held in late May to early June (through Memorial Day weekend) in Kerrville, TX; songwriting; networking; performances.

Lamb's Retreat for Songwriters www.springfed.org Held in November and April in Michigan.

Lotus World Music and Arts Festival www.lotusfest.org Series of events that offer opportunities to experience, celebrate, and learn about the diversity of the world's cultures; named after folk musician Lotus Dickey.

MerleFest www.merlefest.org Held in Wilkesboro, NC in the spring.

MIAC (Music Industries Association of Canada) www.miac.net Trade Show held in August.

Midwest Entertainment Conference www.midwestentertainmentconference.com Keynote speakers; registration; sponsors.

Music in the Parks Music in the Parks www.musicintheparks.com Adjudication festivals for ensembles.

Music Mentor Conference musicmentor.net Held in Orange County, CA in September; "Boot Camp" for the aspiring artist.

Music Midtown musicmidtown.com Held in the spring in Atlanta, GA.

Music Planet www.musicplanet.com/fest.htm Music festival listings.

NAMM (National Association of Music Merchants) www.namm.com Annual conferences; trade shows; concerts; late winter, Los Angeles area; summer, Nashville; International Music Products Association; thousands of exhibitors; all types of music products and services displayed; online program.

Napa Valley Music and Wine Festival www.napafest.com Showcase for songwriters; tickets; links.

National Academy of Recording Arts & Sciences (NARAS) www.grammy.com Check for future showcase opportunities; sponsor showcases for unsigned and independent label rock bands.

National Association for Campus Activities (NACA) www.naca.org Annual conference, showcase, and exhibit hall in mid-February; regional conferences throughout the United States include the Southeast, South Central, Upper Midwest, East Coast, Great Lakes, Pacific Northwest, Heart of America, New England, Far West, Illiana, Wisconsin; showcase music of all genres, comedy, theater, and performance art; membership required.

National Association of Record Merchandisers (NARM) www.narm.com Annual conference, trade show, and showcase; presented by member labels.

NEMO Music Conference nemoboston.com Annual event held in Boston in September; new music showcases.

New Orleans Jazz & Heritage Festival www.nojazzfest.com Annual event held in late April and early May in New Orleans.

Newport Folk Festival www.newportfolk.com Held in August in Newport, RI.

North American Music Festivals www.greatfestivals.com Links to festivals.

North By North East (NXNE) www.nxne.com Annual music conference held in June in Toronto, Ontario, Canada.

North By North West (NXNW) www.nxnw.com Annual music conference, trade show, showcase held in Portland, OR; all music genres.

Northeast Regional Folk Alliance Conference www.nefolk.org Held in November in Philadelphia, PA.

Northern California Songwriters Association or West Coast Songwriters Association www.ncsasong.org Annual Songwriters Conference held in September; networking; seminars; workshops; song critiques; panel discussions.

Ottawa Folk Festival www.ottawafolk.org Held in August in Ottawa, Ontario, Canada.

Philadelphia Folk Festival www.folkfest.org or www.pfs.org Held in August in Philadelphia, PA; always before Labor Day.

Rocky Mountain Folks Festival www.bluegrass.com Held in August in Lyons, CO; Planet Bluegrass.

Sierra Nevada World Music Festival www.snwmf.com Three-day Reggae and World Music festival held in Marysville, CA, in June.

Sisters Folk Festival www.sistersfolkfestival.com Held in Sisters, Oregon.

South By Southwest Music and Media Conference (SXSW) www.sxsw.com Annual conference and showcase held in mid-March in Austin, TX; international talent; all genres.

Strawberry Music Festival www.strawberrymusic.com Held in May on

Memorial Day weekend and in September on
Labor Day weekend in Sonora, CA.

Taxi Road Ralley www.taxi.com Free annual
convention held in Los Angeles; music industry
panels; song and demo critiques; networking.

Telluride Bluegrass Festival www.bluegrass.com
Held in June in Telluride, CO.

*The Association for Recorded Sound Collections
(ARSC)* www.arsc-audio.org Annual conferences
in different parts of the United States.

The Folk Alliance www.folk.org Annual
international folk music and dance conference
held in mid-February; rotate regional locations;
Northwest and Midwest annual conferences;
showcase folk, acoustic, world, ethnic music, and
dance; membership required.

The Great River Folk Festival
www.viterbo.edu/personalpages/faculty/rruppel/fe
st.html Held in August at the University of
Wisconsin, La Crosse, WI.

The Hillside Festival www.hillside.on.ca Held in
July in Guelph, Ontario, Canada.

*The International Association of Fairs and
Expositions* www.fairsandexpos.com Directory
listing county, state, and international fairs and
events in the United States, Canada, and the
world; associate memberships for performers and
agents; directory free with membership.

The Rhythms of the World www.harbourfront.on.ca
Includes the JVC Jazz Festival; mid-June through
September in Toronto, Ontario, Canada.

The South Florida Folk Festival
www.southfloridafolkfest.com Annual event held
in January; folk festivities; songwriting
competition.

The Swannanoa Gathering www.swangathering.org
Held in late July and early August in Ashville,
NC; Guitar and Folkweek.

Tin Pan South www.tinpansouth.com/index.cfm
NSAI annual week-long event held in April in
Nashville; club showcases of songwriters from
everywhere.

Vancouver Folk Festival www.thefestival.bc.ca
Annual event held in July in Vancouver, BC,
Canada.

Walnut Valley Festival www.wvfest.com Held in
September in Winfield, KS.

WestFest www.westfest.net Held in Red River, NM;
Michael Martin Murphy.

Wildflower Arts & Music
www.wildflowerfestival.com Held in May in
Richardson, TX.

Winnipeg Folk Festival www.wpgfolkfest.mb.ca
Held in July in Winnipeg, Manitoba, Canada.

Winter Music Conference
www.wintermusicconference.com Miami Beach,

FL; network with industry professionals; DJs;
radio forums; exhibition area; technology.

Woody Guthrie Free Folk Festival
www.woodyguthrie.com Annual event held in
July in Midwest City, OK.

Copyright, Legal, and Tax Information—Performing and Mechanical Rights—Government Grants

AFM (American Federation of Musicians)
www.afm.org Musicians union; New York
headquarters; how to hire musicians; member
groups; booking agents; member benefits;
history of the organization founded in the 1890s.

*AFTRA (American Federation of Television and
Radio Artists)* www.aftra.com Broadcast/News;
Entertainment Programs; Commercials; Industry
and New Technologies; Sound Recordings: FAQ.

*AKM (Staatlich Genehmigte Gesellschaft Der
Autoren Komponisten Und Musikverlager)*
www.akm.co.at Performing rights organization
of Austria.

APRA (Australasian Performing Right Association)
www.apra.com.au Australasia.

*ASCAP (American Society of Composers, Authors,
and Publishers)* www.ascap.com Performing
rights organization; collects performance
royalties; active members are composers,
lyricists, songwriters, and music publishers;
award-winning Web site; music database;
legislative; licensing; insurance; music business;
catalogs; links; created in 1914 to provide the
essential link between the creators of music and
the users of music; only performing rights
organization in the United States whose board of
directors is made up entirely of writers and music
publishers elected by and from its membership.

Band Radio Contracts
www.bandradio.com/law/samples.html Links to
many different sample music business contracts;
recording, publishing, etc.

BayTSP www.baytsp.com San Jose, CA, based
corporation; developer, patent holder, and
provider of effective means of branding and
tracking online content over the Internet;
software products and services are aimed to deter
theft of online content as well as aid in the
prosecution of those who engage in copyright
infringement.

Better Business Bureau www.bbb.org Online site.

Blue Spike, Inc. www.bluespike.com Information on
digital watermarking.

BMI (Broadcast Music Incorporated)
www.bmi.com Performing rights organization;
music-related links; writer and publisher member
catalogs; licensing information; insurance.

BMI Links to Authors Societies and Performing Rights Organizations Around the World www.bmi.com/international/links.asp A to Z listings.

BUMA (Het Bureau voor Muziek-Auteursrecht) www.buma.nl Performing rights organization of the Netherlands.

California Lawyers for the Arts www.calawyersforthearts.org Nonprofit tax-exempt service organization founded in 1974; provides lawyer referrals, dispute resolution services, educational programs, publications and a resource library to artists of all disciplines and arts organizations.

Canada Council for the Arts www.canadacouncil.ca Art Bank; Public Lending Right Commission.

Catalog of Federal Domestic Assistance www.gsa.gov/fdac Types of assistance; applications; FAQ.

Center for Financial & Tax Planning www.taxplanning.com Tax information.

Central Research Laboratories www.crl.co.uk Information on digital watermarking.

CMRRA (Canadian Musical Reproduction Rights Agency Ltd.) www.cmrra.ca Home page; reproduction rights in Canada.

Copyright Clearance Center www.copyright.com Information on obtaining licenses for copying text.

Copyright Imprints www.mpa.org/agency/framesimp.html Listing of copyright imprints of publishers, both domestic and foreign; based on information submitted by the membership of Music Publishers Association, National Music Publishers Association, and the Church Music Publishers.

Copyright Office of the United States www.lcWeb.loc.gov/copyright Copyright information; copyright law; forms; legislation.

Copyright Resources Online www.library.yale.edu/~okerson/copyproj.html University resources.

Digital Future Coalition www.dfc.org Group formed to help balance the protection of intellectual property and public access to it.

EAU (Eesti Autorite Uhing) www.eauthors.ee Performing rights organization of Estonia.

Electronic Frontier Foundation www.eff.org Civil-rights organization for the online community; general information on copyright; links; articles on issues of debate; freedom of speech rights.

Electronic Policy Network epn.org News and resources from more than 120 research and advocacy organizations.

Entertainment Publisher www.entertainmentpublisher.com Automated contracts for a fee; music industry; film; TV.

Essential Links to Taxes www.el.com/elinks/taxes Tax information.

Federal Government Information www.firstgov.com Federal laws and more; United States government's official Web site.

FedWorld www.fedworld.gov Search for government reports and Web sites.

Find Law www.findlaw.com Legal news; legal professionals; business resources; public and consumer resources; corporate council; student resources; services for lawyers.

Funding for Writing and the Arts www.usartsgrants.bigstep.com Complete directory of all private and government programs which benefit people in writing and the arts.

Future of Music Coalition www.futureofmusic.com Not-for-profit collaboration between members of the music, technology, public policy, and intellectual property law communities; seeks to educate the media, policymakers, and the public about music technology issues; aims to identify and promote innovative business models that will help musicians and citizens to benefit from new technologies; attempts both to address pressing music technology issues, and to serve as a voice for musicians and citizens in Washington, DC, where critical decisions are being made regarding intellectual property rights.

GEMA (Gesellschaft Fur Musikalische Auffuhrungs Und Mechanische) www.gema.de Performing rights organization of Germany.

Government of Canada www.nlc-bnc.ca/window/windowe.htm Copyright information; for book, music, periodical, electronic, and multimedia publishers; support programs; ultimate resource for music and entertainment professionals and consumers; phone, fax, Internet, toll-free numbers, and trade shows.

GPO Access Services www.gpoaccess.gov/index.html Disseminates official information from all three branches of the federal government.

IMRO (Irish Music Rights Organization) www.imro.ie Performing rights organization of Ireland.

Incorporated Society of Musicians www.ism.org UK's professional association for musicians.

International Trademark Association www.inta.org Representing the trademark community since 1878. ·

IP Watchdog www.ipwatchdog.com/copyright.html Copyright law; information; basics; links; industry associations; articles.

KODA (Selskabet til Forvaltning af Internationale Komponistrettighederi Danmark) www.koda.dk/ Performing rights organization of Denmark.

Kohn Music www.kohnmusic.com Copyright law and music licensing on the Internet; links to copyright and music rights clearance organizations; industry resources.

Library of Congress Home Page www.loc.gov Information resources.

MCPS (Mechanical Copyright Protection Society) www.mcps.co.uk UK collection agency.

Media Enforcer www.mediaenforcer.com Fighting online piracy.

Mr. Smith E-mails Washington www.mrsmith.com E-mail addresses of members of Congress.

Music Library Association Guide to Copyright for Music Librarians www.lib.jmu.edu/org/mla/ FAQ; information.

Music Publishers' Association—Copyright Resources www.mpa.org/crc.html Copyright Search Center provides a step-by-step guide to researching the copyright holder or publisher of a piece of music.

Music Rewards Fundraising www.raisemoremoney.com CDs and cassettes from top artists; year-round, holiday, Christian family, Latin, and children's programs; FAQ.

Musician's Intellectual Law and Resources Links www.aracnet.com/~schornj/index.shtml Notes on copyright: new legislation; copyright in compositions; copyright in sound recordings; collection of royalties; mechanical royalties; trademarks and servicemarks; miscellaneous intellectual law links; thoughts on contracts; analysis of recording contract clauses; musician resources; my favorite musician-related links; jazz and music magazines; record company links; booking agents, managers, and music publishers; international venues; American venues; musicians' Web pages.

Musician's Law www.musicianslaw.com Legal issues concerning musicians.

Musician's Union UK www.musiciansunion.org.uk Information on local offices; press releases; FAQs; links; members; gig list; copyright section.

Music-Law.com www.music-law.com Legal issues concerning musicians.

National Endowment for the Arts (NEA) www.arts.endow.gov Learn about work being done by artists and arts organizations across the country; section on helping nonprofit organizations link with federal arts resources; grant applications.

National Endowment for the Humanities (NEH) www.neh.fed.us grant management; apply for a grant; news and publications; search.

National Foundation for Advancement in the Arts www.ARTSawards.org Arts recognition and talent search.

Pacific Music Industry Association www.pmia.org Industry information and development; based in British Columbia.

PRS (Performing Right Society) www.prs.co.uk UK association of composers, songwriters, and music publishers; administers performing rights.

Public Domain Music www.pdinfo.com Lists music in the public domain.

Public Domain Music Works www.pubdomain.com Monthly subscription available; approximately 10,000 hand-picked PD music titles and growing, specially selected by the editors of *Public Domain Report;* search music by title, genre, composer, keyword, lyric, or any word or phrase; updated monthly with hundreds of new titles; Rotating Editor's selection of top 100 PD songs with Real Audio sound clips; subscribers receive unrestricted, password protected access; sheet music offered for thousands of titles; custom copyright research available; copyright forums; articles, tips, tricks, and techniques for practical PD usage.

Quicken Financial Services www.quicken.com Budget and tax planning.

RAO (Russian Authors Society) www.rao.ru Performing rights organization of Russia.

Recording Industry Association of America (RIAA) www.riaa.com Official Web site; copyrights; legislation; technology; Web licensing; censorship; parental advisory; Gold and Platinum awards; links.

Revenue Canada www.ccra-adrc.gc.ca/menu-e.html Tax information.

Rock Out Censorship www.theroc.org Grassroots anticensorship organization; First Amendment rights.

SABAM (Societe Belge Des Auteurs Compositeurs Et Editeurs) www.sabam.be Performing rights organization of Belgium.

SACEM (Societe Des Auteurs Compositeurs Et Editeurs De Musique) www.sacem.fr Performing rights organization of France.

SCALA (Australia Songwriters, Composers, and Lyricists Association) www.senet.com.au/~scala/more.htm Home page.

Secure Digital Music Initiative www.sdmi.org Piracy fighter; secure delivery of digital music across all platforms; press releases; membership requirements; schedule.

SESAC www.sesac.com Performing rights organization; privately owned.

SGAE (Sociedad General De Autores De España) www.sgae.es Performing rights organization of Spain.

SIAE (Societa Italiana Degli Autori Ed Editori) www.siae.it Performing rights organization of Italy.

Small Business Administration www.sba.gov
Government office.
Small Business Taxes and Management
www.smbiz.com Tax information.
SOCAN (Society of Composers Authors & Music Publishers Of Canada) www.socan.ca
Performing rights organization of Canada.
SODRAC Inc. www.sodrac.com Canadian performing rights organization (French).
SoundExchange www.soundexchange.com Collection agency by RIAA to procure royalties from sites that play music in streaming radio format.
Stanford University Libraries Comprehensive Copyright Site fairuse.stanford.edu/ Copyright history; statutes; regulations; treaties; articles; links.
STIM (Svenska Tonsattares Internationella Musikbyra) www.stim.se Performing rights organization of Sweden.
TEOSTO (Bureau International Du Droit D'Auteur Des Compositeurs Finlandais) www.teosto.fi
Performing rights organization of Finland.
The British Phonographic Industry www.bpi.co.uk
British music industry; statistics; links.
The Copyright Website www.benedict.com
Copyright information; all forms and subjects.
The Electronic Frontier Foundation www.eff.org
Defending freedom in the digital world.
The Electronic Privacy Information Center
www.epic.org Devoted to furthering online privacy.
The Harry Fox Agency nmpa.org/hfa.html or www.harryfox.com Mechanical royalties and licenses; searchable database of songs and publishers; current statutory mechanical rate.
The Privacy Rights Clearinghouse
www.privacyrights.org Devoted to furthering online privacy.
The United States Senate www.senate.gov
Information on the Senate.
TONO (Norsk selskap for forvaltning av fremføringsrettigheter til musikkverk)
www.tono.no Performing rights organization of Norway.
United States Nonprofit Gateway
www.nonprofit.gov Directory of information about grants, regulations, taxes, and government services.
UBC (Uniao Brasilera de Compositores)
www.ubc.org.br Performing rights organization of Brazil.
United Nations www.un.org Information about the United Nations.
What is Copyright? www.whatiscopyright.org Basic definitions regarding copyrights; written using the Berne Union for the Protection of Literary and Artistic Property (Berne Convention).

World Intellectual Property Organization
www.wipo.org News and information resources; activities and services.

Country and Western Music—Cowboy Songs—Line Dancing—Western Swing

Academy of Country Music www.acmcountry.com
Awards; news; events; membership; history.
Academy of Western Artists www.awa-awards.org/index.htm Involved in the contemporary cowboy heritage movement; gives recognition to those who excel at writing and performing traditional and contemporary western music and poetry, those who with skill and artistry manufacture the gear of the cowboy trade, those who continue the time-honored arts of campfire and chuckwagon cookery, those who expand and refine the music of western swing, and those who compete in ranch rodeo.
Bill Bader's Line Dance Links
www.billbader.com/line-links.htm Line dance Web sites.
Birthplace of Country Music
www.birthplaceofcountrymusic.org Concerts and events; musical heritage; museum; education.
Canadian Country Music
www.canehdian.com/genre/country.html
Information on country music in Canada.
Club Nashville www.clubnashville.com Directories; radio industry; Nashville music; The Blue Chip Radio Report; Texas music; artists index; extensive resource lists.
CMT Canada www.cmtcanada.com/index.asp
Canadian country music.
Country Charts www.countrycharts.com Interviews; fan clubs; rising stars; artist links; country radio.
Country Legends Association www.clabranson.org
Help save classic country music.
Country Music Association (CMA)
www.cmaworld.com Founded in 1958; first trade organization formed to promote a type of music; now has more than 6,000 organizational and individual members in 43 countries; objectives of the organization are to guide and enhance the development of country music throughout the world; to demonstrate it as a viable medium to advertisers, consumers, and media; and to provide a unity of purpose for the country music industry; awards.
Country Music Association of Australia
www.countrymusic.asn.au Information on country music in Australia.
Country Music Classics
www.countrymusicclassics.com Free weekly newsletter; classic country music.
Country Music Dance Network www.cmdn.net Step sheets; music; artists; new artists; chat and more.

Country Music Hall of Fame www.halloffame.org
   Information on Hall of Fame members; museum;
   programs; music history; *Journal of Country
   Music*; Hatch Show Print.
Country Music History
   thanksforthemusic.com/history/ Information on
   favorite country stars; news; articles on country
   music history.
Country Music Ireland
   www.countrymusicireland.com Ireland's leading
   country music site; artist profiles; contacts;
   albums; updated weekly.
Country Music Media Guide
   www.talentandbooking.com Comprehensive
   reference source guide for the country music
   industry listing contact information for country
   artists, personal managers, booking agents,
   record companies, public relations, clubs,
   casinos, and sponsors.
Country Music MIDI Files and Backing Tracks
   www.seafieldmusic.co.uk Professional quality
   country MIDI files and backing tracks.
Country Music People
   www.countrymusicpeople.com Country music
   magazine; new country, roots, honky-tonk,
   Americana, traditional, acoustic, country-rock,
   old time, bluegrass, Nashpop, cowboy,
   rockabilly, western swing, singer-songwriter,
   alternative.
Country Music Round-Up www.cmru.co.uk UK
   country music magazine online.
Country Music Store www.cmstore.co.uk Over
   4,000 CDs available from stock.
Country Music Television (CMT) www.cmt.com
   Music videos; news; artists; tours; radio; hall of
   fame; top twenty countdown.
Country Review www.CountryReview.com Country
   music reviews of all types; album, artist, and
   concert reviews.
Country Standard Time
   www.countrystandardtime.com Country music
   features, articles, and reviews.
Country Stars www.countrystars.com Artiss; news;
   radio; shop.
Country Weekly www.countryweekly.com Online
   magazine; artist tour dates by state; country
   notes; star stats; history.
Country-Time www.country-time.com Line dances
   online; country dance music CDs for sale;
   homepages for well-known choreographers.
Cowboy Songs
   www.lonehand.com/cowboy_songs.htm Western
   music; history; Pickin' Parlor; old West events.
Cowboy Songs www.mcneilmusic.com/cowboy.html
   CDs; songbooks; historical collections; music
   samples; links; Civil War songs; Revolutionary
   War songs.

Cowboy Songs and Range Ballads
   www.bbhc.org/events/cowboySongs.cfm
   Exhibitions; events; museums; library; store;
   programs and education.
Cowboy Songs and Singers
   www.library.arizona.edu/cowboysongs/ Audio;
   video; books; poetry; issues and activities; links.
Gene Autry Oklahoma Film & Music Festival
   www.cow-boy.com/festival.htm Annual event in
   September at the Gene Autry Oklahoma
   Museum.
Goodwin Music www.goodwinmusic.com Country
   music artists; music; lyrics; sheet music; guitar
   reference; videos; country links.
Greatest Films-Nashville (1975)
   www.filmsite.org/nash.html Detailed review,
   synopsis, and discussion of the film.
Hillbilly Music www.hillbilly-music.com Artists;
   groups; news; press; jukebox; library; reviews;
   publications; music sources; organizations;
   events.
Honky Tonkin' honkytonkinmusic.bizland.com Offers
   a wide variety of Independent music CDs
   including country, Texas, western swing,
   cowboy, bluegrass, alternative country,
   traditional country and honky-tonk along with
   various other genres.
Honkytonk Jukebox www.westerndance.co.uk
   Designed for the western line dancer; good
   selection of difficult to obtain music by
   independent artists from around the world; large
   selection of compilations.
International Country Music Association
   www.radiocountry.org Promotes country
   songwriters and artists worldwide.
Jam! Country Music
   www.caldercup.com/JamMusicCountry/home.ht
   ml Canadian country music news and reviews.
Kickit www.kickit.to/ld/Main.php3 Line dance
   magazine and archive.
Las Vegas Country Music and Cowboys
   www.2steppin.comvegas.htm Country music
   Las Vegas style.
Line Dance Fun www.linedancefun.com San
   Francisco area; streaming MP3s.
Line Dancer Magazine
   www.linedancermagazine.co.uk/ UK line dancing
   magazine; search dances; dance charts.
Nashville City Search nashville.citysearch.com City
   guide, clubs, music, etc.
Nashville Country www.nashvillecountry.com
   Online magazine; legends; rising stars; charts;
   around town; news and views.
North America Country Music Associations, Int'l
   www.nacmai.org Nonprofit international country
   music association to promote aspiring artists,
   musicians, and songwriters through education and

international competition; founded in 1997; Annual Country Music week in March.

PBS Songs of the West
www.pbs.org/weta/thewest/resources/archives/five/songs.htm Songs of the plains; cowboy songs.

Roughstock's History of Country Music
www.roughstock.com/history Country music history; artists from Gene Autry, Roy Acuff, Bob Wills, Hank Williams to Patsy Cline, Lefty Frizzell, Willie Nelson, Garth Brooks, and many others; cowboy music; western swing.

Square Dancing and Line Dancing
members.aol.com/CactusStar/home.htm Dancing deep in the heart of Texas; links.

The Canadian Country Music Association
www.ccma.org/ccmatoday/index.htm Canadian country music industry; events; CCMA Awards archives; Hall of Fame; links to artists; radio stations; magazines; record labels; organizations.

The Dancing Cow Page www.cowdance.com Dancing cows; MIDI music.

The Iceberg
www.theiceberg.com/radio/cowboy_songs/ Internet radio cowboy songs.

The Information Super Dance Floor
www.apci.net/~drdeyne Country western dance instruction, choreography, and music.

The Roughstock Network www.roughstock.com Contemporary country music; audio files; COWPIE archives; chords; sheet music; Country Countdown; charts.

The Western Music Association
www.westernmusic.org Nonprofit corporation whose purpose is the preservation and promotion of the traditional and contemporary music of the Great American West and the American Cowboy.

The Wild West
www.thewildwest.org/cowboys/songs.html Songs and poetry.

Voices West www.cowboysong.comindex.html Cowboy poetry and songs.

Western Swing
http://www.beta.webyoda.com/dumboozle/western/westdex.html History of western swing music.

Western Swing www.westernswing.com Music news and information; links.

Western Swing Journal
members.aol.com/IbeTexan/western.htm Subscriptions; history; players.

Western Swing Monthly wswing.home.texas.net/ Complete and up to the minute listing of dances, shows, festivals and events.

Western Swing Music Society of the Southwest
www.wsmss.com Hall of Fame; history.

Women of Country www.womenofcountry.com Featured artists; album reviews; news; interviews; concert reviews; music store; wallpaper.

Drums and Percussion

A. M. Percussion Publications
www.ampercussion.com Repertoire for percussion recitals and ensembles.

African Rhythm Traders
www.africanrhythmtraders.com/html/drums.html Drums and percussion.

AJs Pro Percussion www.ajpropercussion.com Drummer's resource center.

American Drum www.americandrum.com Online retail store for percussion.

American Drum School
www.americandrumschool.com Drums; instructional drum videos; accessories; free drum lessons.

Audix www.audixusa.com Drum microphones.

Ballistic Drums www.ballisticdrums.com Play feet exactly like hands; free pounding audiotape and report.

Beatboy www.beatboy.com Drum pattern programmers; product info; demos.

Cappella www.cappelladrumsticks.com Drumsticks; practice pads; percussion accessories; timpani sticks; bass drumsticks; tenor sticks; claves; slap sticks; toner boxes.

Clearsonic www.clearsonic.com ClearSonic Panel drum shield and SORBER free-standing sound absorption.

CyberDrum www.cyberdrum.com Online resource for drummers.

Ddrum Drum Module www.clavia.com Ddrum drum module.

Drum Bum www.drumbum.com Gifts and accessories for drummers.

Drum Corps World www.drumcorpsworld.com Drum Corps world history; scholarships; schedules; photos; auctions.

Drum Grooves Publications www.drumgrooves.com Seventy-two page book with CD; fifty play-along songs in many styles with accompanying scores; for beginning through intermediate drummers.

Drum Machine Museum www.drummachine.com Drum machines; links.

Drum Network DrumNetwork.com Developed to help drummers find out about drums, drum tuning, drum sets reviews, and more; on-line drum shop; "today's lick" drum lesson.

Drum Tech www.drumtech.com Drum technology; electronic drums.

Drum Trax www.drumtrax.com MIDI file drum pattern library.

Drum Workshop Inc. www.dwdrums.com Products; artists; information.

Drum! Magazine www.drummagazine.com/html/ Publication for drummers.

Drum-A-Long www.drumalong.com Practice pads; educational kits.

Drumlicks Publications www.drumlicks.com Educational materials.

Drummers Web www.drummersweb.com Links; ads.

Drums and Percussion Music Software www.hitsquad.com/smm/cat/DRUMS_PERCUSSION/ Links organized by platform

Drums on the Web www.drumsontheweb.com Artists; forum; behind the music.

Drums.com www.drums.com Links; lessons; interviews; articles; forums.

Drums.org www.drums.org Information resources and links; global hand drum and dance community.

Drumtech Drum and Percussion School www.drumtech.co.uk Drum school in Europe; for every kind of drummer, beginner to advanced; private lessons; three-month full-time course; one-year diploma; three-year music degree.

Empire Music www.empire-music.com Bongos; congas; Latin percussion; recorders; kazoos; tambourines; rhythm.

Everyone's Drumming Co. www.everyonesdrumming.com Hand drums.

Fat Congas www.fatcongas.com Cajón drums.

Georg Voros www.georgvoros.comindex1.htm Information for drummers of all levels; educational books.

Global Groove www.globalgroove.org Live drums and percussion over ISDN lines; kits set up and ready to go; custom loops.

GrooveMaker www.groovemaker.com IK Multimedia; combination of remixing software and sounds for creating hypnotic, nonstop dance tracks in real time with professional results; groove combinations in every dance style; ready-to-use loops; professional drum grooves; synth pads; sound effects; ambient loops; add-on loop libraries.

Harmony Central—Drums and Percussion www.harmony-central.com/Drums/ Resources; links.

Innovative Percussion Inc. www.innovativepercussion.com Products; education and events.

Kaman Music Corporation www.kamanmusic.com Percussion instruments and more.

Little Drummer Boy (LDB) www.lysator.liu.se/~zap/ldb/ Loop creation software shareware.

LP Music Group www.lpmusic.com Manufacturer of Latin percussion instruments; congas; bongos; udu drums; cowbells; tambourines; maracas.

Ludwig Drums www.ludwig-drums.com Classic Birch Series Drums; Rocker and Accent Series Drums; Educational Percussion Kits; Musser Mallet Percussion Instruments; Timpani and Concert Drums; Selmer 2.0 CD.

Mountain Rythym www.mountainrythym.com Handcrafted percussion instruments; Drums; Ashiko; Djembe; Conga; Simple Twist Tuning System.

Music Room www.musicroom.com/drums.html Drums and percussion songbooks.

Neztech Software www.neztech.com *SequBeat PRO* drum sample sequencing packaging for PC.

Not So Modern Drummer www.notsomoderndrummer.com Drum magazine.

Pearl www.pearldrum.com Departments; forum; artist roster; news.

Percussive Arts Society www.pas.org Music service organization promoting percussion education, research, performance, and appreciation throughout the world.

Porks Pie Percussion www.porkpiedrums.com Products; artists; swag; news; support.

Premier Percussion www.premier-percussion.com Products; artists.

Pro Percussion www.propercussion.co.uk/ Percussion; drums; drum kits; cymbals.

Pro-Mark Corp. www.promark-stix.com2003/ Drums and accessories.

Pure Sound Percussion www.puresoundpercussion.com Blasters; Speedball; Puresound.

Regal Tip www.regaltip.com Drumsticks.

Remixer Drum Loop Archive www.remixer.com/downloads.htm Downloadable drum loops in MP3 and RealAudio format; can convert files to .WAV format.

Remo www.remo.com Drum heads.

Rhythm Band Instruments Inc. www.rhythmband.com Aulos Recorders; Kidsplay; Charlie Horse Music Pizza Rhythm Band Set; Sweet Pipes Recorder Music; Belleplates; Chromaharp.

Rhythm Fusion Inc. www.rhythmfusion.com Wide variety of percussion instruments.

Rhythm Tech www.rhythmtech.com Percussion instruments and accessories.

Rhythms Exotic Afro Percussions LLC www.afrorhythms.com Specializes in the manufacture of Exotic Afro Percussion instruments traditionally found in areas of the Caribbean and parts of West Africa; hard-to-find quality Exotic Afro percussion instruments.

Roots Jam: Collected Hand Drum Rhythms www.alternativeculture.com/music/drumming.htm Music instruction book for African drumming, djembe, and percussion; hand drum lessons, drum rhythms, and drumming tips; easy notation for beginners or advanced drum groups; free samples.

Sabian www.sabian.com Cymbals; accessories; education; artists.

Sheet Music for Keyboard Percussion www.drumspot.comcat121.htm List of items.

Sheet Music for Percussion www.drumspot.comcat62.htm Percussion sheet music.

Sol Drums www.soldrums.com Drums; hardware; company history.

The Drum Club www.thedrumclub.com Online lessons teach students of all ages how to play the drums; each lesson includes RealAudio explanations, video, and play-along MIDI files.

The Overseas Connection www.overseasconnection.com Rhythmkids; Agogo Gongs; Realafrica; Shekeres; Djembes; Djun Djuns; Udu Drums.

Trip Toys www.triptoys.com BioDrummer software drum machine; sixty-two built-in percussion instruments; eighteen different time signatures; ability to import WAV files as percussion instruments.

Trueline Drumsticks www.trueline.com Original T6 Trueline Grip; Natural Diamond Grip; Classic Drumsticks.

Zildjian www.zildjian.com Cymbals; percussion accessories; instructional tips; QuickTime video clips.

Film, Television, and Video Music

A Luna Blue www.alunablue.com Royalty-free stock footage and imagery.

Academy of Motion Picture Arts and Sciences www.oscars.org Academy Awards; events and screenings; awards database.

All Movie Guide www.allmovie.com Guide to films; new in theaters; factoid.

American Film Institute www.AFI.com News and events; catalog; membership; education.

American Movie Classics www.amctv.com Cable channel; guide; the stars; the movies; programming; forum.

Association of Independent Video and Filmmakers www.aivf.org Resources; media advocacy; regional salons; discussion; workshops.

Baseline Hollywood www.baseline.hollywood.com Resource for film and television information; over 1.5 million database records on projects tracked from development to release; cast and crew credits; box office grosses; celebrity biographies; talent contact information; company directories; and industry news; searchable online and updated daily.

BollywoodMusic.com www.bollywoodmusic.com Hindi, Punjabi, Pakistani, Ghazals, Pop, Filmi, and Bhangra songs in RealAudio and MP3 format; over 1,000 songs; complete Indian music site.

Box Office Guru www.boxofficeguru.com Comprehensive box office information.

Box Office Report www.boxofficereport.com Predicted number one film; anticipated rankings.

Boxoffice Online www.boxoff.com Reviews; articles.

Bright Lights Film Journal www.brightlightsfilm.comindex.html Actor profiles; reviews; festivals.

C.A.M. Original Soundtracks www.cam-ost.it Dedicated to Italian and French composers.

Cannes Film Festival www.festival-cannes.com French film event; films; juries; events; awards; archives.

Cinema Confidential www.cinecon.com Current films; news and gossip; trailers; reviews; interviews; forums; gallery.

Cinema Web www.cinemaWeb.com Web site for silent films.

Cinema-sites.com www.cinema-sites.com Links to film industry-related sites.

CineMedia afi.cinemedia.org Film and media directory; over 25,000 links.

Cinemusic Online www.cinemusic.net Film music; reviews; wide variety of scores; audio clip library.

Cinemusic www.cinemusic.de German language score site; reviews.

Classical Music Used in Film www.hnh.comcmuif.htm Pieces heard in films listed in alphabetical order.

Clipland www.clipland.com/index.shtml Online music video database.

CSS Music www.cssmusic.com Libraries on CD; themes for film and TV.

CueSheet.net www.cuesheet.net Film and TV music tip sheet; confidential service, detailing the music licensing requirements of TV/film companies, advertising agencies, etc.

Cyber Film School www.cyberfilmschool.com Web site with instruction, tips, advice, techniques on how to make, produce, direct, shoot, light, and edit TV, films, movies, and videos.

Dawsons Creek Music www.dawsonscreekmusic.com Music and artists from the TV show; featured artists, bands, and songs directory.

Disney Pictures www.disney.com/DisneyPictures/index.html Film industry; studio.

Documentary Educational Resources www.der.org Produce, distribute and promote ethnographic and documentary films from around the world.

Eonline Movies movies.eonline.com Movie information.

Field of Dreams: Film Music on the Internet
www.fod-online.com Online film music
publication.

Film Connection www.film-connection.com On-the-
job training in major film/video studios and
television stations; video clips; news; articles;
film and television resources; tips from hit
directors, editors, and producers; view other
helpful film-related sites; link site.

Film Festival www.filmfestival.be Film Festival
Ghent.

Film Festival Source www.filmfestivalsource.com
Links for film festivals organized by category and
by country.

Film Music www.filmmusic.com SoundtrackNet; the
art of film and television music; new reviews;
new soundtracks; current news.

Film Music Institute www.filmmusicinstitute.com
Offers professional education courses in Los
Angeles, New York, and other locations designed
specifically for the film and television music
industry.

Film Music Magazine www.filmmusicmag.com
Trade publication for the film and television
music industry; comprehensive coverage of
industry news; feature articles; investigative
reporting; event calendar.

Film Music on the Web UK
www.musicweb.uk.net/film/index.htm
Composer profiles; reviews.

Film Score Monthly www.filmscoremonthly.com
Online magazine of motion picture and television
music appreciation.

Film Scouts www.filmscouts.com Independent site
featuring original multimedia programming;
movie trailers and stills; festival coverage;
celebrity interviews; useful information; humor;
reviews; commentary.

Film Site www.filmsite.org/genres.html Lists and
descriptions of film genres.

Film Sound Design-Film Sound Theory
filmsound.studienet.org or www.filmsound.org
Theoretical and practical aspects on narrative
sound effects in film and TV.

FilmFestivals.com www.filmfestivals.com Portal
into the universe of cinema via its actors,
directors, and films being shown at film festivals
all over the world; over 6,000 pages and links.

Film-Makers.com www.film-makers.com Over
2,363 links to film-related Web sites.

Filmtracks Modern Soundtrack Reviews
www.filmtracks.com Reviews of recent motion
picture soundtracks; tributes to modern
composers; information about film music CD
collectibles; recent releases; customer favorites;
links to Amazon.com and E-Bay.com; "Best of
Series" organized by recent years and by decade.

FilmZone www.filmzone.com Previews and facts
about movies; library full of links to homepages;
large film database.

Fine Line Features www.finelinefeatures.com Slate;
spotlight; library; FAQ; shop.

Frame Rate www.framerate.net/ Royalty-free stock
film footage.

*George Eastman House International Museum of
Photography and Film* www.eastman.org
Collects and interprets images, films, and
equipment in the disciplines of photography and
motion picture.

Greatest Films: The Sound of Music (1965)
www.filmsite.org/soun.html Detailed review,
synopsis, and discussion of the film.

Guild of Canadian Film Composers www.gcfc.ca
National association of professional composers
and music producers for film, television, and new
media.

Hindi Movie Songs
www.cs.wisc.edu/~navin/india/songs Hindi
movie songs.

Hollywood Creative Directory www.hcdonline.com
Online data; specials; e-mail names; mailing
labels; lists on disc; site licenses; industry links;
resources; festivals; awards; guilds;
organizations; unions; studios; business; actors;
casting; celebrities; assistants; media; press;
services; music; education; seminars.

Hollywood Network
www.hollywoodnetwork.com/innercircle/
Hollywood Network Inner Circle Dealmaking
Desks.

Hollywood Online www.hollywood.com Movie
information; soundtracks.

Hollywood Reporter www.hollywoodreporter.com
Inside information on film and TV upcoming
projects; online subscriptions.

Hollywood Stock Exchange www.hsx.com Virtual
trading in the movie industry.

Independent Feature Project www.ifp.org Source for
independent filmmakers.

Independent Film Channel www.ifctv.com The
Independent Film Channel (IFC) is the first
channel dedicated to independent film presented
twenty-four hours a day, uncut and commercial-
free.

IndieDVD www.indiedvd.com Independent film
distribution.

Inside Film www.insidefilm.com Film festivals
directory; links; articles.

Internet Movie Database www.imdb.com Favorite
stars and movies, theater and TV show times,
online trailers, movie and trivia games.

Internet Movie Database Pro www.IMDbPro.com
Information resource designed exclusively for
people who work in the entertainment industry;

new content; customizable searches; easy-to-use design; in production; contact listings.

Jeff Rona www.jeffrona.com Information on film music.

Kilima www.kilima.comwelcome.html Intriguing films from a diverse selection of nations; films are listed by country and subject matter; comprehensive information on the films and filmmakers; includes art, music, and literature.

Kiraly Music Network www.kiralymusic.com Orchestral recordings for film made in Hungary.

Lee Holdridge www.leeholdridge.com Official site; audio clips.

License Music www.licensemusic.com Original, precleared songs from over seventy record labels and music publishers; search; listen; download.

Los Angeles Film & Music Magazine www.lafm.com Hollywood resource.

Mandy's International Film and Television Production Directory www.mandy.com Database of television film producers, facilities, and technicians worldwide; current film/TV jobs.

Media Rights www.MediaRights.org Nonprofit organization; helps media makers, educators, librarians, nonprofits, and activists use documentaries to encourage action and inspire dialogue on contemporary social issues.

Megatrax www.megatrax.com Production music for film, TV, ads, multimedia.

MGM www.mgm.com/home.do Studio site.

Michael Kamen www.michaelkamen.com News; interviews; articles; press releases.

Microcinema International www.microcinema.com Short films distribution.

Mining Co. Guide to Classic Movies Classicfilm.about.com Classic films.

Miramax Cafe www.miramax.com Graphics; celebrity information.

Movie Clichés List www.moviecliches.com Hollywood clichés.

Movie Flix www.movieflix.com Large collection of older movies available for viewing online, some free; MovieFlix Plus monthly subscriptions.

Movie Link www.movielink.com Internet movie rentals; Windows only.

Movie Music UK www.shef.ac.uk/~cm1jwb/mmuk.htm Reviews; audio clips; composer information.

MovieFone www.moviefone.com Movie listing guide and ticketing service; local movie show times; tickets; trailers; film reviews; photos; celebrity and more.

Movies with Classical Music www.classicaliscool.com/filmnote.htm Classical music in films sorted by movie title.

MovieSounds www.moviesounds.com Movie listing; sound tools; event sounds; trivia blitz; FAQ.

MovieWeb www.movieWeb.com Internet movie network.

Music Box Theatre's Home Page www.musicboxtheatre.com Chicago's year-round film festival.

Music from the Movies www.musicfromthemovies.com News and updates; reviews; CDs; links.

National Film Board of Canada www.nfb.ca Canadian films; produces and distributes films, audiovisual and multimedia works which reflect Canada to Canadians and the rest of the world.

National Film Preservation Foundation www.filmpreservation.org/sm_index.html Nonprofit organization created by the United States Congress to help save America's film heritage; support activities nationwide that preserve American films and improve film access for study, education, and exhibition.

New Day Films www.newday.com/about/index.html Offers independently produced films and videos that educate and inspire.

Paramount Pictures www.paramount.com Movies and TV.

Score Reviews www.scorereviews.com Current soundtracks review site; composers; blog; features; news.

ScoreLogue Web Magazine www.scorelogue.com Composer interviews; album notes; special features; news; links.

Screen Actors Guild www.sag.com Represents performers.

Screen Archives Entertainment www.screenarchives.com Catalog of regular and rare scores; occasional auctions of collectibles.

Sonic Images Records www.sonicimages.com Soundtrack releases.

Sony Pictures Online www.sonypictures.com/index.html Studio site.

Soundtrack Express www.soundtrack-express.com One of the original score review sites.

Soundtrack Magazine www.soundtrackmag.com Premiere source for film music news, reviews, and interviews.

SoundtrackNet www.soundtrack.net Art and business of film and television music; film scores to pop music that show up on soundtracks; information on composers.

Studio Systems, Inc. www.studiosystemsinc.com Projects, personnel, and production for film; The Studio System; In Hollywood; Scriptlog; information and research for the film and television industries.

SundanceChannel www.sundancechannel.com Promotes indie films; schedule; search; store.

Tamil Film Music Page tfmpage.com Comprehensive resource for Tamil Film Music; discussion forum; song lyrics; streamed live songs; master index of artists.

tdfilm.com www.tdfilm.com Online film resource.

Tennessee Film, Entertainment & Music Commission www.state.tn.us/film Movie locations; music producers; cable channels; video and CD-ROM production, etc.

The Cinematrax Film and Television Music Site www.cinematrax.com Organization founded by film and television composers Northam and Miller; information about *Film Music Magazine* and The Film Music Network; resource links.

The Film Music Network www.filmmusic.net Los Angeles-based organization to help film composers network and learn more about the film music industry; monthly workshop meetings in Los Angeles, New York City, San Francisco, Nashville, and Boston; memberships; magazine subscription; CDs.

The Film Music Society www.filmmusicsociety.org Nonprofit group dedicated to the preservation of film music; news and events; membership; merchandise; resources and links; to increase awareness of the artistic, historical, and commercial value of film and television music; to preserve and restore film and television music scores, manuscripts, orchestrations, recordings, and all related materials; to research, document, and disseminate the histories of film and television music, whether by oral means or by aural, written and/or digital media; to publish scholarly and other journalistic works on subjects relating to film and television music; to foster, encourage and cultivate new musical and journalistic works; to present and promote the film and television music contributions of past, present, and future composers, arrangers, and musicians.

The New York Underground Film Festival www.nyuff.com Call for entries.

The Society of Composers and Lyricists www.filmscore.org Industry forums; technology; performing rights; intellectual rights; seminars; contracts.

The Soundtrack Auction Page www.concentric.net/~Fortytwo/ Soundtrack and movie poster auction and sale site.

The Sundance Institute institute.sundance.org/jsps/site.jsp?resource=pag_ex_home Sundance Film Festival; application; calendar.

The Yorkton Short Film and Video Festival www.yorktonshortfilm.org Dramas; shorts; documentaries; videos; children's films; made-for-TV movies; workshops; food; music; awards; directors; producers; celebrities.

TrackSounds www.tracksounds.com Soundtrack and game soundtrack reviews; interviews.

TV Guides Movies www.tvguide.com/movies Film information; reviews; search database.

Twentieth Century Fox www.foxhome.com Information; film clips.

UCLA Film Scoring Program www.unex.ucla.edu Creative and technical challenges of film scoring; instructors are award-winning composers.

Universal Pictures www.universalstudios.com Production notes; film clips; photographs.

Varèse Sarabande www.varesesarabande.com Historical leader in score releases.

Variety www.variety.com Film; TV; music; news; world; business; legal; features.

Walt Disney Records disney.go.com/DisneyRecords Promotional site for CDs; includes audio clips.

Warner Brothers www2.warnerbros.com/web/movies/index.jsp Information; movie previews.

Welcome to The Sound of Music www.foxhome.com/soundofmusic/som.html Information on the1965 film; historical background; virtual tour of the Van Trapp Estate.

Women in Film www.wif.org Purpose is to empower, promote, nurture, and mentor women in the industry through a network of valuable contacts, events, and programs, including the Women In Film Mentor Program, the award-winning Public Service Announcement Production Program, and the Internship Program.

Women in the Director's Chair www.widc.org Not-for-profit media arts organization dedicated to promoting visibility for women media artists.

Writer's Guild of America www.wga.org Represents writers in the motion picture, broadcast, cable, and new media industries.

Folk and Traditional Music and Instruments—Folk Dancing—Bluegrass

Acoustics Records (UK) www.acousticsrecords.co.uk Virtuoso recordings of Celtic and classical mandolin, Irish accordion, folk songs, and children's music.

AcuTab Publications www.acutab.com Authorized tab transcriptions from the playing of top bluegrass pickers; banjo accessories and software.

American Melody www.americanmelody.com Award-winning recordings of folk, bluegrass, and children's music and stories; audio samples.

ARC Music www.arcmusic.co.uk/ Folk and world music.

Bluegrass Now www.bluegrassnow.com Magazine; festival calendar in each issue; features; reviews; tour schedules; group news.

Bluegrass Unlimited www.bluegrassmusic.com Magazine; annual festival directory; features; interviews; band news; tour schedules.

Bluegrass/Acoustic Music Portal
music.searchking.com Links to information on bluegrass music; associations; bands and artists; festivals; magazines and e-zines; music shops; musical instruments; radio and TV; recording.

Breezy Ridge Instruments Ltd. www.jpstrings.com Strings; hammered dulcimers; guitar products; capos; finger picks; vintage thumb picks; videos; Nuage Gypsy Strings.

Cajun/Zydeco Music and Dance
www.erols.com/ghayman Leading Cajun/Zydeco music and dance Web site; national and international festivals and special events information; regional reporters; bands and artists.

CajunZydeco.net cajunzydeco.net Links to other associated Web pages; schedules and newsletters; bands; festivals and dance camps; dance instructors; online dance instruction; online audio and video; Louisiana culture.

Clarenbridge Harps www.folkcraft.com Amergin; Amergin II; Erin; McClain; Adare.

Country Dance and Song Society www.cdss.org Celebrating a living tradition of English and Anglo-American dance and music since 1915.

Crafters of Tennessee www.crafterstn.com Products; news; history; banjos; mandolins; guitars.

Creativefolk.com creativefolk.com Resources; links; calendar of events nationwide and more.

Cybergrass www.cybergrass.com For bluegrass music enthusiasts; over 175 pages of information; artists; concerts; events; associations; bluegrass magazines; downloadable sound files; links; articles on bluegrass musicians; history of bluegrass.

Deering Banjo Co. www.deeringbanjos.com Banjo manufacturer.

Desktop Banjo www.desktopmusic.com/banjo.html Five-string banjo shareware computer program; learning tool; generates tablature and chords; Windows.

Dirty Linen www.dirtylinen.com Online folk music magazine; tour schedules in each issue; venues and contact information; folk, world music, roots music, Celtic; features; interviews; new release and concert reviews.

Dr. HorsehairMusic Co. www.drhorsehair.com Banjo recordings and instruction books; modern-day clawhammer banjo or frailing style; old-time minstrel banjo stroke style.

efolk Music www.efolkmusic.org/default.asp Folk music; bluegrass; Celtic music; children's music; MP3 downloads and independent CDs.

Encyclopedia of Cajun Culture
www.cajunculture.com Cajun music and culture.

ETSU Bluegrass and Country Music Program
cass.etsu.edu/bluegrass Bluegrass music program at East Tennessee State University.

Fiddler Magazine www.fiddle.com Informative, educational, and entertaining resource for fiddlers, accompanists, and appreciative listeners.

Flea Market Music Inc. www.flea-mkt-music.com Jumpin' Jim's ukulele products.

Folk Corporation www.folkcorp.co.uk UK folk music Web site; links.

Folk Dance Association www.folkdancing.org Calendar; directory; library; camps; cruises.

Folk Den www.folkden.com Roger McGuinn; purpose is to use the medium of the World Wide Web to continue the tradition of the folk process, that is the telling of stories, and singing of songs, passed on from one generation to another by word of mouth.

Folk Image www.folkimage.com Internet DJ's folk music audio Web site.

Folk Music Home Page
www.jg.org/folk/folkhome.html Informative links to folk music sites.

Folk Music Index www.ibiblio.org/folkindex/ Index to recorded sources.

Folk Music Links
Web.ukonline.co.uk/Members/martin.nail/comm erc.htm Links to record companies, publishers, retailers, and artist agents in England.

Folk of the Wood www.folkofthewood.com Acoustic instruments; information; lessons; accessories.

Folk Roots Home Page www.frootsmag.com England's leading roots, folk, and world music magazine; charts; reviews.

Folkcraft Instruments www.folkcraft.com Hammered dulcimers; folk harps.

FolkLib www.folklib.net/ A library of folk music links.

Folklinks.com www.folklinks.com Informative folk and acoustic music Web site.

Folkmusic.org www.folkmusic.org Comprehensive source for folk and acoustic music resources.

FolkWeb www.folkWeb.com Independent folk and acoustic music on CD.

Gold Tone Musical Instruments
www.nbbd.com/goldtone Gold Tone banjos; Gold Tone banjitars.

Guestlist Folk Music Pages
www.guestlist.freeserve.co.uk Extensive directory of UK folk music performers; *Folktalk Magazine*.

Harmonica Lessons www.harmonicalessons.com Complete harmonica source on the Internet.

International Bluegrass Music Association (IBMA)
www.ibma.org Venue, presenter, media, and membership mailing lists available; membership required; events and programs.

International Folk Culture Center www.ifccsa.org U.S., Canadian, and international folk dance and music groups, camps, festivals, institutes, parties, symposia, tours, weekend centers, college and university folk dance and folklore programs, directories, libraries, museum, organizations.

John C. Campbell Folk School www.folkschool.com Held in Brasstown, NC.

Kerrville Music Foundation Inc. Kerrville Directory www.kerrville-music.com Folk festival information; listings of United States and foreign folk venues, folk press, radio stations, newsletters, publications, record companies, agents, managers, performers, and publicists.

Mandolin Bros. Ltd. www.mandoWeb.com Mandolins and guitars.

Musicmaker's Kits, Inc. www.musikit.com Acoustic instrument do-it-yourself kit company; offers audio files of its instruments; catalog of early music and folk instruments.

National Storytelling Association (NSA) www.storynet.org Membership available; directory of organizations; storytellers; workshops; festivals; production companies; publishers of storytelling works; bimonthly magazine; National Storytelling Festival first full weekend in October annually.

Old Town School of Folk Music www.oldtownschool.org Held in Chicago, IL.

Polka Store www.polka-store.com/sheetmusic/index.htm For polka and band lovers; all occasion dance music by all types of polka players, bands, and virtuosos; cassettes, CDs, videos, and tours available.

PrinceGeorge.Com www.princegeorge.com/georgemusic/ Bagpipes, tin whistles, and mandolins.

Recreational Folk Dancing www.recfd.com Information; notes; where to dance; books; music; costumes.

Ridge Runner www.ridgerunner.com Music instruction mail-order company; digital study recorders; instruction videos for guitar, fiddle, mandolin, dobro, banjo, and other instruments.

San Francisco Folk Music Club www.idiom.com/~poet/harmony/ Calendar; local artists; links.

Sheet Music for Harmonica www.harmonicaspot.com/cat67.htm List of items available.

SingOut! Magazine www.singout.org Folk music magazine; annual directory of folk festivals; features; reviews; regular columns; to preserve and support the cultural diversity and heritage of all traditional and contemporary folk musics; to encourage making folk music a part of our everyday lives; tax-exempt, not-for-profit, educational organization.

Sound to Earth Inc. www.soundtoearth.com Instruments; players; dealers; products.

Southeast Celtic Music Association www.scmatx.org Promoting Celtic music in the southwest.

The Folk Alliance—North American Folk Music and Dance Alliance www.folk.org Folk and traditional music; annual conferences held in different locations; membership required; mailing lists available for sale.

The Folk Times www.mybizz.net/~folktimes/ Calendar of acoustic music performances in upstate New York.

The Gumbo Pages www.gumbopages.com New Orleans music and culture.

Traditional Dance in Toronto www.dancing.org Information on traditional dancing in the Toronto area.

Weber Mandolins www.Webermandolin.com Mandolin manufacturer.

World Folk Music Association wfma.net/ Events; folk music links; store.

Guitar and Bass— Acoustic and Electric

12 Tone Music www.12tonemusic.com Guitar and bass *Fretboard Flashcards; Guitar Encyclomedia.*

Acoustic Guitar Magazine www.acguitar.com or www.acousticguitar.com Features; interviews; reviews.

Active Bass www.activebass.com Online bass community.

Alamo Guitars www.alamoguitars.com Tonemonger.

All Jazz Guitar www.alljazzguitar.com Resource and reference site for jazz guitarists.

All Parts www.allparts.com Strings, pedals, parts, cases, etc.

Analog Man www.analogman.com Strings, pedals, parts, cases, etc.

Azola Basses www.azola.com Bug Bass; Mini Bass; Baby Bass; Deco Bass; Jazzman.

Bass Guitar Magazine www.bassguitarmagazine.com Subscribe; gear tests.

Bass Guitar Scale Page www.angelfire.com/id/bass/ Links to scales for bass guitar.

Bass Player www.bassplayer.com Bass guitar magazine; notes; tech; reviews.

Bass Tab Archive www.basstabarchive.com Tab index; submit a tab.

Basslines www.basslines.com Bass accessories.

Blue Book Inc. www.bluebookinc.com Prices and values of guitars.

Charanga Inc. www.guitarcoach.com *Guitar Coach; Electronic Guitar Coach;* award winning CD-ROM series uses groundbreaking technology and proven teaching methods to bring an enjoyable and effective way to master techniques and become a confident and impressive musician.

Chord Melody Guitar Music www.chordmelody.com Chord harmonizations; guitar sheet music and tab books; videos and instructional guitar music in all styles: jazz, classical, rock, country, blues, flamenco, acoustic, religious, and Christmas.

ChordWizard www.chordwizard.com Software for players of guitar, banjo, mandolin, bass guitar, ukulele, bouzouki, and other stringed instruments; free music theory tutorial; Windows.

Classical Guitar Composers List www.musicated.com/CGCL/ Comprehensive list of composers who have composed at least one original score for solo classical guitar.

Crate Amps www.crateamps.com Amplifiers.

Crate Pro Audio www.crateproaudio.com Company; products; support.

Crossroads Guitar www.crossroads-guitar.com Interactive online guitar courses; over 110 one-hour lessons with streaming video, soundfiles, notation, tablature, and text; free MP3 practice tracks, playing tips, introductory lessons, and real-time contact with instructors.

Curbow String Instruments www.curbow.com Home page; custom guitar builder presents procedures to design and develop string instruments; view photo galleries, materials, and features.

Cyberfretbass www.cyberfretbass.com Online lessons.

Daddario www.daddario.com Strings, pedals, parts, cases, etc.

Danelectro www.danelectro.com Guitar manufacturer; guitar accessories; amplifiers; effects; strings.

Dean Musical Instruments www.deanguitars.com Electrics; acoustics; basses.

Desktop Guitarist www.desktopmusic.com/guitar/ Tabulature generator, chord dictionary, guitar tuner, accompaniment player, and MIDI file generator; Windows.

Discount Distributors www.discount-distributors.com Cases and racks.

Dream Guitars & Apparel www.dreamguitars.com Custom instruments; accessories.

Electro-Harmonix www.ehx.com Analog effects for guitar and bass.

Elixir Guitar Strings www.elixirstrings.com Guitar strings; polyWeb coating.

Encyclopedia of Bass Logic www.basslogic.com Instructional text for the electric bass; technique, transcriptions, music theory, and rhythms.

Epiphone www.epiphone.com Division of Gibson Guitar Corp.; acoustic and electric guitars; amplifiers; accessories.

Ernie Ball www.ernieball.com Guitars, basses, and strings.

EVD String Instruments www.evd303.com Variations on traditional acoustic guitars, banjos, and lyres; view custom designs and testimonials.

Experience Hendrix www.jimi-hendrix.com Information on Jimi Hendrix.

Fastfingers www.fastfingers.co.uk Guitar tuition courses covering all guitar styles; courses on compact disk, tape, or video.

Fender Guitars www.fender.com Product catalog; technical support; find date guitar was made with serial number; contests; e-zine.

Fernandes Guitars www.fernandesguitars.com Guitar manufactuter.

Finger Style Guitar www.fingerstyleguitar.com Features; reviews; news.

Flamenco Guitar Transcriptions www.ctv.es/guitar Study of the flamenco guitar throughout the twentieth century; 231 soleares falsetas from the 1900s to the 1990s in standard notation and tablature.

Flamenco World www.flamenco-world.com Site for flamenco music; music and dance videos; CDs; online magazine; interviews and biographies of the world's greatest guitarists and singers.

Flamenco.org www.flamenco.org Flamenco events; classes.

Flat Pick www.flatpick.com Guitar magazine; bi-monthly.

Fodera Guitars www.fodera.com Bass guitars; accessories; electric bass strings.

Fresh Tabs www.FreshTabs.com Guitar tablature.

FretsOnly www.fretsonly.com Online catalog of various educational products for guitar, banjo, mandolin, and violin; by Ashley Mark Publishing Company.

Gary Talley www.garytalley.com Guitar instruction for songwriters; video.

Gas Pedal www.gaspedal.com Forums; hot licks; articles; radio.

Genz Benz Enclosures www.genzbenz.com Products; dealers.

George Furlanetto's Bass www.fbass.com Models; specs; price list; dealers.

George L's Musical Products www.georgels.com Effects; strings; pedals.

GHS Strings www.ghsstrings.com Guitar strings.

Gibson Guitar www.gibson.com Home page; guitar manufacturer based in Nashville; acoustic and electric; strings and accessories; merchandise; music news; references; free online appraisal; dealer directory; auction.

Gig Mate www.gigmate.com Strings, pedals, parts, cases, etc.

GMW Guitarworks www.gmwguitars.com Empire Guitars.

Gretsch www.gretsch.com Guitar and drum manufacturer.

Gruhn Guitars www.gruhn.com Nashville-based vintage guitar dealer; catalog; photo gallery.

Guild Guitars www.guildguitars.com What's new; resources; online store.

Guitar and Bass Guitar Lessons on the Web www.visionmusic.com Guitar education site; free online music lessons for the evolving guitarist or bassist.

Guitar Auction www.guitarauction.com Auction source for used, new, and vintage guitars by Martin, Gibson, Fender, Takoma, and others.

Guitar Base www.gbase.com Gear Mall; guitar and vintage guitar inventory on the Internet; online community; locate dealers; classified ads.

Guitar Center www.guitarcenter.com Guitars; amps; drums; keyboards; software; recording and P.A. gear; DJ and lighting; fifty-seven locations nationwide.

Guitar Chord Calculator www.guitarcalc.com Program shows the correct hand position for every chord; Windows.

Guitar College, Inc. www.guitarcollege.com Home study courses for guitar.

Guitar Concept guitarconcept.home.att.net Guitar lessons online or by United States mail.

Guitar Connection www.guitarconnection.com Sheet music, videos, software, and DVDs.

Guitar Foundation of America 66.223.41.156/index.htm Membership; competition.

Guitar Gallery Sheet www.guitargallerymusic.com Catalog of guitar music and instructional videos; also banjo, mandolin, fiddle, bass, dulcimer, harmonica, penny whistle, autoharp, songbooks, and more.

Guitar Geek www.guitargeek.com Guitar rig database.

Guitar Lessons at Home www.guitar-lessons-at-home.com In-home lessons; transcriptions.

Guitar Lessons at Musiclearning.Com www.musiclearning.com Guitar lessons with play-along MIDI files and RealAudio listening examples.

Guitar Links www.guitarlinks.com Guitar Web site links.

Guitar Magic www.sdgsoft.com Guitar software for both electric and acoustic guitar players; Windows.

Guitar Net www.guitar.net Chord Archive features a different chord every week; Tab Planet; G.E.A.R.; articles.

Guitar Nine Records www.guitar9.com Guitar recordings; books; news.

Guitar Noise www.guitarnoise.com Free online lessons; online college.

Guitar Notes www.guitarnotes.com Guitar links; lessons; MP3s; tabs; shopping; reviews; listings of over 600 guitar dealers; details on how to purchase amps and related accessories.

Guitar One Magazine www.guitaronemag.com Guitar Webzine; tab and notation; MP3s.

Guitar Online www.guitar-online.com Guitar courses online, via e-mail or CD-ROM; videos, scores, and tablatures; MIDI files; online tuner and metronome; English; French; Spanish.

Guitar Player Magazine www.guitarplayer.com Buyer's guide; features; lessons; reviews.

Guitar Playing www.guitarplaying.com Downloads; games; guitarists.

Guitar Pro Manual www.booklocker.com/bookpages/syurtsever.html Self-instruction manual on how to play the guitar; over seventy pages of text and illustrations.

Guitar Simplified www.guitarsimplified.com The "Guitar Barre" method; online sales of a lesson book and a play-along video; for beginners.

Guitar Sounds www.guitarsounds.com The Peter Pupping Quartet.

Guitar Tab Universe www.guitartabs.cc/home.php Lessons; forum; submit song.

Guitar World www.guitarworld.com Electric; features; reviews.

Guitar.com www.guitar.com Guitar guide; chord generator; instructors; artists; MP3; tablature; chat; community.

Guitar4u.com www.guitar4u.com Information on instruction and music theory.

GuitarLessons.net www.guitarlessons.net Guitar lessons taught by a professional guitarist; free 24 hours a day.

Guitarras Manuel Rodriguez & Sons; S.L. www.guitars-m-r-sons.com Classical and Flamenco; Cutaway Models; Cadete and Señorita Models.

GuitarSite.com www.guitarsite.com For guitarists by guitarists; updated daily.

Harmony Central: Bass Resources www.harmony-central.com/Bass/ Links to bass Web sites.

Harmony Central: Guitar Tab www.harmony-central.comGuitar/tab.html Tablature.

Highly Strung www.highlystrung.co.uk Strings, pedals, parts, cases, etc.

Hot Licks Productions www.hotlicks.com Instructional media.

Howling Dog www.howlingdog.com Guitar-oriented software.

International Guitar Seminar www.guitarseminars.com Classes; seminars; FAQ; links.

Jackson Guitars www.jacksonguitars.com Guitar manufacturer; resources.

Jam Bass www.jambass.com Wafer-thin neck back panel for guitars that duplicates the bottom E and A strings fret by fret, voiced an octave lower like a bass guitar.

Jazz Guitar Online www.jazzguitar.com For jazz guitarists; lessons; forum; features; news.

Jean Larrivee Guitars Ltd. www.larrivee.com Guitar manufacturer.

Johnson Amp www.johnson-amp.com Amplifiers.

Just Strings www.juststrings.com Large selection of strings for all string instruments.

Kaman Music Corp. www.kamanmusic.com Ovation; Takamine; Hamer; Toca; Gibraltar; CB.

Ken Smith Basses Ltd. www.kensmithbasses.com Bass guitars.

La Bella Strings www.labella.com La Bella; Criterion; Electrics; Super Steps; Deep Talkin' Bass; Slappers; Pacesetter; Folksinger; Elite Series; Series 2001; Silk & Steel; Kapalua; New Yorkers.

Lakland Basses www.lakland.com Standard; Deluxe; Classic; Joe Osborn Signature; Bob Glaub Signature; Jerry Scheff Signature; Willie Weeks Signature.

Learn to Play Guitar www.guitarcalc.com/learnguitar Free guitar e-book to download; music software.

Levy's Leathers Ltd. www.levysleathers.com Home page.

Martin Guitar Company www.martinguitar.com Guitars; strings; pedals; parts; cases; etc.

Mesa Boogie www.mesaboogie.com Guitar amplifiers; photos; product information; English and German.

Metal Method www.metalmethod.com Video guitar lessons; weekly free lessons include tablature, WAV, and MP3 files.

MetalTabs.com www.metaltabs.com Heavy metal guitar tabs.

Music Theory Course for Guitar www.guitar-jimsuttoninst.comMT.html International correspondence guitar school.

Musical Instrument Makers Forum www.mimf.com Acoustic guitar making; electric guitar building; guitar repair; violin making; online interactive course in instrument making; discussion forum; community for musicians and instrument makers.

National Guitar Summer Workshop www.guitarworkshop.com Held June through August in various locations.

Net Guitar www.netguitar.com Stringed instrument division deals in new and vintage guitars; sales and repair company.

Online Guitar Archive www.olga.net Guitar resources; tablature.

PDS Music www.pdsmusic.com Acoustic and classical guitar lessons offered by international mail order correspondence; free sample lessons.

Pedal Boards www.pedalboards.com Pedal racks.

Pedal Man www.pedalman.com Strings, pedals, parts, cases, etc.

Phantom Guitar Works Inc. www.phantomguitars.com Phantom Guitars; Teardrop Guitars; Mando Guitars.

Picks by the Pound www.picksbythepound.com Guitar picks.

Pignose Amps www.pignoseamps.com Amplifiers.

Play Guitar www.nl-guitar.com Download program to learn how to play guitar; music educational programs for schools.

Play Jazz www.playjazz.com Jazz guitar site.

RainSong Graphite Guitars www.rainsong.com Graphite guitars; RainSong; WS 1000; WS 2000; WS 1100; JZ 1000.

Registry Publications Examination members.aol.com/registrypl/index2.htm Handbooks for electric guitar, classical guitar and bass guitar; books and audiocassettes covering all aspects of guitar from beginners to advanced; performance and improvisation.

Renaissance Guitars www.renaissanceguitars.com Renaissance Guitars and Basses; Rick Turner Guitars; Electroline Basses; Model T Guitars.

Rio Grande Pickups www.riograndepickups.com Pickups.

Sabine www.sabineusa.com Chromatic tuners for all stringed instruments..

Samick Music Corp. www.samickmusicusa.com Guitar manufacturer.

Samson Technologies Corp. www.samsontech.com Strings, pedals, parts, cases, amplifiers.

Santa Cruz Guitar Co. www.santacruzguitar.com Guitars.

Schecter Guitar Research www.schecterguitars.com Custom Guitars and Basses; Diamond Series Guitars; Basses and Seven-String Electrics; Diamond Acoustics; CB-2000.

Self Tuning www.selftuning.com Strings, pedals, parts, cases, etc.

Seymour Duncan www.seymourduncan.com Pickups.

Sierra Steel Guitars www.sierrasteelguitar.com Steel guitars; lap steel; cases.

Smart Sound www.bass-guitar-strings.com Guitar and bass strings.

Sonic Bass www.sonicbass.co.uk Bass guitars.

Spector Design Ltd. www.spectorbass.com Bass guitars and strings.

Stefan Grossman's Guitar Workshop www.guitarvideos.com Comprehensive series of video and audio guitar lessons in a wide variety of styles, featuring world-renowned instructors.

Steinberger www.gibson.com/products/steinberger Headless guitars and basses; company information.

String Letter Publishing www.stringletter.com Publisher of guitar magazines, books, songbooks, and CDs.

String Tech www.stringtech.com Strings, pedals, parts, cases, etc.

Super Guitar Chord Finder www.ready4music.com Learn, search for, analyze, and play guitar chords; Windows.

Tacoma Guitars USA www.tacomaguitars.com Tacoma USA; Olympia.

Talk Bass www.talkbass.comhtml/index.php Reviews; tab; galleries.

Taylor Guitars www.taylorguitars.com Guitar manufacturer based in El Cajon, CA; newsletter.

TCguitar.com www.tcguitar.com *Twentieth Century Guitar* magazine.

Teaching the Folk Guitar www.radioyur.com/yufpub.html Learn to teach basic guitar skills to students of all ages; method for teaching guitar in a group situation; 256-page teaching manual with two cassettes.

The Blues Bible www.onlinerock.com/services/danmc2 Learn to play blues guitar; chord diagrams; lead scale diagrams; slide guitar diagrams; audio examples; information on ordering the CD-ROM.

The Classical Guitar Home Page www.guitarist.com/cg/cg.htm The original Classical Guitar Home Page; created in 1994.

The Natural Approach to Guitar www.thenaturalapproach.com Revolutionary video guitar program; teaches students to see and hear the neck as one unit; no memorizing scales; improvise in any style.

TrueFire.com www.truefire.com Guitar instruction; digital self-publishing and distribution system for guitar instruction; original music, literature, art, and reference materials; available in MP3, pdf, html, and RealAudio formats; content may be purchased for a fee, then downloaded.

VintageGuitar.com www.vguitar.com Guitar magazine.

W. Paul Guitars Inc. www.wpaulguitars.com Timeless Timber guitars and bass guitars.

Washburn International www.washburn.com Acoustic and electric guitars and basses.

Holiday Music

4Hanukkah 4hanukkah.4anything.com Hanukkah history; holiday gift ideas; songs; greetings; Kosher recipes.

All Christmas Music www.allchristmasmusic.com CDs; videos; collections.

All-Yours Free Holiday Greeting Cards www.all-yours.net/postcard/pictures/xmas.html Free season's greetings; animated holiday postcard with music and special effects.

Black History Month, Kwanzaa, and Martin Luther King Day Resources creativefolk.com/blackhistory.html Provides the origins of Black History Month, Kwanzaa, and Martin Luther King Day; links to Internet resources, including recipes, songs, games, and speeches.

Christmas Music on the Web www.kidsdomain.com/holiday/xmas/music.html Links to Christmas music and fun activities.

Christmas World View www.christmas.com/worldview/ Clickable world map with national traditions.

Halloween—History and Traditions of the Holiday wilstar.com/holidays/hallown.htm History and customs of Halloween.

Hanukkahh Celebrations at the Holiday Spot www.theholidayspot.com/hanukkah/ Free Chanukkah wallpaper, recipes, letterhead, music, history, and more.

Happy Thanksgiving www.theholidayspot.com/thanksgiving Greetings; clip art; recipes.

Hatikvah Music hatikvahmusic.com Jewish Music; Klezmer, Yiddish, Ladino, Sephardic, Cantorial, Israeli, and children's holiday CDs, tapes, and videos.

Haunted Halloween members.aol.com/media27/haunted.htm Interactive haunted house file with spooky 2D and 3D animations, pictures, music, and sounds.

Have Yourself a Merry Little Christmas Page www.kate.net/holidays/christmas Large categorized list of Christmas links; holiday music.

Holiday Stuff for Children home.amaonline.com/teacherstuff/holiday.htm Thanksgiving and Christmas sites; arts and crafts, coloring pages; holiday stories.

I Love Wavs www.ilovewavs.com Holiday music files and more.

Merry Christmas www.bishart.com/merry_christmas.htm Celebrate Christmas with holiday links, music and, eToys.

Merry-Christmas.com www.merry-christmas.com/music.htm MIDI files; holiday jukebox.

Merry Christmas Happy Hanukkah—A Multilingual Songbook & CD www.pianopress.com/multilingualsongbook.htm Thirty-two traditional favorites;

piano/vocal/guitar songbook w/CD; lyrics in English, Hebrew, Spanish, German, French, and Latin; RealAudio files.

New Year's Day
www.wilstar.com/holidays/newyear.htm History, traditions, and customs of New Year's Day and how it is celebrated.

Santa Claus Online www.santaclausonline.com E-mail a letter to Santa Claus and he will respond personally; fun and games; holiday music; free clip art; free Christmas cards; toys and much more; listen to Santa read *'Twas the Night before Christmas.*

Santa Land www.santaland.com/songs.html Christmas carols and lyrics.

Sheryl's Holidays Site
www.sherylfranklin.com/holidays Collection of pages and links related to all holidays.

Sleigh Ride www2.acc.af.mil/music/holiday Christmas and holiday season music; in MP3 and RealAudio; United States Air Force Heritage of America Band.

The Holiday Page-History and Customs
wilstar.com/holidays Explains the customs and history of most holidays, including, but not limited to, Christmas, Easter, and New Year's Day; games, graphics, music, and poetry.

Uncle Debi's Holidays
home.wnm.net/~debi/holidays.htm Links to all holidays; message mates; holiday clip art; virtual greeting cards; historical and holiday calendar.

Jazz, Blues, and Swing

4Blues.com www.4blues.com Listen to blues MP3s; read about blues legends, blues festivals, and concert tickets; blues clubs and singers are listed.

A Passion 4 Jazz www.apassion4jazz.net Information; resources; links.

Acoustic Records home.c2i.net/acousticrecords Independent Norwegian jazz record label; artist information; reviews; MP3 samples and more.

Advance Music www.advancemusic.com Jazz Conception; Jazz Workshop Series.

Aebersold Jazz Online www.jajazz.com Producer of play-along disks and educational materials.

All About Jazz www.allaboutjazz.com Reviews and more; guide to jazz.

Alligator Records www.alligator.com Foremost authority on blues music and blues artists; view artist bios and liner notes; online catalog.

Any Swing Goes www.anyswinggoes.com Swing music Web site.

Bird Lives! www.birdlives.com Weekly jazz-zine; sneak previews.

Blue Note Records www.bluenote.com Jazz label; reviews; news; online catalog, artist and tour

information; RealAudio clips; Jukebox StreamWorks audio.

Blues Access www.bluesaccess.com/ba_home.html Current issue; links; subscribe.

Blues Express www.bluesexpress.com TV; records; CDs; DVDs.

Blues for Peace Cafe www.bluesforpeace.com Web radio, blues books, art, CDs, gifts, and more.

Blues Lab www.blueslab.com Youth enrichment programs; after school programs.

Blues News www.bluesnews.com Blues information.

Blues on Stage www.mnblues.com Comprehensive blues guide; reviews.

Blues Paradise-Classic Blues Musicians
www.bluesparadise.com Links to national and regional blues acts; schedule for regional blues venues; festival information and more.

Blues Revue www.bluesrevue.com Magazine site with blues MP3s.

Blues World www.bluesworld.com Calendar; catalog.

BluesNet www.hub.org/bluesnet Articles, photographs, and more; traditional and historical blues artists.

BluesWEB www.island.net/~blues Harp amplifier sound samples; custom-built harmonicas; action and sound.

Camsco Music: Traditional Folk, World, and Blues Music www.camsco.com Traditional blues and folk music of America and the world.

Contemporary Jazz www.contemporaryjazz.com News; releases; reviews; interviews; forums.

Contemporary List of Jazz Links
riad.usk.pk.edu.pl/~pmj/jazzlinks/ Artists; education; radio; links.

Cyberjaz.com www.cyberjaz.com Jazz Web site; hard-to-find and rare recordings.

Dr. Jazz Operations www.drjazz.com Independent radio and print media record promotion firm in the United States; jazz, blues, and world music.

East Coast International Blues and Roots Music Festival www.bluesfest.com.au Australian blues festival.

Electric Blues www.electricblues.com Hundreds of blues CD ratings; biweekly CD reviews with RealAudio, RealAudio Blues Jukebox, and Real Audio Blues links; all artists linked to discographies/soundclips.

Europe Jazz Network www.ejn.it/ Concerts; bulletin board.

Festivals Productions, Inc.
www.festivalproductions.net Founded by George Wein; has been producing music events for over forty-five years; originated outdoor music festivals in 1954 with the Newport Jazz Festival, which continues today as JVC Jazz Festival—Newport, RI; since then, the company has produced festivals all over the world.

Fivenote Music Publishing www.fivenotemusic.com Publishes music books containing jazz improvisation method, theory, and resources for learning and improving skills for beginning through advanced players of treble clef instruments.

Glenn Miller Orchestra www.glennmillerorchestra.com History; personnel; tour schedule; reviews; links.

House of Blues www.hob.com Live concert cybercasts; music news; on demand concert archives; interviews; music reviews; Internet radio; music editorial.

International Association of Jazz Education www.iaje.org Official Web site; *Jazz Education Journal*; annual conference; teacher training institute.

JAZCLASS www.jazclass.aust.com Music lessons on music theory, blues, jazz, improvisation, chords, and scales on all instruments; saxophone technique.

Jazz and Blues www.jazzandblues.org KJAZ radio and Internet radio; program grid; host bios.

Jazz and Blues Report www.jazz-blues.com Reviews of jazz, blues, fusion, and swing music from record labels like Alligator, Rounder, Blind Pig, and more.

Jazz Clubs Worldwide www.jazz-clubs-worldwide.com Organized by continent.

Jazz Corner www.jazzcorner.com Great jazz site with MIDI files, jazz artists Web pages, and other jazz related material.

Jazz in France www.jazzfrance.com/en Concerts; festivals; French Jazz record labels; magazines; forums; music reviews; audio samples.

Jazz Is www.jazzis.com Online retailer of jazz music recordings.

Jazz IZ www.jazziz.com Features; reviews; news; subscriptions.

Jazz Legends jazz_legends.vstoremusic.com The History of Jazz Music Store.

Jazz Master www.jazzmaster.com Information; resources; links.

Jazz Net www.culturekiosque.comjazz Jazz Web site.

Jazz Online www.jazzonline.com Monthly Webzine; news; features; links; artist reviews; Jazz 101; introduction to the world of jazz.

Jazz Promo www.jazzpromo.com Unique independent jazz CDs; MP3s.

Jazz Radio www.jazzradio.org From Lincoln Center in New York City; concert series.

Jazz Review www.jazzreview.com Submit music.

Jazz Roots www.jass.com Early jazz history.

Jazz Roots Rhythms www.jdscomm.comjazz1.html Jazz, soul, blues, gospel, world music; San Francisco and the global music scene.

Jazz Scale Suggester System www.w-link.net/~jsss/jsss.htm Enter jazz chord chart; suggests and explains solo scale possibilities.

Jazz Services www.jazzservices.org.uk/jazzsite.htm UK jazz Web site.

Jazz Stuff www.jazzstuff.com Jazz Web site; artists in residence; news.

Jazz Times Magazine Inc. www.jazztimes.com Club Guide in September issue; night clubs; managers; booking agents; features; reviews; news; photography; subscriptions.

Jazz West.com www.jazzwest.com The Bay Area's online jazz network.

Jazz World www.jazzworld.com Information; resources; links; new faces in jazz; artist network.

Jazz, Blues, Flamenco, and World Music Posters www.arrakis.es/~artstudiohita Limited-edition prints.

Jazzbreak www.jazzbreak.com Jazz guide; history; musicians; fanzine; news.

JazzFM www.jazzfm.com The home of jazz on the Internet.

Jazzharmony.com www.jazzharmony.com Contemporary methods for piano, ear training, chords, and jazz voicings; jazz standard fake books; free monthly chord post; includes teaching and learning tips about chords.

JazzInternet.com jazzinternet.com Jazz resources worldwide; jazz radio; RealAudio sites; "Jazz Club" with message board and chat; resource.

JazzUtopia www.jazzutopia.com Jazz music books, videos, and CDs for listening, practicing, and learning.

Jazzworx! www.jazzworx.com.au Set of learning tools; lesson by lesson on a double CD and book; three-volume series; beginning, intermediate, and advanced.

Montreal Jazz Festival www.montrealjazzfest.com/fijm2003/images/splash/intro.asp?flashPlugin=non In French and English.

Montreux Jazz Festival www.montreuxjazz.com/2003/default.htm Official Web site.

New Jazz Archives www.eyeneer.com/Jazz/index.html Jazz Web site.

New Mexico Jazz Workshop www.flash.net/~nmjw Dedicated to American jazz; premier jazz presenting and education organization.

New Orleans Jazz and Heritage Festival www.nojazzfest.com Schedules.

New Orleans Music Radio: WWOZ www.wwoz.org Listener supported jazz and heritage station for New Orleans and the surrounding region; from blues to jazz, cajun, zydeco, gospel, Brazilian, and Caribbean.

New Orleans Music Resources www.partyhats.com New Orleans music resources; free classified listings; Web radio; mall; music history.

New York Jazz Artist Management www.nyjam.com Representing New York City artists.

Newworldnjazz.com www.newworldnjazz.com Full-service marketing, promotion, and consulting company for the Jazz, Smooth Jazz, and World Music formats; work with over 1,000 radio stations in the United States and Canada.

Open Directory dmoz.org/Arts/Music/Styles/Blues/ Blues links.

Oscar Peterson www.oscarpeterson.com/op Signature CD-ROM project; music book of transcriptions with audio CD; up-to-date personal Web site.

PBS www.pbs.org/jazz/ *Jazz;* film by Ken Burns.

Photographs from the Golden Age of Jazz memory.loc.gov/ammem/wghtml/wghome.html William P. Gottlieb Collection; over 1,600 photographs of celebrated jazz artists; documents the jazz scene from 1938 to 1948 in New York City and Washington, DC.

Pittsburgh Blues Women www.pghblueswomen.com Chicago and New Orleans are known for blues music; many female blues performers are from these cities.

Posi-Tone Jazz World posi-tone.com For jazz enthusiasts; links to tribute sites, legends, and other jazz-related sites.

Real Blues Magazine www.realbluesmagazine.com Guide for blues music.

SaxTrax.com www.saxtrax.com Smooth jazz, traditional jazz, and new age CDs.

Sher Music www.shermusic.com Publisher of jazz educational materials; *The New Real Book;* Brazilian and Latin songbooks.

SkyJazz Internet Radio www.skyjazz.com Jazz in four categories: Big Band, Light & Easy, Straight Ahead, and All Requests.

Smooth Sounds www.smoothsounds.com Contemporary jazz CDs; traditional jazz CDs; new age CDs; video and links.

Sonny Boy Lee's "Ain't nothin' but the blues!" www.sonnyboylee.com Blues artists pages and links to blues music sites worldwide.

Southwest Blues www.southwestblues.com Blues festival.

Stanford Jazz Workshop www.stanfordjazz.org Jazz education.

Swedejazz.se www.swedejazz.se Web site about Swedish jazz.

Texas Blues Music www.texasbluesmusic.com Information about the blues from Texas; blues clubs; guitar maintenance; commentary; flatted thirds and more.

The Blue Highway thebluehighway.com History of and tribute to the blues.

The Blue Zone bluezone.org Blues bands.

The Blues Fake Book www.netstoreusa.com/music/002/HL00240082.s html Fake book of over 400 songs for all "C" instruments; sheet music.

The Blues Foundation www.blues.org Organized and founded in 1980 to promote and preserve blues.

The Jazz Age Page www.btinternet.com/~dreklind/Jazzhome.htm Historical view through the music and events of the twenties and thirties; music clips; biographies.

The Jazz Composers Collective www.jazzcollective.com Musician-run, nonprofit organization dedicated to presenting the works of composers; concert series; newsletter.

The Jazz Pages: Jazz in Deutschland www.jazzpages.com Jazz in Germany.

The Jazz Resource Center www.jazzcenter.org Useful material on jazz theory, voicings, chart transcriptions, and other information.

The Jazz School www.jazzschool.com Specializes in jazz education.

The Jazz Store www.thejazzstore.com Collectible jazz albums and merchandise.

The Jazzserver www.jazzserver.org Interactive jazz database; jazz groups; samples; venues and festivals from all over the world

The JazzSource www.jazzsource.com Comprehensive international resource to the world of jazz.

The Red Hot Jazz Archive www.redhotjazz.com History of jazz before 1930.

The Styles of Jazz www.nwu.edu/WNUR/jazz/styles/ Various jazz styles and other jazz information.

Thelonious Monk Institute of Jazz monkinstitute.com Official site for Thelonious Monk Institute of Jazz; photos and information.

Village Vanguard www.villagevanguard.net Famous jazz club; recording venue; schedules.

What is Jazz? town.hall.org Archives/radio/Kennedy/Taylor/ Four lectures.

Yahoo! Entertainment: Music: Genres: Blues www.yahoo.com/Entertainment/Music/Genres/Bl ues Blues music.

Yazoo Blues www.yazoobluesmailorder.com Deep, gritty, traditional blues; delta blues; acoustic blues; online catalog.

Latin and Caribbean Music — Calypso — Reggae

About Ska/Reggae ska.about.com Information; resources; links.

ART-COM International Latin Music Megastore
www.artcomintl.com/music.htm Online
Hispanic/Latino resource for Latin music CDs
and videos; Latin pop, Latin rap, danza,
flamenco, mariachi, merengue, salsa, tango,
tejano, and more.

Batanga www.batanga.com/sp/default.asp Latin
music Internet radio.

Bembe Records www.bembe.comcgi-
bin/SoftCart.exe/store/index.html?E+scstore
Cuban music record label.

Billboard Latin Music Conference and Awards
www.billboardevents.com/billboardevents/latin/i
ndex.jsp Schedule; finalists and winners; show.

Caravan Music
www.caravanmusic.com/GuideLatinMusic.htm
Guide to Latin music.

*Caravan Music Online Catalog of Latin/Brazilian
Music* www.caravanmusic.com Online mail
order CD catalog; buyers guide for music from
Latin America and beyond; world music genres
covering Brazil, Portugal, Spain, Cuba,
Argentina, Colombia, Argentina, Puerto Rico,
and more.

Caribbean Beat www.caribbeat.com.jm Mission of
the company is to create an Internet environment
to give recognition to the exploits of Caribbean
artists and to satisfy the need for the effective
online promotion and distribution of music
products and services from the Caribbean.

Caribbean Festival www.caribbeanfestival.org
Celebrated during the month of September on the
Labor Day weekend; opportunity for corporations
and businesses to advertise their products and
services by sponsoring various Caribbean
Recording Artists; free to the public; every year
over 75,000 people experience an entire day of
entertainment by leading performers, enjoy exotic
foods, and view arts and crafts; event takes place
on Webster Avenue between 233rd Street and
East Gun Hill Road, Bronx, New York.

Descarga.com
www.descarga.com/db/pages/catalog.html
Artists; journal archives; glossary of terms;

Glossary of Latin Music Terms
aachen.heimat.de/salsa/glossary.htm Definitions
in alphabetical order.

Heartbeat Records www.rounder.com/heartbeat Has
released some of Jamaica's finest quality music,
from ska, rocksteady, early reggae, and dub, to
today's best modern roots and cultural dancehall.

Hispanic Online www.hispaniconline.com Arts and
entertainment.

*Hispano Music and Culture of the Northern Rio
Grande*
memory.loc.gov/ammem/rghtml/rghome.html
Juan B. Rael Collection of religious and secular
music of Spanish-speaking residents of northern

New Mexico; essays in English and Spanish;
RealAudio and WAV files.

Hot Salsa www.chez.com/abri/e/index.htm Archives,
forum, and more.

International Latin Music Hall of Fame
www.latinfame.com Nonprofit organization,
dedicated to honoring those artists and others who
have contributed to and supported the growth of
Latin music around the world.

Jammin Reggae Archives niceup.com Gateway to
reggae music on the Internet; search; sounds;
links.

Just Salsa www.justsalsa.com Web magazine
dedicated to Latin music, dance, and culture.

LaMusica.com stories.lamusica.com Bilingual Latin
music and entertainment site, featuring original
content, music reviews, Web casts, celebrity
chats, concert info, contests, artist interviews,
videos, and online shopping.

LARitmo www.laritmo.com *Latin American Rhythm
Magazine*; interviews; articles; charts.

Latin American Folk Institute www.lafi.org
Nonprofit organization dedicated to building
community through art education and affordable
cultural programs; promotes the art, music, and
folklore of the Caribbean.

Latin American Music Center
www.music.indiana.edu/som/lamc Fosters the
research and performance of Latin American art
music.

Latin Jazz Club www.LatinJazzClub.com Giant
literary cyber-emporium of related music news,
articles, interviews, CD reviews, and
information; virtual online magazine dedicated to
the advancement, education, and historical
preservation of Latin Jazz.

Latin Music Entertainment, Inc.
www.lmeonline.com Licenses, manufactures,
markets, and distributes Latin music on compact
disk and cassette.

Latin Music from Picadillo
www.picadillo.com/picadillo/index0.shtml Latin
music site; Cuban music, salsa, songo, timba,
and guaguanco; complete songs in RealAudio;
extensive press archive in English.

Latin Music Guide
www.latinmusicguide.com/english/index.cfm
Industry publication.

Latin Music Specialists
www.latinmusicspecialists.com Latin music
library for TV, film, and commercials.

Latin Music World www.latinmusicworld.com Mega
store with over 500,000 items.

Latin Pop Music latinpop.vstoremusic.com Latin
pop, ballad, and rock artists and groups; romantic
music of Latino artists.

Latin Real Book, Latin-Jazz
www.shermusic.com/latrealb.htm Contemporary

and classic salsa, Latin jazz and Brazilian music arrangements; exactly as recorded, to help bands play in authentic Latin styles.

Latin Sequences of Miami www.latinosequences.com Cumbia, merengue, salsa, and all Latin rhythms; free catalog; se habla español; over 4,000 Latin rhythm sequences.

Latin/Jazz Reviews www.warr.org/latinjazz.html Reviews of recordings by Latin and Jazz artists.

Latin-Beat.net latin-beat.net/ Latin music, culture, recordings, and shopping; Latin dances; music samples and steps; stars, posters, magazines, leathers, instruments.

Latino Web www.latinoweb.com Latino culture.

LatinWorld www.latinworld.com Articles; travel; adventure; music.

Library of Congress/HLAS Online Home Page lcWeb2.loc.gov/hlas *Handbook of Latin American Studies;* bibliography on Latin America; selected and annotated by scholars.

Music Imports www.musicimports.com/search.asp?7=latin&1= Go&selCriteria=Artist Latin music titles.

Music in Latin America-LANIC lanic.utexas.edu/la/region/music Latin American resources; links.

MusicaPeruana.com www.musicaperuana.com Music of Peru.

Mybodega.com www.mybodega.com/latin_music.htm Latin Music Superstore; rare and hard-to-find imports; rhythms and sounds from the Latin music world; Latino books and foods; Spanish videos and special gifts.

Oasis Salsero www.oasissalsero.com Salsa music Web site; Spanish.

Puro Mariachi www.mariachi.org The Mexican musical genre; conferences; musicians and bands; events.

Reggae Lyrics Archive hem.passagen.se/selahis Reggae lyrics.

Reggae Train www.reggaetrain.com Largest and most comprehensive reggae music portal on the web; visitors reside in 126 countries around the world; free e-mail, festival guide, concert calendar, reggae forum, and more; detailed information on record labels, record distributors, radio stations, music charts, clubs and venues, and publications.

Reggae Web www.reggaeWeb.com/main.htm Reggae resources and information; news.

Salsa Dance Site www.salsadancesite.com Mission is to connect salsa dance lovers and their friends around the world, providing reliable information, services and products.

Salsa Web www.salsaweb.com/home.htm Online magazine; music; artists; videos and more.

Samba Musica www.sambamusica.com Musical instruments and accessories.

Samurai Latino Web www.s-latino.com Informative site devoted to the Latin music of the Caribbean.

Sounds of Brazil www.sobs.com New York City club; World and Latin music; news; calendar.

Tango Reporter www.tangoreporter.com Monthly magazine published in Spanish in Los Angeles, California, with interviews, biographies, CD and book reviews, tango lyrics, milongas, tango news around the world, and more.

Todotango.com www.todotango.com Original tango master recordings; online tango music club featuring unique tango classics.

Trinidad & Tobago Instruments Ltd. www.steelpansttil.com Steel drums; Panland; TTIL.

Tropical Music www.tropical-music.com Newsboard; world music; Cuban music; MP3.

Tropical Music & Pro Audio www.tropicalmusic.com Palmer España; Palmer Pans; Juggs; Biscayne; Starforce USA; Techparts; H. Hoffer; Afrosound.

Music and Health—Healing Music—Recovery Music

12 Step Radio www.12stepradio.com Recovery music streamed 24/7; links to CDs; submit music.

Advanced Brain Technologies www.advancedbrain.com Combines extensive clinical experience with the latest neuroscience and music research to create products, programs, and services that enhance health, learning, and productivity.

Alexander Center www.alexandercenter.com/pa/index.html Alexander Technique for musicians; articles; links.

Alexander Technique www.alexandertechnique.com Systematic guide to information and resources on and off the Internet.

American Music Therapy Association www.musictherapy.org Find a music therapist; career options.

Canadian Network for Health in the Arts (CNHA) Web.idirect.com~cnha/index.html Play It Safe; subscribe; research; links.

Center for Voice Disorders www.wfubmc.edu/voice Information about the causes and treatments of voice disorders; singer's problems.

Crystal Singing Bowls Relaxation Massage Music www.crystalmusic.com Massage relaxation music played on thirty-five pure quartz crystal bowls; for deep relaxation, insomnia, and stress reduction.

Dalcroze Society of America
www.msu.edu/user/thomasna Training programs; biography; articles about Dalcroze Eurhythmics.
Donna Michael www.donnamichael.com Healing music; performances; CDs; workshops; artistic collection of piano and hammered dulcimer recordings.
Ear, Nose, and Throat Information Center www.sinuscarecenter.com Public information brochures; symptoms; self-help; hearing loss.
H. E. A. R. www.hearnet.com Hearing protection; earplugs; referral for hearing help; artist of the month.
Hand Health www.handhealth.com *Finger Fitness* program; help for hands.
Hands On! www.lunnflutes.comho.htm Online newsletter about performance health for flutists; list of performance health clinics; links.
HealingMusic.Net www.healingmusic.net *Love Is a Sound* CDs and books; MidiVox Voice to MIDI products; singing courses; composing and songwriting services; sound healing and music healing techniques and resources.
Healthwindows.com www.healthwindows.com Articles on music and wellness.
House Ear Institute-Hearing Conservation www.hei.org Sound Partner Program; HIP-Hearing is Priceless; research.
Internet Resources on the Alexander Technique www.life.uiuc.edu/jeff/alextech.html Collection of links; articles.
Jana Stanfield www.janastanfield.com Motivational performer; combines music with a message that entertains, inspires, and encourages; mission is to give organizations a "faith-lift."
Karen Taylor-Good www.karentaylorgood.com Healing music; performances; CDs; keynote speaker; workshops; hit songwriter.
Men's Health www.menshealth.comindex.html Online edition of the magazine.
Mental Health Net www.mentalhelp.net Directory of online mental health resources.
Music and Health www.musicandhealth.co.uk/ Links to articles and organizations.
Music Maker Relief Foundation www.musicmaker.org Charity honors and aids traditional Southern musicians over the age of fifty-five who earn less than $18,000 a year.
Musician's Health www.musicianshealth.com Health information for musicians.
Musicians and Injuries eeshop.unl.edu/music Information for musicians with injuries.
Musicians On Call www.musiciansoncall.org Mission is to use music to complement the healing process for patients in healthcare facilities' Bedside Performance Program; CD Pharmacies; Project Playback; Ticket Donations.

Performing Arts Medicine www.ithaca.edu/hshp/pt/pt1/index.html Newsletter; information for the performer and health practitioner; links to resources.
Performing Arts Psychophysiology www.performingartspsych.com Formerly Musician's Stress Management; seminars; workshops; for teachers and performers.
Quantic Music Productions www.quantikmusic.comindex-a.html Music series for relaxation, meditation, and self-healing sessions.
Share Songs www.sharesongs.com Songs of hope, awareness, and recovery for everyone; mission is to use the power of Nashville music to bring attention to the pervasive problem of alcohol and drug abuse; to raise awareness and funds through an album project using songs from recording artists and featuring a song to be recorded by a group of Nashville artists; funds from album sales benefit prevention and treatment programs.
Special Music by Special People www.specialmusic.org Compact disks; MP3 and Quicktime music projects; music composed by people with developmental disabilities.
Spirit, Sound, Music, and Health www.spiritsound.com/spirit.html Resources; links.
Twelve Songs www.twelvesongs.com Songs for each of the Twelve Steps of the A. A. Program.

Music Education—Instructional Media

Acoustic Systems www.acousticsystems.com Practice rooms; instrument storage cabinets.
Adventus www.adventus.com Music instruction software for Windows; *Piano Suite; Ear Training Coach; Musiq; Internet Music Studio.*
All Things Musical www.allthingsmusical.com National music education resource guide.
American Music Conference www.amc-music.com Goal is to build credibility for music and music education, especially at an early age, and to expand that portion of the population that enjoys and makes its own music.
American Orff-Schulwerk Association www.aosa.org Professional organization of music and movement educators dedicated to the creative teaching approach developed by Carl Orff and Gunild Keetman; believe that learning about music—learning to sing and play, to hear and understand, to move and create—should be an active and joyful experience.
Ars Nova Music Software www.ars-nova.com Educational music software; *Practica Musica; Songworks; Kidmusic.*
Association for Technology in Music Instruction www.music.org/atmi Serves as a forum for the

scholarly presentation of technical information by and for specialists in the field of computer-assisted instruction (CAI) in music; delivers such information to an audience of nonspecialists who are users of music CAI.

Berklee College of Music Home Page www.berklee.edu Pragmatic educational approach to jazz, pop, rock, world music, and classical music; Boston, MA.

Blair School of Music www.vanderbilt.edu/Blair/htdocs/ Vanderbilt University, Nashville, TN.

Casa de la Musica www.casamusica.com *Time Signature 2000* Studio Management Software.

Cassette & Video Learning Systems www.cvls.com Music instruction videos, books with CDs, DVDs, tabs, tablature, and lessons for learning on acoustic guitar, electric guitar, bass guitar, rock guitar, blues guitar, keyboards, harmonica, drums, snare drum, banjo, mandolin, violin, and fiddle; free guitar lessons online on video; free banjo lessons online on video.

Children's Music Workshop www.childrensmusicworkshop.com Music education online; links.

Clarus Music, Ltd. www.clarusmusic.com Worldwide K-12 catalog mail order dealer; sell to music and non-music educators.

Coalition for Music Education in B.C. www.bcmusiccoalition.org Music education advocacy information for parents, educational decision makers, and teachers.

College Music Society www.collegemusicsociety.org or www.music.org Annual convention; mailing lists; publications; Music Vacancy List (MVL) weekly e-mail listings; consortium of college, conservatory, university, and independent musicians and scholars interested in all disciplines of music; mission is to promote music teaching and learning, musical creativity and expression, research and dialogue, and diversity and interdisciplinary interaction.

Crown Trophy www.crowntrophy.com Medals and awards for music students.

Dolphin Don's Music School www.dolphindon.com Music education software.

Drill Quest www.drillquest.com Computerized charting software for marching bands.

Eastman School of Music www.rochester.edu/Eastman The Eastman education prepares students artistically, intellectually, and professionally for the rapidly changing world in which musicians now live; ranked No. 1 in the *United States News and World Report* survey of the nation's best graduate schools.

Educational Activities www.edact.com Publishes educational software, children's music, educational videos; early childhood recordings; adult ed and K-12 software.

Educational Cyber Playground www.edu-cyberpg.com Award winning Web site; links to arts and music Web sites; vendor directory.

Educational Programs Network www.educationalprograms.com Adjudication festivals and resources for music educators.

Educator's Music Annex www.educatorsmusic.com Educational supplier.

Edumart www.edumart.com Collection of educational stores and/or school supply distributors in the educational industry.

Electronic Courseware Systems (ECS) www.ecsmedia.com Educational music software company based in Champaign, IL; downloadable demos; developers of music instructional, multimedia, and MIDI software.

eMedia Music www.emediamusic.com Series of instructional software for guitar, piano, bass, and voise; chord dictionary with audio playback; Macintosh; Windows.

Enrichment Works www.enrichmentworks.com Los Angeles schools assembly programs, classroom events, and workshops in the arts.

ER Technologies www.ertechsoft.com Educational music software; *Musica Analytica*.

Exploding Art Music Productions www.explodingart.com Committed to research, promotion, and development of music education; specializing in contemporary music practices, including music technology and rock music.

Expression Center for New Media www.xnewmedia.com Digital visual media and sound arts education.

Happy Note! www.happynote.com/music/learn.html Computer game; allows people to learn how to read music while playing; Windows.

Harmonic Vision www.harmonicvision.com Educational music software; *Music Ace*.

Homespun Tapes Online www.homespuntapes.com Wide selection of music instruction on videos, CDs, DVDs, and audiocassettes for all instruments and styles.

Homework Spot www.homeworkspot.com/theme/classicalmusic.htm Links to classical music sites.

Instrumental Classmates www.instrumentalclassmates.com Meet the Instruments; entertaining musical adventure.

International Schools Service www.iss.edu Providing services to overseas schools and meeting the educational needs of companies abroad.

International Society for Music Education
www.isme.org Serving music educators and
promoting music education world wide.

International Workshops
www.internationalworkshops.org General music;
conducting; piano; strings; jazz improvisation.

Introduction to Music
omnidisc.com/MUSIC/index.html Web-based
course.

Jam Track www.jamtrack.com Music practice jam
tapes and CDs; full band backup for jamming
riffs and licks in many styles; for beginning to
intermediate musicians on guitar, piano,
keyboard, or solo instruments.

K-12 Resources for Music Educators
www.isd77.k12.mn.us/resources/staffpages/shirk/
k12.music.html Valuable resources for music
educators and students of all areas and educational
levels; regularly updated.

Learn About Music www.learnaboutmusic.com
Music education resource and links.

Lessons4you.com www.lessons4you.com Online
music lessons; instructors.

LessonTime www.LessonTime.com Internet service
to help students find music teachers; national
marketing service for teachers; personal profile;
free membership.

Maestro Music Software
www.wrldcon.com/maestro/ Educational music
software.

McGraw-Hill School Division www.mhschool.com
For parents, teachers, and students.

MiBAC Music Software www.mibac.com Products;
theory reference; music instructional software;
MiBAC Jazz and *Music Lessons.*

Mike Mangini's Rhythm Knowledge Online
www.rhythmknowledge.com Rhythm instruction
materials for all instruments.

Mollard Conducting Batons Inc. www.mollard.com
Mollard & Brite Stixs.

Mr. Holland's Opus Foundation www.mhopus.org
Supports music education and its many benefits
through the donation and repair of musical
instruments to underserved schools, community
music programs, and individual students
nationwide.

Murphy Cap and Gown www.murphyrobes.com
Choir robes.

Music Education at Datadragon
datadragon.com/education/ Music education links.

Music Education Council www.mec.org.uk/
Umbrella body for all organizations connected
with music education in the UK.

Music Education Madness
www.musiceducationmadness.com Gathering
place for music educators.

Music Education Online
www.musiceducationonline.org Member-driven
Web site for music teachers, music directors,
performers and parents interested in music
programs.

Music Education Software
www.musicmall.com/cmp/educatin.htm A
variety of music software for learning piano,
guitar, ear training, and music theory.

Music Educator.org www.musiceducator.org Online
community for music educators worldwide.

Music Educators Market Place
www.musicedmarket.com Online retailer of
music educational products.

Music Educators National Conference (MENC)
www.menc.org Official Web site; jobs;
resources; mission is to advance music education
by encouraging the study and making of music
by all.

Music Instruction Software
cctr.umkc.edu/userx/bhugh/musicold.html
Educational software of interest to music teachers
and students; main focus is freely available
software on the Internet that will help students
master the basics.

Music Lessons on Video www.musicvideo.com
Country, bluegrass, blues, jazz, rock, and gospel
instructional music videos.

Music Minus One www.musicminusone.com or
www.pocketsongs.com *Music Minus One;
Pocket Songs; Just Tracks;* participatory
recordings; accompaniment music; play-along
and sing-along for all musicians and vocalists;
popular, classical, jazz, rock, and country.

Music Notes www.musicnotes.net Publishes *Music
You Can Read;* music curriculum for elementary
music teachers, home schoolers, or persons
interested in learning to read music.

Music Reading www.musicreading.com Teaching and
learning tool; sample lessons and mini tests;
CD-ROM.

Music Search www.musicsearch.com/cgi-
bin/search.cgi?QUERY=Educational+Resources
Music educational resources.

Music Simply Music www.musicsimplymusic.com
Helping teachers, parents, and students share the
gift of music.

Music Staff www.musicstaff.com Find a music
teacher; add a listing.

Music Teachers National Association (MTNA)
www.mtna.org Member and program benefits;
convention information; publications; resources;
links.

Music Technology Learning Center www.mtlc.net
Music technology in the schools and at home;
retailer.

Musica www.musica.uci.edu Music and science information; computer archive; research notes and abstracts on the effects of music on the brain; collected by the Center for Neurobiology at University of California, Irvine.

Musical Heritage Network www.si.umich.edu/CHICO/MHN/ Dynamic community of educators, musicians, students and anyone interested in multimedia use and cultural studies; committed to providing online multicultural resources designed for curriculum development; features sound, text and visual materials; although created with K-12 classes in mind, everyone can enjoy intriguing sights and sounds from around the world.

Musical Online www.musicalonline.com/pedagogy.htm Links to information on how to practice.

Musician's Workshop www.musicians-workshop.com Video and audio music instruction since1973.

Musicians United for Songs in the Classroom www.wpe.com~musici/ Nonprofit organization promoting the interdisciplinary use of popular music in education.

Musicianship Basics www.dragnet.com.au/~donovan/mb Music education software for schools and piano teachers; graded ear training and theory activities for all music students; demos for Macintosh and Windows.

MusickEd.com musicked.com Study guides and learning tools for all instruments; membership includes free access to chat rooms and other musical services; online lessons for beginners to professional musicians.

Musicline Publications www.musicline-ltd.com Stage musicals and shows for schools, youth theaters, and amateur groups.

Online Amadeus www.onlineamadeus.com Standard of Excellence software.

Organization of American Kodály Educators oake.org Mission is to enrich the quality of life of the people of the United States through music education by promoting the philosophy of Zoltán Kodály.

PBJ Music www.pbjmusic.com Music education software.

Pedagonet www.pedagonet.com Learning material and resource center.

Peery www.PeeryProducts.com Risers and skirting for performances.

Play Music www.playmusic.com Music instruction software.

Private Lessons www.privatelessons.com Locate a private local music teacher; add teachers' names to the searchable database.

PureGold Teaching Tools www.puregoldteachingtools.com Teaching aids for classroom teachers, private teachers, parents, students, homeschoolers, and music therapists.

Pyware www.pyware.com *3D; Music Office; Amadeus; Drill Quest.*

Quia www.quia.com/dir/music/ Students can test their music knowledge with quizzes, matches, concentration card games, and other activities.

ScholarStuff www.scholarstuff.com Directory of education sites; colleges and universities; educational software; financial aid.

School Music Master www.cmp.net/smm For managing school music program; Windows.

Signature Music Software www.signature5.com *Music Maid.*

Silver Burdette www.sbgmusic.com Music educational materials for the classroom; articles; samples; teacher support.

Singlish www.singlish.com Develop language skills in children through the singing of classic and contemporary folk songs; Volumes 1 and 2 for Pre-K through 2nd grade classroom; helpful for students with limited English proficiency.

Smart Music www.smartmusic.com Access online accompaniments that function as virtual accompanists; *Smart Music* CD-ROM; practice program for woodwinds, brass players, and vocalists.

SmarterKids.com www.smarterkids.com Educational books, audio materials, and software for music teaching.

Songs for Teaching www.SongsForTeaching.com Links to songs used for teaching a variety of subjects; articles; educational lyrics and recordings; tips; store.

Sound Tree www.soundtree.com Music technology services for education; resource guide for music educators.

St. John's College www.sjcsf.edu Founded in 1696; two campuses: Annapolis, Maryland, and Santa Fe, New Mexico; awards Bachelor and Master of Arts degrees; coeducational, four-year liberal arts college; distinctive "great books" curriculum, including music.

Support Music www.supportmusic.com/index-intro.html Public service of the music education coalition.

Suzuki Association of the Americas, Inc. www.suzukiassociation.org Coalition of teachers, parents, educators, and others who are interested in making music education available to all children; provides programs and services to members throughout North and South America; promotes and supports the spread of Dr. Suzuki's Talent Education.

Suzuki Music Academy
www.suzukimusicacademy.com Suzuki Method classical music study; for children two and up.
Suzuki Musical Instruments www.suzukimusic.com Educational musical instruments.
Tapestry www.tapestrymusic.com Music for educators.
Teach Yourself to Play
www.teachyourselftoplay.com Music instructional software.
Teachers.Net www.teachers.net/careers Teacher jobs; employment information.
The Copernicus Education Gateway
www.edgate.com/musichall/educator/ For educators, students, and parents.
The Grove School without Walls
www.dickgrove.com College-level music courses based on the Grove School of Music in Los Angeles, CA; videos, books, CDs, cassettes; correspondence courses.
The Land of Music www.landofmusic.com Tapes and materials for teaching music to young children.
The Practice Spot www.practicespot.com Information about how to practice.
The Technology Institute for Music Educators
www.ti-me.org Nonprofit corporation registered in the State of Pennsylvania whose mission is to assist music educators in applying technology to improve teaching and learning in music.
Thinkquest Internet Challenge Library
www.thinkquest.org/library/cat_show.html?cat_i d=17&cid=1 Online guide to music education.
Tritone Music www.tritonemusic.com Multimedia online music education systems for schools and internet distant learning environments; specialize in incorporating professionally developed content for K-12 with the latest in technology; courses incorporate the use of a specialized MIDI sequencer that allows the user to record and receive an evaluation of their performance.
Understanding Music www.understandingmusic.com Interactive music school.
Voyetra www.voyetra.com Educational and recording music software; *Record Producer; Teach Me Series*.
Watch and Learn www.cvls.com Music instruction videos, books with CDs, DVDs, tabs, tablature, and lessons for learning on acoustic guitar, electric guitar, bass guitar, rock guitar, blues guitar, keyboards, harmonica, drums, snare drum, banjo, mandolin, violin, and fiddle; free guitar and banjo lessons online on video.
Wenger www.wengercorp.com Instrument storage.
Worldwide Internet Music Resources
www.music.indiana.edu/music_resources/mused. html Music education links and online music resources for music educators.

Music History

Academic Info – Music History
www.academicinfo.net/music.html Music history and studies; digital library; musical databases and archives; classical music composers; folk music; jazz resources; music libraries; music organizations and centers.
Basic Music: Your Guide to Music of the Western World www.basicmusic.net Biographies, compositions, and recommended recordings of composers of all genres and styles of music; This Day in Music; musical glossary; musical forms; music and entertainment news.
Classical Music History Timelines on the Web music.searchbeat.com/composer.htm Music history links.
Early Music FAQ www.medieval.orgemfaq Comprehensive information on Medieval and Renaissance; repertory overview; CDs; links.
Encyclopedia Smithsonian
www.si.edu/resource/faq/nmah/music.htm Musical history; artists and exhibitions.
Essentials of Music www.essentialsofmusic.com From Sony Classical and W. W. Norton; basic information about classical music; eras; terms; composers; audio.
Feminist Theory and Music 4
wsrv.clas.virginia.edu/~smp8a/ftm.program.html Bringing feminism into music studies; musicology and gender studies.
Genders OnLine Journal www.genders.org Peer-reviewed academic journal publishing essays about gender and sexuality in relation to social, political, artistic, and economic concerns.
Greek Music Resources
www.webexpert.net/vasilios/grmusic.htm Collection of links to resources on Hellenic music; ancient to modern.
Gregorian Chant Home Page
www.music.princeton.edu/chant_html The Nassau Edition of Gregorian Chant.
History Happens www.ushistory.com Stories from American history on music video.
History Net www.TheHistoryNet.com History on the Internet.
Internet Public Library—Music History
ipl.sils.umich.edu/div/searchresults/?words=musi c+history&where=exhibit Over 1,400 entries; collections finder; learning page.
Library of Congress American Memory Site memory.loc.gov/ammem/amhome.html Collection Finder/Sound Recordings; thousands of historical public domain MP3 files; photos.
Museum of Music History www.zti.hu/museum.htm Located in Budapest, Hungary; Institute for Musicology.

Music History Articles
www.essortment.com/in/Music.History/ Links to many music history sites.
Music History for Music Education
musicandyou.com/musichistory.htm Links; MP3s; sheet music.
Music History Outline .
www.jazzvocal.com/outline.html Breakdown of style periods.
Music History Resources
members.tripod.com~papandr/musicology.html Collection of outlines on music history topics.
Music History Resources
www.nerdworld.com/nw1240.html Information on music history; links.
Music History Titles from CD-ROM Access
www.cdaccess.com/html/pc/63mhis.htm Directory of music history-related CD-ROM titles, including composers.
Music Notes
library.thinkquest.org/15413/?tqskip1=1&tqtime= 0713 Interactive online musical experience.
Music Time Periods
www.plainfield.k12.in.us/hschool/webq/webq89/ Links to information on all style periods.
MUSIClassical.com
www.angelfire.com/biz/acousticdigest/almanac.ht ml Today in classical music history.
Open Directory dmoz.org/Arts/Music/History/ Music history links.
Orpheon www.orpheon.org Museum of historical musical instruments.
Renaissance Dance www.rendance.org Central resource for information on European dance from the fifteenth to early seventeenth centuries.
Smithsonian Institution www.si.edu History of the Smithsonian and the United States.
Stamp on Black History Index
library.advanced.org10320 Inventions and discoveries; works of art; excellence in science, music, medicine, sports; history.
Stylistic Timeline of Music History
www.stevenestrella.com/composers/index.html?s tyletimeline.html Time line by date or name.
The Galpin Society
www.music.ed.ac.uk/euchmi/galpin/ For the study of musical instruments.
The 100 Most Important American Musical Works of the Twentieth Century
www.npr.org/programs/specials/vote/list100.htm l NPR special features cover music from a wide variety of genres—classical, jazz, rock'n'roll, country, R&B, musical theater and film scores; aired on *All Things Considered, Morning Edition*, and NPR's weekend news magazine programs.
The History of Today www.on-this-day.com Daily historical facts and events; music history.

The Internet Public Library
www.ipl.org/div/mushist/ Music History 102; a guide to western composers and their music from the middle ages to the present.
The Music Room
www.empire.k12.ca.us/capistrano/Mike/capmusi c/music_room/themusic.htm Links to many different music history Web sites.
The Use of Music and Dance in Teaching United States History
pw2.netcom.com~wandaron/history.html Successful techniques in teaching history with the use of music and dance.
This Day in Music History datadragon.com/day/ Birthdays; releases; charts; shows and plays.
Those Were the Days, Today in History
www.440.com/twtd/today.html Daily summary of news events, famous birthdays, and hit music that happened on this day in history.
Today in History coach.indiana.net/ What happened on this date in history.
Web Quests—Music History
www.chsdragonband.com/webquests/music_histo ry/ Music history links.
Worldwide Internet Music Resources
www.music.indiana.edu/music_resources/mcolog y.html Musicology and music history links.
Yahoo! Entertainment:Music:History
www.yahoo.com/Entertainment/Music/History Music history.

Music Magazines, E-Zines, Webzines, and Newspapers

Alternative Press Magazine
www.alternativepress.com News; reviews; features; interviews; sound clips.
Bards Crier www.bardscrier.com Weekly guerrilla music marketing and promotion e-zine for the working musician.
BerkleePress www.berkleepress.com Online magazine; publisher.
Billboard www.billboard.com Industry news; interviews; features; reviews; Radio Charts: Hot 100 Singles, Billboard Top 200 Albums, Pop, Country, Hits of the World, Contemporary Christian, Gospel, R & B, Rap, Dance Music, Latin, Blues, Reggae, World Music, Internet and Indie Charts and more; Top Videos; Fun and Games; The Power Book guide to radio and record promotion; online store.
Canadian Magazine Publishers Association
www.cmpa.ca Official Web site.
Canadian Musician www.canadianmusician.com Music of Canada; news; articles; reviews; industry information.
CCM www.ccmcom.com American lifestyle and music magazine.

Chicago Tribune www.chicagotribune.com
   Newspaper.
Circus www.circusmagazine.com Heavy metal.
CNN Interactive www.cnn.comSHOWBIZ/Music
   Music information; celebrities.
Collegiate Presswire www.cpwire.com Press release
   and newswire service.
Crawdaddy www.cdaddy.com United States classic
   rock magazine; interviews; features.
Dotmusic www.dotmusic.co.uk Guide to music;
   news.
Editor & Publisher www.mediainfo.com
   International Year Book: United States Dailies,
   United States Weeklies, and Special Newspapers,
   Canadian Newspapers, Foreign Newspapers,
   News, Picture and Syndicated Services; database
   available on disk or labels.
Entertainment Weekly Online
   www.pathfinder.com/ew Online version of the
   entertainment magazine.
Eworldwire www.eworldwire.com Press release and
   newswire service.
Ezine Universe www.ezine-universe.com E-mail
   newsletter directory.
E-zineZ.com www.E-zinez.com Handbook of e-zine
   publishing.
Fast Forward www.discmakers.comffwd Interviews;
   articles.
Fix Magazine www.fix.com Interviews; articles;
   photos.
Gajoob www.gajoob.com Webzine; articles; links;
   reviews.
Gale Directory of Publication and Broadcast Media
   www.gale.com Annual Guide listing newspapers,
   magazines, journals, radio stations, television
   stations, and cable systems; sold as a three-
   volume set: *Newsletters in Print, Encyclopedia
   of Associations, International Associations.*
Gebbie Press www.gebbieinc.com Publication search
   engine.
Harp Magazine www.harpmagazine.com For those
   passionate about their music.
HotWired www.hotwired.com RealAudio;
   interviews.
Ink Blot Magazine www.inkblotmagazine.com Rock
   magazine; pop culture.
Internet Media Fax www.imediafax.com Press
   release and newswire service.
Internet Professional Publishers Association
   www.ippa.org Association of over 10,500
   professionals involved in New Media and the
   Internet.
Jam! www.canoe.ca/Jam Offbeat entertainment and
   cultural news.
Jelly www.jellyroll.com The "Real Music
   Newsletter"; American roots.

Life www.pathfinder.com/Life Photographs; past
   features.
Live Magazine www.livemagazine.com Online
   magazine.
Live Sound! International Magazine
   www.livesoundint.com Webzine.
Live Update www.liveupdate.com Webzine.
Los Angeles Times Entertainment Section
   www.calendarlive.com Entertainment journalism.
MediaFinder www.mediafinder.com Publication
   search engine.
MediaMagnet www.mediamagnetpro.com Press
   release utility.
Mix Magazine www.mixmag.com Music industry
   resources.
Mixmag/Mixmag Update www.techno.de/mixmag
   UK DJ magazine; news.
MTV Online www.mtv.com Industry news; bands;
   local music.
Music Alive Magazine www.musicalive.com
   Educational resource magazine.
Music for the Love of It
   www.musicfortheloveofit.com Bimonthly
   newsletter for people (and others) who love
   making music; musically literate forum in which
   amateur and professional musicians share
   stimulating ideas, up-to-date technical
   information, and heartfelt enthusiasm for music-
   making.
Music Information www.musicinformation.com E-
   mail subscription service; artist information; new
   releases; tour dates; TV appearances.
Music Industry News Network—Music Dish
   www.Mi2n.com Webzine; industry newsletter;
   links; newswire service for music professionals
   featuring band and record label announcements,
   tour and event dates, digital music news, and new
   releases.
Music Maker Publications Inc.
   www.recordingmag.com *Recording; Musico Pro;
   Playback Platinum.*
Music Universe www.musicuniverse.com Webzine;
   reviews; articles.
Musician www.musicianmag.com *The Musician's
   Guide to Touring and Promotion.*
Musicsearch Magazine Listings
   www.musicsearch.com/NewsRoom/ Music
   magazines are listed alphabetically; brief
   descriptions of content and subject matter.
New Music Weekly www.newmusicweekly.com
   Covers the Radio and Music industry; over
   twenty-four pages; weekly magazine; Web site;
   mail and fax services; built by radio stations who
   "break" the hits first; standard for tracking radio
   airplay nationwide.
New Musical Express www.nme.com Music news
   and gossip.

News Bureau www.newsbureau.com Online press release service.

NewsDirectory.com www.newsd.com Publication search engine.

Newshub www.newshub.com Search news archives.

Newspaper Association of America www.newspaperlinks.com Publication search engine.

NME www.nme.com UK Webzine; indie news; reviews; rock quotes; directory.

Northern Light www.northernlight.comnews.html Archive resource; tool for searching offline publications.

Old Farmer's Almanac www.almanac.com Trivia; folk wisdom.

Parrot Media Network www.parrotmedia.com United States TV Station Directory: printed quarterly; United States Cable TV Directory: printed semiannually; Newspaper Directory: printed semiannually; Radio Directory: printed semiannually; directories priced per issue or per year; subscriptions available for online use; directories updated daily.

Pause and Play www.pauseandplay.com Webzine.

People Online people.aol.com/people Entertainment news; profiles.

Pig Publications www.pigpublications.com Reviews; news; sounds; list of modern rock bands.

Poets & Writers Magazine www.pw.org Webzine.

Pollstar www.pollstar.com Industry news; tour schedules; box office reports; albums sales; radio plays.

Popwire Mag www.popwire.com International music site.

PR News Wire www.prnewswire.com Press release and newswire service.

Pro Audio Review www.imaspub.com *Pro Audio Review; Radio World.*

Publishers Weekly www.publishersweekly.com Online version of the industry magazine.

PubList www.publist.com Publication search engine.

Q www.qonline.co.uk Pop music culture in England; archives.

Radio & Records Online www.rronline.com Industry newspaper; information; facts and figures; links to a wide range of sources including record labels and industry sites; industry news; radio news; reviews; radio charts.

Rocket Fuel Online www.rocket-fuel.com Online magazine.

Rockrgrl www.rockrgrl.com Webzine for women musicians; interviews; reviews.

Rolling Stone www.rollingstone.com Features; CD reviews; music news; e-mail newsletter; MP3 and music video Pick of the Day; message board and more.

Salon www.salon.com Music news.

Sonic State www.sonicstate.com Music industry news.

Spin www.spin.com Music news and information.

Stereophile www.stereophile.com Online magazine.

Talk Music www.talkmusic.com Webzine; *Music Business Daily.*

The American Spectator www.spectator.org Politics and entertainment news.

The GPI Group—A Division of Miller Freeman PSN Inc. www.mfi.com *Guitar Player; Keyboard; Bass Player; Guitar & Bass Buyer's Guide; Music Technology Buyer's Guide; Music Gear Online; Guitar Player Online; Keyboard Online; Bass Player Online.*

The Island Ear www.islandear.com Webzine.

The iZine www.thei.aust.com Entertainment news from Australia.

The New York Times www.nytimes.com Newspaper.

The World's Greatest Music Magazine Online www.qonline.co.uk From the UK's biggest selling music magazine; latest music news and reviews; Gig Guide; quizzes; competitions; chat; database of 17,000 Q reviews.

Time time.com News coverage.

TotalNEWS www.totalnews.com Search news archives.

United States News & World Report Online www.usnews.com News magazine.

URL Wire www.urlwire.com Press release and newswire service.

USA Today Hot Site www.usatoday.com/life/cyber/ch.htm Awards Web site.

USA Today Life www.usatoday.com/life/lfront.htm Entertainment section.

USA Today www.usatoday.com Newspaper.

Virgin.Net www.virgin.net News; reviews.

Viva Music www.vivamusic.com Free music business reports.

Wall of Sound www.wallofsound.com News and reviews; interviews; artist pages; tours; ABC's Go Network.

Weekly Wire www.weeklywire.comww/current/ Archives only.

West Coast Music Review wcmr.com United States Webzine for West Coast music; reviews; interviews; articles; links.

Wired www.wired.com Webzine.

World Press and Media Finder www.escapeartist.com/media/media.htm Publication search engine.

World Wide News Sources on the Internet www.discover.co.uk/NET/NEWS/news.html Guide to international news sources.

Yahoo! Entertainment Summary
www.yahoo.com/headlines/ Entertainment
industry headlines.
ZDNet Music News music.zdnet.com Music news
service; technology update; white papers;
downloads; reviews and prices; wired and
wireless; software infrastructure; hardware
upgrades.

Music on the Internet—
Legal MP3 Download Sites,
Software, and Hardware—
Streaming Audio and Video

101 CD www.101cd.com Download site; MP3.
AltoMP3 Maker www.yuansoft.com CD to MP3
converter or CD ripper; works as a CDDB2-
Enabled ™ CD player; for Windows
9X/NT/2000.
Ampcast www.ampcast.com Rookies; music; videos;
radio; store; Myamp; founded in 1998; dedicated
to introducing and exposing new musicians and
bands as well as providing a forum for the
promotion of more established musical artists.
Apple iTunes www.apple.com/itunes/ Digital music
player; iTunes 4; Music Store; hundreds of
thousands of songs.
Audible.com www.audible.com Download audio
books and more.
Audio 2g audio2g.cjb.net/ Realaudio files; new artists.
Audio Galaxy www.audiogalaxy.com Download site;
MP3; free Web site hosting; indie artists; MP3
search engine; chat.
Audion www.panic.com For Macintosh; MP3s; audio
CDs; streaming Web audio.
Audiopia.com www.audiopia.com Download site;
MP3.
AudioRequest Home MP3 Player
www.request.com/us/ Digital music services.
AudioSoftware.com www.audiosoftware.com Audio
compression software shop; directory; downloads
for MP3 players, encoders, rippers, and utilities;
links to programs used to play, record, make,
copy, and edit audio; MP3 related programs.
AudioTools.co.uk www.audiotools.co.uk Audio tools
and utilities for audio conversion, playback, DJ
mixing, CD audio extraction, sound editing, and
more.
Audiovalley.Com www.audiovalley.com All-in-one
MP3 search engine and legal music downloads.
Auto PC www.autopc.com Windows system for cars;
CDs; CD-ROMs; MP3s next.
Axialis AX-CDPlayer www.axialis.com/axcdplayer
CDDB compatible CD player for Windows 95;
automatically get disk and track titles accessing
CDDB worldwide database through the Internet.
Beatnik www.beatnik.com Audio software solutions.

Benway Doktor www.benway.doktor.co.uk Download
site; MP3.
Berkeley Multimedia Research Center
bmrc.berkeley.edu/projects/mpeg MPEG
information.
BeSonic
www.besonic.com/Home/0,1588,g0r0l0t0o0i0,F
F.html Music; radio; search; shop; news;
community.
Beta Lounge www.betalounge.com Weekly new
music forum in MP3.
Black Diamond Sound Systems
www.blackdiamondsound.com Turn computer
into a virtual recording studio with music
software, including the audio file editing and
MP3 encoding program *TsunamiPro.*
BuyMusic.com www.buymusic.com Windows Media
Player 9 required for legal downloads; all genres;
over 300,000 songs; pay per song or per album;
Top 100 singles and albums.
CD Nature www.cdnature.com Download site; MP3.
City Music www.citymusic.com The Virtual Music
Store; download MP3s; browse.
CL-Amp www4.tripnet.se/~slarti/f_cl-amp_uk.htm
MP3 player for BeOS; makes use of Winamp
skins; many formats supported; MP3; VBR.
Clear Channel cc.com New music network; events;
artists; venues.
CoolPlayer www.daansystems.com/coolplayer
Windows MP3 player with a simple user
interface.
Cornerband.com www.cornerband.com Legal access
to RIAA licensed music; Dallas based.
Creative Labs Nomad Portable Player
www.nomadworld.com MP3 hardware player
manufacturers; portable digital audio players; free
MP3 music downloads; featured artists; digital
audio news; pick a country; information on the
next-generation portable digital audio player.
Customize.org www.customize.org MP3 software
accessories; skins; plug-ins.
CuteFTP www.cuteftp.com Popular FTP program
for transferring MP3 files.
Daily MP3 www.dailymp3.com/main.html Updated
daily; MP3 news; player software; song files;
downloads; links.
DAMP www.damp-mp3.co.uk Full-featured MP3
player for DOS; contains support of PLS and
M3U playlists; has a special visualization option
similar to Winamp's plug-ins.
DC Software fon.fon.bg.ac.yu/~dcolak *Party DJ*
MP3 software program.
Degy Shop www.degyshop.com Download site; MP3.
DFX www.fxsound.com Plug-in for Winamp; audio
enhancing; hi-fi features.
Digital Club Festival www.digitalclubnetwork.com
Online music event.

Digital Music Australia www.digitalmusic.com.au
MP3s; RealAudio; downloads; links.

Dimension Music www.dimensionmusic.com MP3
Web site; artist information; industry news;
links; free MP3 information; forums; chat.

Discosoft www.discosoft.com Player and mixer
software intended for consumer and professional
use; plays, MP3, WMA, MP2, PCM, and MIDI;
working demo available.

D-Lusion www.d-lusion.com/products/index.html
Unique MP3 and soft synthesizer software.

Downloads Direct content.ubl.com/downloadsdirect
Major label and indie artists.

DreamWeaver www.macromedia.comdreamweaver
Web page editor.

Empeg Car Player www.empeg.com MP3 hardware
player manufacturers.

EMusic www.emusic.com Downloadable music site;
listen to song samples before purchasing; buy
only certain songs instead of entire album; MP3s
by known artists for sale; large catalog.

Epitonic www.epitonic.com Source for MP3
recordings; reviewed and selected indie MP3
music; download site.

Ether Stream www.etherstream.com Download site;
MP3.

EvO:R www.Evor.com Interactive music site; free
agent musicians; store; Internet radio.

Experience Music Project www.emplive.com
Seattle-based; 140,000 square foot building
includes interactive exhibits, unique artifacts, and
space for live performances; created to celebrate
the past, present, and future of music; create;
explore; archives; summer camps; museum;
tours; contests.

Extreme Tracking www.extreme-dm.com/tracking
Internet resource.

EZ-Mixer www.ez-mixer.com IK Multimedia;
multifunctional MP3 player/encoder; live
remixing tool which emulates a two-track DJ
mixer with all necessary features to produce
compilation or live remix; like a DJ in a club;
supports the import/export of other audio formats
including Wav, Aiff, QDesign, QuickTime;
direct song ripping from audio CDs.

Fairtunes Winamp Plugin
mi2n.com/press.php3?press_nb=13226 Legal
downloads.

FAQ Archives www.faqs.org Frequently asked
questions.

FireWorks2 www.macromedia:com/fireworks
Graphic utility.

Fraunhofer, Developer of the MP3 Format
www.iis.fhg.de/amm/techinf MP3 reference site;
audio and multimedia technology; licensing;
industry news.

Freeamp Player www.freeamp.org MP3 player
software.

Geiss www.geisswerks.com Winamp plug-in; MP3
light show; visual display to music.

Get Right www.getright.com FTP client.

GiantDisk MP3 Player Project www.giantdisc.com
Contains a selection of free software programs
used to run a home jukebox system through a
computer controlled by a PalmPilot; explanation
on how to set up the system is explained on the
site.

GoldWave www.goldwave.com Sound utility; MP3
recording and editing.

Graphic Artists Guild www.gag.org Graphic design
for album art; weekly newsletter by subscription;
free ads for those seeking artists.

Green Café www.greencafe.com MP3 search
engines.

High Criteria www.highcriteria.com *Total Recorder*
MP3 recording and sound editing software.

High Five www.highfivearchive.com/core/index.html
Archives only.

Host Index www.hostindex.com Web site hosting.

HTML Goodies www.htmlgoodies.com Beginning
HTML.

HTML Headquarters Webhelp.org Introductory
HTML help.

HTML Tutorials in Web Page Design
www.htmltutorials.ca/ Resource.

iBill www.ibill.com Internet billing service.

ID3.org www.id3.org ID3 tag standard.

I-Jam www.ijamworld.com Portable MP3 player.

iMusic www.imusic.com Alternative music; chat
rooms; daily news; tours; reviews; information;
music community; Web sites.

InfoLink Link Checker www.biggbyte.com Tools
necessary to maintain Web site; locate and correct
problem links and pages; utilize statistic reports
to keep a log of site's integrity.

Into Music www.intomusic.co.uk/ Features hand-
picked free download music from independent
musicians, all files are checked to ensure they are
virus free and of good sound quality.

ITunes www.apple.com/itunes/ Music Store with
legal downloads; Import CDs; Smart Playlists;
Sync with iPod; play audio CDs on Macintosh;
convert files on CDs to MP3 format; manage
songs collected; create playlists; tune in to
Internet radio stations; create music CDs.

JukeBytes 1.0 www.jukebytes.00go.com JukeBytes;
have.m3u and .pls playlist inside a jukebox
simulator.

Junkbusters.com www.junkbusters.com Cookie
management tools.

Killer Sites www.killersites.com Web site utility.

Launch.com www.launch.com Download site; MP3; over 4,500 music videos; news; chat; downloadable songs; LAUNCHcast enables members to design streaming audio and video music stations.

Liquid Audio www.liquidaudio.com Streaming audio format; encoded Liquid Audio files or "Liquified" files; supports all leading digital audio formats; CD quality music; downloads.

Listen Smart www.listensmart.com Download site.

Listen.com www.listen.com Rhapsody digital music service; links to online music; guide to legal MP3s; streaming video; free tracks; over 60,000 artists; all genres; reviews; newsletter.

Lycos MP3 Search www.music.lycos.com/mp3 or www.mp3.lycos.com Search engine for MP3s.

MacAmp Player for Mac www.macamp.com MP3 player and encoder software.

MacAst Player for Mac www.macast.com Media player.

Media Wizard www.cdhnow.com/mw.html Powerful and complete multimedia solution supporting all popular audio and video formats.

Megatunes www.megatunes.com Download site; MP3.

Microsoft Media Player www.microsoft.com/windows/ Microsoft audio/video; handles MP3 files and many other audio and streaming formats.

MidiRunner www.midirunner.com Integrated Play Center for MIDI, MP3, Wave, CD-Audio files, and all others WindowsMedia supported sound files; can also be used to create, edit, and load playlists.

MP3 and Wav Converter hammer.prohosting.com~poweryfy Directly converts audio between MP3 and Wav; converts audio digitally, not through the sound card for perfect copies of the originals.

MP3 Audio Player www.yukudr.com/mp3player EasyPEG3; simple freeware application which allows user to play MP3 audio.

MP3 Easy Search www.mp3easy.co.uk Software competitive with Napster.

MP3 Handbook.com www.MP3handbook.com Information on encoding, ripping, editing, and playing MP3s; MP3 and digital music links.

MP3 Music Player www.mp3musicplayer.com MP3 search engine list; find MP3s, songs, and MIDI files; links to download sites.

MP3 Newswire www.mp3newswire.net MP3 news.

MP3 Production Studio Encoder for Windows www.audioactive.com/default.htm MP3 player and encoder software.

MP3 Search www.mp3search.freeserve.co.uk MP3 search engines on the Internet.

MP3 Search.nu www.mp3search.nu MP3 site search engine; gateway to the MP3 community.

MP3 Shopping www.mp3shopping.com MP3 players; news; software; site map; products; links; music; search.

MP3.com.au www.mp3.com.au Australian MP3 Web site; downloads; news; reviews; chat.

MP3Board.com www.mp3board.com MP3 search engine.

MP3Detective cheqsoft.com/mp3detective/index.html Program to search for MP3 music on PC, then play results on default jukebox; makes text and HTML file lists.

MP3Machine.com www.mp3machine.com/database MP3 technology.

MP3Tech www.mp3tech.org MP3 technology resource; MPEG; glossary.

MPEG www.mpeg.org MPEG and MP3 reference site; FAQs; links.

MPEGX.com www.mpegx.com Large guide to MP3 software programs and other related material; listing of various MP3 programs with ratings.

Mpg123 www.mpg123.de Fast, free MP3 audio player for Linux, FreeBSD, Solaris, Hpux, and near all other UNIX systems; decodes MP1 and MP2 files.

Mplayer3 www.mplayer3.com Portable MP3 player; adjust bass and treble.

MPMan F20 www.mpman.com MP3 player.

MPMan Portable Players www.eigerlabs.com MP3 hardware player manufacturers.

MTV www.mtv.com/music/downloads/ Music downloads; join; search.

Music Choice www.musicchoice.com Commercial-free, professionally programmed music channels and digital downloads available on one site.

Music Choice UK www.musicchoice.co.uk Up to fifty CD quality genre specific audio channels; no ads or DJs; available twenty-four hours a day.

Music City www.MusicCity.com Artists; FAQ; links; merchandise.

Music Exchange www.musicex.com Safe sales and licensing of music on the Internet.

Music Link www.musiclink.com/functions/mlmain.php?mlsection=home Provides a new method of payment which incorporates contributions and grants that pay for artists' projects; allows emerging and established artists to enhance their careers and insures fairness and support for diverse access to live music; music education is funded for all communities.

Music Match Jukebox www.musicmatch.com MP3 player and encoder software; download MP3s and demos; for Windows; Shoutcast Internet radio feeds; audio CDs; ten-band graphic equalizer; sort MP3s; auto DJ feature.

Music Net www.musicnet.com Widely distributed digital music service; legal downloads; large catalog; variety of genres; FAQ; stream; download; burn.

Music Now www.musicnow.com Legal downloads; CD quality; commercial free radio stations; MusicNow software; free trial membership.

Music Seek www.musicseek.net Computer audio formats like MP3, vqf, real audio, and more; comprehensive search utility aims to find files.

Musician Assist www.musicianassist.com/archive/ Standard contract language for booking gigs, publishing songs, etc.

Musician MP3 www.musicianmp3.com Free music downloads.

MuzicMan www.muzicman.com MP3 player and organizer; designed for converting a large CD collection to a PC-based stereo system.

Napster 2.0 www.napster.com The new service will offer 99-cent downloads to anyone with a PC; large digital music library with over 500,000 songs.

NCSA: A Beginners Guide to HTML www.ncsa.uiuc.edu/General/Internet/ HTML resource.

Net Burner www.net-burner.com MP3s with a program to burn a CD; put on Web site for others to burn; fully automatic.

Network Solutions www.networksolutions.com Domain name registration.

NEX www.frontierlabs.com Portable MP3 player.

Noizy Land www.noizyland.com Download site; MP3.

Nomad II www.nomadworld.com Portable MP3 player; belt clip.

Ogg Vorbis www.vorbis.com Open, patent-free, professional audio encoding and streaming technology.

One Source onesource.pan.com Distribution system for e-CDs; buy whole CDs or individual tracks; PAN's patent-pending anti-piracy platform Digital Interactive Fingerprinting.

Orbit Music www.orbitmusic.com Custom CDs.

Oth www.oth.net MP3 search site.

Paint Shop Pro www.jasc.com Graphic utility.

Peoplesound.com www.peoplesound.com MP3 download site; new music.

Personal Jukebox PJB-100 www.pjbox.com Portable MP3 player.

Piranha www.piranha.de Download site; MP3.

Planet CD www.planetcd.com Download site; MP3; independent music.

PNC-UK www.pnc-uk.co.uk Rare and collectibles.

Press Play www.pressplay.com Stream; download; burn; FAQ; music; pressroom; leading online music subscription service that offers music fans the widest variety of music, unlimited listening and broad portability options; conceived as an equally held joint venture between Sony Music Entertainment and Universal Music Group (a unit of Vivendi Universal), and launched in December 2001; offices in Los Angeles and New York City; music companies, including BMG, EMI Recorded Music, Sony Music Entertainment, Universal Music Group, and Warner Music Group, as well as numerous independent labels, separately provide their content to *Press Play* on a nonexclusive basis; marketed to consumers through relationships with Gateway, HP, MP3.com, MSN Music, Rio, Roxio, Sony Musiclub, and Yahoo.

Prime Linx Inc. www.primelinx.com Sell chrome plates for automobile with Web site URL.

Projekt www.projekt.com Download site; MP3.

QSound Labs, Inc. www.qsound.com/products Leading audio technology company; software products for 3D audio, virtual surround sound, MP3, and Internet audio.

QuickTime www.quicktime.com or quicktime.apple.com Streaming audio and video format; free download.

RealNetworks www.real.com The Web's first streaming media introduced in April 1995; first to stream audio to the masses; huge installed base of regular users; RealOne.

RealNetworks UK www.real.co.uk Delivers streamed data from Web to computer in real time; information about the technology; samples; free plug-ins download.

Resort Records www.resortrecords.com Label supported free MP3s.

Rhythm Net www.rhythmnet.com Gain exposure and industry recognition; sell songs; international distribution; sell recordings.

RIMPS MP3 Server and Playlist Manager rimps.sourceforge.net Web-based front end; written in PHP to make Apache a streaming MP3 server; facilities for searching; individual song playing; playlist creation.

Rioport www.rioport.com RioPort Audio Manager CD encoder; Diamond Multimedia Pro portable MP3 player; Rio PMP500; online catalog of MP3 hardware and accessories; free downloads.

Round Tower www.roundtower.com Download site; MP3.

Rykodisk www.rykodisc.com Download site; MP3.

Sexy Analyzer www.geocities.com/SiliconValley/Peaks/9546/ Winamp plug-in; visual display of song.

Shanachie www.shanachie.com Independent artists.

Sheer Dance www.sheerdance.co.za Independent music.

Shockwave www.shockwave.com Streaming audio format; Macromedia.

Shoutcast www.shoutcast.com Streaming audio system; broadcast own station; requires Winamp; tutorials.

Sight Sound www.sightsound.com Download site; MP3.

Silk City CD www.silkcitycd.com Download site; MP3.

Software.mp3.com software.mp3.com MP3 information; how to make MP3s.

Sonic Net www.sonicnet.com News; reviews; events; downloads; videos; music directory; contests; radio; artist database.

Sonicle Audio www.sonicle.com WebSynth audio product line; freeware version; new audio file format; support for scalable quality; pluggable decoders; G723, MPeg, AU, WAV.

Sonique Player for Windows www.sonique.com MP3 and audio CD player and encoder software; playlist editor.

Sound Click www.soundclick.com Download site; MP3 and streaming audio; free membership.

Start Up Music www.StartUpMusic.com Selected by The Music Company for Web Development Music technology in the news; dedicated to sharpening the blur of the converging music and technology industries.

StompinGround.com www.stompinground.com Song distribution resource; download site; MP3; unsigned band promotion.

Stream Box www.streambox.com Rich media search engine/portal; over one million free audio and video streams.

Submit It www.submit-it.com/subopt.htm Tips on how to submit URL to search engines.

Super Sampler www.supersampler.com Download site; MP3.

Tactile 12000 www.tactile12000.com MP3 DJ program.

TagMaster dev.tagmaster.se/ Web site utility.

TextAloud MP3 www.nextuptech.comTextAloud Converts any text into voice and to MP3; listen to text, e-mail and Web pages on computer or portable MP3 player.

The List www.thelist.com Where to find Internet Service Providers (ISPs).

The Music Dish Genome Project www.musicdish.com/genome Plan to identify and map the components which make up the online music industry; submit site; downloads.

The Web Reference www.webreference.com Do-it-yourself HTML programming; Web design.

TheCounter.com www.thecounter.com Free Web counter-tracker.

TrueFire.com www.truefire.com Digital self-publishing and distribution system for guitar instruction, original music, literature, art, and reference materials; cross-platform digital formats, including MP3, PDF, HTML, RealAudio, etc.

Tucows music.tucows.com Music Web sites; domain name register.

UltraPlayer www.ultraplayer.com Free Windows audio tool; plays MP3s, WAVs, and CDs; features playing and recording of streaming MP3 broadcasts; assortment of visual plug-ins and skins.

Virtual Turntables carrot.prohosting.com/vtt_overview.shtml Play and mix MP3s; options, effects and tools to aid in mixing of music; DJ software.

Virtual Volume www.virtual-volume.com Interactive record label; European.

Virtuosa Gold www.mp3-converter.com/virtuosa.htm MP3 player and encoder software.

Vitaminic www.vitaminic.co.uk European MP3 site.

Vortex Technology www.vortex.comav.html Streaming audio and video clips.

Web Developers Virtual Library www.wdvl.com Web resource.

Web Monkey www.webmonkey.com Web site utility.

Web Review www.webreview.com Web site utility.

Web Site Awards www.website-awards.net/ Awards Web site.

Web Sticker www.websticker.com Print custom stickers, bumper stickers, decals, and labels with Web site URL.

Web Tunes www.webtunes.com Download site; MP3.

Webopedia www.webopedia.com Look up Web terms.

Winamp Player for Windows www.winamp.com MP3 player and encoder software; from Nullsoft; high-fidelity music player for Windows; supports MP3, CD, and other audio formats; the original Windows MP3 player.

Windows Media www.windowsmedia.com or windowsmedia.microsoft.com Streaming audio format.

WinMP3Locator www.winmp3locator.com Finds any MP3; verifies if files are downloadable; defines server access conditions; integrates with download software.

WinZip www.winzip.com For compressing and decompressing zip files.

Xaudio www.xaudio.com Cross-platform MP3 players; Xaudio Player for Linux.

Xing Technology Corporation www.xingtech.com
Software company that develops MP3 players,
encoders, and rippers; *Xing AudioCatalyst.*

XMMS www.xmms.org X Multimedia System;
open-source MP3 player for Linux and UNIX;
MP3 player and encoder software.

Yahoo Directory: Downloads
dir.yahoo.com/Entertainment/Music/Downloads/
Links to download sites.

ZDNet's Ultimate CuteMX Guide
music.zdnet.comfeatures/cutemx Swap files.

Zebox.xom www.zebox.com Free Web sites.

ZY2000 www.zy2000.com MP3 CD Maker; burn
MP3 files into normal audio CDs; supports
many popular CD recorders.

Music, Print Music, and Music Book Publishers

Alfred Publishing Company www.alfred.com Print
publisher of music education materials, including
software, CDs, cassettes, videos; piano methods.

Archives Music Writing Paper www.daddario.com
Music writing paper; guitar tabulature; stitched
books; perforated books; double folded sheets;
loose-leaf sheets; spiral-bound books; manuscript
pads; archives correcting tape.

Arsis Press www.instantWeb.com~arsis Publisher of
concert and sacred music by women composers.

Artist Pro www.artistpro.com Publications of
interest to musicians; Book/Audio CDs, Videos,
DVDs; magazine.

Association of American Publishers
www.publishers.org Home page; copyright
information for books and text.

Audio Publishers Association (APA)
www.audiopub.org Nonprofit trade association
representing audio publishers, audiobooks, and
spoken audio.

Backbeat Books www.books.mfi.com Books on
contemporary music topics.

Berklee Press www.berkleepress.com Publications
of interest to musicians; Book/Audio CDs,
Videos, DVDs.

Boosey & Hawkes, Inc. www.boosey.com or
www.ny.boosey.com International music
publisher; manufacturer of acoustic instruments;
twentieth-century music; commitment to
performance and music education.

Bosworth Music Publishers
www.demon.co.uk/bosworth Founded in 1889;
pedagogical music publications; Viennese
operetta.

C. F. Peters www.cfpeters-ny.com Print music
publisher; classical editions.

Canadian Publishers' Council www.pubcouncil.ca
Guide to Canadian publishers; index to Canadian
publishing.

Carl Fischer www.carlfischer.com New publications;
retail stores; information for submitting a
manuscript.

Cherry Lane Music Group www.cherrylane.com
Publisher of songs; songbooks.

Classical Sheet Music Publishers and Distributors
www.webcom.com/musics/catalogs.html
Organized by country; links.

Cormorant Press Music Publishers
www.cormorantpress.com Music in attached
catalog is copyrighted; offered as shareware;
permission to play, teach, or copy.

Directory of Music Publishers
http://www.mpa.org/agency/pal.html Large list
of music publishers; links.

EMI www.emimusicpub.com Music publisher.

Encore Music Publishers www.encoremupub.com
Publishers of music for brass, woodwind, and
strings ensembles; publisher of music for the
tuba.

European American Music Distributors
www.eamdc.com European American Music
Distributors Corp. based in Miami, FL.

Frederick Harris Music
www.frederickharrismusic.com Print publisher of
pedagogical materials.

G. Henle USA Inc. www.henle.de/ Urtext Editions;
Musicological Editions; classical music.

G. Schirmer, Inc. www.schirmer.com Print publisher
of classical music; famous yellow/gold covers;
member of the Music Sales Group; details about
composers; catalog listings; premiers; links.

GIA Publications www.giamusic.com Major
publisher of sacred choral music, hymnals, sacred
music recordings, and music education materials.

Hal Leonard Corporation www.halleonard.com Print
publisher of popular and educational music;
software; MIDI disks; books; new music; links;
contact information; company history; search by
title, artist, or category.

Kjos www.kjos.com Piano instruction materials;
band literature.

Koala Publications www.koalapublications.com or
www.learntoplaymusic.com *Progressive;
Introducing; 10 Easy Lessons*; Australian.

Ladyslipper Music by Women www.ladyslipper.org
Publishes a comprehensive catalog of music by
women featuring over 1,500 titles; indie record
label.

Liben Music Publishers www.liben.com
Contemporary orchestral and chamber music;
Double Bass music and recordings.

MediaNews www.poynter.org/medianews Web site for publishers.

Mel Bay Publications, Inc. www.melbay.com Print music for all instruments; CDs, cassettes, videos; method books, especially for guitar and folk instruments.

Music Publisher Sales Agency List www.mpa.org/agency/pal.html Current directory of music publishers; index of publishers' imprints; hypertext links to entries.

Music Publishers and Vendors: The AcqWeb Directory www.library.vanderbilt.edu/law/ Directory of music publishers and vendors; related links.

Music Publishers' Association www.mpa.org Resources; information; links; directories.

Music Publishers' Catalogs www.musicpublications.com Complete searchable database and online ordering site for major music publishers.

Music Sales Corporation www.musicsales.com or www.msc-catalog.com AMSCO; Omnibus Press; Jam Trax; Yorktown Music Press; Oak Publications; Passantino Manuscript Papers; Ashley Music; Ossian Publications.

Music Sales Corporation UK www.musicsales.co.uk Popular titles for guitar, piano, keyboard, and organ; online Internet Music Shop.

MusicEase Software www.musicease.com Music notation and automatic accompaniment software.

Myklas Music Press www.myklas.com Print publisher of pedagogical materials.

National Music Publishers' Association (NMPA) www.nmpa.org Information about music publishing, licensing requirements, copyright laws, editorial standards, and the correct use of printed music; links.

Norton www.nortonmusic.com Publisher of scholarly music books.

Oxford University Press www.oup-usa.org Catalog of over 4,000 titles; education, scholarly, and performance fields.

Peachpit Press www.peachpit.com Publisher of books on computer music technology.

Peermusic www.peermusic.com Music publisher.

Pensacola Publications www.pensacolapub.com Features the Jefferson's *How to Play Black Gospel Music* books.

Piano Press www.pianopress.com Songbooks for piano/vocal/guitar, CDs, CD-ROMs, and music education materials; seasonal items; workshops; poetry; annual writing contest.

Publishers www.sai-national.org/resource/publish.html List of sheet music publishers and distributors on the Internet.

Publishers Marketing Association (PMA) www.pma-online.org Largest nonprofit trade association representing independent publishers of books, audio, video, and CDs; monthly newsletter; resource directory; promotional campaigns.

Publishers Weekly www.publishersweekly.com Online version of the international news magazine for book publishing and bookselling news.

Publishers' Catalog www.lights.com/publisher/ Home page.

Retail Print Music Dealers Association www.printmusic.org Publishers, retailers, and distributors of print music; membership information.

Royalty-Free Music, Inc. members.aol.com/Katzmarek/ Supplier of public domain music; encyclopedia; directory; books.

Scarecrow Press www.scarecrowpress.com Since 1950; large catalog of scholarly music titles; music reference books; academic trade books.

Schott Music www.schott-music.com Publisher of modern classical pieces; composer pages; concert diary; news; sound clips.

Shawnee Press www.shawneepress.com Music print publisher.

Six Strings Music Publishing www.sixstringsmusicpub.com Music instruction books and videos; guitar chords, fingerstyle, bass, playing tips, diagrams, links.

Southern Music Company www.southernmusic.com Established in 1937; distributor of sheet music, music books, and more for over 500 publishers; has published over 5,000 educational works.

Swedish Music Publishers Association www.smff.se Swedish; live music.

The FJH Music Co. Inc. www.fjhmusic.com Ft. Lauderdale-based educational print music publisher; Faber & Faber methods for piano.

Theodore Presser Company www.presser.com Music publisher serving musicians, music educators, and music dealers since 1783; classical editions.

Useful Addresses: Music Publishers www.cmc.ie/addresses/publishers.html Listing of music publisher addresses.

Voice of the Rockies www.voiceoftherockies.com Piano music catalog; sample pages.

Warner Bros. Publications www.warnerbrospublications.com Warner Bros.; CPP/Belwin; Summy-Birchard; DCI Music Videos; REH & SongXpress Videos; Kalmus; Bowmar; Suzuki; Lawson-Gould; Studio P/R; Interworld; Master Teacher Series; Instrumental Classmates; Ultimate Beginner Series; Beyond Basics; Getting the Sounds.

Warner Chappell www.warnerchappell.com International publisher.

Writer's Digest Books www.writersdigest.com Books on songwriting; general writing books.

Yeah Solutions www.yeahsolutions.com Makers of *Music Publisher Pro* software for managing copyrights, royalties, and payments; for artists as well as publishing companies.

Music Resources, References, and Research—Music Links—Directories—Portals

4Trivia.com www.4trivia.com Trivia contests on television, movies, music, etc.

Aardvarks Best of the Web www.stl-music.com/hub.html Links; events; classical and popular music.

About.com Music home.about.com/entertainment Directory of music categories; links.

Amazing Discographies ad.techno.org Discographies; links.

Amazon www.amazon.com/music or www.amazon.co.uk/music Retail site; reference database.

America's Shrine to Music Museum www.usd.edu/smm Home page; index; musical instrument museum and research center located in South Dakota.

AMG All Music Guide www.allmusic.com Database of all recorded music; search by album, artist, or song name; key artists; key albums; music styles; music glossary; music maps; new releases; featured albums.

ArtNet www.artnet.com Samples of art exhibitions around the world.

Basic Music www.basicmusic.net Directory of links to many music categories.

Berklee School of Music Library library.berklee.edu/ Cross-referenced recordings.

Bibliophile www.bibliophile.net Over one million books for sale by independent booksellers worldwide; rare, used, and new books; search by title, author, keyword, subject, language, recent additions, and other criteria; also lists maps, piano rolls, stereoscopic views, and almost very kind of printed material.

BigBook www.bigbook.com Yellow Pages on the Internet of every city in the country.

Bigmouth wwwbigmouth.co.uk Music information in the UK; news; tour dates.

Billboard Directories www.billboard.com Directories: *International Talent & Touring Directory:* artists and their management, performance venues, hotels, and services; *Country Music Sourcebook:* labels, publishers, recording studios, venues, clubs, concert promoters, country artists and managers, radio

stations in United States and Canada; *International Latin Music Buyer's Guide:* "Yellow Pages" of Latin Music contacts in United States, Mexico, Central, and South America.

Biography www.biography.com Based on the popular A&E television series; includes profiles of composers and musicians.

Britannica Online www.eb.com Online version of the Encyclopedia Britannica; articles on music topics.

Center of Web Music Links www.centerofweb.com/music/default.htm List of music links.

Click Music www.clickmusic.co.uk Search portal specializing in music; links; news; celebrities; Internet issues; games.

Compulink www.com/pulink.co.uk/~route66 Information for the musician; news; gigs; bands; composers; producers; magazines; record labels; publishers; links.

CultureFinder www.culturefinder.com/index.htm Calendar of musical events across the United States; music information; news; interviews; online store; purchase tickets online.

Cyber Alert www.cyberalert.com Clipping service for hire; compile information daily on topics of interest; use search engines, forums, and online databases.

DMAs Music Links to Instrument and Vocal Resources www.dmamusic.org Collection of links.

Encarta Online www.encarta.msn.com Online encyclopedia.

Encarta Online Music Links encarta.msn.com/encnet/refpages/SRPage.aspx?search=music&x=19&y=14 Links to music topics.

Entertainment Network News www.enn2.com Directory of entertainment Web sites.

Entertainment-Music www.ntgi.net/ntg/mall/music.htm Over 500 links on all kinds of music.

Faculty of Music: Instrument Collections www.music.ed.ac.uk/collect The Edinburgh University Collection of Historic Musical Instruments; two of the most important collections of historic instruments in Europe.

Getmusic.com www.getmusic.com Links to all genres.

Grace Note www.gracenote.com Information services for digital music and media; includes CD Database.

GuitarLoops www.guitarloops.com Music links.

Harmony Central www.harmony-central.com Information on many musical topics; major collection of resources for the musician; news; communities; software; MIDI; computer music.

How Stuff Works
entertainment.howstuffworks.com/channel.htm?c h=entertainment&sub=sub-music Listing of music-related things and how they work.

Indiana University Library
www.music.indiana.edu/muslib.html William and Gayle Cook Music Library; access to important library catalogs for music in the United States and abroad.

International Alliance for Women in Music
music.acu.edu/www/iawm/home.html Resource on women composers and women in music topics; more than 4,500 pages of archival resources.

Internet Scout Report scout.wisc.edu/ One of the Internet's longest-running weekly publications, offering a selection of new and newly discovered online resources of interest to researchers, educators, and anyone else with an interest in high-quality online material.

Letsfindout.com www.letsfindout.com Interactive encyclopedia.

Library of Congress www.lcWeb.loc.gov/homepage/ Largest music library in the United States.

Music Business Solutions www.mbsolutions.com Resource directory; consulting; articles; books; links.

Music Database www.roadkill.com/MDB/ Search by album title and artist; listeners' reviews and links.

Music Directory of Canada www.nor.com/mbp Listings of artists, agents, managers, labels, festivals, presenters, and other music-related resources.

Music Information Resources
www.library.ucsb.edu/subj/music.html Links to music educational sites, directories, and more.

Music Library Association
www.musiclibraryassoc.org Placement service for music librarians and more.

Music Yellow Pages www.musicyellowpages.com Phone numbers for any music-related company.

Music.com www.music.com Online destination for music lovers; e-mail; weekly e-zine; radio; music news; new releases; music history; birthdays; horoscopes; staff picks; free downloads; custom CDs; free MP3s; 1970s music;1980s music; all genres; indie music; contests and more.

Musical Quotes
www.cybernation.com/victory/quotations/subject s/quotes_music.html Famous quotations.

Musical Web Connections
www.columbia.edu/~hauben/music/web-music.html Large list of music links.

MusicSearch.com www.musicsearch.com Search engine for music only; links to artists, events, industry news, reviews, radio stations, and music publishers.

Music-Sites.net www.music-sites.net Music links directory; music community.

Musreview www.musreview.com Music charts; radio stations; artists; labels; country artists; country music links; record labels; disk jockeys; booking and talent; jazz; links and directories; rock artists; bands; blues; music publishers; Christian and gospel music; recording studios; managers; rap; R&B bands; music stores; musical instruments; music promotion; music news; radio stations; music charts; graphic design; production; MP3/MIDI; classical; songwriters; reviews.

Muze.com www.muze.com Entertainment product information.

New Media Music www.newmediamusic.com Resources for artists and labels; interviews; new products and services; events; music industry press releases.

Open Directory—Arts: Music
www.dmoz.orgArts/Music/ Music-related links.

PC Webopaedia www.pcwebopaedia.com Encyclopedia of computer and Internet information.

Scottie's Music World www.scottiesmusicworld.com Directory of links to artists on the Web; all genres.

Showbiz Data www.showbizdata.com The entertainment search engine.

The American Music Center www.amc.net Resource for musicians and producers; grant information; music directories; artist information and publications.

The Collections of Musical Instruments lcweb.loc.gov/rr/perform/guide/toc.html Library of Congress; illustrated guide.

The Free Music Archive free-music.com Supports free music and artists; alphabetized links to CD sales, e-mail, Web sites, and free music; downloads.

The Instrument Encyclopedia
www.si.umich.edu/chico/instrument/ More than 140 artifacts from the Stearns Collection at the University of Michigan; features musical instruments from around the world.

The Music TOP 10 Sites music.top10sites.net/ Links to music-related Web sites.

The Names of Instruments and Voices in Foreign Languages
www.library.yale.edu/cataloging/music/instname. htm English, French, German, Italian, Russian, and Spanish.

UCLA Music Library
www.library.ucla.edu/libraries/music University of California at Los Angeles music library.

Virtual Museums www.icom.orgvlmp Links to hundreds of museum exhibits around the world; Smithsonian, Louvre, and more.

Voice of the Shuttle
vos.ucsb.edu/browse.asp?id=2722 Music and dance resources.
Web Sites for Music Research
www.lib.unc.edu/music/research/ Compiled by the University of North Carolina; links.
Webring.org dir.webring.com/rw?d=Music Music-related links.
World Art Treasures Sgwww.epfl.ch/berger Art.
World of Mechanical Music Museum
www.mechanicalmusic.co.uk Self-playing musical instruments; antique musical boxes.
World Wide Arts Resources www.wwar.com Comprehensive directory of the arts on the Internet.
Worldwide Internet Music Resources
www.music.indiana.edu/music_resources/ Informational links.
Y2k-Music Co.UK www.y2k-music.co.uk Bands; artists; audio samples; free classifieds; CDs.
Yahoo Directory Music Links
www.yahoo.comentertainment/music Links to music sites on the Internet.
YAV's Music Links
www.yav.com/docs/MusicLinks.html Computer music; MIDI; computer music studios; algorithmic computer music; classical music; opera; music education; composers; music resources.

Music Retailers Online

123Posters www.123posters.com Buy music-related posters online.
Accordion Store www.accordion-store.com/sheetmusic/index.htm For accordion players, bands, and virtuosos; cassettes; CDs; videos; tours.
Alabama Music Inc.
www.alabamamusic.com/Main/Software.htm Sells products from a collection of music software for learning, producing, writing, recording, printing, and scanning music.
Alexander Publishing www.alexanderpublishing.com Self-paced problem/solution instruction; Alexander University Campus Music Store.
Allegro Music www.allegro-music.com Classical, jazz, world, pop, blues, etc.
Amazingcds.com www.amazingcds.com Independent music artists' CDs from around the world; online music store that is listening to original music and accepting all styles of music; see Submission Information page.
Amazon www.amazon.com Music; books; software; reviews; links; Advantage Program for independent publishers and artists.

American Musical Supply
www.americanmusical.com Online retailer.
Artist Direct Superstore www.ubl.com Online retailer.
Audiostreet www.audiostreet.co.uk Online music store; RealAudio samples.
Backtrack Records www.backtrackrecords.com Hard-to-find music; independent; imports.
Barnes and Noble www.bn.com Music; books; software; reviews; links.
Beatmaker.Com www.beatmaker.com The Sound Store; karaoke music CDs, DVD movies, games, educational software, and more.
Blockbuster Online www.blockbuster.com Movie music and video shopping.
BMG Music Service www.bmgmusicservice.com Music club; membership.
Borders www.borders.com Online books and music retailer.
Buy Music Here www.buymusichere.com Online music stores for independent music retailers.
Buy.com www.buy.com Online electronics retailer.
Carvin www.carvin.com Factory-direct music store.
CD Access www.cdaccess.com CD-ROM titles; educational.
CD Baby www.cdbaby.com Online retailer of independent CDs.
CD Now www.cdnow.com CDs; Billboard charts; imports; wide selection.
CD Palace www.cdpalace.com Online retailer.
CD Street www.cdstreet.com Independent CDs.
CD Warehouse www.cdwarehouse.com Retailer.
CD World www.cdworld.com Online store; imports.
Columbia House www.columbiahouse.com Record club online Web site.
Crotchet Web Store www.crotchet.co.uk Ten departments dedicated to classical music, jazz, film soundtracks, and world music; browse latest releases; online database.
CyberMusic Surplus discount-cds.m9b.com Thousands of CDs; discounts available; virtual outlet store for classical, jazz, pop, world, new age, and blues.
Digibid.com www.digibid.com Online auction network; gear.
DVD Express www.dvdexpress.com DVDs; concert videos.
EBopp www.ebopp.com Instruments and equipment.
Emusic www.Emusic.com Legal downloads; MP3 subscription service; free trial.
Encore Music Company, Inc.
www.encoremusic.com Sheet music; music books; accessories; gifts.
Everything English www.everythingenglish.com New and used CDs; English paraphanalia.

Forced Exposure www.forcedexposure.com Online store; reviews of new releases.

Forever Vinyl www.forevervinyl.com Buy and sell vinyl; large inventory.

Friendship House www.friendshiphouse.com Music teaching aids; gifts; novelties; trophies; software; books; CDs.

German Music Express www.musicexpress.com Online CD store; back catalog; singles.

Getmusic.com www.getmusic.com New releases from BMG and Universal.

Global Electronic Music Marketplace (GEMM) www.gemm.com Large catalog of music; combines catalogs of 2,000 discounters, importers, collectors, labels and artists; new, used, hard-to-find, and out-of-print albums.

HMV www.hmv.com Canadian retailer.

Horizon Records www.horizonrecords.net Folk, jazz, blues, world beat, classical, regional, Jewish, Celtic, vintage vinyl.

In Sound www.insound.com Not Top 40 music; chat; photos; audio samples.

Independent Distribution Network www.idnmusic.com/index.html Rare items.

Internet Music Shop www.musicsales.co.uk or www.internetmusicshop.com Order music products online.

Kelly's Music and Computers www.KellysMusicandComputers.com Retailer of audio and computer music products.

K-TEL www.ktel.com Compilations; online retailer; digital downloads.

La Jolla Music www.lajollamusic.com La Jolla, CA; lessons; sheet music; band instruments.

Landphil Records www.novia.net/landphil/indies.html State-by-state list of independent record stores.

Mars Music www.marsmusic.com Online retailer; equipment; software and more.

Mel Bay Links to Music Retailers www.melbay.com/links/stores.asp Links to music retailers in the United States.

Mix Bookshelf www.mixbookshelf.com Distributor of books on music.

Music 123 www.music123.com Online music retailer.

Music and Arts Online CD Catalog www.musicandarts.com Contemporary and historic classical, jazz, and world music recordings.

Music Box World www.musicboxworld.com Specializes in custom music boxes, carousels, fine Italian inlaids, dolls, ballerinas, and children's boxes; choose a tune from alphabetical list of hundreds; virtual museum.

Music Dispatch www.musicdispatch.com Online retailer of products distributed by Hal Leonard.

Music Education Online www.childrensmusicworkshop.com/companies.html Music company links page.

Music for a Song www.musicforasong.com Over 15,000 selections, including out-of-print, cutout, hard-to-find CDs and cassettes; Gold Disks and imports.

Music Gear OnLine musicgearonline.com Large guide to musical equipment including music software, soundware, MIDI, MIDI controllers, effects, signal processors, synthesizers, samplers, recorders, accessories, and more.

Music in Motion www.musicinmotion.com Music education and gift catalog for all ages; music books, videos, audios, awards, teaching aids, posters, bulletin board aids, gifts, software, creative dramatics, multicultural resources, and more.

Music Jackpot www.musicjackpot.com Online connection to online music stores; CDs, tapes, music videos, laser discs, video games, sheet music, and more.

Music Lovers Shoppe www.musicloversshoppe.com Shop for music lovers.

Music Mart www.musicmart.com Online music retailer.

Music Mongers Music & Gifts www.musicmongers.com Sheet music; CDs; songbooks; music instruction; music-themed gifts.

Music Room Music Room www.musicroom.com Online retailer of sheet music.

Music123 www.music123.com Online musical instrument store.

Musichotbid.com www.musichotbid.com Online music auction site.

Musician Store www.musicianstore.com Sheet music; software; musician's gear.

Musicians Friend www.musiciansfriend.com Order all types of music equipment online; music software; Effects Glossary describing various effects; streaming audio demos in RealAudio format.

MusicYo.com www.MusicYo.com Online music store.

Norwalk Music www.norwalkmusic.com Online musical instrument store; links to manufacturer's Web sites; index for every instrument.

Off the Record www.otrvinyl.com Rare and collectible records.

Other Music www.othermusic.com Independent record store; New York City.

Parasol www.parasol.com or www.indies.com Indie CDs and vinyl; new and used; catalog; own labels.

Past Perfect www.pastperfect.com Remastered songs from the 1920s to 1940s.

Preferred Music Retailers
www.allmusic.com/com/amg/music.html Links to retailers.

Pro Audio www.proaudiomusic.com Equipment retailer; links.

Pro Music Find www.promusicfind.com Worldwide marketplace for musicians; instruments; music; downloadable sheet music and files.

Pulse Music www.pulseonline.com Equipment and instruments.

RBP Musician Supply rbpgroup.vstoremusic.com Guitars; woodwind; brass; percussion; instruments for children; large variety of international instruments.

Rockabilia www.rockabilia.com Purchase rock music collectibles online.

Rough Trade Shop www.roughtrade.com Alternative music; used CDs; vinyl; concert listings; tickets; search engine.

Sam Ash Music www.SamAshMusic.com or www.samash.com Online music retailer; equipment.

Seaford Music www.seaford-music.co.uk Classical music retailers; violin repairs and sales; international classical compact disc; sheet music and musical instrumental store based in Sussex, England.

Second Spin www.secondspin.com Buy and sell used CDs.

Sold Out www.soldout.com Purchase tickets online.

Sonicrec.com www.sonicrec.com Collectible vinyl.

Stagepass.com www.stagepass.com Instructional books, videos, software, and MIDI files collections.

Stereo Liquidators www.stereoliquidators.com Stereo equipment.

Streets Online www.streetsonline.co.uk/ Online music retailer.

Tempest Music www.violin-world.com/sheetmusic Sheet music; print music; online store and catalog; music; stringed; bowed; woodwind; brass; piano; percussion instruments; vocal music; novelty; accessories; strings; reeds.

The Federal Trade Commission www.ftc.gov Information on consumer e-commerce protection.

The Music House www.themusichouse.com Online music retailer.

The Music Resource www.themusicresource.com Home page; resources; links.

The Music Stand www.musicstand.com Gifts and novelties for musicians.

The Penoka Collection www.penoka.comd_teach.htm Instruction books, videos.

The Sound Professionals www.soundpros.com Stereo equipment.

Three Rivers www.threeriversmusic.com Music accessories; music stands.

Ticket Web www.ticketweb.com Purchase tickets online.

Ticketmaster Online www.ticketmaster.com Buy tickets to events online.

Ticketmaster UK www.ticketmaster.co.uk UK tickets online.

Tickets.com www.tickets.com Purchase tickets online.

Tower Records www.towerrecords.com CDs; videos; books; records; tapes; sample tracks; *Pulse!* magazine; reviews.

Tower www.tower.com Online music retailer; track listings; RealAudio samples.

Tunes.com www.tunes.com Online music store; track listings; sample sounds; videos; broadcasts; news; links.

Vintage Vinyl www.vvinyl.com 100,000-item inventory; all genres; 1950s, 1960s; imports.

Vinyl 4Ever www.vinyl4ever.com Guitar tab, bass, woodwind, and brass music books; vinyl records; sheet music; scores.

Virgin Megastore www.virginmega.com Online music retailer.

Wax City www.waxcity.com Online retailer; dance music; new releases; audio clips.

Web Tix www.Webtix.com Want ads for tickets.

West L.A. Music www.westlamusic.com Pro gear.

West Music www.westmusic.com Online music retailer.

Wherehouse Music www.wherehousemusic.com Music retailer.

World Music Store www.worldmusicstore.com CDs from around the world.

World Music Web www.worldmusicweb.com Directory of music retailers; classified ads; musician's forum.

World of Music Boxes www.worldofmusicboxes.com Music box designs and mechanical movements imported from Switzerland, Italy, Germany, and the Orient; classic and childrens' collectibles; jewelry boxes; handcrafted gifts.

World Party Music www.wpmusic.com New and used CDs.

World Wide Music www.worldwidemusic.com CDs, cassettes, and more; cover art and sound bites from selected CDs.

Yahoo Directories: Music Retailers dir.yahoo.com/Business_and_Economy/Shopping _and_Services/Music/Instruments_and_Equipmen t/Retailers/ Sellers of instruments and equipment.

Yestermusic www.yestermusic.com Oldies; all genres and decades.

Zzounds www.zzounds.com Online music gear and accessories retailer.

Music Theory and Composition—Notation— Ear Training

A1 Music www.ilovemusic.com Music theory, dance, and music education; compose music, learn chords, scales, rhythm; ear training.

Adult Music Theory www.musicarrangers.com/star-theory Jazzy, classical.

AP Music Theory www.collegeboard.org/ap/music or www.collegeboard.comap/music Teachers' corner; AP music theory credit; placement; advanced standing policies; compact disks.

Camps V4 www.campspro.com/win4/ Music theory software; Windows.

Center for the History of Music Theory and Literature www.music.indiana.edu/chmtl Joint venture of Indiana University's School of Music and the Office of Research and the University Graduate School.

Chord Wizard www.chordwizard.com/theory.html Music theory tutorials.

Complete Chords www.completechords.com Roedy Black's chord posters; products; free information for songwriters; reference charts.

Cope Media www.cope.dk Ear-training software for Windows; aural training of scales, chords, intervals, melody, rhythm, inversions, progressions, etc.

CTHEORY www.ctheory.com International journal of theory, technology, and culture; articles, interviews, and book reviews published weekly.

Dutch Journal of Music Theory sca.ahk.nl/tvm/tvm.html Tijdschrift voor Muziekthoerie.

Ear Trainer www.ilovemusic.com/ear.htm Software program to help musical ear.

Ear Training Expedition www.trailcreeksystems.com Ear-training software for Windows; helps students learn music theory and practice skills with games.

EarMaster www.earmaster.com Ear training software for Windows; intervals, chords, scales, melodies, and rhythms.

EarPower www.earpower.com/earpower.htm Ear-training program to be used as a daily routine; compact and easy to use; many features; for anyone, from the "tone-deaf" person to the professional musician.

Eartraining www.lpeters.de/ Practice intervals, chords, scales, and perfect pitch.

Gary Ewer's "Easy Music Theory" www.musictheory.halifax.ns.ca Free music theory lessons on the Internet; how to write scales, chords, triads, etc.

Good-Ear.com www.good-ear.com Offers ear-training and theory skills.

Hearing and Writing Music www.rongorow.com Professional training; self-study.

I Breathe Music www.ibreathemusic.com Music theory; tips; tutorials; reviews.

Java Music Theory academics.hamilton.edu/music/spellman/JavaMusic Designed to help students of music theory improve their proficiency; basic skills.

Journal of Music Theory Home Page www.yale.edu/jmt Published twice a year, in the Spring and Fall, by Yale University.

MacGAMUT Software www.macgamut.com Music software for ear training.

Metronimo-Educational Musical Games www.metronimo.com Music theory; classic composers; musical culture; instruments of the symphony orchestra; in English and French; Windows.

MIBAC Music Lessons www.mibac.com/Pages/Theory/Main_Theory.htm Music theory reference.

Music Composition Resource www.und.nodak.edu/dept/mcr Sources for composers; books; articles; Web sites; recordings; FAQs.

Music of Cyberworld-Music Theory www.philosophers.org/MusicTheory Music theory Web sites.

Music Study www.musicstudy.com Ear-training and music theory instruction software; Macintosh; Windows.

Music Theory library.thinkquest.org/15413/theory/theory.htm?tqskip1=1&tqtime=0907 Basics of music theory; note reading, intervals, scales, and more.

Music Theory for Songwriters members.aol.com/chordmaps/ Basic music theory links.

Music Theory Online www.societymusictheory.org/mto/ Online resource for music theory.

Music Theory Spectrum www.ucpress.edu/journals/mts Official print journal of the Society for Music Theory; articles and book reviews on topics in music theory and analysis, including aesthetics.

Musicianship Basics users.dragnet.com.au/~donovan/mb/ Music education software for schools and piano teachers; graded ear-training and theory activities for all music students; demos available; Macintosh; Windows.

MusicTheory.net www.musictheory.net Free online music theory lessons; comprehensive.

Myriad Software www.myriad-online.com *Harmony Assistant* and *Melody Assistant*; software programs for computer-assisted tune writing and composition; Macintosh; Windows.

Practical Music Theory—Teoría práctica de la música www.teoria.com Web site dedicated to the study of musical theory.

RhythmTutor members.aol.com/CopperSoft/rhythm.html Music instruction software for PC and Macintosh; learn to sight-read musical rhythm notation.

Richard Daniels Music www.ncp.net/rdm *Theory for the Serious Musician;* seven books on jazz music theory for intermediate to advanced musicians.

Rising Software www.risingsoftware.com Australian software house of music education products; makers of *Auralia* ear-training software; *Musition.*

Rocky Mountain Society for Music Theory jan.ucc.nau.edu/~tas3/rmsmt.html Associated with the Society for Music Theory; regional organization.

Sacred Harp Singing www.mcsr.olemiss.edu/~mudws/harp Information and resources; links.

Shape Note Singing www.fasola.org Shape notes; information and links; print and audio examples.

Sibelius Academy www2.siba.fi/Kulttuuripalvelut/theory.html Music research and music theory.

SMT—Committee on the Status of Women www.wmich.edu/mus-theo/csw.html Society for Music Theory's Committee on the Status of Women Web pages.

Solfege sourceforge.net/project/?group_id=1465 Ear-training software for Linux; requires *Gnome.*

Solomon's Music Theory & Composition Resources music.theory.home.att.net/ Resources for composers; music theory; researchers of music; sound files; analysis; composers and compositions; resources in Musicology, Music Theory, Music Instruction, Music research, notation, recordings, and more.

The Harmonic Metronome www.wholarts.com/music/hm Produces scales and arpeggios, perfectly tuned and perfectly timed.

The Perfect Pitch-Ear Training Super Course www.eartraining.com Ear-training instruction series for musicians of all instruments; CDs.

The Teacher's Apprentice for Music Theory www.creativeware.com/ta.htm Simplifies administrative tasks for the teacher; testing and learning tool.

THEMA www.uga.edu/~thema THEMA stands for (Music) Theory of the Middle Ages; hypertext transcriptions of eighteen manuscript copies of fourteen Latin theoretical treatises on music theory.

Theory www.united-trackers.org/resources/theory/index.htm Serial composition technique; evolved in the twentieth century as the final stage of tonality.

Theory of Music Examination Syllabus www.abrsm.ac.uk/theory.html Theory of Music Examination Syllabuses, Grades 1-8; The Associated Board of the Royal Schools of Music; setting the standards in music examination.

Theory Time www.theorytime.com Comprehensive music theory course; believes that an exceptional music theory course is essential for any music student.

TrackStar:Beginning Music Theory www.scrtec.org/track/tracks/s09756 Lessons created ideally for the youngest of beginners.

Trail Creek Systems www.trailcreeksystems.com Makers of *Ear Training Expedition* software.

Tray Transpose Tool www.simusic.com/traytranspose.html Program that will work with any Windows application to transpose chords into any key.

UCLA Department of Music www.music.ucla.edu Home page; information is available on admissions, courses, faculty, and facilities.

Yahoo! Entertainment:Music:Theory www.yahoo.com/Entertainment/Music/Theory Music theory site.

Musical E-Greetings and Singing Telegrams

1001 Postcards www.postcards.org Large collection of free virtual postcards; cartoons; special occasions; scenic; comedy.

Abby's Good Stuff for Free www.abbys-good-stuff.comgreeting.html Free e-greetings.

American Greetings www.americangreetings.com Personalized greeting cards, printed and electronic.

Animated Greeting Cards with Music members.aol.com/media27/holiday.htm Holiday cards with animation and music.

Applemania Singing Telegrams and Balloons www.tutuguy.com Singing telegrams in Seattle; for parties, birthdays, corporate events, Valentine's day, any occasion.

Awesome Greetings www.awesomegreetings.com Free electronic greetings.

Beat Greets www.beatgreets.com Free music greetings from hundreds of contemporary pop music artists.

Blue Mountain www.bluemountain.com Variety of e-greetings with music; printed greeting cards; poetry books.

CanWebCards www.canwebcards.com Personalized musical electronic greeting cards by e-mail.

Care2 E-Cards www.care2.com/send/categories Free
    animated and musical greetings that help save
    wildlife; over 25,000 greetings.
Compufield www.compufield.net/cards/ E-cards;
    musical greetings.
Egreetings.com www.egreetings.com Hosts free E-
    cards.
Greet2K www.greet2k.com Free greetings for the
    millennium.
Greeting-Cards.com www.greeting-
    cards.comindex.jsp?affiliate_id=01640 Electronic
    greetings.
Hallmark www.hallmark.com Electronic greetings for
    e-mail friends.
Happy Birthday to You
    www.happybirthdaytoyou.com Singing birthday
    cards; personalized, professionally recorded
    versions; all styles.
International Singing Telegrams
    www.intsing.qpg.com Singing telegrams,
    balloon delivery, gift baskets, worldwide flower
    delivery and more.
P.S. I Love You! www.personal-ads-
    network.comPersonalSongs.shtml Personalized
    songs on CD or cassette.
Romantic Cards members.aol.commedia27/love.htm
    Free e-mail greeting cards with animation and
    music; all occasions.
Shopping Center shop001.hypermart.net/cards.htm
    Online personalized, animated, musical greeting
    cards; electronic cards; e-mail greetings.
Singing Phonegrams www.singingphonegrams.com
    Sent anywhere in the world with ten-second
    recorded greeting included.
Singing Telegrams Inc.
    www.singingtelegrams.com.au Delivering gifts,
    poems, balloons, and breakfasts; Sydney,
    Australia.
Singing Valentines www.singingvalentines.com
    Saying "I love you" with a song; available in all
    regions.
The E-Greetings Portal
    www.theegreetingsportal.com Links to e-
    greetings Web sites.
Yahoo Greetings greetings.yahoo.com Send a free
    greeting.

Musical Theater

American Association of Community Theater
    www.aact.org Events and festivals; books; CDs.
American Musical Theater
    www.theatrehistory.com/american/musical030.ht
    ml History.
Applause Tickets www.applause-tickets.com Theater
    and entertainment service; Broadway, Off

Broadway, concert and ballet tickets; sightseeing
    and more in New York City.
Arts and Entertainment at Musical Theater West
    www.musical.org News and information;
    southern California's oldest professional musical
    theater companies; current and past productions;
    tickets; auditions.
Broadway Theater www.broadwaytheater.com
    Theater industry; tickets; reviews; multimedia.
Circle in the Square Theater School
    www.circlesquare.org Professional acting and
    musical theater training at the heart of Broadway.
Concert Tickets www.musicalchairstickets.com
    Ticket agency specializing in all types of tickets
    including concert tickets, theater tickets.
Eldridge Plays and Musicals www.histage.com
    Theater plays and musicals for all occasions; full-
    length plays; one-act plays; melodramas; holiday
    themes; children's and full-length musicals; skits
    and theater collections.
Invisible Sound Design invisible.freeservers.com
    Custom software solutions for the entertainment
    industry; sound design services for musical
    theater.
Learning Technology Institute www.takeiteasy.org
    Musical theater education.
London Theater Guide www.londontheatre.co.uk
    What's playing in London.
Music Theater International www.mtishows.com
    Major Broadway and Off-Broadway shows; youth
    shows, revues and musicals which began life in
    regional theater and have since become worthy
    additions to the musical theater canon.
Musical Stages Online www.musicalstages.co.uk
    Guide to musical theater.
Musical Theater in Europe www.eur.com/theatre
    Almanac; pictures; singers; repertoire; links for
    120+ theaters; search by artist or by work title;
    database includes 500+ titles and 5,000+ singers.
Musical Youth Artists Repertory Theater
    www.myart.org Musical theater for children
    youth artists performers; repertory theater offers
    live stage performances using kids and young
    people in legitimate Broadway plays.
Musical, Opera, Theater, & Music Station
    www.insurance-finance.com/musical.htm Links
    regarding musicals, opera, ballet, and theaters;
    links to top twenty Broadway official and
    unofficial sites; performing arts links.
Musicals 101 www.musicals101.com The Cyber
    Encyclopedia of Musical Theater, TV and Film.
Musicals.Net www.musicals.net Index to many
    Broadway musicals; song lists; synopsises; lyrics;
    discussion forums.
National Alliance for Musical Theater
    www.namt.net/ Service organization for

professional theater, light opera, and opera companies.

Playbill Online www.playbill.com Source of theater information; published by the same company that has printed *Playbill Magazine* on Broadway for over 100 years; international theater news.

Stage Directions www.stage-directions.com Theater industry.

Starbound www3.sympatico.ca/k.widenmaier/ Singing, dancing, and acting tips; sheet music and monologue references.

The American Musical Theater Reference Library www.americanmusicals.com Internet directory for musical theater.

The Definitive Musical Theater Web Site www.musicalshows.me.uk/ News; listings; show database; forum; links.

The Guide to Musical Theater www.nodanw.com World of musical theater.

The Lion King WWW Archive: The Broadway Musical www.lionking.org/musical Brief overview of the Broadway musical; reviews; current Broadway cast list; RealVideo & WAV files.

The Really Useful Company Presents Andrew Lloyd Webber www.reallyuseful.com Site devoted to promoting the musicals and other productions created by Sir Andrew Lloyd Webber.

Theater Development Fund www.tdf.org Nonprofit theater organization for the performing arts.

Theater Net www.theatrenet.co.uk Theater industry; news archives; links.

Theatricopia www.saintmarys.edu/~jhobgood/Jill/theatre.html Links and more for musical theater fans.

University Musical Society www.ums.org News; performances; education.

Whatsonstage.com www.whatsonstage.com UK guide to theater, classical music, opera, and dance productions; news; seating plans; online shop.

Networking—Newsgroups— Mailing Lists—Chat— Career Information— Indie Music Promotion

1212.com-Internet Music Production Guide www.1212.com Search Engine for music sites dedicated to professional musicians, singers, recording studios, sound engineer, and composers around the world. ,

3d Industry Contacts www.3dartist.com3dah/contacts.htm Two-page list of hundreds of software and model/texture publishers and distributors, hardware manufacturers, and book and video publishers.

411 Music www.411-music.com Stringed instruments; search for artists and bands concert schedules; DJ services; duplicating; music business bookstore.

A&R Bandit www.wightweb.demon.co.uk/bandit A&R services for a fee.

A&R Online www.aandronline.com Connect with A&R reps.

A&R Registry www.musicregistry.com A&R Web site.

Acid Planet www.acidplanet.com For users of Sonic Foundry's *Acid* software; self-publish music online.

AFIM (Association for Independent Music) www.afim.org Information; resources; links; membership; formerly NAIRD.

AlMusic www.aimusic.org Advancing independent music.

Allindie.com www.allindie.com Indie artists and labels.

America's Job Bank www.ajb.dni.us Job listings by category and state.

Ampcast www.ampcast.com Highest royalty payment to artists who upload their music on the Internet; introduces new musicians and bands; downloadable MP3s; search the cross-referenced musical archives.

Applause Music Production and Performance Careers www.cnvi.com/applause Tips, tricks, and secrets for a show business, performance, or production career; links.

Ariel Publicity www.arielpublicity.com Publicity at the grassroots level.

Artist Development www.artistdevelopment.com Duplication; design services; promotion.

Artist Direct www.artistdirect.com Artist Web sites; links; search site; superstore; music downloads; music community.

Artist Forum www.artistforum.com Free Web sites; sell CDs.

Artist Launch www.artistlaunch.com Sell indie music; all styles.

Artistpro.Com www.artistpro.com Online community offering free education, training, and information for entire spectrum of audio recording and music production.

Association for Independent Music www.afim.org Annual convention; awards; resources.

Association of Independent Music www.musicindie.com Find a manager.

Audio Grab www.audiograb.com Independent music by genre; packaged players; rippers; encoders for downloading; creating MP3 files; news.

Band Name www.bandname.com Indie music company; register your band's name; classified ads; gigs and more.

Band Radio www.bandradio.com Indie music
company; business sense; resource for labels,
radio, and bands.

Band Store www.bandstore.com Indie music
company.

Band Things www.bandthings.com Web site for
bands.

Band Wear www.bandwear.com Indie music
company.

Bandit A&R Newsletter www.banditnewsletter.com
New music companies seeking acts, songs, and
masters every month; available in United States
and worldwide editions; sample current issue;
success stories file; introductory subscriptions.

Bands on the Web www.bandsontheweb.com Indie
music company.

Bandweb.com www.bandweb.com Web site
solutions for bands and musicians.

Berklee Music
www.berkleemusic.com/school/courses Online
courses; Pro Tools; songwriting; lyric writing.

Best Female Musicians bestfemalemusicians.com
Artist pages grouped by genre; reviews; news.

Big Mama Music www.bigmamamusic.com Indie
music promotion.

Big Meteor Publishing www.bigmeteor.com *The
Indie Music Bible;* free exposure for music-
related site or service; indie link exchange; indie
resource land; submit site.

Bigfoot www.bigfoot.com e-mail lookup service.

BigYellow www.bigyellow.com or
www.bigbook.com Yellow Pages; e-mail
directory.

Bip www.bipbipbip.com Indie music for sale.

British Unsigned Rock Bands www.burbs.org.uk Free
resource for bands; lists artists.

Bryan Farrish Radio Promotion www.radio-
media.com Song/album promotion; syndicated
program promotion; radio interview promotion;
internships.

Business Chops for the Independent
www.succeedinginmusic.net/bcfti/index.html
Interactive workshop that combines a deep-rooted
focus on sound business principles, strategies and
tactics, with a foundation of both artistic
integrity and commercial viability; designed for
the independent producer, engineer, recording
artist, or studio operator.

Business@Home www.gohome.com For individuals
who operate a business from their homes.

Buy Indie Music www.buyindiemusic.com
Independent artist's music and merchandise.

Buzzine www.buzzine.com/indibuzz Indie
submissions.

California Bands www.cabands.com Indie music
company.

*Canadian Independent Record Production
Association* www.cirpa.ca Canadian indies;
resources; links.

CareerPath.com www.careerpath.com Classifieds
from newspapers around the United States.

Careers in Music
spider.georgetowncollege.edu/music/Careers/caree
rs.html Professional areas representing a number
of career possibilities in music.

Careers in Music www.uwrf.edu/music/careers.html
Music major graduates; professional fields open;
careers that recent graduates have entered or that
are available.

Careers.org www.careers.org The Internet's
Directory of Career Directories; access to over
7,500 links sorted by topic and region.

Casino Careers Online www.casinocareers.com
Online resume database; resumes in open access
or confidential format; employment and career
opportunities.

CD Baby www.cdbaby.com Independent CDs for sale;
listed by genre; started by Derek Sivers.

CD Labs www.cdlabs.com CD duplication and
distribution.

CD Review Network www.cdreviewnetwork.com
Purpose of site is to connect reviewer to the
website of any artist on the compilation CD.

CD Reviewers www.cdreviews.com Reviews CDs.

CD Sonic www.cdsonic.com CD-Audio and CD-
ROM duplication.

CD Stands www.cdstands.com Display CD and CD
cover like a trophy.

Coalition of Independent Music Stores
www.cimsmusic.com/index.html Indie music.

College Board Online www.collegeboard.org Help
with exams.

CollegeNET www.collegenet.com Search for colleges
using different criteria.

Community Musician
www.CommunityMusician.com Local listings
for United States cities.

Cool Site of the Day www.coolsiteoftheday.com Cool
picks are archived; links.

Crack the Whip Promotions
www.crackthewhippromotions.com Promotion
for independent artists; news; bands; events.

Creative Musicians Coalition www.aimcmc.com
International organization representing
independent artists and independent record labels;
albums and videos available for purchase;
ongoing dialogue with artists; showcases.

Cybergrrl.com www.cybergrrl.com Entertainment
and informational site to celebrate and inspire
women; technology, music, travel, and books;
focus on profiles of women and women's
personal essays; started by Aliza Sherman who

wrote the book *Cybergrrl: A Woman's Guide to the World Wide Web.*

DemoRama www.demorama.com Reviews CDs.

Diane Rapaport www.dianerapaport.com Author of *A Music Business Primer* and *How to Make and Sell Your Own Recording;* workshops.

Do It Yourself Convention www.diyconvention.com Contests for film, music, and books; events in Los Angeles, Nashville, and New York; news; features; reviews.

Dmusic.com www.dmusic.com Online indie distribution venue.

Duck Music www.duckmusic.com Artists services; Web sites; online consignment CD sales; online tools.

Earbuzz.com www.earbuzz.com Online indie store; 100 percent of profits to the artist.

E-Press Kit go.to/epresskit Electronic press kits; simple, easy, and effective way to promote music.

Faculty of Music-Careers for Music Graduates www.unimelb.edu.au/HB/facs/MUSIC-S11740.html Guide to courses; employment possibilities for music graduates.

Female Musicians and Artists Network www.femmuse.com Shows; calendar; musicians; links; reviews.

FemaleMusician.com www.femalemusician.com Music industry education for young women; indie music company.

Femina.com www.femina.com Searchable directory of exclusively sites for, by, and about women with a special section of sites for girls.

FezGuys.com www.fezguys.com Home page.

FinAid www.finaid.org How to borrow money for education.

Focus Marketing www.focusmarketing.us For independent artists; solutions; resources.

Free Music Classifieds www.freemusicclassifieds.com Home page.

Galaris Musicians Directory www.galaris.com Comprehensive resource on CD-ROM; over 1,200 pages of verified business listings; for musicians and music professionals.

Garage Band www.garageband.com Indie music company; online community created by musicians for musicians.

GearSearch.com www.gearsearch.com New, used, or vintage gear; search by state, instrument, or country; free catalogs available from many of the companies represented.

Get Indie www.getindie.com Indie band distribution.

GetSigned.com www.getsigned.com Music biz advice from leading experts in the industry; indie tools; artist interviews; books; tour booking; interviews; home recording tips; gear reviews;

music law; legal issues; press kits; management tips; playing live; promotion.

Girlmedia.com www.girlmedia.com To help female musicians and girl bands of all styles gain recognition; interviews; contests; live radio broadcast; submissions from new musicians.

Girlmusician.com www.girlmusician.com Designed with the female singer/songwriter in mind; emphasis on the independent recording artist.

Girls Rock 'n' Roll Camp www.girlsrockcamp.org Day camp for girls, ages eight-eighteen, to learn basics of creating and playing rock 'n' roll music on their instrument of choice: vocals, drums, electric guitar, keyboard, or bass.

Go Girls Music www.gogirlsmusic.com Promoting women in music; reviews; new releases; join lists; regional festivals.

Great Music Sites www.greatmusicsites.com Links to featured artists; MP3 stations; genre listings; music reviews; gig alert; open forum; music promotion and more.

GuitarGirls.com www.guitargirls.com Resource and support site for female artists who write, sing, and play guitar; features MIDI, MP3, and Real Audio files; GuitarGirls contest which showcases and promotes independent female talent.

Honky-tonkin www.HonkyTonkin.com No charge to be added to online site; catalog of titles goes out worldwide to wholesale and retail account base; pay per transaction; no returns; no contracts.

Hostbaby.com www.hostbaby.com Web hosting for independent musicians.

Hungry Bands www.hungrybands.com Indie music company; taking submissions.

I Seek You (ICQ) www.icq.com Chat in real time; free program download.

IChat www.ichat.com Software for customized chat rooms.

ICN Music Contacts www.icn.co.uk/music.html Aims to provide access to the music industry for the individual or small company; music contact categories; A & R contacts; CD manufacturers.

Immedia.com www.immedia.com.au/books Music business books catalog; titles dealing with recording, publishing, deals, touring, legalities, business realities, making CDs, setting up a label, songwriting, publishing, performance, and production information relating to a career in the music industry.

Impact Entertainment Group www.impactentertainmentgrp.com Indie music company.

Independent Artists' Services www.idiom.com~upend/ias/index.html Submit URL for a link; plan a tour; links to record labels; online radio stations; list shows on concert calendar.

Independent Bands www.independentbands.com Indie band listings.

Independent Distribution Network www.idnmusic.comindex.html Global indie network; CD catalog.

Indie Band Search www.indiebandsearch.com Run by ModMusic, Long Island City, NY; national contest giving independent musicians, artists, songwriters, and bands a chance to be heard by entertainment professionals and compete for prizes; music of all genres will be accepted.

Indie Biz www.indiebiz.com Indie music Web site; band promotion.

Indie CD Shop www.indiecdshop.com Indie CDs.

Indie Centre www.indiecentre.com Independent label information; creating a label; recording; manufacturing; sales; distribution; promotion; advertising; booking.

Indie Group www.indiegroup.com Indie music company.

Indie Music Forum www.IndieMusicForum.com Annual conferences held around the United States for independent artists and musicians; workshops; seminars.

Indie Pool www.indiepool.com Canadian independent recording artists.

Indie Pro www.indiepro.com Indie music promotion.

Indie Space www.indiespace.com Indie music promotion.

IndieGate www.indiegate.com Indie music Web site; buy CDs.

IndieGirl www.indiegrrl.com Forum for information, networking, and conversation in the realm of independent music from a female perspective; welcomes all female musicians, singers, songwriters, and others in indie music; men supportive of women in music are welcome to join.

Indiego.com www.indiego.com Independent artist and indie record label distribution.

IndieGroup www.indiegroup.com Artist directory.

Indie-Music.com www.indie-music.com Musician's resources; links; Internet primer; bands; education; labels; radio; reviews; studios; tour guide; venues; add URL; mailing list; CDs; mailing list; e-mail; ads; shop; journal; tips.

IndiePromo.com IndiePromo.com Information for independent musicians; resources; links; networking; e-zines; Internet radio; promotion; Web site design; tutorials; reviews; publications.

Indierec.com www.indierec.com Indie music company.

Indy Music www.indymusic.com Submit music.

Infraworks.com www.infraworks.com Secure digital files.

Intermixx www.InterMixx.com/webzine Webzine for independent artists and musicians.

Internet FAQ Consortium www.faqs.org Comprehensive lists of newsgroups.

Internet Relay Chat www.ircle.com (Macintosh) or www.mirc.com (Windows); IRC channels.

IUMA www.iuma.com Independent Underground Music Archive; artists, independent bands, local talent Web pages; publishing and promotion; free MP3 and RealPlayer music track downloads for listening.

JobStar-Specific Career Information www.jobsmart.orgtools/career/ Public library sponsored guide to information for the job search; 1,000 job hotlines; calendar of job and career events; career centers; libraries and more.

Kathode Ray Music www.kathoderaymusic.com Indie music resources; promotion.

KindWeb.com www.kindweb.com Music resources; band links.

Kweevak.com www.kweevak.com Music promotion services; classic rock MP3 downloads.

La Costa Music Business Consultants www.lacostamusic.com Music business advice; songwriting; publishing; artist management; publicity; production; record promotion.

LA Music Awards www.lamusicawards.com LA area awards.

LA Music Productions www.lamusicproductions.com Events in Los Angeles for songwriters and musicians; founded by Leslie Waller; articles; resources; newsletter.

LAMN (Los Angeles Music Network) www.lamn.com News; FAQs.

Local Songs www.localsongs.com Music and songs.

Local Sound www.localsound.com Indie music company.

Master Merchant Systems www.mmscom.net Point of Sale; Barcoding.

Media Omaha www.mediaomaha.com CD duplication.

Meet New Players www.meetnewplayers.com Indie music company.

Modern Postcard www.modernpostcard.com Postcard printing.

Monster.com www.monsterboard.com Search jobs; resume builder.

Musebid.com www.musebid.com Auction Web site.

Music Bargain www.musicbargain.com Free classified music-related ads.

Music Biz Academy www.musicbizacademy.com Resources and books for indie musicians.

Music Biz Coaching www.musicbizcoaching.com Author of *Grow Your Band's Audience;* free newsletter; calls and classes; membership.

Music Builder www.MusicBuilder.com Upload music; statistics.

Music Business Software www.musicbusinessstore.com Professional

Music Business Contracts: 100 music industry contracts; Record Company in a Box: complete record company management software; Tour Manager: manage gigs and complete tours, financial reports, and itineraries; Macintosh; Windows.

Music Careers with Robert Rosenblatt, Esq. www.soloperformer.com/careers/ Music business and legal issues about songwriting, managers, agents, contracts, and performing.

Music Connection www.musicconnection.com Magazine for musicians; music marketplace; free classifieds; find pro players; exclusive directories; detailed industry reference guide in every issue.

Music Contact International www.Music-Contact.com Festivals and events; tours.

Music Countdown www.netmusiccountdown.com Home page.

Music Dish www.musicdish.com Indie music resource; informative music industry e-newsletter; links; career tips; OMI (Online Music Industry Showcase) Award; Music Industry Survey.

Music Distribution www.musicdistribution.com Promote and sell music.

Music for People www.MusicForPeople.org Music workshops.

Music Industry Career Center www.music-careers.com Sponsored by Sweetwater Sound; music industry companies list position openings; potential employees post resumes; free service.

Music Industry Training www.musicit.com/home.asp Offers training and education in the contemporary music industry through on-campus and on-line mediums.

Music Media www.music-media.co.uk UK bands; networking; players needed.

Music Network USA www.mnusa.com Resources for musicians and bands; musicians seeking bands; bands seeking musicians; recording artists; songwriters; music publishers; recording studios; talent agencies; producers and more.

Music Pro Insurance www.musicproinsurance.com Insurance for the musician; instruments; equipment; vehicle; life.

Music Promotion Tips www.musicpromotiontips.com Tips on selling CDs and more.

Music Vision www.musicvision.com Provides publishers with technology solutions to enhance Web sites; provides services to major artists; matches Web sites with advertisers; media technologies; eleven channels.

Music Wizard www.music-wizard.com Music Collection Manager for Windows; manage, edit, and sort records; print professional CD covers with user defined background pictures.

MusicCareers.net www.musiccareers.net/index.php In the studio; on the road; songwriting; education; reviews; interviews; links.

Musician's Phone Book www.musiciansphonebook.com Thousands of listings in over sixty categories; recording studios; record companies; management; purchasing; distribution; FAQ; links.

Musicians Atlas www.musiciansatlas.com Resource for musicians including clubs, venues, and more.

Musicians Contact Service www.musicianscontact.com Contact other musicians.

Musicians Hotline www.musicianshotline.com Networking.

Musicians Institute www.mi.edu Career development center for musicians located in Hollywood, CA; classes; workshops; private lessons; 500-seat concert hall.

Musicians Online www.musiciansonline.com Community of musicians, recording professionals, musical instrument and equipment manufacturers, and record company A&R representatives; artist's showcases; musicians resource and publicity engine; forum for musicians to publicize themselves and their work.

MusiciansPage.com www.musicianspage.com Home page; resources.

Musicplayer.com www.musicplayer.com Resources; networking opportunities; lessons; forums.

Musicpromotion.net musicpromotion.net/ Resources for independent musicians; publications; tutorials; articles; links; newsletter; Web site design; online ordering.

My Music Job www.mymusicjob.com Listing of music industry jobs and internships.

National Band Register www.bandreg.com Database of names and band information; find out if a band name is in use; if not, register it to prevent other bands from using it; free; legal advice for bands; information about CDs by unsigned bands; site's magazine, *GIG*, features music industry news and reviews of unsigned bands.

NetJobs www.netjobs.com Employment guide for Canada and America; technology positions.

New-List www.new-list.com Mail lists and discussion groups.

NewTechMusic www.newtechmusic.com Online music distribution company.

Outer Sound www.outersound.com Over 3,000 pages of material for those in the independent music world; music magazine; reference source; 100 articles offering practical advice to independent musicians and industry personnel; online community for the independent music world; geared to musicians, fans, and the industry.

Overseas Jobs Express www.overseasjobs.com
International job openings and links.
Peoplesound www.peoplesound.com A&R
involvement for emerging bands.
Petersons.com www.petersons.com Online college
and career guides.
PlanetCD www.PlanetCD.com Online store for
independent music; all genres; audio samples;
free newsletter; indie distribution; featured artists.
PlanetJam www.planetjam.com Community of new
music from emerging artists.
Postcard Mania www.postcardmania.com Postcard
printing service.
Postcard Press www.postcardpress.com Bizcards;
postcards.
Professional Musicians www.promusic47.org Radio
promotion; recording studio; CD manufacturing;
practice rooms; instrument insurance; job referral
service; gig assistance; CD mastering.
Promote Yourself www.promoteyourself.com
Musician's guide to the Zen of hype.
Punk Bands www.punkbands.com Indie music
company.
Rainbo Records and Cassettes
www.rainborecords.com Custom CDs, cassettes,
and vinyl.
Rainmaker Publicity www.rainmakerpublicity.com
Indie music promotion company.
REAL Talent Directories
www.angelfire.com/biz/RealPub Publish and
showcase talent, Web site, gig, etc.
Reel Tour www.reel-tour.com TV series dedicated to
the promotion of independent musicians, bands,
and solo artists.
Rock Band.com www.rockband.com Unsigned indie
music.
Show Biz Jobs www.showbizjobs.com Entertainment
professional's network; employers; job seekers.
Sonic Bids www.sonicbids.com Electronic press kits;
subscription fee; drop box.
Sound Click www.Soundclick.com Charts, bands, and
free MP3.
Sound Generator www.soundgenerator.com UK
music site; charts; artists; industry; education.
Spannet www.spannet.org Resource for book-selling
ideas and money-making strategies for
independent presses and self-publishers.
Star Polish www.starpolish.com Store; advice;
community; label management; artist
development; features; resources; Velvet Rope.
Studentreel.com www.studentreel.com Talent search.
Taco Truffles Media www.tacotruffles.com Indie
music promotion by John Dawes, author of *The
Complete Guide to Internet Promotion for
Musicians, Artists, and Songwriters*; Web site
design; resources; tutorials; links.

Takeout Music www.takeoutmusic.com Reviews and
more.
Telephone Directories on the Web
www.infobel.com/teldir/ Links to Yellow Pages,
White Pages, business directories, e-mail address
directories, and fax numbers.
The All Music Network
www.geocities.com/Nashville/3150 Information;
resources; links.
The Buzz Factor www.thebuzzfactor.com Music
marketing tip sheet by Bob Baker; indie music
marketing resources; tips and tools to help indie
musicians market their music on a budget.
The Indie Contact Bible www.indiecontactbible.com
or www.bigmeteor.comicb Resources for indie
musicians; large international list organized by
genre and location; links; sell CDs; available on
disk; lists publications that review CDs and radio
stations that play indie music; all genres.
The Local Scene www.thelocalscene.com
Alternative; indie Web site.
The Palace www.thepalace.com Virtual chat site.
The Tip Sheet www.tipsheet.co.uk Industry
magazine; audio clips.
The Velvet Rope www.velvetrope.com Music
industry information.
The Wonderwall www.beat.co.uk/wonderwall.html
Alternative; indie Web site.
Tile.Net www.tile.net Mail lists and discussion
groups; comprehensive lists of newsgroups.
Tim Sweeney & Associates www.tsamusic.com
Independent artist development company;
promotion; publicity; retail marketing;
distribution network; Internet promotion;
workshops; author of *Tim Sweeney's Guide to
Releasing Independent Records; The Living
Room Sessions; The Complete Guide to Internet
Promotion for Musicians, Artists, and
Songwriters; Tim Sweeney's Guide to
Successfully Playing Live; Tim Sweeney's
Guide to Succeeding at Music Conventions.*
Topica www.topica.com Discussion groups.
Training4music.biz
www.training4music.biz/html/index.php
Products; seminars; forums.
TSI CD Manufacturing www.cdmanufacturing.com
CD and cassette manufacturing.
Ultimate Band List (UBL) www.ubl.com Artist
directory; band Web sites and CDs; resources;
information; music industry-related links.
Umbrellazine www.umbrellazine.com Indie arts.
Village Buzz www.Village-Buzz.com Indie music.
Vision Music USA www.visionmusicusa.com
Booking, management, and promotion
consulting services for independent musicians.
Webgrrls.com www.webgrrls.com Hub for nearly one
hundred Web sites for Webgrrls chapters around

the world; local chapters have gatherings where women meet face to face to talk about the Internet and new media.

Women in Music www.womeninmusic.com Nonprofit membership organization dedicated to promoting the advancement and recognition of women in the music industry; mentoring program.

Wonder Disk www.wonderdisc.net Replication.

World Records www.worldrecords.com Music search engine; add URL; artists; broadcast mail; classifieds; free home pages; music news by the minute; music newsgroup server; video releases; A & R service; download brochure; mainstream artist domains; artist domains; audio companies; download sites and stores; home pages; indie resources; instrument-related sites; music magazines and Webzines; music-style domains; miscellaneous; record labels; recording studios; radio stations; shopping basket.

World Replication Group www.worldreplication.com CD replication; fulfillment; graphics; packaging; video duplication; digital audiocassettes.

World Wide Bands worldwidebands.com Indie music company.

World Wired Productions www.wwpro.com Promotion and positive representation of artists, bands, labels, agencies, and management on every level.

WorldPages www.worldpages.com International phone book; all the phone books in the world combined into one linked site.

Worldwide Online Music Competition www.hitsquad.com/smm/millenium Over $10,000 in prizes with a first prize of over $5,000; professional software, hardware, music equipment, and sheet music that anyone can win.

Writers Net www.writers.net Resources for writers, editors, publishers, and agents.

Writers Online Workshops www.writersonlineworkshops.com Introductory, intermediate, and advanced workshops in a variety of genres; writing tips.

XFM www.xfm.co.uk Alternative; indie Web site.

Y2K Music www.y2k-music.co.uk Online indie music distribution venue.

Zebra Music www.zebramusic.com Music career development; information; tips; links; free monthly e-newsletter.

New Age and Ambient Music

4NewAgeMusic.com www.4newagemusic.com MP3; songs; musicians; labels; retailers.

Amazing Sounds www.amazings.comingles.html New age and ambient music Webzine.

Ambience for the Masses www.sleepbot.comambience Search by label, artist, or type of music.

Ars Electronica www.aec.at/en/index.asp Center; Future Lab; Festival; Prix; Archives.

AstroStar Astrology and New Age Resources www.astrostar.com Eclectic array of astrology and New Age resources; conferences; chat room; astrology; books; Atlantean crystals; romance; twin soul and more.

Backroads Music www.backroadsmusic.com *Heartbeats Catalog*; source for over 6,000 titles of ambient, new age, space, tribal and global sounds, and other music and videos since1981.

Bliss Relaxation CDs www.relaxationcds.co.uk/ New age/spiritual music.

Body-Mind body-mind.com CDs for relaxation, meditation CDs, music and sound frequencies for relaxation, stress reduction, self-healing, meditation, creativity, sleep, relationships, and health; includes nature sounds, dolphins, whales, birds, ambient music, and space sounds.

East West Spiritual and New Age Books and Tapes www.eastwest.com Spiritual and new age books and tapes on the Internet; alternative health and healing; personal growth; self-help; world religions and teachers; mythology; psychology.

Epsilon www.hyperreal.orgmusic/epsilon Ambient music information Web site; links.

Global Stone Music www.globalstonemusic.com Chakras CD; recording studio; artist Kris Stone.

Higher Octave Music www.higheroctave.com Record label; contemporary instrumental music; smooth jazz, new age, ambient, world, and flamenco music.

Invincible Music www.invinciblemusic.com Features yoga music, new age music, therapy music, guitar music, healing music, massage music, and Reiki music.

IVibes www.ivibes.nu/ Electronica music Web site.

Makoche-Native American and New Age Music www.makoche.com Makoche Native American Indian music; label and sound studio; online catalog; ordering; free CD giveaways; RealAudio sampling; concert information.

Music A La Carte www.musicalacarte.net/ New age and world music custom CDs; wide variety of categories, instruments and artists.

Music for a New Age www.mfna.org/index2.html New age music; links.

Music Mosaic www.new-age-music-shop.com New age music compilations by theme; meditation music; healing music; relaxation music.

Narada www.narada.com Record label; new instrumental, jazz and world music; influenced by jazz, world, folk, rock, pop, and classical music.

New Age music-12.hypermart.net/ Browse by subject; general; ambient; Celtic; environmental; independents; lists bestsellers in each category.

New Age Music 101 www.geocities.com/Yosemite/Gorge/7220/ Introduction to New Age music.

New Age Shop www.elysian.co.uk/acatalog/newageshop.htm Music; books; videos; DVDs.

New Age Web Works www.newageinfo.com Invites the new age spiritual, metaphysical, pagan, and alternative health communities to share ideas, products, and service.

New Earth Records www.newearthrecords.com New Age artists, world music, trance, meditation relaxation music, and Reiki.

New World Music www.newworldmusic.com Relaxation, world, Celtic, Native American, and uplifting music.

North Star Music www.northstarmusic.com Music for living.

Obsolete www.obsolete.com Ambient and techno.

One World Music www.oneworldmusic.com Through hands-on music making, this company fosters teamwork, leadership, and innovation in the workplace, promoting cultural change and organizational development.

Only New Age Music www.newagemusic.com Founded by Suzanne Doucet and James Bell to serve the New Age Music industry in all aspects; provides a team of industry professionals and a variety of services, such as general consulting, production, artwork, printing and manufacturing, packaging, marketing, distribution setup, radio promotion, public relations, strategic promotions, national and international licensing, and distribution to New Age Music artists and record labels; operates an online retail store, record label, and music publishing company.

Peaceful Paths www.peacefulpaths.com Enlightening products: books, music, artwork, aromatherapy products, Edgar Cayce Health Care Items, authentic Native American products, candles, Feng Shui items; Gift Pairs and Gift Baskets, and more, all in themes of Spirit and Wholeness.

Quarterlight Productions www.donnamichael.com New Thought keyboard/vocal artist Donna Michael; CDs; bookings; workshops.

Real Music www.realmusic.com/f_main.htm Music for relaxation and rejuvenation; rhythms for lifting the spirit and celebrating life.

Serenity www.serenitymusic.com New age record label; music for massage, Reiki, relaxation, and guided imagery.

Sheet Music Plus—New Age Music www.sheetmusicplus.com/enter.html?s=googleds &t=new+age&e=a Over 100 titles.

Shining Star www.shiningstar.com Music featuring the acoustic guitar music of Bruce BecVar and Brian BecVar, vocals from Aurora Juliana Ariel, Indian and Sanskrit chants from Nada Shakti and chants of the Drepung Loseling Monks and their Tibetan Sacred Temple Music; also featuring the Magic of Healing Music series commissioned by Deepak Chopra.

Spotted Peccary Music www.spottedpeccary.com/artists.php News; releases; listen; artists; order.

Trance Airwaves www.tranceairwaves.com Listen live; submit mix; DJ profiles; forum; chatroom; top ten; links.

Windham Hill www.windham.com Record label; artists on tour; discography.

Wings of Love New Age Guide www.wingsoflove.net Dedicated to providing enlightening gifts, books, music, art and items for living, loving and healing in an effort to bring personal and global balance through creative consciousness with positive thoughts and actions; seeking beauty, wisdom, enlightenment, truth, health, and love.

Yahoo Directory—New Age Music dir.yahoo.com/Entertainment/Music/Genres/New _Age/ Links to Electronica, artists, CDs, labels.

Yahoo Directory—New Age Music Artists dir.yahoo.com/Entertainment/Music/Artists/By_ Genre/New_Age/ Links to New Age artists in alphabetical order.

Patriotic Music, Marches, and Marching Bands

All American Patriotic MIDI Music members.tripod.com~Son_Struck/pmm.html MIDI files of patriotic songs.

America Remembers mp3.about.com/library/weekly/aa091401.htm Patriotic music to honor our nation and its heroes.

American and Patriotic Music my.homewithgod.com/heavenlymidis/USA/ MIDI files of songs.

Anthems and Patriotic Music www.niceflag.com/music.htm Anthems and patriotic music of all countries.

Ceremonial Music Online www2.acc.af.mil/music/ceremonial Ceremonial music in MP3 and RealAudio for all branches of the United States military, veterans, and civic organizations, police and fire departments, scouting, and schools; *National Anthem, Taps,* honors, service songs, marches, bugle calls.

Flags of the Native Peoples of the United States users.aol.com/Donh523/navapage/index.html Photos and histories of Native American flags.

Independence Day wilstar.com/holidays/july4.htm
Links to America's historic documents.
Jack's "MIDI Music" United States of America
www.discoverynet.com~ajsnead/patriotic/usasong
s.html Traditional and patriotic tunes.
March Music Online www2.acc.af.mil/music/march
Forty-two MP3 and RealAudio marches by John
Philip Sousa, Karl L. King, Henry Fillmore, and
others; United States Air Force band site.
Military Women on Sheet Music
userpages.aug.com/captbarb/sheetmusic.html
History of women in the military from the
revolutionary war to the present day.
*Music for the Nation: American Sheet Music, 1870-
1885*
memory.loc.gov/ammem/smhtml/smhome.html
Tens of thousands of songs and instrumental
pieces registered for copyright in the post-Civil
War era.
NIEHS Kid's Pages
www.niehs.nih.gov/kids/musicpatriot.htm
Patriotic songs with lyrics; print an American
flag.
Operation Just Cause Jukebox www.ojc.org/sounds/
Audio files.
Patriotic and Inspirational Songs of America
hometown.aol.com/KidFun101/KidsParties4th/P
g10BPatrioticSongs.index.html Song lyrics.
Patriotic Greeting Cards
www.prairiefrontier.com/pfcards1/patriotic.html
Patriotic multimedia greeting cards by Prairie
Frontier.
Patriotic MIDIS and Marches
www.laurasmidiheaven.com/Patriotc.shtml
Audio files.
Patriotic Music Online
www2.acc.af.mil/music/patriotic User-requested
service; *God Bless America, Battle Hymn of the
Republic, America the Beautiful, Armed
Services Medley*, and more; MP3 and
RealAudio; service of the USAF Heritage of
America Band.
Patriotic Music Page
www.treefort.org~rgrogan/web/flagmusic.htm
Audio files.
Patriotic Songs
www.angelfire.com/tx/scout21/patriotic.html
Audio files and song lyrics.
Patriotic Songs
www.digitaltimes.com/karaoke/singers/patriotic/
Song lyrics.
Patriotic Songs and Hymns ·
www.usflag.org/songs.html Song lyrics.
Prairie Frontier Patriotic Music MIDI Files
www.prairiefrontier.com/pfcards/Xtrapgs/patriotic'
.html MIDI file collection.

Scout Songs
www.scoutsongs.com/categories/patriotic.html
Index of patriotic songs.
*Sheet Music about Lincoln, Emancipation, and the
Civil War*
memory.loc.gov/ammem/scsmhtml/scsmhome.h
tml From the Alfred Whital Stern Collection at
the Library of Congress.
Sheryl's Holiday Site
www.sherylfranklin.com/holidays/ Brief history
of the Pledge of Allegiance; links to other sites
related to the United States flag; Independence
Day.
*Student Travel and Tours for Marching Bands and
Choirs* www.travelgroups.com Student travel and
tour packages for marching bands, choirs, sport
teams, and class trips; includes festivals and
competitions.
The 4th of July Page-Patriotic Fantasy
www.wilstar.com/holidays/july4.htm Uncle
Sam's dream; contains many historic American
documents; listen to patriotic MIDI music.
The Fifties Web
www.fiftiesweb.com/usa/ustunes.htm Patriotic
songs.
The National Flag Day Foundation
www.flagday.org/Pages/PatrioticSongs.html
Patriotic song lyrics.
USA Patriotic Page
www.imagesoft.net/uspatriotic.html Flag,
anthem, and songs.
USAF Heritage of America Band
www.af.mil/accband Calendar, openings, and
audition information; unit/group pages; MP3 and
RealAudio features; songs of the Air Force with
lyrics and history; space themes in classical
music.

Piano—Keyboards—Organ

American Guild of Organists www.agohq.org
Magazines; competitions; convention;
membership; regions and chapters.
American School of Piano Tuning www.piano-
tuning.com Has been training piano technicians
since1958, offering a complete home study
course in piano tuning and repair in just ten
comprehensive lessons.
Anybody Can Play the Piano
www.anybodycanplay.com Books and videos for
beginners as young as three years; information
for parents, piano teachers, and caregivers about
different piano methods.
Baldwin Pianos and Organs www.baldwinpiano.com
Pianos; products and accessories; Baldwin;
Chickering; Wurlitzer; Pianovelle.

Boogie Woogie Press
www.colindavey.com/BoogieWoogie Boogie
woogie piano music.

Casio Inc. www.casio.com Maker of electronic
keyboards.

Chopin Foundation of the United States
www.chopin.org Chopin competitions;
publications and concerts.

Chord Patterns www.chordpatterns.com By
Australian pianist Kevin Fisher; how to form and
spell chords on the keyboard; diagrams.

Church Organ Systems
www.churchorgansystems.com Digital and pipe
combination organs.

Classical MIDI Organ Stop
theatreorgans.com/cmos/index.html Organs;
MIDI.

Classical Piano MIDI Page www.piano-
midi.de/midicoll.htm MIDI and MP3 sequences
for all friends of classical music.

Estonia Piano Factory www.estoniapiano.com
Estonia Pianos.

Fun Brain www.funbrain.com/notes/ Game involving
reading music; Pianomus Platypus.

German Piano Imports LLC www.bluthnerpiano.com
Bluthner; Haessler.

Go Piano www.gopiano.com Free online piano
lessons.

Göteborg Organ Art Center www.hum.gu.se/goart
Study and research into all aspects of the organ;
art and the organ instrument; interpretation of the
music of different periods; improvisation;
research into preindustrial organ building; studies
of sources.

Harpsichord Clearing House www.harpsichord.com
Comprehensive resource for early keyboard
instruments, including the harpsichord, virginal,
spinet, clavichord, fortepiano, or continuo organ
in North America.

History of the Piano www.uk-piano.org/history/
Piano history.

International Piano Festival www.festival-piano.com
Program; press; archives.

International Piano Supply
www.pianosupply.com/ips/ Pianos for sale.

Kawai America www.kawaius.com Descriptions of
products; technical information; download page
has free patch libraries, operating system updates
and sound demos; lists company's pianos, digital
keyboards, home keyboards, and synths; links to
sites containing patches, librarians, and other
information.

Kawai Japan www.kawai.co.jp/english/index.html
Japanese headquarters; home page is in English.

Keyboard Central
angelfire.com/in2/KeyboardCentral/index.html

Learn to play the keyboard, piano, or organ at
home; online lessons and e-books.

Keyboard Coach www.keyboardcoach.com
Instructional CD-ROM.

Keyboard Concepts www.keyboardconcepts.com
Music for keyboards.

Keyboard Education keyboardedu.com Music site for
keyboard players; jazz piano instruction material;
teaching professional melody and harmonic ideas;
fills, run, licks.

Keyboard Player www.keyboardplayer.com Longest
running keyboard magazine in the UK; sample
reviews.

Kurzweil www.kurzweilmusicsystems.com Company
has been acquired by Young Chang; can access
FTP site to download files for Kurzweil
instruments; online catalog; discussion forums;
technical support; links.

*Kurzweil Piano DiscoKnabe Piano, Mason and
Hamlin* www.pianodisc.com Information about
acoustic, digital, and player pianos.

L. Bosendorfer Klavierfabrik GMBH
www.bosendorfer.com L. Bosendorfer pianos.

Letsplaymusic.com www.letsplaymusic.com Learn
to play music through e-mail; piano and
keyboard lessons with an instructor ranging from
beginner to advanced students using MIDI files.

Louis Renner GMBH & Co. www.rennerusa.com
Renner Upright; Grand Piano Actions;
Hammerheads; and Piano Tools.

Lowrey Organ Co. www.lowrey.com Lowrey home
organs.

Luciano's Piano Bar www.piano-bar.com Popular
music in MIDI format played at the piano; easy
listening.

Mason & Hamlin www.masonhamlin.com Mason &
Hamlin pianos.

Music and You www.musicandyou.com Online piano
lessons; beginners to advanced players; jazz,
blues, classical, theory, arranging, and more; free
demo lessons available.

Music for Pianos digiserve.co.uk/musicforpianos
Sequenced MIDI files; includes music by women
composers.

My Piano Lessons www.mypianolessons.com
Online piano lessons.

National Conference on Keyboard Pedagogy
www.francesclarkcenter.org Annual conference;
keynote speakers; teaching demonstrations;
workshops; group forums; technology hubs.

Online Piano Lessons www.medford.net/djsprmain/
Play piano by ear using rhythmic patterns.

Organ Historical Society Catalog
www.ohscatalog.org Catalog sales division of
the organ historical society; sells pipe organ
related books, CDs, videos, and sheet music.

Organ Stop www.organstop.com Keyboards for the home and church organist; customer support materials and activities; large sheet music department.

Organ1st www.organ.co.uk Worldwide mail-order shop; organs; sheet music.

OrganTutor Organ 101 www.organtutor.byu.edu CD-ROM and workbook with sixty-two lessons teaching organ registration, technique, and hymn playing in classical and traditional sacred organ style.

Orgel www.orgel.com Pipe organs; extensive information on pipe organs and organ music; listen to classical as well as modern organ music; RealAudio; virtual photo gallery.

Patti Music www.pattimusic.com Piano sheet music, methods, and classical repetoire; for piano and organ teachers, classical pianists, and organ players.

Perfectly Grand Piano Accessories, Inc. www.perfectlygrand.com For pianists.

Piano—The Movie www.fys.uio.no/~magnushj/Piano/ Information on the movie; links.

Piano 300 http://piano300.si.edu/ Celebrating three centuries of people and pianos.

Piano Home Page www.serve.com/marbeth/piano.html Information for piano teachers.

Piano Lab Online Store www.pianolabs.com Piano parts and supplies.

Piano Lane www.pianolane.com The world of piano at your fingertips.

Piano Lessons Online www.pianolessonsonline.com Interactive piano/keyboard lessons using the Internet and video; for all ages.

Piano Mentor www.piano-mentor.com Online alternative for adult piano students.

Piano Nanny on the Net www.pianonanny.com Online courses using QuickTime movies to teach piano lessons and pop music theory, including some jazz and blues; beginning to advanced levels; free public educational service.

Piano Net www.pianonet.com Official Web site of the National Piano Foundation; comprehensive guide to everything about pianos.

Piano Pal www.piano-pal.com Store and reference for piano books and single sheet music scores; popular, classical, sacred, and educational material.

Piano Passion www.pianopassion.com MP3; links.

Piano Pedagogy Plus www.pedaplus.com Music and resources.

Piano Power www.pianopower.com Endorsed by musicians and medical professionals; book series takes student to new levels of technical and musical proficiency while optimizing time and avoiding injury.

Piano Press Studio www.pianopress.com Piano, keyboard, theory, and voice lessons; recitals; festivals; competitions; MTNA member; original music; publications; newsletter.

Piano Productions www.pianoproductions.com Piano-related materials; publications.

Piano Professor www.pianoprofessor.com Interactive tutorial for learning basic music theory; includes a "Note Tutor" to teach how to read music and identify the corresponding keys on the piano keyboard; Windows.

Piano Quest www.pianoquest.com Used upright and grand pianos.

Piano Spot www.pianospot.com Piano sheet music and accessories.

Piano Supplies www.pianosupplies.com Supplies for the pianist.

Piano Teaching www.pianoteaching.com Nancy and Randall Faber; Piano Adventures; supplementary books; forum; bio; news and events; teaching materials; comments.

Piano Teams www.pianoteams.com Ensemble project.

Piano Technicians Guild Inc. www.ptg.org Find a technician; daily tips; events; merchandise.

Piano Today www.pianotoday.com Online music lesson; subscribe.

Piano Tuning www.pianotuning.com Courses, reference books, and materials for learning how to tune pianos professionally.

Piano Women www.pianowomen.com Women concert pianists.

Piano World www.pianoworld.com Pianos; keyboards; digital pianos; resource for information about the piano; free sheet music; locate a piano tuner, teacher, dealer; e-newsletter; interesting facts about the piano; list of piano movers and pianos for sale; trivia quiz; competitions; links.

Pianodisk www.pianodisc.com Pianodisc; PDS-128Plus; Quiettime GT-360; Knabe; Mason & Hamlin; George Steck Pianos.

Pianomate Co. www.pianomate.com Pianomate.

Pianomouse.com www.pianomouse.com CD-ROM nstructional software; *Music Theory FUNdamentals; Great Composers; Pre-School.*

Pianosoft Express www.pianosoftexpress.com Internet source for Yamaha Disklavier and Clavinova software products.

Pipedreams pipedreams.mpr.orgindex.html Minnesota Public Radio presents live broadcasts of organ music; recordings of show segments online; links to background information; listening tips; organ-related articles.

Piporg-l www.albany.edu/piporg-l Electronic mailing list devoted to pipe and electronic organs, organists, and organ music.

Play Piano by Ear pianomusic.hypermart.net/index.html Learn to play the piano and keyboard by ear, without relying on sheet music.

Play Piano Today www.playpianotoday.com Piano lessons unlimited.

Pro Piano www.propiano.com/index.html Instrument rentals; recital series.

Rhodes Pianos www.badrat.com/rhodes Information; FAQ; downloadable manual.

Roland Contemporary Keyboards www.rolandus.com Roland Corporation; musical instrument manufacturer; product and upgrade information; downloads; includes a section on the history of General MIDI.

Schimmel Piano Corp. www.schimmel-piano.de Schimmel pianos.

School of Music, University of Canterbury www.music.canterbury.ac.nz Christ Church Town Hall pipe organ; follow progress on video clips as the 3,372 pipes were gradually pieced together; learn about how the instrument works.

Sheet Music for Electronic Keyboard www.pianospot.com/cat20.htm List of items available.

Sing Along Piano Bar www.singalongpianobar.com Sing along piano bar.

Smithsonian's National Museum of American History "PIANO 300: Celebrating Three Centuries of People and Pianos" http://piano300.si.edu/ Exhibition celebrating the 300th anniversary of the invention of the piano; composers' manuscripts, tools, photographs, play bills, sheet music, and other memorabilia; highlights museum's internationally distinguished collection of 250 pianos and keyboards.

Steinway and Sons www.steinway.com Factory tour; send a virtual postcard; learn about Steinway and Boston Piano products.

Street Organ www.streetorgan.com Street organ facts; history; makers; music; restoration tips; dedicated to the mechanical organ and its music.

Studiologic studiologic.net/fatar-menu.htm Computer-assisted piano learning systems.

Suzuki Corporation www.suzukipianos.com Digital pianos; portable keyboards; QChord; harmonicas.

Technics www.technics.co.uk Technics pianos, organs, and keyboards.

The Canadian Piano Page www.canadianpianopage.com Information; links.

The Herschell Carousel Factory Museum www.carousels.comhmusem.htm Located in North Tonawonda, NY; area of major

significance to the previous carousel and band organ manufacturing business in America.

The Internet Piano Page www.geocities.com/Paris/3486/ MIDI files of masterpieces.

The Keyboard Studio www.keyboardstudio.com Source for everything in music or computers.

The Pianist www.thepianistmovie.com About the movie; trailer; flash site.

The Pianist's Guide to the Internet www.rainmusic.com/pianomusic/piano.htm Piano links.

The Piano Education Page pianoeducation.org Resource for piano teachers, students, and enthusiasts; over 600 links.

The Piano Place www.pianoplace.com Online catalog; piano books; CDs; videos; software.

The Piano Players Guide to the Internet www.rainmusic.com/pianomusic/piano.htm Complete guide to piano-related Web sites; recommendations include free sheet music, online piano lessons, piano books, and pianos for sale.

The Player Piano Page www.pianola.demon.co.uk/ Information on player pianos or the pianola.

UK Piano Page www.uk-piano.orgmag.html List of UK-based online music magazines.

Used Keyboards www.usedkeyboards.com Find a used keyboard online.

Van Cliburn International Piano Competition-Van Cliburn Foundation www.cliburn.org Information on the competition and foundation.

Weber Piano Co. www.weberpiano.com Weber Piano; Rieger-Kloss Piano; Ridgewood Piano; Sagenhaft Piano.

WM Knabe & Co. www.pianodisc.com Knabe Pianodisk Pianos; Quiet Time Pianos; Knabe Pianos; PianoDigital Pianos.

World Pedagogy Conference www.pianopedagogy.com Annual conference held in October.

Yamaha Corporation of America www.yamaha.com Yamaha music products and more; daily visitation of almost 10,000 people.

Young Chang Worldwide www.youngchang.com Information about products and services; technical help; piano education resources.

Popular Music and Culture—Fashion—Dance Music—Techno—Electronica—Rock 'n' Roll—Oldies—Punk—Heavy Metal

4ClassicRock.com www.4classicrock.com Classic rock bands and artists; listen to music; reviews about the history of classic rock.

70s Traveler Real Audio Music Page
www.70traveler.com Streaming RealAudio of the music from 1970 to 1980.

A Biased History of Glam Rock
www.doremi.co.uk/glam Links and more.

A Brief History of Banned Music in the United States www.ericnuzum.com/banned Selected online chronicle of music that has been banned or censored in the United States.

About Heavy Metal
heavymetal.about.com/entertainment/heavymetal/mbody.htm Hard rock and heavy metal Web site.

Access Place Music
www.accessplace.com/music.htm Music news; reviews; online audio; MP3 files; genres; artists; songs; lyrics; concerts; tickets; CD stores; instruments; references; acoustics; electronics.

All Time Favorites www.alltimefavorites.com Complete entertainment resources.

Armani Exchange www.armaniexchange.com Fashion industry.

Art Rock www.artrock.com Dealer in rock and roll collectibles.

Bazaar www.bazaar411.com Fashion industry.

BBC Pop www.bbc.co.uk/entertainment/popmusic News; features; links.

Beat Boy www.beatboy.com Beat music Web site.

Beat Maker www.beatmaker.com Beat music Web site.

Beatlefest
www.thefestforbeatlesfans.com/Merchant2/merchant.mv The Beatles.

Beatles www.getback.org/beatles.html The Internet Beatles album.

Beatles www.rockmine.music.co.uk/beatwho.html A Beatles who's who.

Beatles Fans Index
beatles.about.com/entertainment/beatles/blalbums.htm The Beatles.

Beatles Sheet Music
www.rarebeatles.com/sheetmu/sheetmu.htm Collecting Beatles sheet music.

Beatles Sheet Music
www.netins.net/showcase/reading/beatsheet.html Currently available sheet music collections; links to find on the Internet.

Beatseek www.beatseek.com Electronica.

Blue Eyes.com www.blue-eyes.com Easy listening music Web site.

British Pop Culture www.sixtiespop.com Music and more.

Bugle Boy www.bugleboy.com Fashion industry.

Canadian Musician www.canadianmusician.com Pop music magazine.

Celebrity Connection
members.tripod.com~jonnykat/celebrity.html Celebrities; musicians, politicians, athletes.

Celebrity Corner www.premrad.com Audio interview clips.

Celebrity Site of the Day www.net-v.comcsotd Links to celebrity sites.

Chronology of San Francisco Rock Music 1965-1969 www.sfmuseum.org/hist1/rock.html Museum of City of San Francisco.

Classic Rock Daily www.classicrockdaily.com Hard rock and heavy metal Web site.

Classic Rock Rules www.classicrockrules.com Links to classic rock bands sites and more.

Club Velvet www.tamboo.com Easy listening music Web site.

CNN Style www.cnn.com/STYLE Fashion journalism.

Comics.com www.comics.com United Media.

Concert in the Sky Diskology www.great-music.net/diskog.html History of pop music; RealAudio samples.

Cover Heaven
freespace.virgin.net/love.day/coverheaven Record cover artwork.

Covers covers.virtualave.net/ Album cover database.

Cross Rock www.crossrock.com Rock music Web site.

Dance Music Home Page
dancemusic.about.com/musicperform/dancemusic/mbody.htm Starting place for exploring dance music on the Internet; dance clubs; artists; contests; interviews; RealAudio; MP3; reviews; links.

Dance Music of the Eighties www.andwedanced.com Home page.

Dancesite www.dancesite.com Tracks available to audio-stream; reviews; news.

Delicious Vinyl www.dvinyl.com Record label; hip-hop; urban.

Disco Music www.discomusic.com Disco music Web site.

Disquiet www.disquiet.com Interviews; electronica.

DJ Rhythms www.djrhythms.com Web resource for dance music.

DJ Union www.djunion.com DJ music and equipment Web site.

DJ.net www.dj.net Amplify your attitude.

Do the Dance www.dothedance.com Los Angeles-based DJ service; all occasions; CDs; videos.

Donna Karan www.donnakaran.com Fashion industry.

Drum and Bass Arena www.breakbeat.co.uk News; reviews; interviews; dance e-zine.

ERock www.erock.net Rock music Web site.

Etnopop.com www.etnopop.com Pop music site.

Eurodance Hits www.eurodancehits.com Information on artists; releases in European dance music; Annual Cyberspace Euro-Energy Awards.

Fansites Database www.fansites.com Database of fan Web sites; all genres.

Fashion Angel www.fashionangel.com Fashion industry.

Fashion.net www.fashion.net Guide to Internet fashion sites.

FirstView www.firstview.com The latest fashions displayed online.

Flash Rock www.flashrock.com Rock music site.

Forever Metal www.thats-metal.de German heavy metal Web site.

George Starostin's Classic Rock Album Reviews starling.rinet.ru/music/index.htm Detailed reviews of 1960s and 70s rock and pop music; ratings; best of lists; etc.

Gianni Versace www.versace.com Tribute to Versace's life and work.

Global Beat www.globalbeat.com Beat music site.

Good Times Mag www.goodtimesmag.com Pop music magazine.

Great Modern Pictures greatmodernpictures.com Photography Web site.

Groove House www.groovehouse.com Groove music Web site.

Guess www.guess.com Fashion Web site.

Hard Rock Cafe hardrock.com Hard rock and heavy metal Web site.

Hard Rock Hotel www.hardrockhotel.com Las Vegas hotel and casino.

Hard Rock Live www.hardrocklive.com Live versions of hits previously unreleased.

Heavy Harmonies www.heavyharmonies.com Metal and hard rock bands.

History of Banned Music www.pathfinder.com/ew/siteoftheweek/0,2028,503,00.html Everything you ever wanted to know about dirty lyrics.

Hyper Real www.hyperreal.org Dance culture site.

Levi's www.levi.com Fashion Web site.

Lilith Fair www.lilithfair.com Official Web site of the concert tour.

Look Online www.lookonline.com Fashion industry.

Losing Today www.losingtoday.com Pop music magazine.

Lumiere www.lumiere.com Slow pages look dazzling.

Made in Italy www.made-in-italy.comfashion/fm.htm Fashion industry.

Media Rocks www.mediarocks.com Rock music Web site.

Metal Edge Online www.mtledge.com Hard rock and heavy metal Web site.

Metal Hammer www.metalhammer.co.uk Hard rock and heavy metal Web site; magazine.

Metal Is www.metal-is.com Metal magazine.

Metal Links www.metallinks.com Hard rock and heavy metal Web site.

Metal Maniacs www.metalmaniacs.com Metal magazine.

Mishatzar www.mishatzar.com Fashion industry.

Modern Rock www.modernrock.com Rock music Web site.

Moonshine Music www.moonshine.com Techno; dance; house; trance; acid jazz; jungle; hardcore; breakbeat; triphop; electronic listening music.

Motion motion.state51.co.uk/ Search resource for dance record shops.

Music and Dance Productions www.musicanddance.com DJ Services; overview.

Music Fan Clubs www.musicfanclubs.org Links to fan club Web sites.

Music Styles by AMG allmusic.com/mus_Styles.html Descriptions of all popular music styles of the twentieth century by professional music journalists.

Music.com www.music.com Affiliate partner of DreamWorks label; free downloads.

Mutha Funkas www.muthafunkas.com Funk music Web site.

NJ Rocks www.njrocks.com Rock music Web site.

Northern UK's Metal Page www.shipley.ac.uk/north Hard rock and heavy metal Web site.

Oldies Music www.oldiesmusic.com History, trivia and charts of the 50s, 60s, and 70s.

Online Rock www.onlinerock.com Rock music site.

Peace Rock www.peacerock.com Collectibles.

Peaceville www.peaceville.com Hard rock and heavy metal Web site.

Pop History Now! www.pophistorynow.com Features a random year in pop history every weekday; covers music, television, movies, news, and politics.

Pop.com www.pop.com Pop music Web site.

Raga Rock www.ragarock.com Rock music Web site.

Rave-Club Info and Electronic Music Links around the World spraci.cia.com.au/ravew.htm Easy-to-use links page.

Recollections www.recollections.co.uk Memorabilia; listed by artists A-Z.

Rhythm Net www.rhythmnet.com Home page.

Rock 108 from Key J www.keyj.com Hard rock and heavy metal Web site; information; news; radio service.

Rock and Heavy Metal Page www.rockworld.ndirect.co.uk Hard rock and heavy metal Web site.

Rock Around the World www.ratw.com Photo library; radio show archive; 1970s.

Rock Daily www.rockdaily.com Rock music Web site.

Rock Music Music Network www.rock.com Guide; streaming audio; online store.
Rock News www.rocknews.com Rock music.
Rock.com www.rock.com Rock music Web site.
Rock.theShoppe.com www.rock.theshoppe.com Rock music Web site.
Rocka.com www.rocka.com Rock music Web site.
Rockabilly www.rockabilly.nl Rockabilly music Web site.
Rockabillyhall.com www.rockabillyhall.com Rockabilly Hall of Fame Web site.
Rockete.com www.rockete.com Rock music Web site.
Rockfest www.rockfest.org Rock music Web site.
Rockhall.com www.rockhall.com Official Web site of the Rock and Roll Hall of Fame Museum located in Cleveland, OH, and now in cyberspace; popular music used in interdisciplinary teaching.
Rockhouse www.rockhouse.de Rock music Web site.
RockinRoll.com www.rockinroll.com Rock music Web site.
RocknRoots.com www.rocknroots.com Rock music Web site.
Rockperry.fi www.rockperry.fi Rock music Web site.
Rusmetal.ru www.rusmetal.ru Rock music Web site.
Seventh on Sixth www.7thonsixth.com Fashion from many designers; the runway scene and designers; links to designers, including Calvin Klein, Hugo Boss, John Bartlett, Perry Ellis, Ralph Lauren, Tommy Hilfiger, and many others.
Seventies Dance Music izan.simplenet.com/70.html Disco Music of the 70s; images; information; lyrics; MIDI; RealAudio clips; links and more.
Simplenet.com ews.simplenet.com/designer Fashion industry.
Speed Garage www.speedgarage.com Dance music; audio files; links.
Spring Groove www.springgroove.com Groove music Web site.
Stone Rock www.stonerrock.com Rock music Web site.
Street Sound ssound.pseudo.com House music and electronica.
Style 365 www.style365.com Directory of fashion Web sites.
Style www.worldstyle.com Fashion industry.
Super Seventies Rock Site www.geocities.com/SunsetStrip/8678 Top hits; photos; links.
The Album Covers Page www.knl.com/albums Artwork.
The Center for Popular Music popmusic.mtsu.edu/ Popular music information and resources.
The Dance Music Resource Pages www.juno.co.uk Complete weekly listing of new UK dance

releases, including catalog numbers and distributor information; future releases; UK dance radio listings; over 500 dance-related links.
The Dark Site of Metal metal.de/ Hard rock and heavy metal Web site.
The Fillmore www.thefillmore.com In San Francisco; famous for booking big names in the 60s; Joplin; Hendrix; Grateful Dead; Jefferson Airplane, and more.
The Gap www.gap.com Fashion site.
The Musical World of Rocky Horror www.rockymusic.org Audio and more; largest Rocky Horror sounds collection on the Internet; images; lyrics; reviews.
The Official George Carlin Web Site www.georgecarlin.com Living comedy legend.
The Space Age Pop Page home.earthlink.net/~spaceagepop Encyclopedia of space age pop, exotica, and lounge music and musicians.
The Wanderer www.wanderers.com/wanderer Oldies Web site.
Tombstone www.tombstone.gr Hard rock and heavy metal Web site.
Tommy Hilfiger www.tommy.com Designer Web site.
Trouser Press www.trouserpress.com Rock magazine; archives online.
Videogame Music Archive www.vgmusic.com 11,000+ game music MIDI files.
Welcome to Vik's Lounge www.chaoskitty.com Easy listening music Web site.
Woman Rock www.womanrock.com Home; features; interviews; reviews; events; radio; message board; links; shop; membership; music resources.

R&B, Rap, Hip-Hop, and Soul

88HipHop.com www.88hiphop.com Current events; reviews; music; videos; links; indie artists.
Aka.com www.aka.com Network of over 125 hip-hop-related sites; links; reviews; digital audio files.
Altrap.com www.altrap.com Hip-hop culture and perspective.
Basically Hip-Hop www.basically-hiphop.com RealAudio on the Internet.
Beatbreaks www.beatbreaks.com Records; tapes; CDs; videos; magazines.
Boomshaka Music www.boomshakamusic.com Hip-hop Web site.
Davey D's Hip-Hop Corner www.daveyd.com Radio shows; visitor polls; boards; newsletters; news.
DJ Rap www.dj-rap.com DJ rap music Web site.
E-Jams www.ejams.com R&B music site; interactive music survey; contests; chat rooms; trivia; music

charts; bulletin boards; links and music information.

Gargantua Soul www.gargantuasoul.com Soul music Web site.

Hip-Hop www.dacrossroadz.cjb.net Hip-hop Web site.

Hip-Hop Directory www.hiphopdirectory.com Hip-hop music; links.

Hip-Hop Elements www.hiphop-elements.com Free subscription to The Elements Newsletter; news; charts; playlists; album reviews; free CD drawing every week.

Hip-Hop Spot www.hiphophotspot.com Interactive Web site; dedicated to helping indie artists achieve their goals; free resources.

HipHopCity.com www.hiphopcity.com Hip-hop directory; top100; add a site; search.

HipHopSite.com www.hiphopsite.com New releases; reviews.

Original Hip-Hop Lyrics Archive www.ohhla.com Large database.

R&B, Hip-Hop, Rap www.cs.ucr.edu/~marcus/music.html Links to related Web sites.

R&B, Rap, Hip-Hop campcaen.engin.umich.edu/showcase/webworkshop/2/r&b&hiphop.html Links to related Web sites.

Rap Sheet www.rapsheet.com Channels; links; community.

Rap Station www.rapstation.com Today in hip-hop.

Rhythm & Blues Foundation *www.rhythm-n-blues.org Home page.*

Rock Rap www.rockrap.com Rap music Web site.

Roland Groove www.rolandgroove.com Groove music Web site.

Soul A Go-Go www.soul-a-go-go.demon.co.uk R&B and 60s soul.

Soul System www.radio101.it/soulsystem/static/chartmenu.asp-date=2003.htm Weekly charts; year-end charts.

Street Jamz www.streetjamz.com Showcasing local and independent unsigned black music.

Support Online Hip-Hop www.sohh.com News section; bulletin boards; music and culture.

The Primer www.theprimer.org.uk Soul Web site.

The R&B Primer Introductory Page www.theprimer.co.uk/ Dedicated to the world of blues and soul music.

The Source www.thesource.com Hip-hop; rap; features; reviews.

The Stax Site perso.wanadoo.fr/stax.site Soul site.

Underground Hip-Hop www.undergroundhiphop.com Streaming audio of singles; emerging artists.

Vibe www.vibe.com Hip-hop and urban music and culture.

Radio, Internet Radio, and Television

2kool4radio www.2kool4radio.com Radio station that plays indie music.

650 WSM (Grand Ole Opry) www.650wsm.com The Grand Ole Opry's very own and first radio station, WSM-AM 650, is now live on the Internet; "Opry Star Spotlight" show with host Matthew Gillian offers songwriters an opportunity to play their songs on the air.

A&E www.aetv.com Arts and Entertainment; program listings and previews.

ABC www.abc.com American Broadcasting Company.

Academy of Television Arts & Sciences www.emmys.org Information on the Emmy awards.

Action Radio www.chez.com/actionradio International Internet radio.

All India Internet Radio www.aiir.com Entertainment and news programs.

American Movie Classics www.amctv.com Classic films.

American Music Channel www.americanmusicchannel.com Internet broadcast network devoted e to country music.

Audiences Unlimited www.audiencesunlimited.com Free tickets to TV show tapings.

Austin City Limits www.pbs.org/klru/austin/ Program featuring original music.

Barrcode www.barrcode.com BCX and BRIAN editing and playout software for radio stations.

BBC Music Live www.bbc.co.uk/musiclive UK's biggest broadcast live music festival; six-day celebration of musical diversity taking place in Glasgow in May.

Beatlock Technology djmixpro.com/beatlock.html DJ *Mix Pro* DJ mixing program for parties and nightclubs or background music; design mixes on headphones while music is playing on speakers.

Black Channel www.blackchannel.de Radio station.

Bravo Cable Network www.bravotv.com Bravo cable television network.

Bring the Noise! bringthenoise.com Radio Web site.

Broadcast Science www.broadcastscience.nl Advanced software for the broadcast industry; automation systems, cart replacement software, and transmission line protection software.

Burli Software Inc. www.burli.com *Newsroom System* integrates newswires, audio feeds, faxes, e-mail, Web access, and more in an intuitive drag-and-drop editing interface.

C-500.com www.c500.com For low-power and college radio stations across the country; consult music charts; join mailing list; view message board.

CBC Television and Radio www.cbc.ca Television and radio Web site.

CBS www.cbs.com Central Broadcasting System.

Cherry Moon www.cherrymoon.com Radio station.

Choice Radio www.choiceradio.com Radio Web site.

Comedy Central www.comcentral.com Humor.

Country Music Television (CMT) www.country.com Country music videos.

DigAS www.david-gmbh.de Digital audio system for broadcast professionals; system modules are a complete package of programs for working with audio material in radio stations.

Disney Channel www.disney.com/disneychannel Family entertainment; Disney movies.

DJ Jukebox www.gammadyne.com/jukebox.htm Playlist generator and MP3 organizer; supports remote control through a LAN; rate each song to ensure favorites are played often.

DJ Mac www.mixthisdjs.com/djsonly.html Software for DJs; allows tracking of shows, income, employees, and clients; free download.

DJ Mix Pro djmixpro.com/djmixpro/djmixpro.html MP3 player and mixer; performs fully automatic quality DJ mixes, including cross-fading and beat matching between songs; screenshots.

DJ Solutions www.greatdjsoftware.com Business management software for mobile disk jockeys, karaoke, or rentals; free demo available.

DJjmixed.com www.djmixed.com News; reviews; downloads.

DMX Music www.dmxmusic.com Digital Music Express (DMX) provides digital music by subscription to businesses and consumers via cable, satellite, and disc.

Dot Music www.dotmusic.com Mainstream music heard on the radio; music news; downloads; online CD store.

DRS—DigiTrax Services www.drs-digitrax.com Producers of video software; teleprompter, video, and video broadcast software.

E! Entertainment Television www.eonline.com Entertainment news.

Fast Channel Network www.fastchannel.com/fastchannel/default.asp Creative channel; traffic channel; asset channel.

FOLK DJ-L www.folkradio.org Lists folk stations; shows; DJs and playlists.

FOX www.fox.com FOX Television Network.

Globalmedia.com www.globalmedia.com Creates e-commerce sites and audio streams for over 100 radio and TV stations; rankings; music videos.

GLR www.bbc.co.uk/london/ Radio Web site; London station.

Hamfests www.arrl.org/hamfests.html Calendar of events run by ham radio operators.

Hard Radio www.hardradio.com Internet radio Web site; hard rock.

HBO www.hbo.com HBO Web site.

House of Blues www.hob.com Internet radio site that accepts submissions.

Industrial-Radio www.industrial-radio.com Radio station.

Intercollegiate Broadcasting System (IBS) www.frontiernet.net/~ibs/ibshome.html College radio.

Internet Radio Linking Project www.irlp.net/ Commercial-free radio.

InterneTV www.internetv.com Internet television in its early stages; music video; film; live music TV; audio channels; pay per view.

Jam Television www.canoe.ca/Television News about TV and other entertainment in United States and Canada.

Jazz 88 Radio www.jazz88.org Radio; world music; jazz.

KCRW www.kcrw.org Eclectic music.

Launch www.launch.com Online radio channel; recommend new music; videos; search engine; store; Webzine.

LesBiGay Radio Chicago www.lesbigayradio.com AM 1240 and 1470; daily show aimed at the gay, lesbian, transgender, and bisexual population; RealAudio.

Live Radio www.live-radio.net/ Extensive radio station list.

Live Radio and Television from Asia broadcast-live.comasia.html Live television and radio broadcasts from China, India, Japan, Korea, Singapore, Thailand, and elsewhere in Asia; music, news, and sports.

Live Radio and Television from Europe broadcast-live.comeurope.html Watch television and listen to radio broadcasts; music; news and sports.

Live Television from around the World broadcast-live.com/television Live television broadcasts are available from a number of countries including Belgium, Croatia, Canada, France, Germany, United States, and the UK from this site.

Live365 www.live365.comindex.live Create an Internet radio station for free.

Loop Recorder www.config.de/LoopRecorder Designed for capturing songs from the radio; loop mode infinitely records up to a specified number of minutes in a continuous loop while scrolling the data.

M4Radio www.m4radio.com Radio Web site.

MediaBureau.com www.mediabureau.com Live and direct Web casts and original content.

Mic Check Radio www.miccheckradio.com Hip-hop radio Web site.

Mix III www.gi-ad.com/GIADsw/MixIII.html Program to play music like a DJ; users can program music styles, rhythms, melodies, and mix a range of audio files.

Much Music www.muchmusic.com Streaming audio and video.

Music Choice www.musicchoice.com Commercial-free professionally programmed music channels and digital downloads.

Music Television (MTV) www.mtv.com Music videos; features.

National Public Radio www.npr.org Home page of NPR.

NBC www.nbc.com National Broadcast Network.

Net Broadcaster www.netbroadcaster.com Source for streaming entertainment; celebrities.

Nick at Nite & TV Land nick-at-nite.com Games; vintage TV.

Nickelodeon www.nick.com Entertainment for young people.

One World Radio TV oneworldradiotv.com Twenty-four-hour world and reggae music; Internet radio; live shows Monday through Saturday, 1 to 5 PM.

Onradio.com www.onradio.com Internet radio.

PBS www.pbs.org Public Broadcasting Station.

Pirate Radio www.pirateradio.com PC-based Internet broadcasting software.

Pseudo.com www.pseudo.com Internet radio; audio; video; chat; message boards.

Queer FM www.lesbigay.com/queerfm News, information, and music for the lesbian, gay, bisexual, and transgender communities.

Radio 1 www.bbc.co.uk/radio1 Radio Web site; RealAudio streams.

Radio 2 www.bbc.co.uk/radio2 Radio Web site; jazz; folk; country.

Radio 3 www.bbc.co.uk/radio3 Radio Web site; classical.

Radio 4 All www.radio4all.org Links to microbroadcasters.

Radio Connection www.radioconnection.com Train for a career in the music industry; on-the-job training in local major recording studios, radio, and TV stations.

Radio Etc. www.radioetc.com Radio Web site.

Radio Free Virgin www.radiofreevirgin.com Download; listen; community; Windows.

Radio Margaritaville www.margaritaville.com Jimmy Buffet's Internet radio Web site.

Radio Moi www.radiomoi.com Radio Web site; MP3 format; create own station; stations; music library; facts.

Radio Promo www.radiopromo.com Radio Web site.

Radio Tower www.radiotower.com Internet radio directory.

Radio X www.radiox.com Information about Internet radio shows.

Radio.Netscape www.radio.netscape.com Radio Web site.

Radiojock.com www.radiojock.comlabels.html Web site for professional broadcasters; production and equipment sources; music; charts; show prep; mix jocks; links to related Web sites.

Radio-Locator www.radio-locator.com Lists U.S., Canadian, European, and other international stations; list of stations that broadcast on the Internet.

RadioTV www.radiotv.com Internet radio site that accepts submissions.

Real Net Radio www.RealNetRadio.com Independent radio station on the Internet; provides unsigned artists with a means of getting their music heard; upload music; maintain custom playlist of music.

RealGuide www.realguide.real.com Comprehensive directory of RealAudio and RealVideo broadcast sites.

Relax Online College Radio Directory www.relaxonline.com/radio State-by-state listing of college radio stations.

Rip-Off Radio thebigripoff.com Plays all music genres twenty-four hours.

Rock'n'Roots www.rocknroots.com Weekly one-hour eclectic music public radio program.

Sci-Fi Channel: Dominion www.scifi.com Science fiction.

Shout Cast www.shoutcast.com Free Winamp-based distributed streaming audio system; thousands of broadcasters around the world.

Spank Radio www.spankradio.com Underground music twenty-four hours.

Special TV Resources www.specialWeb.com/tv Directory of television Web sites.

Spike Radio www.spikeradio.com Global Web radio network.

Spinner www.spinner.com Internet radio site; channels in all genres; free Spinner player; over one hundred stations; artist information.

Streaming Media World www.streamingmediaworld.com Submissions; subscribers.

Sunday Morning Klezmer & Other Jewish Music www.angelfire.com/nj/WBZCFMsndymrnngklz mr An Internet and radio exploration of Jewish music, art, and culture.

Tactile12000 MP3 DJ www.tactile12000.com 3D interactive simulation of a DJ setup; allows users to cross-fade, backspin, and change the speed of full-length WAV and MP3 files; Macintosh; Windows.

Talk Radio News www.talkradionews.com Radio Web site; online version; news from Washington, DC.

Texas Internet Radio www.texasinternetradio.com
Internet radio Web site.
The Groove Box www.groove-box.com Low
bandwidth background music; searching; news.
The History Channel www.HistoryChannel.com
History channel.
The Iceberg www.theiceberg.com Canadian internet
radio.
The Museum of Television and Radio www.mtr.org
Exhibitions; seminars; radio broadcasts;
members; education; information.
Totally Radio www.totallyradio.com New material on
the radio.
TV Guide Online www.tvguide.com Online version
of TV Guide.
TV Show www.tvshow.com Reviewed links site for
everything and anything television related from
all around the world.
Ultimate TV www.ultimatetv.com Schedules and
articles; online magazine covering television.
V Tuner www.vtuner.com Information about Internet
radio shows.
VH1 www.vh1.com Online version of the cable
channel; video hits; popular music; original
movies.
Virgin Radio www.virginradio.com Radio Web site.
Virtual Tuner www.virtualtuner.com Top 500; new
stations; software.
Virtue TV www.virtuetv.com Live Internet video
broadcasts.
Visual Radio www.visualradio.com Online
multimedia service.
Women on Air www.womenonair.com Weekly one-
hour radio series; eclectic mix of female artists
from around the world.
Woofur www.woofur.com Internet radio; independent
music of all genres.
World Radio Network www.wrn.org Live
international newscasts.
Yesterday USA www.yesterdayusa.com Radio Web
site; radio shows from 1920s to 1950s.

Ragtime

20 Ragtime Jazz Classics for Piano
www.netstoreusa.com/music/004/ Ragtime
classics; sheet music.
*Colin D. MacDonald's Ragtime-March-Waltz
Website Welcome Page* www.ragtimemusic.com
Ragtime, march, and waltz MIDI files.
Early Recordings
www.garlic.com~tgracyk/early_ragtime.htm
African Americans early recordings.
John Roache's Ragtime members.aol.com/ragtimers
Ragtime, jazz, and stride piano MIDI sequences;

online catalog for ragtime, stride, and novelty
piano music.
Kansas City Ragtime Revelry
www.sound.net/~garyr/revelry/2.shtml Nonprofit
corporation dedicated to the promotion and
preservation of Kansas City's legacy of ragtime
music.
Music Links www.rtpress.com/links.htm Links to
music sites; ragtime, oldtime, and stride;
American variety stage; vaudeville; entertainment
1870-1920.
National Ragtime and Jazz Archive
www.library.siue.edu/jazz/ Information and links.
Northern Virginia Ragtime Society (NVRS)
www.nvrs.org Mailing list; events; links.
Oleg Mezjuev's Home Page
www.geocities.com/Paris/1790 Ragtime Press
MIDI Music Archive; over one hundred live
recorded MIDI files.
Paragon Ragtime Orchestra
www.paragonragtime.com Professional
organization performing ragtime-era music;
vaudeville hits; silent movie accompaniments;
dance-hall favorites.
*'Perfessor' Bill Edwards Ragtime Sheet Music
Covers and MIDI Files* www.perfessorbill.com
Restored sheet music covers and MIDI files.
Player Piano www.ragtimewest.com Close to one
hundred pages; WAV files; MIDI files.
Ragtime www.northwestern.edu/jazz/styles/ragtime/
Information and resources.
Ragtime Alphabetic Index
www.rtpress.com/titles.htm Alphabetic listing of
song titles and authors; live MIDI performances.
Ragtime for Guitar
village.infoWeb.ne.jp/~ragtime/english.htm
Arrangements for guitar.
Ragtime Home Page www.ragtimers.org Rocky
Mountain Ragtime Festival.
*Ragtime Jazz Vaudeville 1920s Vintage Recordings
on Cassette and CD* www.vintage-
recordings.com Large selection; online catalog.
Ragtime MIDI by Walt E. Smith
members.aol.com/waltesmith/ragtime.htm For
noncommercial use only.
Ragtime MIDI Files by Warren Trachtman
www.trachtman.org/ragtime Ragtime MIDI files
of piano pieces by Scott Joplin, James Scott,
Joseph Lamb, Jelly Roll Morton, Eubie Blake,
and others; Piano Soundfonts.
Ragtime Press MIDI Music Archive
www.rtpress.com Ragtime, blues, stride, and
boogie piano played live by Sue Keller.
Ragtime Rendevous—Ragtime by Mail
www.jazzbymail.com/ragtime.html Online
music store specializing in classic jazz and
ragtime; traditional jazz and Dixieland.

Ragtime Sheet Music Collection
library.msstate.edu/ragtime/ Digital library
collection; search.

Ragtime the Musical www.imagi-
nation.com/moonstruck/albm53.html
Information; cast albums; sheet music.

Ragtime Tunes www.discoverynet.com~ajsnead/
MIDI files.

Ragtime-Blues-Hot Piano
www.doctorjazz.freeserve.co.uk Ragtime piano
music; MIDI files of some of the great ragtime
artists; photographs; document archives.

Scott Joplin International Ragtime Foundation
www.scottjoplin.org Located in Sedalia,
Missouri, the Cradle of Ragtime.

Stomp Off Records
www.stompoffrecords.com/ragtime.html Search
by genre.

Swedish Ragtime Home Page www.ragtime.nu
Ragtime MIDI files; rags written by Swedish,
international, classic, and contemporary ragtime
composers.

The Ragtime Centennial Show www.rrragtimer.com
Online show takes audience back one hundred
years to the beginnings of ragtime.

The Ragtime Ephermeralist
home.earthlink.net/~ephemeralist/ Devoted to the
preservation and dissemination of articles and
items relating to nineteenth- and early twentieth-
century popular music.

The Ragtime Story
www.wnur.org/jazz/styles/ragtime/ragtime-
story.html History of ragtime.

Vaudeville and Ragtime Show
www.bestwebs.com/vaudeville Early ragtime and
vaudeville performers; songs and routines.

Vintage Music-Ragtime Jazz Vaudeville
www.vintage-music.com/ragtime Antique
ragtime; jazz; vaudeville; links.

West Coast Ragtime Society
www.westcoastragtime.com Official Web site.

Western Social Dance
memory.loc.gov/ammem/dihtml/diessay7.html
Ragtime dance.

Record Labels

A Child's Garden of Record Labels
www.mindspring.com~hagar/garden.html
Alphabetical listings.

A&M, Interscope, and Geffen Records
www.amrecords.com Links to artist sites; news;
tours; merchandise; information, including how
to submit a demo; jobs at A&M; tracking down
old records.

All Record Labels allrecordlabels.com Links to record
labels worldwide; over 10,400 record label sites.

Ari's Simple List of Record Labels
recordlabels.nu/index.htm Alphabetical links.

Arista Records www.aristarec.com High and low
bandwidth access; graphics oriented; information
on artists; weekly word section; listen to new
items in RealAudio; audio and video clips; chat.

Association of Independent Record Labels
www.air.org.au National Association of
Australian Owned Independent Record Labels.

Atlantic Records www.atlantic-records.com Label
Web site; artists; news; events; tours.

Band Link www.bandlink.net/labels/a.html
Alphabetical listing of record labels.

Band Radio Directory: Record Companies
www.bandradio.com/dir/Record_Companies/
Record labels.

Blue Note Records www.bluenote.com Jazz;
information; artists; catalog; shopping; new
releases; FAQ; history of the company.

BMG Entertainment www.bmg.com Browse music
by genre; own over 200 record labels; music club
site; order CDs online.

Capitol Records www.hollywoodandvine.com
Current releases; tours; chances to win; listen to
album extracts; join the monthly newsletter;
information about Capitol Studios and gear.

Classical Music Record Companies on the Web
www.search-beat.com/labels.htm The Classical
Music Beat; classical music history Internet
links; classical music history time lines;
composer history resources.

Columbia Records www.columbiarecords.com Record
label; video channel; artist biographies and
schedules; reviews; links.

Cooking Vinyl www.cookingvinyl.com Eclectic
roster.

Curb Records www.curb.com Record label; artist
information; new releases.

Del-FI Records www.del-fi.com Rock 'n' roll
legends; blues.

Deutsche Grammophon www.dgclassics.com
Classical music record label; new releases; tour
dates; new studio.

Dirty Linen's Record Label List
www.dirtynelson.com/linen/special/label.html
Extensive alphabetical listing.

Dreamworks Records www.dreamworksrecords.com
Record label; artist information; new releases.

Early Music Record Labels
www.concerto.demon.co.uk Details of record
labels that issue recordings of early music and
their Web sites.

Edel www.edel.com/index_js.html German company.

Elektra www.elektra.com Individual artists; search
music topics; browse archives; check tour dates;
store; download audio and video clips.

EMI Music www.emimusic.ca Record label; artist
information; new releases.

EMI Records www.emirecords.co.uk Label Web site.

Epic Records www.epicrecords.com Record label;
artist information; new releases.

Geffen Records www.geffen.com Record label; tours;
new releases; artist links.

Google Directory: Record Labels
directory.google.com/Top/Arts/Music/Record_La
bels/ Links by genre.

Hightone Records www.hightone.comindex.html
Independent record label; American roots music.

Hollywood Records www.hollywoodrec.com Artists;
soundtracks; pictures; tracks; videos; tours.

Hyperion www.hyperion-records.co.uk British
classical music label.

Independent Record Labels
www.shef.ac.uk/misc/rec/ps/efi/elabels.html
Outline details and contact information; catalogs
of releases; links.

Independent Record Labels, Links, and Info
members.tripod.com/Hz_dB/labels.html Record
labels.

Info for Artists and Labels
www.racerrecords.com/ArtistsAndLabels.html
Believe in sharing information and in supporting
other folks who are trying to make music
available, whether those people are artists or
other labels.

Island Def Jam www.islanddefjam.com Label site.

Jive www.jiverecords.com Label Web site.

Maverick www.maverickrc.com Information; artists;
forums; owned by Madonna.

MCA Nashville www.mca-nashville.com Record
label Web site.

Mercury Records www.mercuryrecords.com Record
label; artist information; links.

Metal Index: Record Labels
www.metalindex.com/recordlabels.html Record
labels.

Motown www.motown.com Information; music;
featured artists; games and trivia.

MusicMoz
musicmoz.org/Record_Labels/Major_Labels/
Major record label links.

*National Association of Record Industry
Professionals (NARIP)* www.narip.com
Membership; events; industry jobs; news.

Naxos www.naxos.com Classical.

Open Directory: Record Labels
dmoz.org/Arts/Music/Record_Labels/ Links by
genre.

Polydor www.polydor.co.uk Label Web site.

RCA Victor www.rcavictor.com Information; artists.

Record Label Music www.recordlabelmusic.com
Home page.

Record Labels and Companies Guide www.record-
labels-companies-guide.com Resource for record
label and other music company contacts, articles,
news, tips, and more.

Record Labels
directory.google.com/Top/Arts/Music/Styles/Roc
k/Punk/Record_Labels/ Categorized by letter.

Record Labels
www.geocities.com/SunsetStrip/Bistro/5480/labe
ls.html For record labels and companies; submit
link; posts messages from record labels.

Record Labels on the Web www.rlabels.com Over
5,000 links to record label Web pages.

Reprise Records www.RepriseRec.com Record label;
artists; audio files.

Rhino www.rhino.com United States reissue label.

Rounder Records www.rounder.com Independent
record label; Massachusetts based; folk; roots;
ethnic; children's.

Sony Music www.sonymusic.com or
www.sonymusiceurope.com or
www.sonymusic.co.uk Information; artists;
tours; new releases; catalog; news; broadcasts;
multimedia; interviews; music and video clips.

Sun Records www.sunstudio.com Where rock and roll
began; label for Elvis Presley, Jerry Lee Lewis,
Johnny Cash, B. B. King, Roy Orbison, and
others from the Golden Age; history of Sun's
development; information on major artists.

TAXI: Major Record Labels
www.taxi.com/members/links-labels.html
Independent A&R Vehicle that connects unsigned
artists, bands, and songwriters with major record
labels, publishers, and film and TV music
supervisors.

Universal Classics www.universalclassics.com
Rosters of classical labels; artist bios.

Verve Records www.vervemusicgroup.com/verve/
Great jazz artists.

Virgin Records www.virginrecords.com Music
information; technical questions; who to send
demo tapes to; artists.

Walt Disney Records www.disney.com or
www.disney.comDisneyRecords/index.html
Information; pictures; new releases; audio and
video downloads.

Warner Bros. Records www.wbr.com or
www.warnermusic.ca or
www.music.warnerbros.com Feature artists;
company's artists; new releases; job
opportunities; Newswire; artists' message board;
tour dates and information; FAQ; subscribe to
the mailing list; audio and video clips.

World Wide Punk: Punk Labels
www.worldwidepunk.com/labels.html Directory
of punk, hardcore, ska, Oi, and other record

labels; hundreds of record labels, distributors, stores, mail orders, etc.

Worldwide Internet Music Resources
www.music.indiana.edu/music_resources/recind.h tml Record labels, record producers, recording studios.

Worldwide List of Record Labels
spraci.cia.com.au/labels/labelsw.htm Alphabetical list of links to information about record labels around the world.

Yahoo Directory: Labels
dir.yahoo.com/Business_and_Economy/Shopping _and_Services/Music/Labels/ Links to record labels.

Recording

4-Track Recording Tips
members.tripod.com~PROPAC/4track.htm Tutorial; tips on recording; EQ; links to recording equipment manufacturers.

Abbey Road Studios
www.abbeyroad.co.uk/indexpm.html Famous recording studio.

Absolute Sound www.theabsolutesound.com Journal of Audio and Music; articles.

Analog Tape Recorders
arts.ucsc.edu/ems/music/equipment/analog_record ers/Analog_Recorders.html FAQ.

Association of Professional Recording Services (APRS) www.aprs.co.uk UK-based professional audio organization; traditional music studios; project studios; post-production; broadcast; live sound; film soundtracks; duplication; training; leading force within the British music industry; concerned with standards, training, technical, and legal issues; Board of Directors is elected by members; studios can become members; list of associated studios.

Audio Amigo www.audioamigo.com Audio recording; digital home studio equipment; digital; resources; multitrack digital recording software; articles on promotion, home recording, and audio mastering.

Audio Café www.audiocafe.com Reference for audio equipment manufacturers and products; monthly quizzes; reviews; directories of manufacturers; classified ads.

Audio Engineering Society (AES) www.aes.org Professional society devoted exclusively to audio technology; membership includes leading engineers, scientists, and other authorities; membership information; members in forty-seven concentrated geographic areas throughout the world; conferences; links to other audio-related links including audio education and research; audio equipment; audio-related usenet newsgroups; computers and audio; electronic music and MIDI; magazines and publications;

music; musical instruments; professional audio companies; professional organizations; radio and broadcast; search the World Wide Web; test and measurement; submit an audio-related URL.

Audio Forums www.AudioForums.com Audio-related forums.

Audio Institute of America www.audioinstitute.com Train to be a recording engineer.

Audio Recording Center www.audio-recording-center.com Resource for analog, digital, home demo, sound software, studios, and other recording information.

Audio Revolution www.audiorevolution.com Reviews; Audio Video Marketplace.

Audio Seminars www.audioseminars.com Live sound training; system engineering.

Audio Web www.audioweb.com Auction and classified Web site; reviews.

Audio Workshops www.audioworkshops.com Musicians; engineers; producers; sound designers.

Audio World www.audioworld.com Digital music news; articles; industry news.

Digital Domain www.digido.com Site to help audio engineers and musicians make compact disks and CD-ROMs; CD and CD-ROM mastering.

Disk Makers www.discmakers.com Audio duplication company; tutorials; CD promotion; pocket guides; newsletter.

Disctronics www.disctronics.co.uk Manufacturing; United States, UK, and Europe.

Doctor Audio www.DoctorAudio.com Recording Web site.

Electronic Musician www.emusician.com Recording magazine; product reviews; articles; features; resource for musicians interested in personal music production; direct access to music industry and article databases; download past features and reviews.

EQ www.eqmag.com Recording magazine.

Global Express Media
www.globalexpressmedia.com CD reproduction and related services.

Harmony Central: Recording www.harmony-central.com/Recording/ Links to information resources.

Home Recording at About.com
homerecording.about.com/mbody.htm Links to information.

Home Recording Magazine
www.homerecordingmag.com How-to magazine for musicians.

Home Recording Rights Coalition www.hrrc.org Coalition to preserve the rights of those who use home audio and video recording products; legislative issues; digital copyright law; links.

Home Recording www.homerecording.com Equipment reviews; MP3; digital music recording on CDs or hard disks; tutorial for beginners; mailing list; articles on recording and mixing; FAQs on how to get started; active forum; detailed glossary; numerous tutorials.

International Recording Media Association www.recordingmedia.org News; conferences; publications.

Keyboard Magazine www.keyboardmag.com or www.keyboardonline.com Recording information; product reviews; articles; columns.

Live-Audio.com www.Live-Audio.com Recording; study hall; forums.

Mix Magazine www.mixonline.com Reviews; archives; subscriptions; recording; products.

Music Producers Guild mpg.org.uk Information; for professionals.

Musician's Tech Central www.musicianstechcentral.com/library.html Technical information; links.

Muzique.com www.muzique.com Bibliography of books on musical electronics.

National Academy of Recording Arts and Sciences (NARAS) www.grammy.com Organization of recording professionals; presents the Grammy Awards; organizes educational programs; member services and benefits; forum; MusiCares; LARAS; Master Track; Media Center; features; daily news; Grammy winners; Grammy store; Grammy Foundation; chapter updates.

National Association of Recording Merchandisers (NARM) www.narm.com Official Web site; about; members and membership.

Oasis CD & Cassette Duplication www.oasisCD.com Audio duplication company.

Octave.com www.octave.com/en/library.htm Articles on recordable CDs.

Pro Audio Music www.ProAudioMusic.com Audio equipment retailer.

Pro Audio.net www.soundwave.com News; information; discussion groups.

Pro Studio Edition www.discmakers.com/pse Studio newsletter; interviews with engineers; tips.

Prorec.com www.prorec.com Introductory and advanced technology; online music magazine; site index which can be viewed by title, company, product, author, or topic; bookstore; classified ads; active discussion board.

Real Engineers www.RealEngineers.com Audio engineer database.

Recording Career www.recordingcareer.com Los Angeles Recording Workshop; recording engineer school; newsletter; scholarships; job leads.

Recording Connection www.recordingconnection.com Training for engineers.

Recording Industry Association of America (RIAA) www.riaa.com Current copyright infringement and piracy issues; censorship; information; resources; links.

Recording Technology History ac.acusd.edu/History/recording/notes.html History of sound recording; digital technologies and MP3.

Recording Website www.recordingwebsite.com Learn the basics.

Recording Workshop www.recordingworkshop.com Learn the art of recording.

Recording www.recordingmag.com Recording magazine; TAXI newsletter included.

Recording.org www.recording.org Composed of world-class Grammy award-winning producers, engineers and music business enthusiast from around the world; about, how to record music, how to master music, what type of recording tools to use and how to market your music.

Recordingeq.com recordingeq.com Recording Engineer's Quarterly.

Sound on Sound www.soundonsound.com UK high-tech recording magazine; articles and reviews; online forum.

Studio Buddy www.studiobuddy.com Home Recording Helper; self-contained, easy to use database of recording tips designed specifically for people with home studios; free download.

Studio Finder www.studiofinder.com Database of over 5,000 studios by location, equipment, and experience.

Studio Menu www.studiomenu.com Recording site.

Studio Sound www.prostudio.com/studiosound Features from current and past issues are available to read and download.

Sun Studio www.sunstudio.com Virtual tour of the legendary studio; artist bios of those who recorded there.

The Association of Professional Recording Services www.aprs.co.uk Resource for producers and engineers.

The Educational Recording Agency www.era.org.uk/ Recording for educational purposes.

The Encyclopedia of Record Producers www.mojavemusic.com Database of producers.

The Home Recording Web Ring homerecording.com/webring.html Recording, mixing, and more.

The Mastering Board webbd.nls.net/webboard/wbpx.dll/~mastering Audio topics; bulletin board; acoustics.

The Stereo Shop www.thestereoshop.comlinks.htm Large collection of links to manufacturer sites.

Total Recording www.kiqproductions.com Book; Golden Ears Audio Eartraining course for musicians, engineers, and producers.

We Make Tapes www.wemaketapes.com Nashville-based duplicating service.

World Wide Pro Audio Directory
www.audiodirectory.nl Over 10,000
manufacturers and dealers listed; search by
subject.
Yahoo Directory: Recording
dir.yahoo.com/Entertainment/Music/Recording
Information on recording.

Religious and Gospel
Music—Inspirational

1Christian.net www.1christian.net Christian music
network.
A Little Religion and Romance Music
www.greaterthings.com/Music Online MIDI
albums and singles; originals and arrangements
of spiritual, romantic, and patriotic songs,
hymns, anthems, medleys; CD available.
Bible Gateway www.bible.gospelcom.net Bible-
search resource.
Black Gospel Music Clef
www.blackgospel.com/tools/ Dedicated to
providing resources and information for
participants and supporters of black gospel
music.
Black Gospel Music Marketplace
www.blackgospel.com/marketplace/ Products
related to black gospel music; CDs; videos;
books; publications; sheet music; equipment and
more.
CCM Online www.ccmcom.com Christian Music
magazine; radio charts; countdown; Christian
stations reporting.
Ceremony Music Resource Page
www.castle.net/~energize/CMRP/index.html
Selection lists; online sound files; CD retailers;
articles and books, etc.
Choir and Organ www.orphpl.com/choir.htm Music
magazine; religious, secular, choral, reviews,
news, and events.
Christian Answers.Net
www.christiananswers.net/midimenu Christian
background music; TM page; 100+ MIDI files;
floating music menu.
Christian History Institute
www.gospelcom.net/chi/GLIMPSEF/Glimpses/g
lmps089.shtml Slave songs.
Christian Music Place
www.placetobe.org/cmp/central.htm Resources
for writers of Christian music.
Christian Songwriters Group
www.christiansongwriters.com Christian music
songwriters.
Church Assist www.churchassist.com *Worship
Assistant* software.
Church Music Master www.churchmusicmaster.com
Christian music software.

Coalition of Internet Church Music Publishers
www.redshift.com~bowms1/cicmp Dedicated
Christians who compose and publish music for
Christian worship; independent publishers.
Contemporary Christian Music www.ccmusic.org
Directories of Christian music and artists sites;
concert dates.
Country Gospel Guild www.countrygospelguild.com
Members; awards; join; links.
Creation Festival www.gospelcom.net/creation
Christian music festival.
*Education Secretary's Statement on Religious
Expression* www.ed.gov/Speeches/08-
1995/religion.html Guidelines set forth by the
United States Department of Education to clarify
the First Amendment rights and responsibilities
of students, parents, and schools.
Get Christian Music www.getchristianmusic.com
Online Christian music store.
GNMS.COM www.gnms.com Church music,
worship, and drama materials from all suppliers;
large inventory; choir robes.
Godspell—The Musical
www.netpuppy.com/godspell/ Brief summary of
the musical; cast/crew list and production diary.
Gospel Flava www.gospelflava.com Gospel site.
Gospel Music Association (GMA)
www.gospelmusic.org Membership; gospel
music links; resources for writers of Christian
music.
Gospel Music Lessons
www.sensationalgospelmusic.com Gospel music
books and audiocassette tapes for adults and
children.
Gospelcom.net www.gospelcom.net/preview Film
and TV preview Web site.
Harlem Spirituals www.harlemspirituals.com Gospel
and jazz tours.
Heart Songs www.heartsongs.org Christian music;
MIDIs; songs; chat.
Hymns and Spirituals
www.iath.virginia.edu/utc/christn/chsohp.html
Songs; information.
K-LOVE Radio KLOVE.com Contemporary Christian
music heard around the world; listener-supported;
noncommercial.
KXCD www.kxcd.org Commercial-free and
uninterrupted Christian alternative rock;
streaming MP3 station.
Lammas Records www.lammas.co.uk Solo, choral,
and organ music from Britain's cathedrals.
Negro Spirituals www.negrospirituals.com History;
singers; songs; composers.
Negro Spirituals
xroads.virginia.edu/~HYPER/TWH/Higg.html
Article from the *Atlantic Monthly*, June 1867.

Negro Spirituals xroads.virginia.edu/~HYPER/TWH/twh_front.ht ml Hypertext edition; links.

Praise Charts www.praisecharts.com Worship resource center; sheet music to popular worship songs; supplied by a growing network of arrangers.

Reflection Christian Music Resources www.users.zetnet.co.uk/mlehr/reflec/ Original Christian worship music; MIDIs and sheet music available for downloading and use.

Religious Information Source—BELIEVE www.mb-soft.com/believe/index.html Hundreds of informative articles on important words, subjects, and terms in Christianity and other major world religions; source of information for deeper understanding of religious subjects.

Religious Resources on the Net www.religiousresources.org Religious Resources on the Net is a comprehensive, searchable database of religious and Christian Web sites on the Internet. Visitors to the Web site can browse through over one hundred topics or use our search engine to generate a listing of religious resources containing selected words or phrases.

Religious Society of Friends www.quaker.org The official Quaker home page; large listing of Quaker links on the Web; hosting for a number of Quaker groups.

Sacred Harp and Shape-Note Music Resources www.mcsr.olemiss.edu/~mudws/harp.html Describes printed music, literature, recordings, and other related resources.

Sacred Heart www.sacredheart.com/music.htm Religious music.

Sacred Music www.sacredmusic.com Religious music Web site.

Stravinsky's Religious Works www.cco.caltech.edu/~tan/Stravinsky Includes *Symphony of Psalms, Mass,* and *Requiem Canticles*; illustrated biography of Stravinsky's life; listening guide and commentary.

The Almost Definitive Contemporary Christian Music Hot-Page www.afn.org~mrblue/ccm/ccm.html Artist and band links; brief history.

The California Mission Site www.californiamissions.com Histories for each of the twenty-one California Missions; music; color and black-and-white photographs.

The Singing News www.singingnews.com Southern gospel music; features; charts.

The Spirituals Project www.spiritualsproject.org Information on Spirituals, our Mission Statement, Educational Programs, Sponsorship, Projects, Resources, and more.

The World of Christian Music www.worldofcm.com Online magazine of Contemporary Christian music charts; top artists, albums, reviews, etc.

Today's Christian Music www.todayschristianmusic.com Contemporary Christian; live RealAudio feed.

Top Christian Music Titles www.emmanuel.kiev.ua/music_groupE.html Music hit parade of Christian musicians; MP3 songs available for free download.

WeddingMusic2Dance.com www.weddingmusic2dance.com Home page.

Worldwide Internet Music Resources www.music.indiana.edu/music_resources/gospel. html Religious music links.

Worship Music www.worshipmusic.com Christian worship music; praise music media.

Search Engines

About.com www.about.com Human driven search engine.

All the Web www.alltheweb.com Search engine.

AltaVista www.altavista.digital.com One of the top search engines; large database.

AOL.com www.aol.com Web guide; sites for many subjects and interests.

Argus Clearinghouse www.clearinghouse.net Specialty search engine; find music-related search engines.

Ask Jeeves www.askjeeves.com Ask questions; replies with a list of answers about where to find related material.

Beaucoup www.beaucoup.com Specialty search engine; find music-related search engines.

Bigfoot www.bigfoot.com Search for e-mail and Web addresses; Yellow Pages.

Brittanica Internet Guide www.ebig.com Directory; topics and search facilities.

CNet cnet.com/Content/Features/Dlife/ Search Information about search engines.

Copernic for Windows 95 www.download.com/PC/Result/ Search major search engines simultaneously; duplicates automatically removed; results stored in folders; program ranks results; refine search; look for specific words in results; open Web pages; searches are stored.

Disinformation www.disinfo.com Alternative, subculture search engine.

Dogpile www.dogpile.com Multisearch engine; lists up to twenty-four search engines; specify order in which to search.

Euroseek www.euroseek.net European-based search engine; can search in any country, in any language.

Excite www.excite.com Concept-based searches narrow search to relevant sites.

Excite UK excite.co.uk/ Searches UK and European sites.

FinderSeeker www.finderseeker.com Specialty search engine; find music-related search engines.

Google www.google.com Search engine; fast and effective.

HotBot www.hotbot.com Popular search engine; many categories.

Infoseek www.infoseek.com Comprehensive search engine with large database; Web guides; searches newsgroups and other Internet sources; UK site.

Infospace www.infospace.com Many categories including Yellow Pages, White Pages, business listings, personal E-mail addresses; business finder and people finder on UK site.

LookSmart www.looksmart.com Search topics in over 17,000 categories.

LookSmart UK www.looksmart.co.uk Search UK or international sites.

Lycos www.lycos.com Long-established search engine; large, fast, and effective.

Lycos UK www.lycosuk.co.uk Search the UK and Ireland.

Magellen mckinley.com Directory; list of topics; Yellow Pages; People Finder.

Mamma.com www.mamma.com "The mother" of all search engines.

MetaCrawler www.metacrawler.com Meta search engine; search multiple engines.

MetaFind www.metafind.com Meta search engine; search multiple engines.

MetaSearch metasearch.com Goes to six search engines.

NearSite for the PC www.nearsite.com Collects and stores Web pages for offline browsing; set up any number of pages or sites; program automatically downloads; schedule facility automatically updates sites.

PlanetSearch www.planetsearch.com News, finance, and wealth; color-coded bar system indicates rating of sites by each word.

Savvy Search www.savvysearch.com or guaraldi.cs.colostate.edu:2000 Meta search engine; search multiple engines; queries multiple search engines at the same time; indicate number of results wanted; Search Plan ranks nineteen search engines; divides groups by usefulness.

Search Engine Guide www.searchengineguide.com Guide to general and subject-specific search engines, portals, and directories; search the resources by keyword or browse by category.

Search Engine Watch searchenginewatch.com Information about search engines; links to major search engines and others; how to use search engines.

Search Engines Galore www.searchenginesgalore.com All in one search engine directory.

Search.Com www.search.com Search in a range of categories and topics; over one hundred specialty searches listed alphabetically; music entries.

Searching the Web www.hypernews.org/HyperNews/get/www/searching.html Information about search engines, services, directories, software, and articles.

SearchWolf www.msw.com.au/search Search several engines; Web page crawler; compiles lists of files, FTP sites and links; MP3 Wolf scans the Internet for MP3, MIDI, Wave, and other music files and links.

The Big Hub www.thebighub.com Specialty search engine; find music-related search engines.

The Free Encyclopedia www.encyclopedia.com Over 17,000 articles from *The Concise Columbia Electronic Encyclopedia.*

The Internet Sleuth www.isleuth.com Select up to six databases such as news, business, software, Web directories; list of twenty-one categories.

The Mining Company home.miningco.com List of categories; over 500 topics.

The Open Directory www.dmoz.org Human-driven search engine.

The Web Robots Page info.Webcrawler.com/mak/projects/robots/robots.html About the software search engines use to gather information.

TrackerLock www.tracerlock.com Automated service that monitors URL search engine placement.

UK Index www.ukindex.co.uk List of UK sites; search by category.

Ultra Infoseek ultra.infoseek.com Searches the Internet, news, companies, and Usenet data.

W3 Search Engines cuiwww.unige.ch/meta-index.html Lists some of the most useful search engines on the Web; search in list-based catalogs, spider-based catalogs, people databases, and many other search engines.

WebCrawler www.webcrawler.com Search by topic; create personalized search pages; UK site link goes to *Excite UK.*

Yahoo www.yahoo.com First and most well-known search engine and directory on the Internet; list of categories; several search methods.

Yahoo UK www.yahoo.co.uk Search UK and Ireland sites.

Sheet Music —
Historical Collections —
Notation and Transcription Software

About Sheet Music odyssey.lib.duke.edu/sheetmusic/about.html or scriptorium.lib.duke.edu/sheetmusic/about.html Historic American sheet music; what is sheet music?

African-American Sheet Music memory.loc.gov/ammem/award97/rpbhtml From Brown University.

Alley Kat Sheet Music Center www.alleykatsheetmusic.com Discounted sheet music; Broadway; movies; classical; secular; sacred; country; pop; reference; personality; music for fretted instruments; piano; organ; keyboard; instrumental; vocal scores; fake books and more.

Burt & Company Discount Music Supply www.Burtnco.com Large sheet music distributor.

Byron Hoyt www.byronhoyt.com World's largest digital classical sheet music database online with over 100,000 pages of sheet music; traditional and digital sheet music.

California Sheet Music Project www.sims.berkeley.edu/~mkduggan/neh.html Virtual library of 2,000 pieces of sheet music.

CD Sheet Music www.cdsheetmusic.com Complete collections of printable piano works on CD-ROM; the cure for "overflowing piano bench syndrome."

Charles Dumont & Son Inc. www.dumontmusic.com Alfred; Mel Bay; Cherry Lane; CPP/Belwin; International; Kjos; Hal Leonard; Koala; Music Sales; Warner Music; The Ultimate Display Rack System.

Copy Us www.copy-us.com Internet music publishing; sheet music by contemporary composers.

Creative Music www.creativemusic.com Online sheet music store; in-stock inventory.

Demiq Music www.demiq.com Sheet music publisher of choral, instrumental, opera, orchestral classics, and unique new works.

Discount Sheet Music www.netstoreusa.commusic/ Detailed listing of 250,000 songs.

Finale www.finalemusic.com Developer of music software programs, including *Finale*, *Allegro*, and *SmartMusic Studio*; pro-end notation and printing package used by professional music typesetters; current and new products; technical support; FAQ; demos to download.

Free Scores www.free-scores.com Sheet music directory.

Free Sheet Music www.freesheetmusic.net Sheet music search; downloads. .

Free Sheet Music Guide www.freesheetmusicguide.com Guide to free online sheet music.

Green Label Music www.greenlabelmusic.com Buy music in the Green Label format.

Heritage Music Press www.lorenz.com MIDI accompaniment disks; piano methods.

Historic American Sheet Music memory.loc.gov/ammem/award97/ncdhtml/hasm home.html Includes 3,042 pieces of sheet music published in America between 1850 and 1920; selected from the collections at Duke University.

Historic American Sheet Music scriptorium.lib.duke.edu/sheetmusic/ Rare book, manuscript, and special collections library; Duke University.

Home Concert 2000 www.timewarptech.com Follow sheet music on screen; synchronized accompaniment.

International Print Edition www.ipe-music.com Masters Collection; IPE Scores.

J. W. Pepper Music Network www.jwpepper.com/indexb.html Sheet music and music books; music software products; music teaching tools; music distributor specializing in music performance materials for schools, churches, community musical organizations, and home music enjoyment; online ordering.

Keystave www.keystave.com Free public domain sheet music; search by instrument or composer; PDF files; registration.

Koala Publications www.learntoplaymusic.com Instructional materials; Australian company.

MIT Libraries libraries.mit.edu/music/sheetmusic/ Sheet music collection.

Melody Assistant www.myriad-online.com Music notation program; can use with a MIDI synthesizer; comes with bank of internal sounds; *Chord Assistant*.

Music Books Plus www.musicbooksplus.com Online music bookstore.

Music for the Nation memory.loc.gov/ammem/smhtml/smhome.html American sheet music; search by author, subject, or title.

Music Notes www.musicnotes.com Digital sheet music; download and print; music books; classical, piano, guitar, and instrumental; enhanced CDs and DVDs with sheet music.

Music Room www.musicroom.com Sheet music available online.

Music Students www.musicstudents.com Sheet music online.

Musica Viva www.musicaviva.com Free sheet music downloads.

Music-Scores.com www.music-scores.com Free classical sheet music; book and CD recommendations; free music scores and MIDI files; free classical sheet music downloads.

Mutopia Project www.mutopiaproject.org Free downloads.

My Sheet Music www.dalymusic.com Free and "pay and play" music.

National Sheet Music Society www.nsmsmusic.org Sheet music primer; membership information.

New York Sheet Music Society www.johnnymercer.com/nysms.htm or www.nysms.org/ Johnny Mercer Web site; the New York Sheet Music Society; established in 1980; began with a small, dedicated group of collectors.

Nissimo www.nissimo.com Free classical sheet music; view; print.

Notation Machine notationmachine.com Convert files recorded directly from CDs and tapes into sheet music.

Notation Technologies www.notationtechnologies.com *Play Music;* compose, play, print, and e-mail sheet music; entry-level program.

Noteheads www.noteheads.com *Igor;* company dedicated to bringing musicians and publishers together through the medium of sophisticated Internet-oriented music publishing software; head office in Stockholm, Sweden.

NoteWorthy Software www.noteworthysoftware.com *NoteWorthy Composer;* software music composition and notation processor for Windows; create, record, edit, print, and play back musical scores in pure music notation format.

Old and Gold www.oldandgold.com/plus.html Sheet music; songbooks; guitar tabs; records; over a quarter million titles; order online.

Piano Press www.pianopress.com Sheet music for piano/vocal/guitar; world music repertoire guide; seasonal music; CDs; CD-ROMs.

Print Music Online www.printmusiconline.com Print music; sheet music; band methods; instructional videos.

Printed Music Worldwide www.printed-music.com Subscription directory for producers of printed classical music.

Reed Kotler Music www.reedkotler.com *Transkriber.*

Retail Print Music Dealers Association www.printmusic.org Membership; convention; newsletter; copyright information; directory.

Roni Music www.ronimusic.com *Amazing Slow Downer;* intended for musicians wanting to slow down music without changing the pitch.

Score Online www.score-on-line.com Sheet music online.

Seventh String Software www.seventhstring.demon.co.uk *Transcribe* software to help transcribe recorded music; ability to slow down the music without changing its pitch; shareware for Windows or Macintosh.

Sheet Music Archive www.sheetmusicarchive.net How to make PDF files of sheet music; collection available on CD.

Sheet Music Service www.sheetmusicservice.com Sheet music that is hard to find or out of print.

Sheet Music Catalog www.sheetmusiccatalog.com Online retailer; browse by artist.

Sheet Music Center for Collector's of Vintage Popular Sheet Music www.sheetmusiccenter.com Buy, sell, and trade old sheet music.

Sheet Music Collections www.lib.duke.edu/music/sheetmusic/ Collections of sheet music with public access either through a Web page or online catalog.

Sheet Music Direct www.sheetmusicdirect.com or www.smdamerica.com Browse sheet music titles; download and print out for a fee; thousands of titles in many notation styles.

Sheet Music for Piano, Vocal, and Guitar www.biznest.commusic/sheet Publications in book form; singles for piano, keyboard, vocal, guitar, and more; every music style; old hits and artists; today's top performers.

Sheet Music Logistics www.sheetmusiclogistics.com Web management programs for music retailers.

Sheet Music Now www.sheetmusicnow.com Catalog of thousands of pieces of classical sheet music and jazz; download, print and play instantly; exclusive additional information, biographies and background articles.

Sheet Music Online www.sheetmusic1.com Free downloads of public domain piano music; emphasis on music education resources.

Sheet Music Online www.sheetmusiconline.net Free sheet music; sheet music search; downloads.

Sheet Music Plus www.sheetmusicplus.com Sheet music super store.

Sheet-Music www.sheet-music.com Sheet music online.

Sibelius www.sibelius.com Scoring and notation software for Macintosh and Windows.

Sibelius Music www.sibeliusmusic.com/sibeliusmusic_cat/educational/ Large collection of new scores on the Internet.

SongDex.net www.songdex.net/index.cfm Directory of standard popular music in America; sheet music covers; links.

Stanton's Sheet Music Online www.stantons.com Online retailer.

Sunhawk www.sunhawk.com Sheet music in digital and print formats.

The ABC Musical Notation Language www.gre.ac.uk/~c.walshaw/abc/ Language designed to notate tunes in an ASCII format; designed primarily for folk and traditional tunes of Western European origin which can be written on one stave.

The Historic American Sheet Music Project scriptorium.lib.duke.edu/sheetmusic Provides access to digital images of 3,042 pieces of sheet music published in America between 1850 and 1920.

The Lester S. Levy Collection of Sheet Music levysheetmusic.mse.jhu.edu Part of Special Collections at the Milton S. Eisenhower Library of The Johns Hopkins University; comprised of popular American music spanning the period 1780 to 1960; over 26,000 pieces of music are indexed; images of the cover and music are available for pieces of music more than seventy-five years old.

The Sheet Music Addict www.sheetmusicaddict.com Sheet music for the avid collector.

The Sheet Music Company www.sheetmusicco.com/index.php3 Catalog; order online.

The Vivaldi Studio www.vialdistudio.com Music notation software.

Trillenium Music Company & Tunbridge Music www.trillmusic.com On-line catalog of sheet music; located in Vermont's Green Mountains.

UNC—Chapel Hill Music Library www.lib.unc.edu/music/eam.html Nineteenth-century American sheet music.

Vintage Sheet Music Storefront members.aol.com/vinsheets Vintage sheet music.

Virtual Sheet Music www.virtualsheetmusic.com Classical sheet music downloads.

Warner Brothers Publications www.warnerbrospublications.com Sheet music; popular and educational; instructional videos, DVDs, and Book/Audio CDs.

Wildcat Canyon Software www.wildcat.com Software developer; *Autoscore*; *Internet Music Kit* for adding music to Web site; free downloads; technical support.

Songwriting—Songwriting Contests and Camps

Alaska Midnight Sun Songwriters Camp www.songcamp.com/amssc/songcamp.html Held in June in Anchorage.

American Songwriter www.americansongwriter.com Magazine for songwriters; features; interviews; reviews; events listings; Nashville based; lyric writing competition; links.

An Online Course in Songwriting www.euronet.nl/users/menke/songs.html Free online course; links to individual lessons.

Austin Songwriters Group www.austinsongwriter.org Regional songwriters organization.

Baltimore Songwriters Association www.electrobus.com/bsa Regional songwriters organization.

Barbara Cloyd www.barbaracloyd.com Hit songwriter, performer, open mic host at Nashville's Bluebird Cafe, songwriting teacher, consultant, and workshop host; *Ready for the Row* classes, critiques, and consultation for songwriters.

Beaird Music Group www.beairdmusicgroup.com Nashville-based demo studio; Larry Beaird, owner, guitarist; testimonials; online order form.

Beth Nielsen Chapman www.bethnielsenchapman.net Prolific Nashville-based songwriter; career; upcoming performances.

Billboard Song Contest www.billboard.com/bb/songcontest/index.jsp Annual song contest; deadlines, rules; entry form; list of winners.

British Academy of Composers and Songwriters www.britishacademy.co.uk UK songwriters organization; membership; resources.

California Coast Music Camp musiccamp.org Held in July.

Camp Summer Songs www.summersongs.com Weeklong summer camps for songwriters in New York and California started by Penny Nichols; workshops; seminars; critiques; performances; networking; CDs.

Central Oregon Songwriters Association cosa4u.tripod.com Regional songwriters organization.

Chord Coach www.chordcoach.com/songwriting/ Songwriting and chord tips; screen shots.

Chris Austin Songwriting Contest www.merlefest.org/songwritingcontest.htm Annual songwriting contest.

Circle of Songs www.circleofsongs.com Songwriters; live music; workshops; radio.

Club Nashville www.clubnashville.com Radio; artists; songwriting and publishing; record companies; recording and studios; charts; public relations; bluegrass; Americana; Christian and gospel; organizations; publications; archives.

Colorado Music Association www.coloradomusic.org Home page.

Connecticut Songwriters Association www.ctsongs.com Home page.

Cooch Music's Songwriting Contest www.coochmusic.com Amateur songwriting contest; music publisher.

Craft of Songwriting www.craftofsongwriting.com Resources for songwriters; information; links.

Cue Sheet www.cuesheet.net/ Confidential bulletin listing film, TV, and other media projects requiring soundtrack music, composers, songs, library music, or cues; dispatched twice a month by e-mail only to selective subscriber base consisting of music publishers, record labels, music supervisors, composers, songwriters or their managers/agents; researchers based in London and Los Angeles.

Cupit Music www.cupitmusic.com Resources for songwriters.

Dallas Songwriters Association www.dallassongwriters.org Regional songwriters organization; contest.

Denny Martin Music www.dennymartinmusic.com Nashville-based recording and production studio; song demos; recording projects.

Diane Warren www.realsongs.com Prolific songwriter of popular music.

District of Columbia Songwriters Association of Washington www.saw.org Home page.

Eccentric Software www.eccentricsoftware.com A Zillion Kajillion Rhymes and Cliches.

ElectricEarl.com www.electricearl.com/mlinks09.html Songwriting and publishing music links.

Enormous Records Songwriting Contest www.enormousrecords.com/Contest.htm Outlet for singers and songwriters to promote original pop, rock, jazz, country, bluegrass, rhythm and blues, urban, alternative, and more.

Exit In www.exit-in.com Nashville club in Vanderbilt University area; Billy Block's Western Beat; Roots Revival; writer's night.

Fort Worth Songwriter's Association www.fwsa.com Regional songwriters organization.

Frank Brown International Songwriters Festival www.fbisf.com Annual event in Perdido Key, Florida, in November; songwriters; venues; schedule.

Georgia Music Industry Association, Inc. www.gmia.org Home page.

Get Lyrics www.getlyrics.com Full album lyrics.

Glade's Songwriter Page www.zapcom.net/~glade For songwriters.

Goodnight Kiss Music www.goodnightkiss.comcontest.html Janet Fisher; products; contests; newsletter; film and TV placements.

Guild of International Songwriters and Composers www.songwriters-guild.com Member services; copyright assistance; song critiques; demos; publishing.

Harlan Howard www.harlanhoward.com Country music songwriter; hundreds of hits; publishing company in Nashville, TN.

Harriet Schock www.harrietschock.com Hit singer songwriter based in Los Angeles; correspondence courses; workshops; performances; author of *Becoming Remarkable;* CDs; links.

Hitquarters www.hitquarters.com Source of information for songwriters, artists, musicians, and producers; online directory of record company A & Rs, managers, publishers, and producers.

Independent Songwriter www.independentsongwriter.com Online magazine for songwriters.

Inspirations for Songwriters groups.yahoo.com/group/DIFS/ E-newsletter dedicated to songwriters; helpful hints; links; written by Ande Rasmussen.

International Songwriters Association (ISA) www.songwriter.co.uk Songs and songwriting; *The Songwriter* founded in 1967; published by the ISA.

International Songwriting Competition www.songwritingcompetition.com Entry form; rules; judges.

Irene Jackson's Songwriting Workshop www.irenejackson.com Tips; links to relevant sites; post lyrics or discuss songwriting on the songwriting board; tools.

Jai Josefs www.jaijomusic.com Author of *Writing Music for Hit Songs; Secrets of Songwriting Success* CD-ROM; workshops; classes; song critiques.

Jason Blume www.jasonblume.com Tips for songwriters; workshops and seminars; critique service; author of *Six Steps to Songwriting Success* and *Inside Songwriting* (Billboard Books); instructional CDs; one of the nation's most successful songwriters and respected songwriting teachers; songs recorded by *The Backstreet Boys, Britney Spears, Collin Raye, John Berry,* and more.

Jeff Mallet's Songwriter Site www.lyricist.com Large collection of useful links and resources for songwriters; FAQ; updates.

John Brahaney www.johnbraheny.com Los Angeles-based songwriting coach; author of *The Craft and Business of Songwriting;* musician; songwriter; performer; recording artist.

Just Plain Folks www.jpfolks.com or www.justplainfolks.org Created by Brian Austin Whitney; online group of over 25,000 songwriters, recording artists, music publishers, record labels, performing arts societies, educational institutions, recording studios and engineers, producers, legal professionals, publicists and journalists, publications, music manufacturers and retailers; helpful resources including mentor program, chat, bulletin board, e-newsletter; regional and national tours.

Kerrville Folk Festival www.kerrville-music.com Kerrville Music Foundation, Kerrville, TX; song school; New Folk.

Kiss This Guy www.kissthisguy.com Archive of misheard lyrics.

Lamb's Retreat for Songwriters www.jdlamb.com Held in Michigan.

Let's Sing It www.letssingit.com Thousands of lyrics to all styles of music.

Li'l Hanks Guide for Songwriters www.halsguide.com Resources for songwriters; newsgroups; links.

Live on the Net www.liveonthenet.com Venue in Nashville broadcasts nightly show called *Live from the Spoke in Nashville;* over the Internet nightly from 8-9 PM CST.

Louisianna Songwriters Association www.lasongwriters.org Regional songwriters organization.

Lyric Crawler www.lyriccrawler.com Lyrics search engine; more than 120,000 songs.

Lyric Find www.lyricfind.com Search database of over 11,000 lyrics.

Lyricalline Songwriting Resource Forum www.lyricalline.com/theforum/index Resources for songwriters; free e-newsletter; forum; radio show; Q&A; interviews; articles; services.

Lyricist Software www.virtualstudiosystems.com Word processor designed for musicians, songwriters, and poets; includes rhyming dictionary, spell checker, thesaurus, album categorization, and more; download.

LyricPro www.lyricpro.com Software for songwriters; archive song titles and ideas; edit lyrics with a rhyming dictionary; track publishers and submissions; create charts.

Lyrics www.lyrics.com Words to songs.

Lyrics Post www.lyricspost.com Large lyrics database.

Lyrics Review www.lyricsreview.com Submit lyrics to be reviewed.

Lyrics Ring tinpan.fortunecity.com/tripper/811 Song lyrics ring; links.

Lyrics World www.lyricsworld.com Index; links to all of the lyrics available at Lyrics World; songs found in *Top 40 Hits of 1930-1999, #1 Songs of 1930-1999, Top Singles by Decade,* and *Artist Collections.*

Marc-Alan Barnette www.marcalanbarnette.com Nashville-based singer-songwriter; Nashville Tours; workshops and seminars; book *Freshman Year in Nashville;* CDs.

MasterWriter www.masterwriter.com CD-ROM; collection of tools for songwriters; rhyming dictionary with over 100,000 entries; pop-culture dictionary with over 11,000 icons of American and World Culture; dictionary containing over 35,000 phrases, idioms, clichés, sayings and word combinations; *Rhymed-Phrases Dictionary* with over 36,000 entries; *Alliterations Dictionary* in existence; *American Heritage Dictionary* and *Roget's II Thesaurus*; state-of-the-art database to keep track of all lyrics, melodies and information related to the songs written; stereo Hard Disk Recorder for recording melodic ideas; Songuard online date-of-creation Song Registration Service; library of over 250 tempo adjustable MIDI Drum Loops; full-function Word Processing; Mac OS and Windows compatible.

Memphis Songwriters' Association www.memphissongwriters.org Regional songwriters organization.

Merriam-Webster Dictionary www.m-w.comhome.htm Online dictionary.

Minnesota Association of Songwriters www.mnsongwriters.org Regional songwriters organization.

MIT Songwriting Club Index web.mit.edu/songwriting/www/index.html List of songwriting clubs.

Muse's Muse www.musesmuse.com Web mistress Jodi Krangle; large archive of songwriting resources, services, tips, and tools; chat; articles; free E-newsletter; reviews; links.

Music Row www.musicrow.com Information for songwriters; industry news and articles; *Row Fax* tip sheet subscriptions; current listings.

Music Theory for Songwriters members.aol.com/chordmaps Questions about chords; music theory.

Musician's News www.musiciansnews.comsinging/ Singing and songwriting news updates.

Nancy Moran www.nancymoran.com Coaching and consulting; workshops; song critiques; co-author of *The Songwriter's Survival Kit.*

NashCamp Songwriting School www.nashcamp.com Songwriter summer camp in Nashville with pro-writers and music industry professionals; week long session of songwriting workshops; networking; performances.

Nashville Convention and Visitors Bureau www.nashvillecvb.com Visitors and Friends; Meeting Professionals; Media.

Nashville Muse www.nashvillemuse.com Weekly Nashville songwriting and music industry events listings; e-newsletter by Doak Turner.

Nashville Publishers Network www.songpublishers.com Dedicated to networking in the Nashville songwriting community.

Nashville Scene www.nashvillescene.com Entertainment newspaper; back issues; classifieds.

Nashville Song Search www.nashvillesongsearch.com Nashville-based song contest benefiting the Crisis Center; online entry form.

Nashville Songwriters Association International (NSAI) www.nashvillesongwriters.com Nonprofit service organization for songwriters of all levels and genres; based in Nashville, TN; annual Spring Symposium; Song Camps; weekly and regional workshops; free song critique service for members; insurance plans; Songwriter Achievement Awards.

Nashville Songwriters Foundation www.nashvillesongwritersfoundation.com Nonprofit foundation, dedicated to honoring and preserving the songwriting legacy of the Nashville Songwriters Hall of Fame; principal purposes are to educate, archive, and celebrate songwriting that is uniquely associated with the Nashville Music Community.

Nashville Video Showcase www.nashvillevideoshowcase.com Airing on Cable TV Channel 19 Nashville, TN and Cable TV Channel 3 Hendersonville, TN.

NashvilleSongService.com www.nashvillesongservice.com Work with lyric writers worldwide to help them accomplish their songwriting goals.

New Music Nashville www.newmusicnashville.com Radio show; audience and affiliate resources.

Northern California Songwriters Association (NCSA) West Coast Songwriters Association www.ncsasong.org Nonprofit; annual conference in September; networking and performance opportunities; workshops; resources; annual songwriting contest.

Number Chart Pro members.aol.com/numchart/ Software for songwriters; Nashville number system.

Oklahoma Songwriters & Composers Association www.oksongwriters.org Regional songwriters organization; annual songwriting contest.

OneLook Dictionaries www.onelook.com Definitions searched by keyword.

Open Directory dmoz.org/Arts/Music/Songwriting/ Songwriting links.

Pamela Phillips-Oland www.pamoland.com Hit songwriter; lyricist; lyric samples; listen to songs; collaboration discussion group; author of *The Art of Writing Great Lyrics* and *The Art of Writing Love Song*; articles.

Pat and Pete Luboff www.writesongs.com Songwriting coaches; authors of *88 Songwriting Wrongs and How to Write Them;* consultation; instruction; workshops.

Pat Pattison www.patpattison.com Lyric writing instructor; author of several books on writing lyrics; links.

Performing Songwriter www.performingsongwriter.com Magazine; current issue; resource center; festivals; competitions; contact information; DIY product reviews.

Performing Songwriters Boot Camp www.performingsongwritersbootcamp.com Workshops; faculty; application; continuing education seminars.

Pitch This Music www.pitchthismusic.com Nashville-based country music tip sheet; sample; subscriptions.

Pittsburgh Songwriters Association trfn.clpgh.orgpsa Regional songwriters organization.

PublishSongs.com www.publishsongs.com Pitch songs; create an account; add songs; songwriter profile; FAQ; traffic stats.

Ralph Murphy's Laws of Songwriting www.ascap.com/nashville/murphy.html Hit songwriter; ASCAP Nashville.

Rhymer www.rhymer.com WriteExpress Online Rhyming Dictionary; word rhyme; end rhymes; last syllable rhymes; double rhymes; beginning rhymes and more.

RhymeWIZARD www.rhymewizard.com Rhyming software for Macintosh and Windows.

Rhymezone.com www.rhymezone.com Online rhyming dictionary; find phrases.

Roget's Thesaurus thesaurus.reference.com Online version of the thesaurus.

Ryman Auditorium www.ryman.com Nashville venue; original home of *The Grand Ol' Opry*.

San Diego NSAI Regional Workshop hometown.aol.com/sdnsai/myhomepage/index.html Regional workshop focusing on the craft and business of songwriting; monthly meetings; special events with prowriters, authors, and industry guests; song critiques; monthly showcase; networking.

Secrets of Songwriting www.secretsofsongwriting.com Book by Susan Tucker featuring interviews with successful songwriters; essential information and learning tools for songwriters.

Seth Jackson's Songwriting and Music Business Info www.sethjackson.net/ Web site for songwriters; Los Angeles NSAI regional workshop; links.

Singers Looking for Songs www.songmd.com/html/listings/songs.html All genres; contact information.

Software for Songwriters www.musicbusinessstore.com Music contracts; record company software; tour management.

Song Festivals www.songfestivals.com Provides information on the schedules, dates, and locations of many Songwriter Festivals.

Song Planet www.songplanet.com Creation; collaboration; community.

Song Rights www.songrights.com Song rights; legal aspects of songwriting; topics; summary; reviews; ninety-six-page soft bound primer on legal issues facing songwriters.

Songbook.net www.songbook.net Information and resources for songwriters; links.

SongCatalog.com www.songcatalog.com Post and pitch songs online; license songs to film and TV projects.

SongCraft www.songcraft.com Kerrville New Folk winner Mike Brandon; resources; links.

SongCritic.com www.songcritic.com Register; listen and review song lyrics; shop; chat; advertise; FAQ; artist area.

Songfile.com www.songfile.com Harry Fox Agency song licensing; online form.

SongLink International www.songlink.com Tip sheet publication; international listings for all types of music and artists; listings include the artist, label, style of music needed, and contact information for each pitch; pitch instructions.

Songplayer www.songplayer.com Learn guitar and keyboards for songwriters; musical instrument tutor to use with CD collection; uses simple graphics to illustrate, beat by beat, each chord and lick in the song.

Songpluggers.com www.songpluggers.com: Mission is to provide publishers and songwriters with personal and affordable representation in Nashville, Los Angeles, New York, and Canada; monthly retainers are based on numbers of songs.

SongRamp.com www.songramp.com New music community focused on the creative aspects of music; a place where songs and songwriters can advance based upon their merit; much of the site is geared toward creating income opportunities for independent artists and songwriters by bringing them closer to their fans; features designed to allow members to develop relationships with a broad range of people in the industry from fans to record labels; owned and operated by Bondware Inc., an entrepreneurial company based in Nashville, Tennessee.

SongRepair.com www.songrepair.com Songwriter and song development service; song demos; song reviews; Nashville happenings.

Songs Alive www.songsalive.org How to get started in the music business; nonprofit organization dedicated to the nurturing, support, and promotion of songwriters and composers worldwide; founded by Gilli Moon.

Songs for Sale www.songsforsale.co.uk Online music publisher.

Songs Wanted www.songswanted.com Germany's leading song casting publication for professional songwriters and music publishers.

SongScope.com www.songscope.com Online independent songwriter song shopping catalog; open to all songwriters; list individual songs or catalogs; critiques.

SongShop.net www.songshop.net Song finder; news; publishers; authors; register; enables authors and publishers to present songs to the international music business; provides an easy and effective tool for searching specific song material for producers, music managers, and A&Rs.

SongU.com www.songu.com Songwriting courses online; created by Danny Arena and Sara Light, co-authors of *The Songwriter's Survival Kit*; resources; song evaluations; Yearbook Page.

Songwriter Products www.songwriterproducts.com Learning tools; business and career packages; duplication; legal reference materials; supplies.

Songwriter Universe www.songwriteruniverse.com Founded by Dale Kawashima; information; resources; links; services for songwriters; song critiques; seminars.

Songwriters Directory www.songwritersdirectory.com Share talent and market songs; comprehensive reference tool and songwriter database; opportunities for recording artists to find songs, producers to find new music for movies and television and record labels to find new artists.

Songwriters on Songwriting home.earthlink.net/~zollo/song.htm Book by Paul Zollo; Da Capo Press.

Songwriters Resource at Writers Write www.writerswrite.com/songwriting Information for songwriters.

Songwriters Resource Network www.songpro.com News and information for songwriters; current articles on songwriting and the music business.

Songwriters, Composers, and Lyricists Association (SCALA) users.senet.com.au/~scala/homepage.htm Perspectives on songwriting.

Songwriting Articles mattressemporium.com/dave/songwriting.htm Songwriting and lyric writing; articles; links; songwriters toolbox; newsletters; tips and more.

Songwriting Consultants Ltd. www.songmd.com Molly-Ann Leikin; songwriting consultant.

Songwriting Software www.songwriting-software.com Songwriting items, programs, and services designed to enhance songwriting development; explains and shares songwriting software programs, tools, and resources.

Songwriting.org newsome.orgcgi-bin/ultimatebb.cgi Message and lyric critique board.

SongwritingIdeas.com Lisa Aschmann's book *500 Songwriting Ideas for Brave and Passionate People*; bio; CDs; chord charts; lyrics; links.

Steve Seskin www.steveseskin.com Hit songwriter; seven #1 hit songs; performer; songwriting teacher; CDs; gigs; online press kit.

TAXI www.taxi.com Independent A&R Vehicle; connects unsigned artists, bands, and songwriters with major record labels, publishers, and film and TV music supervisors; biweekly listings in all genres; song critiques; related links; free annual TAXI Road Rally in Los Angeles, CA, in November; Michael Laskow, founder.

Tennessee Songwriters Association International www.clubnashville.com/tsai.htm Pitch a publisher night; pro rap night; critique night; legend series; awards banquet.

The Bluebird Café www.bluebirdcafe.com Famous Nashville venue for songwriters; writer's nights; open mic; guest performers.

The Boston Songwriters Workshop www.bostonsongwriters.org Regional songwriters organization.

The Chicago Songwriters Collective www.chicagosongwriters.com Regional songwriters organization.

The Female Singer/Songwriter Web Ring www.geocities.com/sunsetstrip/backstage/9036 For female musicians.

The Great American Song Contest www.GreatAmericanSong.com Entry form; rules; prizes.

The Guild of International Songwriters & Composers www.songwriters-guild.co.uk/ International songwriting organization based in England.

The Hitmaker Archive: Burt Bacharach www14.brinkster.com/hitmaker/ Links; lyrics; guestbook; discography.

The John Lennon Songwriting Contest www.jlsc.com Check for updates on the current year's contest; winners; prizes; print contest application.

The L.A. Songwriters Network www.SongNet.org Network; showcase; links; e-mail group.

The Lyrics Library tinpan.fortunecity.com/blondie/313 Links to many different lyric Web sites.

The Original Songwriters Showcase www.showcaselondon.co.uk London songwriter showcase; weekly.

The Poindexter www.poindexter.com Unfortunately, Rex is no longer with us; he passed away on Jan. 23rd, 2004; condolences to his family and friends and pray that his spirit and music live on.

The Song Site www.thesongsite.com Unsigned songs for artists.

The Songwriters Association of Washington www.saw.org Regional songwriters organization.

The Songwriters Collaboration Network www.songmd.com/html/network.html Hosted by Molly-Ann Leikin; monthly contest; consultation; correspondence course.

The Songwriters Connection www.journeypublishing.com Resources for songwriters; information; newsletter; books.

The Songwriters Guild of America (SGA) www.songwriters.org Membership; SGA songwriter's contract; educational workshops; regional offices and events.

The Songwriters Tip Jar www.songwriterstipjar.com Free e-newsletter; resources; links; forum.

The Stage Hand www.thestagehand.com Songwriters Area; Songwriters Stage; Performers Area; Columnists; links.

The USA Songwriting Competition www.songwriting.net Annual competition; deadline May 31; fifteen categories, including lyrics only; see Web site for updates, contest rules, prizes, winners, and more.

Thesaurus www.link.cs.cmu.edu/lexfn Find the right word(s).

Tune Tools www.tunetools.com Career resources for songwriters; articles; books; interviews; song evaluation; demo service; forum.

Tunesmith.net www.tunesmith.net Song critique forum; seminar info; latest news; Radio Tunesmith; spotlight writers; chat.

UK Songwriting Contest www.songwritingcontest.co.uk/ Entry form; prizes; FAQ.

Unisong: Passport for a Musical Planet www.unisong.com Created by songwriters, for songwriters; to unite a world community bonded by the creation of music; international songwriter resource links; annual international song contest.

Virginia Organization of Composers and Lyricists www.vocalsongwriter.org/index.php Songwriter organization.

Washington Area Music Association www.wamadc.com Regional organization.

Webster's Dictionary www.m-w.com/dictionary.htm Look up words online.

Whole Picture Music www.wholepicturemusic.com J. L. Wallace; credentials; songs; services; talent search; products; music critiquing and production.

Windrift Songwriting competition windriftmusic.com/2003/ Sponsors and prizes; judges; rules; entry form; FAQs.

Write Hit Songs www.writehitsongs.com *Songwriting Kit* Book and CD-ROM; *Arrange 'n Mix.*

WritingSongs.com www.writingsongs.com Writing music; songs; lyrics; information; links.

Yahoo Directory: Songwriting dir.yahoo.com/Entertainment/Music/Compositio n/Songwriting/ Links to songwriting Web sites.

Yahoo Groups: Songwriting dir.groups.yahoo.com/dir/Music/Songwriting?sh ow_groups=1 Join any of a number of songwriting groups.

Your First Cut www.yourfirstcut.com Questionnaire; sample book chapters from *Your First Cut—A Step by Step Guide to Getting There* by Jerry Vandiver and Gracie Hollombe; forum; newsletter; links; news and reviews.

Stringed Instruments — Violin — Viola — Cello — Bass — Harp

About the Violin www.nelson.planet.org.nz/~matthew/cbt.html The violin and its history.

Amateur Chamber Music Players www.acmp.net/ Nonprofit association that facilitates informal playing and singing by people of all ages and nationalities, beginners to professionals; 5,400 members come from every corner of the earth and share the love of making music with others.

American Federation of Violin and Bow Makers www.afvbm.com Members; tips; programs.

American Harp Society www.harpsociety.org Local chapters; awards and competitions.

American School of Double Bass www.asodb.com Clinics; retreat; books; recordings; facilities.

American String Teachers Association www.astaweb.com Member benefits; resources; events; jobs.

American Viola Society www.americanviolasociety.org Membership; local chapters; join.

Berg Bows www.bergbows.com Bows.

Bernard Ellis www.ellisium.cwc.net Handmade early string instruments; supply worldwide to professional and amateur musicians, museums, cultural foundations, and university departments.

Bowed Electricity www.lightbubble.com/bowed/ Electric violin players, makers, and resources.

Cello Classics www.celloclassics.com CDs; news; reviews; distribution.

Cello Heaven www.celloheaven.com Biographies; composers; history and construction; books; lessons; teachers database; image galary.

Cellos2go.com www.cellos2go.com Buying and renting; accessories.

Chamber Music America www.chamber-music.org Membership; programs; events.

Double Bass Links Page www.gollihur.com/kkbass/basslink.html Over 700 links.

Double Bassist www.doublebassist.com Music magazine for double bass teachers, students, players, and makers.

Harpress of California www.harpress.com Harp sheet music, instructional books, recordings, and videos.

International Society of Bassists www.ISBworldoffice.com./ Events; convention; publications.

International Violin Company www.internationalviolin.com Serving the stringed and acoustic industry since 1933; customers include violin and guitar makers, repair people, music stores, schools and universities from around the world.

Internet Cello Society www.cello.org FAQ; What's New; links; newsletter; forums; tips; festivals.

Internet Resources for Double Bass Pedagogy users.lvcm.com/mariani/bass/ Setting up the instrument; fundamentals; right and left hand.

Ithaca Stringed Instruments www.ithacastring.com Home builder of custom guitars, violins, violas, and cellos; product catalog; articles; reviews; contact information.

Johnson String Instruments www.johnson-inst.com Violins, violas, cellos, and their bows; new and antique violins, violas, bows, and cellos; online catalog; repairs and rentals.

Jordan Electric Violins www.jordanmusic.com Electric violins; electric violas; electric cellos; electric basses.

Lashof Violins.com www.lashofviolins.com Care and maintenance of string instruments.

Making a Double Bass homepages.enterprise.net/gwyllum/bass/doubleba ssmaking.html Information; links.

Meisel Stringed Instruments www.meiselmusic.com Meisel; Mittenwald; Mozart; Spitfire; Skyinbow; GIG Stands; Innovation Strings; Pyramid Syntha-Core.

New Directions Cello Association www.newdirectionscello.com/default.html Festival; store; links.

Orchestras www.music.indiana.edu/music_resources/orchestr .html Links to orchestra Web sites.

Otto Musica U.S.A. Inc. www.ottomusica.com Violin bows; violin cases; cello cases; violin strings; violin shoulder rests; violin rosin; violins; cellos; recorders.

PBS Great Performances www.pbs.org/wnet/gperf/shows/artofviolin/artofv iolin.html The Art of Violin; flash video; links.

Perfekt Noten Fingerboard Labels for Violin
www.perfektnoten.com Labels to help reinforce
correct finger positions on the fingerboard.

Rugeri Music Teaching Methods
www.rugeri.com/ru_pub/english/instrumente_e.h
tml Teaching literature for strings.

Shar Music www.sharmusic.com Online violin shop;
sheet music for stringed instruments.

Southwest Strings www.swstrings.com Music
products; strings; sheet music.

String Works www.stringworks.com Violin sales and
rentals.

Stringnet www.stringnet.com String instruments;
violin; viola; cello; bass; bows and accessories.

Strings Magazine www.stringsmagazine.com All
things strings.

Super-Sensitive Musical String Company
www.supersensitive.com Strings and accessories
for bowed instruments.

Suzuki Violin Teachers Central www.suzuki-
violin.com Teachers directory; forum; teaching
points.

Tempest Music www.violin-world.com/sheetmusic
Classical specialist; music and accessories for
stringed instruments.

The Cello Handbook www.cellohandbook.com
Instruction book.

The Cello Page home.thirdage.com/Music/cellomar/
All about the cello.

The Double Bass and Violone Internet Archive
www.earlybass.com Articles; links; resources.

The Harp www.s-
hamilton.k12.ia.us/antiqua/harp.htm Information
on the harp.

The Harp Column www.harpcolumn.com Webzine;
CD reviews; interviews.

The Harp Mall www.harpmall.com Internet link to
the harp world.

The Harp Page www.tns.lcs.mit.edu/harp/harp.html
Harp information; links to harp publications and
events; harps in the news and on the Web.

The Historical Harp Society tns-
www.lcs.mit.edu/harp/HHS/ History;
conferences; workshops; members.

The Internet Cello Society www.cello.org Links to
amateur and professional cellists; cello news
groups, articles, auditions, and job openings.

The Joy of Cello Playing www.wimmercello.com
Harry Wimmer; studio tour; books; links.

The String Pedagogy Notebook
www.uvm.edu/~mhopkins/ Resource for teachers
and performers.

The Viola Web Site www.viola.com Portal for
violists on the Web.

The Violin Society of America www.vsa.to/
Membership; conventions; competitions;
journal.

The Violin Tutor www.theviolintutor.com Practice
software for Windows.

The Virtu Foundation www.virtufoundation.org
Mission is to give every child access to music
through string music teaching programs.

Thomastik-Infeld Vienna www.thomastik-infeld.com
Dominant perlon violin strings.

Viola da Gamba Society of America vdgsa.org Not-
for-profit national organization dedicated to the
support of activities relating to the viola da
gamba in the United States and abroad; society of
players, builders, publishers, distributors,
restorers and others sharing a serious interest in
music for viols, and other early bowed string
instruments.

Violin Acoustics
www.phys.unsw.edu.au/~jw/violindex.html
Basics; publications.

Violin Making www.centrum.is/hansi/ Sound;
construction; care and maintenance; pictures.

Violin Online www.violinonline.com Music and
instruction for all ages.

Violin Scale Charts option-
wizard.com/vsc/violin_scale_charts.shtml Finger
positions for major and minor scales and
arpeggios.

Violin-World www.violin-world.com Stringed
instruments; violin; viola; cello; double bass;
strings; bows; cases; sheet music; online store
and catalog; announcements; classifieds; teachers
directory; sound advice; articles; music jokes.

Virtuoso www.webcom.com/virtvirt/ Practice tools
for string players.

Wood Violins www.markwoodmusic.com Fretted or
fretless vipers; electric violins.

Yahoo Directory: Classical Violinists
dir.yahoo.com/Entertainment/Music/Artists/By_
Genre/Classical/By_Instrument/Violin/ Links to
Web sites.

Zeta Music Systems www.zetamusic.com Violins;
basses; cellos; violas; amps.

Vocal Music—Choral
and Opera—Singing

Academic Choir Apparel www.academicapparel.com
Choir robes.

A-Cappella www.a-cappella.com Order online;
RealAudio.

America Sings www.americasings.org Home page.

American Choral Directors Association (ACDA)
www.ACDAonline.org News; about ACDA;
officers; staff; chapters: divisions, states,
students; *Choral Journal;* national convention;
division conventions; repertoire and standards;
membership form; member services; online
store.

American Karaoke Society www.karaokesociety.com Membership; Labor Day Weekend Talent Search; Karaoke equipment; pictures; Nashville-based.

Anyone Can Sing www.singtome.com Articles and tips; links; advice column; monthly newsletter.

Aria Database www.aria-database.com Quick search; arias; operas; composers; roles; diverse collection of information on over 1,000 operatic arias; for singers and nonsingers; includes translations and aria texts of most arias; collection of MIDI files of operatic arias and ensembles.

Audio-Technica www.audio-technica.com Microphones.

Barbershop Harmony www.spebsqsa.org Locate a barbershop quartet or barbershop chorus; find arrangements and songbooks; purchase CDs and videos.

Center for Voice Disorders www.bgsm.edu/voice/singing.html Singers and singing.

Choir and Organ Classical Music Magazine www.orphpl.com/choir.htm Religious; secular; choral; reviews; news; events.

Choral Clewes Vocal Music Instruction Series www.choralclewes.com For teachers, choral directors, home schoolers, and professional singers.

Choral Music home.att.net/~langburn Information on over one hundred published compositions and arrangements; accompanied and a cappella; mixed and treble; sacred and secular; reviews; performances; repertoire suggestions; ordering tips.

ChoralNet www.choralnet.org Internet launching point for all choral music; collection of links including reference and research resources; database for choral repertoire, events, and performances; news; Web message boards; worldwide directory of choirs on the Web; archives; e-mail lists; support.

ChoralWeb www.choralweb.com Publisher of vocal music and more.

Choristers Guild www.choristersguild.org Home page.

Classical Singer www.classicalsinger.com For singers of classical music.

Classical Vocal Rep www.classicalvocalrep.com Vocal music books.

Classical Vocal Repertoire www.classicalvocalrep.com The Web site of classical vocal reprints.

DigiTech www.digitech.com Vocal harmony and effects processors.

EatSleepMusic www.eatsleepmusic.com Online Karaoke; contests; free downloads; player; links; children's sing-along music.

Global Voices in Song www.globalvoicesinsong.com CD-ROM for vocal music instruction.

Healthy Voice www.healthwindows.com Tips on developing and maintaining a healthy voice.

I'm Not Crazy, I'm Vocalizing! www.vocalizing.com Vocal coach Karen Oleson; VoiceTech; instructional CDs, cassettes, and books.

International Vocalist www.vocalist.org Resource and database for singers.

ISong.com www.isong.com Accompaniment tracks.

Jeannie Deva www.storesonline.com/site/444991/page/69906 Los Angeles voice studios.

Karaoke Scene www.KaraokeScene.com Club directory; articles; forum; magazine.

Karaoke Studio www.koolkaraokestudio.com Software for Karaoke.

KJPro Karaoke Software www.kjpro.com *KJ Pro* Windows program for creating karaoke songbooks.

La Scala lascala.milano.it/ World's most famous opera house.

Learn to Sing! www.inachord.to Voice lessons with Dave and Shalee; eight simple lessons in a four-CD set for men and women.

Lisa Popeil—The Total Singer www.popeil.com Video course for all styles and levels.

MacroMusic's Online Vocal Music Store www.macromusic.com/store/ Vocal music titles; free voice lessons.

Medicine in the Vocal Arts www.bgsm.edu/voice/ Vocal training.

Metropolitan Opera www.metopera.org/home.html Schedules of upcoming presentations and performer bios; online version of the opera quiz.

Metropolitan Opera Broadcasts www.metopera.org/broadcast International radio broadcasts; telecast series.

National Association of Teachers of Singing www.nats.org Home page; membership; resources; links.

Neumann www.neumann.com Microphones.

New York City Opera www.nycopera.com Opera company.

Opera America www.operaam.org Information about opera in the United States; schedules; service organization supporting the creation, presentation, and enjoyment of opera.

Opera Composers lucia.stanford.edu/opera/composers.html For composers listed in the main index there are either complete opera lists, with date and place of premiere or time of composition if known, or links to individual pages providing information.

Opera News www.operanews.com News on opera-related features and events.

Operabase www.operabase.com Schedules; venues; festivals; reviews; links.

Optimal Breathing for Singing www.breathing.com Manual with exercises for the singing voice.

Pocket Songs www.pocketsongs.com Instrumental track sing-along CDs and cassettes of popular music and standards; large catalog.

Primarily A Cappella Catalog www.singers.com Specializing in a cappella recordings, videos, and vocal arrangements in all styles, including vocal jazz, gospel, choral, doo-wop, folk, barbershop, and contemporary.

ProSing www.prosing.com *Top & Country Hits Today; Legends; Monster Hits; Star Disk; Baseline; Sound Choice Pioneer; Music Maestro; Sun Fly; Dick; Vocopro; Gemini; RSQ; JVC; Venturer; Audio 2000.*

Secrets of Singing by Jeffrey Allen www.vocalsuccess.com Vocal method; books; videos; tips; links; order online.

Seth Riggs www.sethriggs.com Camp; resume; clients; instructors; Speech Level Singing.

Showoffs Studio www.nefsky.com For performers; singing classes; workshops; talent showcase.

Shure www.shure.com Manufacturer of microphones.

Sing Your Life www.singyourlife.com Self-teaching manual emphasizing vocal strength and endurance.

Singer Magazine www.singermagazine.com Resources; subscribe; DISCoveries.

Singing for Money members.aol.com/ifsnet/sfmhome.html Singer's resource.

Singing for the Soul www.singingforthesoul.com Singing lessons on tape.

Singing Store www.singingstore.com Everything for the singer; tracks.

Singing Voice www.worldzone.net/music/singingvoice/ Anatomy; history; links.

SongXpress www.songxpress.com Classic Blues; Classic Rock; Modern Rock.

Sound Choice www.soundchoice.com Accompaniment tracks for singers.

The Academy of Vocal Arts www.avaopera.com Academic program; theater.

The Choral Public Domain Library www.cpdl.org Devoted exclusively to free choral sheet music; over 230 contributors and 5,000 scores.

The Gregorian Chant Home Page silvertone.princeton.edu/chant_html Links to chant sites; Medieval music theory sites; resources for chant performance; ecclesiastical, historical, humanistic, and information sciences.

The Metropolitan Chorus www.metchorus.org The 100-voice Metropolitan Chorus presents concerts featuring music of great variety, spanning time from the Renaissance to the twentieth century; strong emphasis on American composers.

The Silvis Woodshed www.channel1.com/users/gsilvis/ Collection of MIDI files and tools to help singers learn

The Singer's Workshop www.thesingersworkshop.com Professional singing coach Lis Lewis; background singing; session singing; The Charisma Factor; tips for the aspiring singer; breath control; articles on preparing for the stage; finding the right voice teacher; Los Angeles-based.

Vocal Instruction www.vocalinstruction.com Extend the range of your voice.

Vocal Music-Choral and Opera library.usask.ca/subjects/music/vocal.html Resource page for choirs and choir conductors; links to American Choral Directors Association; The Aria Database; CHORALNET homepage; Classical MIDI with words; Digital Tradition Folksong (texts of folksongs); Gregorian Chant; International Lyrics Server; Good for folk-song lyrics; Libretto Homepage; Lied and Song Texts page; Metropolitan Opera Broadcasts; Opera Links; Opera Navigation Center; Song Index.

Vocal Power Academy www.vocalpowerinc.com Elisabeth Howard's Vocal Power Method; vocal training; proper breathing techniques; singing lessons; performance workshops; seminars; private lessons; books; CDs; videos.

Vocal Visions www.vocalvisions.net Jazz vocalist and coach Ellen Johnson; workshops; warm-up book and CD; performances.

Vocalist.org www.vocalist.org.uk/index.html Articles; careers; databases; links; resources for singers and teachers.

Voice Lesson www.voicelesson.com Mark Baxter's in-depth knowledge and unique approach to vocal improvement; *The Rock and Roll Singers Survivor Manual.*

Voice Teachers www.voiceteachers.com Find a teacher; add a new teacher; listed by state.

Voice-Craft Electronics Co.; Ltd. www.voice-craft.com.tw Voice-Craft; Dynasonic.

Vorton Technologies www.vorton.com Eat Sleep Music Network; Karaoke.

Yodeling Instructional Video www.yodelers.com Intended to help find natural yodel voice break.

You Can Sing with Impact! www.singwithimpact.com Daily warm-up workout.

World Music—International— Ethnomusicology

200 International Music Links ingeb.org/midimidi.html Links and MIDI files to countries and ethnic music.

4Arabs Music www.4arabs.com/music/ RealAudio files of Arabic music to download; Arabic tapes and CDs; online forum for discussing Arabic music.

Africa Sounds www.africasounds.com Music concerts and cultural events.

Africa1.com www.africa1.com World music radio.

African Music and Dance Ensemble www.cnmat.berkeley.edu/~ladzekpo/ Web site for African music.

African-American Mosaic lcWeb.loc.gov/exhibits/african/intro.html African American history and culture.

Afrojazz www.afrojazz.com Promotes talent, originality, social and cultural respect; alternative and new music from all around the world.

Ancient-Future.Com: World Music Online www.ancient-future.com World music movement; traditional world music education; global music and dance forums.

Arab Music trumpet.sdsu.edu/M151/Arab_Music1.html Major influences; assimilated cultures; Medieval Europe; structure of modern-day Arabic music including maqam and iqa.

Arabic Music Info Source members.aol.com/amisource Resource for Arabic music.

Archives of African American Music and Culture www.indiana.edu/~aaamc African American music; links.

Archives Resource Community archive-india.org Worldwide forum for audiovisual archives of expressive culture.

Arts, Culture, and Music in India www.Webindia.com/india/music.htm Art forms and entertainment in India; classical music and dance, movies, theater, photography; links.

Belly Dance Home Page www.bdancer.com Local features; schedule of dancers; FAQ; educational.

Bhargava & Co. www.indianmusicals.com Indian musical instruments.

Big Sky World of Chinese Musical Instruments www.bigskymusic.com Instruments of the classic Chinese orchestra including four sections: the bowed strings, plucked strings, winds, and percussion.

Blissco www.blisscorporation.com Italian electronic and dance music company; brings together DJs and musicians.

Books on Music of India www.vedamsbooks.com/music.htm Annotated catalog of books on various aspects of music of India; detailed descriptions.

California Newsreel-African American Music and Cultural History www.newsreel.org/aamusics.htm Videos on African American music.

California Worldfest www.worldmusicfestival.com Mission is to present incredible music and dance along with fine food and quality crafts for the whole family; children's program and music and dance workshops are included.

Celtic Music.com www.celticmusic.com Celtic music Web site; MP3s.

Center for Music of the Andes otto.cmr.fsu.edu/~cma/andes.htm Brief history and information about Andean music.

Center for World Music www.centerforworldmusic.org World music center based in San Diego, CA.

Ceolas Celtic Music Archive www.ceolas.org/ceolas.html Celtic music Web site; tunes; tunebooks.

Chandra's-Middle Eastern Belly Dance Supplies www.chandras.com Catalog of Belly dance and Middle Eastern dance supplies; music; costumes and more.

Classical Music of St.Petersburg, Russia www.classicalmusic.spb.ru All about classical music in St. Petersburg; concert halls; musical theaters; musicians; Russian composers; classical MP3; Russian musical links.

Condor Records www.condorrecords.com World music with free audio samples; Andean and Native American music.

Coyne Celtic Imports www.coyneceltic.com Celtic music Web site; bagpipe accessories.

Culturekiosque www.culturekiosque.com Cultural topics; articles in different languages.

Djembe Online www.djembe.dk Scandinavian forum for cross-culture and world music; African and Latin American culture debate; world music record reviews; film and book reviews.

Ethnomusicology Links www.lib.washington.edu/music/world.html Ethnomusicology, folk music, and world music contents.

Ethnomusicology Online research.umbc.edu/eol/eol.html Peer-reviewed multimedia e-journal.

Finnish Music Information Centre www.fimic.fi Finnish music; facts about composers, artists, and groups of contemporary music; folk and world.

Folk Music of England, Scotland, Ireland, Wales, and America www.contemplator.com/folk.html Traditional music; lyrics; tune information; historical background; MIDIs; related links.

France MP3 www.francemp3.com Download site; MP3.

Global Fusion Catalog www.global.fusion.ndirect.co.uk Traditional world music, classical world music, and world fusion music ranging from acoustic English folk, to Latin jazz, to cutting edge dance remixes.

Grooveworks—Art for the Sake of Music—World Music Shirts www.grooveworks.com/shirts.htm Combines music and T-shirt art; African American, Native American, and cultural/political themes on shirts.

Hardanger Fiddle Association of America www.hfaa.org Dedicated to preserving and promoting the Norwegian Hardanger fiddle and related traditions of Norwegian music and dance.

Hawaiian Music 101 tropicaldisc.com/cart/shopcore/?db_name=tropdis k Descriptions of the primary types of Hawaiian music.

Hong Kong Pop Stars huifong.hypermart.net/ Popular music in Hong Kong.

House of Musical Traditions www.hmtrad.com Carry acoustic instruments, accessories, and books from around the world, including rare and exotic instruments.

IMMEDIA! www.immedia.com.au AustralAsian music industry directory.

Indian Classical Music and Dance Kalavant Center www.mightyhost.com/kalavant Works to preserve and help foster growth and innovations in Indian music and dance.

Indian Music Glossary www.chandrakantha.com/tablasite/glossary.htm Glossary of terms used in Indian music.

International Charts d1.dir.scd.yahoo.com/entertainment/music/charts/ countries/ Best selling music in countries all over the world.

International Music Archives www.eyeneer.com/World/index.html Music and musical instruments of the world; articles and pictures; categorized geographically.

Irish Music Box www.dojo.ie/musicbox Online resource for Irish music.

Irish Music Magazine mag.irish-music.net/ or www.mayo-ireland.ie/irishmusic.htm Monthly folk and traditional Irish music magazine from Ireland; published on paper with some articles online.

Irish World Music Centre www.ul.ie/~iwmc University of Limerick; set up in 1994 by Dr. Mícheál Súilleabháin.

Italia Mia-Italian Music www.italiamia.com/music.html Italian music Web sites.

JewishMusic.com www.jewishmusic.com Jewish music books; software; videos.

Kabuki for Everyone www.fix.co.jp/kabuki/kabuki.html Traditional form of Japanese theater.

Lo'Jo www.lojo.org World music, concerts, and press kit; French and English.

M.E.L.T. 2000 www.melt2000.com World music; jazz.

Mathers Museum of World Cultures www.indiana.edu/~mathers/home.html Exhibits, events, and educational programs; learn more about objects from Australia to Zanzibar.

Mondomix—Musiques du Monde—World Music www.mondomix.org Un regard actuel et federateur sur les musiques du monde; retrouvez tous les artistes, les labels, les medias, les concerts, et les festivals de world music.

Moroccan Music www.moroccanmusic.com Music of Morocco.

Music from the Faroe Islands www.framtak.com/fo_music/spaelimen.html CDs; ballads; original music and new arrangements of traditional Faronese tunes.

Music India OnLine www.musicindiaonline.com Updates; mailing list; Real Player G2 required to hear songs listed.

Music of the World www.musicoftheworld.com Independent record label that produces high quality recordings of traditional and contemporary world music.

Musica Russica www.musicarussica.com Russian choral music.

Musical Instruments of the World www.eyeneer.com/World/Instruments/ Brief articles and pictures of various primitive instruments.

Musicanews www.musicanews.com Italian music Webzine.

Musicfinland.com www.musicfinland.com/classical Finnish classical music scene.

NativeWeb www.nativeWeb.org Information of interest to indigenous peoples; seeks to represent all indigenous peoples of the planet.

New Music Express Charts www.nme.com/charts Music magazine from England; cutting edge music.

New World Music www.newworldmusic.com Online retailer of world music CDs.

Oud Home Page www.kairarecords.com/oudpage/Oud.htm Information about the Middle-Eastern lute, oud or ud.

Putumayo World Music www.putumayo.com Established in 1993 to introduce people to the music of other cultures; label grew out of the Putumayo clothing company founded by Dan Storper in 1975 and sold in 1997; known primarily for its upbeat and melodic compilations of great international; CD covers feature the art of Nicola Heindl, whose colorful, folkloric style represents one of Putumayo's goals: to connect the traditional to the contemporary and to create products that people love; combines appealing music and visuals while supporting its releases with creative retail promotions and marketing;

has developed a reputation as one of the industry's most innovative companies.

Rampant Scotland Directory—Music and Dance www.rampantscotland.com/music.htm Scottish music and dance.

RootsWorld www.rootsworld.com Magazine of world music; roots music; music that defies easy classification.

Russian Independent Music www.gromco.com/music/rim Online guide to Russian independent bands and labels; interviews; sound files; news; Russian record reviews; discussion groups; Russian/American dictionary with translations of music terminology.

Scandinavian Indie www.lysator.liu.se/~chief/scan.html Internet guide to Scandinavian independent music.

Swedish Music Festivals www.musikfestivaler.se From spring to autumn there are festivals throughout Sweden; folk music, chamber music, opera, jazz, or choral music; program folder available in Swedish, English, and German.

The Irish Traditional Music Archive www.itma.ie/home/itmae1.htm Reference archive and resource center for the traditional song, music, and dance of Ireland.

The Music of East Asia www.eyeneer.com/World/Ea/index.html Essay analyzing the development of music in this region; emphasis on Chinese music.

The Society for Ethnomusicology www.ethnomusicology.org Founded in 1955 to promote the research, study, and performance of music in all historical periods and cultural contexts; more than 2,000 members from six continents.

The Ultimate Ethnic Musical Instruments Source josh.bakehorn.net/store.html Ethnic instruments.

Traditional World Music Influences in Contemporary Solo Piano Literature www.scarecrowpress.com/Catalog/SingleBook.sht ml?command=Search&db=^DB/CATALOG.db&eq SKUdata=0810833808 "Everything But Bach, Beethoven and Brahms," comprises this *multicultural* repertoire guide for pianists, composers, music teachers and students, world music enthusiasts, and scholars; identifies pieces in the contemporary solo piano literature which show world music influences not traditionally associated with the standard repertoire of Western European art music; includes pieces which use or attempt to emulate non-Western scales, modes, folk tunes, rhythmic, percussive or harmonic devices and timbres.

Traditional World Music Recordings www.medieval.org/music/world.html Quick menu; how to buy.

UK-Dance www.uk-dance.org Mailing list for people to discuss everything to do with dance music culture in the UK.

World Beat Planet www.worldbeatplanet.com World music portal.

World Fusion Music Links www.ancient-future.com/links/index.html Links page for the world music and dance movements; traditional and world fusion music.

World Music www.worldmusic.org Nonprofit organization established in 1990; presenter of global culture, featuring music and dance from the far and near corners of the globe; CRASHarts, Boston's new performing arts series, is a division of World Music, Inc.

World Music Central www.worldmusiccentral.org World music resource; links.

World Music Charts Europe www.wmce.de/ Current charts.

World Music Institute www.heartheworld.org Encourage cultural exchange between nations and ethnic groups; supports traditional music by providing opportunities for visiting and for local artists; presents to the American public the finest in traditional and contemporary music and dance from around the world; collaborates with community organizations and academic institutions in fostering greater understanding of the world's music and dance traditions.

World Music Network www.worldmusic.net/ In-depth information and sound samples of all releases including Rough Guide introductions to music from around the world, fund-raising CDs for Amnesty, Oxfam and New Internationalist, and single artist releases on the Riverboat label.

World Music Press www.worldmusicpress.com Multicultural music books; recordings.

World Music Store www.worldmusicstore.com Multicultural media.

World Music Webcast www.worldmusicwebcast.com Playing music for the global community.

Worldwide Internet Music Resources www.music.indiana.edu/music_resources/ethnic.ht ml National, international, and world music links; extensive list.

Yahoo Directories: World Music http://dir.yahoo.com/Entertainment/Music/World_ Music/ Links to world music Web sites.

5

Tech Talk: Terms A-Z

16x9 or Enhanced for 16x9 Televisions With HDTV (High Definition Television), DVD became the most compatible format with films "enhanced for 16x9 televisions" or "anamorphically enhanced;" HDTV refers to either a digital or analog television set whose aspect ratio is 16:9; extra resolution provided by this kind of transfer can improve an image up to one third; DVDs which are 16x9 enhanced can also be played on regular television sets through a process called "downconverting;" this process adapts the anamorphic image to a standard 4:3 television set; if image of movie appears "squeezed," DVD player is probably set for 16x9 playback for a standard television set; to resolve this problem, with DVD player in "stop" mode, go into basic setup menu and set video option for standard or 4:3 playback.

4-track Cassette multitrack recorder with four tracks.

8-track Cassette multitrack recorder with eight tracks; 1970s car stereo playback device invented by Bill Lear.

A/D Converter Converts an analog sound signal to a digital bitstream.

A2B AT&T's music distribution system.

AAC Advanced Audio Coding; part of MPEG-2; audio compression system with better compression rates than MP3.

AARC Alliance of Artists and Recording Companies.

Absorption Dissipation of sound energy at a surface as the sound changes into heat; absorption of acoustic energy effectively is the inverse of reflection; whenever sound strikes a material, the amount of acoustic energy absorbed, relative to the amount reflected, is expressed as a simple ratio known as the absorption coefficient.

Access Provider Organization that provides access to the Internet via a dial-up account; fee depends on the amount of usage or other individual contract specifications.

Access Speed The speed of an online connection; measured in bits per second (bps); determined by the speed of the modem and the maximum speed allowed by the ISP.

ActiveX Microsoft standard for computer program building blocks known as *objects*.

Ad Banner Graphics that link to an advertiser's Web site; advertisement in the form of a graphic image on the Internet; most banner ads are animated GIF files.

Ad Click The click on an advertisement on a Web site that takes the user to another Web site.

Ad View A Web page that presents an ad or several ads; user may click on after viewing.

ADC Analog-to-digital converter.

Additional Language DVD has a separate audio track with the dialogue dubbed into another language.

ADPCM Adaptive Differential Pulse Code Modulation; a type of digital audio compression that predicts the values of upcoming samples.

ADSL Asymmetric Digital Subscriber Line; technology that transmits data over phone lines faster in one direction than in the other; a type of DSL that sacrifices upload speed for increased download speed.

AES/EBU (**Audio Engineering Society/European Broadcast Union**) **Protocol** Professional transmission protocol that conveys two channels of interleaved digital audio data through a single, two-conductor XLR cable.

AFAIK E-mail acronym meaning "as far as I know."

AIFF Audio Interchange File Format; a type of sound file; a common audio format for the Macintosh; normally uncompressed.

Album Collection of songs with one or more recordings produced as a single unit.

Alignment Adjustment of an analog tape machine's tape head and electronic circuitry to standardize playback and record frequency response and signal levels within industry accepted standards for reasons of compatibility.

Alignment Tape Reference reproduction tape used for aligning analog tape machines.

ALT Alternative hierarchy of Usenet newsgroups.

Amplification Process by which a signal level is increased by a device according to a specific input/output ratio.

Amplitude Distance above or below the centerline of a signal's waveform; the greater the distance or displacement from the centerline, the more intense the pressure variation, electrical signal, or physical displacement within a medium.

Analog In contrast to digital information, which gives precise discrete duplication of each fragment of audio or video information, "analog" refers to the older and traditional method of streaming information for a program directly to the recording format without compression or filtering to ensure the cleanest fidelity; sound or electronic equipment that works with real sound rather than sound that's been transformed into bits and bytes.

Analog Audio Audio represented by a signal that continuously varies; sound that has not been turned into numbers; an analog sound wave can be infinitely variable; digitized sound is limited to discrete values.

Analog-to-Digital (A/D) Converter Device that converts analog signals into digital form.

Anonymous FTP A way of using the FTP program to log on to another computer to copy files without an account on the other computer; enter "anonymous" as the username and the e-mail address as the password.

Applet Small computer program written in the Java programming language embedded in an HTML page; when the page is accessed, the browser downloads the applet and runs it on the computer; applets cannot read or write data onto a computer; applets can only be used if the browser supports Java.

Archive A single file containing a group of files that have been compressed together for efficient storage; must use a program such as PKZIP or Stuffit to get the original files back out.

ARPANET U.S. Department of Defense original ancestor of the Internet.

Article Message someone sends to a newsgroup to be read by those in the newsgroup.

ASCII American Standard Code for Information Interchange; widely used text set that describes up to 255 characters and code points.

ASFS Encoded compressed music file format supported by Virtuosa Gold.

Aspect Ratio Proportional image sizing during enlargement or reduction; expressed as a width-to-height ratio; refers to the length of a movie's horizontal image to the length of its vertical image; a film with a very wide horizontal image, more than twice the size of its vertical height, has an aspect ratio of "2.35:1;" a TV set has an aspect ratio of 1.33:1, so any film presented with a longer horizontal length is in the "widescreen" format; many European and Canadian films have an aspect ratio of 1.66:1, which means only slight black bars are necessary to present the entire film image 1.85:1 is the most common aspect ratio found in theaters and on video, as it adapts easily to all formats; movies filmed in processes called CinemaScope or Cinerama, the aspect ratio may be as wide as 2.55:1.

ASPI A method of accessing a CD-ROM drive; originally developed for SCSI; works well with IDE drives via the ATAPI protocol.

Assistant Engineer Person responsible for microphone and headphone setup, operation of the tape machines, session breakdowns, and for positioning rough mixes on the console for the engineer; larger studios train future staff engineers by having them work as assistant engineers.

Asynchronous Communication that does not depend on two parties talking simultaneously.

ATAPI Protocol used to communicate with non-hard drive IDE devices such as CD-ROMs.

ATM Asynchronous Transfer Mode; high bandwidth technology enabling rapid transmission of large files.

Attachment Computer file attached or "electronically stapled" to an e-mail message.

Attack Initial transient or first part of the envelope of a signal; the beginning of a note.

Attenuate To reduce the signal level.

AU Audio format found on Sun and NeXT computers.

Audio Format Sound recorded on a DVD may be in a number of different formats ranging from mono to Dolby Digital 5.1; the addition of more audio channels as separate streams of sound can increase the realism and dynamic impact of a program.

Audio Spectrum Sound frequencies the human ear can hear, between 20 and 20,000 Hz.

Authentication Technique whereby access to the Internet or Intranet resources requires the user to identify self by entering a username and password; also called "logging in."

Autolocator Feature that enables a specific cue point location on a tape transport to be stored into and recalled from memory; autolocator can shuttle tape to a time point entered by the operator.

Automated Mixdown Enables the console to remember and re-create any settings or changes regarding level and other mix-related functions made by the engineer, while allowing continual improvements until the desired final mix quality is achieved.

Auxiliary Refers to the socket on a sound card that connects with other audio playing devices; also called "line in."

Auxiliary Sends Provide the overall effects or monitor sends of a console; used to create separate and controlled submixes of any or all of the input signals to a mono or stereo output.

AVI Audio Visual Interface; Microsoft graphics standard for compressed movie clips.

Balance Relative level of various instruments within a mix.

Balanced Line Cable having two conductors and a ground connection and often surrounded by a shield; with respect to ground, the conductors are at equal potential but opposite polarity; these lines are often used in professional settings to reduce or eliminate induced noise and interference from external electromagnetic sources.

Bandwidth The measure of a medium's data transfer capability; the transmission capacity of a network or other communications medium.

Bass Trap Used to reduce low-frequency buildup at specific frequencies in a room; low-frequency attenuation devices available in several design types: quarter wavelength trap, pressure zone trap, functional trap, Helmholtz resonator trap.

Baud The number of electrical symbols per second that a modem sends down a phone line; often used as a synonym for bits per second (bps).

BBS Bulletin Board System; electronic message system dialed up directly to read and post messages.

BCC Blind Carbon Copy; BCC addresses get a copy of an e-mail without other recipients knowing about it; usually used for long mailing lists.

Bias Ultrasonic signal mixed with the input signal at the record head of an analog tape recorder to reduce distortion.

Bidirectional (Figure-of-Eight) Microphone Mic sensitive to sounds arriving from on-axis (front) and 180 degrees off-axis (rear); maximum rejection occurring at both sides.

Binary File File that contains information consisting of more than text such as a picture, sounds, a spreadsheet, an archive, or a word processing document.

BinHex File-encoding system popular among Macintosh users.

Bin-Loop High-Speed Duplication High-speed duplication without the duplicated tape being housed in cassette shells; tape is recorded on a reel-to-reel machine; higher quality and better tape handling at high speeds.

Bit Depth Number of bits in a pixel; used to describe a monitor's graphic resolution.

Bit Rate Measured in *kilobits per second* or *Kbps*; number of bits used each second to represent a digital signal; binary digit (either a 1 or a 0); smallest unit of measure for computer data; bits can be *on* or *off* (symbolized by 1 or 0) and are used in various combinations to represent different types of information; amount of data used to hold a given length of music.

Bit(s) Increments of digital data, represented in binary code (0s and 1s); the smallest unit of data in a computer; number of bits corresponds with the amount of information that can be read.

Bitmap Description of images or fonts within a grid of pixels; small dots put together to make a black-and-white or color picture.

BITNET Older network of large computers connected to the Internet.

Black Burst Generator Device that produces an extremely stable timing reference; function of this signal is to precisely synchronize the video frames and time code addresses received or transmitted by every video-related device in a production facility to a specific clocking frequency; process ensures that the frame and address leading edges occur at exactly the same instant in time.

Blumlein Pickup Placement of two coincident bidirectional mics crossed at 90 degrees and aiming 45 degrees left and right of center; named after Alan Dower Blumlein, considered the inventor of stereo.

Board American term for console.

Bookmark Browser feature allowing user to save a link to a Web page; the bookmark is used to return to that page.

Bounce When an e-mail is returned because it could not be delivered to the specified address; returned as "undeliverable" to a bad address.

Bouncing Tracks Commonly used to mix entire performances onto one track, a stereo pair of tracks or several tracks; makes the final mixdown easier by grouping instruments together onto one or more tracks; also opens up needed tape tracks by bouncing similar instrument groups down to one or a stereo pair of tracks, freeing the originally recorded tape tracks for more overdubs.

Boxed Set CD or DVD packages with three or more disks or cassette or video packages with two or more tapes are considered a "boxed set."

bps or **bits per second** Measure of how fast data is transmitted; used to describe modem speed.

Bridge Page Page created to connect a Web site's content and an advertiser's Web site; tracks click-throughs from ad banners.

Broadband Term describing advanced networks that deliver high-speed data access of up to 1,000 times faster than ISDN; used in conjunction with cable modems.

Broadcasting Method of transmitting information; sends the same information to all systems.

Browser or **Web Browser** Software program used to locate and view HTML documents on the Internet; for example, Netscape, Microsoft Explorer.

BTW E-mail acronym meaning "by the way."

Bus Common signal path that routes a signal, throughout a console or connected network, from one or more signal sources to one or more signal destinations.

Byte A set of 8 bits that represent a number from 0 to 255; computer memory is measured in bytes; place for temporary storage of data.

Cable Modem Modem technology that uses standard television cable to deliver increased access speed without a phone dial-up connection.

Cache Hardware or software that speeds up the flow of data.

Cans Slang for headphones.

Cardioid Microphone Common mic pickup pattern designed to attenuate signals arriving 180 degrees off-axis while picking up fully those sounds that arrive at the front on-axis.

Cassette Plastic shell with 1/8 inch analog audio tape in it; invented by Philips in the 1960s; analog format that uses a magnetic film to record audio information.

Cassette Multitrack Recorder Cassette tape recorder, usually with a built-in mixer, with multitrack capabilities; a recording studio in a box.

Cast/Crew Biographies Background information about the actors, directors, and other crew members often included on a DVD.

Categories Motion pictures and other programs each fall under different genres; films may be classified under two or more genres.

CAV Constant Angular Velocity.

CBR Constant Bit-Rate; describes MP3 files where each second of music is compressed to the same size.

CC Carbon Copy. CC addressees get a copy of an e-mail, and the other recipients are informed of this; to send somebody a copy of an e-mail message.

CCIR Center for Communications Research.

CCITT Former name for ITU-T, the committee that sets worldwide communication standards.

CD (Compact Disk) Plastic disk containing optical digital audio information; uses a 44.1 kHz sampling rate with 16 bits of data; uses Pulse Code Modulation (PCM) to convert analog information into digital information.

CDA Compact Disk Audio; refers to the uncompressed encoding method used to store audio on a standard CD.

CD-R Compact Disk-Recordable; a CD that can be recorded only once; drives and media that allow one to make CD-ROMs and audio CDs with a computer.

CD-ROM (Compact Disk, Read-Only Memory or Read-Only Media) Compact disk containing interactive data that can be read by a computer; disk capable of holding as much as 700 MB of any type of computer-based data, including graphics, digital audio, MIDI, text, and raw data; unlike CD Audio disk, CD-ROM is not tied to a specific data format; manufacturer or programmer can specify what is contained on the disk.

CD-RW Compact Disk-Rewritable; a CD that can be recorded and erased multiple times; drives and reusable media that allow one to store data in a CD-like format; cannot be read by normal CD players or CD-ROM drives; most CD-RW drives can also write to CD-R media.

CGI Common Gateway Interface; interface that allows scripts or programs to run on a Web server; CGI-scripts are used to put the content of a form into an e-mail message, to perform a database query, to generate HTML; most popular languages for CGI-scripts are Perl and C.

CGI-BIN Most common name of a directory on a Web server in which CGI-scripts are stored.

Channel In IRC, a group of people chatting together; a major interest area on a service provider one can easily access.

Chanop Channel Operator; in charge of keeping order in a channel in IRC.

Chat Online interactive communication on the Web; "talk" in real time with others in the "chat room"; words are typed instead of spoken; talk (or type) live to other network users from all parts of the world; on the Internet, use Internet Relay Chat (IRC).

Checksum Unique number generated by applying a formula to the contents of a data file; used to determine if a file has been modified or if two files are identical, without directly comparing the files.

Click-Through Rate Percentage of users who click on a viewed advertisement; indicates the effectiveness of the ad.

Client The browser used by a visitor to a Web site; a computer that uses the services of another computer, or *server*.

Client Errors Error occurring due to an invalid request by the visitor's browser.

Client/Server Model A division of labor between computers; computers that provide a service other computers can use are called *servers*; the users are called *clients*.

Clipping The flattening of a waveform peak when it reaches the maximum level.

Closed Caption Most television sets are now designed to include closed captioning, an option which allows dialogue and sound effects to be printed out at the bottom of the screen so the program may also be enjoyed by hearing impaired viewers.

CLV Constant Linear Velocity.

CODEC Compressor/Decompressor; algorithm for encoding and decoding digital information; system to store data in less space.

Color/BW Coloring format; Color refers to items that are displayed in color; BW, B&W, and Black and White refer to items displayed in Black and White.

Commercial Online Service Computer network that offers its members access to its own chat rooms, bulletin boards, and other online features for a monthly fee; for example, America Online, CompuServe, and The Microsoft Network.

Communications Program A program run on a personal computer that enables user to call up and communicate with other computers; a.k.a. terminal programs or terminal emulators.

CompactFlash Small solid-state memory card with an onboard controller; emulates a hard disk.

Compansion Process in which an incoming signal is compressed before it is recorded on tape; upon reproduction, the signal is reciprocally expanded back to its original dynamic range, with a resulting reduction in background tape noise.

Composite Tracks The result of combining the best "takes" from a number of performances that exist on different tracks onto a final single or stereo pair of tracks; is done to "open up" tracks for further overdubbing or to ease the number of mix movements that must be performed during mixdown.

Compress Store a set of data using less space while retaining necessary information.

Compression Method of encoding data to optimize space; technology that reduces the size of a file to save bandwidth.

Compression Ratio (Slope) Ratio of signal dynamic range between the compressor input and output (such as 2:1, 4:1, and 8:1) above the device's set threshold point.

Compressor In effect, an automatic fader; when the input signal exceeds a predetermined level, called the threshold, the gain is reduced by the compressor and the signal is attenuated; reduces dynamic range.

Condenser Microphone Microphone that operates on an electrostatic principle rather than on the electromagnetic principle used in dynamic and ribbon mics; head, or capsule, of the mic consists of two very thin plates, one movable and one fixed; when the distance between these plates decreases, the capacitance increases; when the distance increases, the capacitance decreases.

Constant Bit Rate See CBR.

Control Room In a recording studio, this room serves several purposes; is acoustically isolated from the sounds produced in the studio and surrounding vicinities; is optimized to act as a critical listening environment using critically balanced and placed monitor speakers; houses the majority of the studio's recording, control, and effects equipment.

Cookie Files containing information about visitors to a Web site, including username and preferences; this information is provided by the user during the first visit to a server; the server records this information in a text file and stores the file on the visitor's hard drive; when the visitor accesses the same Web site again, the server looks for the cookie and configures itself based on the information provided.

Country Code The last part of a geographic address, which indicates in which country the host computer is located.

Crossfade A way of using a mixer to overlap the start of one song with the end of another and adjust the levels, creating a smooth transition.

Crosstalk Unwanted leakage of a signal from one channel or track onto another.

Cue Send Auxiliary send used for the musicians' headphone mix.

CUL E-mail acronym meaning "see you later."

Cyberspace The virtual environment of communication created by phone, e-mail, and fax.

Cycle Period in which acoustic or electrical signal varies over one completed excursion of a wave, plotted over the 360§ axis of a circle.

D/A Converter Opposite of an A/D converter.

DAC Digital-to-Analog Converter.

DAE Digital Audio Extraction; ability of a CD-ROM drive to transfer the digital audio information from an audio CD to the computer.

DAT Digital Audio Tape; 4 mm. Cassette; using the correct 44.1 kHz frequency, can send DAT tape to CD duplicator; can be translated direct to CD in the digital mode.

Data Encryption Key String of characters used to encode a message; can only be read by someone with another related key.

Data Transfer Rate The rate that data can be transferred to computers or networks.

DB Decibel; a relative unit measurement for sound.

DB-25 The style of data plug on most modems and serial ports; shaped like a 2-inch-high, thin letter *D* with twenty-five pins; Macs use a smaller, round plug.

dBm Decibels referenced to 1 milliwatt.

dBu or dBv Decibels referenced to 0.775 volt (dBu is preferred).

dBV Decibels referenced to 1 volt.

Decibel (DB) Unit of audio measurement of sound-pressure level (SPL), signal level, and changes or differences in signal level; decibel is a logarithmic (log) mathematical function that reduces large numeric values into smaller, more manageable numbers; calculated as being 10 times the log of the ratio of two powers and 20 times the log of the ratio of two voltages.

Decode To convert a compressed audio file into uncompressed, unencoded digital audio information.

Decompress To convert a compressed audio file into an uncompressed one.

Decompression The process of restoring a compressed file to its original form.

Dedicated Line Leased phone line used exclusively for computer communications.

De-Esser Frequency-dependent compressor used to reduce excessive sibilance ("sss," "sh" and "ch" sounds).

Degaussing (Demagnetizing) Process by which small amounts of residual magnetism are eradicated from an analog magnetic tape head; degauss a magnetic tape head after ten hours of continuous operation.

Deleted Footage Scenes are sometimes cut from a film before its release, either to tighten the pacing of the story or to avoid an undesired MPAA rating; many DVDs feature unused sequences which the makers feel are worthy of preserving; sometimes include "outtakes," better known as "bloopers," with the cast and crew making humorous mistakes on the set.

Delivery Platform End-user platform that plays multimedia or other software.

Delphi Online service that supports text-oriented Internet tools; good for users of older computers and the visually impaired.

Destructive Editing When the audio data recorded on a hard disk is altered and rewritten to disk in such a way that it can't be recovered in its original form.

Dial-Up Temporary connection over a phone line to the ISP computer in order to establish a connection to the Internet; the availability of a phone line for voice or data transmission.

Dial-Up Networking Windows 95 built-in TCP/IP program for connecting to PPP or SLIP accounts.

Diffraction of Sound Sound inherently has the capability to bend around a physical acoustic barrier or go through a hole in the barrier; bends around an object in a manner that will reconstruct the original waveform in both frequency and amplitude.

Digest Compilation of messages that have been posted to a mailing list during the past few days or the past week.

Digital Audio Recording of sound stored as a series of numbers; audio represented by numbers, usually in binary format (1s and 0s).

Digital Audio Extraction (DAE) The process of copying audio data directly from a CD; also referred to as ripping.

Digital Audio Tape (DAT) Compact, dedicated PCM digital audio recorder that combines rotary head technology and PCM digital technology to create a professional recorder with a wide dynamic range, low distortion, and immeasurable wow and flutter.

Digital Console Console in which analog input signals are converted directly into digital data or are directly inserted into the console's chain as digital data, and are distributed and processed entirely in the digital domain.

Digital Mono (DM) Digitally encoded monaural signal (one channel).

Digital Recording Method of converting audio to digital signals so they can be processed and recorded with better equipment that doesn't degrade the sound.

Digital Remastering The transferring of audio to a digital format, used as the new master for duplication; can involve cleaning the original audio (removing pops, hiss, and other unwanted noise), boosting or cutting high, low and mid signals (AKA Equalization), and remixing the separate tracks; quality of the remaster is dependent on the quality of the original recording.

Digital Signal Processing (DSP) The processing of a signal in the digital domain in such a way as to follow basic binary computational rules according to a specialized program algorithm; this algorithm is used to alter the numeric values of sampled audio in a predictable way.

Digital Stereo (DS) Digitally encoded stereo signal; two channels (right and left).

Digitally Controlled Analog Console Console that distributes and processes the signal path in analog form with control over all console parameters being carried out in the digital domain; usually means that the console's control surface containing all the knobs, faders, assignment buttons, and so on, will output its control parameters as digital signals.

Digital-to-Analog (DIA) Converter Device that converts digital signals into analog form.

Digitize To convert analog audio into digital audio by repeatedly measuring or sampling the sound wave.

Direct Injection (DI) Box Box for converting high-level, high-impedance instrument signals to low-impedance microphone-level signals for direct injection into a console mic input.

Directional (Polar) Response Variations in microphone sensitivity versus the angle of sound incidence plotted on a polar graph; the sensitivity on-axis is called 0 dB, and the sensitivities at other angles are relative to that; this chart, known as the polar response or polar pattern of a microphone, shows microphone output with respect to direction and frequency over 360§.

Discography A musician's full catalog of works or recordings in chronological order.

Discrete Surround Sound Multichannel audio output that uses a separate speaker for each individual channel.

Distributor Agency that carries and supplies a product to retailers and end users.

Dither Adding to a signal small amounts of white noise that are less than the least-significant bit or less than a single quantization step, thereby increasing signal-to-error and reducing distortion.

Dithering Method of adding random noise to a digital audio signal to minimize the effect of distortion from quantization.

DNS Domain Name Server or Domain Name System; maps IP numbers to a more easily remembered name; a computer on the Internet that translates between Internet domain names and Internet numerical addresses; also called "name server."

Docking Station Holder used to store a portable MP3 player; is connected to the PC and is used to transfer data to the player from the PC; some recharge the player's batteries.

Dolby Digital (AC-3) This audio encoding format can apply to any number of audio channels on a DVD, ranging from five discrete channels of sound plus an effects channel for the subwoofer (Dolby Digital 5.1) to simple one-channel mono sound (Dolby Digital 1.0); variations exist in between, such as standard Dolby Surround (2.0 or 3.0), which supplies the same audio signal to both of the rear speakers in a home theater setup; Dolby Digital 5.0 is the same as 5.1; separate signals are channeled to the rear speakers; no extra channel for the subwoofer.

Dolby Digital Mono (DDM) Single channel of sound that takes advantage of Dolby's patented noise-reduction process; often used for audio commentaries, interviews, and purposes other than the actual movie.

Dolby Digital Stereo (DDS) System for turning two-channel sound into four playback channels (left, center, right and surround) when played on a home entertainment unit that is equipped with a Dolby Pro Logic decoder; DSS was designed to replicate the movie theater-quality sound in the home.

Dolby Digital Surround 4.1 (DD4) An improvement over DDS; incorporates the four playback channels (left, center, right, and surround), plus an extra channel (the ".1") for rumbling, low-frequency sound effects.

Dolby Digital Surround 5.1 (DD) Current standard for movie theater sound and new movies released on DVD; provides an extra surround channel for a more realistic audio experience (right, left, center and left surround, right surround), plus an additional channel for low-frequency sound effects like explosions and earthquakes.

Domain Name The part of a URL that is user-specific; the specific name that identifies an Internet site; domain names are purchased on a first come, first served basis.

Download Transfer of data from a server to a computer's hard disk; to copy a file from a remote computer to another computer.

Dry Signal Unprocessed signal that doesn't contain reverb or echoes.

DSD (Direct Stream Digital) Analog-to-digital converter, used for recording Super Audio CDs; sample rate of 2.8224 MHz, which can be converted to any industry standard sample rate.

DSL Digital Subscriber Line; technology that increases the capacity of telephone lines.

DST (Direct Stream Transfer) Used in SACD production; lossless compression technique; no data is lost during compression; allows for two programs of content to be printed on the same disk: a two-channel program and a six-channel program.

D-Theater New security encryption system used for newly developed prerecorded D-VHS releases; will support full Dolby Digital 5.1 at a bit rate of 576 Kbps (kilobytes per second), DVD supports it at a 448 Kbps bit rate; D-VHS/D-Theater cassettes are only compatible with D-Theater-equipped D-VHS players; video on D-Theater cassettes are recorded in HS mode; encryption is being employed for content protection; video using D-Theater technology can only be created or duplicated on equipment licensed and approved by JVC; D-VHS/D-Theater cassettes will bear the D-Theater logo, as will all D-VHS players that are D-Theater compatible.

DTS (Digital Theater Sound) Audio format similar to Dolby Digital 5.1; Digital Theater Systems Digital Surround (DTS) was developed to use a lower compression level for the greatest possible fidelity to the separate audio channels of a DVD; decoder is required either externally or in the player; some DVDs include both DTS and Dolby Digital 5.1

tracks, allowing the consumers to choose for themselves; disks only produced in DTS will play on any regular DVD players but will not play back the DTS signal unless a decoder is present.

DTS-CD CD encoded with DTS-formatted sound; regular CD player can play this CD only when a line is run out of the digital output through a DTS-capable receiver; otherwise the audio will come out as static-like noise; CD player's analog output will not work; DVD player is not required since DTS is encoded differently on a DTS-CD than on a DVD; DTS compatible DVD player should be able to read these disks when run through a DTS-capable receiver; multichannel output is 5.1.

DTS-ES DTS technologies containing six channels (left, center, right, back-left, back-center, back-right, and subwoofer) make up this system; three different types of DTS-ES: DTS-ES Discrete 6.1 includes the separate back center channel; DTS-ES Matrix 6.1 hides the back-center channel and sends the back-center audio from the back-left and back-right channels; DTS-ES Neo:6 converts conventional two-channel sound into 6.1 channels.

Dual Layer Many DVDs may contain over four hours of information on a single side due to a process called "dual layer" or "RSDL," which places a semi-transparent extra layer over the same side of a disk; when the player acknowledges the shift from one layer to the next, the layer change may cause a momentary pause in the playback of the film ranging from an instant to several seconds; a DVD with dual layers on both sides of the disk is referred to as a DVD-18.

Duplex Ability to send information in both directions.

DVD "Digital Video Disk" or "Digital Versatile Disk;" video format records information on a disk the size of a compact disk; utilizes digital video and audio compression to store as much as 140 minutes of information on each side of a standard DVD, twice the amount on a dual layered DVD; format allows for special features, such as multiple audio tracks and interactive video options; high-density media, similar to a CD, with a capacity of up to 18.8 GB.

DVD Audio Along with superior image quality, the sound quality of DVD has made the DVD format the most quickly adopted new video format.

DVD Features Commentary: stars and filmmakers talk through the film on a separate audio channel; Deleted Scenes/Outtakes: material left out of an original theatrical release but included on the DVD; "Making Of" Featurettes: Mini-documentaries that show what went on behind the scenes; Alternate Endings: varied endings to appeal to different audiences.

DVD-ROM Content DVD may contain material accessible only through a DVD-ROM drive on a computer; extra features may include written material, Web links, interactive games, or additional amounts of video information.

D-VHS Digital VHS; developed by JVC; a recordable digital VHS cassette that can record streaming digital broadcasts as well as conventional analog broadcasts; selecting different data rates to record will determine the quality of the recording as well as the number of hours that can be recorded onto a D-VHS cassette; D-VHS can hold more data than a DVD and is supposed to have twice the resolution; D-VHS recorders use an IEEE interface or "Firewire" and are fully backwards compatible with the existing VHS formats Super VHS and VHS.

Dynamic Microphone Microphone that operates by electromagnetic induction to generate an output signal.

Dynamic Range The range of signal levels an audio system or piece of audio equipment is able to handle; loudness spectrum from soft to loud.

Dynamics Processing Anything that interferes with the natural dynamic range of the sound.

Easter Eggs Some disks contain hidden extra features which are not advertised on the packaging; these features may be accessible directly from the main or supplementary menu screens hidden icons; others are deliberately difficult to find.

Edit Decision List (EDL) Sequential edit list containing permanent SMPTE time code and related edit information.

Effects Generic name for any electronic box that changes the sound in some way other than EQ or dynamics processing, including reverb, tremolo, flanging, fuzz, chorus, delay.

Effects Send An auxiliary send feeding an effects device.

Electret-Condenser Microphone Condenser microphone that has the polarizing charge stored permanently in the diaphragm or on the backplate; no external powering is required to charge the diaphragm or backplate.

Elm Full-screen UNIX mail reader.

E-mail Electronic mail; message transmitted and sent over the Internet from one person to another, or to a large number of e-mail addresses on a mailing list.

E-mail Acronyms Letter abbreviations of common expressions.

E-mail Address Electronic mail address in the form of user@domain.

EMF Electro magnetic frequency.

Encode To convert data into a specific file format.

Encoder Software or hardware that encodes information.

Encoding The process of converting uncompressed audio into a compressed format.

Encrypted Data files that are stored such that they can't be read without a password or key; process used to create audio files that will only run on the user's player and nowhere else.

Encryption Procedure that scrambles the contents of a file prior to sending it over the Internet; the recipient must have the appropriate software to decrypt the file; security practice of scrambling a file's contents so the information is not able to be read without a software key.

Engine A multimedia software program that displays content and directs interaction.

Engineer Person responsible for expressing the artist's music and the producer's concepts through the medium of recording; an art form because both music and recording are subjective in nature and rely on the tastes and experiences of those involved.

English Dubbed Film originally recorded in another language may be dubbed into English; English-speaking actors perform the lines of the film in place of the original dialogue.

Enhanced CD Audio CD with interactive material contained on the disk to be used on a computer; similar to a CD-ROM.

Enqueue Queue, or place, in a list of items to be processed.

EOT E-mail acronym meaning "end of thread."

EP (Extended Play) Usually contains five or fewer songs; can be considered a long single, or a short album.

EPAC Perceptual audio encoding scheme based on PAC.

EQ Short for equalization.

Equalization Adjusting the relative levels of bands of frequencies to modify or make smoother the frequency response of an audio signal or file; lets the user boost or cut frequencies in any part of the audio spectrum.

Equalizer Frequency-dependent amplifier that enables a recording or mix engineer to control the relative amplitude of various frequencies in the audible bandwidth; lets user exercise tonal control over the harmonic content or timbre of a recorded sound.

Eudora Mail-handling program that runs on Macintosh and Windows.

Expander Device that increases the dynamic range of a signal.

E-zine A magazine that exists in cyberspace.

Fade Slow change in volume; up from silence or down to silence; accomplished manually or by calculation in a DAW or hard-disk recorder; fading in or fading out of a region is a DSP function carried out by calculating the soundfile's relative amplitude over a defined duration.

Fader Linear attenuation device or linear volume control.

FAQ Frequently Asked Questions; document or article that contains the most common questions and answers on a particular subject; e-mail acronym meaning "frequently asked questions."

Feedback The returning of a loudspeaker signal back into a microphone feeding that loudspeaker; excessive feedback results in unpleasant, screaming buildups at particular frequencies.

FIDONET Worldwide network of bulletin-board systems with e-mail access.

Filmography Reference list of the films by a particular actor or director.

Filters A way to narrow the scope of a report or view by specifying ranges or types of data to include or exclude.

Finger A program that displays information about someone on the Internet; the act of getting information about someone on the Internet by using the finger program.

Firewall Specially programmed computer that connects a local network to the Internet and, for security reasons, lets only certain kinds of messages in and out; security architecture between the Internet and a private network that protects the private network from unauthorized access.

Firmware Computer programs that are stored on a piece of hardware.

Flame An e-mail message relaying a nasty or personal attack; to post angry, inflammatory, or insulting messages.

Flame War Two or more individuals engaged in flaming.

Flaming Rude, scolding, or nasty e-mail and newsgroup replies.

Flanging Process whereby a delayed signal is combined with itself undelayed; delay is varied to create continual changes in timbre; also called a comb-filter effect.

Flash Animation software from Macromedia used to develop Web graphics.

Flash Memory Computer memory that does not lose stored data when the power is shut off.

Fletcher-Munson Curves Group of curves that plot the subjective sensitivity of humans to various frequencies at different sound-pressure levels.

Flutter Fast, periodic variation in a tape transport's speed.

Font Comprehensive set of characters in one design or style.

Forms HTML page which passes variables back to the server; used to gather information from users; a.k.a. scripts.

Frame A small chunk of data; specifically on audio CDs.

Freenet Free online system offering local communities information and limited access to the Internet.

Freeware Software that is free.

Frequency Rate at which an acoustic generator, electrical signal, or vibrating mass repeats a cycle of positive- and negative-going amplitude; number of cycles that occurs over the period of one second is measured in hertz (Hz; the perceived range of human hearing is from 20 Hz to 18,000 Hz).

Front End End-user's operational interface to an information system.

FTP File Transfer Protocol; Method of transferring files from one computer to another over the Internet; standard method of sending files between computers over the Internet; a protocol used to transfer files across the Internet.

FTP Server A computer on the Internet that stores files for transmission by FTP.

Fulfillment Service provided by a CD printer, duplicator, or manufacturer that includes warehousing inventory, processing, and shipping orders to customers.

Full Frame Film presented with all visual information available but not requiring letterboxing; can either refer to films made prior to the 1950s which were filmed in a regular square shape and therefore adapt perfectly to the TV format, or to films which are shot with an extra "safety area" at the top and bottom of the image; latter kind of "full frame" presentation, also referred to as "open matte," will contain extra but unimportant picture information compared to a letterboxed version of the same title, usually a more accurate portrayal of the filmmakers' intentions.

Full Screen Movie image fills up the entire television screen; film could have been modified or cropped to fill the screen.

FWIW E-mail acronym; "for what it's worth."

FYI E-mail acronym meaning "for your information."

Gain Amount of amplification in dB.

GAL E-mail acronym meaning "get a life."

Gate Device that fully attenuates a signal that falls below a predetermined threshold level; used to reduce noise or extraneous pickup leakage.

Gateway Device that allows data from one network to access another; a computer that connects one network with another, where the two networks use different protocols.

GB Gigabyte. 1,073,741,824 bytes (2 to the 30th power).

Genre A category of music such as country, blues, jazz, rock, etc.

gHz One billion cycles per second.

GIF Graphics Interchange Format; patented type of graphics file; files in this format end in .gif and are called GIF files or GIFs; common graphics file format on the Internet; can display 256 colors at the maximum (8 bits); mostly used to show clip-art images; photographic images are usually in the JPEG format; GIF 89a standard allows multiple images in one file and can be used to show some animation on a Web site; developed by CompuServe.

Gigabyte One billion bytes or characters of data; 1 Kb = 1,024 bytes; 1 Mb = 1,024 Kb (=1,048,576 bytes); 1 Gb = 1,024 Mb (= 1,073,741,824 bytes).

GKA Government Key Access; United States government proposal to require that encryption software include a way for the government to break the code.

Gopher Internet system allowing user to find information by using menus.

Gopherspace The world of Gopher menus.

Ground Loop Condition that exists in an improper grounding situation, whereby a DC current differential exists between one signal path and another, resulting in 60 Hz or 50 Hz (European) hum.

Handle User's nickname or screen name.

Hard-Disk Recorder System that uses a computer hard disk to record, edit, and reproduce digital data.

Hardware Actual physical parts of computer equipment, as opposed to *software* programs, files, etc.

Harmonic Content Factor that allows user to differentiate between instruments; presence of several different frequencies within a complex sound wave, in addition to its fundamental note; frequencies present in a sound, other than the fundamental, are called partials; partials higher than the fundamental frequency are called upper partials or overtones; overtones play an important part in determining the sonic character of an instrument; harmonics are integral multiples of the fundamental frequency.

HDCD (High Density Compatible Digital) Format of CD encoded with 20 bits of information instead of 16; HDCD player or HDCD receiver is required, but not both, to achieve the full potential of the HDCD encoding; normal CD player will play the CD but will not enhance the sound; HDCD sound has more body and more dynamic range than a normal CD.

HDTV (High Definition Television) Television that offers the highest-quality picture because of its capability to receive all-digital broadcast signals; DVD played on HDTV has a higher resolution, which provides sharper images than a DVD played on a standard television; sound is sharper because audio signal is split up into six channels; because

HDTV has an elongated rectangular screen (16:9), it is tailored for widescreen enhanced movies.

Header The beginning of an e-mail message; To and From addresses, subject, and date.

Headphones Small set of speakers worn on the head that ideally keep outside sounds out, and what the user is listening to from bleeding into the mics.

Hertz (Hz) Cycles per second; used as a measurement of frequency.

Hierarchy In Usenet, the major group to which a newsgroup belongs; seven hierarchies are "comp," "rec," "soc," "sci," "news," "misc," and "talk."

Hiss Broadband tape or amplifier noise.

Hit Single request from a browser to a server; access of a file on a Web page.

Home Page The main page of a Web site; provides an overview; links to rest of site; may contain a table of contents for the site; Web page about a person or organization.

Host The server on which a Web site is stored; a computer on the Internet.

Hostname The name of a computer on the Internet.

Hot Spots Areas of a multimedia display screen that accept user interaction.

HTML Hypertext Markup Language; the standard tool or coding language for creating Web pages; language used to write pages for the World Wide Web; text includes codes that define fonts, layout, embedded graphics, and hypertext links; a way to format text by placing marks or tags around the text.

HTTP Hypertext Transfer Protocol; the way in which Web pages are transferred over the Net; World Wide Web protocol for moving hypertext (HTML) files across the Internet.

HTTPS Variant form of HTTP that encrypts messages for security.

Huffman Encoding Method of data compression that uses shorter codes to represent patterns that are more common.

Hybrid SACDs Disks with a Super Audio layer and a CD layer are called Hybrid SACDs; SACDs (except those by Sony) can be played on regular CD players; SA layer is a semitransmissive layer; normal CD player's laser will read through in order to read the CD layer.

Hyper CD Includes links to a Web site(s) affiliated with the audio content.

Hyperlink Place on a Web page that, when accessed or "clicked," will send the user to a different Web page; often underlined and/or blue.

Hypermedia Method of accessing different media elements (text, graphics, etc.) in an interactive, navigable form.

Hypertext Text that includes hyperlinks to other Web pages; the cross-linking of media, especially texts, for reference purposes; system of writing and displaying text that enables the text to be linked in multiple ways, available at different levels of detail, and with links to related documents; World Wide Web uses both hypertext and hypermedia.

ID3 Format for including informational tags in an MP3 file, allowing multiple players to display information about the song.

ID3 Tag Method for storing data within an MP3 file.

IDE Integrated Drive Electronics.

IETF Internet Engineering Task Force; group that develops new technical standards for the Intenet.

IICS International Interactive Communications Society; organization of multimedia and interface designers.

IKWYM or **IKWUM** E-mail acronym meaning "I know what you mean."

IMA International Multimedia Association; consortium of companies fostering multimedia and interface designers, multimedia standards, and business.

Image Map Graphic that includes embedded spots that link to related files.

IMAX (Image Maximum) This high-quality theatrical format using a large, panoramic screen must be played in a special type of movie theater; for home video, IMAX appears as a full frame presentation with a dense amount of visual detail; this format particularly lends itself to visually driven spectacles, such as scientific or educational films.

IMCO E-mail acronym; "in my considered opinion."

IME E-mail acronym; "in my experience."

IMHO E-mail acronym; "in my humble opinion."

Impedance Opposition of a circuit to the flow of an alternating current.

Impression A page view; every time an HTML document is retrieved; request for a Web page on a server; most server log files count impressions, not "hits," to measure the popularity of a Web site.

Indie Independent; unsigned musician, artist, or band.

Input (I/O) Module Vertical array of controls on a console that relates to a specific input signal.

Instant Relay Chat (IRC) System enabling Internet users to talk to each other in real time.

Interactive Media presentation to a user in which the user navigates content.

Interface Integrated design of a presentation; the ability to operate technology.

Internet Network system that allows global communication; system by which all the computers in the world communicate.

Internet Explorer Popular Web browser from Microsoft; Windows and Macintosh versions.

Internet Phone Program that enables a user to use the Internet to talk to others by using a microphone and speakers, instead of long-distance telephone calls.

Internet Radio Streaming digital audio transmissions over the Internet; can be listened to by those with the compatible receiving program.

Internet Society Organization dedicated to supporting the growth and evolution of the Internet.

InterNIC Internet Network Information Center; keeps track of domain names; a.k.a. Network Solutions; central repository of information about the Internet.

Interrupt Character A key or combination of keys to stop what is happening on a computer.

Intranet Private business network; secure environment to share information within a business and over the Internet; private version of the Internet allowing people within an organization to exchange data using Internet tools.

IOW E-mail acronym meaning "in other words."

IP Address Internet Protocol Address; identifies a computer connected to the Internet; numeric URL; every Internet site has two addresses, the IP address and the URL or domain name.

IRC Chat Real-time text-based chat over the Internet.

ISA Industry Standard Architecture; older type of PC interface (bus) for plug-in cards.

ISDN Integrated Services Digital Network; digital network that permits simultaneous digital voice and data transmission; a type of digital telephone line capable of transmitting combinations of voice and data at up to 128 kbps.

ISO International Standards Organization; group that sets standards for engineering and design concerns.

Isochronous Providing consistent bandwidth to time-sensitive applications.

Iso-Room/Iso-Booth Isolation rooms and the smaller iso-booth are acoustically sealed areas built into and easily accessible from the main studio area; provide improved separation between loud and soft instruments, vocals, etc.

ISP Internet Service Provider; provides Internet access to its members.

ITU-T International Telecommunications Union; sets worldwide communication standards.

IYSWIM E-mail acronym meaning "if you see what I mean."

Jack A connector that receives another connector into it; a.k.a. a socket; generic term for plug-in connectors on audio equipment.

Java Computer language invented by Sun Microsystems; Java programs can run on any modern computer; ideal for delivering application programs

over the Internet; platform-independent programming language; Java-enabled Web pages can include animations, scrolling text, sound effects, and games; many people surf the Web with a Java disabled browser because they don't want to wait for the applet to download; specific programming language that supports enhanced features.

JavaScript Scripting language unrelated to Java; designed by Netscape; embedded into HTML documents.

Jitter Errors introduced into a digital signal because of the seeking inaccuracy of some CD-ROM drives; time-based error caused by varying time delays in a digital-audio circuit path.

Jitter Correction Method of reading overlapping blocks of data from CD-ROMs to eliminate jitter.

JPEG Joint Photographic Experts Group; image compression standard; optimized for full-color digital images; can choose the amount of compression; the higher the compression rate, the lesser the quality of the image has; nearly all full-color photographs on the Web are JPG files; GIFs are used to display clip-art images; type of still-image file found all over the Interet; files in this format end in .jpg or .jpeg and are called JPEG (pronounced "JAY-peg") files.

K 1,000.

Kb Kilobyte 2 to the 10th power (1,024 bytes).

Kbps or **Kb/sec** Kilobits per second; Kilobytes (bytes x 1,024) per second; measurement of the amount of data it takes to make a second of music in an MP3 file.

KHz Thousands of cycles per second.

Kill File File that tells newsreader which newsgroup articles user wishes to skip.

Kilobit or **Kilobyte (Kb)** Rounded a thousand bytes; actually, 1,024 (2 to the 10th power) bytes; 1,000 bytes or characters of data; the smallest unit of computer data storage.

Leader Tape Paper tape that can be spliced into analog audio tape for the purpose of inserting silent spaces, visual separation, and identification for various songs or selections.

Leakage Spilling or bleeding of sound from one instrument onto another instrument's microphone.

Limiter Device used to keep signal peaks from exceeding a certain level in order to prevent the clipping or distortion of amplifier signals, recorded signals on tape or disk, broadcast transmission signals, etc.

Line Level Signal level that is referenced to either +4 dBm (pro) or -10 dBV (semi-pro/consumer; devices other than mics, speakers, and power-amplifier outputs operate at these levels.

Line-In Jack Designed to accept the output from a line-level output.

Line-Level Range of levels found on inputs and outputs of audio equipment.

Line-Out Jack Bypasses the amplifier of a piece of audio equipment.

Link Marked text or picture within a hypertext document, usually underlined or highlighted; one mouse click brings user to another Web page or to another place on the same page; essential in hypertext documents.

Linux Public-domain version of the UNIX operating system; runs on personal computers; supported by enthusiasts on the Internet.

Listproc Like LISTSERV; program that handles mailing lists.

LISTSERV Programs that automatically manages mailing lists; distribute messages posted to the list; add and delete members so list owner does not have to do it manually; names of mailing lists maintained by LISTSERV often end with "-L."

LMK E-mail acronym meaning "let me know."

Location Internet address as displayed on browser; by typing in the URL of a Web site into the location bar of a browser, the browser will take the user to the Web page.

Log File Audit file of hits to a Web server; file that contains recorded events of a computer system, including server access log files, error log files, etc.

Login To enter into a computer system; the account name or user ID that must be entered before user is allowed access to the computer system.

LOL E-mail acronym meaning "laugh out loud."

Lossless Compression Compression methods in which the compressed file can be decompressed into an exact replica of the original uncompressed file; reproduction methods in which the copy is an exact match of the original data; a compression algorithm in which a compressed image's quality is maintained after decompression.

Lossy Compression Compression method that removes redundant or irrelevant information; cannot reproduce an exact copy of the original data; reproduction methods in which the copy is not an exact match of the original.

Lurk To read a newsgroup, mailing list, or chat group without posting any messages; a person who lurks is a "lurker."

Lynx Fast, character-based Web browser with no pictures.

MacBinary File-encoding system popular among Macintosh users.

MacTCP Computer on the Internet that provides mail services.

Mail Server Server of ISP that handles incoming and outgoing e-mail.

Mailing List E-mail-based discussion group on a specific topic; list servers maintain a list of e-mail addresses of subscribers; when an e-mail message is sent to the group, it is copied and sent to all subscribers.

Maintenance Engineer Person who ensures that the equipment in the studio is maintained in top condition, regularly aligned, and repaired when necessary.

Majordomo Like LISTSERV; program that handles mailing lists.

Making Of Behind-the-scenes film or production journal providing a look at the circumstances going on behind the camera during the production of a program.

Masking Phenomenon by which loud sounds prevent the ear from hearing softer sounds; greatest masking effect occurs when the frequency of the sound and the frequency of the masking noise are close to each other.

Master Tape First-generation tape recorded on, generally on a multitrack recorder.

Mastering Process in which the mixdown of a song is transferred to a medium from which it will be replicated, known as the "master;" also includes the cleaning of the audio, tweaking the high, low, and mid signals or Equalization, and boosting the overall volume level; process whereby a number of songs, after being mixed down, are EQ'd, compressed as necessary, and balanced in volume with each other, so that they will sound good when placed together on a CD; processing and transferring of a final, sequenced audiotape to a medium for duplication.

MB Megabyte, 2 to the 20th power (1,048,576) bytes.

Mbone Multicast Backbone; Internet sub-network supporting live video and multimedia.

Megabyte About one million bytes; exactly 1,048,576 bytes (2 to the 20th power), or 1,024 Kb; one million bytes or characters of data.

Memory Card Nonvolatile, solid-state memory; Compact Flash; SmartMedia.

MHz One million cycles per second.

Mic Short for microphone.

Mic In Socket on a sound card designed to have a microphone connected to it.

Microdrive Small hard drive that can be used in place of flash memory in some instances; miniature hard disk made by IBM; about the size of a matchbook.

Microphone Sound goes in one end, electricity out the other.

Microsoft Network, The (MSN) Commercial online service; provides many Internet services, including e-mail, Usenet newsgroups, and access to the World Wide Web.

MIDI (Musical Instrument Digital Interface) Digital communications language and compatible hardware specification that allows multiple electronic instruments, performance controllers, computers, and other related devices to communicate with one another within a connected network; acronym for Musical Instrument Digital Interface; MIDI is a common encoding language that most keyboard synthesizers speak; as used in most recording studios, MIDI files (generally stored on a computer) can be used to force MIDI-based sound modules or sound cards to act as high-tech "player pianos;" many electronic instruments have a MIDI output; standard for connecting electronic instruments and computers; file format used to store the computer equivalent of sheet music, including a list of which notes are played and what instruments are playing.

MIDI Interface Digital hardware device used to translate a MIDI's serial message data into a structure that can be understood by and communicated to a personal computer's internal operating system.

MIDI Machine Control (MMC) Standardized series of transport-related commands that are transmitted over standard MIDI lines from one controller to one or more other MMC-capable devices within a connected system.

MIDI Sample Dump Standard (SDS) Protocol developed and ratified by the MIDI Manufacturers Association that enables the transmission of sampled digital audio and loop information from one sampling device to another.

MIDI Time Code (MTC) Provides a cost-effective and easily implemented means for translating SMPTE time code throughout a MIDI chain as a stream of MIDI messages.

Mil When these letters appear as the last part of the Internet address or URL, it indicates that the host computer is run by the U.S. military.

MIME Multipurpose Internet Mail Extensions; used to send pictures, word-processing files, and other nontext information via e-mail.

MiniDisk Recordable digital format; small disk framed within a thin, plastic casing a little smaller than the computer 3 1/2 inch floppy disk; popular for creating personal mixes to be played on portable MiniDisk players; small, rewritable optical disk designed by Sony Corporation for recording and playing audio; similar to a CD.

MiniPlug Plug used on the end of headphones for portable tape or CD players.

Mirror FTP or Web server that provides copies of the same files as another server; spreads out the load for more popular FTP and Web sites.

Mixdown The final mixing of a recording, mixed down to the essential number of tracks (i.e., two tracks, left and right, for stereo); used to produce the "master" recording; process in which the separate audio tracks of a multitrack tape machine are com-

bined, balanced, and routed through the recording console; volume, tone, special effects, and spatial positioning can be artistically set by the engineer to create a stereo or four-channel mix that is then recorded to a master recording device.

Mixer Device with faders and EQ knobs whose sole function is to control the level of sound from different tracks or inputs.

Mixing All of the sounds that comprise a piece of recorded music are recorded onto separate "tracks;" the sound levels and signal quality (Equalization) of these tracks are then "mixed" together so that all of the sounds complement each other.

Mixing Down Taking the tracks from a recording session, playing them back together, and adjusting the volume, panning, and effects so one can record the final result in stereo to a mixdown recorder.

MLP (Meridian Lossless Packing) Lossless compression technique where no data is lost during compression; used for compressing DVD-Audio files.

Modem MOdulator-DEModulator. Allows computers to transmit information to each other via telephone lines; communications device that converts analog signals to or from digital data for processing by a computer.

Moderated Mailing List Mailing list run by a moderator.

Moderated Newsgroup Newsgroup run by a moderator.

Moderator Someone who reviews the messages posted to a mailing list or newsgroup before releasing them to the public; moderator may eliminate messages that are inappropriate.

Modular Digital Multitrack Recorders (MDMS) Small, cost-effective, multitrack digital audio recorders capable of recording eight tracks of digital audio onto readily available videotape cassettes; called "modular" because they can be linked together in a proprietary sync fashion, with a theoretical maximum limit of up to 128 tracks.

Monitor Speakers used when mixing down, also known as studio monitors; a computer screen.

Mono Program audio is contained within one central channel; one channel sound; monaural; monophonic.

Mosaic Older Web browser.

Moving-Coil Microphone Consists of a Mylar diaphragm of roughly 0.35 mil thickness attached to a finely wrapped coil of wire that is precisely suspended within a high-level magnetic field; when an acoustic pressure wave hits the face of this diaphragm, the attached voice coil is displaced in proportion to the amplitude and frequency of the wave, causing the coil to cut across the lines of magnetic flux supplied by a permanent magnet; an analogous electrical signal of a specific magnitude and direction is generated across the voice coil leads.

MP2 MPEG Audio Layer-II.

MP3 Compression standard for music; almost no loss of quality; popular file format.

MP4 Various audio compression schemes considered to be better than MP3, including AAC.

MPAA Ratings Assigned by The Motion Picture Association of America to designate the appropriate age group for a film; ratings are as follows: "G"—suitable for all audiences; "PG"—parental guidance suggested; "PG-13"—may be inappropriate for viewers under 13; "NC-17"—not suitable for viewers under 17; "R"—not recommended for viewers under 17 without an adult or guardian present; a film designated as "not rated" has not been submitted to the MPAA for a rating; a film referred to as "unrated" usually contains material which was not present in a previous MPAA-approved edition or contains material which is stronger than an "R" rating and may not be suitable for younger viewers.

M P C Multimedia PC; Microsoft trademark specifying a standard of an Intel-based CPU with a CD-ROM player, soundboard, speakers, and pointing device.

MPEG Moving Pictures Expert Group. Compression standard for video in a format similar to JPEG; type of video file found on the Internet; files in this format end in ".mpg"; graphics standard for compressed movie clips; MPEGs are smaller than QT or AVI files; require a powerful processor for playback; standards are labeled MPEG-1, MPEG-2, etc.

MPEG3 MPEG Audio Layer-III; standard of audio compression originally designed for inclusion with compressed video.

MPMan Series of portable MP3 players.

MUD Multi-User Dungeon; started as a Dungeons and Dragons type of game for many players; now an Internet subculture.

Multi-Angle Some DVDs feature the option to change "angles" during playback of a program; multiple angles may be different versions of the same scene, behind-the-scenes footage, or other variations.

Multi-Audio/Commentary Commentary or multi-audio track is an audio option which allows the viewer to hear relevant participants in a film (or critics) share their thoughts and observations on a program; alternate audio may include other features, such as radio programs or audio books.

Multicasting Method of transmitting information allowing multiple users or systems to subscribe to the same stream or channel.

Multimedia Combined use of several forms of media into a product or presentation; field that encompasses the mixed media of text, graphics, MIDI, and digital audio sound for the personal computer.

Multiplexing Technique of combining multiple communications channels at the same time.

Multitimbral Capability of an electronic musical instrument to respond to and output multiple voice patches at one time.

Multitrack Any recording device with one or more tracks that can be separately recorded and played back.

Multitrack Recording Process that provides an added degree of production flexibility to the recording process by enabling multiple sound sources to be recorded to and played back from isolated tracks that are synchronously locked in time; recorded tracks are isolated from one another, so any number of sound sources can be recorded and re-recorded without affecting other tracks.

Music Video Visual programs designed to accompany a song or other musical composition; often include the performer and may or may not contain a plotline.

Mute To turn off or silence an input signal, tape track, etc.

Navigator Web browser from Netscape.

NBC Not backwards compatible.

Nearfield Monitoring Monitoring with a small bookshelf-style speaker on or slightly behind the meter bridge of a console, close to the engineer and producer; ensures that a greater portion of the direct sound mix is heard relative to the room's acoustics.

Net Short for Internet.

Net Surfing Browsing the Internet.

Netiquette Network Etiquette; code of good manners on the Internet.

Netizen Responsible Internet citizen.

Netlag Condition occuring on the Internet when heavy "traffic" slows down the server response time.

Netscape Navigator Web Browser for Windows, Macintosh, and UNIX.

Network Computer Computer that lacks a hard disk and receives all data over a computer network such as the Internet.

Network Wire that allows a group of computers to communicate and share resources; computers that are connected together; local area networks; wide area networks; interconnected networks all over the world form the Internet.

Newbie A newcomer to the Internet.

News Type of Usenet newsgroup that has discussions about newsgroups.

News Server A computer on the Internet that receives Usenet newsgroups.

Newsgroup Discussion group on USENET among those who share a common interest; thousands of newsgroups covering all topics of interest.

Newsreader Program that lets user read and respond to the messages in Usenet newsgroups.

NIC Network Information Center; responsible for coordinating a set of networks so that the names, network numbers, and other technical details are consistent from one network to another.

Niche A dedicated submarket.

Nickname In IRC, the name by which a user identifies him- or herself while chatting.

NNTP Network News Transport Protocol; protocol to transport USENET postings over a TCP/IP network.

Node Computer on the Internet, also called a "host."

Noise Gate Device that acts as an infinite expander, allowing a signal above the selected threshold to be passed through to the output at unity gain and without dynamic processing; when the input signal falls below this threshold level, the device effectively shuts down the signal by applying full attenuation to the output.

Nondestructive Editing Editing a hard disk soundfile by moving pointers without altering in any way the digital audio data originally recorded to disk.

Normalization Process of adjusting the level of a digital audio file so that all songs play at the same volume.

Normalizing Specialized gain-related process that makes the best use of a digital system's dynamic range by automatically determining the amount of gain required to increase the level of the highest amplitude signal to its full-scale amplitude value, and then increasing the level of the selected region or entire file by this gain ratio.

NTSC (National Television Standards Committee) Format developed and still used in the United States; this video format uses thirty frames per second, scanning at 525 horizontal lines per frame.

Nyquist Theorem Theory which states that in order to digitally encode the entire frequency bandwidth, the selected sample rate must be at least twice as high as the highest desired recorded frequency (sample rate 2 x highest frequency).

Objects Data and the computer programs that work with the data.

Offline Not connected to a computer network.

Omnidirectional Microphone A mic that outputs signals received from all incident angles at the same or nearly equal level.

Online Services Online commercial companies, such as America Online (AOL) and Compuserve, that offer Internet and Web access as well as exclusive membership options; connected to a computer network.

Open Tracks Available tracks on a multitrack recorder.

Operational Amplifier (Op Amp) Stable high-gain, high-bandwidth amplifier with a high input impedance and a low output impedance; used as a basic building block for a wide variety of audio and video applications.

OS Operating System.

OTOH E-mail acronym meaning "on the other hand."

Outboard Equipment Signal processing and other devices external to the mixing console.

Outtakes Title contains scenes, such as bloopers, which may not have been included in the original release of the movie.

Overdubbing Enables one or more of the previously recorded tracks to be monitored while simultaneously recording one or more signals onto other tracks; process can be repeated until the song or soundtrack has been built up; if a mistake is made, it is a simple matter to re-cue the tape to the desired starting point and repeat the process until one has the best take on tape.

Overload Distortion that occurs when an applied signal exceeds a system's maximum input level.

Oversampling Process commonly used in professional and consumer digital-audio systems to improve Nyquist filter characteristics, thereby reducing intermodulation and other forms of distortion; effectively multiplies the sampling rate by a specified factor, commonly ranging from between 12 to 128 times the original rate; increased sample rate results in a much wider frequency bandwidth, so a simple, single-order filter can be used to cut off the frequencies above the Nyquist limit; digital samples must be at least double the frequency of the analog signal in order for the digital sample to accurately represent the analog signal; human ear cannot hear frequencies over 20 kHz, therefore, 44.1 kHz is the industry standard for digital sampling, since all frequencies over the 20 kHz digital sample would be inaudible; digital filter that boosts the frequency of the digital sample; boosting the frequency helps the digital sample to be converted to analog more faithfully during playback; the leftover digital frequencies are filtered out so that the signals do not interfere with other electronics.

Packet A chunk of information sent over a network; each packet includes the addresses sent to and from.

Page Short for "Web page" or one single file on the Web; document available by way of the Internet; pages may include text, graphics files, soundfiles, and/or video clips.

Page Views Page Impressions; hits to HTML pages only; access to non-HTML documents is not counted.

PAL (Phase Alternate Line) Developed in Germany and used in the UK and most of Europe; uses 25 frames per second, scanning at 625 horizontal lines per frame.

Pan & Scan When a widescreen film is presented on TV, one option is to fill the frame from top to bottom with the image and then "pan" back and forth across to reveal any necessary information not visible within the square dimensions of the TV set.

Pan Pot Dual-potentiometer that can place a single signal source at any point between the left and right channels of a stereo image, or the left/right, front/back quadrants of a surround sound image.

Parental Lock DVD contains an option to prevent children from viewing certain scenes on a disc; owner can select the age level they wish to block, ensuring that only audiences of a certain age and with access to the code can view the entire film.

Parity System for checking for errors when data is transmitted from one computer to another.

Password Secret code that must be entered after user ID or login name in order to log on to a computer; secret code used to keep things private.

Patch Small program used to change or update another program; file that updates a program by modifying or replacing only the parts of the program that have changed.

Patch Bay Panel that contains a jack corresponding to the input and output of every component or group of wires in the control room; acts as a central point where console signal paths, pieces of audio gear, and other devices can be connected; signal re-router that mounts on a rack, with dozens of jacks on the front and the back.

Patch Cords Short cables used for routing signals through a patch bay; short cable used to connect inputs to outputs on a patch bay.

PCI Peripheral Component Interface; newer type of PC interface (bus) for plug-in cards.

PCM (Pulse Code Modulation) Uncompressed digital soundtrack offers the capacity for either standard left and right stereo playback or a mono soundtrack; analog-to-digital converter used for recording traditional CDs.

PCMCIA Card or PC Cards Personal Computer Memory Card Industry Association; small plug-in card used on notebook computers or laptops to add features such as a modem, network interfaces, and external drives; look like thick credit cards.

PDF File Method for distributing formatted documents over the Internet; requires Acrobat Reader.

Peak Amplitude Maximum instantaneous amplitude of a signal.

Peaking Filter Used to create a peak- or bell-shaped equalization curve in the frequency response that can be either boosted or cut at a selected center frequency.

PERL Practical Extraction and Report Language; powerful computer language; used for writing CGI scripts which handle input/output actions on Web pages.

Phantom Power Power for a condenser mic that comes directly from the console through balanced mic cables by supplying a positive DC supply voltage of +48-V (usually) to both conductors (pins 2 and 3) with respect to pin 1; this voltage is distributed through identical value resistors so that no differential exists between the two leads; the voltage is electrically invisible to the alternating audio signal; DC circuit is completed by connecting the negative side of the supply to the cable's grounding shield.

Phase Degree of progression in the cycle of a wave, where one complete cycle is 360 degrees; waveforms can be added by summing their signed amplitudes at each instant of time; a cycle can begin at any point on a waveform; it's possible for two waveforms having the same or different frequency and peak levels to have different amplitudes at any one point in time; these waves are out of phase with respect to each other; phase is measured in degrees of a cycle (divided into 360 degrees) and will result in audible variations of a combined signal's amplitude and overall frequency response.

Phase Shift Difference in degrees of phase angle between corresponding points on two waves.

PICS Platform for Internet Content Selection; a way of marking pages with ratings about what they contain.

Pine Popular UNIX-based mail program.

Ping Program that checks to see whether a user can communicate with another computer on the Internet; sends a short message to which the other computer automatically responds.

Ping-Ponging Also called Bouncing Tracks.

PITA E-mail acronym meaning "pain in the ass."

Pitch Control Control that varies the speed of a tape transport or the sample rate of a digital audio device, changing the pitch of the reproduced signal.

Pitch Shifting Used to vary the pitch of a program either upward or downward to transpose the relative pitch of an audio source.

PKZIP File-compression program that runs on PCs; creates a ZIP file that contains compressed versions of one or more files; to restore files to former size and shape, use PKUNZIP or WinZip.

Platform Set of operating system hardware and software standards that dictate functionality; the operating system.

Player Computer or device that plays a multimedia program; device or program that decodes and plays digital audio files.

Playlist File with a list of songs for a player to play or select from; list of songs that can be played in succession automatically; sequential list of soundfile regions that can be played as a single, continuous program or sequentially triggered at specific time code addresses.

Plug Connector that gets inserted into a socket.

Plug-in Small program that another program can run, adding functions to the larger program; small piece of software, usually from a third-party developer, that adds new features to another larger software application; computer program added to a browser to help it handle a special type of file; software module that adds functions to a program.

Polar Pattern Polar graph of the sensitivity of a microphone at all angles of sound incidence relative to the sensitivity on-axis.

Polyphonic Capability of an electronic musical instrument to output multiple notes at one time.

Pop Filter Foam or wire screen placed between the mic and the instrument or performer to reduce wind and breath blasts.

POP Post Office Protocol; system by which a mail server on the Internet lets the user pick up e-mail and download it to PC or Mac; Internet protocol used by ISP to handle e-mail for its subscribers; synonym for an e-mail account.

Port Number Identifying number assigned to each program that is chatting on the Internet.

Portastudio Trademarked term of TASCAM referring to their cassette multitrack recorders.

Posting Single message posted to a newsgroup, bulletin board, or mailing list; article published on or submitted to a Usenet newsgroup or mailing list.

Potentiometer (Pot) Rotary gain, pan, or other type of continuously variable signal control.

POV E-mail acronym meaning "point of view."

PPP Point-to-Point Protocol; scheme for connecting a computer to the Internet over a phone line.

Preamp Device that sets the level of an audio signal before it is sent to the main amplifier.

Print-Through The transfer of a recorded signal from one layer of magnetic tape to an adjacent layer by means of magnetic induction, which gives rise to an audible false signal (pre-echo or post-echo) on playback.

Producer Person who handles the scheduling, budgetary, and coordination aspects of a recording project; producer's responsibility is to create the best-recorded performance and final product possible; producer is often chosen for his or her ability to understand the many phases of the overall process of creating a final recorded project, from the standpoints of business, musical performance, and creative insight into recording technology.

Production Notes "Production Notes" feature on a DVD provides a series of screens containing text which details the history of a particular program; these notes are supplemented with details about the cast and crew, as well as anecdotes concerning events during production.

Production Stills "Production stills" are photographs taken during the making of a motion picture or other program; these stills highlight the interaction between the stars and directors or the creation of sets or costumes.

Project Studio Professional-quality recording facility in a home or personal place of business that is used to record the owner's own projects and selected outside projects; not a commercial studio space.

Protocol Set of rules that specifies how data is exchanged; established method of exchanging data over a network or the Internet.

Provider Individual or company that supplies content, supplies, or services.

Proximity Effect Bass boost that occurs with single-D directional mics at close working distances.

Psycho-Acoustic Encoding Lossy digital audio compression based on the properties of human hearing.

Public Key Cryptography Method for sending secret messages whereby user gets two keys: a *public key* given out freely so that people can send coded messages and a *private key* that decodes them.

Pulse Code Modulation (PCM) Common format for uncompressed digital audio that uses fixed length pulses to represent binary data; most common encoding scheme for storing digital data onto a medium with a maximum degree of data density.

Punch-In/Punch-Out The entering into and out of record mode on a track that contains existing program material for the purpose of correcting or erasing an unwanted segment.

Qualified Hits Hits to a Web site that deliver information to the end user.

Quantization Amplitude component of the digital sampling process; in an A/D converter, the process of generating a binary number (made of 1s and 0s) representing the voltage of the analog waveform at the instant it is measured or sampled; rounding of voltage sample values to the nearest integer.

Query String User input to a server on the Internet.

QuickTime Video file format invented by Apple Computer; widely used on the Internet; audio and video encoding and streaming media system; file format for compressing video clips.

Rack Box with metal rails 19 inches apart for mounting electronic equipment.

RAM Random Access Memory.

RCA Plug Standard connector used for connecting audio and video components.

Real Audio Program that allows the user to immediately hear an online audio file; popular standard for streaming audio.

Record Releases that include all collections of recorded material, including albums, compilations, and singles; vinyl-format recording.

Recording Console Device that enables the engineer to mix and control most or all of the device input and output signals that can be found in the studio; console's basic function is to allow for any combination of mixing or control over relative amplitude and signal blending between channels, spatial positioning, or left/right, as well as possibly front/back, routing, or the capability to send any input from a source to a signal destination, and switching for the multitude of audio input/output signals that are commonly encountered within an audio production facility; recording console can be thought of as the recording engineer/producer's color palette.

Recording Studio One or more acoustic environments specially designed and tuned for the purpose of getting the best sound possible when using a microphone pickup.

Red Book Audio Standard format for audio CDs.

Referrer URL of an HTML page that refers to another Web site; link.

Region Code The different areas of the globe have been divided into eight separate regions to accommodate the varying release patterns of movies by the major studios; each DVD player is compatible with a certain region (see below); DVD designated Region 0, "Not Regionally Coded" or "All Region" can be played on any player regardless of its nationality. Region 0: Plays on any DVD player; Region 1: United States; Region 2: Europe and Japan; Region 3: Asian Pacific; Region 4: Australia, New Zealand and Latin America; Region 5: Africa, Russia, and Eastern Europe; Region 6: China and Hong Kong.

Release The final portion of a note's envelope, which falls from the sustained signal level to silence.

Release Time Once dynamic processing has begun, the time taken for a dynamic range changer (such as a compressor, limiter, or expander) to return the signal to 63 percent of its original unprocessed level.

Resistance The opposition to the flow of DC current in a wire or circuit.

Resolution The number of bits used to represent each sample in an uncompressed digital audio signal (e.g., 4.8, 16, or 20 bits).

Return Code The return status of a request which specifies whether the transfer was successful or not and why; 200 = success OK; 201 = success created; 202 = success accepted; 203 = success partial information; 204 = success no response; 300 = success redirected; 301 = success moved; 302 = success found; 303 = success new method; 304 = success not modified; 400 = failed bad request; 401 = failed

unauthorized; 402 = failed payment required; 403 = failed forbidden; 404 = failed not found; 500 = failed internal error; 501 = failed not implemented; 502 = failed overloaded temporarily; 503 = failed gateway timeout.

Reverb Time (RT60) Measurement unit of a room's reverberation; time taken for a reverberated signal, once the initial signal has stopped, to reduce in level by 60 dB.

Reverberation (Reverb) Persistence of a signal, in the form of reflected waves in an acoustic space, after the original sound has ceased; closely spaced and random multiple echoes result in perceptible cues as to size and surface materials of a space and add to the perceived warmth and depth of recorded sound; reverb plays an important role in the perception of music and in proper studio design; reverberated signal can be broken into three components: direct signal, early reflections, and reverberation.

RFC Request for Comment; numbered series of documents that specify how different parts of the Internet work.

Ribbon Microphone Microphone that uses a diaphragm of extremely thin, aluminum ribbon suspended in a strong field of magnetic flux; as sound-pressure variations displace the metal diaphragm in accordance with air-particle velocity, the ribbon cuts across the magnetic lines of flux; this induces a current in the ribbon of proportional amplitude and frequency to the acoustic waveform.

Rip To copy the digital audio information from an audio CD onto a computer.

Ripping Digital audio extraction.

ROFL E-mail acronym meaning "rolls on the floor laughing."

Router Sends data packets back and forth between networks; computer that connects two or more networks.

RSA Patented public key encryption system.

RSN E-mail acronym meaning "real soon now."

RTFM E-mail acronym meaning "read the !#%@$ manual"; suggestion made by those who feel their time has been wasted by asking a question the user could have found the answer to by looking it up.

S/PDIF (Sony/Phillips Digital Interface) Digital protocol adopted for the purpose of transmitting digital audio between consumer digital devices in a manner that is similar to but not identical in data structure to its professional AES/EBU counterpart.

SACD (Super Audio CD) Makes music sound markedly better than a CD; makes full use of a multichannel, multispeaker home theater system.

Safety Copy High-quality analog or digital copy of a production tape or final master recording; should be carefully stored under moderate temperature and humidity conditions.

Sample Single digital measurement of a sound wave; a series of samples is used to make a digital audio recording; segments of existing recorded works being included in a new work.

Sample Rate Number of samples of a sound per second.

Samplefile Computer file that contains sampled audio data.

Sampler Device capable of recording, musically transposing, processing, and reproducing segments of digitized audio to and from RAM.

Sampling Process of taking periodic samples of an audio waveform and transforming these sampled signal levels into a representative stream of binary words that can be manipulated or stored for later reproduction.

SanDisk Compact brand of flash memory storage.

Scene Selection Term for DVD's ability to jump to a specific track or "chapter" on the disk as on an audio CD.

SCMS (Serial Copy Management System) Pronounced SCUMS; system implemented in many consumer digital devices in order to prohibit the unauthorized copying of digital audio at 44.1 kHz or standard CD sample rate; with the SCMS, can make a digital copy of a commercial DAT or CD, but cannot make a copy from that copy.

SCMS Serial Copy Management System.

Scratch Vocal Rough vocal track recorded live along with initial rhythm instruments to help the basic tracks keep in the groove of the song; final vocals can be re-recorded later during overdubs.

SCSI (Small Computer System Interface) Pronounced SCUZZY; sample dump format; bidirectional communications bus used by many PCs and digital devices to exchange data between systems at high speeds.

SDH (subtitled for the deaf and hard-of-hearing) Similar to "closed captioning," but does not require a compatible television set to display the text of dialogue and sound effects within a film; "subtitle" option on the DVD remote activates English subtitles which correspond to the film.

SDMI Secure Digital Music Initiative; an attempt to create a digital audio file format that will be acceptable to the RIAA by eliminating concerns about uncontrolled digital copying.

Search Engine Web tool site that helps user locate information on the Internet; Web site that allows users to search for keywords on Web pages.

SECAM (Systeme En Coleur Avec Memoire) Developed and used in France and other countries with political affiliation; uses 25 frames per second, scanning at 625 horizontal lines per frame.

Sector Pie-shaped section of a disk that holds a fixed amount of data; sectors on CDs are often referred to as frames.

Secure Server Server that uses security measures to prevent access by an unauthorized party.

Secured Transaction Online transaction, often involving a credit card number, that uses security measures to prevent access by an unauthorized party.

Sensitivity Rating Output level in volts that a microphone will produce given a specific and standardized input signal, rated in dB SPL; specification implies the degree of amplification required to raise the mic signal to line level, -10 dBV or +4 dBm.

Sequence Editing Process of editing songs into a final order either in the analog or digital domain; end result of this process is a completed project ready for mastering into a finished, salable product.

Sequencer Digitally based device used to record, edit, and output performance-related MIDI data.

Serial Port Place on the back of a computer where a modem is plugged in; a.k.a. "communications port."

Server Computer that has a permanent connection to the Internet; purpose is to supply information to clients; provides Web site housing and access; designated network computer that stores and manages specific data files; computer that provides a service to other computers known as "clients" on a network.

Server Error Error occurring at the server.

Servo-Driven Fader Resistive attenuator that is driven automatically by a servo motor interface; during the playback of an automated mix, the faders will move on their own, in accordance with the requirements of the mix.

SGML Standardized General Markup Language; formatting language from which HTML was developed.

Shareware Programs that are distributed at no charge by the publisher, but with the expectation that the user will try them and then pay for them if they find the program useful; computer programs that are easily available to try with the understanding that the user will send the requested payment to the shareware provider specified in the program; an honor system; software that can be freely distributed and evaluated but must be purchased if used beyond a certain time period.

Shelving Filter Rise or drop in frequency response at a selected frequency that tapers off to a preset level and continues at this level to the end of the audio spectrum.

Shock Mount Suspension system that isolates a microphone from stand- and floor-borne noises; shock mount built into a mic reduces handling noise.

Shockwave Standard for viewing interactive multimedia on the Internet; advanced multimedia authoring and viewing system.

SHOUTcast Streaming MP3 system developed by Nullsoft; popular streaming audio solution supported by Winamp; often used for Internet radio stations.

SIG E-mail acronym meaning "special interest group."

Signature File Small ASCII text file, up to five lines, automatically attached to the end of an e-mail message; often includes additional information about the author and a hyperlink.

Single Record containing only a few songs, usually the album version of a song plus remixes of the same song; may also contain songs not included on the album, known as B-sides.

Site A place on the Internet; a home page or a collection of Web pages.

Skin File or group of files that creates a different look for a program without changing its function; file that controls the appearance of a program's user interface.

Slate Verbal identification of the song, take, and other identification on the original, master-tape tracks.

SLIP Serial Line Internet Protocol; software for connecting a computer to the Internet over a serial line.

Smart Agent Web monitoring software that alerts users to changes or updates.

SmartMedia Popular standard for flash memory cards; used by MP3 players, digital cameras, and other portable devices; type of memory card with no onboard controller.

Smiley Combination of special characters that portray emotions; hundreds have been invented, but only a few are in active use; a.k.a. emoticons or "emotion icons"; examples follow:

(:)	full face
:-)	happy face with a nose
:)	without a nose
;-)	wink
:(	sad face
:-(	sad face with a nose
[ ]	hug, usually put around

someone's name, for example [Mom]

[[[[ ]]]] big hug

:->	another smile
:-D	said with a smile

SMPTE Time Code Standard method for synchronously interlocking audio, video, and film transports; use of time code allows identification of an exact position on a magnetic tape by assigning a digital address to each specified position; this address code cannot slip and always retains its original location, allowing continuous monitoring of tape position to an accuracy of roughly 1/30th of a second.

SMPTE-to-MIDI Converter Used to read SMPTE time code and convert it into such MIDI-based sync protocols as MIDI time code, Direct Time Lock, or song position pointer.

SMTP Simple Mail Transfer Protocol; method by which Internet mail is delivered from one computer to another; protocol to send and receive e-mail between servers on the Internet.

Snail Mail Mail delivered by the U.S. Postal Service; refers to its slowness in relation to electronic mail.

SO E-mail acronym meaning "significant other."

Soc Type of newsgroup that discusses social topics.

Socket Connector that one inserts another connector into; a jack; logical "port" a program uses to connect to another program running on another computer on the Internet.

Software Programs and information that a computer uses; in contrast to hardware, which are the actual physical parts of a computer.

Solo Monitor function that lets the engineer hear a single instrument or group of instruments without affecting the studio's headphone monitor mix, recorded tracks, or mixdown signal.

Sound Card Internal computer device used to turn computer data into output for speakers, and to digitize audio from outside the computer.

Sound Recording Term that encompasses streaming audio, video, and text.

Soundfile Computer file that contains audio data; rather than being reproduced from a sampler, these files are often played back from a hard-disk-based system.

Sound-Pressure Waves Sound waves generated by a vibrating body in contact with the air, such as an instrument or loudspeaker; sound arrives at the ear in the form of a periodic variation in atmospheric pressure; the atmospheric pressure is proportional to the number of air molecules in the area being measured.

Spam Junk e-mail; a serious breach of netiquette; the act of posting inappropriate commercial messages to a large number of unrelated, uninterested Usenet newsgroups or mailing lists.

Spatial Perception of Direction Capability of two ears to localize a sound source in an acoustic space; one ear is not able to discern the direction from which a sound originates, but two ears can; this is called spatial or binaural localization.

Speaker Polarity (Phase) Speakers are said to be electrically in-phase whenever the same signal applied to both speakers will cause their cones to move in the same direction, either positively or negatively; if they are wired out-of-phase, one speaker cone will move in one direction while the other will move in the opposite direction.

Spider Small piece of software used by search engines for indexing key information.

Splice To join two pieces of analog magnetic tape using a special adhesive, nonbleeding tape called splicing tape.

SSL Secure Socket Layer; Web-based technology that lets one computer verify another's identity and allow secure connections; protocol that allows sending encrypted messages across the Internet; uses public key encryption to pass data between a browser and a given server.

Standard If a film was shot in full frame, it does not need to be altered to fit a television in a standard format; when a theatrical release is filmed in a widescreen ratio it needs to be altered to fit the picture size of a standard television set, a more narrow square-like dimension.

Standing Wave Stationary waveform created by multiple reflections between opposing room surfaces; at certain points along the standing wave, the direct and reflected waves cancel each other, and at other points, the waves add together or reinforce each other; standing waves cause boomy sounding peaks in a room's low-frequency response.

Stereo The program audio is contained in two channels, one for the left and one for the right.

Stereo Surround (SS) A multichannel format that has rear speakers to provide the experience of being "surrounded."

Streaming Audio/Video Technology that allows digital audio or video to play while it is still downloading; system for sending soundfiles over the Internet that begins playing the sound before the file finishes downloading; RealAudio is the most popular.

Streaming Continuous data transport in the order it was sent without duplication.

Studio Company releasing the film may be either a large recognizable Hollywood studio or a smaller independent company; a film may pass from one studio to another for various reasons, such as contractual, financial, and so on, resulting in different studios releasing their own versions of a movie.

Studio Management Businesspeople who are knowledgeable about the inner workings of the music studio, music business, and people; running a studio requires the constant attention of a studio manager, booking department, and competent staff.

StuffIt Mac file-compression program; creates an SIT file that contains compressed versions of one or more files; to restore one of those files to its former size and shape, one uses UnStuffIt.

Submix Grouped set of signals that can be varied in overall level from a single control or set of controls.

Subtitles Text of the dialogue in a program appears at the bottom of the screen when the "subtitle" option is activated on the remote control; usually these subtitles are translations into languages other than the one in which the program was originally recorded (e.g., English subtitles for a French language film, or vice versa).

Suffix The three-digit suffix of a domain can be used to identify the type of organization; .com = commercial; .edu = educational; .gov = government; .int = international; .mil = military; .net = network; .org = organization.

Superbit DVD Alternative product for selected films; is stripped of special features so that the entire disk can be dedicated to the picture and sound of the original theatrical picture; can be encoded at double their normal bit rate and contain Dolby Digital and DTS audio tracks.

Surf or **Surfing** Browsing the Internet.

Surround Program audio is contained in four channels: a center channel for primary dialogue and effects, left and right front channels for music and additional effects, and a monophonic sound channel sent to two rear speakers for dimensional sound effects; surround playback requires a decoder in the audio receiver equipped at the minimum for surround output, or "Dolby Pro-Logic."

Sweetening Overdubbing strings, horns, chorus, and, sometimes, percussion to give added impact to a recorded production.

Sync (Repro) The use of an analog tape machine's record head to play back tracks during the overdub process in order to synchronize with the current tracks being recorded.

Synchronization (Sync) The locking of relative transport or playback speeds of various devices to allow them to work together as a single, integrated system; process of synchronizing overlapping blocks of sectors to eliminate jitter.

Synchronous Communications between two devices at the same time.

Synthesizer Electronic musical instrument that uses multiple sound generators to create complex waveforms that synthesize a unique sound character.

System-Exclusive (Sys-Ex) Messages Messages that enable MIDI manufacturers, programmers, and designers to communicate customized information between MIDI devices; these messages communicate device-specific data of an unrestricted length.

T 1 Telecommunications standard that carries twenty-four voice calls or data at 1.44 million bps over a pair of telephone lines.

Tag Piece of descriptive text embedded into an MP3 system.

Take Sheet Written sheet that notes the position of each take on a tape; comments are written on the take sheet to describe the performance, as well as whether it is a complete take, an incomplete take, or a false start.

TCP/IP Transmission Control Protocol/Internet Protocol; the system networks use to communicate with each other on the Internet; the language of the Internet.

Telnet Program that lets the user log in to other computers on the Internet; Internet protocol that lets a user connect the machine as a remote terminal to a host computer somewhere on the Internet.

Terminal Previously consisted of a screen, a keyboard, and a cable that connected it to a computer; can now use a terminal emulator, terminal program, or communications program.

Tethered System Hardware MP3 playing device designed to stay connected to a computer.

Text File File that contains only textual characters, with no special formatting, graphical information, sound clips, or video; a.k.a. ASCII text files.

THD Total Harmonic Distortion.

Theme Different design for a program's appearance, like a "skin."

Thread Article posted to a Usenet newsgroup, along with follow-up articles, etc.

Three-to-One (3:1) Rule Guideline that states that leakage and phase cancellations can be reduced by keeping the distance between mics at least three times the distance the mics are placed from their respective sound sources.

Threshold of Feeling SPL rating that will cause discomfort in a listener 50 percent of the time and which occurs at a level of about 118 dB SPL between 200 Hz and 10 kHz.

Threshold of Hearing The quietest sound humans can hear: 0 dB SPL; pressure-level reference that constitutes the minimum sound pressure that produces the phenomenon of hearing in most people; equal to 0.0002 microbar; one microbar is equal to one-millionth of normal atmospheric pressure, so it's apparent that the ear is extremely sensitive; threshold of hearing is defined as the SPL for a specific frequency at which the average person can hear only 50 percent of the time.

Threshold of Pain An SPL rating that causes pain in a listener 50 percent of the time; corresponds to an SPL of 140 dB in the range between 200 Hz and 10 kHz.

THX Certified Company and process developed by George Lucas; began as a certification system for movie theaters to ensure the finest and most accurate audio quality; now also refers to a video transfer system by which THX maximizes the optimum visual and audio quality from the available materials and then offers its approval on the final product.

TIA E-mail acronym meaning "thanks in advance."

Time Code A standard encoding scheme for encoding time-stamped address information; used for address location, triggering, and synchronization between various analog, video, digital audio, and other time-based media.

Time Out When a Web page is requested and the server that hosts the Web page does not respond in a certain amount of time, the user may get the message "connection timed out."

Tinted Many silent films were originally exhibited with color tinting added to the prints; scenes were often colored to denote a certain mood; many DVDs of silent films now preserve the original tinting specifications indicated by the film's creators.

Track An entire song.

Track Sheet Sheet that indicates what instrument, or group of instruments, is on each track of a multitrack tape; should always be stored in the box with the reel.

Trailer Preview containing scenes from an upcoming film; an "original theatrical trailer" is the one originally shown to promote the film; a "rerelease trailer" is one shown during a film's return engagement in theaters; a "video trailer" has been designed to promote the film's release on home video; some DVDs also include "TV spots," brief coming attractions designed to be shown as television commercials.

Transducer Any device that changes one form of energy into another, corresponding form of energy; a microphone is an example of a transducer because it converts sound waves into an electrical signal.

Transfer Rate The speed at which data can be transferred.

Transient Response The measure of how quickly a mic diaphragm, speaker, or physical mass reacts to an input waveform.

Triggered Event Digital Audio Automated search and firing on command of a specific file or segment of digital audio data.

Triple-Dub Short way to say "www" when giving a URL.

Trumpet Widely used newsreader program that runs on Windows.

TTFN E-mail acronym meaning "ta-ta for now."

TwinVQ Transform-domain Weighted Interleave Vector Quantization; audio-encoding scheme developed by the NTT Human Interface lab.

UDP User Datagram Protocol; system used for applications to send quick messages.

Unbalanced Line Cable having only one conductor plus a surrounding shield in which the shield is at ground potential; the conductor and the shield carry the signal.

Unicasting Method of transmitting information that uses independent streams or channels to send the same information to multiple users.

Unicode Extension of ASCII that attempts to include the characters of all written languages.

UNIX Operating system developed by AT&T.

Upload Sending files from one computer to another computer through the Internet.

URL Uniform Resource Locator; standardized way of naming network resources; for linking pages together on the World Wide Web; Web address; typed into a browser will access a specific site; means of identifying an exact location on the Internet.

URN Uniform Resource Name; Web page name that doesn't change when the page is moved to a different computer; solution to the broken-link problem.

USB Universal Serial Bus; high-speed interface for personal computers; supports multiple devices.

Usenet System of online message boards available through the Internet; thousands of newsgroups; messages read by using a newsreader.

User Agent Fields in an extended Web server log file indicating the browser and the platform used by a visitor.

User ID Identifier user enters each time a particular service on the Internet is accessed; always accompanied by a password.

User Session Worldwide decentralized distribution system of newsgroups; at least 30,000 newsgroups are available through the Internet.

Uucp UNIX-to-UNIX Copy; old mail system used by UNIX systems.

UUENCODE/UUDECODE Method of encoding files to make them suitable for sending as e-mail.

Variable Bit Rate (VBR) System of MP3 encoding that does not record every segment of the music at the same bit rate.

Velocity of Sound The speed at which sound waves travel through a medium; at 70§F, the speed of sound waves in air is approximately 1130 feet per second (ft/sec) or 344 meters per second (m/sec).

VHS (Video Home System) Invented by JVC; after becoming more popular than the Betamax format, VHS became the standard videocassette format; term "VHS" has become synonymous with "videocassette" and "video," even though "VHS" only refers to the format of the videocassette or format of the home video medium.   ,   ·

Viewer Used by Internet client programs to show files other than text.

Vinyl Large plastic disks, often black, where the audio information is heard by using a needle to "translate" the tiny grooves embedded in the plastic into sound.

Virtual Reality 3D visual computer simulation that responds to inputs.

Virtual Tracking First record MIDI or SMPTE time-code onto one track of recorder using a MIDI sync box; then set up a sequencer with MIDI file; timecode forces sequencer to play MIDI file as tape rolls, so can mix sound from MIDI in directly along with tape tracks.

Virtuosa Gold Player/encoder program for MP3s; encoding that does not record every segment of the music at the same bit rate.

Visit User Session; all activity for one user of a Web site; terminated when a user is inactive for more than thirty minutes; to access a Web page. A visit usually includes several hits.

Voltage Controlled Amplifier (VCA) Amplifier in which audio level is a function of a DC voltage (generally ranging from 0 to 5 Volts) applied to the control input of the device; as control voltage is increased, analog signal is proportionately attenuated; an external voltage is used to change the audio signal level; console automation and automated analog signal processors often make extensive use of VCA technology.

VQF File extension for Twin VQ.

VRML Virtual Reality Modeling Language; Virtual Reality Markup Language; method for creating 3D environments on the Internet; requires a VRML plug-in for browser; standard for designing virtual reality pages.

VT100 Model number of a terminal made in the early 1980s by Digital Equipment Corporation.

Watermarking Method of transparently embedding data in a file to identify the copyright holder.

WAV File Popular Windows format for sound files (.wav files) found on the Internet; common type of audio file, usually uncompressed.

Waveform Graph of a signal's sound pressure or voltage level versus time; waveform of a pure tone is a sine wave.

Wavelength Distance in a medium between corresponding points on adjacent waveform cycles.

Web Page Document available on the Internet.

Web Server Computer that stores and delivers all files for a Web site.

Webmaster The person who is responsible for the Web server.

Widescreen Since the 1950s, motion pictures shown in movie theaters usually feature an image whose width is greater than its height, a rectangle shape; movies filmed in Panavision or Cinemascope are much wider, and this process is often referred to as "anamorphic" due to the type of lens used, or "scope" to be viewed on television, movies must be formatted one of two ways: (1) "Pan and Scan," in which the picture information is chopped off the sides to fit the square shape of a TV and the movie "scans" back and forth when necessary to catch important information, or (2) "Letterboxing," which preserves the original "widescreen" appearance of the film by placing black bars at the top and bottom of the screen; when these black bars are present, you are, therefore, seeing more of the film's image, not less.

Winamp Popular player program for MP3s and other digital audio formats.

Winsock Windows Sockets; standard way for Windows programs to work with TCP/IP; application programming interface by which Windows-based Internet-access programs access the Internet.

WinZip File-compression program that runs under Windows; reads and creates a ZIP file that contains compressed versions of one or more files.

WMA Proprietary audio encoding scheme developed by Microsoft.

World Wide Web Hypermedia system that lets a user browse through information; central repository of information; Internet client-server system to distribute information, based upon the hypertext transfer protocol (HTTP); a.k.a. WWW, W3, or the Web; created at CERN in Geneva, Switzerland, in 1991 by Dr. Tim Berners-Lee.

Wow Slow, periodic variation in a tape transport's speed.

WYSIWYG E-mail acronym meaning "what you see is what you get"; phrase used to explain that what you see on the screen is what you will get on a printout.

X.400 Mail standard that competes with the Internet SMTP mail standard.

X.500 Standard for white pages e-mail directory services.

Xmodem Protocol for sending files between computers; second choice after Zmodem.

XON/XOFF Computer's response when data is coming in too fast; hardware flow control.

XRCD (Extended Resolution CD) JVC invention and trademark, XRCDs are regular CDs with higher sound quality; encoding of disk itself is not what produces higher sound quality; instead, attention is put into the mastering and manufacturing process; mastering is done with 20-bit analog-to-digital conversion with 128 times oversampling, which is then converted to 16 bits during manufacturing while still maintaining its sonic integrity; all of this is done on special JVC equipment; recording is pressed onto a CD where the readable side is coated in aluminum; no special equipment is required to play an XRCD.

YABA E-mail acronym meaning "yet another bloody acronym."

ZIP File File that has been compressed using PKZIP, WinZip, or a compatible program.

Zmodem Protocol for sending files between computers.

Zone Last part of an Internet host name; two letters indicates the country code in which the organization that owns the computer is located; three letters indicates the type of organization that owns the computer.

Bibliography

Althouse, Jay. *Copyright: The Complete Guide for Music Educators*. Van Nuys, CA: Alfred Publishing Co, Inc., 1997.

Bates, Jefferson D. *Writing with Precision*. New York: Penguin Books, 2000.

Besenjak, Cheryl. *Copyright Plain and Simple*. Franklin Lakes, NJ: Career Press, 1997.

Blesh, Rudi. "Scott Joplin: Black American Classicist" in *Scott Joplin Collected Piano Works*. Miami, FL: Warner Bros. Publications, 1971.

Blume, Jason. *Six Steps to Songwriting Success—The Comprehensive Guide to Writing and Marketing Hit Songs*. New York: Billboard Books, 1999.

Bond, Sherry. *The Songwriter's and Musician's Guide to Nashville*. Cincinnati, OH: Writers Digest Books, 2000.

Braheny, John. *The Craft and Business of Songwriting*. Cincinnati, OH: Writers Digest Books, 2001.

Buchmam, Dian Dincin, and Seli Groves. *The Writers Digest Guide to Manuscript Formats*. Cincinnati, OH: Writers Digest Books, 1987.

Burt, George. *The Art of Film Music*. Boston: Northeastern University Press, 1994.

Bye, Dean. *You Can Teach Yourself about Music*. Pacific, MO: Mel Bay Publications, 1989.

Churchill, Sharal. *The Indie Guide Book to Music Supervision for Films*. Los Angeles: Filmic Press, LLC, 2000.

Cool, Lisa Collier. *How to Write Irresistible Query Letters*. Cincinnati, OH: Writers Digest Books, 1987.

Cooper, Helen. *The Basic Guide to How to Read Music*. New York: AMSCO Publications, 1986.

Cupit, Jerry. *Nashville Songwriting*. Nashville, TN: Cupit Music, 1995.

Curtis, Richard. *How to Be Your Own Literary Agent*. Boston: Houghton Mifflin Company, 1984.

Davis, Sheila. *The Craft of Lyric Writing*. Cincinnati, OH: Writers Digest Books, 1985.

Dawes, John, and Tim Sweeney. *The Complete Guide to Internet Promotion for Artists, Musicians, and Songwriters*. Temecula, CA: Tim Sweeney and Associates, 2000.

Dearing, James W. *Making Money Making Music (No Matter Where You Live)*. Cincinnati, OH: Writers Digest Books, 1982.

Delton, Judy. *The Twenty-Nine Most Common Writing Mistakes and How to Avoid Them*. Cincinnati, OH: Writers Digest Books, 1985.

Downing, Douglas, and Michael Covington. *Dictionary of Computer Terms*. Hauppauge, NY: Barron's Educational Series, Inc., 1992.

Editors of *Songwriter's Market*. *The Songwriter's Market Guide to Song and Demo Submission Formats*. Cincinnati, OH: Writers Digest Books, 1994.

Eiche, Jon. *What's MIDI?—Making Musical Instruments Work Together*. Milwaukee, WI: Hal Leonard Publishing Corporation, 1990.

Fries, Bruce, with Marty Fries. *The MP3 and Internet Audio Handbook—Your Guide to the Digital Music Revolution*. Burtonsville, MD: TeamCom Books, 2000.

Gerou, Tom, and Linda Lusk. *Essential Dictionary of Music Notation*. Van Nuys, CA: Alfred Publishing Company, Inc., 1996.

Gibson, James. *How You Can Make $30,000 a Year as a Musician without a Record Contract*. Cincinnati, OH: Writers Digest Books, 1986.

Goldberg, Natalie. *Writing Down the Bones*. New York: Quality Paperback Book Club, 1990.

Goldstein, Jeri. *How to Be Your Own Booking Agent.* Charlottesville, VA: The New Music Times, Inc., 1998.

Guiheen, Annamarie, and Marie-Reine A. Pafik. *The Sheet Music Reference and Price Guide.* Paducah, KY: Collector Books, 1995.

Hamm, Charles. *Music in the New World.* New York: W. W. Norton and Company, 1983.

Harnsberger, Lindsey C. *Essential Dictionary of Music.* Van Nuys, CA: Alfred Publishing Company, Inc., 1976.

Harris, James F. *Philosophy at 33-1/3 RPM—Themes of Classic Rock Music.* Chicago, IL: Open Court, 1993.

Higgins, William R. *A Resource Guide to Computer Applications in Music Education.* Grantham, PA: Messiah College, 1994.

Hill, Brad. *Internet Directory for Dummies.* Foster City, CA: IDG Books Worldwide, 1999.

Hill, Dave. *Designer Boys and Material Girls.* New York: Landford Press, 1986.

Hustwit, Gary. *The Musician's Guide to the Internet.* San Diego, CA: Rockpress Publishing, 1997.

——. *Websites for Musicians.* San Diego, CA: Rockpress Publishing, 2000.

Irvine, Demar. *Writing about Music.* Seattle: University of Washington Press, 1979.

Jamsa, Kris. *Welcome to Personal Computers.* New York: MIS Press, 1992.

Josefs, Jai. *Writing Music for Hit Songs.* New York: Schirmer Books, 1996.

Kasha, Al, and Joel Hirschorn. *If They Ask You, You Can Write a Song.* New York: Simon & Schuster, 1989.

Kimple, Dan. *Networking in the Music Business.* Cincinnati, OH: Writers Digest Books, 1993.

Klavens, Kent J. *Protecting Your Songs and Yourself.* Cincinnati, OH: Writers Digest Books, 1989.

Krasilovsky, M. William, and Sidney Shemel. *This Business of Music.* New York: Billboard Books, 2000.

Kushner, David. *Music Online for Dummies.* Foster City, CA: IDG Books Worldwide, 2000.

Larsen, Michael. *How to Write a Book Proposal.* Cincinnati, OH: Writers Digest Books, 1985.

Levine, John R., Carol Baroudi, and Margaret Levine Young. *The Internet for Dummies.* Foster City, CA: IDG Books Worldwide, 1997.

Levine, Michael. *The Music Business Address Book.* New York: Harper and Row, 1989.

Levitin, Dan. *From Demo Tape to Record Deal.* Van Nuys, CA: Alfred Publishing Company, Inc., 1992.

Linderman, Hank. *Hot Tips for the Home Recording Studio.* Cincinnati, OH: Writer's Digest Books, 1994.

Livingston, Robert Allen. *Music Business Reference.* Cardiff-by-the-Sea, CA: La Costa Music Business Consultants, 1988.

Luboff, Pat, and Pete Luboff. *Eighty-Eight Songwriting Wrongs and How to Right Them.* Cincinnati, OH: Writers Digest Books, 1992.

Maran, Richard. *Creating Web Pages Simplified.* Foster City, CA: IDG Books Worldwide, Inc., 1996.

——. *Internet and World Wide Web Simplified.* Foster City, CA: IDG Books Worldwide, Inc., 1997.

Mash, David S. *Computers and the Music Educator.* Melville, NY: SoundTree, 1996.

——. *Musicians and Computers.* Miami, FL: Warner Bros. Publications, 1998.

——. *Musicians and Multimedia.* Miami, FL: Warner Bros. Publications, 1998.

——. *Musicians and the Internet.* Miami, FL: Warner Bros. Publications, 1998.

McCormick, Scott. *The Musician's Guide to the Web.* Pennsauken, NJ: Disc Makers, 2000.

MENC. *Growing Up Complete—The Imperative for Music Education.* Reston, VA: MENC, 1991.

——. *National Standards for Arts Education.* Reston, VA: MENC, 1994.

——. *The School Music Program: Description and Standards.* Reston, VA: MENC, 1986.

Metter, Ellen. *Facts in a Flash—A Resource Guide for Writers from Cruising the Stacks to Surfing the Net.* Cincinnati, OH: Writers Digest Books, 1999.

Monaco, Bob, and James Riordan. *Platinum Rainbow.* Sherman Oaks, CA: Swordsman Press, 1980.

Muench, Teri, and Susan Pomerantz. *Attention A & R.* Van Nuys, CA: Alfred Publishing Company, 1988.

Murrow, Don. *Sequencing Basics.* Miami, FL: Warner Bros. Publications, 1998.

Nackid, Terri, ed. *The MTNA Guide to Music Instruction Software.* Cincinnati: OH: Music Teachers National Association, 1996.

NAMM. *International Music Market Show Directory.* Carlsbad, CA: NAMM, 2000, 2001.

Newer, Hank. *How to Write Like an Expert about Anything.* Cincinnati, OH: Writers Digest Books, 1995.

Noad, Frederick. *The Virtual Guitarist—Hardware, Software, and Web Sites for the Guitar.* New York: Schirmer Books, 1998.

Northam, Mark, and Lisa Anne Miller. *Film and Television Composer's Resource Guide.* Los Angeles: CinemaTrax, 1997.

Nashville Songwriters Association International. *The Essential Songwriter's Contract Handbook.* Nashville, TN: NSAI, 1994.

Oland, Pamela Phillips. *You Can Write Great Lyrics.* Cincinnati, OH: Writers Digest Books, 1989.

Patterson, Jeff, and Ryan Melcher. *Audio on the Web—The Official IUMA Guide.* Berkeley, CA: Peachpit Press, 1998.

Pattison, Pat. *Writing Better Lyrics.* Cincinnati, OH: Writers Digest Books, 1995.

Pickow, Peter, and Amy Appleby. *The Billboard Book of Songwriting.* New York: Billboard Publications, 1988.

Poe, Randy. *Music Publishing.* Cincinnati, OH: Writers Digest Books, 1997.

Prendergast, Roy M. *Film Music—A Neglected Art.* New York: W. W. Norton Company, Inc., 1977.

Rabin, Carol Price. *The Complete Guide to Music Festivals in America.* Great Barrington, MA: Berkshire House, 1990.

Rachlin, Harvey. *The Songwriter's and Musician's Guide to Making Great Demos.* Cincinnati, OH: Writers Digest Books, 1988.

——. *The Songwriter's Handbook.* New York: Funk and Wagnells, 1977.

Randall, Robin, and Janice Peterson. *Lead Sheet Bible.* Milwaukee, WI: Hal Leonard Publishing Company, 1997.

Randel, Don. *The New Harvard Dictionary of Music.* Cambridge, MA: Belknap Press of Harvard University Press, 1986.

Rapaport, Diane S. *How to Make and Sell Your Own Recording.* Englewood Cliffs, NJ: Prentice Hall, 1992.

Rudolph, Thomas E. *Teaching Music with Technology.* Chicago, IL: GIA Publications, Inc., 1996.

Rudolph, Thomas, Floyd Richmond, David Mash, and David Williams. *Technology Strategies for Music Education.* Wyncote, PA: Technology Institute for Music Educators, 1997.

Russell, William. "Notes on Boogie Woogie" in *Frontiers of Jazz,* ed. by Ralph de Toledano. New York: Ungar Pub., 1962.

Schock, Harriet. *Becoming Remarkable for Songwriters and Those Who Love Songs.* Nevada City, CA: Blue Dolphin Publishing, Inc., 1998.

Schuller, Gunther. "The Future of Form in Jazz" in *Saturday Review,* January 12, 1957, 62.

Sharp, J. D. *Home Recording Techniques.* Van Nuys, CA: Alfred Publishing, Inc., 1992.

Skolnik, Peter L. *Fads.* New York: Thomas Y. Crowell Company, 1978.

Stanfield, Jana. *The Musicians Guide to Making and Selling Your Own CDs and Cassettes.* Cincinnati, OH: Writers Digest Books, 1997.

Stangl, Jean. *How to Get Your Teaching Ideas Published.* New York: Walker and Company, 1994.

Starr, Greg R. *What's a Sequencer?—A Basic Guide to Their Features and Use.* Milwaukee, WI: Hal Leonard Publishing Corporation, 1990.

Stern, Jane, and Michael Stern. *Encyclopedia of Pop Culture.* New York: Harper Perennial, 1992.

Stewart, Dave. *The Musician's Guide to Reading and Writing Music.* San Francisco: Miller Freeman Books, 1999.

Trubitt, David. *Managing MIDI.* Van Nuys, CA: Alfred Publishing Company, Inc., 1992.

Tucker, Susan, and Linda Lee Strother. *The Soul of a Writer.* Nashville, TN: Journey Publishing, 1996.

Underhill, Rod, and Nat Gertler. *The Complete Idiot's Guide to MP3: Music on the Internet.* Indianapolis, IN: Que Corporation, 2000.

Uscher, Nancy. *Your Own Way in Music—A Career and Resource Guide.* New York: St. Martin's Press, 1990.

Waterman, Guy. "Ragtime" in *Jazz,* ed. by Nat Hentoff and Albert McCarthy. New York: Rinehart & Co., Inc., 1959.

Waugh, Ian. *Music on the Internet (and Where to Find It).* Kent, U.K.: PC Publishing, 1998.

Webb, Jimmy. *Tunesmith—Inside the Art of Songwriting.* New York: Hyperion, 1998.

Westin, Helen. *Introducing the Song Sheet.* Nashville, TN: Thomas Nelson, Inc., 1976.

Whitmore, Lee. *MIDI Basics.* Miami, FL: Warner Bros. Publications, 1998.

Williams, David Brian, and Peter Richard Webster. *Experiencing Music Technology—Software, Data, and Hardware.* New York: Schirmer Books, 1996.

Williams, Robin. *The Little Mac Book.* Berkeley, CA: Peachpit Press, 1993.

Wills, Dominic, and Ben Wardle. *The Virgin Internet Music Guide Version 1.0.* London: Virgin Publishing Ltd., 2000.

Zollo, Paul. *Beginning Songwriter's Answer Book.* Cincinnati, OH: Writers Digest Books, 1993.

About the Author

Elizabeth C. Axford (B.A., Music, University of Illinois, Urbana-Champaign; M.A., Musicology, San Diego State University) is an independent piano instructor and freelance writer living in Del Mar, California. She is an active member of the Nashville Songwriters Association International (NSAI), serving as regional workshop coordinator in Miami, FL (1990-1992) and San Diego, CA (1992-present). She is also a member of the California Association of Professional Music Teachers (CAPMT), an affiliate of the Music Teachers National Association (MTNA), ASCAP, NARAS, SCBWI, and TI:ME.

Ms. Axford has been teaching piano, keyboard, music theory, and voice to students of all ages, levels, and backgrounds since 1984.

She has attended or produced over one hundred songwriting, music industry, and piano pedagogy seminars and conferences in San Diego, Los Angeles, Nashville, Miami, Dallas, and Orlando. Ms. Axford is a published songwriter and arranger of piano music as well as a published poet.

She is the author of Keyboard articles written for www.Indie-Music.com, and her column "Songwriting and the Web" has appeared in the NSAI Newswire.

Other publications by Ms. Axford include *Traditional World Music Influences in Contemporary Solo Piano Literature* (Scarecrow Press, 1997), *Merry Christmas Happy Hanukkah—A Multilingual Songbook and CD* (Piano Press, 1999), and *The Art of Music—A Collection of Writings, Volumes 1 and 2* (Piano Press, 2001, 2003).

Born in Van Nuys, California in 1958, Ms. Axford has lived in six different states, including California, Texas, Illinois, New Mexico, Kansas, and Florida.